THE
AMERICAN
COLLEGE
TOWN

THE
AMERICAN
COLLEGE
TOWN

Blake Gumprecht

UNIVERSITY OF
MASSACHUSETTS PRESS
AMHERST AND BOSTON

LC 2008024533
ISBN 978–1–55849–813–6

Designed by Richard Hendel
Set in Scala with The Serif Bold display type by dix!
Printed and bound by Sheridan Books, Inc.

Library of Congress Cataloging-in-Publication Data

Gumprecht, Blake.
The American college town / Blake Gumprecht.
    p. cm.
Includes bibliographical references and index.
ISBN 978–1–55849–671–2 (cloth : alk. paper)
1. Community and college—United States.
2. University towns—United States.   I. Title.
LC238.G85 2008
378.1'030973—dc22
                                2008024533

British Library Cataloguing in Publication data are available.

Publication of this book has been assisted by a generous grant from
Furthermore: a program of the J. M. Kaplan Fund.

To Zeke: Now we can go to Sweden

The local is the only thing that is universal.

—*William Carlos Williams*

CONTENTS

PREFACE

In 1986, jobless and my meager savings nearly gone, I drifted back to the college town where I had earned a bachelor's degree three years before, Lawrence, Kansas. I had abruptly quit my job at a small newspaper in Arkansas when I clashed with an editor who had learned his management techniques in the Army. Taking that job was the latest in a series of stupid moves that sent my life into a downward spiral. My difficulties began a year before, when I quit my job at an independent record label in Minneapolis and naively went in search of the ideal small town. Over the next twelve months, my life unraveled. I went from West Virginia to New York to North Carolina to Chicago, back to Minneapolis, then to Montana, Louisiana, and Arkansas, each wrong decision assuring that the next would be even more desperate. My family lost track of me and friends learned to write my phone numbers in their address books in pencil.

Lawrence was a refuge for me when I returned, but like a refugee, I never considered it a permanent home. A handful of my less ambitious college pals still lived there. I found an inexpensive attic apartment and got back my old job filling vending machines on the University of Kansas campus. Lawrence is the quintessential college town. I loved it as an undergraduate, but returning to a college town after you graduate can be alienating because it looks the same but all the faces have changed. I soon felt out of place. I grew to resent students, who seemed spoiled and badly behaved. The professors were aloof and condescending. Living as an adult in a college town when you're not a student or professor can make you feel old and dumb. I came to distrust college towns because they didn't seem like "real" places. I left when an old friend in the music business offered me a job in Nashville.

Yet the few months I spent back in Lawrence were more important to shaping my worldview than I realized at the time. That was when I started to think about college towns as distinctive places. I recognized their differences more than I had as an undergraduate. Despite my newfound ambivalence toward college towns, I was happier and felt freer during that time than I have since. I could live cheaply, yet the amusements were comparable to those of a big city. Life was easy, yet stimulating. No one cared that I was not living up to my potential, since college towns are full of such people. The economics of a college town made it possible for me to behave with little concern for the future. It was not until years later, after I'd lived in enough "real" places, woken to an alarm clock every morning, and followed the same yellow line to a job as thousands of other people, that I realized what annoyed me about college towns upon my return to Lawrence in fact represented their greatest virtue. College towns are unlike other places, but that's a good thing.

My first exposure to a college town came while I was growing up in Wilmington, Delaware. My family lived in a boring-as-hell 1960s suburb, but we were five miles from the college town of Newark, home to the University of Delaware. I began to spend more time there after my mother entered graduate school. Newark was a different world for a suburban kid like me. I often accompanied my mom and had free run of the town and campus. Newark had a long Main Street lined with bars, book and record stores, restaurants, and small shops. It had an all-night diner and a movie theater that showed foreign films. Wonderland Records had black light posters in the window and sold drug paraphernalia in back. The Stone Balloon and Deer Park Tavern were student bars that sounded as exotic as a Shanghai opium den to a teen forbidden to enter. The campus held its own attractions. We swam in the indoor pool and went to movies at the student center. The university library made the public library near my house seem grossly inadequate. At the far end of campus were the football stadium and field house. I was obsessed by sports as a kid and went to games often. Compared to where I lived, Newark was a lively place.

I moved to Lawrence in 1977 to attend the University of Kansas. Newark is inseparable from the larger Wilmington metropolitan area; it had a Chrysler assembly plant and a sizable non-university workforce. The student body included many commuters. But Lawrence when I arrived was a cultural island, dominated by KU and college life. It was unlike any place I had known, and I took to it immediately. It had the comfort and convenience of a small town but without the insularity and conservatism. It had a compact downtown where you could buy almost anything. It didn't have a shopping mall (still doesn't). There was a family-run department store, an ancient hardware store that stocked one of everything, two movie theaters, and Drake's Bakery, where I ordered a waffle and two eggs every Saturday for a year. But it also had a college town flavor. Sunflower Surplus seemed staffed solely by old hippies and sold bikes, Levis, and outdoor gear. There was a record store where I bought my first Mekons record. The Town Crier stocked the English music weeklies. Lawrence Opera House smelled like beer and booked Iggy Pop and Muddy Waters. There were multiple bookstores and head shops.

Lawrence was full of kids like me, away from home for the first time and testing our freedom. My roommate in the dorm was a townie, and from him I learned what it was like to grow up in a college town, with its greater freedoms and easy access to beer, drugs, and sex. I learned how to drink from a dozen out-of-control freshmen from Atchison, Kansas, who lived with me on the eighth floor of Ellsworth Hall. My transformation intensified after I moved off campus. I figured out how to cut classes but still get good grades, and take the easy route around requirements by enrolling in "pud" classes. A buddy persuaded me to buy the first Clash album. I began to work at the college radio station and hang out at Off-the-Wall Hall, which booked local bands and offbeat touring acts. I went to KU to study journalism, but eventually a career as a reporter came to sound hopelessly square to me. It was my experiences in Lawrence that sapped me of that ambition.

As is true of most students in college towns, my life took place largely off campus.[1] I lived in one run-down old house that had a living room floor that tilted thirty degrees. A friend and I shared another house that was flea-infested. One day when my roommate filled the kitchen sink to do a week's worth of dishes, a dead mouse floated to the surface. Later, I moved to an apartment above a store downtown, nearer the places I spent my time. I stopped daily at Exile Records. I spent nights at Off-the-Wall Hall and nearly all the rest of my waking hours at KJHK. School began to recede in my mind. I created a radio program called *Alternative America* that played only obscure American rock 'n' roll at a time when few people paid attention to such music. I published a fanzine that featured interviews from my show. I helped book shows at Off-the-Wall Hall by bands such as the Replacements and Black Flag. I stopped taking classes. Eventually, I finished my degree, but didn't care enough to attend commencement. When Twin/Tone Records offered me a job in 1983, I left Lawrence and moved to Minneapolis. Most of what I learned in college I learned in town, not in classes.

I share my story because it is the seed from which this book grew. My time in Lawrence shaped my ideas about college towns. What I first tasted in Newark and swallowed whole in Lawrence strongly influenced how I approach the subject. I didn't live in a college town again for more than a decade, but my life continued to operate tangent to such places. I spent much of my time at Twin/Tone Records talking to radio stations and record stores in college towns. The alternative American music scene that emerged in the 1980s could not have developed without the supportive network for independent music that was strongest in places like Amherst, Massachusetts, and Ann Arbor, Michigan. After I left the music business, I continued to visit college towns with my record-executive wife. I began taking frequent driving trips, meandering down two-lane roads in the spirit of William Least Heat Moon and Jane and Michael Stern.[2] I stopped in college towns like Eugene, Oregon, and Arcata, California. I began to see a commonality to such places and felt an affinity for them.

In 1995, I moved to the college town of Norman, Oklahoma, to enter the Ph.D. program in geography at the University of Oklahoma. Moving to Norman rekindled my interest in college towns. I had spent the previous decade following my wife around the country—first to Chicago, then to Southern California. I bounced from one career to another. Pursuing a doctorate was a marital compromise, but also presented an opportunity to escape Los Angeles. My wife stayed behind when I went to Oklahoma. I visited Norman before deciding to attend OU. The campus and surrounding neighborhoods are tree-covered and idyllic, the antithesis of the state's image, and convinced me more than anything that the faculty said to attend OU. I lived in Norman for five years: two years by myself before returning to Los Angeles long enough to have a child, and then three years with my wife and young son. Norman was a different sort of college town from Lawrence—it lacked Lawrence's bohemian air, and its downtown was desolate—but my life was very different by then, too.

We bought a brick Tudor revival house two blocks from campus in a neighborhood of cozy bungalows and occasional student homes. I loved that I could ride my bike to my office in five minutes. The campus was my son's playground, full of endless possibilities for recreation and exploration. The tavern most popular with faculty and graduate students was a short walk away. We had a giant backyard, with a big pecan tree, complete with tree house and tire swing. The senior professor in my department lived over our back fence. My adviser lived four blocks away. A young faculty member lived on the same street, and our kids became kissing two-year-olds. A new hire from France bought a house nearby. I knew a half-dozen grad students who lived within walking distance. So many students and faculty lived in the vicinity that we often held impromptu get-togethers on Fridays in our backyard. It was an ideal life that I wish I could have continued forever, but universities rarely hire their own graduates these days.

My life in Norman inspired me to contemplate college towns as a research topic. I was struck again by how exceptional they are. Norman stood in sharp contrast to the rest of Oklahoma. Oklahoma City may be the ugliest city on earth and its airport, as a microcosm of city and state, was always a shock on return trips home. The drive from Oklahoma City to Norman is obscene in its tackiness. Once we exited Interstate 35, however, then drove east toward campus, the houses grew older and the tree cover thicker. By the time we reached home, it felt like Camelot. College towns, even one as conservative as Norman, are comfortable yet cosmopolitan. Norman was equally tolerant of cowboys, storm chasers, and Rudolph Anaya theorists with ambiguous sexuality. I could get into an argument at a bar about almost anything. I felt free to dress, think, and behave as I pleased. I could plan a trip to Afghanistan with a Kiowa Indian who spoke fluent Burmese. I could subscribe to the *New York Times* or borrow a book from a library a thousand miles away. I could find vegetarian options at most restaurants, and no one looked at me as if I was strange when I said I didn't eat meat. Almost everyone we knew was from someplace else. Departmental parties were like a mini–United Nations. I could see the number one–ranked college football team in America five minutes from my front door or hear a singer from the Metropolitan Opera. But I could also lie on a campus lawn with my son and watch the clouds drift by or wade knee deep in a river with nobody else around. Some of what made Norman attractive I could find in a big city. Some of what made it special I could find in a small town. Nowhere but in a college town could I find such a mix of sophistication and simplicity. Nowhere but in a college town could I find so many like-minded people in such a small place. Nowhere but in a college town could such a diverse group of people feel so at home.

Although I have spent much of my life in and around college towns, my perspective has also been shaped by the other types of places in which I have lived. Many academics spend their entire adult lives in college towns. I have met second-generation professors who have never lived in any other type of place. But I have lived in suburbia, small towns, state capitals, and big cities. Living in such places has made me better comprehend the distinctiveness of college towns. Growing up in a soporific subdivision made me appreciate Newark's college town funkiness. Working as a reporter in Rochester, New York, and Long Beach, California, made me see Lawrence differently when I returned. Living in Minneapolis, home to one of the largest universities in the country, taught me that a big city dilutes the impact of a university. I moved from there to a succession of even larger cities, which made me long for the compactness of a college town. My first teaching job was at the University of South Carolina in Columbia, a mid-sized urban area and state capital. Columbia suffers from many of the same problems as larger cities and possesses few of the qualities of a college town. We bought a house as close to campus as we could, but it was too far to walk or bike to work easily. Faculty and students lived all over the place, many far out in the suburbs, so there was little socializing outside work. The campus had none of the magnetism of the OU campus. I don't live in a college town now either—that was a compromise to a marriage that no longer exists—but the University of New Hampshire, where I work, is located in the college town of Durham, and that was part of the attraction of the job.

Looking back, I now realize that I began researching this book a quarter-century ago when I was an undergraduate and an aspiring reporter living in Lawrence. I wrote a three-part series for the student newspaper that examined the potential impacts of a proposed increase in the state's drinking age. That series devoted significant attention to the possible impacts on the state's college towns, and one article surveyed the effect of drinking-age changes on college towns in other states. I wrote several articles about a former student activist and state legislator known as "Marijuana Mike," which acquainted me with the peculiar political culture of college towns. Most of my college town research was informal. I lived in Lawrence's student ghettos, hung out in its rock clubs and record stores, observed eccentrics like the "Tan Man" who sunbathed shirtless on campus even in winter, and first came to appreciate many of the features of college towns that define them in my mind.

Years later in Oklahoma, while taking a graduate seminar in environmental history, I decided to investigate legends about the tree-planting efforts of the first university president, who helped transform Norman from a treeless prairie town into an attractive community known for its verdant campus and shaded streets. My research about tree planting in Norman made me think more generally about college towns. I looked to see what else had been written on the subject. I searched in vain for books about college towns in the United States. I looked for articles. I was astonished by how little serious research had been conducted about them. There are books about company towns, mill towns, cattle towns, and black towns, but not a single major work had ever been published about the American college town.[3] While much has been written about colleges, their campuses, student life, and related subjects, writers act as if colleges exist in a vacuum, as if the lives of students and staff do not extend beyond the college grounds. What little research has been conducted about college towns has been narrow in scope, ephemeral in its findings, or has used college towns as case studies for topics that have no relation to those attributes that make them unusual.[4] A book has been published about university towns in Great Britain and Germany, but even its author acknowledges that college-dominated communities are more prevalent and distinctive in the United States than in Europe. Others, too, have recognized the deficiency in writing on the subject. The literary critic Henry Seidel Canby wrote seventy years ago, "Surely it is amazing that neither history, nor sociology, nor fiction, has given more than passing attention to the American college town, for surely it has had a character and personality unlike other towns." Nearly four decades later, the cultural geographer Wilbur Zelinsky observed that the geography of college communities is "almost totally terra incognita."[5]

Why has so little research been conducted about college towns, particularly when so many authors and scholars live in such places? I blame it on academic far-sightedness and the natural human tendency to overlook what is all around us. Research on local topics is perceived in academe as parochial and counterproductive to building a national reputation necessary to earn tenure and promotion. But I have also found that professors who live in college towns are often oblivious to those characteristics that make them unusual. Many wrongly assume that a college town is little different from the county seat just down the road. Perhaps because of my background in journalism, where reporters are pushed to always be on the lookout for a "scoop," I am drawn to subjects that are comparatively unknown and about which little has been written. When I discovered that no book had ever been published about the American college town, I decided to write one.

College towns are exceptional places, worth knowing and worth knowing about. They are an essential component of American geography. They are part of what makes life different in these United States. They reflect the singular nature of American higher education and the indelible characteristics of American culture. They are distinctive, memorable, lively, and ever-changing. Millions of people have lived or gone to school in college towns. Memories of the college years, like my own, are often intertwined with recollections of such a place. College towns, as a result, possess a prominent image in the American mind. For all these reasons, they deserve far greater attention than they have received. This book seeks to redress past neglect of this subject by creating a portrait of the college town. It will identify the distinguishing attributes of college towns, examine why they have developed as they have in the United States, and explore in depth several characteristics that make them distinctive.

As I began working on this book, I wrestled with how best to portray the college town in all its complexity. I considered organizing the book historically, like most of my research, but decided that approach would not adequately capture the contemporary personality of college towns. I thought about focusing on the internal geography of college communities, examining distinct districts such as the campus, the college-oriented shopping area, and characteristic residential neighborhoods, but decided against that approach because it ignored other important traits. I contemplated taking a landscape perspective like my mentor Bret Wallach, focusing on the visible elements of college towns, but rejected that idea because part of what makes college towns compelling cannot be seen or touched. I also considered organizing the book according to the types of college towns that exist, but discarded that approach because it emphasized differences between college towns rather than their unity as a type of place.

Ultimately, I decided to employ a thematic organization that incorporates elements of all those approaches. Following an introduction, eight chapters each explore a theme that is a substantial feature of college town life and together, I believe, capture the essence of what makes the college town distinctive. A final chapter considers the future of college towns. Though the book is organized thematically, individual chapters take a historical approach and the entire book shows a strong landscape perspective. The different types of college towns that exist are discussed in chapter 1, while other chapters examine identifiable areas found in most college towns. Choosing themes was difficult. I considered more than three dozen possible topics. Many that I didn't choose warrant research on their own, and most are covered in some way in this book. But as the first detailed study of college towns, my book must necessarily be selective. The themes I chose strongly reflect my own experiences and the ways that I approach the study of places.

Each of the eight thematic chapters focuses on a single college town as an example. I chose a case study approach because it permitted me to explore each theme in greater depth than would have been possible if I had attempted a national-scale examination of the same subject. I believe strongly in the value of local research because it is particular places that give geography its personality and meaning. I agree with William Carlos Williams that "the local is the only thing that is universal," and it is that philosophy that guides my own research, which is intensely local.[6] Producing a work that is national in scope using a case study approach—particularly one with eight case studies rather than the usual two or three—proved to be labor-intensive and caused this book to take longer to complete than originally anticipated. I spent months researching each of the themes and towns in addition to reading more generally about higher education, student life, campus design, and related topics. I traveled to each of the case study towns for one to two weeks to do archival research, interview residents, and conduct field examinations. I made follow-up research trips to five towns.

The towns that are the focus of thematic chapters were chosen because they exemplify the topic under consideration. They are intended to be typical, not unusual. In each case, I could have chosen many other towns in which to explore the same theme. I had previous personal experience with three of the towns, which influenced my choices. Others I selected partly because I developed valuable contacts in those places. Some I picked in part because good published sources exist about them. I decided against focusing a chapter on the college town with which I have had the deepest long-term relationship, Lawrence, partly because I feared that my personal feelings about the city and what it has become would undermine my ability to write objectively about it. But Lawrence is present in every chapter of this book—explicitly as a source of anecdotes and comparison, or implicitly because it strongly shaped my perspective. All of the case study towns are home to big universities. I chose to focus on college towns with large universities because the distinguishing characteristics of college towns are most pronounced in such places. But the themes explored are present to varying degrees in all types of college towns, big and small, even if they are not present in every one. Not all of the themes are unique to college towns, but nowhere but in college towns are so many evident in a single place and nowhere but in college towns are they expressed with such intensity.

The case study towns were drawn from a longer list of sixty college towns about which I conducted secondary research. Those sixty towns (fig. 1.3) are representative of the diversity of college towns. They range in size from Eugene, Oregon, with a 2005 population of 144,515, to Langston, Oklahoma, with a population of 1,688.[7] I chose towns from all parts of the country. In all, thirty-four states are represented. I chose towns that are home to a variety of college types—public research universities, private liberal arts colleges, land-grant institutions with their agricultural and applied-science orientation, regional state universities, church-affiliated colleges, and historically black colleges.[8] I also included three cities that are parts of major urban areas, even though they are less strongly influenced by a collegiate culture than isolated college towns—Cambridge, Massachusetts, because it was America's first college town; Berkeley, California, because it has been so important to American history and culture; and Claremont, California, because of my own familiarity with it.

Along the way, people have questioned my choices, wondering why their favorite college town was not on my list. But the study towns are not intended to be a subjective selection of the best college towns. Nor does my list only include towns where a collegiate influence is greatest. Some of the study towns I knew personally before I began this project. Others I had visited. A few have been home to friends or colleagues. I have tried to read town and college histories for each of the study towns, along with any periodical articles I could find. I have visited as many as possible. I have visited forty-five of the study towns and more than 150 college towns in all. In each of the case study chapters, I have included examples from other college towns to show that the theme explored is also present elsewhere.

In the process of writing this book, I conducted more than two hundred interviews, took two thousand photographs, and amassed enough material to fill three file cabinets and a six-foot-long bookshelf. The work required was overwhelming at times. In retrospect, it was a foolish project to attempt in the initial years of an academic career when the time available for research is limited. But my faith in the project and the way I chose to approach it has never wavered. This book has changed my life in both good and bad ways. It has taught me much about myself. I hope readers learn from it, come to a better understanding of college towns they know because of it, and are entertained by it. I hope it brings college towns the attention they deserve and will inspire others to study and write about them.

THE
AMERICAN
COLLEGE
TOWN

DEFINING THE COLLEGE TOWN

The American college town is a unique type of urban place, shaped by the sometimes conflicting forces of youth, intellect, and idealism, that has been an important but overlooked element of American life. The hundreds of college towns in the United States are, in essence, an academic archipelago.[1] Similar to one another, they differ in fundamental ways from other cities and the regions in which they are located. They are alike in their youthful and comparatively diverse populations, their highly educated work forces, their relative absence of heavy industry, and the presence in them of cultural amenities more characteristic of big cities. They are typically more liberal than towns without prominent colleges. They tend to be more tolerant of unusual behavior and supportive of unconventional ideas. Some have become centers for high technology development. The attributes of the institutions located in college towns and the people who live in these places, furthermore, breed unusual landscapes—the campus, fraternity row, the college-oriented shopping district, and more.

What is a college town? I consider as a college town any city where a college or university and the cultures it creates exert a dominant influence over the character of the town. This definition is deliberately imprecise because I do not believe there is a clear distinction between a college town and a city that is merely home to a college. They vary along a continuum. I will focus on towns where colleges are clearly dominant. I will not devote significant attention, for example, to cities such as Austin, Texas, that are home to big universities but are also state capitals. State governments, their employees, and related activities exert a strong influence. Similarly, I will say little about big cities that are home to universities or separately incorporated college communities like Tempe, Arizona, that are part of larger urban areas, because the socioeconomic diversity of such places dilutes the influence of a college. Although Austin and Tempe possess some of the attributes of college towns, particularly in areas closest to campus, what makes the college town as I envision it different is that the impact of a collegiate culture is concentrated and conspicuous. Small cities like Ithaca, New York, and Manhattan, Kansas, are defined by colleges and all that go with them.

The degree to which a college shapes the life of any place can be evaluated in a variety of ways, but none is sufficient to enable us to determine unequivocally which cities are college towns and which are not. There are places most people would agree are college towns. Charlottesville, Virginia (fig. 1.1), springs immediately to mind. There are many other places that clearly are not college towns. New York City, for example, is not one, despite occasional attempts to market it as such. But what about the large number of places that fall somewhere between those extremes? Is it possible to measure college town-ness? I would argue no, but there are methods to gauge from a distance the extent to which a college influences a place and so can give us a sense. In my view, the best barometer of a college's influence is the ratio of college students to overall population. I would argue that if the number of four-year college students equals at least 20 percent of a town's population, then a collegiate culture is likely to exert a strong influence. The 20 percent threshold is somewhat arbitrary, but it is based on my knowledge of numerous places I consider college towns and the ratio of students to population in those places.[2]

But we need more to go on than that, because there are many places that meet the 20 percent requirement that I would not consider college towns. They may be part of larger urban areas. They may be so tiny that they aren't really towns by any common definition of the word. We could consider other statistical measures to fine-tune our assessment. We could use data on the share of the labor force that works in education or the population that lives in group quarters such as dormitories, as Brian Berry did when he attempted to classify college towns. We could look at the portion of land area within a city occupied by colleges or universities, as Edmund Gilbert did in his study of university towns in Europe.[3] We could consider the median age or the percentage of adult residents possessing a doctoral degree. Indeed, we could create a complex matrix of characteristics a city must possess to be considered a college town, but that would suggest this process is more scientific than it should be.

I chose to keep it simple and include on a provisional list of college towns all places that meet the 20 percent enrollment-to-population threshold, but also had an urbanized area population in 2000 of less than 350,000 (a college town can't be too large), were nucleated urban areas that were physically separated from any larger city (to exclude suburbs and cities that are part of bigger urban agglomerations), possess a distinct identity apart from

FIGURE I.I. *The Corner, a college-oriented shopping district across from the University of Virginia campus in Charlottesville. Photograph by the author, 2002.*

other places, and are perceived as college towns. Most of those requirements are somewhat subjective. I based my decisions on my own knowledge and research. When in doubt, I examined U.S. Geological Survey maps, collected Census data, conducted periodical and Internet searches, and consulted reference sources. In 2000, there were 305 U.S. cities that met all those requirements (fig. 1.2). There are probably more cities that should be considered college towns, but do not meet the 20 percent threshold (e.g., Grinnell, Iowa) or are located in large metropolitan areas (such as Berkeley, California). Not all my sixty study towns met the requirements, though my parameters were conservative and intended to exclude places about which there may be disagreement rather than include any place that might be considered a college town.

Ultimately, whether a city is a college town is in the eye of the beholder. You may consider a city to be a college town that I do not and visa versa. That's okay. My purpose is not to create a definitive system for classifying college towns. I am more interested in understanding and explaining what makes college towns distinctive.

DISTINGUISHING CHARACTERISTICS

Much of what makes college towns unusual and interesting cannot be quantified in any meaningful way, and most of this book will take a humanistic and historical approach, but data on the socioeconomic characteristics of college towns confirm that they are fundamentally different from other places and from the United States as a whole. To begin, therefore, I will identify several distinguishing features of college towns that are measurable and significant, using data from the sixty study towns (fig. 1.3) as proof. Though some of these attributes are also present in other places, college towns are exceptional because most possess a majority of these traits, not just one or two, and because several are most strongly felt in towns where colleges are large relative to the size of the community.

College towns are youthful places. The migration to college towns every fall of new students and the exodus each spring of graduates makes college towns perpetually young (fig. 1.4). The average median age in the study towns in 2000 was 25.9 years old, ten years younger than the median for the United States.[4] More than one-third of study town residents on average were aged 18 to 24. Some of the study towns were even more youthful than the group. In Oxford, Ohio, home of Miami University, two-thirds of all residents were 18 to 24. Because college town residents are young, they are also less likely than the general population to be married. Just 38.0 percent of study town residents 15 and over, on average, were married in 2000, compared to 54.4 percent for the nation.

College towns are highly educated. Because most academic appointments require a Ph.D. and many universities have large graduate student enrollments, college towns are among the most educated places anywhere. Adult residents in the study towns were on average twice as likely as the U.S.

(opposite)
FIGURE 1.2. *There were 305 cities in the United States in 2000 where enrollment in four-year colleges was at least 20 percent of the population and met other criteria suggesting they are college towns. Map by the author. For a complete list, go to http://scholarworks.umass.edu/umpress/.*

College Towns in the United States

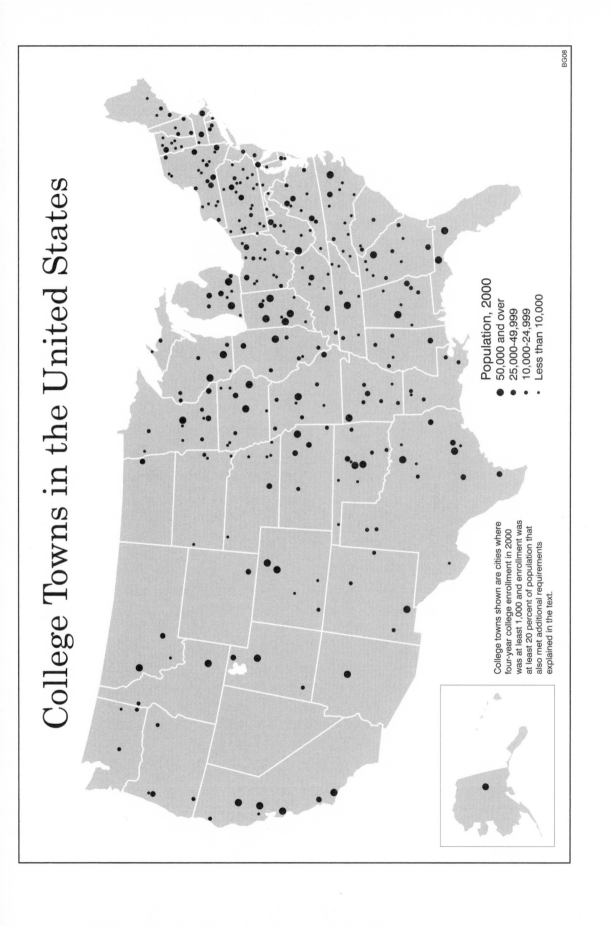

Population, 2000

- 50,000 and over
- 25,000-49,999
- 10,000-24,999
- Less than 10,000

College towns shown are cities where
four-year college enrollment in 2000
was at least 1,000 and enrollment was
at least 20 percent of population that
also met additional requirements
explained in the text.

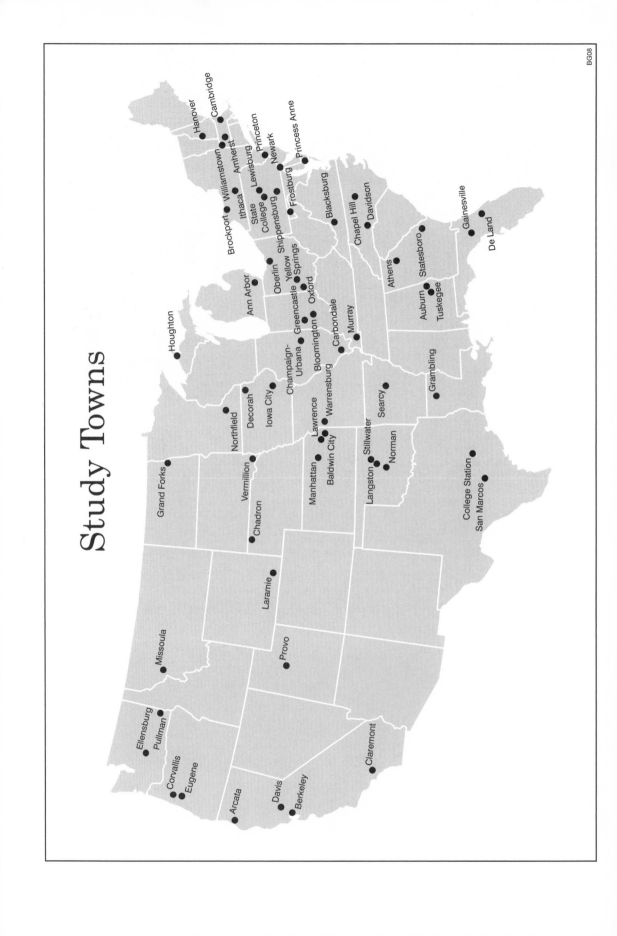

Study Towns

Hanover
Cambridge
Williamstown
Amherst
Princeton
Lewisburg
Newark
Princess Anne
Ithaca
State College
Frostburg
Brockport
Shippensburg
Blacksburg
Chapel Hill
Davidson
Gainesville
De Land
Oberlin
Yellow Springs
Ann Arbor
Greencastle
Oxford
Athens
Statesboro
Houghton
Champaign-Urbana
Bloomington
Carbondale
Murray
Auburn
Tuskegee
Decorah
Iowa City
Lawrence
Warrensburg
Searcy
Grambling
Northfield
Manhattan
Baldwin City
Langston
Stillwater
Norman
Vermillion
Grand Forks
Chadron
College Station
San Marcos
Laramie
Missoula
Provo
Ellensburg
Pullman
Claremont
Corvallis
Eugene
Arcata
Davis
Berkeley

FIGURE I.4.
*College towns are
youthful places,
as this scene of
students jello
wrestling at a
fraternity party
in Ithaca, New
York, suggests.
Photograph by the
author, 2000.*

population in 2000 to possess a college degree and six times more likely to hold a doctorate. Almost half of study town residents 25 years and older on average were college graduates. Nearly 7 percent possessed a Ph.D. The educational differences between college towns and other places are most dramatic in small towns with elite colleges. In Hanover, New Hampshire, home of Dartmouth College, three in four adults were college graduates, 42.6 percent held a graduate degree, and 14 percent possessed a doctorate.

The educational level of college towns is reflected in other ways. Data on public library circulation and the presence of bookstores suggest college town residents read more for pleasure than the general population. Per capita public library circulation in 2002–03 in study towns for which data were available was 50 percent higher than in the United States. Bookstores were also more abundant per capita in the study towns than they were nationwide. The study towns averaged ten bookstores for every 100,000 residents in 2002. Nationwide, there were 3.8 bookstores per 100,000 residents. Berkeley had twenty-two bookstores (fig. 1.5). Gainesville, Florida, seat of the University of Florida, had fifteen.[5]

(opposite)
FIGURE I.3. *The sixty study towns that were the focus of research. Map by the author.*

FIGURE I.5.
*Moe's Books
in Berkeley,
California, one
of more than
twenty bookstores
in that city.
The presence of
unusual numbers
of bookstores is
evidence that
college towns
are more highly
educated than
other places.
Photograph by
Syzmek Surma,
2007; used with
permission.*

College town residents are more likely to work in white-collar jobs. Although a
few college towns still possess factories, most college towns have little heavy
industry. In many, such as Bloomington, Indiana, manufacturing declined
dramatically following World War II, as college enrollments increased, college towns became more dependent on education for their economic survival, and civic leaders grew more selective about the types of businesses
they sought to attract. Workers in the study towns on average were half as
likely as the U.S. population to work in manufacturing in 2000; just 7.2
percent did so. Nearly half of study town residents on average worked in

managerial and professional jobs in 2000. More than a quarter were employed in education in 2000, three times the national rate. Many college towns resemble company towns in that a large percentage of adults work for a single employer. Southern Illinois University, for example, employed more than 5,000 people on its Carbondale campus in 2005, half the total labor force of the city.[6]

College towns are comparatively affluent. By most measures, college towns are prosperous and unusually stable economically. The median family income in the study towns in 2000, for example, averaged nearly $10,000 higher than similarly sized urban places nationwide.[7] Because colleges are supported by state appropriations, endowment income, and tuition revenues that fluctuate less than the economy, college towns are somewhat insulated from economic downturns. Indicative of the economic stability of college towns were their low unemployment rates as the country emerged from its most recent recession. In April 2002, the five metropolitan areas with the lowest unemployment rates in the country, and thirteen of the top twenty-six, were small cities with major universities, such as College Station, Texas, and Charlottesville, Virginia. Further evidence that college towns are less susceptible than other places to economic crisis came in 2007, when the subprime-lending fiasco threatened to plunge the United States into another recession. University cities were discovered to have fewer high-cost home loans than other urban areas. College towns also perform well by other measures. Retail sales per capita in the study towns in 2002, for instance, averaged 20 percent higher than in the nation as a whole. As the U.S. economy shifts to knowledge-based industry, college towns are also well positioned for growth. Employment grew 20 percent faster in the study towns on average than in the country during a recent twelve-month period.[8]

These numbers do not tell the whole story, however. Per capita income in college towns is comparatively low because many students do not work or work low-wage, part-time jobs. Poverty rates in college towns are unusually high for that reason, though these numbers are deceptive since they do not likely consider all income sources. Nearly one quarter of study town residents in 2000 on average lived below the federal poverty line, twice the national rate and higher than chronically depressed regions such as Appalachia. Although some students are truly poor, poverty data do not accurately reflect the well-being of students, since many are supported by families. More troubling is the presence in college towns of unusual concentrations of unemployed or underemployed college graduates, typically the partners of professors, so-called trailing spouses. Colleges offer high incomes for professors and administrators, but career options for other college graduates in college towns are often limited.[9]

College town living costs, especially for housing, are high. Because family incomes in college towns are high and local governments are sometimes restrictive about development, living can be expensive. The overall cost of living in the study towns in June 2005 averaged 2.4 percent higher than the country. Housing costs averaged 4.5 percent higher. Those numbers are somewhat deceiving. They are unduly influenced by a few college towns where living costs are especially pricey. Living costs are greatest in college towns with elite colleges, particularly those within commuting distance of big cities, such as Princeton, New Jersey, and Boulder, Colorado. The average house price in 2005 was $628,000 in Princeton and $546,350 in Boulder. Most college towns are more reasonably priced. A Coldwell Banker survey in 2005 found that home prices in fifty-nine markets with major universities—including many college towns—were 19 percent less than they were nationwide. Prices are cheapest in isolated college towns like Manhattan, Kansas, where the average home price was $185,850. Many academics aspire to live in an Ann Arbor or a Berkeley, but a professor's salary, comfortable but rarely huge, buys more in less desirable college towns.[10]

College towns are transient places. Going away to college is a rite of passage that has deep roots in American culture, particularly among the middle and upper classes, and is one characteristic that distinguishes U.S. higher education from that in the rest of the world. Every year, millions of American teenagers leave home to attend college. Students also move frequently while in school and usually leave college towns as soon as they graduate. Professors, too, are relative gypsies, because universities rarely hire their own graduates and academic culture encourages scholars to study at multiple institutions. Moving vans and U-Haul trucks are probably a more common sight in college towns than in any other type of place. One-third of heads of households in the study towns in 2000, on average, had moved in the previous fifteen months, 75 percent more than in the nation overall. Study town residents on average were twice as likely as the U.S. population to have lived in a different state five years before. In most college towns, the majority of the population is from somewhere else. In Chapel Hill, site of the flagship campus of the University of North Carolina, nearly two-thirds of residents in 2000 were born in a different state.

Transience produces one of the most striking features of college town life. Because students arrive on campus in fall, return home at Christmas, travel at spring break, and leave every summer, college towns display a predictable seasonality. The pulse of a college town rises and falls with the academic calendar. In August, college towns come back to life after a sleepy summer as students return for the fall semester. Traffic mounts. Cars line up near dormitories. Rental trucks back up on lawns. The thump-thump-thump of a distant student stereo replaces the hum of cicadas. Sorority pledges parade from house to house near campus. Businesses that cater to students make last-minute preparations. Parking spaces fill. There's a palpable energy to a college town at the dawn of another academic year as freshmen learn their way around and year-round residents readjust to life in a city of youth.

Christmastime is the busiest season in most places, but not in college towns, which turn desolate after final exams end in December. College towns tend to empty more completely at Christmas than even in summer. Sometimes it seems the only people who remain are foreign students, marooned at a single dormitory kept open by the university. College towns at Christmas can seem as deserted as a coastal town after a hurricane evacuation. The vacation exodus is repeated to a lesser degree in March at spring break. Later in spring, the ebb and flow that began in August reverses direction as students leave for the summer. The movement of students is more gradual at the end of the school year. Graduating seniors stick around for commencement, which stimulates a short-lived resurgence in activity as parents and relatives descend upon campus. A few underclassmen remain in town longer, enjoying the laziness of life in a college town without classes. College towns turn trashy at the end of the school year, when curbs are piled high with beer-stained couches, broken furniture, old computers, and the Wal-Mart remains of the undergraduate existence. The archaeologist could learn much about youth culture on trash day in May in any college town.

A college town in summer is like a beach resort in December. The pace of life slows. Businesses shorten their hours or close completely for weeks. Traffic diminishes. Permanent residents finally get around to chores they put off while the students were still in town. The grass grows long in front of fraternity houses, and weekend nights are quiet again. The campus is in a state of hibernation. Administrative offices are run by skeleton staffs. The library closes at 5 p.m. Faculty wear sandals and go to campus an afternoon or two a week, if at all. Apartments empty. Summer subleases are cheap and plentiful. Most of the town looks abandoned, newspapers yellowing on lawns. The college radio station is off the air in mid-afternoon. Bars and restaurants are uncrowded, but more congenial as a result. Year-round residents revel in the quiet of a college town in summer and curse when students return.

College town residents are more likely to rent, live in apartments, and have room-mates. With their high concentrations of transient residents, college towns provide a lucrative market for landlords. College town residents are less likely to own their homes and more likely to live in multi-unit dwellings and group housing, such as dormitories and fraternities, than the overall U.S. population. Turnover of rental housing in college towns is so frequent that "For Rent" signs are often left up year-round (fig. 1.6). Seven in ten U.S. residents in 2000 lived in owner-occupied housing, but more than half of study town residents on average were renters. Most lived in apartments. Nearly 20 percent of study town residents lived in group quarters, compared to 2.8 percent nationally. Reflecting the fact that many students seek to lower their costs by sharing housing, residents of the study towns were three times more likely than the U.S. population to have roommates.

College towns are cosmopolitan. Because colleges attract students and faculty nationally and internationally, college towns can seem as worldly as big cities. They are more ethnically diverse than other small cities. Asians, for example, were twice as common on average in the study towns in 2000 as they were in small urban areas in general. One in thirteen study town residents on average was born outside the United States, nearly triple the percentage in all metropolitan areas with fewer than 100,000 residents. In one quarter of study towns, the foreign-born population was 10 percent or more. In Champaign-Urbana, Illinois, home to the University of Illinois, Asians made up 9.4 percent of the population and 12.4 percent of residents were born outside the United States. Illinois students in 2004 came from 120 foreign countries. Because of their cultural diversity, college towns tend to have a greater variety of ethnic restaurants. A single block in Bloomington in 2000 had restaurants featuring cuisines from Morocco, Thailand, Eritrea, China, India, Italy, and Tibet.[11] At the same time, college towns are home to smaller percentages of blacks and Hispanics than other urban areas, which reflects the lower incomes and educational attainment of those two groups.

College towns are unconventional places. Because of their unusual demographics, many college towns are full of eccentrics, activists, and others who reject mainstream values (fig. 1.7). Some college towns revel in their excep-

FIGURE I.6.
*Rental properties
in college towns
are often aimed at
a single market, as
this student house
in Brockport, New
York, indicates.
Photograph by the
author, 2002.*

tionality. Residents of Ann Arbor call the city twenty-seven square miles "surrounded by reality."[12] T-shirts in Boulder urge locals to "Keep Boulder Weird" and ads on buses in Denver market the city as "Close in . . . but still far out."[13] Eccentricity is difficult to calculate, but several measures do suggest the unconventional nature of college towns. College town residents are less religious than the general population and more likely to walk or bike to work. They are more likely to listen to public radio, vote for left-wing political candidates, and shop at food cooperatives.

Nationwide, more than half of U.S. residents in 2000 claimed to be

affiliated with one of 149 religious groups. Residents of study town counties, however, were 25 percent less likely to belong to an organized religion. Six of the thirteen metro areas in the United States with the lowest rates of church membership were college towns. In Corvallis, Oregon, seat of Oregon State University, just 22.6 percent of the population was religious.[14] Although college town residents are less likely to belong to organized religions, many who do not belong to religious groups nevertheless consider themselves spiritual. As Alice Evans wrote in an essay on religion in Eugene, Oregon, where just 24.5 percent belonged to organized religions, "many . . . may be on a spiritual search, but few search in church."[15]

Public radio stations capture such a small portion of radio audiences in most places that their ratings are excluded from Arbitron ratings distributed to media. The leading National Public Radio outlet in Chicago, for example, captured just 2 percent of radio listeners in 2005. But public radio stations are often the most popular stations in college towns and capture five to ten times the audience share they do in big cities. Public stations were the number one–ranked stations in 2005 in Ann Arbor; Athens, Georgia; Missoula, Montana; and Arcata, California. WUOM, the NPR outlet in Ann Arbor, attracted 13.9 percent of listeners in its market in 2005, a remarkably high number in an industry in which ratings leaders often capture only 5 percent of listeners.[16] In college towns like Ann Arbor, public radio listenership is so high that conversations around the water cooler are more likely to be about what people heard on *Morning Edition* than *The Howard Stern Show*.

College town residents are also more likely than the general population to bicycle or walk to work, which reflects an environmental awareness and desire to be physically fit that are characteristics of an educated populace. Study town workers in 2000 were five times more likely on average to walk to work—one in five workers did so—and six times more likely to commute by bicycle than the overall U.S. population. In Ithaca and State College, Pennsylvania, more than 40 percent of workers walked to work. Nationwide, less than 3 percent did. In Davis, 14.4 rode a bike. College town voters are more likely to support liberal political candidates. In 2000, residents of study town counties voted for Ralph Nader at nearly twice the rate of the nation. College towns are also more likely than other types of places to possess food cooperatives, many of which emerged from the 1960s protest movements that were strong in college towns. Forty percent of the study towns possessed a food co-op in 2005. Even tiny Chadron, Nebraska, home of Chadron State College, had one.[17]

Quality of life in college towns is high. College towns are known for having lively downtowns, picturesque residential neighborhoods, unusual cultural opportunities for cities so small, ample parks and recreational facilities, safe streets, and good schools. They rank high on lists of the best places to live, retire, and start a business.[18] Quality of life, like idiosyncrasy, can be difficult to quantify, but several measures substantiate the idea that college towns are desirable places to live. Every year, *Expansion Management* magazine rates all public school districts in the United States. In 2005, fifteen of the twenty-five metropolitan areas that had the highest-rated schools were college towns. College towns are also healthy places. Twelve of the 27 metropolitan areas with the lowest cancer mortality rates in 2003 were college towns.[19]

AN AMERICAN INSTITUTION

College towns are largely an American phenomenon. Nowhere else in the world are there so many communities that are so dominated by colleges and universities as there are in the United States. In most countries, higher education institutions are located predominantly in large cities and national capitals.[20] In Europe, birthplace of the university, the oldest and most prestigious institutions of learning are located chiefly in cities like Paris, London, and Rome, and regional centers too economically diverse to be considered college towns in the American sense. There are but a handful of exceptions, including Tübingen and Marburg in Germany, Pisa and Siena in Italy, Cambridge in England, and St. Andrews in Scotland. Several cities that were once strongly shaped by education, such as Oxford, England, have grown too large and complex to be considered true college towns. Oxford, for example, is an auto manufacturing and publishing center. It has a sizable immigrant underclass, higher crime rates than the rest of England, and is the focus of a county with a population of more than 600,000.[21]

In Latin America, universities are concentrated in megacities such as Mexico City, Rio de Janeiro, and Buenos Aires. Mexico City is home to ten major universities with combined enrollments of 450,000 students. The only small city in Mexico where college enrollment equals at least 20 percent of population is Chilpancingo, better known as the capital of the state of Guerrero than as a university city. Similar patterns are evident in Asia and Africa. Neither China nor Japan has a single city where college enrollment is at least 20 percent of population. In Africa, Nsukka in Nigeria and Stellenbosch in South Africa are among a small number of cities that meet that requirement. Outside Europe and North America, most universities were founded comparatively recently, so colleges have had less time to shape the urban personality than they have in Europe and the United States. Tubārao in Brazil, for example, meets the 20 percent threshold, but the university there was not founded until 1967, and the city is known as a coal-mining town. Australia has the greatest concentration outside Europe and North America of cities where enrollment is at least 20 percent of population.

Bathurst, Armidale, Lismore, Toowoomba, and Ballarat all meet that criterion and are considered university towns.

Even in Canada, the country that most resembles the United States in its history and government, college towns are rare. Nearly all of Canada's government-supported universities are located in provincial capitals or major urban areas. Only two cities that are home to universities with enrollments of at least 5,000 students—Waterloo and Kingston, both in Ontario—would be considered college towns as conceived here. Those Canadian municipalities where colleges exert the greatest influence are small towns that are home to small colleges, such as Wolfville, Nova Scotia, and Sackville, New Brunswick. But even those towns are less shaped by colleges and all that go with them than many college towns in the United States, because, as Henry Srebrnik has noted, the all-encompassing collegiate culture so common in the United States is largely absent. "In Canada," he writes, "students treat their institution as they might a company where they work: they arrive on campus, attend classes, and go home."[22]

There are probably more college towns in the United States than in the rest of the world combined. Several factors help explain why college towns are more common. First, the sequence of college development versus urban development has been different in the United States than elsewhere. In Europe, cities preceded universities. Many of Europe's oldest universities emerged organically in locations where scholars and students gathered over time. Intellectuals were drawn to cities because they were the focus of economic, political, and cultural life. Large-scale settlement of North America, in contrast, occurred long after the emergence of the university idea, and colleges were founded as settlement spread westward across the continent, often at the same time towns were founded. Many colleges were established before significant urban development had taken place in an area.[23]

The size of the United States and its cultural diversity have also resulted in a profusion of college towns. The large land area and dispersed nature of settlement meant more colleges were needed to serve a scattered population. The architects of the U.S. system of government sought to recognize the size and diversity of the country by creating a federal-type democracy in which significant power is delegated to local governments. Today, each state controls its own higher education system, which has contributed to a multiplication of colleges. America's religious diversity has also been important. From the beginning, the country was populated by people belonging to a remarkable range of denominations. Each wanted its own college and, because the country was large, they wanted at least one in every state.

College founding, writes Donald Tewksbury, was integral to the "spiritual conquest of the continent." This was especially significant because 85 percent of colleges founded before the Civil War were established in conjunction with church groups.[24]

The most common explanation of why the United States has so many college towns has been the perception that college founders believed that a quiet, rural setting, away from the evils of city life, was the only proper environment for learning. Influential in spreading this idea was the fact that the first college founded in North America, Harvard College, was founded by graduates of Oxford and Cambridge universities, both unusual in Europe because they were residential universities located apart from big cities. Though Harvard's campus has since been subsumed by the Boston metropolitan area, it was founded a significant distance from Boston in seventeenth-century terms—eight miles by horse. Harvard was established in 1636 in Newtown, a struggling village, which was then renamed Cambridge (fig. 1.8). Although Harvard's founders left no record of why they chose Newtown, Samuel Eliot Morison has argued that they "brought with them from Oxford and the ancient Cambridge a definite vision of a university site" and Newtown more closely matched that image than any other site in the colony. Located beside a river like Oxford and Cambridge, the town occupied a "spacious plain" and "could be envisaged as the seat of a university that might vie with alma mater Cantabrigia in beauty, if not learning." Harvard's founders sought to create a college according to the Oxbridge model in which students would study, eat, sleep, and worship in a close community, an ideal that would have been more difficult to achieve in a larger city. Newtown, furthermore, had not been tainted by religious controversies that had divided Boston. The town's minister, in fact, later suggested that the main reason colonial leaders chose Newtown for the college was because it had been "kept spotles[s] from the contagions of the opinions." The desire to limit outside influences has been a justification for locating colleges in small towns and rural areas ever since.[25]

Harvard graduates and their disciples who inherited a belief in the superiority of a secluded setting went on to found numerous colleges and influenced other college founders. Alumni unhappy with Harvard's drift from Congregational orthodoxy in 1701 founded Yale University, which operated first in two small towns on the Connecticut coast before settling in New Haven. Yale converts to Presbyterianism in 1746 founded Princeton University in New Jersey. The college had no campus at first, holding classes in Elizabeth and Newark. But its trustees sought an isolated location for its permanent home, one that was "more sequestered from the various temptations attending a

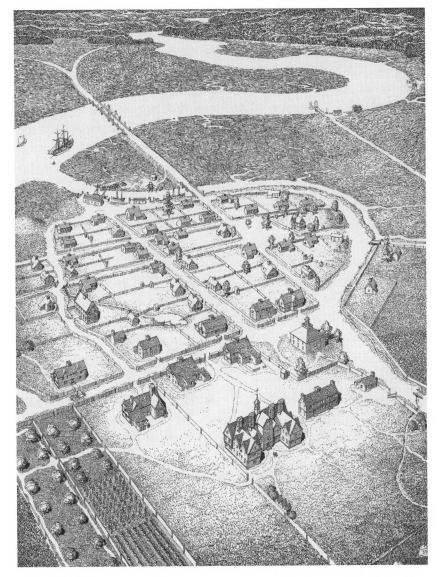

promiscuous converse with the world." In 1752, they chose Princeton over New Brunswick, a larger city that was an early transportation hub. Yale and Princeton each became the "mother" of colleges for their denominations, their graduates helping birth many colleges as settlement spread west. Yale graduates helped found at least sixteen colleges before the Civil War. A historian of the Presbyterian Church claimed Princeton alumni were instrumental in establishing twenty-five colleges.[26]

Harvard, Yale, and Princeton implanted a preference for residential education that sought to shape the total person, which became a hallmark of

American higher education. In doing so, they also encouraged the location of colleges in small towns because it was easier for faculty to control students in such places. Five of six permanent colleges founded by Presbyterians and nine of ten established by Congregational interests during the colonial era were founded in small towns or the countryside. Anti-urban sentiments also shaped the placement of state universities. State leaders in North Carolina, for example, stipulated that the University of North Carolina be founded at least five miles from any seat of government. Not everyone believed in the virtues of remoteness, however. Episcopalian college founders showed a preference for city locations, founding Columbia University in New York and the University of Pennsylvania in Philadelphia. Nearly all Catholic colleges were located in big cities. As the United States industrialized and urbanized, advocates for city colleges became more vocal, arguing that the country's future leaders would be better prepared if they were educated in population centers. "If the young man is to live in the city," asked Charles Francis Adams, Jr., "is it quite wise to bring him up in the country's sweet seclusion?" [27]

The influence of anti-urbanism on the locational decisions of college founders has been overstated, however. The booster mentality that characterized early town development in the United States was probably more important in explaining why so many colleges were founded outside big cities. As Daniel Boorstin has observed, even the smallest of villages imagined itself as the "Athens of the West" and many town leaders believed no community could be complete without a college. Local communities actively pursued colleges as a way to assure their future, offering land, money, and buildings to persuade colleges to locate in their town. Yale, for example, relocated to New Haven when that city constructed a building for the college and gave it a prime piece of real estate across from the town green. Trustees who decided where to locate Princeton may have been looking for a bucolic site far from the temptations of urban life, but they chose Princeton because local landowners offered trustees 1,000 pounds, ten acres of cleared land for a campus, and 200 acres of woodland for fuel. [28]

Most colleges established before the Civil War, David Potts has argued, were "essentially local enterprises" that owed their origins and early support to the town in which they were located. Religious groups provided sanction, he writes, but little else at first. Denominational influences were more limited than is often supposed because colleges had to appeal to a wide constituency to survive. The process of founding a college was often initiated locally by civic leaders who recognized the benefits a college could bring. A college could supply teachers to local schools. The college president might also serve as the town minister. Lectures and concerts on campus would enhance local cultural life. Students would require lodging and supplies, so would inject money into the economy. Civic leaders organized to pursue a college, then solicited support from a religious body or tried to persuade an existing college to relocate, just as a city today might recruit a corporation. Most of the costs to underwrite a college were raised locally. "The fundamental element in college-founding," Potts writes, "was the alliance forged between college promoters and a particular town or county."[29]

Competition between towns for colleges intensified following the Civil War, when state governments became the prime agents of college founding. Stanley Brunn has commented that "aside from the state capital, the state university was probably the second most important political prize a city or region could be awarded." States encouraged localities to bid for colleges, and they were customarily awarded to the town that offered the most lucrative package, regardless of whether it was the best site. The University of Missouri, for example, was placed in Columbia, far from the state's population centers, after local residents outbid citizens of six other counties by offering the state $82,381 in cash and $35,540 in land. Texas chose a site near Bryan as the location for the state's agricultural college, now Texas A&M University, when a merchant offered 2,250 acres for a campus, even though opponents said soils in the area were among the worst in the state. Back-room deals and unethical behavior were common in contests for colleges. Town leaders in Lawrence bribed legislators deciding where to locate the University of Kansas for $5 a vote. A group trying to persuade the Illinois legislature to locate the University of Illinois in Champaign was accused of providing $12,000 in free wine and food to legislators. Big cities may have been less likely to enter the bidding for colleges because they were more economically diverse and not so desperate to find ways to guarantee their survival. Roger Geiger has argued that bidding for colleges favored small or medium-sized towns over large cities because "boosterism could be most readily mobilized" in smaller communities.[30]

A 1923 study of the factors shaping the placement of state teachers colleges found that 70 percent of such colleges were established in municipalities that had donated sites or money. Harry Humphrey, author of the study, was critical of how the location of most teachers colleges had been determined. Many had been "offered to the highest bidder," he said, "quite irrespective of its merits as a suitable location." Political factors, he argued, were "probably the largest influence." In many states, the placement of schools closely followed the preference of the political party in power. In New York, for example, the legislature in 1889 approved seven new teachers schools, but a Democratic governor vetoed six, approving only the one that had been proposed by a member of his party. Often, a powerful individual unduly influenced the process. In Virginia, for example, a college was awarded to Harrisonburg, hometown of a state senator who was chairman of the finance committee. In many states, legislative acts authorizing the creation of colleges required that any municipality awarded a school must provide land, buildings, or money, and sometimes all three. In a few states, laws explicitly required colleges to be awarded to the city that offered the greatest inducements. Humphrey recommended that states implement more scientific procedures for locating colleges and eliminate the practice of accepting donations from towns. "Wisdom and forethought as to locations are very frequently sacrificed to the political expediency of the hour," Humphrey wrote. "Society and the state are the losers."[31]

Most states did become more systematic in how they decided where to locate colleges after World War II. Many earlier decisions had proven unwise because colleges were unevenly distributed or inconvenient for most people. Pennsylvania, for example, placed its largest state university in the center of the state, far from the state's two biggest cities. Pennsylvania State University, when it opened in 1859, was four miles from the nearest village and twenty-two miles from the nearest railroad station. State College, the town that grew up around the university, is less isolated today, but still fits the description of an early Penn State president who called it "equally inaccessible from all parts of the state." Partly in response to its remoteness, the university in the 1930s began creating satellite campuses around the state and now has twenty-four branch campuses.[32] Most other states have also implemented strategies to make their colleges more accessible. The largest state universities established since World War II are located in big cities, not college towns.

DIVERSITY AMID LIKENESS

Although college towns share many attributes, their individual personalities vary. The varying nature of college towns is partly a function of regional cultural differences and local circumstances, but most strongly reflects differences in the character of the schools located in them. Colleges differ in size, mission, the degrees and fields of study they offer, entrance requirements, tuition costs, and the extent to which they regulate the lives of undergraduates. Colleges attract students and faculty who reflect those differences and who, in turn, shape the character of the towns in which they are located. I will describe six types of college towns that can be differentiated according to school type and discuss regional differences in college towns that exist.[33]

College towns with flagship state universities. College towns like Iowa City and Chapel Hill are home to large, state-supported, research universities that are referred to as flagship state universities because they are the biggest universities in their states and receive the largest share of government higher education funding. They have significant graduate student populations, recruit faculty and students internationally, expect professors to be productive scholars, and are strongest in the liberal arts, especially the social sciences and humanities. They draw most of their students from major urban areas. College towns that are home to flagship state universities tend to be larger than other college towns, more cosmopolitan in their demographics and business mix, and liberal in their politics. Their populations are highly educated, intellectually ambitious, ethnically diverse, and earn high incomes. College towns with flagship institutions tend to stand out most conspicuously as cultural islands. Drive a few miles outside Athens, Georgia, with its well-known music scene, vegetarian restaurants, and funky student neighborhoods, and you quickly realize how much of anomaly Athens is in the Deep South. Bloomington stands out in much the same way in Indiana, Lawrence in Kansas, and Eugene in Oregon.

Because of the nature of their populations, college towns with flagship universities are more likely than other college towns to have bookstores that cater to non-mainstream tastes, lively arts scenes, ethnic restaurants, and movie theaters showing offbeat films (fig. 1.9). Studies have found that faculty in the social sciences and humanities are more liberal than those in the physical and applied sciences, so such college towns are more likely to support left-leaning candidates and causes. Voters in study towns that are home to flagship universities were more likely than those in other types of college towns to have voted for liberal Democrat George McGovern in the 1972 presidential election and Ralph Nader in 2000.[34] Residents of such towns also tend to be open-minded and suspicious of convention. They tend to be more tolerant of gays and less religious. Homosexuals are more common in flagship university towns like Bloomington and Eugene than in the country as a whole.[35] Just 36 percent of residents in study town counties with flagships on average belonged to organized religious groups in 2000.[36] Residents of flagship college towns also tend to be worldly and aware. They are more likely to read the *New York Times*. A greater percentage of households in Iowa City read the newspaper in 2000 than did in

FIGURE I.9.
*College towns
that are home
to flagship
universities are
more likely than
other university
communities
to have movie
theaters showing
foreign and
independent
films, such as
this theater in
Champaign,
Illinois.
Photograph by the
author, 1999.*

Boston or Philadelphia.[37] Because many students come from far away and so are unlikely to go home on weekends, such college towns tend to be more socially active seven days a week. All of these characteristics make college towns with flagship universities desirable places to live for educated, liberal, hip young people and older adults. But that allure combined with high incomes mean living costs can be expensive. The median home sales price in 2004 was $298,500 in Chapel Hill and $227,000 in Missoula.[38]

College towns with land-grant universities. Towns like College Station and Stillwater, Oklahoma, are home to schools that were founded as land-grant colleges to provide agricultural and mechanical education to rural and working-class populations. In numerous states, the land-grant and flagship university are one in the same. College towns that are home to such universities tend to be hybrids. But twenty-one states have separate land-grant and flagship universities. Although flagship and land-grant institutions have become increasingly alike as agricultural education has diminished in importance, most land-grants retain a strong rural orientation. They draw a large portion of their students from small towns and rural areas because of the long association between farmers and land-grants. At land-grant Kansas State University, for example, nearly two-thirds of in-state undergraduates in 2001 came from non-metropolitan counties. At the University of Kansas, in contrast, nearly 80 percent came from metro areas.[39] Reflecting the continued perceptual distinctions between land-grants and flagships, KSU is still known as "Silo Tech" and KU as "Snob Hill." The greater allegiance rural dwellers maintain for land-grants is also reflected in their support for sports teams. Whenever I drove country roads in Oklahoma, the sports schedules displayed in rural and small-town businesses were those of Oklahoma State University, the state's land-grant, even when I was near the University of Oklahoma campus.

Land-grant universities are distinct from flagships in other ways that influence the character of college towns. Land-grants emphasize applied fields, with large percentages of faculty and students in engineering and agriculture. At Kansas State, nearly one in five undergraduates in 2002 majored in engineering or technology fields. Ten percent majored in agriculture. At the University of Kansas, in comparison, just 6 percent of students majored in engineering (it has no programs in agriculture). More than half of KU students were in the College of Liberal Arts and Sciences, and three-quarters of them majored in the social sciences or humanities. Because of the characteristics of land-grants and their students, college towns that are home to such schools tend to be more conventional than flagship towns. They are less likely to possess vegetarian restaurants, skateboard shops, and other indicators of college town weirdness. Residents of study towns with land-grants vote more conservatively than the nation as a whole. Suggesting those differences, a resident of West Lafayette, Indiana, home to land-grant Purdue University, refers to it as the "East Germany of college towns."[40] At the same time, foreign-student enrollments are greatest in the applied sciences, so land-grant college towns have higher foreign-born populations than any other type. In Blacksburg, Virginia, and Pullman, Washington, one in ten residents in 2000 was born outside the United States.

College towns with regional state universities. Warrensburg, Missouri, and Statesboro, Georgia, are examples of college towns that are home to regional state universities that began as "normal" schools and evolved into teachers colleges. While most former teachers colleges have expanded their missions and many have become universities, teacher training remains the focus and graduate programs are limited in size and scope.[41] Research is comparatively unimportant and faculty have heavy teaching loads. Students are lower in quality.[42] When they were founded, many teachers colleges were designated to serve a particular district within a state and, because most states possess several such colleges, they draw the majority of their students from the immediate area. Many go home every weekend. They hang out with the same kids they did in high school. At Central Missouri State University, for example, one-third of undergraduates in 2001 were in the College of Education, and nearly 60 percent came from counties within fifty miles of the school's Warrensburg campus.[43] Because of these characteristics, towns with regional state universities lack the intellectual climate and cultural sophistication of other college towns. Cities with regional state universities have student-oriented bars (fig. 1.10) and neighborhoods full of student rentals, but the impact of a collegiate culture is less conspicuous, and they tend to be more representative of the regions in which they are located than other types of college towns. Liberals and gays feel out of place. Bookstores are rare. Student life is less varied. For all these reasons, towns with regional state universities tend to be muted in their college town flavor.

College towns with private colleges. College towns like Williamstown, Massachusetts, and Oberlin, Ohio, that are home to private liberal arts colleges are elite enclaves that have changed much less than other college towns over the last century. With their unhurried tempo and rarified atmosphere of an academic village, many project the air of the quintessential college town of literature and movies. Private colleges are smaller and more expensive than other types of schools, more selective in admissions, attract a larger percentage of students from out of state, and exert greater control over the lives of undergraduates. They have larger endowments and pay their faculty higher salaries. All these characteristics help explain why college towns with private colleges are different from other college towns and more extreme in many attributes.

Compared to other college towns, study towns with private non-religious colleges had the highest family incomes and home values, lowest unemployment rates, and greatest concentration of physicians and bookstores, and spent more on public schools. Residents of such towns were more likely to have been born in another state, speak a language other than English, walk to work, and be gay or lesbian. In Hanover, New Hampshire, for example, median family income in 2000 was nearly $100,000, average price of a single family home in 2005 was nearly a half million dollars, library circulation was three times the national average, and the town spent 40 percent more than the U.S. average per student on its schools. At many private colleges, students are also expected to live on campus until they graduate. Town and gown are less integrated as a result. At Williams Col-

FIGURE I.IO.
*Although the
college town flavor
of cities that are
home to regional
state universities
is muted, many
possess dense
concentrations of
student-oriented
bars, such as this
strip in Platteville,
Wisconsin.
Photograph by
Terry Williamson,
2006; used with
permission.*

lege in Williamstown, for example, 93 percent of students in 2003 lived in college-owned housing.[44] At most state universities, in contrast, two-thirds to three-quarters of students live off campus. Private colleges have also grown more slowly than state universities since World War II and place less emphasis on athletics. As a result, towns with private colleges lack the high-rise dormitories, massive sports complexes, dense concentrations of bars and cheap restaurants, and block-upon-block of student rentals typical of big university towns.

College towns with religious colleges. Church colleges attract students and faculty who are more religious and conservative, and less cosmopolitan, than are found in other types of schools, and they shape the college towns where they live. No college town is more unusual in this regard than Provo, Utah, home of Mormon-controlled Brigham Young University, where students are prohibited from drinking coffee and alcohol, and the university maintains strict dress and grooming codes.[45] Provo was the most religious urban area in the United States in 2000.[46] Bars and coffee houses are much less common in Provo than other college towns. Provo is the antithesis of Berkeley or Ann Arbor. Eighty-six percent of Provo voters supported George W. Bush in 2004. Other college towns with church schools exhibit similar, if less extreme, attributes. Residents of study towns containing church colleges were more likely than those in other college towns to be white and religious, and less likely to be gay or have voted for McGovern or Nader. Bookstores were less common than in any other type of college town.[47] In towns like Searcy, Arkansas, home of Harding University, the impact of a collegiate culture is comparatively inconspicuous and, because church colleges usually have small enrollments and most students live on campus, that impact is often invisible except in areas near the college.

College towns with historically black colleges. Towns such as Tuskegee, Alabama, and Grambling, Louisiana, that are home to historically black colleges stand in sharp contrast to other college towns because most black colleges are underfunded and their students are relatively poor. The visitor to any black campus or college town is struck by how destitute these places seem compared to other university communities. Black college towns, in fact, are exceptions to many of the characteristics that distinguish college communities. The four study towns that are home to black colleges are small, poor, ethnically homogenous, and less educated than other college towns. Economic conditions in black college towns reduce the market for businesses. Langston University in Oklahoma has 3,000 students, but the town of Langston in 2005 had only three retail businesses—a restaurant, liquor store, and dollar store—despite the fact that the nearest city of any size is twenty minutes away. Retail sales per capita in Tuskegee were one-fifth what they were in Missoula or Greencastle, Indiana. Tuskegee's downtown is deserted and full of vacant buildings. Novelist V. S. Naipaul visited the city on a trip through the South and was disturbed by the disparities between Tuskegee and the nearby college town of Auburn, home to Auburn University. Tuskegee, he observed, was "small and poor, black-poor, with nothing of the life and money of the white university town of Auburn, just twenty miles away."[48]

Regional differences between college towns do exist, but they are less pronounced than differences that can be attributed to college type.[49] College towns in the Northeast, for example, tend to be more prosperous, educated, cosmopolitan, and liberal than other college towns, characteristics that reflect the historic strength of private liberal arts colleges in the region. College towns in the South, typical of the region, have high black populations, few Asians or foreign-born residents, and fewer gays and lesbians than other college towns. Residents are more conservative and read less. College towns in the Midwest are more parochial than other college towns. They are overwhelmingly white and the least diverse in the geographic origins of their residents. College towns are less common in the West because the region was settled later, after the period when church competition stimulated a proliferation of colleges. The West has also experienced its greatest growth since World War II, when states became more systematic in choosing college locations. Many state universities in the West were placed in large urban areas. College towns in the West mirror regional attributes. They have high Asian, Hispanic, and foreign-born populations, but few blacks. They are the least religious and most liberal compared to college towns in other regions, and have the highest concentrations of homosexuals. Reflecting the westward movement of the population and immigration patterns, college towns in the West are also experiencing the greatest growth.

Since moving to New England, I have discovered that the region possesses a peculiar variety of college town I have encountered nowhere else. Four of six flagship universities in New England are located in small villages where the population is smaller than the enrollment of the college. Many students and professors live elsewhere and commute to campus. These villages are less self-contained than other college towns and have small downtowns. Durham, New Hampshire; Orono, Maine; Kingston, Rhode Island; and Storrs, Connecticut, share these attributes, but are different from college towns elsewhere that are home to universities comparable in size. I first noticed this in Durham, where I teach. When I interviewed for a job at the University of New Hampshire, I was shocked when I asked students in a class how many lived in Durham and nobody raised their hand. Few UNH employees live in Durham either.[50] Many Durham residents, moreover, have no connection to the university. Downtown Durham is tiny and contains few businesses that would appeal to anyone over age twenty-five. Compared to other college towns, Durham is all college and no town.

In this context, I was surprised to learn that for years UNH maintained an unwritten policy that faculty were expected to live in Durham and even developed a residential area for professors still called the Faculty Neighborhood. UNH abandoned this policy after World War II when enrollment exploded and demand for housing outstripped supply. In other college towns, university growth stimulated residential and commercial development, but that did not happen to a significant degree in Durham. Why not? And why are four of New England's flagship college towns so different from those elsewhere? Some have suggested that the small size of New England flagships is the reason, but that fact hasn't stifled normal college town development in places like Laramie, Wyoming. The best explanation offered to me came from Stephen Hornsby of the University of Maine, who suggested that because New England's flagships were founded 250 years after European settlement that the region's urban network was already fixed, which may have made it more difficult for emergent college towns to compete.[51] Durham, Orono, Kingston, and Storrs are all within thirty miles of larger cities. The two New England flagship towns that are more full-bodied college towns—Amherst, Massachusetts, and Burlington, Vermont—possessed colleges much earlier. Still, that explanation does not satisfactorily justify why other New England flagship towns have grown more slowly than the universities located in them and why they still attract little development.

The individual personalities of college towns are also shaped by their proximity to big cities and the urban character of the areas from which they draw students. College towns in states where most people live in large urban areas, such as Massachusetts and California, tend to be more sophisticated, cosmopolitan, and dynamic than those elsewhere. College towns in states where big cities are absent, such as Mississippi and North Dakota, tend to be more conservative, sedate, and homogenous. These differences help explain why Athens, Georgia, has developed a reputation as a cultural mecca, while college towns in other southern states have opposite images. The University of Georgia in Athens draws most of its students from Atlanta. College towns that are near big cities also tend to be comparatively cosmopolitan because the schools located in them attract students and faculty who desire access to big-city attractions. This helps explain why Athens and Ann Arbor are decidedly more hip than isolated State College or Fayetteville, Arkansas. As Michael Bérubé notes, in remote college towns like State College, hunters and devout Christians are as common as vegetarians or Noam Chomsky devotees.[52]

A SHORT HISTORY OF THE COLLEGE TOWN

The history of college towns in the United States can be divided into five periods, each of which parallels a definable era in the history of American higher education. Key developments in the history of education and the distinguishing features of college towns during each period are summarized here to establish a framework for understanding why the college town has developed its distinctive personality.

Setting the foundation (1636–1775): Beginning with the founding of Harvard College in Cambridge in 1636, the colonial era established the foundation for an American system of higher education. That included a preference for residential education, which encouraged the founding of colleges in small towns when settlement spread west. Although Cambridge is still perceived as a college town, only three of nine permanent colonial colleges were established in towns that are college towns today as conceived here—the College of William and Mary in Williamsburg, Virginia; Princeton University in Princeton, New Jersey; and Dartmouth College in Hanover, New Hampshire. It seems unlikely that any of these towns were true college towns during the colonial period, because enrollments were small and these early colleges were insular in character. None had enrollments greater than 175 students. They operated like boarding schools. Students were younger than they are today, their lives were tightly regulated, and they spent nearly all waking hours on campus. As a consequence, the influence of a collegiate culture on these incipient college towns was limited.[53]

Harvard's enrollment did not rise above 100 until more than seventy-five years after its founding, and in 1771 it still had only 124 students. Cambridge remained a farming village, but also began to attract wealthy residents who earned their incomes in Boston. William and Mary was established six years before Williamsburg was made capital of Virginia, but it was the town's status as capital of a vast colony that shaped its early personality. Perhaps in Hanover we see the best evidence of a college town beginning to take shape. Dartmouth was founded in a "wilderness," but four years later, in 1773, Hanover had 342 residents, plus 90 students. A visitor reported that "several tradesmen and taverners are settled round the college in good buildings." There were two taverns, one "good" and one "bad." Student drinking has posed problems for college towns since the birth of the university, and Hanover's difficulties in that regard began immediately. Dartmouth's first president tried to stop the sale of liquor to students, but the owner of the "bad" tavern refused to cooperate, and student drunkenness was common. The president's efforts to halt the sale of liquor "threw Hanover into a turmoil." In the "guerilla warfare" that followed, the tavern owner at one point broke down the college gates.[54] In such events, we see the beginnings of the college town as we know it.

Proliferation of colleges and college towns (1776–1861): More than two hundred colleges were founded in the United States between the American Revolution and the Civil War. College enrollments increased 2,500 percent from

1800 to 1860, and the percentage of young males who attended college, though still small, more than doubled. Most of the new colleges were affiliated with religious groups. The first state universities were also established during this period, a development that intensified after Congress began granting land to states to fund colleges. Twenty-one state colleges were in operation by the Civil War, though most did not gain significant public support or funding until later. Many operated like private colleges, forced to rely on tuition and donations, and differed little from denominational colleges. The greatest growth in colleges occurred west of the Appalachians, and by 1860 the Midwest enrolled more students than any other region. Antebellum colleges were conservative, most following a classical curriculum that included ancient languages and moral philosophy, and relied on the recitation method of teaching, though a few began to experiment. The first "normal" school, predecessor to the teachers college, was established in 1839, and the earliest agricultural college was chartered in 1853. Most colleges were single-sex institutions, which shaped the character of student culture. Gradually they began to attract more economically diverse students, not just the sons of the wealthy. Many were poor, worked their way through school, and could not afford college housing, so resided off campus, which stimulated greater interaction between town and gown.[55]

Nearly 40 percent of colleges founded during this period were established in cities that are still college towns today. Many of the best known college towns—including Amherst, Chapel Hill, and Ann Arbor—first acquired colleges during this time. Nevertheless, most cities with colleges would not have been considered college towns by contemporary standards before the Civil War. Enrollments remained small. Only one of the study town colleges, Oberlin, had an enrollment of greater than 1,000 in 1860 and just three study towns are known to have reached the 20 percent enrollment-to-population threshold by that date. Few cities relied on colleges for their economic survival. Farming was the lifeblood of Williamstown, Massachusetts. Athens, Georgia, was a cotton processing center and had more slaves than students. Student lives were still tightly regulated, so their influence on town life was minimal. Students at Davidson College, for example, were forbidden to leave campus without permission, make noise during study hours, drink, possess a weapon, or swear. As enrollments increased, however, colleges began to exert a greater impact. A bookstore was established in Williamstown in 1848 (fig. 1.11), which a historian called "the first major influence of Williams College on the business character of the town." The first social fraternities were founded and, in Hanover, began occupying rented rooms above stores on Main Street. Town-gown tension also

FIGURE I.II.
*The opening of
this bookstore in
Williamstown,
Massachusetts,
in 1848 was the
first evidence that
Williams College
was exerting
an influence on
the town. Used
with permission,
Williamstown
House of Local
History.*

increased, most often incited by student drinking. Student riots erupted in numerous university towns. In Ann Arbor, fights broke out when unruly students were thrown out of two restaurants and returned with a mob. One student was held for ransom.[56]

Diversification and democratization (1862–1945): While small colleges that had limited influence on urban life characterized the first 225 years of American higher education, college enrollment in the postbellum period grew faster than at any other time in history, new types of institutions emerged, and a collegiate culture began to strongly shape college towns. Hundreds of new colleges were founded. By 1940, there were more than 1,700 colleges in the United States, six times as many as existed prior to the Civil War. College enrollment grew 9,000 percent, stimulated by growth in the number of high schools, a rise in the proportion of women attending college, and the increasing importance of professional education. The percentage of young people who attended college quadrupled in the first three decades of the twentieth century. Much of the growth occurred at new types of colleges. Congress in 1862 enacted the Land-Grant College Act, which provided land to states to fund the establishment of agricultural and technical colleges. Black colleges were founded across the South after the

Civil War. Two-year normal schools were transformed into four-year teachers colleges. But the most important development of the era was the rise of the university and the growth of graduate education. By the end of the period, the multipurpose university that dominates contemporary higher education had taken shape. In the process, universities grew increasingly large and complex. The splintering of academic life helped fuel a growth in extracurricular activities, such as fraternities and intercollegiate athletics, which caused concern among educators and prompted Princeton President Woodrow Wilson to comment that "the side shows . . . have swallowed up the circus." Colleges still believed they had a responsibility to act in place of parents—in loco parentis. In an effort to tighten their rein, they built dormitories and student unions, hired deans of men and women to oversee non-academic aspects of student life, and implemented ever-more legalistic student regulations.[57] But as enrollment grew and more students were forced to live off campus, administrators began to lose control, and student life began to spill into college towns.

The college town emerged as an identifiable type of urban place in the years before World War II. Nearly 70 percent of colleges in contemporary college towns owe their origins to this period. Enrollment increases meant that students and faculty made up an increasing portion of town populations. Three-quarters of the study towns reached the 20 percent enrollment-to-population threshold during this time. The University of Kansas quadrupled in size in the two decades before 1910. "After having housed a university for forty years," write James Shortridge and Barbara Shortridge, "Lawrence became dominated by it." The average study town population nearly doubled between 1870 and 1940, the greatest growth of any period. The increasing influence of colleges over college towns became evident in a variety of ways. Rising student populations led the development of rooming houses and prompted families to construct an extra room they could rent to students. Developers discovered that faculty represented a lucrative market and began building homes marketed explicitly to professors. Faculty enclaves such as Cayuga Heights in Ithaca and Carle Park in Urbana were developed during this period. College town shopping districts also began to exhibit their distinctive flavor. Residential streets near the University of Illinois, for example, were converted to commercial use, and Champaign's Campustown shopping district came into being. The first student bars opened after prohibition was lifted in 1933. The earliest glimpses of college town liberalism also began to appear, particularly during the depression years of the 1930s. Berkeley police arrested eighteen war protestors in 1935.[58]

Explosive growth and dramatic change (1946–1973): No period transformed colleges and college towns more than the quarter century following World War II. Though the changes were greatest in the 1960s, the forces that stimulated the shocks of that decade began soon after the war, when veterans flooded campuses. Congress enacted the GI Bill of Rights, which guaranteed a free college education to veterans. Enrollments surged and demand for housing in college towns outstripped supply. Countless colleges imported surplus military barracks to provide emergency housing. Students lived in poultry barns, water towers, even tugboat deckhouses. The direct impact of veterans was short-lived—most graduated by the early 1950s—but their indirect effect was long-lasting. Many were the first in their families to attend college, and they influenced siblings and later their children to pursue a college education. The percentage of young people attending college tripled during the period. A college degree came to be required for most well-paying careers. Veterans were also older than other college students and had little tolerance for the traditional aspects of student culture. The "big dance" and rules that required freshmen to wear beanies disappeared. Regulations governing student behavior grew less restrictive. Drinking became widespread, and the number of student bars increased. "'Joe College' had gone off to war . . . [and] did not return," said one observer. Some have suggested that veterans paved the way for the student protest movements that rocked campuses two decades later. A graduate of Washington State University said "the 1940s were the beginning of the 1960s" because students in the immediate postwar years were the first to seriously question teachers, rules, and convention.[59]

The arrival on campuses of veterans and, subsequently, the baby boom generation stimulated a prolonged expansion in American higher education. Nationwide, college enrollment grew every year from 1951 to 1975, increasing fivefold in the process. Comparatively few new four-year colleges were founded, however, and most were established in major urban areas rather than college towns. Four-year colleges grew in size more than quantity. Many state universities were transformed into large, impersonal institutions with sprawling campuses, giant lecture classes, and big football stadiums. Enrollment at the University of Massachusetts, Amherst, for example, grew from 787 in 1943 to 24,128 thirty years later. Colleges were perpetual construction zones for three decades. Housing shortages prompted the federal government to provide loans to colleges to build dormitories, and many came to house a greater percentage of their students. Graduate programs grew faster than undergraduate enrollment, as colleges hurried to hire faculty to teach the hordes of students but also because universities expanded their research activities. World War II and the Soviet launch of the Sputnik satellite in 1957 stimulated increased government funding for research. Technology industries began to sprout near some campuses, and universities developed research parks to encourage commercial development of academic innovation. Land-grant colleges expanded their missions as agricultural education declined. By 1957, 60 percent of enrollments at land-grant Auburn University were in the liberal arts. Former teachers colleges were transformed into general purpose universities. The study town colleges that grew fastest during this period, in fact, were regional state universities like Georgia Southern University, whose enrollment increased tenfold from 1940 to 1970. Many college towns with such universities reached the 20 percent enrollment-to-population ratio during this time. Population of the study towns doubled between 1940 and 1970.[60] Colleges came to dominate college towns as never before.

The most critical changes occurred outside the classroom and increasingly off campus in college towns. Students demanded greater freedom, became politically active, and created student cultures that were the antithesis of the rah-rah campus life of an earlier age (fig. 1.12). They pushed for an end to in loco parentis regulations and other rules governing their lives. Differential regulations for female students were gradually eliminated and coed dorms created. Curfews, dress codes, and restrictions on visitation between men and women were abolished. Students gained the right to bring cars to campus and drink alcohol in dorms. Fraternity membership plummeted. Activist students also turned their attention off campus, participating in civil rights marches, campaigning for women's equality, and protesting the Vietnam War. Protestors blocked city streets in college towns and firebombed stores. After the voting age was lowered to eighteen in 1971, students and young faculty also began to reshape college town politics, electing progressive candidates and helping implement progressive policies. Marijuana was decriminalized in Ann Arbor and Eugene. A hippie was elected justice of the peace in Lawrence and performed gay marriages. More than any other cause, the anti-war movement inspired young people to reject conventional ways of life and stimulated the rise of a counterculture. Young people grew their hair, adopted blue jeans and T-shirts as the anti-establishment uniform, and showed increasing preference for drugs over alcohol. Many students moved off campus, and they transformed areas near universities into "cities of youth." Families and conventional businesses relocated. Single-family homes were converted to student rentals. Student ghettos and campus-adjacent business districts became "alternatives" to "straight society." Bookstores stocked *The Anarchist Cookbook*. Movie theaters screened

FIGURE I.I2. *Young people gather outside a popular student bar near the campus of the University of Kansas in Lawrence, 1970. Lawrence became known as "Baghdad on the Kaw" because of the vibrant countercultural scene that developed there.* Lawrence Journal-World *photograph; used with permission; University Archives, Spencer Research Library, University of Kansas.*

X-rated movies and foreign films. Young people started record stores and vegetarian restaurants. College towns began to attract young people who weren't students, prompting University of California President Clark Kerr to warn that a "deviant" subculture was emerging near campuses. Youth culture became so divorced from the rest of American society that during this period college towns developed into iconoclast islands.[61]

Retrenchment and reinvention (1974–present): The mood on college campuses changed abruptly after the U.S. government in 1973 discontinued the military draft and withdrew all remaining ground troops from Vietnam. No longer did young people stay in college to avoid military service. Enrollment growth slowed, then declined in 1976 for the first time in twenty-five years. Enrollment began inching up a few years later, but most growth occurred at commuter universities and two-year colleges in big cities. Average enrollment at study town colleges, which tripled from 1940 to 1970, grew only 21 percent over the next three decades. Student culture was transformed. No longer facing the prospect of war, but worried by rising oil prices and economic uncertainty, young people were more conservative, career-oriented, and hedonistic than their predecessors. Student life in college towns revolved around alcohol. Fraternity membership rebounded. Streakers replaced hippies, and giant fraternity beer bashes became more common than protests. The movie *Animal House,* released in 1978, symbolized the student culture of the era. The decline in activism prompted one student of the period to remark that going to college in the late 1970s was "like coming to town the day after the circus leaves."[62]

Falling enrollments and changing public attitudes about higher education posed financial challenges for institutions. Many Americans lost faith in colleges during the 1960s, perceiving student unrest to be a more serious problem even than the Vietnam War. That made it easier for politicians to cut higher education funding in the recessionary years that followed. The percentage of public university budgets that come from state allocations has steadily declined. Colleges have been forced to become more entrepreneurial. As U.S. government and private sector funding for academic research grew, universities began to look to research grants as one way to make up for budgetary shortfalls. After Congress in 1980 gave universities ownership of patents resulting from federal research grants, many universities created technology transfer offices in an effort to seek commercial applications for faculty innovation. Universities have also become ever more aggressive at marketing to attract students and donations. As part of that strategy, many have spent increasing amounts of money to construct high-profile buildings that have limited relation to an institution's academic mission—student centers, recreation complexes, arts facilities, sports arenas, and the like.[63]

College towns have continued to evolve, partly in response to changes in higher education, but also as a result of demographic, economic, and social shifts. Once the housing crisis stimulated by post–World War II enrollment growth passed, colleges reduced their spending on housing construction. Over time, a larger portion of students came to reside off campus, stimulating the growth of student housing districts and student-oriented shopping areas. Undergraduates also began arriving in college towns with more money, thanks to a decade-long economic expansion that began in 1991. Developers have built high-end rental housing aimed at affluent undergraduates. Expensive coffee shops and clothing boutiques have replaced the used record stores and head shops of an earlier period. The freedom of students, meanwhile, has created headaches for city and university officials. Student drunkenness has grown. Drinking shifted off campus to fraternity houses and rental housing after Congress in 1984 enacted legislation requiring states to raise the drinking age to twenty-one. At first, the number of bars declined, but they have grown in number in recent years as the average age of students has risen. Students are staying in school longer, and some are undoubtedly doing so to perpetuate a lifestyle of partying and sleeping till noon. Colleges have sought to regain some control over student lives by extending judicial codes to include off-campus behavior and notifying parents when minor students misbehave.[64] College town governments have also employed a range of tactics intended to restrain undergraduate behavior, including noise ordinances, tighter liquor law enforcement, and restrictions on the number of people who can live in rental houses.

Although enrollment growth has slowed at America's colleges and universities, college town populations have grown faster than other cities and the nation as a whole. In fact, sixteen college towns have grown large enough since 1994 to be designated metropolitan areas by the U.S. government—one quarter of all new metro areas in the country.[65] Several factors explain these seemingly contradictory trends. College graduates are now more likely to stay in college towns after they earn their degrees, because they enjoy the college town lifestyle but also since career opportunities in them have increased. College towns have also been discovered by lifestyle migrants and retirees, who are drawn by their youthful vigor, cultural opportunities, and small-town charm. High-tech businesses have begun to locate in college towns with elite universities to take advantage of campus-based research. Such developments have made college towns less dependent on colleges and more socioeconomically diverse. They have also stimulated other changes. Residential development has intensified and home prices have risen. College town shopping districts now appeal to professionals as well as students. As college towns have grown, they have become less isolated, acquiring interstate highway connections and commercial air service. An educated elite class, predominantly liberal in its politics, is now numerically dominant in many college towns and controls civic life to a greater degree than ever before. College towns have become more integrated into contemporary American life while retaining their inherent distinctiveness as urban places.

THE CAMPUS AS A PUBLIC SPACE

2

One of the most distinctive attributes of the American college town is the college campus, an island of green punctuated by monumental buildings, site of a diverse range of educational and social activities. In many ways, the campus is the focus of life in the college town, much as the central business district was in the pre-automobile city or the shopping mall is in suburbia. Campuses often function like self-contained cities, with residential areas, restaurants and bookstores, recreational facilities, concert halls, sports stadiums, park-like green spaces, and busy calendars of events. They are a hub of activities that serve not only students and staff, but the larger population of a town and region. As such, the campus is both an environment for learning and a public space.

The college campus is largely an American invention. The belief that colleges should be set in an open and verdant landscape, often according to formal plan, originated at Harvard College and has been followed almost without exception at every college and university founded since. In Europe, the earliest universities did not even possess their own buildings. Instruction took place in the homes of teachers or in rented facilities. Even after European universities began to acquire their own properties, they were often scattered throughout a city. The closest European kin to the American campus was found at Oxford and Cambridge universities. But the grounds of the Oxford colleges resembled monasteries, with buildings set close together around a courtyard. Cambridge, ever influential in the development of American higher education, broke from this model. Reflecting new ideas in urban planning that were emerging in Europe at the time, Cambridge's Gonville and Caius College, founded in 1557, was built around a courtyard that was open on one side.[1]

Where the typical European university was cloistered and inward-looking, the American college campus, in the words of the architectural historian Paul Venable Turner, has been "extroverted and expansive."[2] The tradition of placing buildings far apart in an open landscape had its origins in concerns that were both pragmatic and philosophical. The earliest buildings at Harvard were made of wood, not brick, unlike most European universities, so fire was an ever-present danger. Separating them reduced the risk that fires would spread. But Harvard's founders also believed in the Puritan ideal of community and felt the college should be an integral part of the town that surrounded it. The distinctly American notion that college should be a total experience, not limited to the classroom, has also shaped campus development. From the beginning, European universities housed only a small percentage of their students, and still today devote comparatively little attention to extracurricular activities.[3] University is seen as a place for teaching and study. Students are generally expected to house, feed, and entertain themselves. American colleges and universities, in contrast, spend millions of dollars to maintain their campuses and provide a range of activities and facilities for students, staff, and people with no direct connection to the university.

The campus of the University of Oklahoma in Norman is typical (fig. 2.1). Sprawling across 2,000 acres, it has long been recognized as an oasis in the region and is active day and night, year-round. Indicative of the varied uses of the American campus, the OU grounds include parks, formal gardens, a duck pond, an eighteen-hole golf course, a large hotel, and an airport. There are restaurants, bookstores, cappuccino bars, and convenience stores. Feature-length movies are shown regularly in the student union. Rotating exhibits are featured at campus art museums, and concerts are held several nights a week. A museum of natural history, annual medieval fair, and sporting events draw more than a million people to campus each year. Once students leave town for the summer, children of all ages invade the campus for cheerleading camps, debate competitions, and the like. The university spends more than $1 million annually to landscape its grounds. The popularity of the campus with the public also impacts nearby areas in Norman, encouraging commercial development on surrounding streets and making campus-adjacent residential areas among the most desirable places to live in town.

The variety of activities that take place on campuses makes clear that they serve many purposes that have little direct connection to the formal educational mission of a college or university. This is especially true of campuses located outside big cities, because metropolitan institutions often face greater security concerns and demand for their facilities that force them to be less welcoming. Campuses in smaller cities and towns, in contrast, tend to be open and inviting, and help to make the college town a distinctive type of urban place. This chapter will examine the multifaceted role of the

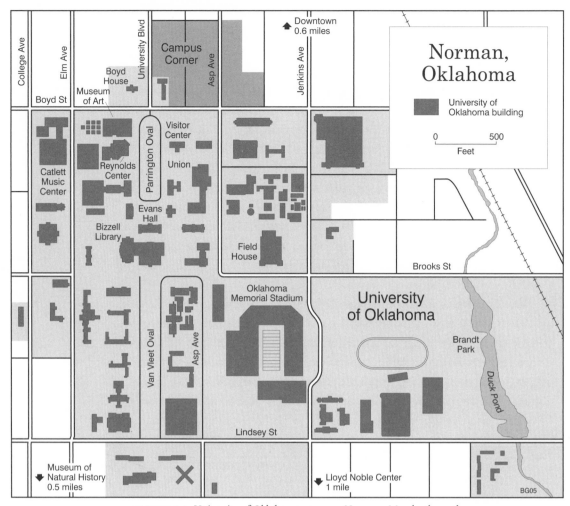

FIGURE 2.1. *University of Oklahoma campus, Norman. Map by the author.*

Oklahoma campus as a way to demonstrate the centrality of the campus to college town life.

THE CAMPUS AS A PARK

The belief that a college campus should be green and wooded has a deep heritage in Norman and other college towns. It says much about the value placed on campus green spaces that trees were planted on the University of Oklahoma grounds even before the university hired a single faculty member or began constructing its first building. The school's first president, moreover, is often remembered more for his tree-planting efforts than for building the university into a respected institution. Over the years, the

Oklahoma campus has become one of the most popular public spaces in the region, its shaded walks and colorful gardens an attraction to visitors, a magnet for Norman residents, and a favorite memory of alumni.

Norman was a college town almost from its inception, although it was not planned as such. It was one of four towns platted along the tracks of the Atchison, Topeka & Santa Fe Railroad in what is now Oklahoma after the U.S. government announced that a portion of Indian Territory not assigned to any tribe, the so-called Unassigned Lands, would be opened to homesteaders on April 22, 1889. Norman grew in a hurry after the opening and by nightfall of its first day was a tent city with a few hundred residents. In subsequent months, settlers began to transform the prairie town into a market center. Norman was named the county seat and became site of the first cotton gin in Oklahoma Territory. By the following year, it had two banks, two newspapers, three hotels, an opera house, a Methodist women's college, and, according to the first census of the city, 787 residents.[4]

The Oklahoma legislature selected Norman as site of the territorial university in December 1890, though the first classes were not held until two years later. Town residents donated a forty-acre parcel one-half mile southwest of the railroad depot for a campus and, in December 1891, the Board of Regents issued a request for proposals for the design of a university building. Two men who owned lots north of the campus each donated a narrow strip of land so a road could be laid out leading to the campus. The contract for construction of the building was issued in March 1892. That same month, residents held a meeting downtown to plan for the planting of trees on campus on Arbor Day. A rare March snowstorm prevented planting that day, but a member of the Board of Regents came to town that week anyway to coordinate the design of the grounds. Plans for the layout of the campus were adopted, a citizens committee was appointed to survey the land, and once the survey was completed, trees were to be planted. A separate committee oversaw planning for the street that was to connect the town and university. It was to be bordered on both sides with trees. Warm weather soon returned, and several hundred trees were planted on campus on the rescheduled Arbor Day in April. One week later, construction began on the first building.[5]

David Ross Boyd, first president of the University of Oklahoma, arrived in Norman in August 1892. A considerable legend has developed about Boyd's tree-planting efforts in Norman.[6] At times he is portrayed as a Johnny Appleseed of the Plains. Boyd himself perpetuated this notion in later recollections, though many of his statements do not hold up to scrutiny. Recalling the view from the railroad depot the day he arrived, he later said: "As far as I could see, looking to the southwest toward where the university now stands, there was one vast stretch of buffalo grass. Not a tree or shrub broke the interminable monotony of that hard-pan desert."[7] Newspaper accounts show such statements had little basis in fact. Numerous trees had been planted on campus and in town before Boyd's arrival, and many of those had survived and even thrived. Still, there can be no denying the importance of Boyd in transforming the campus and the infant town. Largely through his work, Norman became known throughout Oklahoma and elsewhere for its trees.

Born and raised in a part of Ohio his brother described as "heavily timbered country," Boyd came to Oklahoma from Arkansas City, Kansas, where, as school superintendent, he helped organize a citywide beautification program that anticipated his tree-planting activities in Norman.[8] With registration at the university scheduled to begin less than a month after his arrival, Boyd had little time for tree planting at first. But soon after school opened in September, his thoughts turned to the campus. "I was fresh from my tree planting experience in Arkansas City," he later wrote, "and could not visualize a treeless university seat." He convinced the Board of Regents to allocate $70 to purchase 1,000 trees and, in the spring of 1893, numerous elm and ash trees were planted on campus and along University Boulevard. That June, the *Transcript* observed that "university avenue is blossoming as the rose."[9]

About this time, Boyd purchased a lot just north of campus and began building a house. That fall, he planted thousands of trees on the university grounds and around his home site. Boyd apparently purchased the trees with his own money because of insufficient university funds. He cultivated shade and fruit trees around his home and laid out a five-acre nursery on the campus. There he began tending the seeds and seedlings that would supply the university for years to come. Boyd continued to plant trees every spring and fall, and the campus nursery grew progressively larger. In 1897, more than 2,000 trees were planted on campus, and the following spring 13,000 were set out. The *Transcript* estimated in 1898 that there were 40,000 small trees growing in the nursery.[10] Other schools in dry regions, such as the University of Kansas and the University of Wyoming, also had individuals who believed like Boyd that the planting of trees was essential to the making of a university.[11]

Photographs and descriptions of the campus illustrate how thoroughly it was transformed by the planting of trees. A photo of the university in 1893 shows a solitary two-story building standing in a grove of newly planted elms in an otherwise empty field (fig. 2.2). In a photo taken seven years

FIGURE 2.2. *First building at the University of Oklahoma in 1893 (top) and 1900, after trees planted had experienced significant growth. Used with permission, Western History Collections, University of Oklahoma.*

later, elm and maple trees have grown so tall that only the top of the building can be seen. Similarly, a photo of the president's home in 1895 shows a few leafless seedlings. In an image taken about 1898, the president's home is barely visible amid the flourishing elms. Though the university at first was essentially out in the country, a half mile from the settled part of Norman, the campus began to attract townspeople. "If you are seeking for some real downright enjoyment," wrote the *Transcript*, "take a walk or drive out university way."[12]

Nothing better exemplified the changes the campus underwent than the metamorphosis of University Boulevard. It was designed as a grand entranceway, with elms planted on both sides, a parkway lined with trees down the middle, and a wooden walk on one side. In early photos, the elms provide little shade and appear to be struggling against the hot Oklahoma sun. But as the years progressed, the trees grew taller and fuller, and what was originally a dusty horse path became a shady lane. By 1900, the trees planted on each side of the walkway met overhead, making "The Walk" a favorite spot for a stroll by students and townspeople. An Oklahoma City newspaper called the street "one of the most attractive in Oklahoma."[13]

It was under Boyd's leadership that one of the most revered public spaces on campus, the Parrington (or North) Oval, was first conceived. Like many other American colleges, Oklahoma was repeatedly beset by fires in its early years. In 1903, the university's only building burned to the ground. In the wake of the fire, Vernon Louis Parrington, a professor of English literature, created a plan for future development of the campus. Most of the plan was never implemented, but Parrington's proposal for the campus core formed the basis for the North Oval, later renamed in his honor. It called for University Boulevard to be extended into the campus, where it would encircle an oval-shaped open area. University Hall, then nearing completion, was to sit at the head of the oval, and future academic buildings were to encircle the open area.[14] Eventually, eight buildings were constructed there. The picturesque Parrington Oval, with its inviting lawn, stately trees, and old buildings, remains the symbolic center of the campus.

Parrington was also the first to suggest that Oklahoma adopt Collegiate Gothic as its preferred architectural style, arguing in a detailed proposal submitted to the Board of Regents in 1908 that "it is the single style in the whole history of architecture that bears the academic stamp."[15] Parrington made his recommendation after studying the campus plans of twenty-five universities. His conclusions reflected a growing popularity of Collegiate Gothic nationwide. The style, which first appeared at a few eastern colleges in the 1880s and spread coast to coast over the next quarter century, was inspired by the architecture of Oxford and Cambridge universities. As Peter Ferguson and his coauthors observed in their study of campus development at Wellesley College, Collegiate Gothic "made reference to a documented past and provided reassurance in a period of rapid social change."[16] Oklahoma's second president, A. Grant Evans, hired the architectural firm of Shepley, Rutan & Coolidge, which had designed buildings at Harvard, the University of Chicago, and Stanford University, to develop a long-range plan for the campus. The architects recommended the university adopt the Classic architectural style for its buildings. With Parrington's endorsement of Collegiate Gothic fresh in their minds, however, the Board of Regents asked the architects to provide two sets of drawings, one in Classic and one in Collegiate Gothic. Despite the architects' continued insistence that the Classic style best fit the university's needs, the Board of Regents chose Collegiate Gothic.[17]

The selection of Collegiate Gothic was a critical decision in the making of the campus because, as the architectural historian Carolyn Sorrels has observed, it is the Gothic buildings on campus that help to create "a sense of place that is uniquely the University of Oklahoma." Townspeople and others drawn to campus are attracted not just by the trees and green spaces, but by the distinctive structures that frame the campus landscape. More than a dozen buildings on campus were built in variations on Collegiate Gothic, distinguished by its rising turrets, pointed arches, divided windows, and ornate detailing (fig. 2.3). The most striking of these, including Evans Hall and Bizzell Library, were constructed of red brick in a style known locally as Cherokee Gothic, a phrase supposedly coined by the architect Frank Lloyd Wright when he visited the campus in the 1950s. Recognizing the symbolic importance of the early structures, the current president, David Boren, has reinstituted Collegiate Gothic as the preferred architectural style for the campus, albeit in a modernized form. Even the football stadium has been retrofitted with a Gothic façade.[18]

Over the years, the university expanded the scope of campus landscaping, reflecting a new formalism that took hold at American colleges and showed the influence of Beaux-Arts planning ideas popularized by the 1893 World's Columbian Exposition in Chicago. Oklahoma's third president, Stratton D. Brooks, was the first to hire a trained gardener to oversee the campus. Trees continued to be planted, but formal gardens were also developed. Ivy was grown on campus buildings. The topsoil on the Oval was replaced and scrubby lawns were resodded with Bermuda grass. Flowering shrubs, such as crape myrtle and hydrangea, were introduced. In the process, the university became a destination. An Oklahoma City newspaper in

FIGURE 2.3. *Bizzell Library, one of more than a dozen buildings constructed on the Oklahoma campus in the Collegiate Gothic style. Used with permission, Western History Collections, University of Oklahoma.*

1920 called the campus "the garden spot of the Southwest" and reported that "hundreds of Oklahoma City residents have formed the habit of driving to Norman Sunday afternoons" to visit the campus.[19]

The campus grew in size as the university's enrollment increased, encompassing 167 acres by 1926. As demand for classroom space escalated, Oklahoma's fourth president, William Bennett Bizzell, initiated a plan to develop a second oval directly south of the original. A new library was placed at the head of an axis that looks south and mirrors the North Oval, an approach that also showed a desire to apply Beaux-Arts principles to an existing campus. After World War II, eight classroom buildings were built around the South Oval (later renamed Van Vleet Oval), all in a modern style that marked a sharp break from Collegiate Gothic. In 1930s, the university acquired sixty acres that it developed first for athletic fields and a golf course, and later as Brandt Park, a popular destination for students and townspeople because of its duck pond.[20] The campus today includes 2,000 acres, but it is the central campus that was in place by 1940, measuring slightly more than 200 acres, that remains the focus of public activity.

While dust storms in western Oklahoma were drawing national media attention during the 1930s, numerous projects were initiated to beautify the campus and create new public spaces, many of them the result of federal government worker relief programs. In 1936, Works Progress Administration laborers planted grass and trees in what became Brandt Park. They built a stone fence around the park and erected a dam on a stream that ran through the site, creating the duck pond. WPA projects also enabled beautification of the South Oval, where workers created a sunken garden lined with flowers and enclosed by a stone wall, and laid out a series of gardens that run half the length of the oval. Now planted every spring with red petunias and each summer with chrysanthemums that bloom during football season, these gardens have become a signature feature of the campus. WPA workers also planted 300 evergreen trees, one hundred shade trees, and more than 6,000 hedge plants, and created the popular formal gardens between Bizzell Library and Adams Hall. Depression-era recovery projects paid for similar campus improvements at Oklahoma State University and the University of New Mexico.[21]

Landscaping on American college campuses has generally followed one of two design philosophies. Many colleges have sought to emulate the informal and naturalistic park designs of the landscape architect Frederick Law Olmsted, designer of New York's Central Park, who also created numerous campus plans, including ambitious proposals for the University of Massachusetts and the University of California, Berkeley, which were never implemented but influenced later designers. Other campuses are more formal in approach and European in their influences, full of geometric spaces, each flower, shrub, and tree deliberately placed. Drawing on the work of French landscape architect André Le Nôtre and the palace gardens at Versailles, such designs view the campus as a work of art where nature, in the words of Richard Dober, is to be "controlled and contained."[22] The Oklahoma campus was informal at first. Most of the trees planted by David Ross Boyd were placed without plan. After the university hired a gardener to oversee the grounds, however, the campus took on a more formal appearance it has retained to the present and in places suggests the Beaux-Arts principles of symmetry and axiality. Although some campus spaces, including most of the Parrington Oval and Brandt Park, are informal in arrangement, with trees and grass as the dominant landscape elements, most of the campus is highly controlled and manicured.

In time, the landscaping of the campus came to be institutionalized, as much a part of the administration of the university as maintaining its buildings and infrastructure, as important to its image as the faculty or football team. Caring for the extensive lawns and gardens took a small army of workers. The hot and dry Oklahoma climate meant much of the campus had to be watered artificially, particularly in summer. Flowers were planted every spring, replaced in summer, and moved to greenhouses before the first frost. Campus greenhouses produced about 30,000 plants a year. As the campus grew in size, the number of workers required to maintain the grounds increased. In 1947, the landscape department had fifteen workers. By 1971, the number had risen to fifty-two.[23] No one ever seemed to question whether campus beautification was the most appropriate use of university funds.

Interest in the campus has waxed and waned with university budgets and depending on who has been president. The post–World War II years were a period of tremendous growth for America's universities, as the flood of veterans and, later, the arrival of baby boomers caused enrollments to rise exponentially.[24] The need for new faculty and buildings meant aesthetics were often sacrificed and money was diverted from less critical programs, such as landscaping. The financial situation at American colleges deteriorated in the 1970s, as the nation plunged into recession and college enrollments leveled off. Student protests and changing campus mores undermined public confidence in higher education, which led to further budget cuts. The appearance of the campus suffered as a result. Trees that died were not replaced. Lawns dried up under the relentless Oklahoma sun. Hedges went untrimmed and gardens sprouted weeds. The newer areas of campus were bare and windswept. Landscaping staff was cut from fifty-two to thirty-seven.[25] "The campus looked absolutely terrible," remembered one resident.[26]

The campus once again became a focus of administrative attention with the arrival of Bill Banowsky as president in 1978. Banowsky had created Pepperdine University's dramatic campus overlooking the Pacific Ocean in Malibu, California, and, soon after his arrival in Norman, the administration announced plans to spend $80,000 on campus improvements. Additional landscaping staff was hired. New gardens were created and others that had languished were restored. Some 10,000 flowers were planted. The South Oval lawn was resodded and the sunken gardens renovated. Automatic sprinkler systems were installed. Old buildings were sandblasted. In justifying the improvements, a university vice president, said, "The campus ought to be a nice place for people to visit. It makes them more proud of the institution." In 1981, Banowsky initiated a tree-planting campaign he named the David Ross Boyd Tree Planting Program. Some 3,000 trees were planted, most of them on the newer, south campus.[27]

No president since Boyd has devoted more attention to campus beautification than the current president, a former U.S. senator and Oklahoma governor, David Boren. He initiated a figurative sculpture program that has produced campus statues of Oklahoma leaders such as Congressman Carl Albert and several larger-than-life artworks, including four by American Indian artist Allan Houser. One, an eleven-foot-tall bronze statue called *May We Have Peace,* which shows an Indian reaching toward the sky, was placed prominently at the entrance to the North Oval. Boren also created programs to enhance campus green spaces. He began the program to replant the South Oval flowers twice a year. He transformed the entrance to the North Oval, which now spells out the university name in chrysanthemums. As part of an ambitious fund raising program, he raised $3.2 million to endow six campus gardens, thus assuring future funds for their maintenance.[28] He has also supported efforts by the botany department to label trees on campus and turn it into an arboretum, something that has been done on many college campuses.[29] In 1996, Boren declared his intention to make the campus "in essence the 'Central Park' of the metropolitan area."[30]

A few critics have argued that Boren has placed aesthetics above academics in importance, but naysayers are in the minority. His morning walks around campus with his wife Molly have become legendary locally and on several occasions have inspired substantive changes to the campus, such as a program to fill forty-seven niches in campus buildings with statuettes of major figures in the school's history. Boren has sought to draw people to campus by installing benches, erecting fountains, restoring class memorials, and placing historical markers in front of most campus buildings. Many of the improvements have been funded by private donations. Donors, for example, can have a bench erected on campus in their name for $1,500. More than 250 benches have been installed under the program. Boren also created a Visitor Center, which offers tours of campus and publishes an eighteen-page *Historic Campus Guide*.[31]

Norman residents and university alumni attest to the value of the campus and its varied uses as a park (fig. 2.4). One man who grew up in Norman said the "first tree I ever climbed was on the OU campus."[32] Another remembered building a toy battleship out of orange crates when he was a boy and sailing it on the Brandt Park duck pond.[33] The campus has always had a strong allure for the parents of young children, who can learn to walk or ride a bike without the fear of cars. "My children grew up running around the campus," said one parent.[34] Part of the attraction of the campus for people who came to Norman to attend college was that it was different from that to which they were accustomed. Carol Burr, editor of Oklahoma's alumni magazine, came to OU as a student in 1959 from Blackwell, Oklahoma. "I was awestruck," she said. "This was something outside my realm. The buildings were big. It was beautiful. It just had that wonderful collegiate feel, like something I read about in books [or had] seen in movies."[35] I lived three blocks from campus with my wife and young son while I was in graduate school. Campus was where I pointed my son's stroller when we could not get him to sleep. We played football on the North Oval, hide-and-seek in the shrub-enclosed labyrinth east of Bizzell Library, and fed the ducks at Brandt Park. It was the campus more than anything else that made Norman a special place we never wanted to leave.

Compared to the campus, Norman's city parks are bare and unattractive, appealing chiefly for their athletic fields and playground equipment. Even on spring days, they sit empty for hours on end. But the campus is a popular spot in all seasons. In spring, visitors flock to the South Oval to see thousands of red petunias in bloom. On weekend days, campus walks are busy with bicyclists and rollerbladers. Couples stroll hand-in-hand across lush lawns. Children ride bikes with training wheels near the library. Students throw Frisbees on the North Oval, while others sunbathe nearby. Musicians

(opposite)
FIGURE 2.4. *Child plays on tree-lined walk behind Evans Hall, University of Oklahoma. Photograph by the author, 2001.*

practice in view of the Brandt Park duck pond, which draws scores of visitors on weekends. On football game days, alumni come early to walk the grounds. Even in winter, the campus is used. When it snows, for example, a hill in Brandt Park provides the best sledding in town. A longtime Norman resident who lives three blocks from campus says she and her husband use the campus "practically every day of our lives" and commented that living near the university is like living "next to the most beautiful park." [36]

Other campuses have served similar roles. The campus of the University of California in Berkeley has been called "one of the most precious public parks in an increasingly built-up urban area," while a longtime resident of Newark, Delaware, commented that without the University of Delaware campus, "there would be no park" in the city. A woman who grew up in State College, Pennsylvania, wrote that the Penn State University campus was "our special park and playground." Reflecting years later in the local newspaper, she said, "The college golf course was there for us to take walks on, the horticulture woods were fine for our picnics, the cow barns and sheep barns were our zoo, the dairy building our ice cream parlor. We had Easter Egg hunts in the campus woods. How possessive we children felt about everything, the tree-lined walks and the front wall on College Ave., so perfect to sit on. When our parents took us for Sunday walks through it, or when we played and rolled on the grass and down the hills on our own, the campus was always gloriously ours." [37]

The Oklahoma campus also serves as the site of a variety of recreational activities, formal and informal. The university swimming pool, which opens on Memorial Day after most students have gone home for the summer and closes on Labor Day shortly after they return, is essentially a public pool. City soccer leagues play their games on campus. An eighteen-hole campus golf course is the city's largest and most lavish, complete with pro shop, dining facilities, and corporate meeting rooms. Over the years, the university has sponsored a wide variety of athletic camps for children. Campus tennis courts, softball diamonds, and other facilities are utilized by town residents in the same way that public facilities are in non-college towns. Some have suggested that the campus relieves city governments in college towns like Norman of part of the responsibility to provide parks and recreational facilities for their residents. [38]

THE CAMPUS AS A SOCIAL AND CULTURAL CENTER

College campuses also serve as social and cultural centers for the college towns in which they are located. They host concerts, plays, and sporting events. They possess museums and sponsor other activities that draw people from the community. Campus ballrooms, banquet halls, and auditoriums provide venues for a diverse range of social events. In big cities, activities that occur on campuses are part of a larger social and cultural mix, but in college towns the campus is often the primary provider of culture, entertainment, and spaces for interaction. Campuses host events comparable in quality and quantity to those found in major metropolitan areas. As such, college towns like Norman often act as regional centers of culture, unusual in their amenities for cities of their size.

Probably the first activity to draw significant numbers of non-university people to the Oklahoma campus was college football. OU played its first football game in 1895. A field was laid out on the northwest corner of campus and, according to one report, "a large crowd watched the game."[39] Vernon Parrington, who had played football at Harvard in an era when the Ivy League was the center of the college football universe, became the school's first non-student football coach two years later. It was Parrington, according to a historian of OU football, who "lifted from obscurity" the football program. In the process, football began to attract attention off campus and throughout the region. A game on Thanksgiving 1897 drew 400 people. Enrollment at the university that year was 433, so it is likely that some in the crowd were non-students. Two years later, the start of a game had to be delayed to allow spectators from Oklahoma City and other nearby towns to reach campus.[40]

College football, geographers John Rooney and Richard Pillsbury have observed, was the "first intercollegiate sport to bloom as public entertainment" and has continued to grow in popularity. Oklahoma now regularly draws more than 80,000 people to its games. The university built its first football stadium, Boyd Field, in 1905. It had bleachers capable of seating 500 people. A year later new bleachers were added, and 1,100 people, twice the university's enrollment, attended a game. Under Bennie Owen, who coached the team from 1905 until 1926, Oklahoma became a nationally recognized football power and football became, in the words of Harold Keith, "the great driving force of college life in Norman." But it was equally popular among townspeople and other Oklahomans, who soon outnumbered students in the grandstand. Football weekends became the most important dates on local social calendars in Norman and other college towns. In Blacksburg, Virginia, for example, betrothed couples would consult the Virginia Tech football schedule before setting a wedding date.[41]

The first section of the present Oklahoma football stadium was built in 1925 and its construction was part of a nationwide trend. At least fifty-five colleges built football stadiums in the first decade after World War I, many of them motivated by increasing public demand for seats.[42] Oklahoma Memorial Stadium has been expanded several times since then because of the success of the Sooner football program. The most recent expansion came in 2003, when 8,000 seats were added, bringing capacity to 81,207. Only 11,000 of those who attend games are students and staff. The rest come from Norman and beyond. Other sports also draw significant numbers of spectators. In 1928, a 5,000-seat field house was built. That season, the basketball team went undefeated and "crowds packed the new Field House night after night." The men's and women's basketball teams now play at the 12,000-seat Lloyd Noble Center, built in 1975. Wrestling, baseball, and women's softball also draw large crowds. No other activities draw more people to campus at one time than do college sports. Louis Geiger argues in his history of the University of North Dakota that athletics "became a kind of public service as well as a major instrument in [a] University's relations with the public, of considerably more weight in some influential circles than the standards of instruction."[43]

The second critical early development that drew the public to campus was the building in 1918 of Holmberg Hall, whose 2,000-seat auditorium provided a venue for lectures, concerts, plays, and other events. Talks by scholars and other dignitaries, concerts by touring musicians, and live theater drew students and faculty, but also townspeople, in Norman as in other college towns.[44] A concert series in 1922, for example, brought to campus a soprano from the Metropolitan Opera and a French pianist. Events seemed to have been scheduled as much with faculty and the public in mind as students. In fact, students protested that the acts brought to campus were too "high brow" in nature. They walked out of performances by the opera singer and pianist, and the student council later approved a resolution calling for the university to present "more popular stuff."[45]

As the university and Norman, like colleges and college towns nationwide, grew following World War II, the number and variety of events on campus increased. A "Celebrity Series" in the 1940s brought to campus best-selling novelist Sinclair Lewis, tap dancer Paul Draper, and singer Burl Ives. Over the years, other campus buildings also hosted major events. The field house has been the site of concerts by Johnny Mathis and the Moody Blues. Rock bands such as the Rolling Stones and Van Halen have played at the football stadium, which in 1984 even hosted a monster truck rally. The Lloyd Noble Center has featured a wide range of touring performers, from Elvis Presley to ZZ Top. Such events have little relation to the educational mission of a university, but produce revenue.[46]

Campus concert halls and theaters provide local residents access to high-quality arts and entertainment events of the sort normally associated with big cities. The same Norman resident who climbed his first tree on the OU campus took his first date to a concert by the Prague Symphony at Holmberg Hall.[47] A woman who grew up in Norman said seeing a campus performance of *The Magic Flute* as a five-year-old "instilled a life-long love of musicals."[48] The College of Fine Arts sponsors a wide variety of educational programs for children, which expose Norman residents to the arts at a young age and, in some cases, have exerted a lasting influence. Both children of history professor David Levy, for example, grew up to pursue careers in music, an interest they first developed while attending youth programs on campus.[49] Residents of other college towns also expressed the view that campuses provide cultural opportunities that greatly enhance the quality of life and add value to real estate nearby.[50]

In recent years, universities nationwide have spent increasing amounts of money to build high-profile cultural facilities designed as much to impress the public as to further the educational mission of the university. Although Oklahoma's Holmberg Hall was celebrated upon its opening, it came to be viewed less favorably as it aged because its acoustics were inferior to those of more modern facilities. A 1965 campus plan called for the construction of a new concert hall that could seat 2,000 to 3,000 people. A lack of funds delayed construction for nearly two decades, but the first phase of Catlett Music Center was completed in 1986. Indicative of the larger public purpose that campus cultural facilities have come to acquire, OU President Frank Horton said upon the building's completion, "This new facility represents a cultural center not only for our campus but also for the community and the state."[51]

The concert hall at Catlett Music Center (fig. 2.5) was not completed until 1998 because private contributions to the university slowed when Oklahoma's oil boom went bust. It was not completed until after David Boren, ever conscious of the university's public image, became president. Boren initiated a fundraising campaign that paid for completion of the $14-million second phase of the project. The addition includes a 1,018-seat concert hall, a 125-seat recital facility, and an open hall that houses a pipe organ. The concert hall opened with much fanfare in 1998. Opera singer Marilyn Horne was the featured performer on opening night. The School of Music now sponsors three concert series that bring touring performers to campus, in addition to a busy schedule of faculty and student recitals. The Catlett Music Center hosts 300 to 350 concerts a year, and it is emblematic of the public purpose of campus music programs that the school has

FIGURE 2.5.
Concerts at Catlett
Music Center,
completed in
1998, draw large
numbers of visitors
to the Oklahoma
campus.
Photograph by the
author, 2000.

on staff a full-time "coordinator of audience development." Seventy percent of those who attend concerts in its three concert series have no university affiliation. Six years after Catlett Music Center was completed, Holmberg Hall was renovated and expanded, the acoustics in its concert hall modernized, and it was renamed the Donald W. Reynolds Performing Arts Center after its chief benefactor.[52]

While the sports stadiums and concerts halls are the sites of high-profile cultural and entertainment events, the Oklahoma Memorial Union emerged as an important social center for local residents on its completion in 1928. The Union when it opened had a cafeteria, ballroom, auditorium, pool hall, bowling alley, soda fountain, and seventeen rooms for overnight lodging. While the building was intended as a "meeting ground for undergraduates," it soon began to attract the public because it possessed facilities unavailable elsewhere. The ballroom was the site of weddings and high school proms. The cafeteria attracted hordes of football fans on game days. High school students hung out at the pool hall. Conferences, banquets, and short courses were held in its meeting rooms. During one four-month period in 1935, ninety-one banquets and luncheons were held there.[53]

The Union was expanded in 1951. The new facilities were designed even more with the public in mind. The cafeteria was doubled in size. On a single football game day, it served 10,000 people. A new restaurant, the Ming Room, was added. Decorated in a Chinese motif, it offered table service and four-course dinners, and was intended as anything but a student hangout. An Oklahoma City newspaper called it Norman's "favorite local restaurant." An auditorium was added on the main floor. It hosted speakers and motion pictures. The ballroom was enlarged and added to the concert facilities on campus, hosting touring performers such as Louis Armstrong. The renovated Union boasted a wider range of meeting facilities than any other site in Oklahoma.[54]

Hosting political rallies, Lions Club meetings, Chamber of Commerce breakfasts, and Dale Carnegie short courses, the Union served the same purpose that a convention center or major urban hotel does today. "You had meetings all day long everyday," said James "Tuffy" McCall, the Union's food director from 1960 to 1965. The Union was a favorite place for Norman residents to eat in an era when dining out was still a special occasion and restaurants were not ubiquitous as they are today. Its cafeteria was such a popular destination for residents after church that local churches staggered the times of their services to avoid overloading the Union at any one time. The cafeteria would add a third serving line and special items to its menu, such as hand-carved roast beef. "That was a big deal," said one lifelong Norman resident.[55]

The Union relinquished some of its role as a meeting place as Norman grew, restaurants were built, and Oklahoma City developed a convention center. Conferences and meetings still take place on campus, but most are held at the Center for Continuing Education on the south campus, far from the campus core. Student use of the Union decreased as classes shifted to new buildings on the South Oval and high-rise dormitories were built further south. Shortly after taking over as president, David Boren announced plans to renovate the Union in hopes of restoring it to the center of student life. To some degree, the changes have also brought the public back to the Union. The renovated ballroom, for example, has again become popular for banquets, dances, and weddings. In justifying the $11.5-million renovation, Boren acknowledged the building's public role. "In many ways," he said, "the Union is the real community center for both the University and the city of Norman."[56]

Like most major universities, Oklahoma also has several museums that attract visitors from off campus. Typically, such museums were begun to showcase student work or augment classroom activities but developed a more public mission over time. The Natural History Museum at the

University of Kansas, for example, has become the most visited tourist attraction in the state. A Museum of Art was founded on the Oklahoma campus in 1936. The roots of the museum go back to 1915, when Oscar Jacobson joined the faculty and was asked to build a School of Art. Jacobson organized the first exhibition of Oklahoma art on campus the next year and became known as a champion of American Indian art and mentor for a group of Indian artists known as the Kiowa Five. The museum's collections grew in size and stature when it acquired two major collections from the federal government that included works by American artists such as Georgia O'Keeffe and Edward Hopper. In 1971, the museum moved into the newly constructed Fred Jones Jr. Museum of Art.[57]

The art museum was not considered one of the campus's front-line attractions, however, until 2000, when it received a $50-million gift of French Impressionist art. The Weitzenhoffer Collection includes thirty-three works by Monet, Renoir, Van Gogh, and others. The museum rushed to put the works on display and, over the two months they were first exhibited, "broke every [attendance] record we have," according to the museum's director. Some 33,000 people came to see the collection in two months. The university then doubled the size of the museum to provide permanent exhibit space for the collection. Although the collection was taken off display after its initial exhibition, attendance remained high because of the attention the gift has brought. Before the donation, typical annual attendance was about 20,000. In 2001, even with the Weitzenhoffer Collection in storage, attendance was three times that. Officials estimate that 80 percent of the museum's visitors have no university connection.[58]

Driving south from Kansas on Interstate 35 or west from Tulsa on the Turner Turnpike, motorists pass the usual array of roadside billboards. One, however, stands out: It advertises the Sam Noble Oklahoma Museum of Natural History on the OU campus (fig. 2.6). The building of that museum and its popularity provide a final example of the role of the campus as a public space. The museum's roots are older than the state of Oklahoma. In 1899, the territorial legislature authorized the establishment of a museum on campus. The museum was given space in the university's first building, but the following year fire destroyed the building and the museum's collections. In 1904, the museum was reopened in the newly constructed Science Hall, but over the next four decades, as its collections grew larger and more diverse, it moved repeatedly and its materials came to be scattered across campus. Twice the Oklahoma legislature allocated funds for the building of a new museum, but both times the money was reallocated for other uses. It was not until 1947 that the museum obtained

FIGURE 2.6.
*Billboard along
Interstate 35
promoting the
Sam Noble
Oklahoma
Museum of
Natural History
on the University
of Oklahoma
campus.
Photograph by the
author, 2001.*

its own building, an old ROTC building far from the campus core. It was given storage space in two adjacent structures—a former horse stable and an ROTC "gun shed," which were little more than garages.[59]

By 1953, the Stovall Museum of Science and History, as it was named that year in honor of a former director, had collections worth $2 million, including 100,000 invertebrate specimens and 10,000 rocks and minerals. It had separate rooms devoted to zoology, ethnology, geology, Plains Indians, and Oklahoma history. The museum came to serve an important public role: Officials in 1956 estimated that 92 percent of its visitors came from off campus. But as its collection grew, the museum ran out of space. By 1961, it was able to display less than one-tenth of one percent of its archaeological, paleontological, and botanical specimens. That year, officials presented to the Board of Regents one more proposal to build a new museum. Like earlier proposals, it went nowhere. A parade of museum directors was stymied in their efforts to obtain funding for a new building. One called the museum's facilities "abysmal."[60]

Michael Mares, who came to the museum as a curator in 1981 and became director two years later, quickly discovered what his predecessors had learned, probably contributing to their departure—a museum whose chief clientele was the public was not a priority for the university in an era of declining budgets, increasing scholarly specialization, and a growing emphasis on externally funded research. Promised hires never happened. The museum's budget was cut. Mares claims one president "unilaterally gave the museum away to another city; I read about it as I opened the morning paper!"[61] Another suggested the museum auction some of its collections to raise funds for a new building. Unable to convince the university administration of the merits of the museum, Mares tried a different strategy. He sought to build public support and hoped through the public to pressure the state and university to build a new museum.

The museum created an outreach program, and, over the next two decades, traveling exhibits "reached almost every town in Oklahoma," according to Mares. He began giving backroom tours to influential individuals. In 1988, he used a grant to publish a 72-page book, *Heritage at Risk*, which sought to draw attention to the quality of the museum's collections and the poor conditions in which they were kept. The museum had only 4,000 square feet of exhibit space. Its collections were stored in attics and spare rooms all over campus. Roofs in its buildings leaked. It lacked fire protection and environmental controls necessary to preserve aging materials. The fire department told museum officials that the former horse stable that held the bulk of its collections were so hazardous that a fire would destroy them in seven minutes. In 1990, the museum unveiled plans for a new 300,000–square-foot building that would cost more than $30 million. Seeking to convey the value of the museum in terms Oklahomans could understand, Mares predicted the new museum would "draw more people annually than OU football."[62]

In response, Norman residents created two citizen groups to advocate for the building of the new museum. They went door to door collecting signatures to place on the election ballot a bond initiative to raise $5 million toward its construction. In 1991, Norman voters approved the bond referendum by a 2–1 margin. The bonds were contingent on the state providing $15 million and the university raising $15 million in private donations. The following year, Oklahoma voters approved a higher education bond issue that provided $15 million. Two years later, the Samuel Roberts Noble Foundation donated $10 million, the largest gift in university history. Several smaller donations provided the remaining funds. Construction of the new museum was assured when David Boren, shortly after becoming president, agreed to provide additional funds to boost the budget for the project to $42.5 million.[63]

The museum opened in 2000 and immediately became the most popular attraction on campus. Nearly 300,000 people visited during its first year. The location of the museum, the design of its facilities, and the nature of its exhibits reveal much about its purpose. The building is located on the extreme southwestern part of campus, far from the academic core, but convenient to major highways. The museum was also located in the less developed south part of campus so there would be ample space for parking. It has a gift shop and restaurant. It can be rented for weddings. In 2001, it staged an exhibition on OU football. The museum seems designed more with children in mind than any other group. A thirteen-foot-tall bronze mammoth is especially popular with kids. There are dinosaurs galore. Children can dig for fossils in the "Discovery Room" or attend summer camp at the museum. An estimated 50,000 school children visit the museum every year as part of school tours. Youngsters can even have birthday parties at the museum.[64]

THE CAMPUS AS SYMBOL

The question I have, for the most part, avoided until now is "why?" Why must a campus be pretty? Why must it be spacious and park-like? Why must its buildings be grand? Why must it have football games, concerts, and museums that seek to entertain and enlighten not only students and faculty, but the public? Why, indeed, should a college or university be more than a school? Why can't a campus merely be functional, with utilitarian buildings and parking lots out front, like a high school? Why, in short, should the campus be a public space, a meeting ground, and a cultural center for the college town? The reasons are many and varied.

At one level, the campus is a symbol of the college as a place apart, "separated from the great world," in the words of one early American college president. The French urban planner Le Corbusier, after visiting several U.S. campuses in the 1930s, observed that "the American university is a world in itself, a temporary paradise, a gracious stage of life." College is a place for learning, personal growth, and free intellectual inquiry, where pragmatism is viewed by many with hostility, and there are no time clocks (except in the cafeteria kitchen and the janitors' quarters). Never mind that college to most students today is vocational and a college degree a requirement for entrance into the upper echelon of our services-based economy. Colleges and universities are still built upon utopian beliefs about the value of a liberal education and the importance of scholarly self-discovery.[65]

College campuses reflect those attitudes. Campuses were designed to emulate nature and to be "beautiful and uplifting." Henry David Thoreau, writing about Williams College, set in the Berkshire Mountains of western Massachusetts, observed that "it would be no small advantage if every college were thus located at the base of a mountain." Princeton University's Woodrow Wilson argued that college required a "secluded" setting. Paul Venable Turner has observed that "the romantic notion of a college in nature, removed from the corrupting forces of the city, became an American ideal."[66] In this spirit, the campus is seen as a refuge, a contemplative space, a place where thinkers can think and dreamers can dream. That the average student is more likely to use the campus as a place to nap between classes and few faculty have time to sit under an oak tree in quiet introspection is no matter, because it is these older ideas that still shape campus planning. We expect a college campus to look different from other places.

The campus landscape has been central to the identity of the University of Oklahoma from the beginning. David Ross Boyd could not conceive of a treeless campus and went to great effort to make "a thousand trees grow where none had grown before." Exactly why Boyd felt it necessary to beautify the university grounds is not clear. Nearly all records from his first eleven years as president were lost in a fire. Late in his tenure as president, Boyd wrote to a territorial senator, "I find almost as much pleasure in the development of a tree as in enjoying it after it is grown."[67] Perhaps from that statement we can infer that Boyd gained the same sort of satisfaction from trees that a teacher derives from seeing a student develop. But, more than likely, he was simply following a template for campus design already well established. Even in more naturally wooded regions, tree planting has been integral to place making on college campuses, as Lisa Chase demonstrates in her study of campus development at Smith College and Kit Anderson shows in her essay about the University of Vermont campus green.[68]

Boyd and the presidents who followed him have also recognized the symbolism of the campus, especially its trees (fig. 2.7). Boyd regularly used tree metaphors in his speeches and is credited with the design of the university seal, which depicts a sower scattering seeds in an empty field against a horizon of bushy trees. President Bill Banowsky, who created the David Ross Boyd Tree Planting Program on campus in the 1980s, said, "The act of tree planting symbolizes the university's high academic mission, for both education and tree planting imply vision and deferred gratification. Operating an institution of higher learning is like planting an oak tree which gives shade to people who come along generations later." The meanings humans ascribe to trees are many and varied. Yi-Fu Tuan has observed that the preference of many people for a park-like landscape can be traced back

The Way To College

For catalogue and full particulars
Address,
DAVID R. BOYD, Norman, Okla.

FIGURE 2.7. *The symbolic importance of trees is demonstrated by the University of Oklahoma seal (above), designed by the school's first president, David Ross Boyd. The university made a tree-lined walk the focus of its advertising in 1904. Seal used with permission, University of Oklahoma; advertisement from* University Umpire, *June 1904.*

to the savannas of Africa, "the warm nurturing womb out of which the hominids were to emerge." Simon Schama argues that the human attachment to trees represents a desire "to find in nature a consolation for our own mortality."[69]

The campus and its buildings are also intended to influence. Campus trees and gardens are meant to instill in students an appreciation for beauty and refinement (fig. 2.8). Campus buildings, at least in the pre–World War II era, were designed to awe, but also to educate, for, as the campus planner Richard Dober has succinctly argued, "buildings teach, too." Oklahoma's Vernon Parrington, in trying to convince the Board of Regents to adopt Collegiate Gothic, wrote, "Personally I feel that we talk too much about a big university and too little about a beautiful university. If we hope to educate cultivated men and women we shall do well to surround them with those things which will inspire a wish for culture. If there is any spot that should be made homely and honest and beautiful, it is a school." The decision to establish Collegiate Gothic as the style for campus buildings, furthermore,

allowed young American universities like Oklahoma to establish instant tradition. As Woodrow Wilson noted in making a similar decision at Princeton, Gothic forms "added a thousand years" to the school's history.[70]

William Bennett Bizzell, Oklahoma's fifth president, came to Norman in 1925. Under his leadership, the university built nine buildings in the Collegiate Gothic style, including the library that bears his name. Bizzell also initiated the landscaping plan for the South Oval that still defines that space today. Demonstrating the larger purpose of campus green spaces and buildings, Bizzell said in a speech in 1932, "This campus is one of the beauty spots in Oklahoma. Every tree, shrub, and flower has been planted with loving care in a way to promote a sense of the beautiful. The buildings and equipment . . . have been designed to create a love for truth and appreciation for goodness." That David Boren has resurrected Collegiate Gothic as the campus architectural style and has planted trees, fountains, and statues all over the campus testifies to the resiliency of such ideas. Even at the dawn of the twenty-first century, the college campus is seen to provide, in the words of David Littlejohn, "an image of humaneness and order to impressionable young people."[71]

University archives are filled with high-minded pronouncements about the value of campus landscapes, but, truth be told, the campus also has very practical purposes. Every university president knows that a handsome campus, lively cultural programs, and top-ranked athletic teams can be as important as a first-rate faculty for drawing students, pleasing alumni, and attracting donations. Ernest Boyer, longtime president of the Carnegie Foundation for the Advancement of Teaching, reported in 1987 that 57 percent of college students surveyed by the Carnegie Foundation visited at least one campus before deciding where to enroll, and he argued that "the appearance of the campus is, by far, the most influential characteristic during campus visits." He observed that "when it comes to recruiting students, the director of buildings and grounds may be more important than the academic dean." The language used by universities in planning campus landscapes echoes this view. A recent campus master plan for the University of Massachusetts, Amherst, says, "The vision is to create a campus that is a five-star attraction . . . a garden in the valley that attracts the top students and best faculty."[72]

The use of the campus in student and faculty recruitment is not new. In defending his ambitious plans for the University of Virginia campus and fearing his designs would not be completed, Thomas Jefferson wrote, "Had we built a barn for a college, and log huts for accommodations, should we ever have had the assurance to propose to [a] European professor . . . to come to it? To stop where we are is to abandon our high hopes, and become suitors to Yale and Harvard for their secondary characters." Although the original architects of the University of Oklahoma were never so lofty in their aspirations, college catalogs included detailed description of the grounds from the school's earliest years. "The campus and approaching boulevard have been set out in trees," said one, "which have already attained a size to render the spot one of the most pleasing in Oklahoma." In 1904, the university began running advertisements that featured a photo of the tree-lined walk that was one of the most popular spaces on campus under the headline "The Way to College." No other details were provided.[73]

Techniques for marketing colleges to prospective students have become ever more sophisticated. Like most universities, Oklahoma now publishes an annual "viewbook" it sends to high school students. These glossy, full-color brochures are light on text and heavy on image. Increasingly, college is marketed in the same way as any other high-priced product, using graphic devices designed to make "buyers," in this case prospective students, want to be part of what they see. Campus buildings and greenery are central to creating an image of the university. One recent Oklahoma viewbook, for example, features fifty-one color photographs on eight pages. Only five show students engaged in activities that are clearly educational in nature. Nine focus on campus trees, gardens, and buildings. Seventeen show students socializing. Six show sporting events. The overall impression is that college is fun and exciting. As students turn increasingly to the World Wide Web to acquire information about colleges, universities have created websites that depict college life in much the same way. Invariably, the photograph on a university's main web page shows a bucolic campus scene or students having fun. The Oklahoma site for prospective students includes a "Flash" preview that features constantly changing images of six campus scenes. No students or classrooms are anywhere in sight.[74]

Attractive and lively campuses create memories and build loyalty among students, who become alumni, who, if successful, may become college donors. The campus and its amenities are central to the "selling" of the university to alumni and a larger public. Campus scenes are regularly featured in Oklahoma's alumni magazine. The university now publishes a calendar featuring full-color photos of the campus. David Boren has sought not only to beautify the campus, but to endow it with landmark status by erecting statues and placing historical markers in front of campus buildings. The OU Visitor Center sells Christmas ornaments, pen and ink drawings, and notecards featuring artistic renderings of the campus. Not surprisingly, all the buildings featured are Collegiate Gothic structures built before World War II. The drab postwar structures where present students spend most of their time are conspicuously absent from the image the university seeks to project. As Todd Gitlin has observed, the best view of such modernist campus buildings is often from the inside looking out, where you cannot actually see them, so they rarely are the view a university promotes.[75]

Campus cultural facilities also serve an important public relations purpose. In trying to persuade the university to build a new museum of natural history, an official in 1944 argued that such a museum could help dispel "the prevalent idea that the university is run by a group of snobs and atheists." Both the museum of natural history and the Weitzenhoffer Collection at the Fred Jones Jr. Museum of Art have been featured in public service announcements for the university aired on national television during Oklahoma football games. An Oklahoma City investment banker who worked for ten years in the university's development office emphasized the importance of campus amenities to fundraising. "If you don't have nice facilities," he said, "it's very difficult to attract gifts and financial support from people who are used to nice surroundings."[76]

In the competition for students and money, the campus and its amenities are also sometimes used as surrogates for a university's academic programs. It is much easier to promote the beauty of the campus than to make the public appreciate the value of a professor's specialized research. Concerts and museums have an infinitely wider appeal than what goes on in the classroom. David Boren's efforts at image building are clearly working if the attitudes of undergraduates are any indication. I asked 200 undergraduates in a lecture course to explore the campus and write about their reactions. Almost all were laudatory in their comments, and few questioned whether beautification was an appropriate use of university funds. A remarkable number made a connection between the look of the campus and what they perceived as the academic prestige of the university. Their attitudes were well represented in the words of an undergraduate writing in a local newspaper. "A little mist on a grey fall day transforms the old Bizzell Library into one of the most beautiful places in the world," he said. "Why would anyone ever want to go to Harvard when we have those kinds of structures in Norman?"[77]

Finally, the Oklahoma campus and its public attractions serve as a potent symbol for the college town of Norman and the state. The success of OU football has arguably drawn more attention to the state than any other activity. Oklahoma historian William Savage has argued that the university first sought to build a top-ranked football team as a way to counter the negative image of the state created by John Steinbeck's 1939 novel, *The Grapes of Wrath*. Campus museums, concerts, plays and other events have a similar purpose, even if their profiles are not as high. Max Weitzenhoffer, a Broadway theater producer whose parents bequeathed the Weitzenhoffer Collection to the university, said, "It was their way of showing the nation that Oklahoma has an interest in art and culture."[78]

Norman has long promoted the university's facilities as its own, and campus attractions help foster positive town-gown relations. In the years before Oklahoma became a state, several cities challenged Norman's status as seat of the territorial university. In the face of such threats Norman civic leaders viewed the beauty of the campus as its greatest asset and best defense. "The trees growing about the university," wrote the town's newspaper, "would be the strongest argument against its removal." Campus amenities have figured prominently in booklets and brochures published to promote the city ever since. The cover and first six pages of a 2003 Norman visitors guide, for example, are devoted to campus attractions. When, within the span of a year, the new museum of natural history opened, the art museum was bequeathed the Weitzenhoffer Collection, and OU sports teams won two national championships, a local newspaper columnist remarked that Norman was the "envy of the state" and said the convergence of events "made for chest-thumping pride throughout the city."[79]

The important public role that the University of Oklahoma campus plays in Norman is representative of the larger purpose campuses possess in college towns. The campus is a park. It is a cultural center and meeting place. It is a symbol for the college, the town, and, in the case of public institutions, the state. College officials use the campus and its attractions to promote the school, recruit students, and build goodwill with alumni, residents, benefactors, and government officials. The characteristics of campuses at U.S. colleges and universities, particularly those located in small cities and towns, stand in sharp contrast to the role physical facilities play at higher education institutions in other countries. The campus is very much a public space, and its status as such is one of the defining traits of the American college town.

FRATERNITY ROW,
THE STUDENT GHETTO,
AND THE FACULTY
ENCLAVE

One college town. Three neighborhoods. Three very different images. South of the Cornell University campus in Ithaca, New York, dilapidated old frame houses split into student apartments hug the street. Couches sit on porches, which are permanently affixed with "Now Renting" signs. Empty beer bottles line railings. A few newer high-rise apartments, equipped with game rooms, high-speed Internet access, and other amenities desired by today's college students, tower above sidewalks crowded with young people day and night. West of campus, the landscape is more spacious and the buildings more pretentious. Gothic, Tudor, and Italianate mansions occupy large lots. Greek letters mark their entrances. Spires rise toward the sky. The windows of one have been covered with paper to hide secret rituals inside. Red plastic cups from a fraternity keg party litter the lawn of another. North of campus, single-family homes predominate. Stone pillars mark the entrance to the separately incorporated village of Cayuga Heights. Architect-designed houses, dignified and understated, sit far back in landscaped yards, shrouded in foliage. Few people are visible, and the quiet is broken only by the occasional sound of lawn machinery. Rolled-up copies of the *New York Times* lie on flagstone walkways.

The college town residential mosaic is one of its most striking features and reflects the unusual demographics and social differences of college communities. College towns are highly segregated residentially. Faculty and other long-term residents seldom want to live near undergraduates because of the different lifestyles they often lead. For students, the college years represent their first chance to live relatively free from adult interference, so they, too, prefer to live among their own. Dissimilarities within the student body, particularly between members of Greek-letter societies and so-called independents, further fragment the residential landscape. Although faculty are less concentrated residentially than students, they have shown a tendency to cluster in architecturally distinctive neighborhoods near campus. These preferences have led to the emergence in college towns of three distinct types of residential districts—the Greek-housing area sometimes called fraternity row, the student rental district often known as the student ghetto, and the faculty enclave. In order to establish why such districts developed and how they have changed, I will examine the origin and evolution of examples of each in Ithaca.

Ithaca (fig. 3.1) is home to two four-year colleges, Cornell University and Ithaca College. I will focus on residential districts near Cornell because its impact has been more pronounced than its younger and smaller neighbor. Cornell was founded in 1868, its campus laid out atop a plateau that overlooks the city and Cayuga Lake, one of the Finger Lakes. Growing quickly to become one of the largest and most prestigious private universities in the United States, Cornell has come to exert a profound impact citywide. Ithaca College's influence is more localized and less conspicuous. Founded in 1892 as the Ithaca Conservatory of Music, it did not offer bachelor's degrees until 1926. For most of its history, it lacked a cohesive campus, its facilities scattered throughout downtown Ithaca. It did not develop its current campus on what is known locally as South Hill until the 1960s. Like other private, undergraduate-oriented, liberal arts colleges, Ithaca College houses the majority of its students on campus and has no off-campus fraternities, which limits its residential impact. Ithaca College faculty, moreover, seem as likely to live near Cornell as Ithaca College, drawn by the greater campus amenities of a research university.[1]

Like other college towns, Ithaca has come to be more strongly influenced by its colleges over the years. When Cornell was founded, Ithaca was a growing manufacturing town. By the turn of the twentieth century, its factories made boats, glass, pianos, guns, clocks, paper, and typewriters. In the early 1900s, factories were developed that made adding machines, bicycle chains, airplanes, and later automobile parts.[2] After World War II, however, college enrollments grew rapidly and manufacturing's share of employment declined, with most of the city's old-line industries eventually closing.[3] Students and faculty came to make up an increasing share of Ithaca's population. Today, education is overwhelmingly Ithaca's biggest "industry." Cornell and Ithaca College together employ more than 11,500 people in the city, and nearly half the labor force in 2000 worked in education, compared to 3.5 percent in manufacturing. Since 1960, combined enrollment at Cornell and Ithaca College has doubled to nearly 26,000,

(opposite)

FIGURE 3.1. *Ithaca and vicinity, showing the location of the West Campus Greek housing district, the Collegetown student rental housing area, and the faculty enclaves of Cayuga Heights and Bryant Park. Map by the author.*

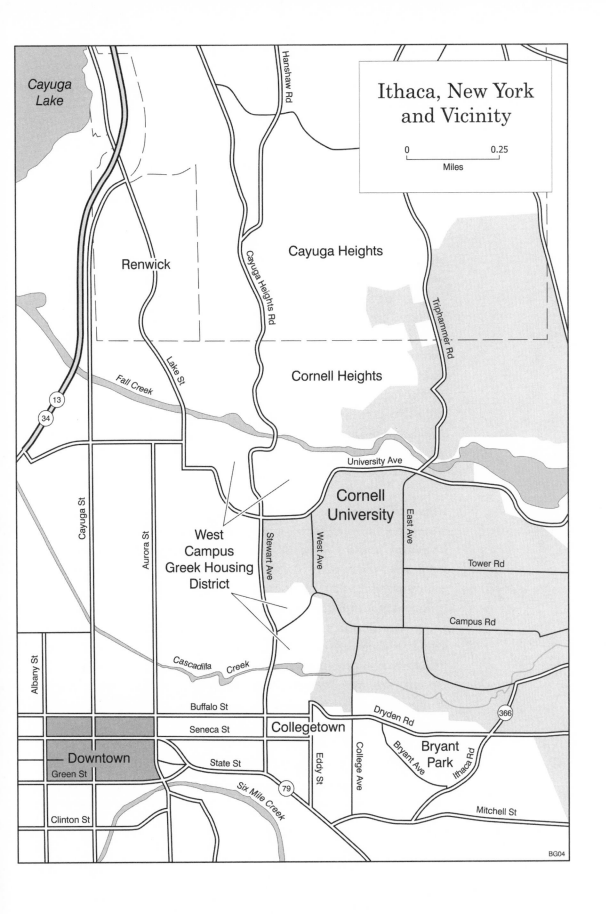

Cayuga
Lake

Ithaca, New York
and Vicinity

0   0.25
Miles

Hanshaw Rd

Cayuga Heights

Renwick

Cayuga Heights Rd

Cornell Heights

Triphammer Rd

Lake St

Fall Creek

13
34

University Ave

Cayuga St

Cornell
University

East Ave

Tower Rd

Aurora St

West
Campus
Greek Housing
District

Stewart Ave

West Ave

Campus Rd

Cascadilla   Creek

Albany St

Buffalo St

Seneca St

Collegetown

Dryden Rd

366

Eddy St

College Ave

Bryant Ave

Bryant
Park

Ithaca Rd

Downtown

State St

Green St

79

Six Mile Creek

Mitchell St

Clinton St

BG04

while the city's population has remained about the same. In 2000, 55 percent of the city's residents were college students. As Ithaca's colleges have grown, the housing needs of students and faculty have increasingly shaped the city's urban landscape.[4]

FRATERNITY ROW

At non-commuter colleges, undergraduates are normally required or strongly encouraged to live in university-owned residence halls on campus for at least their freshman year. After freshman year, students begin to sort themselves out according to their interests and lifestyles. Away from home and perhaps lost in a university many times larger than their high school, some choose to postpone independence and formalize their social lives by joining a fraternity or sorority. In most college towns, fraternity and sorority houses are concentrated in one or two areas. Often, several line a single street, which is typically called fraternity row. Examples include Webster Avenue in Hanover, New Hampshire; Dubuque Street in Iowa City; and Colorado Street in Pullman, Washington.

With their classical or Greek-revival mansions and the unusual traditions and active social lives of the people who live in them, the fraternity district is a landscape unique to college communities. Raucous parties pour from fraternity houses on weekend nights. Pledge week rituals, formal dances, and the building of homecoming floats are local spectacles. Fraternity houses can make bad neighbors, which helps explain why they are often concentrated and located apart from other residential areas. Contrary to popular perception, fraternity houses at most universities are privately owned and located off campus.[5] While most Greek organizations voluntarily submit to regulation by universities, college officials do not exert the same degree of control over them that they do over on-campus dormitories.

Although membership in Greek letter societies is declining and some elite private colleges, such as Williams College in Williamstown, Massachusetts, have abolished their Greek systems altogether, fraternities and sororities remain an integral part of student culture in most college towns. Greek life tends to be most important at big state universities and private colleges. At large state universities, typically one-quarter to one-half of undergraduates pledge. At some private colleges, such as DePauw University in Greencastle, Indiana, three-quarters of undergraduates join.[6] While fraternities and sororities have long been criticized for their elitist (and sometimes bigoted) selection processes, dangerous hazing rituals, cliquish behavior, excessive drinking, and anti-intellectual attitudes—indeed, it is hard to find non-critical accounts of Greek life—they can serve a useful purpose for students who require greater social interaction.[7] "For a certain kind of boy at a certain tender age, fraternity is simply a given," wrote the novelist Richard Ford, who pledged Sigma Chi at Michigan State University. "A go-along guy, who wants friends. A guy with standards he can't understand. For this kind of boy conformity is a godsend. And I was that kind of boy."[8]

Conversations with fraternity members at Cornell reduced my own innate hostility toward Greeks, fostered as an undergraduate and later as a faculty member living near several Oklahoma fraternity houses. The interests and motivations of fraternity members are different from mine, but they seem no less academically oriented than most undergraduates. They are simply people who, Helen Lefkowitz Horowitz has noted, "need a ready-made group life with a clear identity" and are willing to sacrifice personal freedom, privacy, and time to get that. Simon Bronner has observed that Greek organizations act as surrogate families. When asked why he preferred to live in a fraternity rather than an apartment, one Cornell Greek member replied, "Because I don't want to live with just two guys. I want to live with thirty or forty. Anytime I'm home, there's somebody around to talk to." Others spoke of a desire to perpetuate the sort of camaraderie they first experienced in the locker room. "All my best friends in high school were the kids on my sports teams," said one. "Now they are all the guys that I live with."[9]

Ithaca does not possess a single fraternity district or fraternity row like some college towns. Most fraternities and sororities are located on the west side of the Cornell campus or in one of two suburban areas north of campus, Cornell Heights and Cayuga Heights. The Greek houses north of campus are relatively spread out and interspersed with single-family homes. I will focus on the West Campus Greek housing district, since fraternity houses are more concentrated and conspicuous there than elsewhere, and because the area has been home to fraternities for the longest period. The West Campus area is home to twenty-three fraternity houses and one sorority house (fig. 3.2). Most of the houses were built in the late 1800s or early 1900s. Many have been occupied by the same organization for a century or more. The majority of Cornell's most elite fraternities are located in this area. Most of Cornell's sororities are north of campus, and thus outside the focus area, because they developed later.

Fraternities were an outgrowth of the campus literary societies that emerged on college campuses in the late 1700s in response to the conservative nature of higher education at the time. Most colleges were religiously oriented and had classical curricula that emphasized memorization and

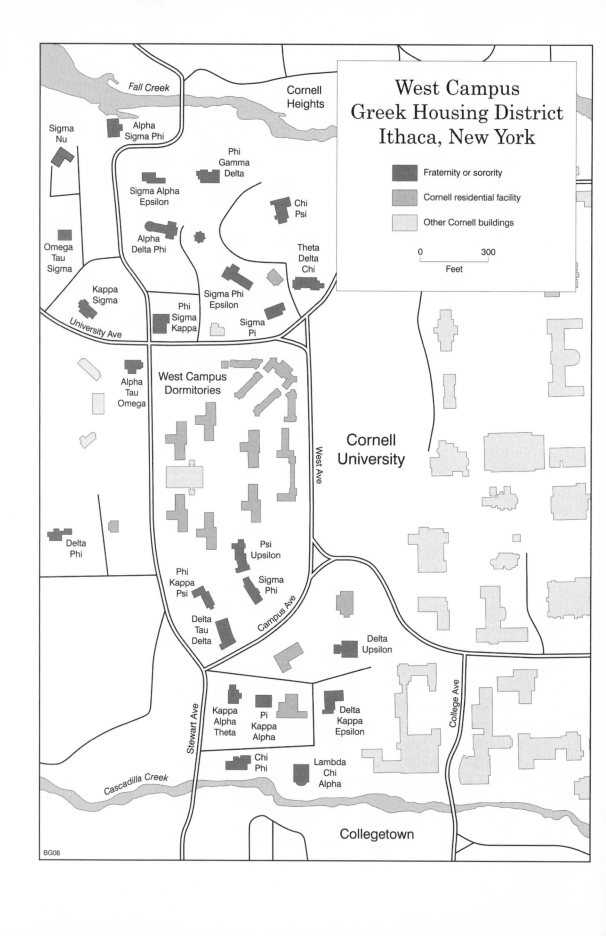

West Campus Greek Housing District Ithaca, New York

Fall Creek

Cornell Heights

Sigma Nu

Alpha Sigma Phi

Phi Gamma Delta

Chi Psi

Sigma Alpha Epsilon

Alpha Delta Phi

Omega Tau Sigma

Theta Delta Chi

Kappa Sigma

Sigma Phi Epsilon

Phi Sigma Kappa

Sigma Pi

University Ave

West Campus Dormitories

Alpha Tau Omega

West Ave

Cornell University

Delta Phi

Psi Upsilon

Phi Kappa Psi

Sigma Phi

Delta Tau Delta

Campus Ave

Delta Upsilon

Stewart Ave

College Ave

Kappa Alpha Theta

Pi Kappa Alpha

Delta Kappa Epsilon

Chi Phi

Lambda Chi Alpha

Cascadilla Creek

Collegetown

Fraternity or sorority

Cornell residential facility

Other Cornell buildings

0   300
Feet

BG08

recitation. It was in literary societies that students found an environment that nurtured free intellectual inquiry. Literary societies sponsored debates on the issues of the day and built libraries that often surpassed college book collections in size and scope. The first fraternity established in the United States, Phi Beta Kappa at William and Mary in 1776, was also intellectual in its purpose, but from the beginning fraternities had a social component. As colleges liberalized their curricula and took over some of the functions of literary societies, the purpose of fraternities became chiefly social. There were other important differences between the literary societies and fraternities. Where literary societies were inclusive in their membership and democratic in their intentions, fraternities were selective and secretive. In time, most fraternities also developed a residential component.[10]

By the time Cornell University opened in 1868, fraternities had replaced the literary societies in importance on most college campuses and had largely forsaken their intellectual roots. They had become gentlemen's clubs that sought only the most urbane young men for membership. They provided fellowship and institutionalized the long-standing college traditions of drinking, smoking, card playing, and singing. They grew, in the words of the historian Frederick Rudolph, because they "offered an escape from the monotony, dreariness, and unpleasantness of the collegiate regimen." Cornell welcomed fraternities from the start. Its first president, Andrew Dickson White, had been a fraternity man at Hobart and Yale, and he spoke publicly about the virtues of fraternities on numerous occasions, arguing that they encouraged responsibility on the part of their members and calling them "the best substitute possible for the family relation." In Cornell's first year, seven fraternities were founded.[11]

Fraternities have long served an important housing function at American universities such as Cornell, which opposed the construction of dormitories initially. White was adamant in his belief that students would be better housed in private homes or fraternities, saying that dormitories were breeding grounds for "carelessness, uproar, and destruction." Still, the Cornell campus in its early years was isolated from the main part of Ithaca, sitting atop a steep hill that remains a difficult climb even in good weather. As a consequence, the university had little choice but to provide rooms for students and faculty at first. As new classroom buildings were constructed, rooms were set aside for student residences, but as the

(opposite)

FIGURE 3.2. *Ithaca's West Campus Greek housing district is home to twenty-three fraternities and one sorority. Map by the author.*

demand for educational facilities grew, these were gradually eliminated. The first dormitory for men was not built until 1914. Rising enrollment and demand for student housing stimulated the growth of the Greek system at Cornell and elsewhere. Fraternities came to house an increasing portion of undergraduate men. Sororities developed later, but have never been as numerous as fraternities because American colleges and universities were predominantly male during the prime period of Greek society development in the late 1800s and early 1900s. Female students were so outnumbered at Cornell that fraternities regularly bused in undergraduates from nearby women's colleges for big party weekends until the 1960s.[12]

Cornell's first fraternities rented meeting rooms above businesses downtown, as they did in other college towns. Few college societies anywhere in the country had their own buildings before the Civil War. The newly founded Psi Upsilon became the first Cornell fraternity to have its own house and to locate near the Cornell campus when it rented a two-story structure in 1876 at the corner of Buffalo and Quarry streets in a neighborhood that became known as Collegetown. The next year, Delta Kappa Epsilon rented at a house nearby. In 1878, Alpha Delta Phi became the first fraternity to build its own chapter house in the area. One by one, fraternities migrated from downtown up the steep hill, East Hill, which separates Ithaca's central business district from the Cornell campus. The steady migration of Greeks reflected a general shift in student housing. Collegetown emerged as Ithaca's preeminent student-housing district. Fraternity and non-fraternity men alike took their meals in Collegetown boarding houses. In time, however, animosity between Greeks and independents prompted most fraternities to relocate. As early as 1868, the independents had organized in opposition to fraternities, one critic calling them "the foulest blot on college life."[13]

The story of the Cornell chapter of Alpha Delta Phi is useful in explaining why this geographic shift took place and how separate Greek housing districts emerge in college towns. Alpha Delta Phi, begun at Hamilton College in 1832, was the fourth fraternity chartered at Cornell. Shortly after its founding in 1868, members rented rooms in downtown Ithaca, near those of several other fraternities. Soon after Psi Upsilon and Delta Kappa Epsilon rented houses near campus, alumni of Alpha Delta Phi mounted a campaign to raise money to build a house. They raised $12,000 and purchased a lot on Buffalo Street about halfway up East Hill. The lot was ideally situated because at the time most Cornell students lived downtown and walked up Buffalo Street to campus, passing by the Alpha Delta Phi house.

The two-story brick chapter house was completed in 1878 and provided housing for sixteen brothers.[14]

Three developments shifted the geographic focus of fraternity life and motivated Alpha Delta Phi to seek a new home. In 1881, Cornell began the practice of allowing fraternities to lease land on campus to build chapter houses. Then, in 1888, a bridge was built across Cascadilla Creek at Stewart Avenue, providing easier access from the west side of campus to Collegetown and central Ithaca, which encouraged the building of homes and fraternity houses in the area. Within a few years, three fraternity houses were built on the central campus and several more were constructed on the west side, some on campus lots, others on privately owned parcels. Finally, in 1893, a street railway was built from downtown to campus along State Street, eliminating most of the pedestrian traffic that had passed in front of the Alpha Delta Phi house on Buffalo Street. These changes served to isolate Alpha Delta Phi. "Buffalo Street . . . is now quite deserted," wrote the fraternity's alumni secretary in 1900, "and for some years the chapter has labored under the disadvantage of being out of the direct line and a considerable distance from the center of student life." The migration of independents to rooming houses in Collegetown, meanwhile, spurred an exodus of Greeks from the neighborhood. In 1893, Alpha Delta Phi had been one of thirteen fraternities in the area. By 1900, only three remained.[15]

Though Alpha Delta Phi was the first fraternity to build its own house, in the intervening twenty years it had become run-down and was smaller and less opulent than several newer fraternity houses. If Alpha Delta Phi was to compete for the most sought-after pledges and retain its prominence in campus life, it needed a new house in a new location. Student members first wrote alumni urging them to build a new house in 1895. In 1899, the fraternity's alumni board appointed a committee to consider its options. By this time, Cornell was under control of a new president, Jacob Gould Schurmann, who was critical of the Greek system and discontinued the practice of granting fraternities leases of campus land. Without the option of building on campus, Alpha Delta Phi considered four sites for a new house, three in Collegetown and one on the west side of campus. In a move indicative of the growing divide between Greeks and independents, it rejected all the Collegetown sites, dismissing one because of its proximity to "a number of cheap, unattractive buildings" and another, located near several rooming houses on Heustis Street (now College Avenue), because "it has a Heustis Street atmosphere as distinguished from a campus atmosphere." With its seedy rooming houses and unsanitary boarding houses that three years later were blamed for an outbreak of typhoid, Collegetown was becoming, in every sense of the term, Ithaca's student ghetto, and the status-minded fraternities wanted no part of it.[16]

Alpha Delta Phi in 1900 chose a site on the west side of campus, but away from most of the fraternities in that area. By this time, there were seven fraternities located on the west side of campus just north of Cascadilla Creek. Another stream, Fall Creek, formed the northern boundary of campus. Five years before, the Chi Psi fraternity had purchased the famous McGraw-Fiske mansion, which sat on thirty acres on the south edge of Fall Creek, opposite the northwest corner of campus (fig. 3.3). Built in 1881 for Jennie McGraw, daughter of one of Cornell's founders, the McGraw-Fiske mansion was Ithaca's most extravagant residence and one of the most famous mansions in upstate New York. Styled after a French chateau and designed by William Henry Miller, who designed more than seventy buildings in Ithaca and on the Cornell campus, including nine fraternity houses, it had sweeping views of the campus, town, and Cayuga Lake, and cost a reported $300,000 to build. After McGraw died, the land on which the mansion sat was subdivided into smaller lots, and, over the next decade, many were sold to fraternities. This became the next major fraternity building area. In 1899, Phi Kappa Psi built a house next door to Chi Psi. A year later, Alpha Delta Phi purchased the largest of the lots carved from the McGraw-Fiske estate, five acres just below the Chi Psi house.[17]

The Chi Psi house set a standard of luxury that other Cornell fraternities sought to emulate. In fact, Alpha Delta Phi alumni worried about choosing a site nearby, fearing they would be forever "overshadowed." They also worried that the site was too far from the center of student life. Two factors enabled them to overlook these disadvantages. The Ithaca street railway was extended along Stewart Avenue in front of the site they were considering, making the area more accessible and stimulating the building in the vicinity of several "fine residences by professors and leading business men," a class of people more compatible with the fraternity's own social aspirations than the independents in Collegetown. Moreover, the fraternity had learned "from reliable sources" that Cornell planned to build several men's residence halls across from the site. Although the fraternity wanted no part of the "Heustis Street atmosphere," the dormitories would house freshmen, the source of future fraternity pledges.[18] What better place to showcase the attractions of fraternity life?

Rather than try to copy the gothic grandeur of the Chi Psi house, Alpha Delta Phi hired Chicago architect George Dean, a student of Frank Lloyd Wright, who designed the house in the Prairie School tradition of his men-

FIGURE 3.3.
*The Chi Psi frater-
nity purchased
Ithaca's famous
McGraw-Fiske
mansion in 1881,
establishing a
standard of luxury
that other Cornell
fraternities sought
to emulate. Used
with permission,
Division of Rare
and Manuscript
Collections,
Cornell University
Library; Carol
Sisler Papers,
Collection 4925.*

tor (fig. 3.4).[19] Seeking to distinguish it still further from Chi Psi, Alpha Delta Phi built a separate initiation chamber—a windowless, nine-sided, star-shaped structure designed for the fraternity's secret initiation rituals. Scott Meacham in his study of fraternity architecture in Hanover has argued that "the air of mystery that surrounds the fraternity came to inform the look of the buildings these organizations built." Alpha Delta Phi's chapter house and initiation chamber were completed in 1903, and a year later the value of the property was assessed at $20,000, making it the second most valuable fraternity house in Ithaca. About the same time, two other fraternities purchased land on the former McGraw-Fiske estate and began building houses. A third fraternity purchased a private home nearby. Within a decade, there were ten fraternity houses in the vicinity. There were thirteen more located further south, on the north edge of Cascadilla Creek.[20] In 1914, as expected, Cornell built the first of fifteen men's residence halls in between the two Greek housing areas. They provided a steady stream

FIGURE 3.4.
Alpha Delta Phi chapter house, built in 1903 on land subdivided from the McGraw-Fiske estate. Used with permission, Alpha Delta Phi at Cornell University.

of new initiates to nearby fraternities and stimulated the building of other chapter houses in the vicinity.

At Cornell and elsewhere, as Helen Lefkowitz Horowitz has noted, Greeks dominated the formal aspects of student life. They were disproportionately represented in student government. They were the editors of the student newspaper and the yearbook. They were the cheerleaders and stars of athletic teams. Their parties and dances were the most important events on local social calendars and were covered on the society pages of newspapers. Fraternity men were wealthier and more conservative than the student body as a whole, and their chapter houses were sumptuous mansions designed to symbolize the status of their residents, with great bay windows, wide verandas, grand staircases, oak-lined dining rooms, and stone fireplaces. The *Saturday Evening Post* called Cornell's chapter houses "the very apex of sybaritic luxury." [21] Cornell's early fraternities were also exclusively white and Christian, which stimulated the development of minority Greek organizations. The first black fraternity in the United States, Alpha Phi Alpha, was founded at Cornell in 1906, though it does not appear to have had a chapter house, its members living together in a rooming house on State Street. A Jewish fraternity, Zeta Beta Tau, was established on campus the following year. It established chapter houses first in Collegetown and later in Cornell Heights.[22]

Cornell's Greek system, like those at other universities, grew with the institution, eventually becoming one of the largest in the United States. By 1925, there were eighty fraternities and sororities, and chapter houses had spread north into the Cornell Heights neighborhood and the separately incorporated village of Cayuga Heights. The lure of fraternity life and the contrasts between the Greeks and their opposites, the studious but socially inept "grinds," were well illustrated in Charles Thompson's novel *Half-way Down the Stairs*, set in Ithaca. The book's protagonist, a self-described "grubby little jerk from Philip, Mass.," arrives in Ithaca at one of the West Campus dorms, expecting ivy-covered grandeur only to find a "dirt and tar-paper shack, which was crouched with nine or ten like it under the shadow of two great brick fraternity houses." The houses belonged to Psi Upsilon and Sigma Phi, still today among Cornell's most elite fraternities.[23]

"Well, I dropped my bags on the stoop of this hovel, and looked up at the fraternity houses," recalled the novel's central character. "They were huge, with diamond panes and lattice windows and about fifteen chimneys apiece. Each one had a cool flagstone terrace, and on one of these terraces a bunch of people were having a party. They were tall brown boys and girls in skirts and cashmere sweaters, in light flannels and white bucks, and they looked like something out of the Philip Yacht Club. They were drinking what looked like orange juice; they moved in and out of wide French doors on the terrace, and inside someone was playing good cocktail piano. I stood there and watched them for a long time, fascinated." After a while, one of the fraternity men wandered over to a wall, gazed over the town, then looked down at the dorms. "There was a funny mixture of reactions on his face. He saw my suit and my shoes and my long hair and my beat-up cardboard suit-cases, but it wouldn't have bothered him if he hadn't caught the look on my face. I guess he saw pure envy there, and a bitter kind of lust. . . . I wanted to be up on the Sigma Phi terrace with the pretty boys and pretty girls."

Fraternities have experienced alternating periods of expansion and contraction, support and criticism. Many closed during World War II and struggled to regain their previous stature in a postwar era during which veterans dominated campus life. Fraternities boomed again during the 1950s once the veterans graduated—two-thirds of Cornell freshmen pledged in mid-1950s—only to come under attack in the non-conformist sixties. Membership declined and some two dozen fraternities and sororities at Cornell closed. The Greek system became less exclusive. Fraternities nationwide were pressured to eliminate discriminatory clauses in their charters and to actively recruit ethnic and religious minorities. In 1968, Cornell's board of trustees instituted a policy requiring all Greek groups to comply with an anti-discrimination pledge. The conservatism of fraternities stood in sharp contrast to the tenor of the times. When militant blacks occupied the Cornell student union in 1969, for example, members of the Delta Upsilon fraternity broke into the building to try to remove them. Some faculty at Cornell and elsewhere called for the abolishment of the Greek system, which one report called "an absurd anachronism." Few colleges ever acted on such recommendations, perhaps because, as one Cornell report found and observers elsewhere have noted, a disproportionate share of the most generous alumni donors to colleges and universities are fraternity men.[24]

The campus protests of the 1960s led to the eventual elimination of many university regulations governing student behavior, which, along with the raising of the legal drinking age and the popularity of the fraternity movie *Animal House*, spurred a revival of Greek life in the 1980s. As state after state raised its drinking age to twenty-one (New York did so in 1985), fraternities assured undergraduates continued access to alcohol and made chapter houses once again the center of campus life. Fraternities became, in the words of Simon Bronner, "underage drinking clubs." Nationwide, fraternity membership nearly doubled between 1980 and 1986. Membership mushroomed even on liberal campuses such as the University of California, Berkeley. The number of fraternities and sororities at Cornell grew from fifty-two to sixty-five in a decade. Giant fraternity parties rocked the West Campus Greek housing district every weekend. One Greek alumnus described the 1980s as Cornell's "*Lord of the Flies* period," an era when fraternity parties advertising 125 kegs and drawing three thousand people were common. Other college towns witnessed a similar explosion in fraternity parties. A fraternity-sponsored beer bash in Pullman in 1988 attracted thirteen thousand people.[25]

Growing concern in recent years over student drinking, the sexual conduct of fraternity members, injuries caused by hazing, and continued criticism that fraternity membership practices are elitist and even discriminatory have prompted colleges to again try to rein in the Greeks.[26] Some institutions, such as the University of Oregon, have banned alcoholic beverages from chapter houses. Cornell has imposed many new restrictions on Greek social activities. Open parties are now prohibited: All events must be by invitation only, and sponsors are required to have a guest list at the door. Chapters must hire a licensed caterer for all events where alcohol is served and must have five "sober monitors" for every two hundred guests. Parties

FIGURE 3.5.
*Students use
a funnel while
drinking at a
Cornell University
fraternity party.
Photograph by the
author, 2000.*

must end by 1 a.m. Rush and pledge functions must be dry. Conversations
with fraternity members indicate that the regulations are more a nuisance
than a deterrent, and are routinely ignored or circumvented (by such ploys
as making up a guest list composed of the entire student body). Drinking
is still a central component of Greek life and student cultures in general
(fig. 3.5). Large parties are still common, with the fraternities on West Campus taking turns holding the biggest events. Underage drinking is still
widespread. Hazing is still practiced, though dangerous rituals are rare.[27]
Cornell's fraternities and sororities, like Greek organizations nationwide,
also remain overwhelmingly white. While all have eliminated discriminatory membership policies in their bylaws and now have minority members,
they are still less diverse than the student body as a whole.[28]

Changing attitudes toward fraternities are having an impact. Nationwide, fraternity membership declined 30 percent between 1990 and 2000.
At the dawn of the twenty-first century, "Greek life is . . . a tough sell," according to Richard McKaig, director of the Center for the Study of the College Fraternity at Indiana University. At Cornell, membership fell 4 percent
between 1996 and 2005. There were five fewer chapter houses in 2005
than a decade before. Cornell fraternity members refer to the time before
the new social rules were implemented as "the good old days." Fraternity
upperclassmen increasingly live out of chapter houses, often in so-called
fraternity annexes in Collegetown, where the social rules cannot be

enforced. Occupancy in chapter houses fell 20 percent from 1996 to 2005. Nevertheless, Greek life remains an integral part of student life at Cornell, which had forty-seven fraternities and twenty-one sororities in 2005. More than one-quarter of undergraduates were members.[29] The continued importance of fraternities and sororities, and the prominence of their chapter houses in the built environment (fig. 3.6), suggest that the fraternity district will remain a distinctive attribute of college towns well into the future.

THE STUDENT GHETTO

For as long as there have been fraternities and sororities, there have been undergraduates who have reviled them, resented their importance, and lived their college years outside their sphere of influence. Many prefer to rent large houses near campus with friends or live in apartments. Campus-adjacent neighborhoods are often dominated by such rentals. Most college towns of a certain size have at least one neighborhood near campus that is home almost exclusively to undergraduates. Informally, it is often called the student ghetto and is characterized by dilapidated houses, beat-up couches sitting on porches, cars parked on lawns, and bicycles chained to anything that won't move (fig. 3.7). It is the result of what happened to many campus-adjacent neighborhoods when enrollments mushroomed following World War II, colleges became less able to house their students, landlords saw an opportunity, and homeowners sought refuge from the influx of young people. Such neighborhoods often filtered down from faculty and other more well-to-do permanent residents as the housing stock deteriorated.[30]

Neighborhoods such as University Hill in Boulder, Colorado; College Park in Gainesville, Florida; and the Collegetown district in Ithaca are locally notorious and the frequent subject of proposals by government officials seeking to control their spread and improve their appearance. Many college towns have sought to slow the expansion of such neighborhoods by imposing regulations intended to discourage the conversion of single-family homes into rental properties. Couches on porches are so central to the image of the student ghetto that an entrepreneur in Ithaca created a poster that is a parody of tourist posters such as "The Doors of Dublin." It features thirty-three photos of couches and other indoor furniture on Ithaca porches above the banner "Couches of Collegetown." Some see the proliferation of couches on porches as less benign, however. The City Council in Boulder recently implemented an ordinance prohibiting upholstered furniture outdoors in response to several riots on University Hill in which couches were burned.[31]

FIGURE 3.6. *The Chi Phi fraternity house is perched prominently overlooking the Cascadilla Creek gorge in Ithaca's West Campus Greek housing district. Photograph by David Rice, 2007; used with permission.*

FIGURE 3.7. *Typical student ghetto rental house in the Collegetown neighborhood, Ithaca. Photograph by the author, 2000.*

In its origin and evolution, Ithaca's Collegetown neighborhood is in many ways representative of student-rental districts in college towns nationwide. Collegetown did not exist when Cornell opened its doors in 1868. Most residents of Ithaca lived on the "flats" that extended southward from Cayuga Lake. Ithaca's central business district developed along State Street, and most homes were located north of it. There was but a scattering of private homes on East Hill, adjacent to the Cornell campus. Most of the area was occupied by small farms and woods. The first significant building on East Hill was a cotton mill built in 1827 by Otis Eddy, for whom one of the major streets in Collegetown is named. The mill was torn down in 1866 and replaced by a five-story stone building, Cascadilla Place, a hospital based on the water cure, which also failed. Cornell leased Cascadilla Place, converting it into a dormitory for students and faculty. It became the nucleus around which the neighborhood grew. Collegetown developed organically in response to undergraduate demand for housing, the student-dominated district expanding outward as Cornell's enrollment increased.[32]

When Cornell opened, students had three choices in where to live. Cascadilla Place provided room and board for 104 students, plus twelve faculty members and their families. It was abhorred by professors and students alike. It had outdoor privies and gas lighting. It had running water, but the system rarely worked. There were no baths. The manager of the dining room kept a pigsty out back. Cornell's first president, Andrew Dickson White, who lived in Cascadilla while his home was being built, called it "an ill-ventilated, ill-smelling, uncomfortable, ill-looking alms house."[33] Another seventy-five students lived in the university's first academic building, Morrill Hall. Everyone else had to live down the hill in central Ithaca and walk a mile to campus, climbing the steep, four hundred-foot hill upon which the university stands. The walk to campus was so exhausting that an early professor placed a stone bench about halfway up Buffalo Street to provide weary climbers a place to rest.[34]

White opposed the building of dormitories, insisting undergraduates would be better off rooming in private homes, a view that echoed the attitudes of a growing number of university presidents.[35] "Large bodies of students collected in dormitories often arrive at a degree of turbulence," he said, "which small parties, gathered in the houses of citizens, seldom if ever reach."[36] By necessity, some space was set aside in the first university buildings to house students, but as enrollment grew, student rooms were converted to academic uses. By 1875, there was living space for only about fifty students on campus, nearly all of that reserved for women students. By this time, Cascadilla Place had reverted to private control. The building of rental housing near campus lagged behind demand. For the first five years, the majority of students lived in central Ithaca, many forming clubs so they could reduce expenses by leasing an entire house. Cornell's first student newspaper, the *Era*, urged Ithaca residents to "wake up" and "furnish accommodations—at reasonable prices and within reasonable distance of the University halls." So desperate were students for housing near campus that a group of twenty students was granted permission to build a cottage on the university grounds. Later, David Starr Jordan, who became the first president of Stanford University, joined with several classmates to build a wood "hut" on campus, near the president's house.[37]

Finally, in the late 1870s, several large, frame rooming houses were built on Eddy Street and Heustis Street, now College Avenue (fig. 3.8). Rents were cheaper than Cascadilla. By 1889, there were fifty-nine residences in Collegetown. Enrollment at Cornell had topped one thousand, making it one of the largest universities in the country. That year, the *Era* appealed to the city to extend its streetcar line to campus, claiming that the lack of transportation served to "isolate the university" and caused rents in Collegetown to become "abnormally high," a common complaint in student rental districts to the present day. The streetcar line was extended to campus in 1893. In time, businesses began to spring up in Collegetown to serve students living in the rooming houses. The largest rooming houses were located along Heustis Street, most of them, in the words of Cornell's historian, "cheap, ugly, and hazardous." Four of these houses alone accommodated almost sixty students. In 1903, a private dormitory, Sheldon Court, was built opposite the main entrance to Cornell. It housed 135 students, the Triangle Book Store, a doctor's office, and a restaurant known as Mother's Kitchen.[38]

There were few restaurants in Collegetown because most students, independents and Greeks alike, took their meals in private boarding houses. Few fraternity houses had dining rooms at the time. There was but one food facility on campus, a hot dog wagon called the Sibley Dog. In 1900, "everybody ate at boarding houses," according to Romeyn Berry. Some were run by homeowners such as Martha Lucas Warren, who bought a house on Linden Avenue when her husband died and began offering meals. A few years later, she bought a five-story rooming house on Heustis Street. There, she fed one hundred students three times a day and rented rooms. In most boarding houses, students bought weekly meal tickets that entitled them to three meals a day. To save money, some students formed boarding clubs. They would persuade a homeowner to cook and serve meals in her house. The student organizers would supply the food and recruit boarders. Berry argued that many fraternities began as boarding clubs. "The congenial

FIGURE 3.8.
Rooming houses built in the 1870s along Heustis Street, now College Avenue, in Ithaca's Collegetown neighborhood.
Used with permission, Division of Rare and Manuscript Collections, Cornell University Library; Archive Photograph Collection, No. 13-6-2497.

table of one year became the private alcove of the next," he wrote. "When gaps appeared about the board, the survivors took thought to fill them with pleasant persons of their own selection. The table gave itself a name and something like a self-perpetuating organization followed." [39]

What happened to the boarding houses? In Ithaca, change was stimulated by tragedy. The boarding houses were unregulated by the town or university and "some of them were pretty squalid," said Berry. The cheapest presented a health hazard. In 1903, thirty-nine Cornell students died from an outbreak of typhoid, which some blamed on unsanitary conditions in the boarding houses (others suspected the city water supply was contaminated). That year, Psi Upsilon fraternity added a dining room and, before long, all the fraternities had kitchens. Cornell responded more slowly. In 1910, the student newspaper published an exposé on the boarding houses, claiming conditions had not improved. It found that food was "satisfactory" in only four of thirty-two Collegetown boarding houses. It reported that it was common practice for boarding houses to re-serve food that was returned to the kitchen uneaten, and also found that plates were routinely cleared but not washed before they were used again. The following year, the city health officer, acknowledging some boarding houses were "exceedingly dirty," recommended they be inspected regularly. Finally, in 1911, Cornell opened a cafeteria on campus. Restaurants, subject to greater regulation, became more common. Construction of apartment buildings also increased nationwide, which put pressure on landlords to provide kitchens. Within a few years, most of the boarding houses closed.[40]

The student-housing district grew and grew. Year by year, new houses were built on the north-south streets leading to campus. Between 1904 and 1910, twenty new houses were built along Heustis Street. In 1912, the Cornell alumni magazine reported that it was lined with rooming houses "clear to State Street." Eventually, new east-west streets were developed, and one by one houses were built along them. The Cook family, Ithaca's leading florists in the early 1900s, owned a large tract between Huestis and Eddy streets, upon which they had an orchard and several greenhouses. Catherine Street and Cook Street were built through this tract. Over the next twenty years two dozen houses were built on the two one-block streets, and the last of the greenhouses was removed. By 1930, most of present-day Collegetown was built up. Houses furthest from campus were initially occupied by families, who may have rented an extra room to students, but over time these too were converted to rooming houses and later apartments. The Collegetown commercial district also expanded. The parts of Heustis Street, Dryden Road, and Eddy Street closest to campus came to be lined with restaurants, bookstores, grocers, barbers, and other businesses catering to students.[41]

As Cornell students began to sort themselves out residentially according to lifestyle differences, Collegetown developed a decidedly different character than the Greek-housing district between Fall and Cascadilla creeks. Where the fraternity houses were expensive and palatial, the rooming houses were, in the words of Morris Bishop, a Cornell student and later a faculty member, "light, flimsy structures of wood or of loathsome chocolate-colored Ithaca mud." Bishop mapped the geography of the rooming houses in a 1912 article in the *Cornell Era*. The most desirable—and expensive—were located on the hill leading to Collegetown. "The dweller here need never be ashamed of his address," Bishop wrote. The quality of housing quickly deteriorated east of Eddy Street, an area he referred to as "The Great Rooming-House Belt." "Rooms here are cheaper," he wrote, "but as ever you must pay for cheapness. Many . . . are small, bare, and insecure against the invasion of our famous February weather. Here live the small army of hard-working, persevering men who must fight for their education, and who face privation and discomfort that they may forge a weapon with which to hew their way in their world." In 1913, a student committee reported that most of the Heustis Street and Dryden Road rooming houses were "crowded" and many were "fire traps," and recommended the university regularly inspect the rooming houses. The following year, Cornell began inspecting all rooming houses annually and providing freshmen a list of inspected houses. Anecdotal evidence suggests that the program did little to improve conditions.[42]

Where the best of the fraternity houses were home to the undergraduate elite, Collegetown housed students who were at the bottom of the Cornell "caste system," according to Bishop. They were, he wrote fifty years later, "a vast plebian mass, the independents, the outsiders, the pills, the poops, the drips." Where the fraternity district was Cornell's country club, Collegetown was its tenement district. It also became Ithaca's Left Bank, particularly after World War II, when Cornell ceased to be a workingman's university, and living in the "sweet little slum of rooming houses" became an affectation of the wanna-be proletariat. "The Collegetown crowd—well, they're the bohemians," wrote Charles Thompson in *Halfway Down the Stairs*. "They dress a la Greenwich Village and they're actors and writers and musicians and that sort of thing. I always thought they were a ratty bunch."[43]

As Cornell's enrollment grew following World War II, the student-housing district expanded. Enrollment nearly doubled between 1940 and 1965, as veterans flooded campuses and baby boomers began to enter college. The proportion of high school graduates attending college tripled in the first three decades after the war. Like most American universities, Cornell devoted increasing resources to dormitory construction, building seven residence halls capable of housing 1,200 students in the 1950s alone, but the number of students living off campus grew even faster. The nature of student accommodations also changed, as the postwar student sought more room and greater freedom. Students came to prefer apartments, and gradually most of Collegetown's rooming houses were converted.[44] As demand for off-campus housing increased, many single-family homes in Collegetown were also turned into apartments. Landlords could outbid families as houses came on the market. The lifestyle differences between students and older adults also pushed families out. Block by block, Collegetown turned from a mixed neighborhood into a student-dominated district. At the time, it was also a predominantly male neighborhood, as female students were required to live on campus or in sororities, as they were at many American colleges.

Collegetown became the center of Ithaca's countercultural scene during the 1960s, a period one writer later called the neighborhood's "Golden Age." As enrollments grew and the contrasts between undergraduates and the rest of the population intensified, student-housing districts in college towns developed a culture all their own. They were, in the words of the sociologist John Lofland, "cities of youth." The anthropologist William Partridge called one such neighborhood in Gainesville "the hippie ghetto." Deposed University of California President Clark Kerr wrote in 1967 that increasing numbers of non-students were gravitating to such neighborhoods, drawn by campus cultural programs, political activities, and a sense of freedom. "Left Banks are now found around a few of the great American universities," he wrote. "They will be found around more, and they will grow in size." It was in Ithaca's Collegetown that Richard Fariña, confidante of Bob Dylan and brother-in-law of Joan Baez, set his quintessentially sixties novel, *Been Down So Long It Looks Like Up to Me*. Vladimir Nabokov reportedly wrote *Lolita* in a Collegetown apartment at 205 Quarry Street. There were poetry readings at the Cabbagetown Café. Gays and bikers hung out at Morrie's bar. "Eight Miles High" drifted out of apartment windows. A paved parcel at the corner of Eddy Street and Dryden Road was set aside as "People's Park."[45] Street people skinny-dipped at a reservoir nearby. "Collegetown," wrote a contemporary observer, "is, and always has been, the fertile soil in this area for writing, partying, rioting, speech-making, and messing up and getting off."[46]

In the early seventies, however, a "wave of heroin" arrived in Collegetown and the mood began to sour. In 1971, a reputed drug dealer was murdered in a Collegetown parking lot. Junkies ruled the streets, according to one writer. The grassy slope behind Cascadilla Place became the favored spot to smoke marijuana. Drug deals "were going on all the time" on Eddy Street. LSD was commonplace, with hangers-on "'laying hits' on anyone who walked by."[47] In May 1972, following an anti–Vietnam War rally on campus, a crowd tried to set fire to the Collegetown branch of the First National Bank, but it would not burn. Two days later, police seeking to break up a block party on College Avenue triggered a four-hour melee during which partygoers threw bottles, cans, and rocks at police. Twenty-nine people were arrested and twenty others injured, including ten policemen. Police in riot gear used tear gas to disburse the crowd.[48]

By this time, the housing stock in Collegetown had deteriorated. Little new housing had been built in a half-century, and existing housing was poorly maintained. The most run-down buildings were fire and health hazards. "It was dirty, cockroach infested," said Sean Killeen, who represented the neighborhood on the Ithaca Common Council.[49] As enrollments increased, a housing shortage developed on campus, which heightened demand for housing off-campus. The greatest growth was in the female enrollment, which doubled between 1965 and 1975 while male enrollment stayed about the same. In response to protests against differential regulations for coeds, which grew out of the nationwide student power movement, Cornell's administration gradually eliminated rules requiring female students to live on campus, which escalated demand for rental properties in Collegetown. Demand exceeded supply in the areas closest to campus, so rents rose. Because students were a captive market, landlords often did little to improve their properties. The situation grew so bad that in 1965 students put up tents on campus to protest poor housing conditions in Ithaca. Cornell implemented a detailed code for student rental housing and, in 1966, began requiring students to live in university-approved housing. In 1969, the Ithaca Tenants Union was formed; it called on Cornell to build more residential facilities on campus and pressured the city to strengthen its building codes and increase enforcement. Rent strikes became widespread.[50]

A columnist in the Cornell student newspaper in 1975 lampooned the poor conditions of Collegetown housing, telling the story of his search for a place to live. He visited one apartment on Eddy Street, which he described as "a street of singular charm and ugliness, punctuated by garbage cans and parking meters." He went on: "The landlord, an unfriendly and unshaven man with an apron, showed me into the flat which had a bedroom, kitchen and water closet and all slanting ten degrees off the horizontal. The table was nailed to the floor and the landlord told me the only problem with the flat was when Sally upstairs washed her twelve blue jeans and washing machine B overflowed, but there was plastic in the closet to catch the drippings." He visited another apartment on Buffalo Street. "The landlord led me up the stairs [which] creaked with the poverty that makes a great writer and my heart beat faster and my pencil weighed heavy in my pocket. The door to the flat led to the kitchen which led to the bathroom which led to the bedroom where the light from the gabled window lit all three rooms because they were in a straight line. . . . The window had a crack in it where I could stuff my socks. Bad apartments make good writers so I signed the lease and I was happy."[51]

Collegetown has undergone profound changes over the last quarter century. City officials began to press for the redevelopment of the neighborhood in 1968. The following year, a city-sponsored urban renewal plan called for the heart of Collegetown to be demolished and replaced with a massive, multi-purpose development. It recommended construction of a large building on College Avenue that would include 375 apartments, 600 parking spaces, retail on the first and second floors, two movie theaters, a restaurant, and nine floors of office space. It also called for the construction of six to eight high-rise apartment towers, the tallest eighteen to twenty-one stories. The plan went nowhere because, as Ithaca planning director H. Matthys Van Court said, "it was too big" and "unfinanceable." Countless proposals were debated over the subsequent decade, but little real change took place until the 1980s. In 1981, Cornell, which had worked with the city on various redevelopment proposals, decided to build a $16.5-million performing arts center in Collegetown, and to renovate Cascadilla Place and Sheldon Court, originally a private dormitory, to provide additional student housing.[52]

Cornell spent $40 million on various Collegetown projects and, in the process, stimulated the transformation of the neighborhood. Today, large apartment buildings, the tallest of which is nine stories, line both sides of Dryden Road (fig. 3.9). Several other apartment buildings were built on College Avenue and Eddy Street. "It's like a mini-Manhattan," observed one local businessman.[53] The city encouraged development by temporarily suspending building height limits and parking requirements. Over a ten-year period, more than a dozen apartment buildings, capable of housing 1,700 people, were built, replacing crumbling old wood-frame houses battered by a century of undergraduate living. All the new apartment buildings are geared to students. The building boom is representative of changes that are taking place in student-housing districts in college towns nationwide. A prolonged period of economic prosperity meant students were arriving at college with new cars and more money for housing. Landlords in Ithaca and elsewhere discovered that student tastes had changed. Where undergraduates in earlier periods would snap up cramped and dingy apartments in beat-up old houses, a new breed of students prefers modern buildings with greater amenities, while still wanting to live close to campus. Developers such as Houston-based Sterling University Housing have recognized this market niche. Sterling has built amenity-rich student housing—intended as a cross between a dormitory and apartments—in more than thirty college communities. Its properties typically include fitness centers, volleyball courts, hot tubs, game rooms, and high-speed Internet. They provide a roommate-matching program and offer individual leases by the bedroom. Universities have also sought to keep students on campus by improving residential facilities and providing a greater range of housing options.[54]

Jason Fane, Ithaca's biggest landlord, built three of the apartment build-

FIGURE 3.9.
*Large, modern
apartment
buildings now
line Dryden Road
in Collegetown,
indicative of the
changing nature
of college town
rental districts.
Photograph by the
author, 2000.*

ings on Dryden Road. All are fully furnished, air conditioned, with dish-washers, microwave ovens, and Ethernet connections. One even has a doorman. Fane also owns a number of older Collegetown houses divided into student apartments. He has watched student-housing tastes change over the last quarter century. In 1975, he remarked that students "aren't interested in aesthetics." Twenty-five years later, however, he observed that students "are looking for quality." They want apartments that are "clean, fresh, new," "close to campus," with "the latest technology," "superb ser-vices" and "views." "Basically," he concluded, "students want pretty much the same thing as the tenant in a new high-rise tower in a big city." Rental rates have skyrocketed as a result of the new development. A one-bedroom apartment in Fane's newest building, Collegetown Center, is $1,405–$1,485 a month. Parking costs another $175 a month. Studio apartments in the 312 College Avenue building, which has a mini-theater that residents can reserve, study rooms, and a concierge, are $1,140–$1,365 a month.[55]

The expensive new buildings have increased the population density, stimulated new retail development, and created, in effect, two Collegetowns. There were nearly two thousand more people living in the neighborhood in 2000 than there were twenty years before, an increase of 125 percent. Population density is now comparable to Brooklyn or San Francisco. Not surprisingly, the population is young, most are students, and nearly all are renters. Anyone over age thirty stands out. In 2000, the median age was 21.7 years old, 90 percent of residents were college students, and 97 percent of housing units were rentals. Collegetown is also increasingly Asian, reflecting a rise in the enrollment of Asian students at Cornell. Asians made up 30 percent of the neighborhood's population in 2000, a proportion three times higher than in 1980.[56] Many of the new apartment buildings include retail on the first floor, and the character of businesses has changed dramatically in recent years. Collegetown is now filled with restaurants, bars, coffee houses, and other businesses catering to the wealthier students who live in the new buildings. There are seventeen different restaurants, including six different varieties of Asian cuisine.

Farther from campus, however, Collegetown remains much as it has been for fifty years. The lower ends of Eddy Street, College Avenue, and nearby streets are still lined with large frame houses full of student apartments, many of them approaching one hundred years old. The houses on Catherine, Cook, and Blair streets are smaller, but are likewise packed with students. Rents are cheaper than they are in the new buildings. Since the 1960s, the student-housing district has expanded down East Hill and east into the Bryant Park neighborhood, as rising enrollments and elimination of regulations requiring female students to live on campus increased demand for rentals. Collegetown remains Ithaca's student ghetto and still meets the definition of a ghetto as a neighborhood where a particular group lives in relative isolation from the rest of the population, but parts of the area no longer fit the aesthetic characteristics that such a designation suggests. Collegetown, like student-housing districts in university communities nationwide, is changing.

Although professors are less concentrated residentially than they once were, and are scattered throughout university communities like Ithaca, most college towns have at least one older neighborhood near campus that has resisted the invasion of undergraduates and is home to large numbers of professors. Often these neighborhoods were marketed directly to faculty. In Norman, Oklahoma, one such neighborhood was actually platted as Faculty Heights. The faculty enclave is a neighborhood of classic homes and tree-lined streets, where residents vigilantly seek to preserve the area's character and prevent incursions by students (fig. 3.10). John Jakle, in a study of Urbana, Illinois, found that University of Illinois faculty were concentrated in that city's Carle Park neighborhood and observed that professors were more likely to own houses that were architecturally distinctive as a way to set themselves apart as an "educated gentry class." Gorman Beauchamp, in a portrait of Burns Park, a faculty enclave in Ann Arbor, Michigan, noted that residents of such neighborhoods are more likely than inhabitants of other areas to own a passport, subscribe to the *New York Review of Books*, and espouse liberal causes, and less likely to go to church or fly the U.S. flag. "Ah yes, Burns Park," Beauchamp wrote, quoting a faculty colleague, "where they vote left and live right." [57]

Ithaca has at least two faculty-oriented neighborhoods, Cayuga Heights and Bryant Park. Cayuga Heights, north of the Cornell campus, is the more elite of the two, its lots larger, its homes more expensive, and, as a result, is home to high percentages of tenured and emeritus faculty. Nearly two-thirds of adult residents in Cayuga Heights in 2000 held graduate degrees, and one-quarter possessed a Ph.D., the highest percentage of any place in the country. Bryant Park, adjacent to the south side of the Cornell campus and convenient as well to Ithaca College, was developed about the same time, but its lots are smaller, its homes less grandiose, and its location less desirable. Where Cayuga Heights looks out on picturesque Cayuga Lake, Bryant Park abuts the student-dominated Collegetown district. While Cayuga Heights has traditionally been home to large numbers of senior faculty, Bryant Park is more affordable and, as a result, has been popular with younger faculty buying their first homes. One longtime resident of Bryant Park, a Cornell economics professor, said, "I always tell my students that the proletariat professors live in [Bryant Park] and the affluent ones live in Cayuga Heights." [58]

In the early years after Cornell was founded, most faculty lived on campus—first in Cascadilla Place alongside students and later in houses

FIGURE 3.10.
*Entrance to
Cayuga Heights,
one of two major
faculty enclaves
in Ithaca.
Photograph by the
author, 2000.*

built on the university grounds. Because the campus was isolated from the rest of Ithaca, Cornell's trustees permitted faculty to build houses on land leased from the university, a practice once common in college towns. A faculty enclave in Durham, New Hampshire, in fact, grew out of a University of New Hampshire program to lease land to professors for home construction as demand for housing intensified following World War II. The area actually carries the name of the Faculty Neighborhood.[59] At Cornell, the first two faculty cottages were built in 1871 and eventually thirty-four faculty homes were built on campus. Cornell President White supported the program because he believed "commodious, convenient, and attractive" homes would make professors less likely to leave Cornell. "Even the presence of an attractive little veranda or bay-window," he said, "may hold a wife against advanced salary for her husband elsewhere." After the turn of the century, as Cornell's enrollment began to rise, there came to be increasing pressure for the land upon which the houses were built. One by one the faculty houses were purchased, demolished, and replaced by academic buildings, and faculty moved off campus. This change stimulated residential development nearby. In fact, the only subdivisions developed in Ithaca between 1888 and World War I were built on East Hill in areas convenient to the Cornell campus.[60]

Ithaca's first faculty enclave was Cornell Heights, located between the Cornell campus and Cayuga Heights, on the north edge of the Fall Creek gorge. An unnamed writer in the Cornell student newspaper first recognized the residential potential of the area one year after the university's founding. In an article calling for the construction of housing for students near campus, the writer appealed to the owner of the land north of Fall Creek to "at once throw a bridge across that stream as near as possible to the University edifices, cut up his property into building lots, and forthwith erect as many inexpensive but substantial residences as can be built." A few years later, Franklin Cornell, son of university founder Ezra Cornell, likewise recognized the attractions of the area, observing, "the land across the gorge is the grandest and best in this country for residences." He had a different clientele in mind than the student writer, however, predicting that one day "the campus people will burst across the gorge . . . and make those lands the choicest in Ithaca."[61]

The lack of a bridge across the deep gorge inhibited development of the area for a quarter century. Finally, in 1896, a group led by Edward G. Wyckoff, son of a wealthy Ithaca businessman, announced plans for the development of Cornell Heights on seventy-seven acres north of Fall Creek. Wyckoff purchased a controlling interest in the Ithaca Street Railway so that the streetcar line could be extended to the area. Two bridges were built across the gorge just before the turn of the century, enabling the street railway to be built through the Cornell campus to Cornell Heights and back. From the outset, Wyckoff envisioned Cornell Heights as an elite residential area catering to faculty and businessmen, "without the encroachment of commercial interests or students."[62] Several streets were named for early Cornell professors. Announcement in 1904 that three buildings in the new College of Agriculture would be constructed a short walk from Cornell Heights increased demand for home sites in the area. Most original residents were Cornell faculty, who walked to campus or rode the streetcar.

An unwelcome development in 1906, typical of the forces that trigger neighborhood change in college towns, squelched Cornell Heights's emergence as Ithaca's premier faculty enclave. That year, Sherman Peer donated his Cornell Heights house to the Alpha Zeta fraternity. The move enraged

Wyckoff, who threatened legal action against Peer for violating the terms of his deed. "You are aware as to the efforts we have always made to the end of keeping fraternities from occupying houses on Cornell Heights," Wyckoff wrote his lawyer. "These young men are causing considerable annoyance in the neighborhood." Cornell Heights's proximity to campus made it increasingly difficult to keep out students, and gradually faculty began to relocate. In 1912, Cornell built the first of several women's dormitories in the area. Two years later, Wyckoff himself gave up, selling his estate to the Phi Kappa Psi fraternity. Before long, several other homes were bought by fraternities and sororities and converted into chapter houses. Many faculty who sought to escape the invasion of students looked north.[63]

Cayuga Heights held many of the attractions of Cornell Heights without its major disadvantages. Sitting atop the same plateau as the Cornell campus, it is at the same elevation as the university grounds, a desirable characteristic in hilly and snowy Ithaca. It overlooks Cayuga Lake, and its gently rolling topography meant many home sites would have lake views. While it was convenient to the Cornell campus, it was not so close that it faced the same pressure from student housing (though fraternities were later built on its southern edge). Because it is separately incorporated, it has also been better able to control what goes on within its borders. The nucleus around which Cayuga Heights developed, two parcels totaling 616 acres north of Cornell Heights, just beyond the Ithaca village limits, was purchased about 1901 by Jared Newman, Edward Wyckoff's attorney, and Charles Hazen Blood, Newman's law partner. Newman and Blood hired Boston landscape architect Warren Manning to design the subdivision. Influenced by the picturesque residential designs of Frederick Law Olmsted, Manning laid out Cayuga Heights with irregular-sized home lots and curving streets that followed the contours of the landscape. White pines and other trees were planted according to formal plan.[64]

Development of Cayuga Heights was slow at first. Newman built a summer home there in 1903. In 1909, he built a year-round residence, a large, Mission-style house that marked the entrance to the district. His brother-in-law built a house in the Prairie style nearby. Two years later, Sherman Peer, who precipitated the transformation of Cornell Heights when he donated his house to a fraternity, built a Gustav Stickley–designed house next door to the Newman home. By the end of that year, there were twenty-one houses in the tract. In 1913, Newman began to promote Cayuga Heights more actively. He named the first area that was subdivided White Park, after Cornell's first president. He advertised home sites in the *Cornell Alumni News*, which circulated to faculty on campus. He envisioned Cayuga Heights as a village of "cultured families" and predicted it would become "the finest residential section in Ithaca." To keep out "undesirable elements" he refused to allow real estate agents to sell home lots on his behalf. Deeds prohibited fraternities and commercial enterprises. House designs had to be approved by the developers.[65]

Newman saw Cornell faculty as his preferred clientele. In a letter to a Chicago real estate broker in 1920, he noted that Cornell professors were to receive "very large" salary increases that year. Many of them, he observed, "are on the lookout for homes and a goodly portion of them turn their attention in this direction." To distinguish Cayuga Heights from Cornell Heights, he noted that there "isn't a single boarding house in the entire village" and "the lots are larger and the outlook finer." By February 1921, there were fifty-six houses in Cayuga Heights. "Three-fourths of the residents," he wrote, "are in some way connected with the University." Newman's correspondence is filled with sales pitches to professors. In one, he encourages Professor John Parson, bothered by fraternities near his Ithaca home, to look to Cayuga Heights for relief. In trying to interest Professor W. W. Fisk in a large parcel, Newman wrote, "it seemed to me it was just what a University man might want."[66]

From the beginning, Cornell faculty exerted a disproportionate influence on civic affairs in Cayuga Heights. All but two mayors since 1923 have been Cornell professors. Frederick Marcham, a professor of history, was mayor for thirty-two years. Faculty and their spouses have occupied a majority of seats on the village governing board over the years, and their attitudes, particularly the desire to prevent developments that would attract students, have shaped policy. Marcham led a successful 1954 campaign against annexation by the city of Ithaca, which he feared would bring Cayuga Heights the student-related problems that plague campus-adjacent neighborhoods in the city. The village rejected proposals for the building of a restaurant with a tavern because of the worry that the tavern would attract students. In the 1970s, it thwarted an attempt by Cornell to build a dormitory in the village.[67] Cornell professors have also shaped life in Cayuga Heights in other ways. Education-minded residents paid special attention to the Cayuga Heights School, founded in 1924. Many faculty spouses taught there. One longtime resident observed that the influence of faculty families on the operation of the Cayuga Heights School was so great that it "was practically a branch of Cornell . . . a kind of private school adjunct to the Cornell faculty."[68]

The Cayuga Heights School went only through eighth grade, so older students had to attend Ithaca High School. When village teenagers went down the hill to attend high school, they sometimes found their new class-mates had preconceived notions about people from Cayuga Heights. Residents from other parts of Ithaca were less highly educated, more blue collar. Cayuga Heights inhabitants were perceived as bookish, cultured, and aloof. "With unfamiliarity grew contempt," said John Marcham, son of Cayuga Heights's longtime mayor. "One day when I had to leave a school activity early to catch a bus to the Heights, a friend was incredulous. 'You're not one of *them*, are you?' was just the way he put it." Indicating the light-hearted tension that existed between hill dwellers and those who lived on the "flats," intramural teams at Ithaca High School composed mostly of Cayuga Heights residents were sometimes known as the Cayuga Heights Sophisticates.[69]

Bryant Park was developed about the same time as Cayuga Heights by the same developer. Its emergence as a faculty enclave followed a similar path. The land upon which the neighborhood developed had been a wheat farm and fruit orchard owned by Solomon Bryant. Following his death, three of his children in partnership with Jared Newman subdivided forty-five acres of the property into 161 building lots. The Bryant tract began immediately east of the rooming houses in Collegetown. The growth of the neighborhood was stimulated by the development of the New York State College of Agriculture. In 1904, the state legislature created the college and placed it under the control of Cornell. Within a few years, it became the largest college on campus. The sale of lots in Bryant Park began in 1908. Lots sold more quickly than they did in Cayuga Heights, in part because parcels were less expensive, but also because Bryant Park was less isolated. By 1914, one third of the lots in Bryant Park had been sold, many of them to professors. Most of the lots in Bryant Park were built upon before World War II and development began to spread east to the city limits. A 1941 report said that 477 Cornell employees lived in the area, nearly half of them staff members in the College of Agriculture.[70]

The design of the subdivision, the nature of promotional materials, and the characteristics of deeds make clear that developers sought to establish Bryant Park as a faculty enclave. The initial announcement of the sale of lots noted that the tract was "within three minutes walk of the campus bridge." Bryant Avenue was cut diagonally across the slope of the tract to create a nearly level road, "so that it would not be necessary to go up hill to reach the University campus." To distinguish the subdivision from Cornell Heights, the announcement pointed out that Bryant Park "is much nearer to both town and campus." With the College Avenue rooming houses so close, developers imposed deed restrictions designed to prevent student housing from expanding into Bryant Park. Deeds prohibited commercial enterprises and the sale of liquor. They forbade more than one house from being built on any lot, to prevent homeowners from erecting separate rental properties. Some deeds also included a statement that any house built "shall be planned and erected for use as a home, and not for the purpose of keeping roomers."[71]

Like their counterparts in Cayuga Heights, faculty in Bryant Park have been unusually active in civic affairs. When the Bryant Park Civic Association was formed in 1923 to mount a campaign for the building of a school in the neighborhood, thirty-five of forty-seven people who signed their names in support of the organization were Cornell employees or their spouses. Four of five members of the group's original board of directors had Cornell connections, and ten of its first fourteen presidents were faculty. Although neighborhood organizations are common today, the Bryant Park group was the only such organization in Ithaca at the time. The nature of its activities, moreover, showed a strong imprint of academic culture. The group regularly formed committees—on schools, streets, zoning, parking, parks, bus service, and other issues of the day. It produced detailed and remarkably sophisticated studies on matters of neighborhood concern, in order to better present the group's views to city officials. One such report in 1946 was actually written on Cornell University stationery.[72]

Ithaca was essentially fully developed residentially by 1950 and has seen little single family housing construction since then. The city's population actually fell by 3,000 people between 1950 and 1970, though it has rebounded since that time because of the tremendous growth of Collegetown and rising on-campus student populations at both Cornell and Ithaca College. Most single-family housing development since 1950 has taken place outside the city limits, in suburban towns like Lansing, where a shopping mall was built in 1974, and Dryden. Cayuga Heights has also grown. It annexed an area north of the original village in 1953, quadrupling its size and more than doubling its population in the process. Most of the homes in the newer part of the village were developed after World War II and are smaller and more typically suburban in character than those further south. In 1994, a retirement community catering to Cornell faculty and alumni was developed in this area.[73] As the Ithaca area has suburbanized, faculty have become more residentially dispersed. Nevertheless, Cayuga Heights and Bryant Park have maintained their status as faculty enclaves to varying degrees.

Bryant Park today is a mixed neighborhood, about half owner-occupied houses and half rentals. Some blocks are inhabited mostly by faculty families; others are dotted with student houses. As Cornell's enrollment grew in the 1960s and 1970s, the student-housing district spilled east into Bryant Park. Those streets closest to Collegetown have significant student populations. Most of the neighborhood is zoned for single-family homes, but some houses have apartments, or were rentals before current zoning classifications were implemented. The threat that Collegetown will further encroach on Bryant Park is an ever-present fear of non-student residents. "You always have to be vigilant," said one resident, the wife of a Cornell professor, echoing the sentiments of homeowners in campus-adjacent neighborhoods in college towns nationwide. "You don't want to live next door to an undergraduate student house. One property, one bad apple, can cause a whole flight."[74]

Bryant Park has been able to retain its character as a faculty enclave in the face of such threats because its current residents, like original homebuyers in the area, have been politically adept, a trait that reflects the presence of so many highly educated people in the neighborhood. Homeowners pay particular attention to real estate activity. If a house comes on the market, the Ithaca Common Council representative for the neighborhood will telephone the real estate agent to make sure he or she knows the zoning for the area and to encourage the agent to seek family buyers. If someone applies for a zoning variance, a potential precursor to conversion of a single-family house to a rental property, homeowners will quickly organize to oppose the application.[75] "When a situation that makes the neighborhood potentially vulnerable comes up . . . the word spreads very quickly and, before you know it, the phones are buzzing," said a longtime resident. "There will be a meeting at somebody's house, and, if necessary, a small army will march down the hill to the city council chambers. We come in large numbers and we're pretty savvy about how to play the political game. There's a level of sophistication that I think academics are able to bring to bear on these things that allows them to fight these kinds of fights."[76]

Why do professors seem more likely to live close to their place of employment than other workers? Numerous residents of Bryant Park and Cayuga Heights spoke of a desire to be able to walk to work. Academics tend to work more irregular hours than employees in other industries, and are more likely to go to their offices at night and on weekends, which makes convenience desirable. Faculty are also drawn to college campuses because they possess amenities—concert halls, museums, recreational facilities, park-like green spaces—that other workplaces do not. Joel Savishinsky, who teaches at Ithaca College but chooses to live near Cornell, is a case in point. "I don't work [at Cornell], I don't teach here, but I subscribe to the theater series," he said. "I can walk to the performing arts center. I love the fact that I can walk out my front door and in five minutes be up at the graduate library at Cornell. I love having Cornell next door."[77]

Alison Lurie, in her novel *The War between the Tates*, set in a thinly disguised Ithaca in the turbulent sixties, captures the peculiar flavor of college towns and the fractured nature of their social environments. She writes about the book's protagonist, a political science professor: "Brian had known for some time that he and his colleagues were not living in the America they had grown up in. It was only recently though that he had realized they were also not living in present-day America, but in another country or city-state with somewhat different characteristics. The important fact about this state . . . is that the greater majority of its population is aged eighteen to twenty-two. Naturally, the physical appearances, interests, activities, preferences and prejudices of this majority are the norm. . . . Cultural and political life is geared to their standards, and any deviation from them is a social handicap." In college towns, faculty like Brian may govern the classroom, but their influence is less significant off campus. "Like a Chinaman in New York, [Brian] looks different; he speaks differently. . . . He likes different foods and wears different clothes and has different recreations," writes Lurie. "Naturally he is regarded with suspicion by the natives."[78]

It is those differences that also shape the residential mosaic of college towns like Ithaca. Young people are dominant, but they are not distributed evenly across the city. Undergraduates live apart from permanent residents, both by choice and because year-round residents do all they can to keep them out of their neighborhoods. Some students live in fraternity and sorority houses. Some live in the beat-up old rentals of the student ghetto. Still others prefer the expensive new apartment buildings that are indicative of the changing face of college communities. Faculty and undergraduates work and play in close proximity, but they rarely live near one another, "by silent consent from both sides," as one longtime Cayuga Heights resident observed.[79] The distinctive character of college town residential districts is one aspect of life in the American college town that helps give it its unusual personality and contributes to making it a unique type of urban place.

CAMPUS CORNERS AND AGGIEVILLES

4

Walk through downtown Burlington, Vermont, around the square in Oxford, Mississippi, or along Telegraph Avenue in Berkeley, California, and you begin to notice an idiosyncratic similarity to these places that reflects the distinctive demographics of college towns. College town business districts, like residential areas in college communities, strongly reflect the presence of unusual concentrations of students and highly educated adults. Whether in Georgia or Oregon, whether in a college town that is home to a big state university or a small liberal arts college, you will find a similar mix of stores, the same sorts of restaurants, a familiar street life. If you visit enough college towns, you will eventually discern a predictable sameness, a sort of informal franchise of offbeat shops, student-oriented bars and restaurants, and businesses that cater to the unconventional tastes of professors.

Two principal differences distinguish college town commercial districts from the business districts of non-college towns—certain types of businesses are more numerous than they are in other cities of similar size, while other businesses cater primarily to the needs and desires of a campus population, so are rarely found in other small cities. Businesses that are more numerous in college towns include coffee houses, bookstores (there are thirteen within a fifteen-minute walk in Ann Arbor, Michigan), pizzerias, bike shops, record stores, copy shops, and ethnic restaurants. Because college is the first time many young people can drink legally (or at least easily), the most conspicuous difference is the large number of bars per capita. There are twenty-one bars in a six-block area of the Aggieville district in Manhattan, Kansas, and fifty-six in downtown Athens, Georgia.[1]

College town shopping areas also strongly reflect the ever-changing tastes of young people and the comparatively unorthodox orientation of many academics. Businesses that are somewhat unique to college towns among small cities because of their unusual demographics include movie theaters showing independent and foreign films, art galleries, live music venues, natural foods stores, T-shirt shops (there were a half dozen in Norman, Oklahoma, the last time I visited), juice bars, and outdoor recreation suppliers. Vegetarian restaurants, such as the Grit in Athens or the ABC Café in Ithaca, New York, may be more common per capita in college towns than any other type of place. As a vegetarian, I long ago learned that it is possible to drive coast to coast without having to rely on a diet of bad pizza and chain restaurant salad bars. It's simply necessary to play hopscotch from one college town to another. A distinctive, albeit noncommercial attribute of campus-adjacent districts is the presence of student-oriented religious organizations, such as the Baptist Student Union, the St. Thomas More Catholic Student Center, and the Wesley Foundation.

Although college town business districts exhibit a degree of regularity, they are by no means identical. One way they differ is in their proximity to the college campus and their role within a city's larger commercial environment. In some college towns, business districts have developed adjacent to campuses that are separate from a city's downtown. Most college towns have some stores or bars near campus, but only in a few have such areas developed a unified identity and acquired a name. Examples include The Corner in Charlottesville, Virginia; Campustown in Champaign, Illinois; and Campus Corner in Norman. Separate campus-adjacent shopping districts may have developed because downtown was too far from campus for students to travel regularly in a pre-automobile age. The Kansas State University campus in Manhattan, for example, is more than a mile from the city's downtown. The original road from campus to town was unpaved and impassable much of the year. In the late nineteenth century, a bookstore, laundry, and barbershop were developed adjacent to campus to serve student needs. From these beginnings, Manhattan's Aggieville district grew organically into a thriving business area (fig. 4.1).

The attributes of college town business districts also vary according to the nature of the schools they serve. Sometimes this is a consequence of the size of a school. College towns that are home to small colleges, for example, show a more limited influence of campus cultures because they lack a campus population of sufficient size to support esoteric enterprises. The characteristics of a college's academic programs and its student population also play a role. College towns that are home to regional state universities, which offer a limited range of majors and draw most of their students from nearby, do not possess the range of businesses of college towns that are home to research universities. A college town like Warrensburg, Missouri, for example, includes student-oriented bars, but not an independent record store or an art gallery. There also tend to be dramatic differences between

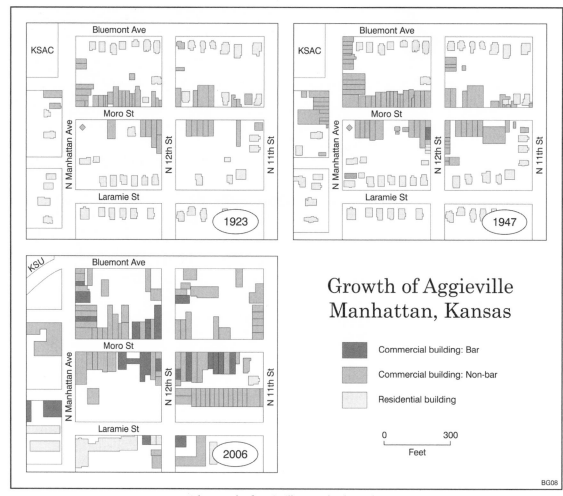

FIGURE 4.1. *The growth of Aggieville. Map by the author.*

the business districts of college towns that are home to flagship state universities and those that are home to land-grant institutions, because of their different demographics and curricula. Massachusetts Street in Lawrence, location of the University of Kansas, is a very different place from Aggieville in Manhattan, site of the land-grant Kansas State. Lawrence has fewer bars and a more cosmopolitan mix of hip businesses.

In order to demonstrate how college town business districts came to acquire their distinctive attributes, this chapter will examine the origins, evolution, and contemporary character of Manhattan's Aggieville district (fig. 4.2). It will also provide occasional comparisons between Aggieville and downtown Lawrence as a way to offer some insight into the differences that exist between college town business districts.

FIGURE 4.2. *Varney's Book Store, which opened in 1908, has grown to occupy one-half block in Aggieville and has become the district's most prominent business. Photograph by the author, 1999.*

THE EMERGENCE OF AGGIEVILLE

Probably the first business activities to take place near the campus of Kansas State University in Manhattan were informal in nature. Homeowners in the area rented rooms to students and provided meals before there were dining facilities or dormitories on campus. The university was founded in 1863 as Kansas State Agricultural College under the provisions of the federal government's Morrill Act, which offered land grants to states to support the creation of colleges that would provide agricultural and mechanical education to rural and working-class citizens. The original campus was located three miles west of Manhattan on the former grounds of a small Methodist college. In 1871, the town of Manhattan purchased 160 acres of farmland adjacent to the city as an incentive for the college to move closer to town, and four years later the college moved to its present site. Because the new campus was nearer Manhattan, no provisions were made initially to provide food or housing for students. The first dormitory on campus was not built until 1926.[2]

Even in its new location, the college was out in the country. The center of campus was two miles from Manhattan's railroad station, and the earliest academic buildings were one mile west of the nearest residential neighborhood. For the first few years, most students roomed in town and walked to campus every day. In time, professors and others began to build homes southeast of campus and offer room and board to students for a fee. A photo of the campus taken from present-day Aggieville in 1885 shows scattered houses amid farmland (fig. 4.3). Professor George Failyer built a house at the corner of Eleventh and Moro streets, now in the center of Aggieville. Professor H. M. Cottrell built a home catty-corner to it and rented rooms to female students. In the 1890s, chemistry professor J. T. Willard built a home on the south side of Moro Street, and engineering instructor O. P. Hood erected a house where Moro meets Manhattan Avenue. At the time, the area southeast of campus that became Aggieville seemed destined to become a faculty enclave rather than a commercial area.[3]

Exactly when the first formal business developed in Aggieville is unknown. The Aggieville Business Association today claims the district originated in 1889. That claim is based on a letter a Manhattan physician wrote to a local newspaper in 1950. The physician said his father built a small structure behind the family home on Manhattan Avenue about 1889 to house a laundry run by a student named Hanson. The laundry, he wrote, also stocked school supplies and second-hand books, and housed a barber shop. While the story may contain elements of truth, it seems unlikely it happened so early. The first college newspaper includes no mention of the operation, even though it printed "news" of less significance, along with announcements about new businesses. A student newspaper included an ad for a College Barber Shop, which was located near the college entrance and acted as an agent for a downtown laundry, but not until 1897. Making the physician's story seem more unlikely is the fact that the paper in 1899 published an ad announcing the opening of Hansen's Laundry, located north of the College Barber Shop.[4] It seems too much of a coincidence for another laundry operated by someone named Hansen (though spelled differently), and located adjacent to a barbershop, to have been in business in the same area in the same period. The physician was fourteen years old when he said the laundry began and more than fifty years passed before he spoke about it to a newspaper, so he probably conflated the events in his mind.

Regardless of whether the story is true, the pivotal early development that stimulated the growth of Aggieville was the establishment in 1899 of a cooperative bookstore and dining hall by a group of students. If college officials had been successful in their efforts to operate a bookstore on campus, Aggieville might not have developed as it did. For the first thirty-five years

of the college, students had to travel to downtown Manhattan to buy books. Three stores on Poyntz Avenue sold textbooks. The trip downtown, however, was long and often muddy. None of the roads had yet been paved. A horse-drawn coach service traveled between campus and downtown, but the trip took thirty minutes. The college, in response, opened a bookstore and dining hall on campus in July 1898. The bookstore, according to a college historian, "was warmly approved by students, and as warmly disapproved by local book dealers."[5] Republican business leaders in town insisted the college should not compete with private businesses, still a familiar refrain in college towns today. Critics charged that under the control of a Populist Board of Regents, the college had become "a school of socialism."[6]

The campus bookstore became a casualty of changing political leadership in the state. In November 1898, Kansans elected a Republican governor and majority Republican House of Representatives. The governor replaced four Populist members of the Board of Regents with Republicans, giving the GOP control of the board. In June 1899, the Republican board removed KSAC president Thomas E. Will and most of his allies on the faculty. Soon after, they closed the bookstore and dining hall. Students petitioned for the bookstore and dining hall to be reopened, arguing that the closing of the dining hall forced students to rely on expensive and less convenient private boarding houses. The regents agreed to reopen the dining hall with limited service but not the bookstore. Efforts to start campus bookstores faced similar difficulties in other college towns. In Warrensburg, Missouri, for example, a store operated by the YMCA to provide low-cost school supplies to students opened in a university building in 1910, but was shut down three years later as a result of pressure from the local business community.[7]

Claiming the closing of the bookstore on the Kansas State campus allowed downtown book dealers to raise their prices, a group of students in September 1899 formed the Students Co-Operative Association and opened a bookstore in a two-room building just beyond the college gate. The co-op also established a boarding club that offered students meals in a nearby house. "Our object is to cut down the expense of a college education," the group said in one of its ads. The dining hall offered board for $1.75 a week, compared to $2 at private boarding houses, and quickly became the "largest club in town," according to the student newspaper. The bookstore sold textbooks, stationery, supplies, and uniforms, and offered used books on consignment. Students in other college towns also founded cooperative businesses as a way to reduce expenses. Undergraduates at Harvard, for example, created the Harvard Cooperative Society in 1882; the Harvard Coop remains the biggest bookstore in Cambridge today and a major presence in Harvard Square.[8]

The Students Co-Operative Book Store became the nucleus around which Aggieville grew. Soon after it opened, J. W. Harrison established the College Grocery on Bluemont Avenue. By 1902, the Co-Operative Book Store outgrew its original quarters and leased a new building on Moro Street. This marked a slight move southward of the student district, owing perhaps to lower real estate prices on Moro. Property was cheaper on Moro because the area was prone to flooding, while land along Bluemont, one block north, was better drained and the street became principally residential. In 1903, the Harrison grocery followed the bookstore to Moro Street. Sensing a geographic shift in the student market, Joseph "Guy" Varney, owner of a downtown bookstore, purchased land on Manhattan Avenue between Moro and Bluemont and in 1908 opened the College Book Store on the site. That same year, the Students Co-Operative Book Store built the first brick building in Aggieville (fig. 4.4). There were seven businesses in the area, including the College Tailor Shop and the College Campus Restaurant. The district gradually came to be known as Aggieville after the KSAC athletics teams, which like those at other land-grant colleges were nicknamed Aggies because of the college's agricultural orientation.[9]

FIGURE 4.4.
*The Student
Co-operative
Book Store, which
opened in 1899
and moved to this
brick building at
the corner of Moro
and Manhattan
Streets in 1908,
was the key
development
that stimulated
the growth
of Aggieville.
Photograph
from 1912* Royal
Purple, *student
annual at Kansas
State Agricultural
College.*

The next critical early development in the growth of Aggieville was the opening in 1909 of a streetcar line that connected the Union Pacific Railway depot and the college. The first streetcar line ran along Moro Street and Manhattan Avenue through the heart of Aggieville on its way to the campus. A second streetcar line was built along Vattier Street, two blocks north of Moro. Students praised the development, the *Students' Herald* remarking that "the long walks through the slush and mud will not be experienced any longer and much time will be saved." Although the streetcar lines could have slowed Aggieville's growth by making downtown more accessible, the opposite occurred because the streetcars opened up new areas near Aggieville to residential development, thus expanding the market for businesses in the district. In 1910, the area immediately west of Aggieville was annexed by the city and began to be developed for homes.[10]

Aggieville's transformation from an incipient faculty enclave into a student-oriented business district was assured in 1912 when J. T. Willard, dean of the science faculty, sold his home on Moro Street, the last large single-family home on the block. The house became the site of the RTC Club restaurant. The Aggieville Laundry, the first business to carry the Aggieville name, was built next door. By this time, businesses occupied most of the north side of Moro Street from Twelfth Street to Manhattan Avenue, where Moro ends. Residential development in the area intensified as the college grew, enabling students to live closer to campus and heightening demand for goods and services in Aggieville. Enrollment at KSAC doubled between 1902 and 1912 to nearly 3,000. Rooming houses came to line Bluemont Avenue and Laramie Street, which parallel Moro Street. Businesses gradually spread to the south side of Moro, then east to Eleventh Street, and north along Manhattan Avenue toward the campus.[11]

By 1913, there were twenty-three businesses in Aggieville and the *Mercury* called it a "thriving college suburb." The Varsity Shop sold men's clothing, sporting goods, cadet uniforms required by male students, and college novelties. The Bungalow Store specialized in supplies required by the sewing and cooking classes at the college and became known as "The Coed's Store." The College Book Store sold drafting instruments and college jewelry in addition to textbooks. The Aggieville Bakery supplied numerous student boarding houses in the area. Several Aggieville businesses were branches of downtown stores. One of those, Palace Drug Store, built a pharmacy and soda fountain on Manhattan Avenue and advertised itself as the "students' hangout; no freshman barred."[12]

Following World War I, Aggieville and the residential districts that surrounded it experienced "the biggest building boom Manhattan has ever known," according to a local newspaper. By 1923, there were sixty-eight businesses in the district. All the streets between downtown and campus came to be lined solidly with homes, many of them housing a student or two. Aggieville had six restaurants, five grocers, four laundries, three barbers, and three shoe repair shops. The College Book Store expanded, building a two-story brick building on Manhattan Avenue that still houses Varney's Book Store. Proof that Aggieville was displacing downtown as the principal business district for students and others living in the area, a postal substation and telegraph office were established there and, in 1923, the district got its first bank. That year, the *Morning Chronicle* published a special edition about Aggieville in which it called the district a "city of youth." Although non-students shopped there, its story was the story of the students who walked its streets, hung out in its soda fountains, and ate in its cafes. "The college life is the essence of the life of Aggieville," the paper said.[13]

Aggieville began to develop a nightlife to supplement its daytime activities in 1915 when Harrison's Grocery built a two-story brick structure on Moro Street that featured a dance hall on the second floor. Without a student union or ballroom on campus, the dance hall became the site of most major college social events, including "varsities" and fraternity parties. In fact, in 1919 a college committee on student affairs ruled that students were forbidden to attend dances other than those held every Saturday at Harrison's Hall. The dance hall, which later became known as the Avalon Ballroom, was equipped with a stage and a dance floor supported by 1,300 railroad car springs to provide greater strength under the weight of large crowds. Dances at the Avalon Ballroom drew such big crowds that the city of Manhattan in 1940 restricted attendance at "official college dances" to 750 persons. Adding to the nighttime activities, a movie theater, the Miller Theatre, opened in 1926 where Moro Street meets Manhattan Avenue.[14]

The centrality of Aggieville to student life at Kansas State (fig. 4.5) was well demonstrated in the pages of the *Royal Purple*, the student yearbook. The yearbook observed in 1932 that there were several distinct types of students at the college, including the Bookworm, the Beau Brummel, the Fraternity Man, and the Campus Hero. One of the types it identified was the Aggieville Student. "Some young people come to college to hang around Aggieville with the gang," it wrote. "Aggieville Students are not interested so much in courses as in loafing and throwing the bull and the coco-cola, the laboratory fee for which is anything from a nickel to two bits in the pocket and a 'line.' 'C'mon, let's go to Aggieville'; 'Where you going?' 'Oh, down to Aggieville.' The words ring through halls and along walks more times a day than the stock greeting, 'Whaddayusay?'"[15]

Although Aggieville today is known more for its student-oriented bars than anything else, that was not the case until comparatively recently. Kansas became the first state to amend its constitution to prohibit the sale of alcoholic beverages when it did so in 1880. As a result, there were no bars in Aggieville until after Congress repealed prohibition in 1933 and Kansas voters four years later approved the sale of 3.2 percent beer. The first Aggieville bar was the Shamrock Tavern, better known as Slim's, which opened on Twelfth Street in 1937. Serving "good chili, sandwiches, drinks," it called itself "The Aggieville Oasis."[16] There were no other bars in Aggieville until after World War II and comparatively few until the late 1960s.

FIGURE 4.5. *Student life at Kansas State Agricultural College revolved around Aggieville, as shown by this parade in 1938. Used with permission, Department of Special Collections, Kansas State University Libraries.*

A QUINTESSENTIALLY COLLEGIATE PLACE

Aggieville continued to expand following World War II, as enrollment at Kansas State increased, first because of the flood of veterans that invaded college campuses following the war to take advantage of free tuition offered by the GI Bill and subsequently because of the arrival at colleges of the baby boom generation. Enrollment quadrupled in the first two years following the war and increased every year from 1951 to 1981, growing by an average of 500 students per year. In 1959, the college became Kansas State University. Stimulated by enrollment growth, twenty new businesses opened in Aggieville between 1944 and 1946. The last houses on Moro Street were replaced with businesses and the remaining vacant lots developed. Commercial development also intensified along Manhattan Avenue and Twelfth Street. The business district expanded westward along Anderson Street, on the south edge of campus. Eventually, scattered businesses also sprang up along Bluemont, Laramie, and Eleventh streets and the boundaries that define Aggieville today began to take shape.[17]

In the first two decades following World War II, Aggieville was a decidedly more wholesome, innocent, and familial place than it is today, the center of a collegiate culture straight from the pages of *Life* magazine. Fraternities and sororities still dominated student life. Varsity athletes were the big men on campus, and pep rallies before key games drew large crowds (fig. 4.6). Reaching adulthood in a period of prolonged economic growth, undergraduates saw little reason to question the mainstream values of their parents. KSAC did not build a permanent student union until 1956, so Aggieville largely served that purpose. Aggieville was where students ate, shopped, socialized, and celebrated. Manhattan and Moro streets grew so crowded by 4 p.m., according to an Aggieville barber, that "you couldn't walk down the street."[18]

Students bought their textbooks and school supplies at the Campus Bookstore, successor to the Students' Co-operative Book Store, or the College Book Store, which had green sidewalks out front.[19] College men got their haircuts at the Varsity Barber Shop, while female students got the latest hairdos at the Campus Beauty Parlor. They had their clothes laundered at College Cleaners. Male undergraduates fresh from the farm bought their first suits at Woody's Men's Shop. Yeo & Trubey Electric stocked the popular records of the day. Students danced to Matt Betton and his Orchestra at the Avalon Ballroom. They saw the latest Hollywood movies at the Sosna Theater and later the Campus Theater, as the Miller Theatre became known. Thousands filled the streets of the district on the first weekend of the school year when merchants sponsored the "Aggieville Jamboree."[20]

Most students still lived off campus in rooming houses and private homes, so many took their meals in Aggieville restaurants, which offered weekly meal tickets. Restaurants gradually supplanted private boarding houses as the places most undergraduates who did not live in dormitories or fraternities ate. They were especially busy at lunchtime, the student yearbook noting in 1950 that "café lunch hour lines are sometimes so long as to be impossible." The area near the campus had more than a dozen restaurants, including the AV Snack Shack, Wildcat Grille, Mar Café, and Dolly's K-Lunch. Others were popular gathering places after movies, dances, and sporting events. Brownie's Coffee Shop, for example, sold five-cent hamburgers "by the sack." The Orange Bowl Confectionary was known for its chili dogs.[21] The opening in 1956 of the K-State Union, which included dining facilities, led to the demise of several Aggieville restaurants. As

FIGURE 4.6.
Student life in
college-oriented
shopping districts
like Aggieville
was decidedly
more wholesome
in the 1950s than
it would be a
decade later, as
shown by this
pep rally in front
of the Campus
Book Store. Used
with permission,
Department
of Special
Collections,
Kansas State
University
Libraries.

dormitories with dining facilities were built on campus and apartments with kitchens began to replace rooming houses, the nature of Aggieville's restaurants changed. They became less oriented to the daily diets of undergraduates and more specialized. The opening in 1960 of Aggieville's first two pizzerias was indicative of this change.

The College Canteen on Anderson Street, across from the campus, was the preeminent student hangout until the building of the union. The Canteen was originally developed on campus in 1918 to serve members of the Students' Army Training Corps during World War I. It grew so popular that in 1924 the dean of women complained that students were skipping chapel to go to the Canteen. That same year, the state ordered the college to close the Canteen. Its operator erected a new building across from campus and reopened it there. With its soda fountain, jukebox, and pinball machines, the Canteen was the place students went before, after, and, sometimes, instead of class. The campus "jelly joint," it was for many undergraduates, according to the student newspaper, "their favorite class, 'jelly lab.'" The Canteen boasted in ads that it was "one class you couldn't cut gracefully."[22] It closed about 1959 in the face of competition from the new K-State Union.

Aggieville had three bars by 1951, but they were less popular than they later became because at the time sorority women were forbidden from entering Aggieville's taverns and even independent female students were rarely seen in them. Female students at the time faced much greater restrictions on their activities than males, formally and informally. They were prohibited from leaving town without permission, had to be in their rooms by 10 p.m. on weeknights, and were allowed to wear pants on campus only if the temperature fell below freezing. "A girl was looked down on if she was seen in a pub," a female student from the era later recalled.[23] Indeed, Aggieville in the 1950s possessed a gendered geography. Not only were women not found in the bars, but they were rarely seen in the Hole-in-One Recreation Club, a pool hall, or in the Orange Bowl, which offered gambling on football games.[24] The social prohibition against female students visiting Aggieville taverns gradually broke down, although it was unusual to see unescorted females in a bar well into the 1960s. Still, as women came to invade these former male domains, bars increasingly became the focus of student social lives, which may have contributed to the demise of earlier hangouts like the Canteen.

The most popular student bar in Aggieville for forty years was Kite's (fig. 4.7), named for its owner, Keith "Kite" Thomas, a former major league baseball player and star athlete at K-State who bought the Shamrock in 1948. Kite's became the quintessential college bar, with knotty pine walls, vinyl booths, pinball machines, a jukebox playing the Kingston Trio, and Schlitz on tap. It became even more self-consciously collegiate in character after Kite later sold the bar, its new owners covering its walls with college pennants and photos of K-State sports heroes. Kite's was popular because its owner had a magnetic personality, regaling fresh-faced students and alumni alike with stories of his athletic exploits at Kansas State and years playing professional baseball. He called everyone "coach."[25]

Aggieville acquired two more bars by the mid-1960s and, in time, as in college towns nationwide, each came to serve an identifiable niche of the population. Kite's became known as a Greek and jock bar, in part because Kite hired fraternity men and KSU athletes to work there. He also sought to appeal to women and about 1964 moved the entrance to Kite's so women could reach the back room without having to parade by the bar. In 1960, Kite purchased a bar on Manhattan Avenue and turned it into the Dugout. The Dugout attracted primarily non-Greek undergraduates, known as

GDI's—"god damn independents." Located on the opposite end of Twelfth Street from Kite's was Aggie Lounge, which drew a "cowboy crowd." Few students ventured to the east end of Moro Street, location of the Tap Room, which was a "less reputable place," according to one longtime resident.[26]

Campus-adjacent shopping districts like Aggieville have long been the site of both planned and impromptu sports celebrations. Pep rallies were staged before big games in front of the Campus Book Store. Homecoming parades passed down Moro Street on their way to campus. Students celebrated big wins by lighting bonfires in the middle of the intersection at Twelfth and Moro streets. Kansas State was notoriously uncompetitive in football until relatively recently, so the most notable celebrations came in association with basketball games or after rare football victories over its archrival, the University of Kansas. Occasionally, then as now, celebrations got out of hand. In 1956, for example, fans celebrating a basketball victory over Kansas that gave KSAC the conference championship lit a bonfire in the street and obstructed firemen trying to extinguish the blaze. Two firemen were injured and two fire trucks damaged. Two years later, fans chopped down two telephone poles to feed a bonfire after KSAC beat KU.[27]

Aggieville until the 1970s was also a full-service shopping area, a second downtown for Manhattan in an era before suburban shopping centers. It had a supermarket, multiple pharmacies, a hardware store, florists, a newsstand, and numerous clothing stores. There were realtors, insurance agents, dentists, and car repair shops. There was a branch of a downtown department store and Duckwall's, a variety store chain. There was even, briefly, a Crosby car showroom and a boat dealer. "You could get anything you wanted here in Aggieville," said one longtime business owner.[28] Aggieville ceased to function as a one-stop shopping district as suburban shopping centers developed, chain stores spread, residential areas nearby lost their non-student population, and the sixties counterculture transformed Aggieville.

BONGS, BELL-BOTTOMS, AND BIG-ASS BARS

On December 13, 1968, arsonists set fire to Nichols Gymnasium on the Kansas State University campus. Built in 1911, it had once been home to the Wildcat basketball team, had long been the site of course registration, and was the scene of many college dances. A north wind fanned the flames and pressure in water lines proved insufficient to fight the fire, so the building was destroyed. A year later, arsonists destroyed the Manhattan Country Club and a downtown restaurant. Nobody claimed responsibility for the fires, nor was anyone ever convicted for setting them. Although university officials and local residents said that the fires were the work of a few extremists or the often-blamed "outside agitators," these events nonetheless symbolized that the sixties had come to Manhattan.[29]

To be certain, Manhattan was no wheatfield Berkeley. That distinction belonged to Lawrence, ninety minutes to the east, which activists liked to call "Baghdad on the Kaw" (Kaw is a local nickname for the Kansas River). Lawrence was under a near-constant state of siege in the late 1960s and early 1970s. Activists torched the student union, and two men were killed by police. Rebellion centered on a block-long collection of bars, shops, and student apartments immediately north of the KU campus that included the Abington Bookstore, the Gaslight Tavern, and the Rock Chalk Café, which had on its menu "fascist pig burgers."[30] Typical of college towns with landgrant universities, Manhattan was conservative by comparison, so much so that when President Richard Nixon searched following the 1970 killings at Kent State University for a college from which he could speak to the nation's students, he chose KSU. Although a few in the crowd heckled Nixon and his speech received strong criticism in the student newspaper, most of the 15,000 who attended were respectful and supportive. He received an "almost ear-splitting reception" when he entered the building, and his speech was interrupted twenty to twenty-five times by applause. Kansas State was ridiculed in the national press for the fawning reception it gave to the embattled president.

The countercultural scene in Manhattan was small and subdued compared to other college towns. Kansas State did have a chapter of the militant Students for a Democratic Society. As on other campuses, protesters tried to interfere with an ROTC review, but were pelted with manure and eggs. Following the Kent State killings, two thousand people gathered for a peace protest in front of the administration building. Doves were released into the air, but classes were not canceled. Students grew their hair and virtually overnight went from wearing button-down shirts and pressed slacks to tie-dyed T-shirts and bell-bottoms. A few joined communes. Students created the University of Man as an alternative to traditional classes on campus. One student in 1970 estimated that "there probably still aren't 100 genuine radicals in town." As Calvin Trillin observed in the *New Yorker*, "At Kansas State, it is not always easy to tell if a pair of faded bluejeans is a symbol of the counter-culture or a leftover from the farm."[31]

The social upheaval of the era was most evident in Aggieville, and its influence persisted long after the campus protests ended. Transients and long-hairs began to hang out on the streets and complained of harassment by police. They adopted Me & Ed's, a tavern on Manhattan Avenue, as their favorite bar. "The hippies were just everywhere, hundreds of them on the sidewalks, sitting on the curbs," recalled Alvan Johnson, a Manhattan police officer at the time and later director of the Riley County Police Department. The changes were unwelcomed by business owners. Aggieville, according to Bernie Butler, who has operated a Pizza Hut on Moro Street since 1960, "was starting to step out of bounds. We had an element in Aggieville that wasn't what we thought Aggieville ought to be. We had long hair. We had the group that don't trust anybody over thirty. They would sit on my doorsteps and wouldn't let anybody through. I had the [police] chief come down with his wife one time and this little fourteen-year-old girl called the chief an MF and his wife a cunt." [32]

Contributing to the changing mood in Aggieville was the gradual dismantling by the university of in loco parentis regulations and other rules that had long governed student life. In 1965, ROTC was made optional. Curfews that had required female students to be in their rooms by 10 p.m. in the 1950s were pushed ever later and eventually eliminated. Where in the past the university had sought to separate male and female residences, building its men's dorms on the west side of campus and its women's dorms on the east, in 1969 it established a coed dorm. [33] The loosening of student regulations reflected larger societal trends that also impacted Aggieville. Women demanded equality and gained new rights. The stigma against women entering bars disappeared, so the center of student social lives shifted. The Pill encouraged sexual promiscuity, and sex began to be discussed openly. Young people had greater freedom than ever before, and they flaunted it in Aggieville.

Several new businesses opened in Aggieville and elsewhere in Manhattan that reflected the new youth culture. The Door was one of several head shops. Located down an alley between two buildings, it sold pipes and other drug paraphernalia, incense, and bell-bottoms, and featured a peace sign in its ads. The Whitewater Leather Co. on Manhattan Avenue, a non-profit cooperative, sold vests, beadwork, and "stash bags." Some of the businesses were student owned. An archaeology major opened Chocolate George, named after a member of the Hell's Angels motorcycle gang, which sold erotic teas, pillows, and crafts. The transition of businesses was often suggestive of changing tastes. Brownie's Coffee Shop, for example, was replaced by Earthshine, a clothing store that promised a "cosmic experience." Not all of the businesses catering to the counterculture were located in Aggieville. The Treasure Chest downtown sold black lights, peace symbols, and, oddly, guns. A health food store opened on Third Street.

The Experimental Light Farm, a bar on the edge of town that featured live music, had enclosed cubicles with pillows on the floor and aluminum foil on its walls for light shows. "Come to dance or just groove," said its ads. All of these businesses were short-lived.[34]

Some longtime Aggieville businesses changed with the times. Ballard Sporting Goods, which had long specialized in sweatshirts bearing fraternity insignias, began to sell jeans. Varney's Book Store stocked records by the Mothers of Invention and Jimi Hendrix, carried local underground newspapers like the *Mushroom*, and sold a dozen or so copies of the *Anarchist's Cookbook*. Waggoner's clothing store advertised shirts with "the liberated look." In a move emblematic of changing sexual attitudes, the Campus Theater began to screen sexually explicit films. In September 1969, for example, it sponsored a late show of the X-rated Swedish movie *Inga*, which featured nudity, masturbation, lesbianism, and copulation, and was advertised as "so graphic I could have sworn the screen was smoking." Such changes were not restricted to college towns with big universities. In Chadron, Nebraska, home to tiny Chadron State College, the only movie theater in town began screening X-rated motion pictures, prompting protests by the women's club and church groups, and igniting a controversy that drew national media attention.[35] Clearly, the clean-cut and rah-rah attitudes of an earlier era were fading.

Aggieville was also the center of Manhattan's drug scene. Marijuana, LSD, and amphetamines were the most widely available narcotics. The Manhattan Police Department had two undercover narcotics detectives, and they spent most of their time in Aggieville. "Heck, it wasn't anything on a Friday night to arrest twenty or thirty people," recalled Alvan Johnson, one of the detectives.[36] A Drug Education Resource Center, a sort of consumer's clearinghouse for information on the potency and safety of drugs on the local market, operated briefly on Bluemont Avenue, across the street from Aggieville. A string of underground newspapers with names like the *Miscreant* and *Roach* were published out of a Bluemont apartment building and included reports on the drugs available in town provided by the center. A typical report read:

> All the so called THC analyzed has turned out to be PCP—a horse tranquilizer. An overdose of PCP can make you feel sick, tense, and throw up. A heavy overdose can kill you. . . .
>
> Yellow Acid—About 0.5 cm diameter and 0.3 cm deep. Recently around town. Turns out this is good clean LSD with a trace of inert ingredients.

Brown Mescaline—Small tab 0.6 cm by 0.5 cm. As I said mescaline can't be found—this is LSD and PCP. It's your trip, take care. . . .

Heroin—White powder. Very, very little around town. Checked out to contain insignificant amount of heroin or none at all. Negative test for methadone. We're not sure what it is as yet.[37]

Several long-standing Aggieville businesses that catered to non-students did not survive the period and, symptomatic of the changing social attitudes, were replaced by bars. Duckwall's Variety, which had operated on Manhattan Avenue since 1926, closed in 1972 and was replaced by the Dark Horse Tavern. College Cleaners, an Aggieville fixture since the 1940s, also became a bar. Courson Chiropractic gave way in time to Auntie Mae's Parlor. Dodd's Furniture was replaced by the Jon, which used toilet seats as bar stools. Ira Haynes, who owned an Aggieville barbershop for sixty-two years, said it was the changes that took place during the 1960s that forced many old-line businesses out and turned Aggieville into a student-dominated district. "It all started changing during the hippie days," he said. "I think that's what drove a lot of the town residents away and made this area more of a college hangout."[38]

The most enduring impact of the 1960s on Aggieville was an increase in the number and size of the bars and the growing importance of the bar scene to student life. The number of bars increased from three in 1960 to eight in 1970, thanks to the new permissiveness and ever-increasing enrollment at the university, which doubled during the decade to nearly 14,000. New bars opened up throughout the seventies and early eighties. In 1978, Aggieville had thirteen bars, five of them private clubs that were permitted to serve hard liquor (Kansas approved the creation of private clubs in 1965). By 1982, eighteen bars and restaurants in Aggieville possessed liquor licenses. The minimum age for consuming 3.2 percent beer in Kansas at the time was eighteen, so most students could drink. Aggieville became known as a bar district. It was, according to the *Kansas City Times*, "where boy and girl meet beer."[39]

Long after the smell of marijuana dissipated, the bars remained. Peace and love gave way to drunken debauchery. More bars meant increased competition, which stimulated price wars. Bars featured endless promotions designed to pack their rooms and increase consumption. Women drank free on ladies night. Kite's and Mr. K's advertised nickel drafts to attract customers on Tuesdays. Bars featured "drink and drown" nights, where patrons paid a fixed price for all they could drink. Fraternities had drinking contests with rival houses and sponsored "Chug-a-Thons" to benefit charity. The name of one bar captured the new morality: It was called Mother's Worry, and its logo featured a devil's pitchfork. Long-term residents watched warily, and parents tried to keep their kids away. Dan Walter, who grew up near Aggieville, said, "In the early 1960s, my mom would have no trouble with me as a young boy riding my bike to Aggieville to get a pop and hang around. In the 1970s and 1980s, parents did not want their children to go to Aggieville. It was a student place and it was wild."[40]

Aggieville's bars grew in size to accommodate demand. The most popular were big places that drew huge crowds on weekends. Terry Ray, a long-time employee at Kite's, bought Kite's and Mr. K's in 1969. Two years later, he purchased a dance studio next to Kite's and enlarged the bar. It was Ray who developed Kite's K-State theme. He mounted a stuffed Wildcat above the bar, installed purple booths (KSU's colors are purple and white), and hung dozens of pictures of Wildcat athletes on the wall. He also nearly doubled the size of Mr. K's, evicting a restaurant, and bought the former Me & Ed's Tavern next door, which he turned into Rocking K, a country bar. In the late 1970s, Ray opened Aggie Station, a private club. Other Aggieville bars, such as the Dark Horse and Jon, were also large. Brothers, located in the former Avalon Ballroom, could hold four hundred people. The bar business had become big business. "We made a lot of money," said Ray, who became known as the "Mayor of Aggieville."[41]

Drinking ceased to be a weekend-only phenomenon. Fraternities and sororities held house meetings every Wednesday and adjourned to Kite's afterwards. Thursday was, well, almost the weekend, so it too became a big party night. On Fridays, happy hour started at lunchtime. Representatives from individual fraternities or a floor in the dorms would arrive at lunch to save a table for the rest of the group. By 4 p.m., the most popular bars had a line of people waiting to enter. We "had people waiting a half a block to get in all night," said one bar operator.[42] The overflow filled the streets and sidewalks of Aggieville, which resembled a block party. Students went "jiffing," as bar-hopping was known. Enforcement of the minimum drinking age was lax because most undergraduates were old enough to drink, so Aggieville became a destination for teenagers from throughout the region.

The social geography of Aggieville's bars remained largely as before, if spread among a greater number of locations. Kite's was still the most popular Greek bar. Mr. K's was the leading independent drinking hole. The Dark Horse Tavern (fig. 4.8) attracted "dormies" and developed a reputation as "the place where normal people went." Mother's Worry was Aggieville's first disco bar, opening soon after *Saturday Night Fever* took America by storm in 1977. Rocking K remained Aggieville's most popular country bar.

FIGURE 4.8. *Bars became the focus of student life in college towns during the 1970s. Here students play a popular drinking game of the period at Aggieville's Dark Horse Saloon. The game revolved around the CBS television series* The Bob Newhart Show. *Participants took a drink every time someone on the situation comedy said "Hi Bob." Used with permission, Department of Special Collections, Kansas State University Libraries.*

Auntie Mae's Parlor attracted graduate students and older undergrads. Aggie Lounge was Aggieville's preeminent townie bar, drawing working-class Manhattan residents. Aggie Station was a private club where you had to be twenty-one to drink, so it drew single adults a few years out of college. Bars in other college towns exhibited a similar geography. In Pullman, Washington, for example, Cougar Cottage and Rusty's were Greek bars, grad students hung out at Rico's, and the underage students traveled across the state border to Rathskeller's in Pullman's sister college town of Moscow, Idaho, where the minimum drinking age was nineteen.[43]

As Aggieville became a bar district, sports celebrations turned increasingly raucous and occasionally violent. In 1972, 3,000 fans celebrating K-State's first football win over rival KU in eighteen years filled the streets of Aggieville, setting bonfires in the street, damaging street signs, and throwing full beer cans at police. After one man was arrested for assaulting a police officer, someone in the crowd yelled, "Kill the pigs, let's start a riot." In 1978, again following a KSU football victory over KU, the celebration was even more destructive. Windows of several stores were broken, and fights erupted in the streets. Five people were arrested.[44] The disturbances in Aggieville reflected developments in college towns nationwide. Campus-adjacent bar districts have posed increasing problems for local police and university officials, whose ability to regulate student behavior has diminished since the 1960s.

In recent years, student celebrations have careened out of control in numerous college towns, often in conjunction with sporting events. In 2003, for example, eighty-seven people were arrested and twenty-three injured in Durham, New Hampshire, when students went on a rampage after the University of New Hampshire hockey team lost in the national championship game. In Boulder, Colorado, eighteen people were arrested and four injured in 2001 when fans celebrating a University of Colorado football victory filled the streets of the city's University Hill district, lighting seven fires, damaging cars, and tearing down streetlights. A detailed study of disturbances in college communities found that the number of disturbances that were not related to protests has increased fivefold since the 1980s.[45]

Aggieville's two most violent sports-related disturbances occurred in 1984 and 1986, following Kansas State football wins over Kansas. Both schools had such bad football teams at the time that the annual game between them was "like the Super Bowl," according to the editor of a KSU fan publication. In October 1984, 6,000 to 8,000 people jammed Moro Street after KSU defeated KU 24–7 (fig. 4.9). As day turned to night, many became drunk and a few turned malicious. They overturned a car, broke store windows, uprooted street signs, and attempted to steal radios and nightsticks from police. Twenty-four were arrested and twenty-six, including seven officers, were injured. The most frightening incident took place shortly after midnight, when a crowd surrounded a group of police officers at Twelfth and Moro streets, shouted obscenities and threw bottles at them, then chased the officers north to Bluemont Avenue and then south on Eleventh Street. Most of the officers were able to escape, but five were trapped by a mob in front of a garage, where the crowd took turns throwing rocks and bottles at them, like a "dodge ball game elementary kids play against a wall," according to one eyewitness. The week following the violence, which police and the media called a riot, the Manhattan City Commission formed a task force to study how to prevent future mayhem.[46]

The two schools next played in Manhattan in 1986. Government and university officials urged fans to act responsibly, but made few substantive

FIGURE 4.9. *Thousands of revelers jam Moro Street in Aggieville in October 1984 after Kansas State University beat archrival University of Kansas in a football game. The celebration later turned violent. Twenty-four people were arrested and twenty-six people were injured. Used with permission, Department of Special Collections, Kansas State University Libraries.*

changes. As it turned out, the events of 1984 acted as an impetus for greater destruction. "Riotville" T-shirts were sold and, as KSU defeated KU 29–12, one fan in the stands held up a sign that read "Riot II." After the game, fans tore down a goalpost in celebration and carried it to an Aggieville bar. By nightfall, 6,000 people swarmed Moro Street. Drunken revelers climbed atop buildings, one woman doing a striptease, others pouring beer on the crowd below and throwing bottles and cans. Celebrants on the street threw bottles and cans back at them, breaking windows. By night's end, nearly

every business on Moro Street had sustained broken windows; some forty shop windows were shattered in all. Some stores were looted. About 1 a.m., a crowd overturned a Volkswagen Beetle parked in front of the Varsity Theater and set it afire (fig. 4.10). Twenty-two people were arrested. Aggieville businesses sustained $70,000 in damage.[47]

Because of a scheduling irregularity, the two schools played in Manhattan again the next year. This time, police increased their presence in Aggieville and implemented several changes designed to reduce the potential for violence. Reinforcements were brought in from as far away as Wichita. More than 250 officers patrolled the city, double the size of the combined forces of the county and university. The city enacted an ordinance prohibiting possession of hard containers on game days. Aggieville was closed to automobiles, and an eight-foot fence was erected around its perimeter. Anyone who wanted to enter had to pass through one of five gates, where security checked for bottles and cans. No problems were reported following the game, which ended in a tie, or in subsequent years. Aggieville, in fact, has not experienced any significant disturbances since 1986, a period during which KSU's football program has been transformed into one of the nation's best. Although victory celebrations still draw large crowds to Aggieville, all have been peaceful, perhaps because, as Bill Felber, executive editor of the *Manhattan Mercury*, observed, "We got used to winning. The culture changed."[48]

Aggieville also grew to encompass a larger area as enrollment at the university continued to increase. Beginning in the 1960s, businesses began to replace residences on the south side of Bluemont Avenue, extending the district one block further north. In 1969, the district expanded south one block when a shopping center was built on Laramie Street. In 1978, the city implemented a new land-use plan that defined the boundaries of Aggieville and directed future growth. The plan recognized Bluemont Avenue and Eleventh Street as the north and east boundaries of the district, but allowed expansion on both sides of Laramie Street and west to Fourteenth Street. By 1985, a small shopping center, liquor store, and bar were built on the south side of Laramie. Two years later, a shopping center was constructed on Anderson Avenue, behind Varney's Book Store and across from campus.[49] With these new projects, Aggieville reached its current state of development.

THE CHANGING FACE OF AGGIEVILLE

In retrospect, the Aggieville riots of 1984 and 1986 can be seen as the last gasps of a hedonistic era, vanquished by the rise of a new social conservatism and the fear of AIDS. A columnist in the student newspaper went so far as to say that the 1986 riot was "the night Aggieville died."[50] In the years since, college administrators, government officials, and parents have tried to regain control over student conduct off campus. Student binge drinking and other self-destructive behaviors have come under increasing scrutiny.[51] At the same time, the shopping and eating habits of American consumers have undergone radical changes. These factors have combined to transform Aggieville and other college town business districts yet again. Aggieville today has a bipolar personality. Its retail sector has declined, while food and drink establishments have increased in number. It has become what some call an "entertainment district."

The single most important factor that has reshaped Aggieville and other college town business districts over the last two decades has been the raising of the minimum age for drinking alcoholic beverages. President Ronald Reagan in 1984 signed into law a bill that required states to raise their drinking age to twenty-one within two years or lose part of their federal highway funds. The following year, the Kansas legislature raised the drinking age for 3.2 percent beer to twenty-one. The minimum age was already twenty-one for stronger beer and liquor, while consumption was limited to private clubs. The state also enacted regulations that prohibited bars from staging promotions intended to increase alcohol consumption. Happy hours were banned, and bars were prohibited from running "all you can drink" specials. Kansas voters two years later approved a constitutional amendment permitting the sale of liquor by the drink in establishments open to the public, allowing Kansans for the first time to buy a drink without having to join a private club.[52]

The impact of the raising of the drinking age on Aggieville was devastating. Business at Kite's, Aggieville's most successful bar, "dropped off 50 percent the first week, and went down further," according to its owner, Mike Kuhn, who purchased Kite's and Mr. K's from Terry Ray in 1984. Kuhn lost the bars the next year when he was unable to make loan payments. In time, numerous bars went out of business. In 1987, Mr. K's and Brothers, two of Aggieville's most popular bars, closed. The Dark Horse Tavern shut down the following year, its owner reporting that the new drinking age "cut 70 percent of my customers." By 1988, the number of bars in Aggieville had dwindled from eighteen before the raising of the drinking age to just five. The *Manhattan Mercury* wondered, "Where have all the kids gone?" Signaling the end of an era, Kite's shut down in 1993 because of liquor law violations and did not reopen.[53]

Terry Ray, Aggieville's biggest bar owner during its peak years as a student beer-drinking district, got out of the bar business, later filed for bankruptcy, and moved to Jackson Hole, Wyoming, where he owns an art gallery. Ray first sold his five bars in 1984, before Reagan signed the new law. He sensed a changing attitude toward student drinking a few years earlier when Kansas conservatives, led by the Rev. Richard E. Taylor, Jr., mounted a drive to raise the drinking age in the state. Ray formed the Kansas Retail Beer Association to fight the proposal, and he and Taylor often testified on opposite sides of the issue at the state capitol. "He used to sit there and point at me," Ray recalled. "He'd say, 'Lookie there, there he is, the biggest drug dealer in the state of Kansas. It isn't marijuana. It isn't cocaine. It's 3.2 beer.'" Ray regained control of his bars within eighteen months of selling them when the buyers defaulted on their loans. All were losing money. He sold them again one at a time and left Manhattan in 1989. "It was not a fun time," he said. "Business was bad."[54]

If the raising of the drinking age dealt a staggering blow to Aggieville, the opening of a suburban-style shopping mall in downtown Manhattan in 1987 was a potent follow-up punch that weakened the district further. The opening of the mall epitomized changes occurring in the Manhattan retail landscape since the 1960s, all of which reflected national trends. Shopping had suburbanized along with residences. Manhattan got its first suburban shopping center, Westloop Plaza, in 1963. By the 1970s, suburban shopping centers had developed on every side of town. Although city officials blocked efforts to build a "cornfield" mall on the outskirts of the city, the downtown mall had the same impact, driving stores on Poyntz Avenue out of business and shifting the focus of shopping.[55] National chains began to displace locally owned stores. Discount department stores like Wal-Mart also changed shopping habits. The more recent arrival of "big box" retailers like Home Depot and Staples has intensified these trends.

As a result of these and other changes, Aggieville ceased to be a full-service business district. Duckwall's variety store closed its Manhattan Avenue location about the same time Wal-Mart came to town in 1972. Aggieville lost its last grocery store by 1977. By that time, chain supermarkets existed in three newer shopping centers. In 1978, Palace Drug Store, which opened in Aggieville in 1913, stopped filling prescriptions, unable to compete with three suburban pharmacies. About 1982, Keller's Department Store closed its Aggieville branch. Aggieville Hardware, a fixture on Moro Street for a half century, closed about 1984, soon after a True Value hardware store opened in Westloop. Wal-Mart has also captured a significant share of the hardware market. Aggieville had two movie theaters until the late 1990s, when both closed in the face of competition from home video and two suburban multiplexes.[56]

The opening of the mall, the Manhattan Town Center, also stimulated an exodus of businesses from Aggieville and cut sales of stores that remained. "When the mall opened up, Aggieville really got sucked terribly," said Gwyn Riffel, a Manhattan developer. Clothing and shoe stores were hit the hardest. One women's clothing store moved to the mall and another closed. Sales at Woody's Lady's Shop "dropped dramatically." Woody's Men's Store, where generations of K-State men were fitted for their first suits, closed when its owner died. Several other stores also closed. By 1992, one-fifth of the storefronts in Aggieville were vacant. The student newspaper reported that there were "hard times in Aggieville."[57]

Since that time, Aggieville has recovered from the impacts of the higher drinking age and changes in the Manhattan retail environment by catering more directly to the campus population. It's hard to imagine many of the businesses in Aggieville today existing in a non-college town of similar size. It's also hard to conceive of most of them surviving elsewhere in Manhattan. Other than bars and restaurants, student-oriented businesses include Varney's Book Store, which now occupies a full block; On the Wild

Side, a store specializing in the cultural products of the 1960s (love beads, lava lamps, Grateful Dead paraphernalia); and Acme Gift, which stocks a self-consciously kooky collection that includes Strawberry fluffer-nutter, Jesus ashtrays, and handbags straight from the pages of *Instyle* magazine, and whose typical customers, according to its owner, are "twenty-year-old tanned blonde women . . . lots of sorority girls."[58] As in almost every other college town in America, there are also tattoo parlors, copy shops, coffee houses, and video game dealers that could not survive without the student trade. Businesses that cater to an older educated clientele, such as graduate students and faculty, include Dusty Bookshelf, a used bookstore; and Olson's Shoes, the only local dealer for the college town staple, Birkenstock. Varney's and Ballard's Sporting Goods also do a strong business in KSU clothing and souvenirs.

Like other older business districts in cities nationwide that have successfully adapted to changes wrought by the suburbanization of shopping, Aggieville also has fewer retail stores and more restaurants than ever. The number of restaurants increased from eight in 1980 to twenty-one in 2007, not including bars whose main business is alcohol but also serve food.[59] Although Aggieville and Manhattan do not possess the diverse restaurant choices of college towns like Lawrence or Ann Arbor that are home to flagship universities, with their more cosmopolitan populations, its restaurant mix does show a strong influence of the college market. It has three pizzerias, three restaurants offering variations on Mexican food, two Chinese restaurants, one specializing in spicy chicken wings, and, owing to eternal student demand for cheap and quick food, nine sandwich shops and fast food restaurants.

In the last decade, Aggieville and other college town shopping districts have also experienced an infiltration of chain businesses as entrepreneurs discover the campus market. Although student-oriented districts include fewer chains than malls and suburban centers, and in some college towns chain stores have encountered hostility,[60] numerous chains have emerged that have targeted college towns because they represent definable and concentrated markets that can be reached relatively cheaply. Many of these chains are not immediately recognizable as such, but a traveler among college towns begins to notice that businesses that first appeared to be one-of-a-kind are actually what might be called college town chains. A few chains that initially focused on college towns have since spread more widely. The most famous of these are Domino's Pizza, which initially located in college towns near dormitories (it opened in Aggieville about 1982), and Kinko's, the copy shop that grew large producing "course packs" for college classes and serving student needs (it came to Aggieville in 1981).[61] Other national chains, such as the Gap, Starbucks, and Urban Outfitters, have a significant presence in college towns.

In Aggieville, most of the chains are restaurants. This is partly due to local factors, but also reflects the fact that college students eat out more often than the general population. Among the chain restaurants that have targeted college towns and have opened in Aggieville are Jimmy John's Gourmet Sandwiches, begun in the college town of Charleston, Illinois; Pita Pit, established near Queen's University in Ontario but located chiefly in U.S. college towns; Gumby's Pizza, created in Gainesville, Florida, by two fraternity brothers; Buffalo Wild Wings, begun near Ohio State University; and Chipotle Mexican Grill. Aggieville has not yet attracted any of the chain retail stores that have begun to appear in college towns, merchants say, because it lacks sufficient parking. In 2004, the city, university, and business groups joined to fund a study to examine the feasibility of building a parking garage in the area.[62]

Recent changes in Aggieville also reflect shifts in the geography of housing. Aggieville became more student-oriented as enrollment at KSU grew, families living nearby moved to the suburbs, and the houses they left were converted to rental properties to meet student demand. From 1986 to 2006, enrollment at Kansas State grew by more than 5,600 students. During the same period, the university built no new dormitories, so the student housing district in Manhattan has grown outward in every direction. Developers are also tearing down houses and replacing them with multi-unit housing. Since 2004, a sixty-four-unit apartment building was constructed on the south side of Aggieville and a seven-story condominium complex was built one block north of the district. The student population near Aggieville will likely continue to grow because the city in 2003 approved new zoning for twenty-two residential blocks in the area to encourage construction of high-density housing.[63] Changes in Aggieville echo shifts that have occurred in college towns nationwide, whose business districts were more like the downtowns of non-college towns until the student population mushroomed following World War II.

The most surprising change in Aggieville over the last decade has been the slow return of the bars, which runs counter to the logic of what was supposed to happen after the drinking age was raised to twenty-one. The number of bars increased from five in 1992 to twenty-one in 2007, not including those businesses that have liquor licenses but whose principal business is food. In all, there were twenty-five bars and restaurants in 2007 that served alcohol, plus two liquor stores and three convenience stores that sell beer.[64] Aggieville has become a bar district again, albeit with a different character than before and without the recklessness of an earlier era. How could this be? The raising of the drinking age was expected to exclude most KSU undergraduates because traditionally they did not reach age twenty-one until their senior year.

Several factors explain Aggieville's rebirth as a bar district. Enrollment at Kansas State increased by nearly one-third from 1985 to 2006, so the number of undergraduates old enough to drink grew. College students nationally are also staying in school longer than ever before; just one-third of bachelor's degree recipients in 1999–2000 earned their degree within four years of graduating from high school. Faced with the prospect of entering the work force, college students increasingly seek to extend the fun of their college years as long as possible. Officials at the University of Georgia in Athens, with its lively nightlife, have even proposed increasing tuition and cutting scholarships for students who take longer than four years to earn a degree. At Kansas State, the percentage of undergraduates who took five years to earn their degree increased from 24.8 percent for students who entered school in 1991 to 28.0 percent for those who entered in 2000. More students took five years to earn a degree than four years. This change has caused the average age of students to rise. In fall 2004, more than half of KSU undergraduates were old enough to drink.[65]

Although state and local authorities have increased enforcement of the drinking age and bars face stiff penalties if caught serving underage drinkers, many young people who are under twenty-one are drinking. As Michael Moffatt observed, "Liquor lubricate[s] undergraduate partying, and restoring the minimum drinking age to twenty-one . . . did nothing to alter this fact." From 1998 to 2003, the Riley County Police Department cited an average of 381 minors a year for purchase or consumption of alcoholic beverages, most of them in Aggieville. Those numbers do not include minors cited by the state's Alcohol Beverage Control division. Technology has made it easier than ever for minors to acquire convincing fake IDs. "They're kids, they're smart, they're going to figure out how to get in," said Rusty Wilson, Aggieville's most successful bar owner in recent years.[66] But Aggieville's bars have also changed and adapted to a different market. Most work to appeal to adults older than college age. Until 2004, they were required to derive 30 percent of their sales from food, so many have a significant restaurant business. Although there are a greater number of bars today than there were before the drinking age was increased, those numbers are deceiving because most are smaller than many that existed before the law was changed.

FIGURE 4.11.
*Rusty's Last
Chance has been
the most popular
student bar in
Aggieville since
the raising of
the minimum
age for drinking
to twenty-one.
Photograph by the
author, 2002.*

The most popular Aggieville bar in the post twenty-one era has been
Rusty's Last Chance (fig. 4.11). Rusty Wilson, who began working in Aggieville bars as a KSU sophomore in 1983, bought the bar from Terry Ray in
1989. Last Chance, at the time, was "a dog," according to Wilson. It was located in a former gas station on Moro Street; the area where the gas pumps
once stood was a patio. Wilson added a second patio behind the building,
which became Rusty's Outback. He tripled sales the first year to $1.2 mil-
lion, and the business continued to grow after that, building a following
by featuring almost nightly promotions. "There's always got to be something going on," Wilson said. "Whether it's a band or a free giveaway or
T-shirts or a swimsuit contest or throw balloons off the roof or smash a car."
In 1997, *Playboy* named Rusty's one of the top college bars in the United
States. Reflecting Rusty's dominant position in the new Aggieville, when
KSU beat football power Nebraska for the first time in three decades in
1998, fans tore down a goal post, carried it to Aggieville, and deposited it on
Rusty's roof.[67]

Rusty's has grown ever larger, so much so that a columnist in the KSU
student newspaper called it an "empire" and jokingly compared Wilson to
Star Wars villain Darth Vader. In 2000, Wilson opened Rusty's Next Door,

Aggieville's first smoke-free bar. Two years later, he expanded in the opposite direction, opening Rusty's Other Side, a pool hall. "Like the blob, it will ooze all across the city, devour it, and leave behind a stench of stale beer, fryer grease, and cheap perfume," remarked the columnist. There are now four Rusty's bars and all are connected, so patrons can move between them without ever having to leave the premises. "My whole idea," Wilson said, "[was] by the time you get through the whole complex, it's going to be 2 in the morning and you didn't have a chance to go to another bar." He expanded his holdings further when he bought the 12th Street Pub in 2003 and resurrected Kite's Bar and Grill. He also opened a T-shirt shop that sells shirts and souvenirs bearing the logos of Aggieville bars, past and present. He sold Last Chance in 2004 after turning forty years old to concentrate on the smaller, more sedate Kite's. "It's a young man's business," he said.[68]

The four Rusty's bars have muddied the social geography of the Aggieville bar scene because they draw a diverse mix of people. Rusty's Last Chance attracts mostly students, but equal parts Greeks, independents, and others. Smoke-free Rusty's Next Door draws an older fraternity crowd. Rusty's Outback attracts mostly non-students and is especially popular with smokers. Kite's has regained its status as a fraternity bar. Older Greeks also go to Porter's, which was developed initially as a martini bar. Auntie Mae's Parlor books more live bands than other Aggieville bars, many of them underground acts on the college circuit, so it attracts scruffier undergraduates and culturally aware grad students. O'Malley's Alley draws a similar crowd because it has Guinness on tap and stocks many imported beers. The Purple Pig, as its name suggests, is a sports bar that has built on the success of K-State's football team. The bar that most strongly reflects the older demographic of the current bar scene is Rock-A-Belly Tavern. With its glass block walls and chrome, it attracts a hipper, better-dressed crowd that includes academics and Manhattan professionals. Aggie Lounge, Aggieville's only remaining beer-only tavern, still has a reputation as a townie bar.[69]

Because of the large number of bars, Aggieville has a very different character after dark than it does during the day, like student-oriented districts in college towns all over. Tension has long existed between the district's daytime and nighttime businesses. Illustrative of this fact is that a history of Aggieville published in 1989 by the Aggieville Business Association to commemorate the district's 100th anniversary includes remarkably little coverage of Aggieville's bars, despite the central role they have played in establishing its contemporary identity. Dan Walter, the book's author and textbook manager at Varney's, said the exclusion was deliberate, in part because bar owners at the time were less likely to participate in the activities of the Aggieville Business Association, or they would "sign up for committees and never show up. They [were] just kind of irresponsible." Walter, who identifies himself as a Christian and non-drinker, also said he "did not want to glorify drunkenness" and questioned the morality of bar owners. "What is it inside a person that chooses to make their living by selling alcohol?" he asks. "What does that do to a person inside? When I think about the effect it has on people, the things that they do, drunk driving, the damage it does to people physically.. . ."[70]

Although Walter's views are more extreme than those of other Aggieville merchants, the belief that there are too many bars in the district and that they sometimes have a detrimental effect on daytime businesses is widespread and representative of attitudes in many college towns. Merchants grow accustomed to bar patrons using their buildings as urinals and cleaning up vomit on their doorsteps. It is part of doing business in Aggieville that every now and then a window will be broken by drunken revelers. Merchants complain about the music that blares day and night from Rusty's. It is the bars that shape the image of Aggieville. A comment in the K-State student newspaper, presumably by a non-student, illustrates the friction that exists. "You really know the students are back," said an anonymous writer, "when you have to dodge all the puke on the sidewalks of Aggieville."[71]

There is an ever-present fear among non-bar owners that when a retail or service business closes that yet another bar will take its place. Recent history, including the growth of Rusty's, has proven this to be true. Since 2004, bars have replaced an art gallery, a pet store, and a video game retailer. When a pizza parlor and a hair salon closed on Moro Street, the bars next door expanded to fill those spaces. "If another bar opens and puts up K-State memorabilia I'm going to throw up," Diane Meredith, owner of the Dusty Bookshelf and Acme Gift, said. Gwyn Riffel, a Manhattan developer who owns Aggieville properties that house nine businesses, said whenever one of his properties becomes available he is approached by someone who wants to open a bar. "Always," he said. He has refused to lease his properties for that purpose, though he has allowed properties that were bars when he bought them to remain bars. He grew frustrated in his attempts to help turn Aggieville into a more diverse business district. "There is an endless cycle [of] young guys going to college, get out [and decide], 'I want to open a bar,'" he said. "For whatever reasons, they think Aggieville needs more bars. I think it has so much potential, but it is just too difficult to take it to another level."[72]

The proliferation of bars also highlights differences between Manhattan and the nearest of its college town brethren, Lawrence. City officials and community leaders in Lawrence regularly hold up Aggieville as the example of what they do not want downtown Lawrence to become.[73] The "fear of imitating Aggieville" has even guided public policy. In order to slow the spread of bars downtown, Lawrence now requires new bars and restaurants holding liquor licenses to derive at least 55 percent of their gross receipts from the sale of food.[74] Voters in Manhattan and Riley County, in contrast, voted in 2004 to eliminate a requirement that 30 percent of bar receipts must come from food sales. Occasionally, too, Manhattan residents and KSU students wonder why the city and Aggieville can't be more like Lawrence and its downtown. "Aggieville," commented a student newspaper columnist, "cannot compete."[75]

Manhattan, today as in 1969, is a very different place from Lawrence and those differences are most conspicuous when Aggieville is compared to Massachusetts Street, Lawrence's principal downtown street. Some of those differences can be explained by differences between the two schools. As a land-grant institution, KSU has long drawn a large percentage of its students from small towns and rural areas, while most KU students come from cities and suburbs. Because land-grant colleges were created to provide agricultural and engineering education, KSU's academic programs are more applied than those of KU, where most students major in the liberal arts. Studies have found that students and faculty in the applied sciences are more conservative than those in the humanities and social sciences.[76] Those differences are reflected in the ways residents of the two cities shop, what they eat, and where they go in their free time. Not all differences between Aggieville and Lawrence can be explained by institutional differences, however. Lawrence has a larger population than Manhattan and has become a bedroom community for Kansas City and Topeka. Lawrence does not have a shopping mall or separate campus-adjacent shopping district. Government and community leaders in Lawrence have aggressively worked to strengthen its downtown for years.[77]

When you walk along Massachusetts Street, the contrasts between downtown Lawrence and Aggieville are immediately apparent. Lawrence has a more exotic variety of food choices—Korean, Middle Eastern, Latin American, Indian, Indonesian, world fusion, sushi, and tapas restaurants, two artisan bakeries, and a twice-weekly farmers market. Aggieville has only Chinese, Mexican, and Cajun, and Manhattan's only Indian and progressive Italian restaurants went out of business. Despite its large number of bars, Aggieville does not have a brew pub or micro-brewery, perhaps because, as Rusty Wilson said, "The kid from Colby is going to drink a Bud Light. He couldn't give a rat's ass about spending more money on a micro-brewed beer."[78] Downtown Lawrence also offers a greater variety of shopping choices. Lawrence has two general-interest bookstores that specialize in new books, while Aggieville has none. Lawrence has two independent record stores; Aggieville has been unable to sustain such a store since the 1980s. Lawrence is also more supportive of the arts. Its downtown has a half dozen venues that book original music several nights a week. No bars in Aggieville consistently book live music. Lawrence has numerous art galleries. Aggieville's only gallery closed and was replaced by a bar. Lawrence's Liberty Hall books independent and foreign films seven nights a week, while the only effort to screen non-mainstream movies commercially in Manhattan failed. In general, Lawrence is funky and bohemian; Aggieville is provincial and beer-guzzling. In hip college towns like Lawrence, the aroma of incense is never far away, while in comparatively conservative districts like Aggieville, you're more likely to smell stale beer and vomit.

Some sense of the differences between Manhattan and Lawrence can also be gained by examining the characteristics of businesses that have locations in both cities or that have been related in some way. Kief's Records in Lawrence supplied records to an Aggieville record store, Sound Shop, from 1974 to 1986. Steve Wilson, Kief's manager, said Lawrence record buyers were quicker to support new and adventurous musical acts, were more likely to purchase high-priced imports, and bought more classical music, while sales at Sound Shop were more mainstream. Dusty Bookshelf, a used bookstore that originated in Aggieville, opened a Lawrence store in 1996. From the day it opened, the Lawrence store sold more books and carried titles on a more esoteric range of subjects, reflecting the more diverse tastes of Lawrence readers. Diane Meredith, the store's owner, has also noticed that "the books in Lawrence are usually in rougher condition. They're smellier." Wilson, a Lawrence native with a typical Lawrence arrogance about Manhattan and Kansas State, suggested that may be because Lawrence residents "actually . . . read the books they resell."[79]

Yet for all their differences, Aggieville and Massachusetts Street in Lawrence are more alike than they are different, more similar to one another than they are to shopping districts in Topeka or Tonganoxie, Kansas. It is telling that Dusty Bookshelf has thrived in Aggieville and Lawrence, but its attempt to open a store in Wichita, most definitely not a college town, failed. Aggieville and Lawrence, despite their differences, both possess abundant bars, coffee houses, offbeat shops, and several of the same student-oriented chain restaurants that have targeted college towns. With their demographic similarities, college towns all over possess business districts that reflect the unusual nature of their populations and, as a result, stand apart from commercial areas in other cities. Youthful and eclectic, unusually cosmopolitan for towns of their size, with more bookstores and bars per capita than other cities, the business districts of college towns display a free-spirited distinctiveness that helps explain why the American college town is a unique type of urban place.

5

ALL THINGS RIGHT AND RELEVANT

The lands along America's interstate highways are normally the most placeless of spaces, anonymous corridors that look the same from Florida to Washington state. Chain restaurants. Motels. Truck stops. Driving along Interstate 80 in California's Central Valley en route to the college town of Davis, however, I encountered a series of billboards unlike anything I had seen previously in my interstate travels. There were four billboards placed at equal distances like the old Burma Shave signs. The first showed a toad climbing over the billboard and asked: "Why did the toad cross the road?" Subsequent signs answered the question: "To live in Davis because it's green, safe, and nuclear free."

Early for a meeting on the University of California, Davis, campus, I noticed a traffic circle, but this one was different from the ones I curse all over New England because it was built for bicycles. It seemed like a preposterous idea because most bicyclists I know pay attention to traffic laws only when necessary for their own safety. I watched with amazement, however, as every single bicyclist went around the circle, exactly as they were supposed to do. Rush hour in Davis is when endless streams of bicyclists travel to the university campus each morning—not just students but staff and aging professors. As I prepared for a research trip to Davis, two people offered me the use of a bicycle during my stay.

A farmers market is not normally considered a political place, but everything about the Davis Farmers Market exudes the left-of-center character of a college town. One of the first producer-only farmers markets in California, it was organized in 1975 to support area farmers experimenting with organic growing methods and provide residents a place to buy food not produced by agribusiness.[1] The farmers market has evolved into a community meeting place that embodies the Davis way of life. Many farmers post signs saying their produce is "certified organic." Exotic fruits and vegetables are common. One end of the market is set aside for groups promoting every imaginable cause. I met two lesbians distributing fliers on a documentary film about the Boy Scouts' ban on homosexuals. Another group was promoting an upcoming election initiative, while others gathered signatures for petitions.

All over Davis I encountered symbols that demonstrate this town stands apart in the comparatively conservative Central Valley and suggest how different college towns are politically from other places. On the UC Davis campus, hundreds of cardboard tombstones had been erected by critics of Israel's treatment of Palestinians. The marquee at the Varsity Theater announced a film about Mexico's Zapatista rebels presented by the Davis Working Group on Globalization. In the window of a downtown newsstand were magazines like *Mother Jones* and *Slow Food*. At city hall, a choice parking space was reserved for electric vehicles and a sign in a garden announced that the city stopped using chemical pesticides in 1995. Another sign beside the entrance prohibited smoking within twenty feet of the doorway. Davis was one of the first cities in the United States to ban smoking in all public places, even outdoors.[2]

Davis (fig. 5.1) is typical of a certain kind of college town where liberal politics are mainstream, moderate Democrats are considered conservative, and Republicans are lonely. College towns are unusual politically because faculty and students tend to be more liberal than the rest of the population.[3] This is most true in college towns that are home to flagship state universities and elite private colleges because they attract faculty and students who are cosmopolitan and intellectually ambitious, and they have strong programs in the social sciences and humanities. In that sense, Davis is an anomaly, because UC Davis began as an agricultural school. But it was also a pioneer in organic farming and developed one of the first ecology programs in the country. Moreover, enrollments in the liberal arts surpassed those in agriculture after UC Davis was made a general campus of the University of California in 1959. The town was transformed as the university evolved.

Over the years, Davis has declared itself a nuclear-free zone, the nation's first pro-choice city, and a sanctuary for Sandinista refugees. The Davis City Council officially opposed the Vietnam and Iraq wars. It was one of the first U.S. cities to implement curbside recycling. The city has sought to encourage alternative forms of transportation, building more than one hundred miles of bike routes. It has enacted restrictive growth regulations to slow sprawl. Davis has been called "the City of Cooperatives" because it has a food co-op that competes with mainstream supermarkets, arts and child care cooperatives, and a range of co-op housing opportunities. Davis is also famous for its political quirkiness. When construction of an overpass

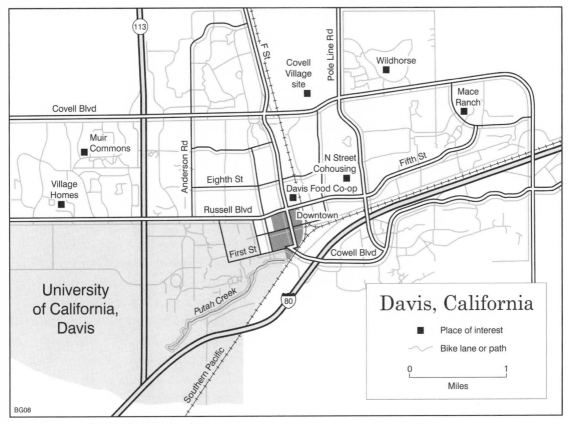

FIGURE 5.1. *Davis. Map by the author.*

threatened the migration route of frogs, the city built a tunnel under the road for them. Such incidents prompted a Pennsylvania newspaper columnist to label Davis "the weirdness center of the world."[4] A local newspaper columnist who has made a career of lampooning the city's liberal image calls it "the city of all things right and relevant."[5] Others have called it the "People's Republic of Davis." College towns elsewhere have acquired similar nicknames.

College towns all over have become blue islands on the increasingly red political map of the United States. Many have long histories of progressivism. Oberlin, Ohio, was an important stop on the Underground Railroad. Chapel Hill, North Carolina, was the first predominantly white city in the South to elect a black mayor. Ann Arbor, Michigan, decriminalized marijuana possession. Activists in Ithaca, New York, devised an alternative currency system to encourage residents to patronize locally owned businesses. Arcata, California, created an innovative marsh and wildlife sanctuary that naturally cleans the city's sewage. Cambridge, Massachusetts, was the first city in the country to accept marriage applications from same-sex couples. Few cities have such a deep liberal tradition as Berkeley, California, which elected a socialist mayor in 1911, created the first listener-sponsored radio station in the nation, and was site of one of the earliest large protests against the Vietnam War. But even comparatively conservative college towns tend to be more progressive than nearby places. Searcy, Arkansas, home to Harding University, for example, was one of the first cities in the state to voluntarily integrate its schools.[6]

The left-leaning character of college towns is also evident in election results. Davis voters preferred liberal George McGovern over Richard Nixon in the 1972 presidential election. They rejected Proposition 13, California's infamous taxpayers' revolt, in 1978. In 1994, they voted against Proposition 187, the anti-immigrant initiative that won an overwhelming statewide victory. In the 2000 presidential election, Davis voters preferred Democrat Al Gore to Republican George W. Bush by a two-to-one margin. Even more telling was that Green Party candidate Ralph Nader received nearly 10 percent of the vote. Other college towns have exhibited similar patterns. McGovern received his greatest support in college towns like Ann Arbor and Chapel Hill. Support for Nader in 2000 was even more heavily concentrated in university communities. Although Nader received less than 3 percent of the vote nationally, he won 25 percent of the vote in Amherst, Massachusetts, and 19 percent in Missoula, Montana.[7]

The political culture of college towns began to shift in the 1960s, as students and faculty who came of age during the Vietnam War era began to make up an increasing share of college town populations. This was a period of great growth in higher education, which necessitated the hiring of huge numbers of faculty. Most were young and many had been radicalized by the civil rights and anti-war movements. They soon outnumbered their older, more conservative colleagues and began to influence students and local politics. The balance of power in college towns shifted further in 1971, when eighteen-year-olds won the right to vote. The next year, with many students voting for the first time, a liberal coalition of candidates wrested control of the Davis City Council from the business interests that had long dominated local politics. Leftists also won elections in Berkeley, Ann Arbor, and other college towns. Policies became more self-consciously liberal as a result. The revolutionary tide also impacted other aspects of college town life. Free clinics were started. Cooperatives were created to circumvent the capitalist system. Experiments in living arrangements flourished. Although the liberal influence diminished over time, the sixties left a permanent imprint on the political fabric of college towns.

This chapter will trace the emergence of a progressive political culture in Davis as a way to analyze the unusual politics of college towns. It will examine several episodes and issues that have been important to the city's political transformation and are suggestive of the city's liberal tradition. It will also consider the sometimes contradictory meanings of progressivism in college towns like Davis.

MAKING BIKE CITY, U.S.A.

Though the origins of progressive Davis are generally traced to a 1972 City Council election, hints that the city was undergoing a political metamorphosis are evident even earlier. Shifts in the city's political culture have been closely linked to changes at UC Davis. The institution was established in 1909 as the University Farm to augment facilities of the University of California's College of Agriculture, based in Berkeley. Davis was an unincorporated farm town, with about twenty-five homes and a few businesses. The University Farm offered short courses to working farmers and a three-year agricultural program to farm boys who had completed grammar school. Berkeley agriculture students also sometimes spent a semester there. In 1922, a four-year degree program was initiated at Davis.[8]

If UC Davis had remained strictly an agricultural school, the town would likely never have developed its progressive reputation. The seeds of change were planted when the college began offering bachelor's degrees and hired faculty in non-agricultural fields. In 1922, the first courses in literature were offered. The earliest history classes were taught in 1936. Even so, Davis remained very much an agriculture college. Students could not major in anything but agriculture. Reflecting the rural roots of most professors and students, Davis was a deeply conservative town. Davis merchants and "aggie" faculty dominated civic affairs. So close was the connection between business and government that in 1941 the Chamber of Commerce used the mayor's office for its headquarters.

Developments following World War II transformed the campus and town. As veterans flooded colleges and California's population exploded, UC Berkeley experienced overcrowding, so the state decided to expand other campuses. In 1951, a College of Letters and Science was created at Davis. Within three years, it offered degrees in nineteen fields. Then in 1959, UC Davis was designated a general UC campus. By 1964, enrollments in Letters and Science outnumbered those in agriculture three to one. Shifting demographics stimulated change off campus. In 1958, the first woman was elected to City Council, an event UC Davis sociologist John Lofland calls a "turning point" in local politics. A year later, a political science professor, one of the "newcomer cosmopolitans" according to Lofland, won a seat on the council.[9]

Controversy over a proposal in 1956 to build a tomato cannery in the city signaled an awakening of the Davis electorate. A decade before, a development of this sort would have received little opposition, but a citizens group quickly formed to oppose it. Although the plant was enthusiastically supported by the City Council and Chamber of Commerce, critics argued it would be "a public health menace and an all around headache." The issue so divided Davis that it was placed on the election ballot four times in a year, though it won approval every time and the cannery opened in 1961. Still, the presence of a sizable opposition and the contentious nature of the debate marked a change in the political mood of the city. It was Davis newcomers, especially faculty in the College of Letters and Science, who led the opposition.[10]

One of Lofland's "newcomer cosmopolitans" was Frank Child, hired to chair the UC Davis Department of Economics in 1962. Another was Dale Lott, who joined the Department of Psychology in 1965. Child earned his Ph.D. at Stanford University and taught in Massachusetts, California, and Michigan before moving to Vietnam in 1959 to participate in a U.S. government educational program. He had lived in Europe during World War II. It was there he met his wife, Eve, a professional dancer. Lott was born on a government bison range in Montana and earned his Ph.D. at the University of Washington, where he was a student activist and chaired the campus chapter of the American Civil Liberties Union. Child and Lott had lived overseas and traveled extensively. They were antithesis of the parochial "aggie" faculty that had long dominated local politics. They instigated efforts to create bike lanes in Davis, the first significant example of progressive public policy in the city.

The Childs lived in Saigon as fighting intensified across Vietnam. Fearing for their lives, Eve left in 1960 with their four children, moving to the Netherlands, while Frank stayed. It was in the Netherlands that Eve became an avid bicyclist. "Everybody rode bicycles," she said. "People didn't just bicycle for recreation. They actually used their bikes for practical transportation." Inspired by that experience, the Childs sold their second car when they moved to Davis and bought six bicycles. Frank rode his bike to work. Bicycles had long been popular in Davis, which is ideally suited for bikes because it is flat and warm year-round. Dale Lott also rode his bike to campus, buying a used bike for $5 soon after he moved to town.[11]

Bike use was common at UC Davis because, like many agricultural colleges, it had a large campus. As early as 1910, a bicycle had been supplied to the superintendent of the University Farm. Bike riding increased during World War II because of gasoline rationing, and remained popular after the war. Seeking to build on the Davis bike tradition, Chancellor Emil Mrak in 1961 directed architects "to plan for a bicycle-riding, tree-lined campus." In response, the university closed the central campus to automobiles, developed bike paths separated from pedestrian walkways, and created bicycle parking lots. The closing of the central campus to autos stimulated even greater bicycle use.[12]

As enrollment and population increased, however, conflict between automobiles and bicycles developed. Traffic intensified, and bike riders began to worry about their safety. Frank and Eve Child suggested to Davis's police chief that the city create separate right-of-ways for bicycles on city streets. The police chief thought bike lanes could be created on a few secondary streets, but said it was unfeasible to do so on major thoroughfares. Undeterred, Frank wrote a letter that was published in the local newspaper, warning that the Davis bike-riding tradition would disappear if something were not done to protect bicyclists. Dale Lott read that letter, which "got me all excited," he said. Child and Lott, along with their wives, formed a citizens group to advocate for the creation of bike lanes in Davis. They proposed a network of bike lanes on existing streets and presented their ideas to the City Council. "Most of the members stared at us incredulously," Lott recalled.

The group then initiated a petition drive calling for the creation of bike-only lanes on most major streets. Their efforts faced criticism from residents and city officials. One resident argued that gas taxes and auto license fees paid for roads so cars should have priority and dismissed the group's proposals as "nostalgic." City engineers opposed the plan because state and federal vehicle codes did not allow for bike lanes on public streets. City officials also feared that the city would be legally liable if there were collisions between autos and bicycles. Still, the group collected 1,500 signatures and presented the petitions to City Council. "This time the stares weren't incredulous," Lott said, "they were hostile."[13]

With two seats on the Davis City Council up for election in 1966, the bicycle group sought the support of candidates. One of them was Maynard Skinner, who like Child and Lott, represented the new Davis. Director of UC Davis's study abroad program, Skinner grew up in the college town of Boulder, Colorado, had studied overseas, and directed Peace Corps projects in Asia. He was worldly and liberal. The Citizens Bicycle Study Group invited him to meet with members. Skinner, who rode his bike to campus, endorsed the bike lane proposal and incorporated it into his campaign. A second candidate, Norm Woodbury, also pledged his support and even created a round campaign poster that attached to a bicycle wheel. Both Skinner and Woodbury won election. As John Lofland has noted, "the old order was passing."[14]

The election of Skinner and Woodbury gave bike lane supporters a majority on the council. At the first City Council meeting after the election, Skinner introduced a motion to establish bike lanes on three streets as a test project. Council approved the motion. "We danced out of city hall," Lott said. Bike lanes were eventually created on forty blocks. Plans to create a more extensive bike network, however, ran into difficulty when the city attorney discovered that placement of bike lanes on streets violated the state code. City officials persuaded two state representatives to introduce a bill in the California legislature to change the code. Once the bill was approved, City Council authorized an additional seven miles of bike lanes, plus five miles of bike paths separated from roadways.[15]

Davis was the first city in the United States to create bike-only lanes on city streets (fig. 5.2).[16] By 1968, there were 18,843 bicycles registered in Davis (population 20,100), which, a local historian wrote, "surely makes Davis the bicycle capital of the United States." Recognizing the importance of bicycles to the city's image, Davis that year adopted a new logo featuring a high-wheel bicycle. A survey in 1971 found that 60 percent of UC Davis students and 25 percent of employees commuted to campus by bicycle. The city's status as a college town was critical to its becoming a bicycle pioneer. Students are more likely than older adults to ride bikes because they are more physically active, but also because universities discourage students from driving cars to campus. Professors are more likely to commute by bicycle than the general population because as intellectual curious people they tend to be receptive to alternative ideas. College town residents are also comparatively politically adept because they are highly educated. The success of the bike lane movement encouraged future activism. Bike lanes, said Lott, were "a kind of model" that helped "people think 'well, gee, this is a town where you can do stuff.' "[17]

Davis developed many transportation engineering standards for bicycles later adopted more widely and implemented innovations rarely seen elsewhere. It is believed to be the first city in the world to install bike traffic circles, which were developed at thirteen spots on the UC Davis campus. Numerous bicycle undercrossings were built under roads. Bike-only left-turn lanes were created at several intersections. In 1990, the city installed the first bicycle traffic signal in the country, and eventually they were erected

FIGURE 5.2.
*Davis in 1966
became the first
city in the United
States to create
bike lanes on its
streets. Used by
permission, City
of Davis.*

at six intersections. Davis also devised standards for bikeway widths, curvature, and grades. They were distributed widely and helped Davis establish an international reputation as a bicycling leader. Standards first developed in Davis were later adopted by the state of California and the Federal Highway Administration.[18]

Over time, the building of bikeways and other bicycle facilities became institutionalized in Davis. The city created a full-time position for a bicycle coordinator and established a Bicycle Advisory Commission. The city's General Plan has become ever more specific in its requirements for bicycles. The 2001 General Plan requires that bike lanes "be provided along all collector and arterial streets." Home developers have come to understand that if they want to build in Davis, they have to provide bike lanes and bike paths. Apartment builders must provide two bike parking spaces for each apartment. New and expanding businesses must install bike racks. The city's bike network is so extensive that Davis schools no longer provide bus service for children. By 2006, the city had 50 miles of bike lanes and 53 miles of bike paths. Ninety percent of collector and arterial streets had them. The League of American Bicyclists in 2005 named Davis the most bicycle-friendly city in the nation (fig. 5.3). Fourteen of the seventeen most

FIGURE 5.3. *The number of bikes parked around buildings on the University of California, Davis, campus attest to the heavy bike use in the city. Photograph by the author, 2001.*

bike-friendly communities were college towns or small cities with prominent universities.[19]

Although Davis still possesses an international reputation as a bicycling city, bikes are less pervasive than they once were. Several factors have contributed to a decline in bike use. The city has grown substantially in area, so is less bikeable. Rising home prices have forced many students and faculty to live elsewhere. College students are less environmentally conscious than earlier generations and more affluent, so are more likely to own cars. UC Davis bike coordinator David Takemoto-Weerts also blames the popularity of the university's bus service, the success of which partly reflects the city's progressive heritage. Nevertheless, the changes are relative. The percentage of Davis workers who commute by bike declined from 21.6 percent in 1990 to 14.4 percent in 2000, but bike use is still far more prevalent than in the rest of the country, as it is in other college towns. Just 0.4 percent of U.S. workers in 2000 commuted by bicycle, compared to 7.1 percent in Corvallis, Oregon, and 5.3 percent in Gainesville, Florida.[20]

A second development that anticipated the dramatic changes in Davis politics was the creation of a recycling program. As the emergence of the city's bike culture demonstrated, progressive ideas were not necessarily new ideas. Sometimes it is necessary to look back to move forward. Recycling was widespread in the United States until the early twentieth century. The reuse of everything from rags to steel to kitchen waste, historian Susan Strasser has observed, was "inherent to production in some industries, central to the distribution of consumer goods, and an important habit of daily life." The spread of municipal trash collection, the advent of disposal packaging, and rising affluence stimulated a decline of recycling, although it regained popularity during times of depression and war.[21]

Recycling is now promoted chiefly for its environmental benefits, but the birth of recycling in Davis, like the creation of bike lanes, had nothing to do with the environmental movement, though support of the city's progressive community was critical to its growth. The city's recycling program, in fact, predates the first Earth Day, April 22, 1970, generally considered the birth date of the modern environmental movement. It began even more inauspiciously than did efforts to create bike lanes. Richard Gertman, a UC Davis graduate student who created the program, would not have been considered one of the "newcomer cosmopolitans." He studied paleontology and hoped to become a college teacher. Gertman was president of the campus geology club and was looking for a way to raise money to finance club activities. "We really needed some cash," he said.[22]

Gertman and his fellow geology club officers obtained eight Salvation Army donation boxes that the organization was removing from Davis. They placed them at local schools, then announced that residents could drop newspapers at the boxes. The program began the first week of April 1970. The Davis program was part of a nationwide movement, though its founders were unaware of that at the time. All across the country, environmentally aware young people were starting voluntary recycling centers. An estimated 3,000 such programs were organized in the months surrounding the first Earth Day. The young activists were influenced by publications like the *Whole Earth Catalog* and *Mother Earth News*. The geology club program was not the only recycling program in Davis. About the same time, the Ecology Club at Davis High School began collecting aluminum cans.[23]

But geology club members did not share equally the labor required to run the recycling program, and Gertman soon grew frustrated. In response, he founded the Recycling Committee of Davis in September 1970 to take over the program. It ceased to be a fundraising vehicle. Through his recycling activities, Gertman was gradually transformed into an environmentalist. He never finished his Ph.D. and made recycling his life's work. He began to recognize that recycling had non-monetary value. "It had become something different," he said. "It was a worthwhile activity that needed to continue." In February 1971, the program was expanded to include bottles and cans.[24]

Disposable glass bottles became popular during the 1960s, which increased the volume of glass destined for landfills. Between 1960 and 1970, the percentage of soft drinks produced in refillable containers declined by half. The shift to disposables drew the ire of environmentalists, who in 1970 dumped mounds of non-returnable bottles at Coca-Cola's headquarters in protest. Gertman became politically active to address the issue. In fall 1971, he organized a campaign that resulted in the Davis City Council enacting the first bottle deposit ordinance in California. The beverage industry opposed the ordinance and threatened to stop distributing bottled drinks to Davis. The City Council withdrew the ordinance when Coca-Cola agreed to haul cans and bottles collected by the Recycling Committee to buyers. The Davis bottle law anticipated efforts by several states. In 1972, Vermont and Oregon approved laws requiring beverage producers to distribute drinks in returnable bottles.[25]

Bob Black, a former UC Davis student body president and activist who ran for City Council in 1972, proposed in his campaign that Davis establish a curbside recycling program. Although numerous groups around the country had organized recycling drop-off centers, few cities had curbside recycling. The college town of Madison, Wisconsin, is believed to have been the first U.S. city to institute curbside recycling when it did so in 1968. After Black was elected, he encountered resistance to curbside recycling from people who thought it would be expensive. In response, he initiated a survey of residents, asking if they would be willing to pay more for garbage collection to support curbside recycling. "The results came back rather dramatically," Black said. "Yes, people want that and they'd be willing to increase their garbage rates by a significant amount."[26]

The survey results reflected Davis's changing demographics and shifting political climate, all of which were stimulated by developments at UC Davis. The city's population tripled between 1960 and 1972, pushed higher by rising university enrollments. Many of the newcomers were students and faculty in the College of Letters and Science. UC Davis in 1966 formed an Institute of Ecology. Two years later, it created the Graduate Group in Ecology to offer degrees in the field. The College of Agriculture underwent profound changes and in 1967 was renamed the College of Agricultural and Environmental Sciences. The university also lent support to the Recycling Committee when in 1972 it allowed the group to set up a full-time recycling center on campus land. That same year, the group incorporated as the nonprofit Resource Awareness Committee of Davis.[27]

Davis implemented mandatory curbside recycling of newspapers in 1974 (fig. 5.4). Recognizing that high participation in the program was essential to justify the cost, Black devised an ordinance that made it illegal for residents to mix newspapers with the rest of their garbage. The City Council approved the ordinance, which imposed a $5 penalty for each violation, though no one was ever fined. In implementing curbside recycling, Davis was at the leading edge of a national movement. The number of curbside recycling programs in the United States grew from two in 1970 to 118 in 1974. The Davis program was unusual in that it made recycling mandatory. In November 1974, the recycling program began picking up cans and bottles, making it one of the first cities in the nation to collect multiple types of recyclable materials. Two years later, the city's garbage contractor, Davis Waste Removal, built a recycling processing center and took over curbside recycling collection. Participation had grown, and once skeptical city staff had come to see the merits of recycling. "A lot of people, when we first started, felt that this is a college student fad thing and it's not going to last," said Gertman, who was then hired as the state's first recycling coordinator. "We'd proven that we were a real program." [28]

Three years later, Gertman became Davis Waste Removal's first full-time recycling coordinator and began expanding the recycling program. It began recycling cardboard. It installed a magnetic can separator. It started purchasing wine bottles, initiated a program to collect white paper from offices, and purchased a grinder to make compost from yard waste. One of the company's owners, a former UC Davis professor, invented a machine that scoops yard waste placed directly on the street rather than in bags, which slow the composting process. Davis Waste Removal also developed a specialized recycling truck. Techniques such as these are now common, but Davis was consistently among the first to try such ideas. By 1981, 30 percent of waste produced in the city was recycled or composted. Five years later, Davis was honored for having the best curbside recycling program in the United States.[29]

Davis's recycling program became a model for communities throughout

FIGURE 5.4.
*Newspaper
collection box
used by Davis's
pioneering
curbside recycling
program, circa
1974. Photograph
by Richard
Gertman; used
with permission.*

California. Gertman applied what he learned in Davis elsewhere. As recycling coordinator for the California Waste Management Board, he developed legislation to provide funding for communities to establish recycling programs. In 1985, he was hired by the city of San Jose to create a recycling program and modeled it after Davis's program. The Davis system was later spread more widely when Waste Management, the nation's largest garbage removal company, purchased the San Jose company that operated the city's recycling program. It became the basis for Waste Management's recycling division. Davis has continued to be a recycling leader. In 1994, for example, it became the first city in California to recycle aerosol cans. By 2001, the city was recycling 53 percent of its refuse.[30]

THE REVOLUTION OF 1972

As we have seen, individuals have been crucial to making Davis into a progressive city. Without Frank and Eve Child, along with Dale and Donna Lott, Davis might never have become "Bike City U.S.A." Maynard Skinner helped them gain support for their ideas within city government. Richard Gertman transformed Davis into a recycling leader. Each of these people possessed characteristics that are unusually common in college towns. Born and raised elsewhere, they are highly educated, politically adept, and willing to work for change. No individual provides greater insight into the metamorphosis of Davis than Bob Black, who was elected in 1972 to the first of two terms on the Davis City Council, served as mayor for two years, and later won a seat on the Yolo County Board of Supervisors. His story parallels changes that have occurred in Davis political life from 1965 to the present.

Born in Chicago in 1946, Black moved to the San Francisco suburbs with his family when he was ten years old. His father was a construction superintendent for Bechtel Corp. Black's parents were Republicans. They took him in 1962 to see Richard Nixon, who was campaigning for governor. He shook Nixon's hand. In high school, Black came under the influence of several young teachers he now describes as Kennedy Democrats. Black's changing politics spurred conflict at home. He remembers telling his mother that one of his teachers said the Russian people were better off under the Soviet Union than they had been under the czars. Bob's father overheard him and stormed into the room, threatening to report the teacher as a communist. Foreshadowing his future activism, Bob was active in student government as early as elementary school.

When Black entered UC Davis in September 1964, it was a comparatively conservative university. The town was "apolitical," he said. Black's radicalization occurred a year later, when he attended a speech on campus by *Ramparts* magazine editor Robert Scheer, who urged students to protest the Vietnam War. Immediately after that speech, Black became an active participant in the anti-war movement. He became the undergraduate spokesman for the UC Davis chapter of the Vietnam Day Committee and led an anti-war march to Travis Air Force Base. In 1965, Black was elected to the executive council of student government. It had long been dominated by Greeks and was chiefly concerned with extracurricular activities such as homecoming. "I quietly slipped in there," Black said. But opposition to the war and student activism on other issues was growing, even on conservative campuses.[31]

In 1966, Black was elected UC Davis student body president on a "mandate for radical change." He pushed to create the student-run Unitrans bus system. Under his leadership, UCD student government created an Experimental College that today offers non-credit courses on subjects ranging from composting to Tarot card reading. It started a student-run coffee house. It created an arts festival that has evolved into the annual Whole Earth Festival and established a program that published student ratings of Davis apartment buildings. "My platform was one of moving away from the rah-rah activities," Black said, "[and] addressing issues that were vital to the actual day-to-day lives of students."[32]

One year after he was elected student body president, Black abruptly quit school. Frustrated by what he saw as the increasing irrelevance of his classes in a country torn by war and racial strife, he stood up in the middle of a sociology midterm, walked to the front of the room, and wrote on the blackboard, "How long will we indulge these absurdities? I quit." He dropped his exam in the trash and did not return to school for five years. He first worked as a migrant farm laborer in Oregon. Once he saved some money, he moved to Mexico. The assassination of civil rights leader Martin Luther King in 1968 prompted him to return to the States. That same year, Robert Kennedy was shot, protestors and police clashed at the Democratic convention, and more than 14,000 U.S. soldiers were killed in Vietnam. "It seemed like America was coming apart," Black explained. "I decided I needed to reconnect with my politics." He went to work for a nonprofit organization educating poor and minority children in Pennsylvania. In 1969, he returned to Davis, where he helped found a health food store.[33]

Davis in 1969 was a different place than when Black entered UC Davis. Enrollment at the university had nearly tripled. The city population had doubled and was projected to grow to 240,000 by 2010. Residents were concerned about the rate of growth. The campus had become politicized, as casualties in Vietnam grew and student protests spread. Davis students in May 1969 boycotted classes and marched through downtown after UC Berkeley seized control of a park created by activists. In April 1970, students staged sit-ins in the administration building. After four anti-war protestors were killed at Kent State University, two Molotov cocktails were thrown into the ROTC building. But Davis was peaceful compared to Berkeley. It is remembered as "the quiet campus." An effort to start a UC Davis chapter of the radical Students for a Democratic Society failed.[34]

The U.S. government created an unprecedented opportunity for political change in college towns when it lowered the voting age from twenty-one to eighteen in 1971. Equally important to altering the balance of power in college towns were court rulings that authorized college students for the first time to vote in the towns where they went to school rather than where their parents lived. After the voting age was lowered, two local activists approached Black and suggested he run for Davis City Council. They felt his notoriety as an activist student body president would help him win the youth vote, but Black was reluctant. "I said, 'Gosh, I'm not a student,'" he recalled. "'I'm not really respectable.' You've got to remember, I walked out of a university class."[35]

Black eventually chose to run for City Council because he was concerned about Davis's rapid growth. The city added 2,000 residents in 1971 alone. That same year, city officials approved 6,000 additional housing units. "I had been experiencing [a] sense of unease as I observed Davis losing its small-town character," he said. "It takes a while to put that into a political context, that these are political decisions being made to allow this to happen." He talked with leaders of the Davis Democratic Club about running. Three seats on the five-member City Council were up for election in 1972, but only one incumbent chose to run. The three openings, lack of incumbents, lowering of the voting age, and the city's changing political climate made local progressives think they could take control of the City Council if they worked together. Maynard Skinner, the most liberal member of the council, helped organized a series of meetings with other like-minded residents. Eventually they decided the best way to achieve their goals was to run a slate of three candidates. "This town was ready to change," Skinner said.[36]

The group chose three candidates intended to appeal to different segments of the electorate. All agreed it was essential to select a candidate who would attract students. Black was the obvious choice. They also agreed to choose a candidate who would appeal to working-class Democrats and selected British-born Richard Holdstock, an environmental health and safety officer at UC Davis. Skinner called him "my favorite Trotskyite." All agreed, too, that the slate must include a woman. They selected Joan Poulos, an attorney and wife of a UC Davis law professor. The candidates each ran independent campaigns except on campus, where they took out joint advertisements and distributed campaign signs promoting all three.[37]

The campaign exposed a deep divide in Davis politics. Harry Miller, a UC Davis 4-H specialist, was the incumbent and represented the old guard of Davis politics. He and jewelry store owner Fred Pearson were backed by the business community. Black ran the most radical campaign, warning voters that "Davis is at a turning point." The focus of his campaign was controlling growth. He called for a freeze on approval of development applications. He also proposed implementation of a composting program, adoption of affirmative action in city hiring, and the development of guidelines for "ecologically sound house design." Many of Black's ideas represented dramatic departures for city government, long concerned chiefly with schools, streets, and other basic needs. Students became actively involved in the campaign. UCD student government organized a registration drive that signed up 6,400 new voters. In addition, a UC Davis student organized a petition drive that placed on the ballot a referendum demanding withdrawal of U.S. military forces from Southeast Asia.[38]

The election results stunned almost everyone. Poulos, Holdstock, and Black won landslide victories, and the peace referendum was endorsed by 76 percent of voters. So shocking were the results that the *Los Angeles Times* published a front-page story about the election. Support for coalition candidates was greatest in student-dominated districts, but analysts later observed that the progressive slate so dominated the election that all three candidates would have won even without the student vote. Poulos, Holdstock, and Black were sworn into office one week later in a ceremony that was a powerful symbol of change (fig. 5.5). It began with the three outgoing council members posing for a cameraman. They were a picture of conventionality. All wore coats and ties. They were clean shaven, their hair closely cropped. The new members were then sworn in. Holdstock wore an anti-war button on his lapel. Poulos was only the second woman elected to City Council, so her mere presence was a statement about the new Davis. Black wore loud striped pants. His beard and mustache were unkempt, and his bushy hair flowed in front of his head like a wave. "It was a visual representation of the change," said a member of the group that organized the progressive slate. "It was very potent and very charging."[39]

The new City Council immediately signaled how differently it would interpret the function of local government. On the night the new members were sworn in, it approved a motion by Black allowing city workers two hours off with pay to attend a Vietnam War moratorium rally at UC Davis. Three weeks later, City Council took its second foreign policy action, proclaiming a "peace day" in response to a decision by President Nixon to mine North Vietnamese ports and bomb Hanoi railroads. Although Davis and other college towns have been ridiculed for establishing policies on issues over which they have little control, Black said such efforts represented a deliberate attempt to redefine the role of local government. "If the people of Davis are concerned about ending the Vietnam War," he said, "then why wouldn't they want their City Council to speak for them in that regard?"[40]

Black went even further in expressing his opposition to the war. On the "peace day" declared by City Council, he joined an anti-war protest that blocked the Southern Pacific Railroad tracks that pass through Davis and was arrested (fig. 5.6). The protest began on campus. Later, protestors marched to Interstate 80, where they blocked traffic for twenty-five minutes. Under the threat of arrest, they headed for the Southern Pacific depot.

FIGURE 5.5. Davis City Council in 1970 (top) and in 1972, after two liberal candidates and a woman were elected to the council. Used with permission, City of Davis.

FIGURE 5.6. *Police arrested sixty anti-war protestors, including newly elected Davis City Council representative Bob Black, when they blocked the Southern Pacific Railroad tracks that pass through Davis in 1972. Used with permission, Special Collections Department, University of California Library, Davis.*

About 150 protestors interrupted rail traffic for six hours in an effort to halt the transportation of "war materials," with many, including Black, sitting on the tracks. Two hours later, police arrested sixty protestors who refused to move. Black drew "thunderous applause" when he was arrested.[41]

City Council also quickly addressed local issues. It enacted a two-year moratorium on the approval of development applications while the city drafted a new General Plan.[42] The council also gave citizens significant input in developing the General Plan, appointing 110 residents to ten committees. The new General Plan was approved in 1973 and strongly showed the influence of an activist council. It imposed significant limits on growth and recommended that the city's population not be allowed to exceed 50,000 by 1990. City Council in 1969 had projected a 1990 population of 75,000. The main tool for slowing growth was a housing allocation system that authorized the city to specify the maximum number of housing units that could be approved each year. Between 1975 and 1982, nearly half of all housing units proposed were rejected. Davis was only the second city in California to institute growth control.[43] Other college towns were also pioneers in that regard. Eugene, Oregon, in 1972, sought to limit growth by establishing an urban service area boundary, beyond which it refused to provide city services. Boulder in 1976 imposed strict limits on housing construction, restricting growth in the number of housing units to 1.5 percent a year, and has continued to be a growth-control innovator.[44]

Black calls the 1973 Davis General Plan "a masterpiece of community development." Although many ideas in the plan have since gained wider acceptance, there is much about it that made it unusual at the time. In order to maintain air quality, for example, it called on the city to engage in planning that "de-emphasizes the use of the automobile." It advocated creation of a "continuous system of interconnected bikeways in and out of the city." The plan encouraged use of native and drought-tolerant plants in landscaping, adoption of alternatives to pesticides, and restoration of habitats eliminated by development. It recommended enactment of laws restricting use of disposable bottles and cans, implementation of curbside recycling, and revision of city codes to require buildings to be energy-efficient. It seems doubtful many other small city general plans at the time would have formally defined terms such as "ecosystem" and "sprawl."[45] Those that did were probably college towns.

Other City Council actions also reflected a new progressive posture. In 1975, it approved an energy conservation building ordinance, becoming the first city in the nation to enact such a law. Even before the 1973 Arab oil embargo, which forced Americans to become more energy-conscious, local environmentalists convinced the council to provide $15,000 so they could study ways in which buildings could be made more efficient. The energy ordinance requires houses to face north-south in order to benefit most from the sun's warming rays and prevailing breezes. It requires windows to be shaded in summer, limits the extent of windows, imposes minimum insulation standards, and requires roofs and exterior walls to be light in color to limit absorption of solar energy. The ordinance drew international attention. President Jimmy Carter praised the city's efforts to conserve energy in an address to the nation. "If you're a university community," Black told *Newsweek*, "you . . . have the responsibility to experiment, to step out and take risks."[46]

The liberal takeover of the Davis City Council has had crucial long-term consequences. A belief in growth control is firmly ingrained in the city's psyche. Bicycles and recycling are defining elements of local culture. The changes that occurred also encouraged greater citizen participation in politics. Few cities possess such an active citizenry. Serving on city committees is compulsory for many. Time set aside for public comment at City Council meetings, perfunctory in most places, is a key forum for public opinion and acts as a springboard for public office. A reporter once remarked that "Davis is the only town where people go to city hall the way people in other towns go to the movies." Two-term mayor David Rosenberg says that "being mayor of Davis is like being mayor of a town of 50,000 mayors." All of these characteristics derive from the city's status as a college town, populated by people who are highly educated, engaged, and believe in the value of debate. But carrying out the business of government can be difficult for the same reasons. During the administration of one progressive mayor, City Council meetings averaged more than six hours in length and often dragged on past 2 a.m. The most recent General Plan revision took eight years and cost $1 million.[47]

Progressives and moderate Democrats have controlled the Davis City Council ever since 1972. Newspaper columnist Bob Dunning refers in jest to the city's "twenty-seven Republicans." The percentage of voters registered Republican declined from 36.7 percent in 1970 to 19.7 percent in 2005.[48] Lacking a meaningful Republican opposition, Democrats differentiate instead between "progressives" and "moderates," but these terms are rarely applied consistently. In truth, most Davis "moderates" would be considered liberal anywhere but in a college town. Again, the case of Bob Black is suggestive. After serving two terms on City Council and two more on the Yolo County Board of Supervisors, he moved in 1998 to rural northern California, where he is Del Norte County counsel. Black is as idealistic and liberal as ever, but in a 2005 Davis election he endorsed a proposal to build a large housing development outside the city in what became the most contentious election in city history. In the process, he found himself on the opposite side of the issue from many contemporary "progressives." Self-proclaimed "progressives" have become ever more extreme in their views, making Black look moderate by comparison and raising questions about what it means to be progressive in a college town.

The liberal character of college towns is reflected not only in government policies and election results, but in the progressive nature of businesses and organizations. Davis, like other college towns, is home to an unusual variety of institutions created to provide a public good or offer alternatives to established ways of doing things. In 1972, for example, a local doctor founded a free clinic to provide medical care to drug addicts and others who could not afford private physicians. Today, it operates seven clinics in five cities and treats 80,000 patients a year. Volunteers also created the Short Term Emergency Aid Committee, which offers housing, clothing, and money to low-income residents, abuse victims, and others. Davis Community Meals provides free meals to the needy twice a week and operates a homeless shelter, while the local chapter of Food Not Bombs offers free vegan meals weekly in a city park.[49]

The Davis Food Co-op (fig. 5.7) is the most prominent alternative institution in Davis, and its success demonstrates the degree to which liberal ideas have become mainstream values in college towns. Food co-ops are more common in college towns than in any other type of setting. More than one-third of all U.S. cities that had food co-ops in 2005 were college towns.[50] The Davis Food Co-op is one of the most successful in the United States, and its 27,000–square-foot store is the largest west of the Mississippi River. It competes directly with mainstream supermarkets. Successful co-ops have also influenced natural foods chains like Whole Foods and Wild Oats, which began in the college town of Boulder. But the Davis Food Co-op, like other co-ops, is more than a store. It was founded to give residents access to products not available in conventional groceries, but also to provide an alternative to buying food in profit-driven supermarkets. For its most loyal customers, the Davis Food Co-op represents their political beliefs put into action in everyday life. It is an important meeting place and venue for distributing information and building support for liberal causes.

The roots of the Davis Food Co-op are similar to those of many so-called new wave cooperatives. They are called "new wave" to distinguish them from hundreds of cooperatives founded during the Great Depression, which were less radical in their intentions than later co-ops. All cooperatives trace their ideological origins to Rochdale, England, where a group of striking weavers and artisans in 1844 opened a cooperative store to provide staples to strikers at low prices. By the 1860s, there were more than four hundred co-ops in England. Most "new wave" co-ops grew out of the counterculture move-

FIGURE 5.7.
The Davis Food Co-op, the largest food cooperative west of the Mississippi River, has become the most prominent alternative institution in Davis and serves as a meeting place for local liberals. Photograph by the author, 2001.

ment of the late 1960s and early 1970s. Activists frustrated by their inability to achieve sweeping political and social change sought through the creation of food co-ops, communes, and alternative media to carve lifestyles outside the mainstream. Some 5,000 to 10,000 food co-ops were established in the United States during the period. The founding of food co-ops reflected a newfound interest in ecology and nutrition, disenchantment with commercial health food stores, and opposition to the food industry. Co-ops, one writer commented, are "businesses with a conscience." [51]

Like many other co-ops, the Davis Food Co-op began as a buying club, an effort by a group of UC Davis students to pool their money so they could purchase natural foods in quantity. The leader of the group was Ann Evans, later elected to two terms on the Davis City Council. Evans grew up in Berkeley, where her mother was a school teacher and her father was president of a credit union affiliated with the Berkeley Co-op. Growing up in the most liberal of college towns shaped Evans's world view. Her parents were politically active, and she worked on city council campaigns as a teenager. Evans enrolled at UC Davis in 1968, majoring in nutrition. She fell in with a crowd of radical agriculture students, many of whom started organic farms in the area. They protested against corporate agriculture. Evans read

Frances Moore Lappé's influential book, *Diet for a Small Planet*. She became a vegetarian and moved into an old house with three like-minded friends. The house operated as a co-op. "All of us were fairly political," Evans said. "We gardened together. We ate together. It was a whole philosophy."[52]

Evans and her housemates joined with several other student co-ops to buy cheese, dry goods, and other food they couldn't grow themselves directly from wholesalers. Davis had a health food store, Natural Food Works, started by Black and others in 1969. Evans shopped there occasionally, but "I didn't share their economic philosophy. It wasn't a non profit. It wasn't community owned." When several student co-ops closed for the summer, those that remained could no longer meet the minimum purchase requirements of wholesalers. So Evans and three friends organized a buying club, which they called the People's Food Conspiracy. By 1976, the buying club had grown to include three hundred households, but as it grew, fewer people were willing to put in the time to make it work, and Evans feared it would collapse. "You reach a certain point where you can't sustain on a volunteer basis," she said. She and several other leaders decided to open a store. "We were very clear that it would take the same amount of energy," she explained. "And we could feed many, many more people."[53]

Group members raised $4,000 to open a store. Someone discovered a bulk dog food store was going out of business. It was a raw space, with one door and a garage-like interior, but rent was cheap. Members did all the work themselves to outfit the store. They built the shelves and counter. The boyfriend of Evans's roommate did the plumbing. Evans oversaw applications for city approval and painted the first sign. "A lot of people put in incredible amounts of time—just gave their lives—to open that store," Evans said. The group changed its name to the Davis Food Co-op, and the store opened in December 1976. It was cramped, incomplete in its selection, and inefficient in its operation. The space was so small that two people could not pass each other in the aisle if either was wearing a backpack. Shipments had to be sorted on the sidewalk. Management was haphazard. Volunteers who worked a half-day each week ran the store. There was no paid staff. Member households were required to work two hours a month. The Co-op remained unincorporated. "People fought incorporation," Evans remembered, "because they thought, 'Oh god, we're going to be too normal.'" Despite these shortcomings, membership grew and within two years, the Co-op had 750 member households.[54]

Like many young co-ops, the Davis Food Co-op refused to carry certain products on political grounds. It honored all United Farm Workers' boycotts. It boycotted Nestlé products because the company's sale of baby formula in poor countries was blamed for high infant mortality rates. It refused to stock yellowfin tuna because fishing resulted in the deaths of dolphins and other marine mammals. As the Co-op grew more financially viable, it began to stock a greater variety of conventional products, which some members opposed. Evans recalled that when the Co-op decided to stock white sugar, one member "was just about ready to lay down and die." Disagreements reflected differing motivations members had for joining. One early member said about half of members joined because the Co-op's prices were cheaper than supermarkets, but the other half did so "to destroy the capitalist system."[55]

The Davis Food Co-op moved to a larger store in 1978. It also adopted a new logo that symbolized its political stance featuring a fist holding a carrot encircled by the slogan "Food for People, Not for Profit." The new store was three times larger than the original. The move prompted other changes. The Co-op increased the member work requirement. It hired its first paid employees and later hired a "resource coordinator" to oversee daily operations. In 1979, the Co-op expanded into an adjacent space and began the process to incorporate. In order to obtain credit from wholesalers, it reorganized its management. Paid employees took over most ordering. But policy meetings became increasingly contentious. Some members felt the Co-op devoted too much shelf space to packaged foods. Members in response decided against increasing space for packaged products in the larger store and instead to double the selection of bulk foods. Bulk foods sections—which offer lower prices than packaged foods and reduce reliance on disposable materials—have long been a distinguishing feature of co-ops.

Controversy became commonplace as the Co-op grew, but that tendency emphasized a basic fact of life about college towns: Highly educated people tend to be opinionated and vocal. Over time, many of the Co-op's leaders came to recognize that incorporation was necessary to protect members from legal liability. They also believed incorporation would provide the Co-op greater credibility and enable it to reduce taxes by offering patronage refunds. The Co-op incorporated in 1978, but was only a paper corporation at first. A separate association controlled the Co-op's assets. When the corporation's board of directors moved to merge the corporation and association, the chair of the Co-op's newsletter committee objected, insisting the proposal constituted a "takeover" by the corporation board. She seized the Co-op mailing list, placed it in a safe deposit box, and protested to the local newspaper. The meeting at which the proposal was debated turned into a "four-hour marathon" of "heated discussion," but members eventually approved the merger. Incorporation was finally completed in 1981.

The next major Co-op controversy developed over a proposal to move to an even larger location, inspired by continued sales growth. When Safeway vacated a 20,000–square-foot store in central Davis in 1980, the Co-op's board of directors proposed that it take over part of the space. Proponents argued that the larger store would enable the Co-op to enhance its visibility, offer a wider range of products, and boost sales by being located near other retailers. Critics of the plan feared that continued expansion would require prices to be raised, undermine the Co-op's identity, and reduce the role of members in daily operation. The Co-op board in November 1981 asked members to vote on whether to borrow $95,000 to finance the move and sign a lease. Organized groups on both sides of the issue produced campaign flyers to influence other members. Even the decision on whether to hold the election by mail or at a membership meeting was controversial. The proposal was rejected. Co-ops in Davis and elsewhere have long been split between members who believe strongly in the virtues of smallness, volunteer labor, natural foods, and alternative lifestyles and others who think co-ops have more to gain by achieving economies of scale and becoming more professional.[56]

Before long, however, those who believed bigger is better gained control and have shaped Co-Op policy ever since. Change was partly motivated by necessity. Although sales and membership continued to grow, an audit in 1982 showed the Co-op had been losing money for two years. In response, management increased the store's markup. They hired paid cashiers for busy times. They began to actively market the Co-op and bring in more products found in mainstream supermarkets. The changes helped the Co-op become profitable again by the end of 1982. Expansion once more became an issue the following year. The Co-op's building had proven increasingly inadequate. It was not designed as a grocery, and its electrical system had been pushed to its limits. The old Safeway store again became available. Because of improvements made by the store's previous occupants, the move would be less expensive than before. The prospect of moving also became more attractive because the Co-op's finances and the national economy had improved. In January 1984, the Co-op members overwhelmingly approved the proposal.[57]

The new store nearly killed the Co-op, but leaders now say it would not have survived without the expansion. The store was 11,000 square feet, more than double the size of the old store. The added space created opportunities, but also posed challenges. The Co-op could stock a greater variety of products and keep larger quantities on shelves. A full-service meat counter was added. The Co-op began carrying products like cat food and light bulbs. For the first time, it was possible for customers to do all their grocery shopping at the Co-op. But rent was much higher, and added inventory increased costs. Few staff members had experience operating a larger store. The situation grew more grim that fall when Safeway told the Co-op it must lease the remainder of the 22,000–square-foot building or vacate. Unable to afford to move, the Co-op agreed to the new lease, which increased its monthly rent by $5,000. Despite the added space and inventory, Co-op sales actually declined. Membership fell for the first time in its history. Losses mounted. The store's longtime general manager quit. The Co-op's reputation in the community deteriorated. "It was the worst of times," said David Thompson, a longtime Co-op board member and Evans's husband. The Co-op, he said, was "near death." [58]

The organization recovered, but to do so it had to fundamentally alter the way it is managed and reinvent itself as an upscale supermarket with a natural foods emphasis. In 1985, it eliminated the member work requirement, which discouraged people from joining. Member work was made voluntary, and working members are charged less. In 1986, the Co-op hired its first marketing manager, who developed more aggressive marketing strategies and sought to better define its market niche. When it was revealed that Washington apples sprayed with the pesticide Alar posed a health threat, for example, the Co-op advertised that its apples were pesticide-free. In 1987, the store hired a new general manager, who put in place a new management team. They initiated a study of the Co-op's pricing structure, which revealed that its prices to all but working members were more expensive than conventional supermarkets. In response, they persuaded members to change the organization's bylaws to restructure its pricing system. [59]

The changes enabled the Co-op to become profitable again by 1989, and it has been profitable ever since. Between 1986 and 2004, sales grew an average of 10.8 percent a year and now average more than $1 million a month. Sales growth has been strongly related to membership growth, since 80 percent of money spent at the Co-op is spent by members. Since 1989, membership has more than tripled, and the Co-op in 2005 had 8,115 members, roughly one-sixth of the adult population of the city. No other organization in Davis has so many members, and few groups anywhere can claim such a large percentage of a local population in their membership. Buoyed by its success, the Co-op in 1988 bought its building. In 1997, it expanded to 25,000 square feet and remodeled the entire store. [60] It is now the second largest retailer and biggest private employer in downtown Davis.

The Davis Food Co-op grew to be one of the most successful co-ops in the nation by moving ever closer to the mainstream. Symbolic of that shift, in 1988 it abandoned the carrot-and-fist logo for one that is professionally designed and decidedly less provocative. "The raised fist in the '60s was a widely understood symbol of idealistic militancy," wrote two staff members in justifying the change. "People [today] are more likely to associate raised fists . . . with senseless gang violence." The greatest evidence that the Co-op has changed is in the store itself. The 1997 renovation gave it a sleek and modern appearance. The interior is bright, colorful, and clean, a sharp contrast to the drab and dingy character of early co-ops. The store has a bakery, large meat department, huge selection of beer and wine, demonstration kitchen, cosmetic counter, and computer station for customers. Although the Co-op stocks fair-trade coffees, free range meats, and countless soy products, it also carries many products you would have never found in a co-op thirty years ago, such as Coca-Cola, Clorox, and disposable diapers.[61]

Like most cooperatives, the Davis Food Co-op has become less political over time. In its early days, members voted to ban many products. Although the Co-op newsletter is filled with complaints that it sells Starbucks coffee, genetically modified foods, and even toy guns, members have not approved any product boycotts since 2000. Today, the Co-op emphasizes education over dogmatism, preferring to let customers decide what they will purchase. It carries fish, for example, that has been endangered by overfishing or caught using ecologically destructive methods, but recently began a labeling program that indicates whether a fish is "sustainable." Although it will stock almost anything conventional supermarkets carry, it has a policy against advertising products containing artificial flavors or coloring. "It comes down to what our members want," said general manager Eric Stromberg.[62]

Co-op leaders say all these changes have been essential to the institution's survival. Most successful cooperatives have gone through a similar evolution, while others that deliberately stayed small and ideologically pure have gone out of business. Even the Berkeley Co-op where Ann Evans shopped as a child, once one of the most successful co-ops in the nation, closed in 1988. As the popularity of organic and healthy foods grew, co-ops lost their market niche. Now chain supermarkets carry organic produce, bulk foods, and tofu. "Almost all of the existing cooperatives had to make the decision at some point," said David Thompson. "Were they going to be a museum of natural foods and inefficient cooperation and then close down? Or were they going to be a community-oriented business and just figure out how to be smarter about how to do it all? They had to recognize they were in a competitive world."[63]

The Co-op still differs from conventional supermarkets in fundamental ways. Members make all major policy decisions. The board of directors is composed entirely of members. Members can still initiate product boycotts. All profits are reinvested in the organization, donated to community groups, or returned to members. Members can still work to reduce their costs (only about 3 percent do). The Co-op also exhibits its progressive ideals in other ways. It sponsors an annual holiday meal for needy residents and benefits for local social service nonprofits. It helped bring members of a Peruvian coffee cooperative to town to speak. It visits Davis schools to teach children about nutrition, organic agriculture, and cooperatives. In 2004, the Co-op installed a solar roof designed to provide 6 percent of its energy needs.[64] The pages of its monthly newsletter also strongly reflect a liberal world view, with articles about "Indie Foods," fair trade, and "the Politics of Chocolate." The Davis Food Co-op still embodies alternative values that epitomize the distinctive political culture present in many college towns.

CREATING COMMUNITY THROUGH NEIGHBORHOOD DESIGN

Davis has also been the site of a wide range of housing experiments. The most famous is Village Homes, which broke all rules for suburban design when it was developed in 1975. Conceived by the husband and wife team of Mike and Judy Corbett, it was envisioned as an environmentally friendly residential community. Houses are clustered on small lots to encourage interaction and create open space. Structures are oriented in a north-south direction to make them energy-efficient, and many were equipped with active solar energy systems. Streets are narrow and lined with trees to slow traffic and facilitate natural cooling.[65] Over the years, Village Homes has attracted international attention and drawn countless visitors, including French president François Mitterrand and actress Jane Fonda.[66]

Village Homes appears less remarkable today than it once did, however. It occupies too much land for the number of people who live there. Its homes are nondescript and look dated. Many of its solar features have fallen into disuse. Two Davis housing experiments that have attracted less attention but better reflect the unusual personality of college towns are the city's two pioneering cohousing communities, Muir Commons and N Street Cohousing, the first two developments of their kind in the United States. Cohousing is an approach first conceived in Denmark that seeks to combine characteristics of communal living with the privacy of a single-family home. As with food cooperatives, cohousing is more concentrated in college towns than in any other type of setting. A directory compiled by a national cohousing group in 2005 showed that 36 percent of U.S. cities with cohousing were college towns.[67]

Muir Commons and N Street Cohousing grew out of a long-standing local interest in cooperative housing. UC Davis students developed the Davis Student Cooperative Union in 1966. Students also created the cooperative Baggins End, fourteen geodesic domes built on campus by residents in 1972. Co-op houses also flourished off campus. Kevin Wolf, an environmentalist who is the driving force behind N Street Cohousing, enrolled at UC Davis in 1975 and moved into an off-campus co-op two years later. In 1980, he moved to a co-op at 716 N Street, which became the nucleus around which the N Street community emerged. Linda Cloud, who organized the first public meeting about cohousing in Davis, had lived in a co-op in San Francisco. Wolf and Cloud met while working to protect the Stanislaus River and later married. In 1986, they bought a house on N Street, which they turned into a co-op.[68]

One of the individuals who helped get Muir Commons off the ground had tried to initiate a similar project a decade before. Developer Virginia Thigpen, who had worked for Village Homes designer Mike Corbett, first heard about cohousing in the 1970s from a friend whose brother lived in a Danish cohousing community.[69] In that development, all houses were clustered on one part of the site. The rest of the land was left open. Residents shared meals nightly at a common house. "It met my ideals just straight up and down," Thigpen said. She suggested to the owners of an undeveloped parcel in Davis that they allow her to develop a similar community on the site. They agreed, but the project was never built because so little was known about cohousing in the United States. "I didn't really know how to go about developing it," Thigpen said. That changed in 1988 when two Berkeley-based architects, the husband-wife team of Kathryn McCamant and Charles Durrett, published *Cohousing: A Contemporary Approach to Housing Ourselves*, the first book in English on the subject.[70]

Exactly how Muir Commons originated is subject to debate. There is, moreover, a rivalry between Muir Commons and N Street over which developed first. Cloud read the McCamant-Durrett book and in 1988 invited the authors to Davis to give a presentation. Wolf says Cloud then called a meeting for people interested in starting a cohousing community in Davis, which became Muir Commons. Wolf and Cloud later pulled out of the Muir Commons planning group, deciding instead to transform N Street into a cohousing community. Thigpen remembers what happened differently. She was a partner with Ridge Builders Group, which set aside a portion of a new subdivision for affordable housing to satisfy city affordable housing requirements. Davis was one of the first cities in the nation to implement "inclusionary housing" policies that require developers to build affordable housing. Four of the first seven cities in California to enact inclusionary housing policies, in fact, were small cities with major universities. Davis's inclusionary housing program, however, had proven to have limited long-term impact because it lacked regulations governing the resale of affordable units. Thigpen, in response, sought to devise a way to make housing permanently affordable. "I thought the only way to make housing affordable over time is to do something in the design of it that makes it somehow less appealing to everybody," she said. "Cohousing seemed like the perfect thing." She said she was already contemplating developing a cohousing community when she attended the McCamant-Durrett presentation.[71]

One characteristic of cohousing as defined by McCamant and Durrett is that residents participate in the planning and design of the community. Future residents of Muir Commons were actively involved in every step of the process. Ridge Builders donated the land. Thigpen formed Muir Woods Development to act as developer. McCamant and Durrett were hired by the resident group to facilitate planning. The group met often with the developers and architects to work out details. It made all decisions by consensus rather than a majority vote, which increased the time planning took. Meetings were so frequent and time-consuming, Thigpen said, that "I must have spent $10,000 on babysitting." Thigpen's role in the process diminished over time because residents had an inherent distrust of developers. Planning took two years and was so contentious that some would-be residents quit.[72] Construction began in November 1990. The first residents moved in the following summer (fig. 5.8). Muir Commons was the first cohousing community built for that purpose in the United States and drew national media attention.[73]

Another distinguishing feature of cohousing communities is that they should be designed to encourage interaction among residents. This is achieved primarily through the layout of the site and creation of common facilities. Muir Commons' twenty-six homes encircle a park-like green space. The green space includes common gardens, a Ping-Pong table, and playground. Parking is restricted to the edge of the site. The most important common facility is the common house, which McCamant and Durrett consider "the heart of the cohousing community."[74] Muir Commons' 3,668–square-foot common house includes a kitchen and dining area that can seat sixty people. Meals are shared several nights a week. The common house also includes a sitting room with fireplace, exercise room, TV room, office, laundry room, and guest room for overnight visitors. Other common

FIGURE 5.8.
*The original
residents of Muir
Commons in 1991,
when it became
the first cohousing
community built
for that purpose in
the United States.
Photograph by
John Trotter,
Sacramento Bee,
September 4,
1991; used with
permission,
Sacramento
Archives &
Museum
Collection Center.*

facilities include a woodworking and auto repair shop, hot tub, and composting bin. Residents share use of tools and a lawnmower.

The extensive common facilities enabled individual houses to be built smaller than most single-family homes. Houses range in size from 808 to 1,381 square feet. Kitchens are compact because it was assumed residents would eat often in the common house. The common laundry room negates the need for every house to have a washer and dryer. The guest room reduces the necessity for homes to have an extra room for visitors. The common house serves many functions that typically take place in private homes. Residents read newspapers or watch TV there. Kids play in the exercise room. One resident compared individual homes to "the bedrooms in a house. We do our hanging out outside or in [the common house]." Sharing of everything from laundry facilities to lawnmowers reduces unnecessary duplication of property. Other features reflect the environmental concerns of residents. In 2002, Muir Commons installed a solar energy system on the common house that is designed to supply 70 percent of its electricity.[75]

Cohousing developments are legally similar to condominiums, although cohousing residents are more actively involved in management of the community than condo owners. Muir Commons residents own their houses and share ownership of common areas. Like condo owners, they pay monthly dues. Each adult is expected to cook one meal and clean after two meals each month. They serve on one of twelve committees. Each adult serves on a work team responsible for maintaining part of the common facilities and must participate in periodic workdays. They are expected to help clean the common house once a quarter and take minutes periodically during meetings. Decisions are still made by consensus. If residents cannot agree, an issue can be brought to a vote, but there has never been a vote in the history of the community.[76]

Muir Commons in 2005 had eighty-six residents, including thirty-seven children. There has been considerable turnover since the beginning, but current residents say the turnover has been beneficial. Some members of the original resident group, they say, had personalities that made them less well-equipped to live there day to day. "A lot of the original owners came with expectations," said one resident. "They had this idea and they were going to make this idea work. They worked really hard. Then it was done and, to the degree that it met their expectations, they were happy or not. But the people who have come in, who bought their houses, looked around and said, 'Hey, this is a cool community. I think I want to live here.' They didn't come with that same set of expectations." Decision-making and requirements of residents have become more relaxed. Common meals are less frequent. There are fewer meetings. Decisions are often delegated to committees. Controversy is less common.[77]

I spent an evening at Muir Commons and shared a meal with residents. I spoke with a couple while they cooked in the common house. Others drifted in, many stopping to chat. Dinner was a revelation, not because of the food but because it displayed an effortless amiability rare in contemporary American life. Conversation was relaxed and lively. Family members did not always sit together, some eating with friends. At one point, everyone stopped eating to applaud the cooks. Later, the group sang happy birthday to a resident. Afterwards, I strolled outdoors. Residents passed frequently, many pausing to talk. Everyone was friendly. Children roamed in packs. It was a warm evening, so one parent pulled a kiddy swimming pool to the playground, positioned it under a slide, and draped a running hose over the top of the slide. Kids slid down the improvised waterslide with giddy excitement.

Despite the arduous planning process, the considerable demands on residents, and continued turnover, Muir Commons has clearly fulfilled its goals. "We have a blend of privacy and community," said one early resident.

"I like running into people in a casual way," said another. Not having to cook dinner every night leaves more time for family and other activities. Parents are especially fond of Muir Commons. There are always other children around. Because the common area is surrounded by homes, most parents allow even youngsters to wander freely. Almost every home has children, so parents share child care duties informally. There's little need to hire a babysitter. "To have other adults that you can trust to help take care of your children and set an example for them is important to me," said a mother. "Maybe it doesn't take a village, but it certainly helps to have one."[78]

N Street Cohousing (fig. 5.9), considered the first retrofit cohousing community in the United Sates, began to take shape even before planning for Muir Commons started. Wolf lived in the co-op house at 716 N Street from 1979 until 1986. He bought the house in 1984. Wolf and his housemates shared meals, took turns cooking and cleaning, and planted a garden that contained forty species of edible plants. The house is located in a neighborhood of nondescript tract homes separated by tall fences. "We'd look over the backyard fence," Wolf said, "and we'd dream 'Gosh, wouldn't it be great if we could take over [the house next door] and have the two back yards united?'" In 1986, that dream became reality when he and Cloud bought the adjacent house. Residents then tore down the fence between them. Owners of two other neighboring houses joined the community by 1988. Each time a house joined, the fences around it were torn down. The removal of fences became an important symbolic act in making the community. Residents also began to regularly share potluck dinners.[79]

All the while Muir Commons was gaining national attention, N Street Cohousing grew incrementally and organically, beneath the media radar. By the time Muir Commons was completed in 1991, N Street Cohousing had ten dwellings. Most houses in the neighborhood were rentals, which meant turnover was high, but made it easier to recruit new houses into the community. When a house came up for lease, community members recruited tenants interested in joining the community. If a landlord decided to sell a house, they would mobilize to help like-minded people obtain loans to buy it and circumvent rules that made it difficult for people with little money and few assets to purchase real estate. Wolf recalls that the owner of one of the houses told him, "The bankers and the lawyers and the real estate agents wrote the rules about owning property. You need to figure out the rules of the game and make them work for your own ideals." Wolf added, "I had this sense that the revolution was going to take a long time. Maybe I should try to figure out this capitalist system and make it work for what I believed in."[80]

FIGURE 5.9.
*Residents of
N Street
Cohousing tore
down the fences
that separated
adjacent houses
every time a new
house joined
the community,
creating a large
common area that
includes gardens,
a children's
play area, and
a chicken coop.
Photograph
by Graham
Meltzer; used
with permission.*

Although the houses in N Street joined yards and shared gardens, meals, and tools, the McCamant-Durrett book gave residents the idea that they could have shared indoor space too. Residents in 1991 converted the original house at 716 N Street into a common house. They gradually added other shared facilities, including a bike rack, washing machine, computer, and children's play area. They built a chicken coop that straddles multiple properties to get around city regulations that prohibit more than six chickens on any lot. As that strategy suggests, N Street has been more subversive in its methods than Muir Commons. By 2005, N Street Cohousing grew to include nineteen residences on seventeen lots that were home to forty-three adults and sixteen children. Twelve homes were owner-occupied, seven were rentals. N Street has negotiated options on all the landlord-owned properties, so it has first right of refusal if the houses are sold. As the community grew, the original common house became inadequate, so in 2005 it was torn down and a larger common house erected on the same lot. The new common house was equipped with solar panels designed to provide all the house's electrical needs.[81]

N Street Cohousing differs from Muir Commons in several important ways. N Street has more rentals, which Wolf feels is beneficial because renting allows people to decide whether they like living in the community before they buy and the turnover of tenants injects new blood into the group. Incomes of N Street residents are lower and home prices more affordable. N Street has fewer rules, meetings, and committees than Muir Commons. Members are not expected to cook as frequently and are required to work only eight hours a year. Although backyards of contiguous properties have been joined, all land is individually owned, a vestige of the fact that the block was not built as cohousing. To address that weakness, N Street has been rezoned by the city as a planned development, which enables the community to restrict what property owners can do with their property. Owners, for example, are prohibited from erecting fences. N Street also tries to blur property distinctions by placing shared facilities so they extend across property boundaries. Most parcels include at least one shared facility.[82]

Residents of N Street as a group are more extreme in their political views and show greater environmental consciousness than Muir Commons residents. One reason Wolf and Cloud discontinued their involvement in Muir Commons was because it was to be built on undeveloped land, so contributed to sprawl. N Street has encouraged densification through the enlargement of homes and building of second units, which is less environmentally destructive and lowers housing costs. To make this possible, N Street reduced setback requirements and eliminated limits on second units. N Street has also adopted rules that prohibit homeowners from blocking the solar access of neighbors. In a statement redolent of the differences between the two communities, a Muir Commons resident said he originally considered joining N Street because "they were more hip and a more Grateful Dead kind of contingent," but his wife preferred Muir Commons because its residents "are cleaner, more organized, and a little more anal."[83]

GROWTH CONTROL AND THE CHANGING MEANING OF PROGRESSIVISM

Although Davis, like other college towns, is home to many inventive individuals who have pushed the city to implement progressive policies and helped create a diverse range of alternative institutions, the story of Davis liberalism is not monolithic. John Lofland has observed that liberal control of local politics even during the city's most progressive period, the fifteen or so years following the 1972 election, was "precarious." Lofland and his wife Lyn Lofland have also criticized Davis progressivism as "superficial." City policies and voter behavior, they argue, have strongly reflected the class identity of Davis residents, who are overwhelmingly white, affluent, and family-oriented. Davis liberals, they note, have been most active on issues related to the environment, peace, and local control, but have been less supportive of ideologies generally associated with the left such as civil rights and economic justice.[84]

There is ample evidence to suggest that support for liberal causes in Davis has been unreliable, selective, and motivated more by selfishness than concern for a larger public good. Davis voters have never elected a Hispanic or African American to the City Council. In 1980, voters rejected a gay rights initiative. Although the City Council six years later enacted a civil rights ordinance that provides protection based on sexual orientation, local homosexuals say they face discrimination and hostility. Davis has also shown little interest in helping the poor. The City Council enacted a rent control ordinance in 1979, but it was declared unconstitutional, and the city never tried to implement rent control again. The city's recent affordable housing policies favor middle-income residents. Unlike college towns such as Bloomington, Indiana, and Corvallis, Oregon, Davis has not sought to implement a "living wage" law.[85]

There is no better window into the clouded history of Davis progressivism and the sometimes hypocritical nature of college town liberals than growth control. Growth control was a radical notion when introduced by Bob Black and others in 1972. Over time, however, growth control has taken on a different meaning, and I will argue that it is no longer a progressive philosophy. Davis was only the second city in California and among the first in the nation to implement growth control in 1973 when it began specifying the maximum number of housing units it would approve each year. It established a grading system for all development proposals and regularly rejected development applications. The beliefs that local governments could say no to builders, limit growth, and dictate how a city would develop were all progressive ideas at the time. Growth control in Davis achieved its goals. It slowed population growth, reduced urban encroachment onto farmland, and kept Davis compact and self-contained.

Growth control nonetheless has remained the dominant political issue in Davis and has become ever more divisive. It has been a more prominent issue in Davis than in other college towns because the city is located in a state that never seems to stop growing and is near enough to a big city to attract commuters. Other college towns within commuting distance of large cities, such as Ann Arbor and Boulder, have also experienced growth pressures. Opposition to growth says much about the priorities of college town liberals. Writing about Ann Arbor, Gorman Beauchamp observed: "When living in a nest of tenured radicals, it is useful to recall how much more tenured they are than radical."[86] Liberals oppose growth so fervently because it threatens their quality of life. They may join the ACLU and affix anti-war bumper stickers to their cars, but the issues over which they are most willing to fight are those that impact them personally.

In enacting the city's first growth-control policy in 1973, the Davis City Council pursued a moderate growth strategy, permitting the population to grow just under 4 percent a year and setting a 1990 target population of 50,000. Over time, growth opponents forced the city to grow even more slowly. In 1982, voters approved a ballot initiative that pushed back the 50,000 population target to 2000. But limiting the number of houses that could be built also caused home prices to rise because demand exceeded supply. Some people began to criticize the city's growth policies. "Davis has developed into a closed, elitist yuppie town where only people with a certain income range can afford to live," said a UC Davis professor. Columnist Bob Dunning observed that "the way we've structured the town, we may as well have a wall around it—a wall to keep the unwashed masses out." He sarcastically suggested that the city form a commission to create a "profile of the perfect Davisite" and only recruit as new residents people who fit the profile. "Anyone with anything less than a Ph.D. is clearly unacceptable," Dunning wrote, "unless [they] can present proof of purchase of at least ten solar panels or two Volvos in the last year."[87]

Others argued, however, that Davis was growing faster than nearby cities (fig. 5.10) and California as a whole, despite growth control. The city's population increased from 27,850 in 1973 to 40,450 in 1985, an increase of 45 percent (3.8 percent a year). The county population grew 10 percent during the same period. Davis, like other college towns, was becoming a victim of its success. With its highly rated schools, extensive parks and bike network, compact downtown, and progressive reputation, it was beginning to attract lifestyle migrants from Sacramento and even San Francisco. Voters, in response, elected City Council candidates who were increasingly anti-growth. But growth control ceased to be strictly a progressive ideology and appealed to voters across the political spectrum. The most conservative council member during the period, in fact, was a longtime growth-control advocate.[88]

The city's rigid position on growth backfired. In 1984, developer Frank Ramos sought city approval to build a technology park on 94 acres just east of the city limits. Ramos was required to obtain city approval because the parcel was within the city's "sphere of influence," a legal designation in California for land adjacent to a city over which it has authority. Ramos also unveiled a master plan for 434 acres adjacent to the technology park site, which included housing, an industrial park, and a conference center. Because the second parcel was outside Davis's sphere of influence, Ramos was not required to obtain city approval for those plans. Fearing that the larger plan would undermine the city's growth policies, officials ordered an environmental impact study of the entire project. The study confirmed the worst nightmares of city officials and residents. It estimated the project would add 3,340 residents to the area. In May 1986, the Davis Planning Commission and the City Council both rejected the application unanimously. Most

FIGURE 5.10.

Davis has grown rapidly since the 1960s, as shown on this map depicting areas annexed to the city, which has prompted the city to implement ever-more stringent growth control measures. Map by Bruce Boyd; used with permission, City of Davis.

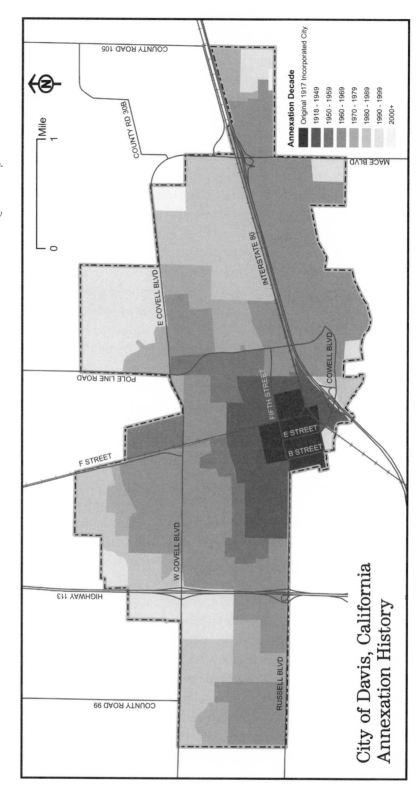

City of Davis, California
Annexation History

residents supported that decision. In June 1986, voters approved a ballot initiative calling on the city to "grow as slow as legally possible."[89]

Ramos in response turned his back on Davis and sought approval from Yolo County for the part of his project located outside the city's sphere of influence. This move forced city officials to negotiate with Ramos if it wanted to exert any control over the project. In May 1987, the city, county, and Ramos agreed to a compromise. In order to prevent other developers from using a similar strategy, the city then negotiated with the county the Davis-Yolo Pass-Through Agreement, which requires the city to "pass through" to the county a portion of its tax revenues so long as the county does not approve any development in a large area surrounding Davis. In 1989, voters approved Ramos's Mace Ranch housing development, which included 1,515 units, and the development was annexed to the city. All the new housing pushed the city's population above 50,000 in 1994, six years ahead of schedule. Bob Black insists Davis grew faster than it would have grown if the city pursued a more pragmatic growth-control policy. "The anti-growth horse was ridden too hard," he said.[90]

Population growth in Davis stimulated by the building of homes changed the city demographically and politically. New homes in places like Mace Ranch were too expensive for many who already lived or worked in Davis, so attracted commuters employed in Sacramento and beyond. The newcomers were more conservative than longtime residents and, like commuters everywhere, tend to be less active in civic affairs. UC Davis continued to grow, adding more than 11,000 students and staff between 1978 and 1990, but increasingly they were forced to live elsewhere. These changes help explain why in 1990, progressives lost the City Council majority they had held since 1972, an event the *Davis Enterprise* called "a significant turning point in Davis politics." Moderate Democrats controlled the council for the next decade and approved still more development. The biggest project was the 800-home Wildhorse subdivision. Davis added nearly 14,000 new residents in the 1990s.[91]

Heightened development provoked a strong reaction from progressives and other growth opponents. Some of their efforts were symbolic, but others substantially retarded growth. Even newcomers in suburbs like Mace Ranch and Wildhorse began to oppose growth. In the process, an alliance developed between progressives and conservatives. In 1997, voters rejected for the fourth time a proposal to widen an underpass between Interstate 80 and downtown. To growth opponents, the underpass was "a symbol of the community's small town atmosphere." Then in 2000, voters approved a referendum that requires voter approval of any development proposed outside the city limits but in the city's planning area. In the same election, progressives regained a majority on City Council. That enabled them to strongly influence a new General Plan, completed in 2001, which called on the city to cut its annual growth rate to 1.43 percent. Critics contended the plan did not allow sufficient growth to provide housing for people already living or working in the city and failed to accommodate planned growth at UC Davis. Frustrated by the city's refusal to allow housing to meet its needs, UC Davis is building a mixed-use project on campus that will house 3,500 students, plus 500 employees and their families.[92]

Although opposition to growth came to represent a new conservatism in local politics, the city's efforts to provide affordable housing show it can still be a policy innovator. Recognizing that growth control has the potential to increase housing prices by reducing supply, Davis in 1973 became one of the first cities in the nation to implement inclusionary housing policies, which require developers to provide low-cost housing. It achieved this by giving preference to development proposals that included affordable units. Four years later, the city mandated that one-third of all housing units in new developments be affordable. But the original program failed to fulfill its goals, so the city has repeatedly strengthened its requirements. In 1987, it began requiring that 25 percent of new, for-sale homes be affordable to low- and moderate-income households and obligated buyers to meet income requirements. The new rules also required 35 percent of new rental units to be permanently affordable. Home prices continued to rise, however, making it difficult for even the middle class to afford a house in Davis, so in 2003 the city mandated that an additional 20 percent of new, for-sale homes be affordable to middle-income buyers. Now nearly half of all new, for-sale homes must be affordable. The city also imposed resale controls that limit appreciation.[93] An affordable housing expert said that Davis's inclusionary program is "one of the best, if not the best, in the country."[94]

The first test of citizen review over development proposed outside the city came in 2005 when a group of longtime local developers proposed building the biggest housing development in Davis history immediately north of the city. The Covell Village project was to include 1,864 housing units, a commercial center, parks and wildlife habitat, a fire station, school site, and amphitheater. The City Council approved the project in 2005, but it also had to win the support of voters. Developers filled the project with features intended to appeal to an enlightened college town population. Compact, pedestrian-oriented, and with homes and businesses built in close proximity, it was promoted as a model of "new urbanism." Plans called for an old-style business district to face a village green. One-fifth of the housing was designated for low- and moderate-income households. Developers proposed creation of a cohousing community. Covell Village also incorporated numerous environmental features, including a nature corridor, eight miles of bike paths, and solar panels on every home. Developers also agreed to preserve 776 acres of farmland north of the site and create a 124-acre wetland. Growth opponents were unmoved, insisting all the perks disguised a project that was too large and beyond the means of most Davis residents. They insisted it would clog Davis streets, overtax its sewage plant, endanger government finances, and alter the local way of life. Voters resoundingly rejected the project by a 60–40 percent margin. Political observers say Covell Village was defeated by such a wide margin because progressives and conservatives alike opposed it.[95]

Debate over Covell Village exposed the fault lines in Davis progressivism and emphasized the degree to which the meaning of the term has changed. Covell Village would have been considered an innovative and desirable project almost anywhere but Davis. It would have added significantly to the city's affordable housing stock, enabling a greater number of Davis workers and UC Davis students to live in the city and reducing energy consumption and air pollution associated with commuting. Covell Village was full of progressive amenities. Its mix of residential and commercial uses and comparatively high population density fit the vision Davis residents have of their community as expressed in the city's General Plan. By rejecting Covell Village, Davis voters will encourage developers to build elsewhere and, in the process, contribute to sprawl, air pollution, energy consumption, and farmland conversion because developers will not have to meet the same standards they do in Davis.

Ironically, Covell Village was endorsed by many prominent progressives, including former City Council members Bob Black and Ann Evans, co-op promoter David Thompson, and cohousing advocate Kevin Wolf. Self-proclaimed progressives who opposed Covell Village did so because it offered little to them and threatened what they prize. Davis growth opponents have become so extreme in their views that they have come full circle, their attitudes now coinciding more with the beliefs of conservatives than old-line progressives. Once upon a time, growth control in Davis was part of a progressive philosophy that also gave birth to bike lanes, recycling, the Davis Food Co-op, and multiple housing experiments. Growth control as it is practiced in the city today has ceased to be a progressive ideal, because it is founded on opposition to change. "Growth control in the seventies . . . was used to encourage innovation," Black said. "Today, it's just used to shoot things down."[96]

Self-proclaimed progressives who fought Covell Village with unprecedented fervor have become ever-more strident in their beliefs and intolerant of anyone who does not think like them. Eileen Samitz, one of the leaders of the Covell Village opposition, is typical. She moved to Davis in 1976 and fell in love with the city because it was a "cute little college town" and "very safe." She helped organize the campaign to require a citizen vote on development outside the city and contributed to the growth policies in the 2001 General Plan. Samitz believes "every city has a maximum size it can be and still function and be a pleasant place to live." Davis, she says, has nearly reached that point and should not be permitted to grow beyond that. She dismisses politicians who advocate moderate growth as "developer Democrats." Village Homes creator Mike Corbett, who helped design Covell Village, is "a sellout." Cohousing organizer Kevin Wolf "is not playing with a full deck." She no longer considers Bob Black a progressive and resents that he rendered an opinion on Covell Village since he no longer lives in the city. Samitz warns that continued growth would turn Davis into "an inner city" and says the building of "malls and stuff like that" would increase crime.[97] She sounds an awful lot like the conservatives she abhors.

The changing meaning of growth control in Davis exemplifies the peculiar character of college town politics and the sometimes contradictory nature of college town liberals. They talk like liberals, support liberal causes, and vote for liberal candidates, but when their own well-being is endangered they behave remarkably like conservatives. They become reactionary, intransigent, and hostile. But the conflict over Covell Village also underscores the exceptional nature of college town politics. College town residents in Davis and beyond are unusually politically active. They are engaged and involved. They are opinionated, informed, vigilant, and uncompromising. Little escapes their attention. Even the smallest of issues—the paving of an alley, the renaming of a street, the arrest of a vagrant—inspire indignation, debate, proposals and counter proposals. To survive in such an environment, politicians and public officials in college towns must be cool under fire and quick witted. You can't get away with much in a college town.

PARADISE
FOR
MISFITS

College towns, like the schools located in them, are transient places. Young people come to them to pursue an education and leave
once they earn their degrees. For most of the history of American higher
education, this model held true for nearly all young people who attended
college at residential universities. They went away to college naïve and irresponsible, and graduated four years later more mature and self-confident.
They moved to cities and suburbs, began careers, got married, and started
families. If they ever returned to the college town of their youth, it was to
attend football games or alumni gatherings, and remember their college
years. You were not supposed to stay in a college town after you graduated.

The dynamics of college town life began to change in the 1960s. College enrollments grew rapidly as the children of the baby boom reached
college age. Colleges and universities were forced to expand their faculties,
and many of the new professors were more liberal than their predecessors, having earned their degrees in an era of war protests and civil rights
marches. They influenced their students. College students, meanwhile,
looked around them and saw a world in the throes of convulsive change.
Heroes were gunned down. Politicians were proven corrupt. Large corporations began to shape life in profound ways. To some young people, the
American dream began to look like a nightmare. They started to question
the conventional path of career, marriage, and family. Some quit school.
Others saw in college towns an opportunity to create alternative ways of life
outside the American mainstream. They opened coffee houses and formed
rock 'n' roll bands. They got low-pressure jobs in places like the university
library, and worked only when necessary in order to survive.

College towns came to offer a permanent escape for a wide variety of
eccentrics—artists, musicians, writers, hippies, punks, slackers, tattooed
Gen-Xers. Many went away to college with traditional aspirations of becoming teachers, lawyers, businessmen, and the like, but were changed in some
fundamental way by what they encountered in a college town, abandoned

those goals, and remained in the cities where they went to school, or later returned when they discovered they missed the college town life. The college years are widely acknowledged as a rite of passage and a time of individual awakening, but too often what happens in the classroom is given exclusive credit for this. Away from home for the first time, thrust into communities where young people are dominant, exposed to an eclectic mix of lifestyles and cultures at a time in their lives when they are impressionable, some students are changed forever. Often the experiences that trigger such life changes occur not on campus, but in the nightclubs, coffee houses, and roach-infested student apartments so characteristic of small cities with major universities. Life in college towns has the ability to transform young people in ways that have little to do with formal higher education.

This is most common in college towns that are home to flagship state universities like Lawrence, Kansas, and Athens, Georgia. Such universities typically have strong programs in the arts and humanities that attract young people who see college as more than just a path to a nine-to-five job. They come into contact with like-minded individuals and, soon, something larger begins to coalesce. They form bands, organize poetry readings, sponsor film series, hang out, discuss ideas. Eventually creative communities emerge. College towns provide conducive settings for people who wish to follow non-traditional life courses because they offer relatively cheap rents, lots of flexible, low-wage jobs, and a constant influx of new people with new ideas. Some also attract individuals with no formal connection to a university who are drawn to their unusual ways of life. Those who remain in college towns and live unconventional lifestyles are never numerically dominant, but, because many are creative, they shape life in college towns to a degree disproportionate to their numbers.

I first recognized the ability of college towns to permanently capture young people who came to them to go to school as an undergraduate at the University of Kansas. There were the "old hippies" who hung out at the Crossing, sixties burnouts who, to our punk rock eyes, had changed little since the student union was torched in 1970. There was Bill Rich, who published a local music fanzine and started a record label. There was James Grauerholz, who moved to New York when he graduated but returned to manage the affairs of beat novelist William Burroughs (and persuaded Burroughs to relocate to Lawrence, which says much about the eccentric magnetism of college towns). There was Steve Wilson, who grew up in town but remained after most of his classmates moved away, still manages a record store three decades later, and refers to Lawrence's ability to swallow its young as "the Wakarusa Triangle" (after a river south of town). There were also people of my generation who remained in town after they stopped going to school, such as Fred Fatzer, who grew up in Kinsley, Kansas, moved to Lawrence to attend KU, dropped out after one semester, but stayed in town for several years working in restaurants and playing in bands. Eventually, he moved to New York, got a record contract, adopted the stage name of Freedy Johnston, and developed a successful music career.

Athens (fig. 6.1) is similar to Lawrence in many ways. Both are cultural islands in comparatively conservative states, though the Athens music scene is better known and, in fact, world famous. The people who helped create that scene were originally students in the University of Georgia's Lamar Dodd School of Art. Music was something they did for kicks when they put down their paintbrushes. Eventually, others became involved. Today, Athens is a bohemian pocket in the South (fig. 6.2). Many of those who have advanced the city's reputation as a cultural mecca came there to attend college but never left. Members of now famous rock 'n' roll bands like the B-52's and R.E.M. did not set out to become pop stars. Such bands were a natural outgrowth of the nurturing environment for experimentation that exists in many college towns. As R.E.M. drummer Bill Berry once remarked, "It's funny; I came to school to grow up and do something right, but I just said 'fuck' it and I threw myself into the band." [1] Many others followed similar paths. Over time, Athens became, in the words of one writer, "a paradise for misfits." [2]

College towns all over are home to creative individuals who found their place in a college town. Like Athens, Chapel Hill, North Carolina, became nationally known for its music scene, thanks to the success of bands like Superchunk and the presence of independent labels such as Merge Records. Iowa City and Missoula, Montana, have acquired reputations as literary enclaves, developments stimulated initially by the presence of creative writing programs on campus, but over time both cities have developed writing scenes that have a life beyond the university. College towns such as Charlottesville, Virginia, and Boulder, Colorado, have developed vibrant visual arts scenes. Several of the activists who helped transform Davis, California, into a liberal college town came to the city to go to college and stayed. Many other college towns are home to loose collections of eccentric and free-thinking individuals who may be unknown outside the area or region, but nonetheless inject vitality into a community. [3]

To examine why some young people who go away to college never leave or return to the towns where they went to school, and to consider how it is that certain college towns develop into bohemian islands, this chapter

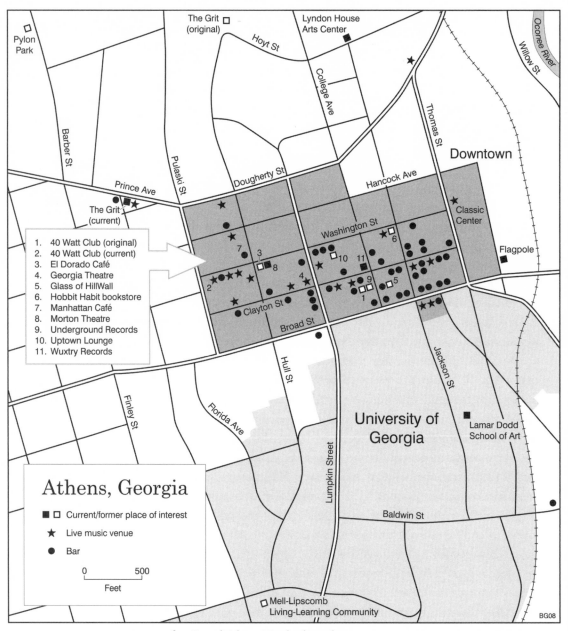

The Grit □
(original)

Lyndon House
Arts Center ■

Hoyt St

College Ave

Pylon
Park □

Barber St

Pulaski St

Prince Ave

Dougherty St

Hancock Ave

Thomas St

Downtown

Oconee River

Willow St

The Grit ●■★
(current)

Classic
Center ★

Flagpole ■

1. 40 Watt Club (original)
2. 40 Watt Club (current)
3. El Dorado Café
4. Georgia Theatre
5. Glass of HillWall
6. Hobbit Habit bookstore
7. Manhattan Café
8. Morton Theatre
9. Underground Records
10. Uptown Lounge
11. Wuxtry Records

Washington St

7
3
8
10 11
6
2
4
9
1
5

Clayton St

Broad St

Hull St

Finley St

Florida Ave

Lumpkin Street

University of
Georgia

Jackson St

Lamar Dodd ■
School of Art

Baldwin St

Athens, Georgia

■ □ Current/former place of interest

★ Live music venue

● Bar

0   500
Feet

□ Mell-Lipscomb
Living-Learning Community

BG08

FIGURE 6.1. *Central Athens. Map by the author.*

FIGURE 6.2.
Sidewalk scene on College Avenue in downtown Athens, epicenter of the college town's alternative community. Photograph by the author, 1999.

will profile six individuals who came to Athens to attend the University of Georgia but now call the city home, plus one who was drawn by the city's music scene. These individuals were chosen from a longer list of nineteen people I interviewed in depth who came to Athens to attend college but stayed—captivated by its verve, openness, and free-spirited lifestyle—or moved there for similar reasons. There are many more people in Athens who fit that description.[4]

CHANGEFUL TIMES

Athens was a very different place when Pete McCommons, editor and publisher of the alternative weekly *Flagpole*, enrolled at the University of Georgia in 1958. McCommons (fig. 6.3) grew up in the small town of Greensboro, Georgia, a cotton mill town thirty-four miles south of Athens. He had been coming to Athens since he was four years old, when his parents drove him up Highway 15 to have his tonsils removed. His family occasionally went to Athens for Georgia football games. During his four years in college, however, McCommons seldom ventured into the town. "Athens hardly existed for me a student," he later recalled. He lived in a dormitory his freshman year, joined a fraternity as a sophomore, lived in the Phi Delta Theta house

FIGURE 6.3.
*Pete McCommons,
editor and
publisher of
Athens alternative
weekly* Flagpole,
*who came to
Athens to attend
college in 1958
and still calls
the city home.
Photograph by the
author, 1999.*

through the end of his junior year, and continued to take meals there until
he graduated. He rented a house as a senior, but his social life revolved
around the fraternity and a Methodist student group on campus. "This was
a typical Southern party school—football and fraternities," McCommons
said. Athens at the time had no student bars. There were only two restaurants downtown and perhaps four others in the entire city. Female students
were still required to live on campus. "It was a dead, dark, deserted town,"
he said.[5]

Like most undergraduates of the era, McCommons left town upon graduation. He graduated in 1962 with a degree in political science and moved to New York, entering graduate school at Columbia University. He returned to Athens in 1968 to marry an artist from Georgia he had met in Manhattan. They moved to Athens so she could pursue a master's degree. When they arrived, they discovered that the university and town had changed. Enrollment had doubled to more than 20,000. The curriculum had been expanded and many new graduate programs added. In 1962, Georgia elected a pro-education governor, who greatly increased state funding for higher education. State allocations to the university nearly quadrupled over six years, and in 1967 alone the university hired 450 new faculty members, most of them young and liberal. "When we came back here," McCommons recalled, "the campus was just transformed. There were kids that were excited by what these young professors were talking about. The whole campus was just unlike what we had ever experienced here before. It was incredible."[6]

The sixties had arrived in Athens, however late. In 1967, a chapter of the radical group Students for a Democratic Society was formed. The following year, five hundred students marched on the university administration building, demanding an end to regulations that imposed greater restrictions on female students. After four student protestors were killed at Kent State University in 1970, 4,000 Georgia students marched to the president's home, demanding classes be canceled. UGA was closed for two days. Athens was not Berkeley, however. A confederate flag still hung in front of the Kappa Alpha fraternity. Five thousands students signed a petition in support of U.S. involvement in the Vietnam War. But times were changing. In 1970, a Presbyterian minister named Frank Hutchinson arrived in town and became an advocate for local blacks. Unable to gain coverage from Athens's daily newspaper, Hutchinson began publishing a weekly newsletter called the *United Free Press*. McCommons became involved and got his first taste of alternative media. "We were classic, well-meaning white liberals," he said.[7]

McCommons never earned a degree from Columbia, but upon his return got an administrative job with the Institute of Government at the University of Georgia. He also became active in local politics, helping the Democratic Party elect a slate of delegates to the national convention in Miami in 1972 that, he said, "was a little left of McGovern." Later that year, when the university administration contemplated eliminating coed dorms in response to criticism from conservatives, McCommons joined a sit-in in the president's office. When protestors refused to leave, thirty-three of them, including McCommons, were arrested for trespassing. Most pleaded guilty to avoid jail time, but McCommons and seven others refused. They were convicted, fined $1,000 each, and placed on probation. They became known as "the Athens Eight." A year later, McCommons lost his job when his contract was not renewed, ostensibly because he lacked a Ph.D., but more than likely because of his involvement with the sit-in.

Out of work, McCommons joined with a friend, Chuck Searcy, to found Athens's first true alternative newspaper, the weekly *Athens Observer*. He cashed in his retirement from the university and borrowed $900. McCommons and his wife had divorced, but they remained friends, and the newspaper used her art studio as an office. By that time, the Vietnam War was winding down. Young people no longer needed to stay in school to avoid the draft. Many quit, but stayed in town. Some started businesses and, in the late 1960s and early 1970s, several businesses that catered to non-mainstream tastes opened downtown, including the Hobbit Habit bookstore; Underground Records; Glass of HillWall, a head shop; and the El Dorado Café, a vegetarian restaurant.[8] "It was a time when a significant off-campus community had begun to develop," McCommons said. "People were going to school and dropping out for a while and working and going back. There was the beginning of what has become the Athens scene. There was a niche there that we sensed, the beginnings of an alternative market that wasn't being served by the daily papers."

The first issue of the *Observer* was published in January 1974. Because McCommons and Searcy were active in local politics, it made an immediate splash. "We had a real deep understanding of who was who and what was what," he said. "We knew all the players and they knew us. It gave us an immediate presence." The paper made no money at first. Advertising paid for printing costs, but McCommons lived off his retirement. "We had trade outs with restaurants," he said. "We would swap them an ad for lunch. We lived on barter and hand to mouth." The *Observer* offered free classified ads, which helped it become established outside the liberal community. Within two years, it was financially secure. In 1976, it converted to paid circulation. The next year, Searcy joined the administration of President Jimmy Carter, but returned when Carter lost his bid for reelection. He and McCommons then converted the paper to twice weekly publication, which, McCommons said, "almost killed the *Observer*."[9]

By 1986, McCommons was burned out. He sold the *Observer*. With a few thousand dollars in the bank, he holed up at home and wrote two mystery novels, but they still sit in a drawer. He had remarried. He and his wife had a daughter. His wife worked, which paid the bills. When his savings ran low, he began working odd jobs and writing freelance. In 1992, he was asked to return to the *Observer* as publisher. At the time, he was selling ads for a used car magazine, so "I jumped at the chance." In six years, the paper had gone through three owners and had lost its edge. Circulation had declined. "It's so odd," McCommons said. "For years, it was *the* alternative paper in town. And then it became nothing much." He bought a minority share in the newspaper, but never was able to gain the degree of editorial control he desired, so he quit a year later. In 1994, he was hired as editor of *Flagpole*, a weekly tabloid that had been started in 1987 to cover the city's growing music scene, but was on "shaky" financial ground and had begun to expand its coverage beyond music.[10]

Flagpole, so named because it claimed to be the "color bearer" of the Athens music scene, represented the new Athens. The B-52's and the novelty hit "Rock Lobster" put Athens on the musical map. The subsequent success of R.E.M. turned Athens into a hipster destination the *Washington Post* called "Liverpool South."[11] People actually began to move to Athens with the dream of becoming rock stars. McCommons was fifty-four years old when he took over *Flagpole*, perhaps the oldest editor of an alternative weekly in the country. He was twice as old as anyone else at the paper. He took the job on the condition he be allowed to buy stock in the publication and eventually became majority owner. From the beginning, younger staff members have sometimes been wary of his leadership; he'll turn seventy in 2010. "I have really had to fight the perception that I am the old guy who owns it," he said. "They don't understand I just haven't grown up."

Under McCommons's leadership, *Flagpole* was transformed from a music tabloid into general-purpose alternative weekly that is a respected source of news and commentary, accepted enough by mainstream Athens that free copies sit on the front desk at the Holiday Inn. It has a weekly circulation of 16,000 and a readership comparable to Athens's daily newspaper. In 2001, McCommons won a national award for political commentary from the Association of Alternative Newsweeklies. Like many who have remained in college towns long after their college days, McCommons never made a conscious decision to stay in Athens, but got "caught in its web." "I just never really hit a point when I was free of obligations or commitments," he said. "And I like it here. It really is an oasis as far as Georgia is concerned. We forget that just over the county line people see things a lot differently."[12]

McCommons's story parallels the histories of alternative press pioneers in college towns nationwide. One of the most influential Vietnam-era underground newspapers, the *Berkeley Barb*, was started by Max Scherr, who earned a sociology degree from the University of California, remained in Berkeley, worked as a lawyer and union organizer, and owned the Steppenwolf Bar before founding the *Barb* in 1965. One of the individuals who founded the Madison, Wisconsin, underground paper, *Free for All*, was a University of Wisconsin dropout, Tim Wong, who stayed in town. The *Athens News* in Athens, Ohio, was started in 1977 by a twenty-three-year-old former Ohio University campus activist, Bruce Mitchell, who continues to publish the paper today. The *Missoula Independent* was founded by Erik Cushman, who moved to Montana to go to college, promoted rock shows in town, didn't want to leave when he earned his degree, and ended up staying fifteen years. He might still live in Missoula if he hadn't been "fired by the fucker" to whom he sold the newspaper.[13]

Four decades after returning to Athens with no intention of staying, McCommons is deeply rooted and will remain. He lives in an old Victorian house in the city's Normaltown neighborhood. A few years ago, he daydreamed of leaving, perhaps retiring to Greenwich Village. He missed the vibrancy of a big city, but no longer. He recognizes his story is not unusual and that college towns have the ability to seduce young people who move to them to pursue a degree. Athens, McCommons once wrote, "can draw you in, make you lose your bearings, start you playing in a band or staying up late listening to one, detour you off the fast track, turn you toward quiet rides in the country, early morning breakfasts, noon awakenings." McCommons is wise and critical, his southern drawl belying his liberalism, but turns reverent when the city is the subject. "Athens," he observed, "can show you a better way to live and then make you realize that there aren't a lot of other places where you can live this way. Soon you'll face the choice of leaving Athens to succeed or staying here to get by."[14]

A GOOD PLACE TO BE UNAMBITIOUS

Where McCommons is a comparatively public figure who has shaped Athens in discernible ways while carving his own path, John Seawright is representative of a different type of personality also abundant in certain kinds of college towns. Shadowy figures unknown by name to most local residents, they are a constant presence and legendary to a small segment of the population. Unwilling to sacrifice personal freedom in order to pursue a career, they work only to survive, doing odd jobs that will leave them the time and energy to explore their individual obsessions. College towns, with their cheap rents, employment flexibility, and tolerant attitudes, provide a refuge for such people.

FIGURE 6.4.
*Iconoclasts like
John Seawright
have found their
niche in college
towns like Athens.
Photograph by
Terry Allen; used
with permission.*

One of my best friends from my Lawrence days was such a character. Steve Greenwood came from Boston (or so he said), looked like Joey
Ramone (of the archetypical punk band the Ramones), didn't know how to
drive, rarely woke before noon, and dreamed of moving to Sweden where
he figured through twisted logic he would be out of reach of nuclear war.
He helped wrest control of the college radio station from the old hippies and
turned it into a station known for playing weird bands first. In the process,
he amassed a giant record collection (which he slowly sold to pay the rent),
developed a musicologist's knowledge of obscure pop music, acquired a
taste for marijuana brownies (he couldn't tolerate smoke), and worked various clerical jobs at the University of Kansas, but only long enough to sock

away enough money so that he wouldn't have to work for a while. Questioning, sarcastic, but usually with a sly grin on his face, like Seawright he died relatively young, and left those who had come under his spell numb and grasping for words to try to convey his importance to those who didn't know him.[15]

Seawright (fig. 6.4) was born in Toccoa, Georgia, in the foothills of the Blue Ridge Mountains, the son of an itinerant Methodist minister. His family moved frequently when he was young. In 1968, when Seawright was eleven, they moved to Athens, just as the sixties counterculture was arriving. He and his friends liked to hang out on campus, but Seawright's parents were strict. "I didn't get out of the house too much," he recalled. He did occasionally go to see rock bands on campus or to a big show at the Coliseum. By the time Seawright entered high school, an alternative commercial culture was emerging in Athens, and every Saturday he would go downtown to the Hobbit Habit bookstore, which stocked "your whole gamut of sixties and early seventies stuff," he said. "Good literature, but also every kind of possible political psychedelic manifesto and leftist writings. That was an education for a lot of kids."[16]

When Seawright was fifteen, his family moved to Washington, Georgia, where he finished high school. But Athens had made an impression, and he began to plot his return. "I was in exile for a year," he said. "A lot of my friends were messing up, doing a lot of dope, being sent off to reform school." He told himself he was going to "play it real straight, get a scholarship, [and go] back to Athens." He graduated from high school in 1973 at age sixteen and enrolled at UGA. He lived his freshman year in the honors dorm, the Mell-Lipscomb Living-Learning Community, which he described as "an important nodal point for everything that happened" over the next decade. The following year he moved into a run-down Athens house with friends. He majored first in art, then English, but music came to define his life. Hanging around several downtown record stores, he discovered artists like Patti Smith and the Stooges. Like McCommons, Seawright noticed an important attitudinal shift underway. "You didn't really have a Spartacist youth league with red arm bands, but there was a definite major shift that took place here," he said. "There were deep changes that happened."[17]

Upon earning his bachelor's degree in 1977, Seawright entered graduate school at the University of Chicago, but he stayed only one year and never earned a degree. "I missed being in Georgia," he explained. "I'm very, very located in northeast Georgia. I have a really strong attachment to the place."

He moved back home with his parents and taught high school for a year. Then he followed some of his college pals to New York. Three years before, the B-52's had become favorites of New York's downtown music scene and, with their help, another Athens band, Pylon, made a splash in Manhattan. Their success spurred a steady migration of young Athens residents to New York City.[18] But Seawright returned after a year. "I just couldn't make a living," he said. "I had all kinds of jobs. It was just more trouble than it was worth. It's not my style: The great adventure of just doing your laundry. It was all too much for me."

Seawright moved back to Athens to stay in 1980. He got a job with the U.S. Census Bureau, trying to track down rural residents who had failed to return their Census forms. "Usually there was a reason," he said. When that job ran out, he went to work in the mailroom of the *Athens Banner-Herald*, where he met Mike Mills and Bill Berry, who had helped form R.E.M. a few months before. Over the years, he had a variety of "typical Athens just-above minimum wage" jobs. He worked at the library and as a proofreader for a law firm. He managed a publishing company for a local poet. In the 1990s, he began writing procedural manuals for machine operators, earning for the first time, he said, "something resembling middle-class money." He got married, and he and his wife, a massage therapist, secured a loan and planned to buy a home. But his wife was killed in a car crash three days before they were to close on the house. "I was really on the cusp of becoming, as I call it, a citizen," he said. "That disappeared."

Like many Athens and college town lifers, Seawright came to be defined not by a career, but by what he did when he wasn't working for pay. He wrote poetry, though he never published anything outside Athens. He did read two of his poems in the 1986 film documentary, *Athens, Ga., Inside/Out*. He became involved in a number of short-lived literary magazines. With some friends, he started the Rat and Duck Playhouse. Commercial space in Athens was cheap at the time, so they rented the second floor of a run-down building and staged three to four productions a year. He also helped initiate weekly poetry readings at a local bar. While researching the life of his great-grandfather, who was found dead in an Alabama ditch, Seawright became fascinated with a number of lesser-known figures in Georgia history. He began spending his free time poring over old newspapers on microfilm in the basement of the University of Georgia library. Eventually, he began writing a history column for *Flagpole* and occasional articles for magazines like the *Oxford American*.

Writers have long shown an affinity for college towns, partly because teaching is the only way many can earn a living, but also because university communities possess good libraries and bookstores, and an appreciation for the literary life. Innumerable writers who never pursued teaching careers have also chosen to live in college towns. Some first moved to them to attend school, while others simply came to prefer the college town life. Emily Dickinson spent her entire life in Amherst, Massachusetts. Oxford, Mississippi, was home to William Faulkner and inspiration for his fictional town of Jefferson. Ken Kesey lived for three decades on a farm outside Eugene, Oregon, where he attended college. Jon Krakauer, author of *Into Thin Air*, grew up in Corvallis, Oregon, and later moved to Boulder, where he was a "climbing bum" and began his writing career. Numerous well-known writers have passed through Missoula, Montana, and some have stayed, including Neil McMahon and James Welch. New England's many college towns are sprinkled with writers. Novelist Jodi Picoult makes her home in Hanover, New Hampshire. Jamaica Kincaid resides in Bennington, Vermont. Augusten Burroughs, author of *Running with Scissors*, is one of many writers who live in Amherst and the five-college area of western Massachusetts, a region so abundant with authors and bookstores that the *New York Times* called it "the Valley of the Literate." [19]

John Seawright never made significant money from writing, but Athens made it possible for him to survive and pursue his varied interests. He lived cheaply, renting an old house where the landlord allowed him to reduce his rent by doing work around the property. He rolled his own cigarettes. His clothes were worn. "I'm comfortable here," he said before his death. "It's a nice place. I'm not extremely ambitious. I'm doing stuff that I enjoy doing that I really can't do anywhere else. [I have] access to the library, the documents there and the newspapers. I have a really close community of very good friends. That's what's important for me. I don't feel a real intense pressure as if say I was living in Atlanta. [Athens is] a good place to not be extremely driven, which I'm definitely not." Seawright died in 2001 from a brain aneurysm. Tributes were published in *Flagpole* for the next month. A memorial was held at the Manhattan Café, an Athens tavern where Seawright had spent many nights. An exhibition at the Lyndon House Arts Center was dedicated to his memory. Athens singer Vic Chesnutt, a close friend, "kinda lost it," attempting suicide and winding up in a coma. He recovered. [20]

When Michael Lachowski moved to Athens in 1974, he planned to stay for two years. Raised in Stone Mountain, Georgia, an Atlanta suburb, he graduated from a Catholic high school and intended to enroll in art school, but decided to attend the University of Georgia for two years before transferring to the Atlanta College of Art. "I had this strong realization that I was living a sheltered life," he said. "I wanted to go to a common people's school." He attended UGA through the end of his sophomore year. "I finished my exams early and had like five more days in the dorm," he recalled. "I went out and bought seven paperback books and a bottle of vodka. I just hung out on the grass outside the dorms, read books and drank Bloody Marys, and slowly said goodbye to everybody. When I left, I didn't think I'd ever be back." [21]

But like McCommons and Seawright before and many since, Lachowski returned to Athens, drawn back that fall by friends he'd made at school and kept there by an evolving set of circumstances and a growing social network. Today, he operates a commercial graphic design company, publishes a fashion magazine, and is an esteemed visual artist. He also finds himself moving ever closer to the city's mainstream, serving on Chamber of Commerce committees and rubbing shoulders with civic leaders. But in an earlier time, Lachowski was part of a new generation that helped transform Athens from a sleepy college town into a city known around the world for music. He was a founding member of the band Pylon, which helped cement the city's reputation as a breeding ground for innovative sounds. It happened almost by accident, a scene created by people who weren't musicians, who didn't know how to play their instruments at first, and only did what they did as a way to have fun in a college town where, if you didn't like football or weren't in a fraternity, you had to create your own.

Hurrying back to Athens just before fall quarter began in 1976 and re-enrolling at the University of Georgia, Lachowski was able to rent a room in an old house with an art school friend of his, Randy Bewley. He lived in that house (fig. 6.5) for the next ten years, never paying more than $100 a month for his share of the rent. "It was the beginning of the lifestyle that I still live now, which has remained almost intact since the fall of 1976," he said, "both for the style of house I lived in and the roughness of the house, being like three decades behind the times in terms of creature comforts." In the nearly three decades since then, Lachowski has remained a renter and has lived at only three different addresses, all of them old houses with "bad plumbing, bad wiring." Cheap accommodations are rare in contemporary Athens, but were ubiquitous twenty-five years ago and are crucial to understanding why the Athens music scene was able to develop. They made it possible for young people like Lachowski to live cheaply, work sporadically, and have plenty of time to create.[22]

The B-52's came and went, relocating to New York. Their impact was in showing those who followed how easy it could be. But it was Lachowski and his cohorts who created the long-running music scene for which Athens is known. He and Bewley were music fans and took turns buying the latest records from New York and Europe. They subscribed to *New York Rocker*, which charted Manhattan's burgeoning new music scene. Watching the rapid rise of the B-52's, they decided it would be fun to form a band, play New York once, get their picture in *New York Rocker*, then break up. Lachowski found a bass at a yard sale, Bewley bought a guitar at a pawnshop, and together they learned to play in a studio space Lachowski rented above a sandwich shop downtown. "It was a time of a lot of wide-open wonder about the potential of everything," Lachowski recalled. "I got wrapped up in the whole lifestyle of living off campus and being in art school and having a million friends and going to a million parties."[23]

One day when Lachowski and Bewley were banging away on their instruments, Curtis Crowe, who had leased two floors above the sandwich shop and turned them into artist studios, overheard them. It was on the third floor of that building that Crowe had thrown a Halloween party in 1978, nicknaming the space the "40 Watt Club" for its primitive conditions. The name stuck and the 40 Watt Club, in a succession of locations, became Athens's most important rock club. Bewley and Crowe first met at that Halloween party. When Crowe heard Lachowski and Bewley practicing later that winter, he went downstairs and asked if he could join them on drums. They auditioned a series of singers, settling on Vanessa Ellison, an art school graduate who had stayed in town and worked at J. C. Penney. The band that became Pylon practiced together for the first time on Valentine's Day 1979 and debuted in public at a party the next month. "I didn't realize it at the time," Lachowski said, "but I was getting on a train that wasn't going to stop. It was a real wild and crazy ride."

Lachowski finished taking classes that spring, graduating a year later. He got a job working weekends as a laborer at a DuPont textiles plant on the edge of town, discovering he could make enough money working two eight-hour shifts on weekends that he wouldn't have to work the rest of the week. Pylon's singer Ellison got a job there too. Lachowski had no long-term plans and was having too much fun to leave Athens. "I didn't really have a strong sense that graduating from college was a precursor to getting a job," he ex-

FIGURE 6.5. *Michael Lachowski rented this house with a friend when he returned to Athens in 1976 and lived there for the next decade, never paying more than $100 a month rent. The availability of cheap housing nurtures the development of alternative communities in college towns. Photograph by the author, 2003.*

FIGURE 6.6.
*Michael
Lachowski (right
front) and his
band Pylon
perform at the
original 40 Watt
Club in Athens,
1978. Photograph
by Jimmy
Ellison; used
with permission,
Michael
Lachowski.*

plained. "Most of my friends didn't think so. I didn't think so. I didn't care."
Pylon continued to practice. That spring they played a party, and Ellison invited Fred Schneider of the B-52's. Afterwards, they gave Schneider a demo
tape, which he took to New York and played for a club booking agent. Pylon
was invited to play at the trendsetting Manhattan nightspot Hurrah as the
opening act for the Gang of Four, a highly touted English band.[24]

Like the B-52's, Pylon (fig. 6.6) was an instant underground hit. Influential *Interview* magazine writer Glenn O'Brien devoted half his review
of the Gang of Four show to Pylon. Soon after, Atlanta-based DB Records,
which released the B-52's' surprise hit "Rock Lobster," agreed to put out
a single by the band. Pylon opened for the B-52's in New York's Central
Park. In October 1980, the band released its debut album, *Gyrate*, to rave
reviews in New York and England. London's ultra-hip *New Musical Express*
called the album "one of the year's most fundamental rock and roll celebrations." Pylon was featured on the cover of *New York Rocker*.[25] Lachowski and
Ellison quit their jobs so the band could tour. Meanwhile, back home in
Athens, Barber Street, where Lachowski lived, became the epicenter of the
party-based Athens music scene. Members of a half-dozen bands, including
R.E.M. and Love Tractor, lived on the street. Next door to Lachowski's house
was a vacant lot that became the favorite party spot. They strung up lights

and set up speakers. It was dubbed Pylon Park, and Lachowski's answering machine became the clearinghouse for party information.

Pylon released a second album in 1982, but broke up the following year when the band began to feel increasing pressure to record and tour. "When we formed and the whole time we were together, we kept saying we were going to only do it as long as it was fun," Lachowski explained. Earlier, he had helped the owner of Pylon's record label open an Athens branch of his Atlanta record store. When Pylon disbanded, Lachowski increased his hours at the store. He gave little thought to leaving Athens. He had a steady girlfriend in town. When the record store closed in 1984, he painted houses for his landlord, and then got a job at a bike shop. "I saw two choices," Lachowski said. "What kind of career are you going to pursue or what kind of town are you going to live in? So I was willing to pick the town, the quality of life and figure out how to do the work around [it]." Pylon reformed in 1988, encouraged by the success of bands like R.E.M., and made a new album. But it broke up again three years later.[26]

Over the years, Lachowski has continually reinvented his life and been involved in a dizzying array of activities, partly because of the fluid nature of his creativity and partly to survive in a city where, as in other college towns, if you don't work for the university, opportunities for meaningful employment are limited. After Pylon broke up the second time, he went back to work at the bike shop. He assisted University of Georgia film professor Jim Herbert on two R.E.M. videos. He took a class taught by Herbert on Super 8 film, which inspired him and some of his classmates to create the Flicker Film Society, which screened films once a month at an Athens nightclub. For several years, Lachowski's only means of financial support was as a club disc jockey, making $500 to $1,000 a night. After hearing Africa Bambaataa's "Planet Rock" on the street when Pylon was in New York, he became captivated by electronic dance music. He began making party tapes and, in 1988, the 40 Watt Club persuaded him to DJ a dance night at the club. It was so successful that it became a regular feature.

Lachowski's most enduring activity and his primary source of income today is as a commercial graphic designer, an endeavor that began, like so much he has done, by chance. Once at a wedding he ran into an old friend who was an admissions officer for a small college. After Lachowski told him of his film work, he was persuaded to create a TV commercial for the school. "That turned into another job and another one and another one," he said. Before long, "I had developed a sideline career as a one-man ad agency." When he stopped doing work for the college in 1996, Lachowski opened Candy, a creative services agency. "I really had to decide who can I

FIGURE 6.7.
*Michael
Lachowski, now
in his fifties,
has continually
reinvented his
life in the more
than three
decades he has
lived in Athens.
Photograph by the
author, 2003.*

work for in this town and be happy about myself," he said. "Athens is growing, [but] the job opportunities here are still very constrained. I finally concluded that the only way I could do it would be to work for myself and start
a business." Lachowski designs everything from websites to billboards. His
clients have included R.E.M., retailers like the coffee house Jittery Joes, and
the Mental Health Association of Northeast Georgia.[27]

Now in his fifties, Lachowski (fig. 6.7) is still defining who he is and
seems genetically incapable of standing still or doing only one thing. To

keep his hand in music, he opened a Candy retail store that sold mostly dance records to DJs. When the market for dance music diminished, Candy began to stock clothing. It became the exclusive local outlet for Diesel jeans and sold $25 designer T-shirts. Clothing gradually displaced music as the store's primary business. Trained as a photographer, Lachowski has also continued to make art. In 2001, for example, he exhibited *Size Life,* a series of semi-erotic, life-size portraits of shirtless young men. In 2005, he staged a major retrospective at Athens's Lyndon House Arts Center. A year later, he had a themed show in Charleston, South Carolina. He's also become active in the community. He was a member of the steering committee for the city's bicentennial celebration. He volunteered to do an ad campaign for a candidate for the Athens-Clarke County Commission. He was appointed to a Chamber of Commerce committee on arts and technology business. Those efforts, he said, are not part of any deliberate strategy, but are "the result of being at a certain age and the people who think I have something to offer are in different positions now, in positions of power." [28]

I made my first research trip to Athens in 1999, but because work on this book has taken so long, I've had to re-interview many of my Athens contacts repeatedly. As I made final revisions to this chapter, I interviewed most of the featured individuals for fifteen to twenty minutes by phone, but my conversation with Lachowski stretched over three hours. His life had changed dramatically. As always, he bubbled with ideas. In 2005, he closed his Candy retail store, which was "hemorrhaging money." Relieved of the stress the store inspired, he said the period since has been "idyllic, calm, peaceful—very enjoyable, very manageable." His *Size Life* series stimulated an increasing interest in fashion-type photography and, in 2004, he won a *Surface* magazine competition and published a photo spread in the magazine. One of the models in that spread was a local slacker named Atom. Lachowski began to regularly photograph Atom and created the *Atomlook* photo series, which he exhibits primarily on the World Wide Web, with a different photo posted each day. The website also sells prints, a limited-edition book, and a keychain slide viewer containing an Atom photo. [29]

As *Atomlook* suggests, Lachowski's art and business activities are converging. In 2006, he started a modeling agency called Natural Purity that seeks to represent models in the Atom mold: young, slim, fresh-faced, and without attitude or conventional model looks. Then in 2007, he began publishing *Young, Foxy, and Free,* a quarterly fashion and art magazine (the name is meant to be silly). Glossy and colorful, the magazine is entirely visual and provides an outlet for Lachowski's photos and the work of other artists. The magazine is available all over Athens and in a few hip stores throughout the South. Lachowski has also joined with five other local artists to form a design collective. They won a commission to produce an Athens bus shelter and are designing an outdoor cigarette disposal device for Keep Athens-Clarke County Beautiful. Music is also a constant. Lachowski is half of a disc jockey duo with the playfully pornographic name of Cumbrella. In 2004, Pylon reunited and has played several shows in Athens. New York label DFA Records in 2007 reissued the band's debut album, long unavailable. Lachowski's involvement with Pylon's re-formation seems uncharacteristically backward-looking, but he agreed to participate because of his relationships with other band members.[30]

Viewed in broad terms, Lachowski's life is remarkably similar to its contours thirty years ago—dynamic, inventive, and economically marginal. His financial situation was so precarious as his clothing store struggled that his home telephone was disconnected. He was also forced to close his design office and now works out of his apartment. Lachowski has occasionally contemplated leaving Athens, frustrated by its small size and limited potential. But that has passed, and he remains drawn to Athens because of the social network he has built over the years and the creative community for which the city is known, but also because of the natural rhythms of the place—the climate, the angle of the sun, the wisteria that blooms every spring, the hypnotic din of cicadas in summer. Once when returning home from New York by train in March, he was discouraged to see that the wisteria had begun to bloom while he was gone. He resolved to never again leave Georgia from March till May. Athens isn't as cheap as it once was. He wishes the city had more of a visual arts scene and watches warily as Atlanta grows closer every day. Still, the small piece of the earth that is Athens is Lachowski's social and ecological niche, and he now doubts he could survive anywhere else.[31]

TOTALLY IN LOVE WITH A DEAD MAN

Some people, like McCommons and Lachowski, were fundamentally changed by their experiences in a college town. Others, such as visual artist Joni Mabe, did not necessarily undergo a significant personal transformation, but found in a college town a combination of small-town comfort and big-city sophistication where weirdness is welcome. Mabe is a kook, albeit a funny and endearing one, with a hillbilly accent straight out of *Hee-Haw*, who shocked her professors in art school and has made her name documenting her private obsessions in public.[32] She is best known for her *Traveling Panoramic Encyclopedia of Everything Elvis*, a mind-boggling collection of original Elvis Presley–inspired art and memorabilia that for twelve years toured the world in an eighteen-wheel truck. Mabe is one of those rare artists who has bridged the arcane and the popular. Her work has been featured in *Art Forum* and *TV Guide*. She has works in the permanent collection of the Museum of Modern Art in New York, but has also appeared on *The Howard Stern Show*. Years after her work first gained international attention, she still lives in a bungalow at the end of a gravel road in Athens that she first rented as an undergraduate.

Born in Atlanta, Mabe (fig. 6.8) grew up in the small north Georgia town of Mount Airy, where her father owned a jukebox and pinball distributorship and was mayor for twenty-one years. As a first grader, she won an art show at the library, beating out several adults. She's been cutting and pasting, drawing and painting ever since. She moved to Athens in 1975 to attend the University of Georgia, though the town was hardly new to her. Her parents began bringing her to football games when she was six. She had regularly visited her older sister in the Zeta Tau Alpha sorority. In high school, she and her friends would go to Athens to drink. Mabe majored in printmaking, and drawing and painting, but almost immediately found herself at odds with her professors. "They would tell me, you can't do this, you can't do that, don't mix this and that," she recalled, "so that's what I would do."

Mabe's life changed dramatically on August 16, 1977, the day Elvis Presley died. She was at home in Mount Airy for the summer, preparing to return to college. She was outside washing her International Scout, listening to the radio, when she heard the news. Until that time, her musical tastes ran more toward Lynyrd Skynyrd and Aerosmith, but after Presley's death was announced, the radio station played nothing but Elvis for the rest of the day, not only his hits, but also obscure ballads and gospel songs, most of which Mabe had never heard before. "I became obsessed," she said. "It was like, you fall in love and it's intense and you can't think of nothing else and you're crazy and everything seems absurd." That night, she started making Elvis art, cutting out pictures from supermarket tabloids. The following week, she made her first Elvis lithograph. She began trading her Elvis artwork to collectors for Elvis memorabilia. "I was totally in love with a dead man," she said.[33]

Graduating from UGA in 1981, Mabe spent the summer in Italy and then returned to Athens for graduate school. She courted controversy and attracted media attention with the first of three shows she staged as part of the requirements for the master of fine arts degree, an exhibit entitled *Ten*

FIGURE 6.8.
*Joni Mabe, "The
Elvis Babe," is
typical of the
sort of eccentrics
who are drawn
to college towns.
Photograph by
Mikel Yeakle; used
with permission.*

Men I've Slept With, which featured a series of life-size nude body prints she made by covering each man with petroleum jelly and having him lie face down on a large lithographic plate. The show was shocking even by art school standards. "I've had several faculty members just look at me and turn away," Mabe said at the time.[34] Her second show as part of her master's program was *The Elvis Room,* precursor to her traveling Elvis show. She wallpapered a room with images of Elvis, displayed a series of Elvis scrapbooks she'd made, installed a plaster Elvis bust, and set up one of her father's jukeboxes, which played Elvis continuously.

Her final and most controversial exhibit as a graduate student was entitled *Me, The World, Shit, Phalluses, Hair, Jesus: Concerns,* which included, among other images, a print of DaVinci's *Last Supper* juxtaposed with cutouts of nude men. It created an uproar more for the way it was promoted than for its content, however. Mabe plastered flyers all over town featuring an advertisement clipped from a men's magazine in which porn star John Holmes, his genitals exposed, promoted a penis enlarger, under the headline "Hope for Small Men." The chairman of the art department ripped the posters from the walls of the Visual Arts Building. Mabe received a written reprimand from her major professor. She got such a kick out of the faculty's response that she framed the letter of reprimand and displayed it in the show. During her oral examinations, one faculty member asked her what her art was about. She replied, "Sex and death." Her major professor stood up, patted her on the head, and said, "Go back to Mount Airy, little girl." Then he walked out of the room.[35]

Mabe went instead to New York, serving as an apprentice for a year at the Center for the Book Arts. She liked New York so much she considered staying, putting down a $50 deposit on a studio. But just before Christmas, while walking down Broadway, she came upon a man on the sidewalk who had just fallen from a tall building. "I said to myself, 'I need to get home,'" she recalled. "You don't know who you are until you go somewhere else and see yourself and see yourself back where you came from and what you're about. I realized what a product I was of this region." She returned to Athens, where she has lived ever since, moving back into a house she rented from an art school professor. She bought the house the next year.

Back in Athens, making Elvis art and collecting Elvis memorabilia began to occupy most of Mabe's time. She first exhibited her Elvis collection professionally in 1984 in Atlanta with a show entitled *I Wanted to Have Elvis' Baby, But Jesus Said It Was a Sin.* She purchased a wart removed from Presley's wrist. On a trip to Graceland, she found a toenail in the green shag carpeting that she calls the "Maybe Elvis Toenail." Her art includes Elvis shopping bags, Elvis lithographs, an Elvis prayer rug, and a coat covered with 3,000 Elvis buttons. In 1985, she began touring the collection, which includes 34,000 pieces, taking it as far as London. In 1996, she published a book, *Everything Elvis*, which features reproductions from her collection. She has since stopped touring the Elvis museum, instead installing it permanently on one floor of her grandparents' home in Cornelia, Georgia, not far from her hometown. She bought the house in 1993, restored it (it is now listed on the National Register of Historic Places), and turned it into the Loudermilk Boarding House Museum. She sponsors an Elvis festival there every August and is planning to open a "B&E" (Bed & Elvis) in a room modeled after Elvis's Graceland bedroom that fans will be able to stay in overnight.[36]

Mabe's Elvis museum is an extract from a larger collection, *The Museum of Obsessions, Personalities, and Oddities,* that she has also occasionally taken on the road. It includes dirt from Harry Houdini's grave, holy water from the Jordan River, and cat fur balls. Her obsessions have also resulted in commissions to create art for permanent display. In 1996, in conjunction with the Atlanta Olympics, she created twelve large glitter portraits of southern icons, such as Patsy Cline and Tennessee Williams, which are displayed at Atlanta's Hartsfield International Airport. Most of her income today comes from her museum, the "Big E" festival, and private art commissions. She created a glitter portrait of blues legend Robert Johnson, for example, for a California bar. Her Athens house is filled with the detritus of her life and work. An arts publisher who visited her home said, "I couldn't decide where art stopped and life began."[37]

Mabe's art has been exhibited in thirty states and fourteen countries. She has traveled widely, lecturing at museums and conferences. Why does she still live in Athens? "Because I have so much junk!" she said. "Can you imagine moving this?" Why not Mount Airy or Cornelia, where she now spends several days a week? "Cornelia is a different world than Athens," she said. "My artwork, the naked men and the *The Last Supper*? What would be the point of me doing that to that town? It's conservative. It's a small, little town." What about Atlanta? "Athens is so much better. Atlanta's too big. It's sort of like a mini–New York." But why Athens? "My friends are here," she said. "There's a lot of smarts here. It has a lot of intelligent people, that are worldly, have been places and come back here. You can throw out some subject and somebody's going to know something about it. There's so many people here that I've known forever who haven't left. It's home, I guess."[38]

STUMBLING INTO SUCCESS

By the time Jessica Greene graduated from high school in Atlanta in 1981, college had become what you did after high school for children of middle-class suburbanites, even if, like Greene, you had no idea what you wanted to do. Like her sister Barrie two years before, Greene moved to Athens and enrolled at UGA. Unlike Jessica, Barrie had a career plan. She majored in political science and intended to go to law school. Once in Athens, however, she became immersed in the city's music scene. In time, she married (and later divorced) Peter Buck, guitarist for R.E.M., and became owner of Athens's premier rock 'n' roll nightclub, the 40 Watt Club. Like Jessica, she came to Athens to attend college but never left.[39]

Athens was changing when Jessica arrived. She knew about the B-52's. She bought the band's debut album in high school. R.E.M. had just released its first single. Two Athens clubs were booking new music on a regular basis. The mainstream media had discovered Athens music. Jessica fell in with the same crowd as her sister. School became secondary. She chose to major in art during her sophomore year after taking a ceramics course. "I really took to it," Greene said. "I had a good time. Then it's like, hey, I can get a degree in this?!? Sure! I didn't know what the hell I was going to do with my life." [40]

Greene met her husband, Ted Hafer, shortly after he moved to Athens in 1985 at age twenty. Hafer, who died in 2007 of an apparent suicide, was among a new breed that moved to Athens not to attend college, but to be in a band. Athens changed Hafer, who grew up in Potsdam, New York. He became a strict vegetarian. He became politically aware. He joined a band, eventually becoming bass guitarist for a group called Porn Orchard that released two albums. "Moving here exposed me to all kinds of cultural things that I wouldn't have seen where I lived," he said. "That was a real turning point in my life. I was really concerned about the environment. I became really zealous and extremist about things. I met a lot of people rapidly, a lot of people that made me go, 'wow,' and look at myself in a different way." [41]

Greene and Hafer met when he helped her move into a house north of downtown, around the corner from where he lived. The house was located in a small neighborhood isolated by the North Oconnee River on one side and railroad tracks on the other. "It was a real neat little community, just five or six households of like-minded people," Greene recalled. "That was the beginning of hanging out with a certain crowd. Ted had three other roommates. Next door there were a couple of guys and down the street a couple of girls. [There were] four guys on the corner. And we just all hung out together. We'd wake up on Saturday morning, meet in the middle of the street. We'd just go swimming or go out and eat a late breakfast. We all became pretty good friends. That was the beginning of, hey, this is a fun place to live." [42]

Greene earned a bachelor of fine arts in 1986, but had no desire to leave Athens. As a student, she worked part-time at the university library and, when she graduated, was able to turn that into a full-time job. "It was just fun living here," she explained. "I just couldn't imagine packing up, moving somewhere, just for some job. The thought of dressing up and going on some job interview was the worst thing I could imagine. I was just willing to float along as long as I could." She worked at the library for another year, but quit when working at a desk from eight to five became "torture." She worked a series of low-wage restaurant jobs. Her mother began to pressure her to pursue a career, suggesting she become an art teacher. She thought of enrolling in graduate school. "But it all came back to what do you do after that?" she said.

In 1988, a friend of Greene's asked her if she wanted to a buy a half-share in a coffee house and vegetarian café called the Grit for $500. She said yes. The Grit had opened two years before in an old railroad station north of downtown. Its facilities were primitive: The kitchen had a crock pot, a hot plate, a toaster oven, a plastic cooler, and an avocado-green stove.[43] It opened at seven in the evening and closed after the bars shut down. Mostly, the Grit was a hangout for musicians and others hipsters, "townies" as they are called locally (distorting the traditional meaning of the term), who stayed for hours drinking coffee. "We were not making any money," Greene recalled. She had to work part-time jobs just to keep the Grit afloat. The location was less than ideal. It was located near a public housing project and was burglarized frequently. It was also in the same building as a fraternity bar, which sponsored a "Zoo Night" every Wednesday that was so rowdy that the Grit decided to close on that night. Then a sports bar opened next door. The owners coveted the Grit's space so they could expand and, in hopes of driving it away, verbally abused the Grit's customers. They were "awful, awful people," Greene said. "We were pretty tough girls, but nobody wanted to come there." She stayed with it, she said, because, "I was doing my own thing. That was it."

Today, the Grit (fig. 6.9) is an Athens institution, a popular vegetarian restaurant with a reputation far beyond the city's borders. To succeed, the Grit first had to move. In 1989, Greene approached Michael Stipe, singer for R.E.M. and a Grit regular, asking him if the restaurant could move into an old building he had purchased on Prince Street. Stipe agreed and spent thousands of dollars renovating the structure in collaboration with Greene's architect father (contrary to rumor, Stipe does not own the restaurant though he does still own the building). The Grit moved into the new location in 1990. Greene worked three other jobs initially, reinvesting most of her earnings in the restaurant. The new location had a full kitchen. The Grit instituted table service and expanded the menu. Eventually, Greene began taking a salary of $100 a month. In time, she was able to quit her other jobs. The Grit grew slowly but steadily. "We didn't know what the hell we were doing," she said, "but somehow it worked."[44]

The Grit owes part of its personality and at least some of its success to the Athens music scene. Musicians and their friends were its earliest customers. Over the years a disproportionate share of its employees have been in bands, attracted to the Grit as a place to work because of the owners' willingness to provide flexibility in their schedules to allow them to pursue their music. Hafer was one of those musicians at first. He worked there off and on. "I quit several times," he said. "I quit out of frustration with the way things were going. For a long time, this place was kind of in limbo, where the food was pretty good but the service was bad." He returned full time about 1993. He and Greene married the following year and became joint

FIGURE 6.9. *The Grit, a popular vegetarian restaurant and alternative institution in Athens. Photograph by the author, 2003.*

owners of the Grit. They made a conscious effort to improve the service, produce food in larger quantities, strive for greater consistency, and appeal to a broader spectrum of the population—to become, in Hafer's words, "a real restaurant."[45]

The strategy worked, and the Grit grew ever more popular. In 1998, it expanded, doubling in size. It now employs fifty people. It is a successful business in conventional terms, but it achieved success without bank loans or business plans, and retains a casual air and funkiness that reflect its location in a college town. In the process, the lives of Greene and Hafer became more traditional. They bought a house. They had two children. Both gave up being vegetarians. A few years ago, an Athens book publisher approached Greene and Hafer about writing a cookbook. They were reluctant at first, but eventually agreed. *The Grit Cookbook* was published in 2001 and has sold 30,000 copies, which Greene finds especially ironic because "I was never like a cook or anything," she said. "I just fell into it."[46] To be sure, vegetarian restaurants exist in non-college towns and people living in other types of places stumble upon what they do in life. But college towns, with their cheap rents and bohemian sensibility, provide an unusually fertile ground for dreamers and, with their uncommon concentrations of like-minded people, increase the likelihood that businesses such as the Grit will succeed.

Reviewing the cookbook, the *New Yorker* called the Grit an "indie rock Moosewood," after America's most famous (quasi) vegetarian restaurant, located in another college town, Ithaca, New York, whose cookbooks provided inspiration (and recipes) when the Grit was starting out. Moosewood was also founded by people who moved to a college town to go to school but stuck around. Five of Moosewood's seven founders attended Cornell University or Ithaca College. Other college town vegetarian restaurants were also founded by former students. Jan Gillie graduated from Virginia Tech in Blacksburg, wandered around the country for a few years, then returned to found Gillie's, the city's first vegetarian restaurant. Elaine Ramseyer attended Southern Illinois University in Carbondale, relocated to Los Angeles, sold real estate in New York City, but moved back to Carbondale and helped transform the Longbranch Coffeehouse into a vegetarian cafe. Melissa Murphy, who grew up in conservative Casper, Wyoming, earned a degree in international studies from the University of Wyoming in Laramie, left the state to enter graduate school, but returned to Laramie a decade later and founded Sweet Melissa's, a vegetarian oasis in cattle country.[47]

While Athens has become a supportive environment for eccentrics of all sorts, it is best known for its music, and it remains more possible for musicians to support themselves through their art than it is for other creative people. Visual artists complain that even though the city has more galleries than ever, nobody actually buys art in Athens. Media have reported about a growing literary scene in the city, but few writers can support themselves from writing alone. An increasing number of musicians, however, do make a living from their music. A recent report estimated that 1,800 to 2,000 people are employed in the music industry in Athens, and while those numbers exaggerate its economic importance, the sheer number of bands and clubs demonstrates the vitality of the city's music scene. *Rolling Stone* called Athens "the alpha and omega" of college music.[48]

The growth of the Athens music scene since the 1970s has transformed the city, especially downtown. When the B-52's played their first show in 1977, it was at a party. The only bars that booked music specialized in southern boogie and folk music. Only gradually were clubs willing to take chances on bands playing other styles. With the colossal success of R.E.M., however, everything changed. As recently as 1993, there were twelve bars in downtown Athens. By 2008, there were fifty-six bars downtown and three dozen clubs in the city booking live music. There were more than five hundred bands. Athens has become a destination for aspiring musicians seeking to launch their careers. Artists in bands such as Olivia Tremor Control and the Drive-By Truckers moved to Athens because of its music scene. "My friend Brandon brought me over one evening from Atlanta," said Drive-By Truckers singer Patterson Hood. "I thought it kicked ass and moved here less than a month later."[49]

The Athens music scene has also influenced many young people who came to the city to go to college. The story of acclaimed singer-songwriter Vic Chesnutt (fig. 6.10) illustrates the powerful role music has played in remaking the lives of individuals who came to Athens with traditional aspirations. Chesnutt grew up in rural Pike County, Georgia, an hour south of Atlanta, where his father worked as a baggage handler for Eastern Airlines. Though his dad worked in the city, they were country folk. His parents were deeply religious, raised chickens and pigs, and had gardens of okra, peas, and tomatoes. Chesnutt trapped rabbits before school. He hunted and fished. The closest town was Zebulon, a county seat and cotton mill town. Chesnutt worked in a mill during high school, cleaning cotton from the

FIGURE 6.10.
*Singer and
songwriter Vic
Chesnutt captured
the peculiar
charms of college
towns like Athens
when he said,
"It's just a little
small town in the
South, and it's a
bohemian freak
show in other
ways." Photograph
by the author,
1999.*

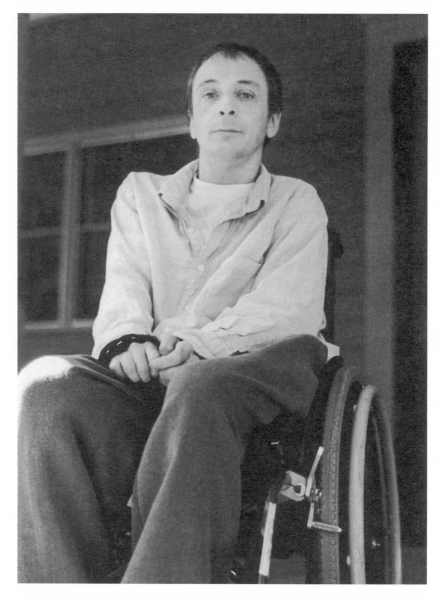

ducts, "the worst job you can imagine," he said, "crawling through a pitch black dark. I had asthma, so it almost killed me every day."[50]

Chesnutt made music from an early age, inspired by a grandfather who was a semi-professional country singer. He wrote his first song, called simply "God," at age five. When he was nine, he began playing trumpet. At thirteen, he rejected religion and began listening to rock 'n' roll. His parents bought him a guitar for Christmas in 1980 to help him get over the death of John Lennon. When he was sixteen, Chesnutt joined a cover band.

He hung around a record store in nearby Griffin. When he graduated from high school in 1982, he enrolled at a junior college a half hour from home. The following year, on Easter Sunday, Chesnutt got drunk, fell asleep at the wheel of his Chevrolet Chevette, and flipped it into a ditch.[51] The accident left him partially paralyzed and confined to a wheelchair. After undergoing rehabilitation he moved briefly to Nashville with a friend, then, in 1984, relocated to Athens.

At the University of Georgia, Chesnutt majored in English and planned to become a school teacher. Athens was a revelation for Chesnutt, who went to see a band his first night in town and, by his own account, went out every night for the next seven years, "hanging out and yakking, drinking and yakking." He began meeting people—painters, sculptors, poets, and musicians. The experience transformed him. "I was struck at how opposite of Pike County it was," he said. "People [were] talking about art and not hunting or fishing or racist ideas, or their Baptist beliefs. I met a million people who had something to talk about. It was very inspiring to me. I was so excited that I thought it was like Paris before the First World War."[52]

Chesnutt had no interest in playing music himself at first. His accident, moreover, undermined his ability to play guitar, though eventually he super-glued a pick to the "push cuff" he used to push his wheelchair and began to relearn how to play.[53] Late one night, friends coaxed him into playing a few of his songs. The next day, they got him a gig at the Uptown Lounge. He formed a band with some friends from Griffin called the La-Di-Das. Eventually, he stopped going to school. That happened one night when he took acid before going to a Latin class. "It traumatized me so much I never went back to school," he explained. "I was sitting there and the teacher was talking—'wah, wah, wah,' just like [on] *Charlie Brown*. Somehow I realized that he was looking right at me. I looked around and everybody was looking at me. I realized he's talking to me. But I couldn't understand a word he was saying. I took my books and left."

When the La-Di-Das broke up, Chesnutt began playing solo. About 1988, he began performing every Tuesday night at the 40 Watt Club, playing a different set of songs every week. Michael Stipe, singer for R.E.M., heard him and asked him if he wanted to record some of his songs. "I realized," Stipe said, "that what he was doing had reached a point where if it hadn't been put down on tape, it might get lost forever and he might never go on from there."[54] They recorded and mixed twenty-one songs in ten hours. Stipe persuaded a friend who owned a Santa Monica, California, independent record label to release the recordings. The resulting album, *Little,* was released in 1990. The primitive musings of Chesnutt became an immediate leftfield hit among new music cognoscenti.

Chesnutt, who had never played outside Georgia, began touring. Caught up in the rock 'n' roll life, he moved to Los Angeles, where he met actor Harry Dean Stanton, producer Van Dyke Parks, and Exene from the legendary punk band X. It was a whirlwind, but after seven months Chesnutt had enough. "I had to get out of there," he said. "There was just too many cars. It's just insane. I couldn't stand it anymore." He moved back to Athens. "Life here was easy and that's what I liked," he said. "It's a small town, so people would help you out. I couldn't be that drunk downtown in Atlanta. Somebody would have taken me and put me in a basement somewhere, sodomized me in a little cage. Here the cops would help me back to my van. It was a very caring small town like that. To me, it fit perfect. There was culture, but five minutes outside of town, you're back in the country again." [55]

More than any other group, rock musicians have shown a penchant for living in college towns, partly because the college years are an especially fertile period for rock band formation, but also because university cities are key nodes in the alternative rock universe and possess the clubs, radio stations, and record stores essential for launching a rock 'n' roll career. Countless bands and musicians have gotten their starts in college towns, and many stayed even after they became successful. Chapel Hill is still home to members of the db's, Superchunk, and Southern Culture on the Skids. Gainesville, Florida, gave birth to the bands Less Than Jake, Against Me, and Sister Hazel, and all three are still based there. Cultural icons Phish formed at the University of Vermont, and band members still live in Burlington. Green Day was founded in Berkeley, California, and continues to call the city home. Producer Butch Vig, who has worked with everyone from Nirvana to Jimmy Eat World, grew up in a small town in Wisconsin, earned a degree from the University of Wisconsin, but chose to stay in the college town of Madison, where he founded the successful band Garbage and still operates Smart Studios.[56]

In Athens, Vic Chesnutt is one of many who stayed in town to make music after their college days ended. One of the more unusual musical success stories of the last quarter century, he has made eleven solo albums and two albums in collaboration with Athens band Widespread Panic. Caustic, unpolished, but with a wry sense of humor and a razor-sharp wit and sounding like nobody else, he is a musician's favorite. In fact, the album that gained him the greatest notoriety was not one of his own but a tribute album that featured Madonna, the Smashing Pumpkins, and others singing his songs. He was also the subject of a documentary by filmmaker Peter Sillen and even appeared in actor Billy Bob Thornton's Academy Award–winning motion picture, *Sling Blade*. Recording on low budgets and often touring without a band, he has been able to make a living from his music. He bought a house in Athens's Cobbham neighborhood. He quit drinking ("I killed my liver") and rarely goes out anymore, preferring to stay home to read or write. But Chesnutt acknowledges that Athens has been a nurturing environment, a sort of "womb, a place where I grew from my fetal rock 'n' roll state into a full-blown human."[57]

PROTECTING THE "FREAKS"

It was Chesnutt who once said about Athens, capturing the dualistic quality of college towns, "It's just a little small town in the South, and it's a bohemian freak show in other ways."[58] Members of the Athens creative community are fond of calling themselves "freaks," but whether the city will remain a haven for eccentrics may depend on economics and politics. Real estate prices in Athens have skyrocketed, pushed ever upward by increased demand for housing and the willingness of newcomers to pay more for a place to live. Those changes have been stimulated by the migration to the city of Atlanta-bound commuters, the growth of the university, and a new state scholarship program that provides B-or-better students free tuition and leaves them more money to spend on rent.[59] Like other college towns, Athens has experienced rising tension between homeowners and renters as the university has grown. Efforts by government officials to address the situation brought into focus the links between housing prices and the development of college towns as eccentric enclaves.

One reason college towns have become attractive to musicians, writers, and other "freaks" is because they have lower rents than big cities. By renting run-down old houses and splitting costs with roommates, creative people can live cheaply and work less, allowing more time for their art. Chesnutt, for example, said he never paid more than $80 a month rent through the 1980s. When I interviewed Andrew Rieger, singer in the band Elf Power, he paid $160 rent for his share of a four-bedroom house that reeked of cat litter. As rents rose, the need to have roommates became even more critical. Between 1990 and 2005, median monthly rent in Clarke County more than doubled to $659 a month. Rent for an older house near downtown of the sort preferred by Athens bohemians is typically more than $1,000 a month.[60]

Like other college towns, Athens has an ordinance that limits the number of unrelated people who can live in a house. Such regulations are intended to preserve the quality of life in neighborhoods inhabited primarily by families. In Athens, no more than two unrelated people can live in a house in areas zoned for single-family housing, but that ordinance has been difficult to enforce. In response to complaints by homeowners, the Athens-Clarke County Commission in 2003 sought to implement a new ordinance to make it easier to enforce occupancy limits. Under the ordinance, landlords would have been required to register their properties, pay an annual registration fee, and file an affidavit identifying the occupants of each rental unit and their relationships to each other.[61]

The proposed ordinance pitted the usual adversaries in college town housing battles against each other (landlords vs. neighborhood groups, students vs. permanent residents) but also brought out a contingent usually absent from local politics—the artistic community. Rising rents had already caused some local artists and musicians to consider leaving Athens.[62] Tighter enforcement of occupancy limits promised to push living costs upward. A musician who shared an $800-a-month house with three persons would have to pay twice as much if he could only have one roommate. The proposed ordinance was hotly debated for months. Four public hearings attracted standing-room-only crowds. Debate reached a crescendo as commissioners met to vote on the ordinance. Nearly one hundred people spoke at the meeting, which dragged past midnight. Among them were a surprising number of scruffy and tattooed sorts who looked as though they were more accustomed to spending their nights at the 40 Watt Club than City Hall.

"Our creative community defines our town in many ways," said one person who spoke against the proposed ordinance. "Many of the artists and musicians in Athens were drawn here by affordable rents in comfortable neighborhoods and the promise of receptive audiences. This rental registration program will 'out' many of these talented, creative, valuable and peaceable citizens as criminals. Many will find it necessary to take on full-time jobs to make ends meet and neglect their art and music. Many more will very likely abandon Athens."[63] Another speaking against the proposal noted the irony that Athens was considering the ordinance at the same time it was preparing to host Athfest, an annual music festival. "Is it right," he asked, "that we brag about this segment of the population while simultaneously passing laws that make it impractical for them to continue to live here?"[64] A third, who claimed to represent the city's "freak community," was more blunt. "If passed, this ordinance will have a disastrous affect on

Athens diversity," he said. "The weirdoes will leave."[65] In any other type of place but a college town would the protection of "weirdoes" become a significant part of the public debate? In any other type of place, would a sizable coalition develop to defend the right of a segment of the population to *not* have to work full time?

The ordinance was approved, only to be voided when Georgia's governor signed legislation prohibiting the registration of rental property. Athens-Clarke County commissioners immediately rewrote the ordinance to side-step the law. Under the new ordinance, although landlords would not have had to register properties or pay a registration fee, both landlords and tenants would have been required to sign a document declaring who lives in a rental property and the relationships of all tenants. The impact on tenants would have been the same as the original ordinance. Pete McCommons of *Flagpole* was the most vocal public opponent of the various plans. "Our government," he wrote, "is killing our music community. The two-person limitation is too tight. Until that manacle is loosened our flow of creativity will ebb and the spirit that nourishes this special life in our community will atrophy." In August 2003, the Athens-Clarke County Commission approved the revised ordinance, but four months later a Clarke County judge declared it unconstitutional.[66]

It may already be too late. Preparing to return to Athens as debate over rental registration raged, I sought to interview a few creative individuals under age thirty who came to Athens to go to college but never left. A surprising thing happened: I could not find anyone who fit that description. Could it be that Athens is already too expensive for a younger generation of musicians and artists of the sort that made the city famous? Could it be that government efforts to tighten enforcement of occupancy limits would have only confirmed a trend economics began? Or was my inability to locate any younger people a simple reflection of the fact that creative people in their twenties are still in the process of becoming? Will someone like Drek Davis, a visual artist who remained in town after earning an art degree in 1998 but five years later was thinking about leaving, still be in Athens a decade later?[67]

The future of Athens as a creative center may be in doubt. The continued growth of the city's music scene would seem to argue against that view, but music in contemporary Athens has become an industry in the true sense. It is no longer simply something to do. One longtime local musician has suggested that Athens, when rents were still cheap and nobody aspired to rock 'n' roll stardom, was like innocent and idyllic Bedford Falls in the movie *It's a Wonderful Life*, but has turned into Pottersville, the decadent and sinful town of George Bailey's nightmares.[68] Athens may become a victim of its own success and its day in the spotlight may be passing, but so long as university communities are home to young people with fresh ideas who wish to live apart from the American mainstream, and so long as some of those places have cheap rents and plenty of low-wage jobs of the sort necessary to sustain creative people, college towns will continue to be nirvana for misfits of all sorts.

STADIUM
CULTURE

One of the most conspicuous differences between higher education in the United States and that in other countries is the greater importance of intercollegiate athletics at U.S. colleges and universities. Stadiums and arenas dominate campuses. Athletic departments have annual budgets that dwarf those of academic units. Games draw spectators from great distances and are televised coast to coast. Coaches are paid higher salaries than university presidents, student athletes are national celebrities, and the marketing of college sports paraphernalia is a billion dollar business. Sporting events are also a central component of student life at American colleges and universities and sometimes overshadow the educational purposes of an institution. When is the last time undergraduates camped overnight in the cold to get the best seats for a professor's lecture? College sports as they are played and celebrated in the United States have no equivalent elsewhere in the world, where college athletics tend to be participatory activities intended for all students, emphasize fitness and recreation more than competition, and are largely intramural in character or comparatively small-time.

Nowhere is the significance of intercollegiate athletics more apparent than in college towns because of the sheer magnitude of major college sports relative to the small size of such cities. If the number of stadium seats is compared to population, college towns possess more seats per capita by far than any other type of place. In some college towns, the football stadium holds more people than live in the entire city. Stadiums are often the most prominent features on the landscape and the first structures you see when you approach a college town. Tens of thousands of fans descend upon towns for games. Such regular pilgrimages are economic boons and can leave a permanent imprint on the built environment and way of life. College sports impact college towns in ways that often go unrecognized. They affect government budgets and influence transportation planning. Big games are important events on local social calendars, preferred seats are status symbols, and the outcome of games shapes the moods of residents. Because major sporting events carry the names of the towns where they are played far and wide, the identities of a college town and a university's athletic teams are often intertwined. College towns are many things—bohemian islands, elite enclaves, and liberal outposts—but they are also among our most sports-obsessed places. One-quarter of the cities in a major sports magazine's recent ranking of the one hundred best sports cities in the United States were college towns.[1]

The personalities of many college towns have been shaped in part by big-time college sports. Auburn, Alabama, is one such town. Typical of the region in which it is located, Auburn (fig. 7.1) is a football town. If you have ever been in a football town on an autumn weekend when a game is to be played, you cannot ignore it and will never forget it. When I used to have to wend my way through the semi-drunken hordes on game days to get to my office at the University of Oklahoma, the whole experience seemed the antithesis of what higher education is supposed to be about, part of what Murray Sperber calls "beer and circus," the strategies universities employ to keep students (and the public) entertained while allowing the quality of education to decline.[2] But I could not help but also be intrigued. The electricity that permeated my college towns on a football Saturday was tangible. I have experienced game days in State College, Pennsylvania, and Athens, Georgia. I used to be a sportswriter: I've sat on press row at the NCAA basketball tournament, interviewed major leaguers around the batting cage at Yankee Stadium, and covered the Rose Bowl. But nothing could prepare me for a football weekend in Auburn or the degree to which life in Auburn revolves around sports.

As such, Auburn presents an extreme example, but nonetheless provides a useful lens for examining the ways in which college sports can impact college towns. This chapter seeks to show the important role intercollegiate athletics have played in shaping college towns. To achieve this, I will describe a typical football weekend in Auburn, analyze the historical development of Auburn football and its evolving impact on the local way of life, and assess the contemporary significance of sports in the town.

THE FOOTBALL WEEKEND

Compared to other college towns with major state universities, Auburn is relatively small, with a two-block downtown and students making up nearly half of the 50,000 residents. Indicative of the importance of sports, Auburn's football stadium is large. It holds 87,451 people and dwarfs all

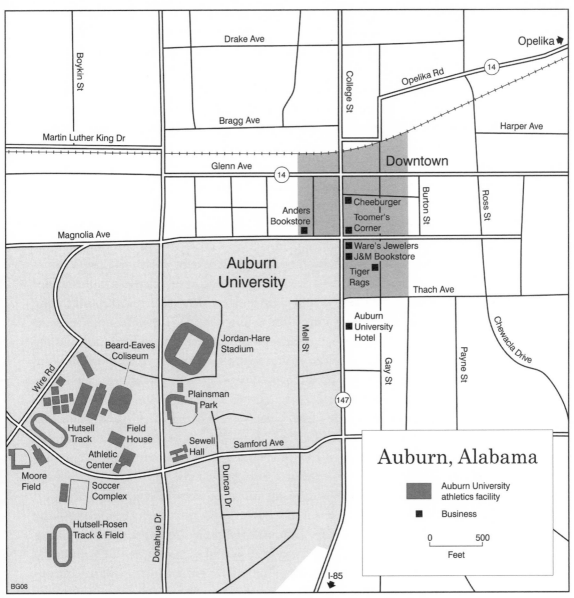

FIGURE 7.1. *Auburn and athletic facilities on the Auburn University campus. Map by the author.*

other buildings on campus. On six-to-eight weekends a year, the town is transformed. Fans begin to arrive a week before each game, so what would appear to be an isolated event gradually consumes the period from August to December. In truth, football season never really ends in Auburn. The actual season culminates with the January bowl games (in a good year). But that is followed by the recruiting season, which some argue is more important than the season itself because it determines future success. Not long after the recruiting season ends, spring practice begins and fans assess the prospects for the coming year. Spring practice culminates with the annual A-day intersquad game in April, when as many as 40,000 people have turned out to see the Auburn football team play itself. Practice resumes in July or August, and the season usually begins on the Saturday before Labor Day.

My first visit to Auburn on a football weekend was in 1999. Auburn was coming off a turbulent season in which its head coach had quit after five games amid allegations that a high-powered banker and Auburn trustee had single-handedly forced him to resign. Auburn finished 3–8, the Tigers' worst record since 1952. Five years before, another coach had resigned and Auburn had been placed on probation after a former player revealed he had received payments from coaches.[3] When I traveled to Auburn in October 1999, the football team had a new coach and a 2–3 record. I arrived the Thursday before the game, following the orange Tiger paws painted on U.S. 29, the main highway into town. Already, motels were filling and the town was buzzing with activity. Even though I had made my reservations months in advance, the closest room I could find was ten miles away from the city along Interstate 85. Auburn's recent troubles and mediocre start had done little to dampen enthusiasm. Since then, Auburn has regained its place among college football's elite—winning three-quarters of its games since 2000, going undefeated in 2003, and playing in January bowl games five times—but the behavior of Auburn fans when the team was losing was even more telling about the power of college sports in college towns.

On College Street downtown, fraternity and sorority members were painting store windows to inspire their team to victory (fig. 7.2). Employees of J&M Bookstore, Anders Bookstore, and Tiger Rags were busy restocking their shelves with T-shirts and hundreds of other items to which the Auburn logo had been affixed. Special shirts are printed for each game. Tiger Rags even sells "season tickets," giving fans the opportunity to reserve a complete set of a season's shirts so they won't risk arriving to find shirts for a particular game sold out. Merchants all over town were preparing for the invasion of fans. An entire window at Ware Jewelers was devoted to Auburn

FIGURE 7.2. *Fraternity and sorority members paint store windows in downtown Auburn in an effort to inspire the Auburn University football team to victory. Photograph by the author, 1999.*

paraphernalia. Inside there were Auburn earrings, decanters, even crystal emblazoned with the school's logo. The produce section of a grocery store far from campus was decked in orange and blue, Auburn's colors, with football-shaped Auburn balloons flying above the produce section. John Bale has called the ubiquitous symbols of college sports teams on display in college towns the "popular icon[s] of a latter day religion."[4]

On campus, motor homes were arriving and fans were setting up tables and tents. To many, tailgating is as important as the game itself. Indeed, what makes game day in a college town such a spectacle is not what happens on the field on Saturday, but all that leads up to and follows the game, what John Rooney and Richard Pillsbury have called "a school-oriented culture fest."[5] I have met tailgaters who set up on campus, spend the weekend socializing, but never actually go to the game. I have met people who live within walking distance of the stadium but drive RVs to campus for football weekends. Many Auburn fans have been parking in the same spot for years. Locals drove to campus the Monday before a game, pounded four stakes into the ground, and connected them with colored ribbon.[6] In the unwritten rules of Auburn football etiquette, that reserved the spot. Out-of-towners asked local friends to do the same for them, or, if they had children who were Auburn students, assigned them the task. Fans have been known to buy old cars, park them near the stadium, and leave them there all season. When they arrive in town for a game, they relocate the car across town and park their RV in the spot. One-third of fans who attend Auburn games, and stay somewhere other than home, do so in motor homes.[7]

On Friday morning, what began as a trickle of early-arriving fans turned into a steady stream as the day progressed. The Auburn Grille, its walls lined with framed photos of Auburn sports heroes, was busy.[8] On the menu: Tiger (potato) skins, an Aubie chicken sandwich (named for the Auburn mascot), and War Eagle wings (for the Auburn battle cry). Next door at the University Barbershop, the owner was selling the last four squares on his weekly football pool. In the window, below the words "Cracked Pecans for Sale," were painted the scores of Auburn's wins over archrival Alabama. Nearly every store on College Street was filled with sports memorabilia. There were framed football jerseys in Cheeburger, clippings from Auburn's undefeated 1993 season on the walls of the Traditions sandwich shop, a giant photo of legendary coach Ralph "Shug" Jordan at the Big Blue Deli. Everything in town, even the Compass Bank ATM, was done up in orange and blue. Friends and strangers passing on the street did not say "hello" or "good morning," they exhorted "War Eagle!" the Auburn battle cry. As Al Reinert observed in his analysis of high school football in Texas, "It is a

FIGURE 7.3.
*Auburn fans fill
downtown and
throw toilet paper
over tree branches
and streetlights
at Toomer's
Corner following
every Auburn
home football
win. Photograph
by Todd Van
Emst; used with
permission.*

truer measure of their values than art or war or politics: the way they choose to declare themselves."[9]

Toomer's Drugs, kitty-corner to the campus, had ordered 2,000 extra rolls of toilet paper in preparation for an Auburn victory. Following every football win, fans pour into the intersection that connects the town and campus, and throw toilet paper in the trees (fig. 7.3). On this October morning, toilet paper still dangled from trees from Auburn's last win, a month before. Nearby, one beer truck after another unloaded its cargo in front of downtown bars. After noon, traffic began to back up at major intersections. Because of limited parking, the university turns over nearly the entire campus to football traffic. With the exception of a few sacred spots, such as the area in front of the university's first building, fans can park anywhere they want, even on campus lawns. By Friday evening, there were RVs all over campus. Fans milled about, introducing themselves to their weekend neighbors, greeting old friends, and trading good-natured barbs with fans of Mississippi State University, the weekend's opponent.

There is a social geography to tailgating. The lots at the basketball arena and the grove in front of Allison Laboratory drew an older crowd, content to set up quiet picnics under the awnings pulled from the roofs of their motor homes. Groves Amphitheater nearby, in contrast, was full of students and young adults. SUVs and late model pickups were more common than RVs. Six-foot-long barbecue grills had been hauled to the site. Rock music wafted through the air. Everyone seemed to have a beer in hand (despite university rules forbidding drinking on campus), and they moved freely between parties.[10] Auburn is near enough to its Southeastern Conference opponents that most games draw eight to ten thousand fans from the opposing school. Many travel to all their team's road games, arriving in motor homes or converted buses of the sort used by touring entertainers.[11] To show their allegiance, they raise school flags atop plastic poles. From a distance, the horizon of opposing flags, with each school claiming particular territories, suggested a battlefield scene.

Campers awoke Saturday morning to the sound of the Auburn marching band practicing in the distance. Ticket scalpers staked out ground at major intersections. One, standing in the rain at the corner of College and Glenn, told me he'd been there since 4 a.m. He'd driven from Atlanta with relatives, and each took a position at a different spot around town. Supporters of Mississippi State drove through downtown ringing cowbells. An orange and blue Volkswagen bus, decorated with an airbrushed Tiger and Auburn stickers, flying four Auburn flags and emblazoned with the words "Planet Auburn," circled through town, blasting the Allman Brothers from speakers mounted on top. Retired alumni strolled hand in hand down College Street. Fans poured in and out of stores, carrying bags of souvenirs. Crowds were especially thick in front of J&M Bookstore, where high school students painted Tiger paws on the faces of children for $1, and Toomer's Drugs, which sells a wide range of souvenirs and dispenses its famous lemonade, but no longer fills prescriptions.[12] Tailgaters cooked vats of jambalaya and giant racks of barbecue chicken. They set up buffet tables with enough potato salad and coleslaw to feed an army. They mounted satellite dishes on the roofs of motor homes, which were connected to big-screen TVs placed under awnings. Kids played football in front of Langdon Hall. Almost everyone wore orange and blue. One T-shirt read: "Auburn football is life."

Pregame festivities culminated with "Tiger Walk" (fig. 7.4), a tradition that began in the 1960s but intensified in 1989 when Auburn hosted archrival Alabama at home for the first time. Fans lined Donahue Avenue from Sewell Hall to cheer the team as they walked from the athletic dorm

FIGURE 7.4.
"Tiger Walk" has become a game-day tradition in Auburn. Fans line Donahue Avenue to cheer the football team as it walks from the athletic dormitory to Jordan-Hare Stadium before each game. Photograph by the author, 1999.

to Jordan-Hare Stadium to dress for the game. An estimated 20,000 fans jammed the street before the 1989 Alabama game. During my visit, fans began to congregate an hour beforehand. One fan rode a unicycle up and down the street. Fathers held young girls dressed in cheerleader outfits on their shoulders. Adults acted like children, giddy with anticipation. At 9:15 a.m., buses carrying the Mississippi State football team inched their way through the crowd, blaring the anthem "We Will Rock You," and igniting the ire of Auburn fans in the process. Soon after, someone heard the first notes of the Auburn marching band and yelled "Here they come!" The crowd packed the street so tightly that it was almost impossible to see the football players as they walked past. As John Egerton has observed, football in college towns like Auburn is "celebrated with all the ritual and pageantry and spectacle of a High Church ceremony."[13]

I missed the opportunity on my first football trip to Auburn to witness the most unusual of Auburn's traditions, the toilet papering of Toomer's Corner. I left the stadium with three minutes remaining in the game and Auburn leading 16–3 so that I could see all of the postgame celebration downtown. But Mississippi State scored three times in the final three minutes, and Auburn lost the game in a collapse so maddening that it incited fights between Auburn fans afterwards. Two years later, however, I saw Auburn upset the University of Florida, the first time it had ever defeated a team ranked number one in the nation at Auburn. Thousands stormed the field after Auburn's kicker booted the game-winning field goal in a blowing rain with eleven seconds remaining. They rocked the goal post until it fell, then marched to Toomer's Corner, chanting, "It's great . . . to be . . . an Auburn Tiger . . . yes, it's great . . . to be . . . an Auburn Tiger. . . ." Soaked to the skin, hundreds filled downtown streets, covering the trees with toilet paper, and celebrating into the night.

HISTORICAL DEVELOPMENT

Experiencing an Auburn football weekend today makes it surprising to learn that for years Auburn was such a small town that the football team played most of its games elsewhere. The growth of the town has paralleled the growth of the university and its athletics program. And though it is impossible to say what role football has played in that growth, it has undeniably been a factor. There is little doubt Auburn would have fewer motels, restaurants, and stores hawking souvenirs if Auburn University sports teams were not so successful. A successful athletics program helps to raise the profile of a university and, in the process, can stimulate enrollment growth. Enrollment growth, in turn, yields population growth.

Rightly or wrongly, many young people first learn about a college because of athletics, not academics. Major college football teams like Auburn are on TV almost every week. College athletes are media stars. As a youngster growing up in Wilmington, Delaware, during the years when quarterback Pat Sullivan and receiver Terry Beasley propelled Auburn to among the nation's best college football teams, I proudly wore a replica Auburn football jersey. I was no different from millions of other kids who came to know Auburn for its football team. College administrators will tell you, furthermore, that applications for admission surge the year following a championship season in a major sport.[14] Eight of the ten biggest single-year enrollment increases at Auburn since 1950 in percentage terms have come within two years of a season in which the football team was ranked in the top ten in the country or played in a major bowl game.[15] Winning sports teams can enhance the image of a higher education institution more than any number of Nobel Prize winners or National Merit Scholars. Legendary scientist Vannevar Bush, who helped develop the atomic bomb and guided U.S. government science policy during and after World War II, once told the president of Pennsylvania State University that "there are three ways to build a great university. You can build a lot of buildings. You can build a football team. Or you can build a faculty."[16]

The growth of athletics at Auburn and elsewhere has been dependent upon three factors—regular success on the field (or in the arena), the presence of a few unusually successful coaches, and the support of alumni. Auburn played its first football game in 1892, beating the University of Georgia in a game that is considered the first interstate college football game in the South. But it was not until a young Irishman named Mike Donahue came to Auburn to coach the football team in 1904 that the school (officially called Alabama Polytechnic Institute but always known colloquially by the name of the town) began to be recognized for football. Donahue had played quarterback at Yale University under Walter Camp, considered the father of college football. Football was still a relative novelty in the South, imported from the North following the Civil War. During Donahue's eighteen years as coach, Auburn won three-quarters of its games, went undefeated twice, and captured three southern championships.

College athletes, unlike those in pro sports, come and go, staying only a few years. Those universities known for their sports programs, and those college towns whose personalities have been shaped by college sports, are those where legendary coaches have established winning traditions and filled stadiums. In football, think Bud Wilkinson at Oklahoma or Bo Schembechler at the University of Michigan. In basketball, think Bobby Knight at Indiana University or Dean Smith at the University of North Carolina. Although academics are loath to admit it, successful coaches can have a dramatic impact on a university and the town in which it is located. Football coach Joe Paterno has been so important to the development of Penn State and the growth of State College that a local magazine tried to imagine, à la *It's a Wonderful Life*, what the city and university would be like if Paterno had never become coach. It imagined a downtown full of boarded-up buildings and empty storefronts, and a university with half its current enrollment, a crumbling library, and a meager endowment. As a well-known sports odds maker once told a football booster club at the University of Alabama, "Anytime you can name the head of a university before you can name the head coach, you've got a problem at that football program."[17]

Still, football during the days of Mike Donahue was decidedly small-time. Auburn did not even have a stadium. What few games it scheduled on campus were played on its practice field. Every fall, ten rows of bleachers, capable of holding 700 people, were erected on one side of Drake Field. Auburn played one or two home games a year, typically against small schools like Mercer or Oglethorpe. The town in 1910 had a population of 1,408, plus

700 students. It had no paved streets and only one hotel. Football games on campus could not produce sufficient revenues to attract big-name opponents. Auburn was so ill-prepared to accommodate visitors that when it did have a home game, special trains had to be arranged so out-of-town fans could get home the same night. API scheduled most of its "home" games in cities like Birmingham, Montgomery, and Columbus, Georgia. With few games in Auburn, fans followed their team on the road. After API beat Georgia in Atlanta in 1913, a newspaper reported that "upwards of one thousand loyal adherents of the Tigers were speeding back across the Alabama line, almost delirious with the joy of the Tigers' achievement."[18]

As important to the growth of Auburn athletics as coaches like Donahue have been the alumni. To alumni, then and now, college sports represent a way to stay connected to their alma mater and rekindle the memories of the college years. It may be difficult to keep track of the academic accomplishments of a university after you have graduated and moved away, but you can still follow the football team and bask in the reflected glow of its success.[19] As colleges and universities became larger and their curricula more diverse, furthermore, athletics became a means for bringing together an increasingly fragmented student body. As the historian Frederick Rudolph has noted, "If every man did not take the same courses, at least he had an opportunity to cheer for the same team."[20] Alumni give college sports a marketing advantage over professional sports. Every spring at a large state university like Auburn, 5,000 or so students graduate and become alumni, typically the most fervent supporters of a school's athletic program. Every fall, several thousand new students arrive on campus, and many of them are soon indoctrinated into the stadium culture.

As Donahue built a winning tradition, alumni rallied around the team. Every fall, an entire issue of the alumni magazine was devoted to football. After Auburn won consecutive conference titles in 1913 and 1914, the *Auburn Alumnus* came to be so filled with sports news that at times it resembled a sports magazine. Alumni recognized early that if Auburn's sports teams were to remain competitive, its facilities would have to be improved. It says much about the priorities of alumni that the Alumni Association's first fundraising campaign was organized not to raise money for a new library or academic building, but to build a gymnasium to house the basketball team and provide training facilities for the football and baseball teams. The $50,000 Alumni Gymnasium was dedicated in 1916. The connection between alumni and athletics became more explicit in 1924 when homecoming festivities were switched from spring commencement to fall to take place in conjunction with a football game. Auburn's first homecoming game was held that October. Additional bleachers were erected at Drake Field for the occasion. The Atlanta and West Point Railroad arranged special trains to handle the crowds. An overflow crowd of 5,000 people watched Auburn defeat Clemson College 13–0. The student newspaper reported that "there were more souls in Auburn than have ever been here before." [21]

The successful homecoming, however, obscured a growing discontent among Auburn football fans that foreshadowed future battles between athletics and academics at Auburn and elsewhere. Events leading to the resignation in 1927 of Auburn's president, Spright Dowell, would say much about the growing power of athletics and alumni even in this embryonic stage in the development of college sports. Dowell, who took over as president in 1920, sought to correct what he saw as an overemphasis on intercollegiate athletics. He halted special treatment of athletes, refusing to give them preference for scholarships and campus jobs, and requiring them to meet normal academic and disciplinary standards. In 1922, Dowell suspended five football players for academic problems. Soon afterwards, coach Donahue resigned and a month later accepted the head coaching job at Louisiana State University. Almost immediately, alumni around the state began to call for Dowell's removal. [22]

The football program went into a downward spiral after Donahue's departure, as Auburn lost more than two-thirds of its games over the next eight seasons. In 1923, Dowell wrestled control of the athletic department from the semi-autonomous Auburn Athletic Association, a group controlled by alumni, coaches, and boosters, placing it under jurisdiction of the college. He refused to raise the athletic department budget and required coaches to teach more classes, reducing the time they could spend with varsity athletes. Dowell further raised the ire of football boosters when he redirected athletics revenues to help pay for the construction of academic buildings on campus and expressed opposition to holding pep rallies in Langdon Hall. After the football team lost its last four games in 1924, a group of Birmingham alumni held a mass meeting at which they demanded the president's resignation. Other alumni groups around the state soon joined the call.

Five years of football-inspired turmoil came to a head in 1927. The decisive event came just before the season, when Dowell expelled quarterback Frank Tuxworth for drinking. Without Tuxworth, Auburn was humiliated in its opening game, losing to tiny Stetson University. The following week, it was defeated by Clemson for the first time in two decades. Auburn failed to score a point in either game. A "Bolsheviki uprising" occurred on campus the day following the Clemson loss, as students began to organize to seek Dowell's ouster. They sent representatives to Birmingham and Montgomery to enlist the support of alumni. The final blow came the following Friday, when, during a pep rally, coach Dave Morey unexpectedly resigned. That night, students went on a "wild rampage" in the town. They built a bonfire and posted placards saying "To Hell With Spright." Four weeks later, Dowell resigned. He blamed criticism over his handling of athletics as the most important factor influencing his decision. College football historian John Sayle Watterson wrote about the Dowell incident, "In the oft-repeated struggle between educational values and big-time football, the hunger for football victories had won out." [23]

Not surprisingly, Auburn's next president was a football fan. Soon after taking office in 1928, new president Bradford Knapp declared in the alumni magazine, "Football is a great game. I love it because it is so much like the great game of life." He pledged to return Auburn football to its previous stature. "We have a long, up-hill job on athletics, especially football," he wrote. "Let us not be dismayed. We can and we will win with united effort." As part of that effort, Knapp initiated a drive to build a 10,000-seat football stadium he hoped would enable Auburn to play at least half its games on campus. In justifying the plan, he argued that playing so many games on the road put the football team at a competitive and financial disadvantage and disrupted the academic life of the college, since many students followed the team out of town for big games. Two alumni donated $20,000 to launch the stadium drive. The move to build a stadium was part of a nationwide explosion in campus stadium construction that began after World War I. During the 1920s, at least fifty-five colleges built new football stadiums. [24]

Under Knapp's presidency, the football program began to rebound. In 1930, Knapp hired Chet Wynne, a former Notre Dame All-America, as head coach. In his second season, Wynne coached Auburn to its first winning record in five years. The following year, led by All-America tailback Jimmy Hitchcock, Auburn went 9–0–1 and won the Southern Conference championship. The impact on the town was palpable. "These are happy days in the 'loveliest village of the plains,'" wrote an Associated Press reporter. "The sun shines brightly now. The black clouds have sailed away. The Plainsmen have pounded back to the top flight of Southern football. In this little town folks take their football seriously. Talk starts and ends with football. Everyone knows his neighbor and all join in the chatter around the corner drug store or on the post office steps. They like to go out and watch the players practice in the afternoon, sit along the sidelines, chew grass stems and second guess. An injury to a gridder hurts them almost as if it was one of their kin." [25]

The Great Depression slowed the drive to build a stadium, but efforts were revived after successful seasons in 1935 and 1936 and Auburn's first appearance in a bowl game, the Bacardi Bowl in Cuba. Alumni in 1937 launched a campaign to raise money to build a stadium, a field house with locker rooms for the football team, and a running track. Efforts were boosted by a report that the football team traveled 11,297 miles in 1936, playing games in San Francisco, Detroit, New Orleans, and Havana, plus other cities closer to home. It played just one game in Auburn. Work on the stadium began in 1937, but a lack of funds delayed construction of a grandstand. With the stadium incomplete, the team was forced to play thirty-two straight games on the road over the next three years. A $160,000 loan from the federal Public Works Administration enabled construction to resume in 1939. A concrete grandstand with redwood benches capable of seating 7,338 spectators and wooden bleachers that could hold another 5,000 people were completed in November of that year.[26]

The stadium (fig. 7.5) was dedicated on Thanksgiving Day 1939 with a game against Florida. It was also homecoming. In anticipation of large crowds, temporary bleachers were erected to boost capacity to 15,000. Local Jaycees mounted a drive to "fill every seat" and sought volunteers in every county in Alabama to sell tickets. Merchants were urged to put up window displays to celebrate the occasion and were asked to open until noon the day of the game, even though it was Thanksgiving. The *Lee County Bulletin* published a fourteen-page special issue commemorating the event. It was filled with ads from businesses across Alabama congratulating Auburn on its new stadium. The dedication was a front-page story every day the week of the game in the *Daily News* in neighboring Opelika, which predicted it would be "the greatest day in the history of Auburn."[27]

Local leaders worried how Auburn would accommodate a crowd that was predicted to be three times as large as the city's population. Tickets had been purchased from as far away as Louisiana, Ohio, and Massachusetts. There were but two hotels in town, with fewer than one hundred total rooms. The only public restrooms were at two gas stations. Fans began arriving the day before the game, and a large crowd turned out for a pep rally that night. The next morning, the streets of Auburn were "jammed at an early hour." Food stands were erected in front of stores on College Street. A crowd of 13,000 people attended the game, which ended in a 7–7 tie. Local businesses got their first taste of what future football weekends would mean. The crowd was so large that it spilled over into Opelika, which reported that "hundreds of dollars" were spent at local hotels, cafes, and gas stations. "One café owner said he turned away more people than he served," reported the *Daily News*, "so huge were the crowds that packed his place."[28]

Homecoming weekend became the biggest social event of the year, with residents hosting gala parties and merchants competing for prizes for the best-decorated windows. But the stadium did not have the intended effect, as homecoming was often the only game played on campus. Auburn continued to play major opponents in big cities and log so many miles by train that one writer remarked that its slogan ought to be: "Join the Auburn football team and see the United States." Auburn's stadium was small by the standards of the day. API could draw much larger crowds in Columbus, Birmingham, and Atlanta. "We could still make more money playing in the bigger stadiums on the road," said Jeff Beard, the athletic department's business manager.[29] Auburn was not unique in this regard. Florida regularly scheduled games in Jacksonville, Miami, and Tampa. Oklahoma played big games in Oklahoma City and Dallas. Penn State long played archrival the University of Pittsburgh in Pittsburgh every year. The University of Oregon played many of its games in Portland.

Despite the fact that Auburn played most of its games on the road, football became central to the life of the college and the town. With so few games at home, fans turned out in large numbers to watch the team practice. It was not unusual for several hundred people to turn out on a fall afternoon. Businessmen would close their offices early. Students and faculty would head over after classes. The team traveled by train, and it became a tradition for students and townspeople to gather every Thursday to see the players off and greet them upon their return (fig. 7.6). A pep rally would be held on campus or downtown, then the marching band and cheerleaders would lead the team and crowd to the train station. Nearly the entire student body and many townspeople would gather at the railroad depot. Many fans, too, would travel to the games. Railroads scheduled "War Eagle" specials. Students who could not afford train fare hopped a freight or hitchhiked. Auburn would empty the weekend of a game.[30]

Special events were held in conjunction with big games. Students built floats and marched in their pajamas for the annual "Wreck Tech" parade before the team boarded a train to Atlanta to play Georgia Institute of Technology, better known as Georgia Tech. A "Beat the Bulldogs" parade preceded Auburn's game with Georgia. When Auburn played far from home, the Tiger Theater downtown sometimes erected a giant board painted like a football field in front of its movie screen and charted the course of the game via telegraph, moving a football-shaped marker across the field with each play. Films of Auburn games occasionally replaced the regular Hollywood features on the big screen. Postgame celebrations were also common. After Auburn beat Alabama in Birmingham in 1950, a thousand cars poured into downtown Auburn. They soaped "War Eagle" and the score of the game on car windows and burned Alabama's elephant mascot in effigy under the traffic light at the intersection of Glenn and Magnolia.[31]

To some degree, the local obsession with football reflected a regional fascination with the game. As John Rooney and Richard Pillsbury have noted, "Football and the South are virtually synonymous. Nowhere is the sport-place bond stronger." The American brand of football was born in the North, but the South adopted the sport as its own and it became a defining attribute of southern culture. Scholars of the South have argued that football enabled the perpetuation of the southern belief in rugged masculinity in an age when industrialization was forcing many people off the land. Football victories over northern opponents, such as the University of

FIGURE 7.6.
*Fans greet the
Auburn football
team at the town's
railroad station,
1955. Used with
permission, Media
Relations Office,
Auburn Athletic
Department.*

Alabama's historic upset of the University of Washington in the 1926 Rose
Bowl, enabled the South to restore a sense of honor lost in the Civil War
and to attain a degree of respectability even as its traditions were being torn
apart.[32]

Annual rituals surrounding sporting events and spontaneous celebrations of important victories were central components of collegiate culture
in college towns nationwide. Oklahoma fans, like those in Auburn, regularly saw the football team off at the train station. They, too, held an annual pajama parade downtown (as did students at the University of Kansas
and the University of California, Berkeley). Big wins inspired impromptu
celebrations on Main Street. In Bloomington, Indiana, parades following
significant Indiana University basketball wins drew larger crowds than a
visit by the president of the United States. In State College, students built
celebratory bonfires in city streets, making off with fences, outhouses, and
anything else made of wood to provide fuel. Then, as now, celebrations
sometimes turned violent. In Ann Arbor, Michigan, police had to use tear
gas to disperse a crowd of 2,000 football fans in 1937 when they marched

downtown and stormed the Michigan Theater, vandalizing the facility and injuring a police officer.[33]

Two factors enabled Auburn to finally begin scheduling more of its games on campus—the post–World War II expansion of the university and the arrival of football coach Ralph "Shug" Jordan, who became the winningest coach in school history. Enrollment mushroomed following the war as veterans took advantage of the free tuition offered by the GI Bill. By 1948, enrollment reached 7,660, double its prewar high. Auburn's football stadium was expanded that year to accommodate increased demand for tickets. A new grandstand was built on the east side of the field, raising capacity to 21,290. With the added capacity, Auburn in 1950 hosted three games on campus for the first time since 1922. It also began selling season tickets for the first time.[34]

In 1951, Auburn hired Jordan to replace Earl Brown. Under Brown, Auburn won but three games in three years and finished 0–10 in 1950, its worst record ever. Auburn's decline created such turmoil in the state that two days after his inauguration in 1951, Alabama governor Gordon Persons, an Auburn alumnus, declared that the school needed a new coach. Money was also an issue, as the poor performance of the football team had reduced gate receipts. Auburn's president, Ralph Draughon, had initially come to Brown's defense, but after Jeff Beard, athletic department business manager, reported the department was $100,000 in debt, Brown was fired. Beard was promoted to athletics director, and his first major action was to hire Jordan, an Auburn graduate. Jordan, an assistant coach at Georgia, played three sports at Auburn and had been its basketball coach and an assistant football coach before the war. Together, Beard and Jordan set out to rebuild the athletic program. First, they sought to regain the support of alumni. That summer, they traveled the state, attending as many as five alumni meetings a week, "Shug trying to sell football," Beard said, "and me trying to sell tickets."[35]

Auburn finished 5–5 in Jordan's first season and fell to 2–8 in 1952, but over the next eleven years won more than three-quarters of its games, finished the season ranked in the nation's top twenty teams eight times, and went to four bowl games. The town of Auburn would never be the same again. Enrollment at API steadily increased. Football attendance grew ever larger. Homecoming games drew standing-room-only crowds. In 1954, the game attracted 25,000 fans, 4,000 more than the stadium's listed capacity. The next year the stadium was enlarged to seat 34,000. In approving the expansion, Auburn's board of trustees justified the project by saying that the added capacity "would permit API to negotiate for games with almost every member of the Southeastern conference."[36] In 1955, Auburn played four games in Auburn for the first time in the modern era, including two against conference opponents.

Season tickets began to be in such demand that college donors and alumni were given preference for the best seats. Ninety percent of season ticket holders were alumni. The growing crowds taxed the city's ability to accommodate visitors. Army MPs were called into help patrol. The Chamber of Commerce set up information booths along highways leading into town to distribute maps showing routes to the stadium. Local residents were urged to leave their cars at home. There were still only four hotels and motels in Auburn. Responding to the growing demand for lodging, a group of local businessmen, including the former sports publicity director at the college, announced plans in 1955 to build a Holiday Inn. Although football alone could not explain this development, the economic windfall it provides has enabled Auburn to support more hotels than other cities its size. But the impact of football on the town was more than economic. Indicative of the growing penetration of football into all aspects of local life was a 1955 appearance by Fob James, Jr., Auburn's star halfback (and future governor of Alabama), at a special Sunday night service at the First Methodist Church. The pastor delivered a sermon entitled "The Game and the Goal of Life."[37]

Auburn's most successful season came in 1957, when it went 10–0 and was awarded the national championship by the Associated Press. Auburn did not go to a bowl game, however, because a year earlier it had been placed on probation for paying two recruits, a charge Jordan steadfastly denied over the years. That fact did little to dampen the enthusiasm of Auburn supporters. In the scrapbook full of stories on Auburn's undefeated season, probation is rarely mentioned. Five thousand people jammed downtown Auburn after the national championship was announced, then paraded to Jordan's home one and a half miles away. A week later, 12,000 people turned out for presentation of the national championship trophy. Afterwards, a parade was held downtown and a banner proclaiming Auburn national champions was raised above College Street. Schools canceled classes for the day. Athletics had come to dwarf academics in importance. The same year Auburn won the national championship, two of its engineering programs lost their accreditation.[38]

Auburn went undefeated again in 1958 and over a three-year period won twenty-four straight games. Having restored a winning tradition, Athletic Director Beard then set out to persuade those opponents API had traditionally played at neutral sites to come to Auburn. Georgia, Auburn's oldest opponent, was the first to give in. The Auburn-Georgia game had traditionally been played in Columbus. For eight years, Beard tried to persuade Georgia officials to move the game to campus sites. Finally he succeeded, and the game was played in Auburn for the first time in 1960.[39] Auburn that year played five games on campus for the first time since 1907. To meet demand for tickets, Hare Stadium was expanded, its capacity increased to 44,500. But even the enlarged stadium was too small for the Auburn-Georgia game. More than 46,000 people, the largest crowd to watch a football game in state history, saw Auburn beat Georgia 9–6. That year, API officially took the name of the town in which it is located, changing its name to Auburn University.

The football team continued to win, university enrollment continued to increase, the town of Auburn continued to grow, and the stadium periodically had to be enlarged. The next expansion came in 1970, raising capacity to 61,261.[40] The expansion made possible the movement of Auburn's annual game with Georgia Tech entirely to campus sites. Quarterback Pat Sullivan and receiver Terry Beasley propelled Auburn back among the top teams in college football. Coming off a 9–2 season in which it finished tenth in the nation, Auburn in 1971 scheduled six games at home for the first time ever. In 1973, the stadium was renamed Jordan-Hare Stadium, making it the only stadium in the country named for an active coach. Then in 1974, the University of Tennessee agreed to visit Auburn for the first time. The game drew a record crowd of 64,293. The following season was Jordan's last. During his twenty-five years as coach, 40,000 seats were added to the stadium and annual attendance increased 683 percent.

No one seems to know exactly when tailgating became an integral part of Auburn football weekends, but it was probably a response to growing traffic and a shortage of restaurants. Auburn was still very much a small town in the 1970s, with a population of just over 20,000. Most people who attend Auburn football games come from outside the area, and the city was ill-equipped to move crowds three times as large as its population in and out of town in a hurry. Auburn's thirty or so restaurants, while sufficient to handle demand most of the year, could hardly accommodate crowds of 60,000. So fans came early, brought a picnic, and stayed late, waiting for traffic to clear. Motor home use increased in response to the limited availability of motel rooms (and, perhaps, as Warren St. John suggests, a shortage of bathrooms). In 1975, Auburn had five motels; Opelika had nine. As traffic intensified, people came earlier and stayed longer. Tailgating became more elaborate. The number of night games increased because of television, making it more difficult for out-of-town fans to return home the same day. What once was a single-day phenomenon was gradually transformed into a multi-day event. The football weekend has become, in the words of the literary scholar Edwin Cady, "a *fiesta*, a communal and ritual party, a blowout at which you are authorized to take a moral holiday from work, worry and responsibility." [41]

College football grew more popular during the 1980s, boosted by the growth of cable television and expanding TV coverage of games. Before 1983, Auburn had never been on TV more than twice during a regular season. By the end of the 1980s, the majority of its games were televised and many were telecast nationally. [42] Under Pat Dye, who took over as coach in 1981, Auburn rebuilt the reputation it lost after Jordan retired. In his second season, Dye recruited a nineteen-year-old from Bessemer, Alabama, named Bo Jackson. Jackson won the Heisman Trophy, awarded to the best college football player in the country, four years later and became one of the most popular athletes of all time. He helped Dye build a program that finished among the nation's top twenty teams for nine straight seasons. Under Dye, Auburn finished in the top ten five times, won four conference titles, and played in January bowl games six times. It was Dye, people say, who changed expectations in the town of Auburn and among Auburn supporters. Fans went from wanting to win to expecting it. Any season with fewer than eight wins, without a conference championship, without an invitation to a major bowl or a top ten ranking came to be viewed as failure.

As can hardly be surprising by this stage in the story, Auburn's football stadium grew still larger during Dye's twelve years as coach. John Rooney and Audrey Davidson have commented that the steady expansion of college stadiums is "analogous to a freeway: the more lanes one builds, the more traffic one generates." An upper deck was added to the west side of the stadium in 1980, raising capacity to 72,169. Indicative of the growing importance of big money in college sports, 1,008 sheltered seats were installed for major athletics donors. Demand for tickets soared during Jackson's four years at Auburn. In 1984, Auburn sold out all its home games, averaging 75,037 a game. After the season, an upper deck was built on the east side of the stadium, increasing capacity to 85,214. This time, seventy-one enclosed luxury suites, priced at $20–48,000 a year, were added. Although the $15-million project was funded entirely from athletics department revenues, it highlighted the growing tension between athletics and academics at Auburn and elsewhere. Auburn lagged behind other state universities in faculty salaries and its budget for academics, but athletics spending was extravagant. [43]

Athletics facilities have come to occupy ever-expanding real estate in most college towns, and the building of such structures, Ronald Smith has argued, has become part of the competition between universities for prestige. At Auburn, much of the southwest quarter of campus is taken up by sports facilities and athletics department offices. The events that take place at such facilities create a bond between people and place. As Karl Raitz has observed, they are a "source of civic pride and a symbol of victory and accomplishment." They are the sacred sites of the sporting world. In a society where sports have eclipsed religion in popularity, stadiums and arenas have become, in the words of Michael Novak, "our cathedrals." Major stadiums, he writes, are "storied places. Universes of tales. One sits in them surrounded by ghostly ancestors, as at the Mass one is surrounded by the hosts who have since Abraham celebrated a Eucharist."[44]

Cities other than college towns have large stadiums, universities with big-time sports programs, and professional sports teams that play to sellout crowds. So why are sports any more important in college towns and why are they so central to understanding the distinctive nature of many college communities? For one thing, the size of sports facilities and the crowds that attend games in college towns are much larger relative to the size of the communities. Auburn's Jordan-Hare Stadium now seats 87,451 people (it was expanded again in 2000, 2001, and 2004), meaning there are two seats for every resident of the city. If Yankee Stadium were that large relative to the size of New York, it would hold 16 million people (it holds 57,545). In college towns, a much larger portion of the population pays attention to local sports. As Michael Oriard has noted, many college towns lack symphonies, skyscrapers, and other civic symbols of major metropolitan areas. "Football's local importance tended to be inversely proportional to the community's size and status," Oriard writes. In college towns like Auburn, "the football team became the chief source of local pride."[45]

The 1985 expansion of Jordan-Hare Stadium was used as leverage to enable Auburn to win the one scheduling prize that had so far eluded it, a prize that has had a major economic impact on the city. Auburn had moved all its neutral-site home games to campus except its annual game against archrival Alabama. The game had been played at Birmingham's Legion Field since 1948, when the series resumed after a forty-one-year interruption.[46] Tickets for the game were split evenly between the schools, with Auburn fans on one side of the stadium and Alabama fans on the other. But Legion Field is a second home to Alabama, which plays several games there each year. It is much nearer to the Alabama campus in Tuscaloosa than Auburn (56 miles v. 187 miles). As a result, it never felt like a neutral site to Auburn. The expansion of Jordan-Hare made it larger than Legion Field, so the argument could no longer be made that playing the game in Birmingham gave a greater number of fans the opportunity to see what in any year is the single biggest event in a football-crazed state. It is no coincidence that Auburn's board of trustees approved the expansion on the Monday following Auburn's 1984 loss to Alabama. Alabama had won twenty-five of thirty-seven games between the schools in Birmingham, and Auburn fans had long felt that if they could just get Alabama to Auburn they could win more often.

The importance of the Auburn-Alabama game to fans of the two schools cannot be overstated. Marriages have broken up and business partnerships dissolved because of it. It is more important than any bowl game. No coach can expect to keep his job if he cannot win it. Even retired Auburn athletic director David Housel, ever the preacher about the benefits of college athletics, acknowledges there is a "sickness in this state about the game."[47] With the contract stipulating that the game be played in Birmingham due to expire in 1987, Dye sought to move it to campus sites. Alabama refused at first, threatening to drop Auburn from its schedule if it continued to push for the change. The city of Birmingham, claiming the game injected $17-to-$20 million a year into its economy, filed a lawsuit against both schools seeking to have the game played permanently at Legion Field. The state legislature threatened to intervene. In April 1989, a compromise was reached. Alabama agreed to come to Auburn that year on the condition that the game be played in Birmingham in 1990 and 1991.

Able to include Alabama in its season ticket package for the first time, Auburn sold 75,000 season tickets in 1989, 15,000 more than the year before and the maximum number it could sell because of commitments to visiting teams. The buildup leading to the game was intense. Tickets sold for as much as $500 each. All 1,200 motel rooms in the area were booked months in advance. "This is the biggest thing that ever happened . . . to the little town of Auburn," said one resident. Auburn coach Dye said, "The biggest thing . . . is not who wins or loses. The biggest thing for Auburn is that it is being played in Auburn." The next morning, 20,000 fans lined Donahue Drive to cheer the Auburn football team as it walked to Jordan-Hare Stadium. The largest crowd in stadium history and a national television audience watched Auburn defeat Alabama, 30–20 (fig. 7.7). After the game, coach Dye likened the experience to the fall of the Berlin Wall. "Auburn people were let out of bondage," he said. Local officials estimated the game injected $8 million into the area economy, equivalent to $14 million in 2008.[48]

FIGURE 7.7. *A record Jordan-Hare Stadium crowd of 85,319 watched Auburn defeat Alabama in 1989, the first time the two archrivals played in Auburn. Used with permission, Special Collections & University Archives, Auburn University Libraries.*

CONTEMPORARY IMPACT

How important is football to the town of Auburn? It depends on whom you ask. In any college town, there are many who hate what football represents and for whom the huge crowds are a nuisance. "I get the schedule every fall," says one longtime resident, "so I know when to stay home."[49] City officials, ever anxious to diversify Auburn's economy and expand its tax base, will tell you the significance of football is overrated. "Auburn . . . is a lot more than football," says longtime Auburn city manager Doug Watson.

When told of my intention to write about the impact of football on the city, Jan Dempsey, Auburn's mayor for eighteen years, frowned. "I'm sorry you chose Auburn . . . for that," she said, sighing. "It's wearying for that to be the thing we're thought about the most."[50]

But Watson acknowledges it took a postgame traffic jam to convince a state government official to push for the widening of College Street from downtown to Interstate 85. And Dempsey admits football so governs the mood of residents that when she was mayor she would change the agenda for city council meetings if Auburn had lost the Saturday before, postponing action on any controversial issues. "The whole town gets down when Auburn loses," she says. Football also impacts the city's finances because one-third of the local sales tax goes to the city government. The four months with the greatest sales tax revenues are those in which football is played (though the return of students for fall semester and Christmas season also play a role). Consequently, when officials sit down to create the city budget, they make sure to bring a football schedule. If Auburn is to host Alabama, they'll bump up projected tax revenues by $50,000. They take a hit if Auburn has a disappointing season.[51]

The economic impact on local businesses is great. A 1996 study found visitors who travel to Auburn to attend sporting events spent $27 million annually. Adjusted for inflation, that would mean sports fans inject $37 million into the local economy every year.[52] More recent research found that people who attend Auburn football games spend an average of $223 a day on lodging and other purchases, not including tickets, and stay in town an average of 1.8 days. Eighty-four percent of 75,000 season ticket holders live outside the Auburn area. Those numbers underestimate the full impact of Auburn's athletics department, which if it were a business would be the second largest private employer in the city. It employs 150 people full time, has an army of part-time workers, and supports 400 scholarship athletes, who are in essence employees (it pays their tuition, room, and board). Athletics revenues increased from $19.6 million in 1993 to $37.5 million in 2001, thanks to increased television revenues and rising donations spurred by greater demand for tickets.[53] The athletics department is also one of the most active developers in town. In recent years it has built a women's athletic center, a swim complex, a softball stadium, and an indoor tennis facility. It has enlarged the baseball stadium and renovated the basketball arena. All those projects pump money into Auburn's economy.

To businesses in college towns like Auburn, football season can be as critical in determining financial success as the Christmas season is to merchants in a non-college town. Businesses that benefit most are motels,

FIGURE 7.8.
*Stores and
restaurants along
College Street in
Auburn depend
on business
generated by
Auburn University
athletics.
Photograph by the
author, 2001.*

restaurants, and stores selling Auburn merchandise, particularly those on College Street (fig. 7.8). When I visited Auburn in 1999, the general manager of a motel across the street from campus told me the motel sold out for football weekends by March. The motel raised its rates 250 percent for those weekends and required a two-night stay. Every January, the motel sent out "season contracts" to its regular customers. Some had been staying in the same room on game days for twenty-five years.[54] The Auburn University Hotel and Conference Center does not even take reservations for football season. Regular customers are given the option at the time of the last game of the season to renew for the next year. Room rates are more than double their normal price. Demand for accommodations is so great that two condominium complexes have been built that are marketed to wealthy fans who want to assure themselves a place to stay six to eight football weekends a year.[55]

On game day, College Street restaurants have more business than they can handle. Long lines stretch down the sidewalk from Mellow Mushroom pizzeria. The Auburn Grille was so crowded during my visit that it eliminated its breakfast menu, offering only a buffet, and using an abbreviated menu for lunch and dinner. The owner admitted he was not a football fan, but decided to retain the sports theme when he bought the restaurant because football season "helps us catch up on bills the rest of the year." Ware Jewelers may do a month's worth of business on a single football weekend. J&M Bookstore, one of three stores downtown that specializes in Auburn souvenirs, does 50 percent of its annual sales on game days. The store stocks 6,000 different items featuring the Auburn name, logo, or one of its two mascots. When Auburn wins, says Trey Johnston III, J&M's owner, "there's more beer drank, there's more T-shirts purchased, and there's more money given to churches on Sunday."[56]

Football permeates all aspect of life in Auburn and its impact is year-round. My most recent visit to the town was in mid-winter 2002, a month following a disappointing season. Even then, football was the most common topic of conversation. Its presence was still felt almost everywhere I went. Auburn football was featured on the front of the sports section of the local newspaper every day that I was in town. Embedded in the sidewalks downtown are more than fifty markers that make up the Tiger Trail, Auburn's version of the Hollywood Walk of Fame, which honors its greatest sports heroes. There are dozens of businesses with Tiger, War Eagle, or sports motifs in their names. Flags bearing the Auburn logo fly from homes. "War Eagle" is painted on mailboxes. On campus, Auburn's photographic services department does a steady business selling reprints of sports photos. Even in the bowels of the Auburn University library, the sort of place you would think would be immune to the local obsession, staff members in the Special Collections Department field a steady stream of calls about sports.

Football shapes the emotions of this college town. I encountered it on the pages of the student newspaper. "Welcome to Auburn," wrote the columnist in a back-to-school issue. "I hope you like football." I saw it in the eyes of a man who ran a tailor shop on College Street for sixty-nine years. "Football changed Auburn," he said. Only those who wish Auburn was something else try to downplay its importance. David Rosenblatt, a Missouri native and historian by training who came to Auburn in 1976 to work in the university library, has watched the pulse of the town rise and fall with the success of its football team. "You can't," he says, "write the history of this city without sports, without football." As Gregory Stone has observed, sport can be "a unifying force for those communities it represents."[57]

While the case of Auburn represents an extreme example of the impact college sports can have on college towns, similar stories could be told to varying degrees for other college towns, from State College to College Station, Texas, and from Gainesville, Florida, to Eugene, Oregon. Each university and town has its sports traditions and history. In general, the impact is greatest in the South and more conspicuous in college towns where football is the most popular sport, because football crowds are larger, games are played on weekends when fans have more free time, and the game-day experience is more prolonged. But basketball has also helped to shape the character of college towns. A resident of Chapel Hill, North Carolina, recently remarked that the culture of that town is "so interwoven in the ethos of college basketball" that if the sport was eliminated it "would probably crumble into a ghostly dust." Even in a place like Eugene—hippie town, anarchist center, the very antithesis of Auburn—college athletics are an important influence. "Sports is our most shared spectacle," observed a Eugene writer. "Sports have helped define the kind of community we are." [58] As comments like this attest and the Auburn story clearly demonstrates, college sports can play an important role in the making of place in the American college town.

HIGH-
TECH
VALHALLA

To the outsider, Ann Arbor, Michigan (fig. 8.1), appears to be two different cities. On and around the University of Michigan campus, it seems like any other college town. "The Diag" is the focal point of campus, where activists distribute leaflets and students gather between classes. Shaded walks lead to buildings that are quintessentially collegiate. Across from campus, bookstores, coffee houses, and other businesses typical of college-oriented shopping districts line State Street, which bustles with activity late into the night. Surrounding the campus and downtown are endless blocks of rumpled old rental houses characteristic of student ghettos all over. Nearby is Burns Park, Ann Arbor's faculty enclave, comfortable, cosmopolitan, and politically correct.[1] All is as expected in the American college town.

Away from downtown and the campus, however, a second Ann Arbor reveals itself. All college towns lose some of their idiosyncratic flavor as you move farther from campus, but the contrasts are particularly dramatic in towns like Ann Arbor that have experienced significant high technology development. When I traveled to the city in 2001, the differences were jarring and made me worry that college towns like it were losing some of their distinctiveness. Driving across Ann Arbor my first day in town exposed its bi-polar personality. The area was experiencing a boom in research park development. Construction crews were creating new industrial spaces with redundant fiber optics lines and other features desired by tech-savvy entrepreneurs. Already there were ten research parks along State Street just south of the city limits. Most were full of nondescript buildings occupied by companies with brave new world names—Xitron, Beyond Interactive, Esperion Therapeutics.

As I drove south on State Street, one research park stood out. The car rental tycoon Warren Avis developed Avis Farms Research and Business Park, saying he wanted it to include only "go-go, high-tech, really exciting" companies. Well landscaped, with volleyball courts, picnic areas, and walk-

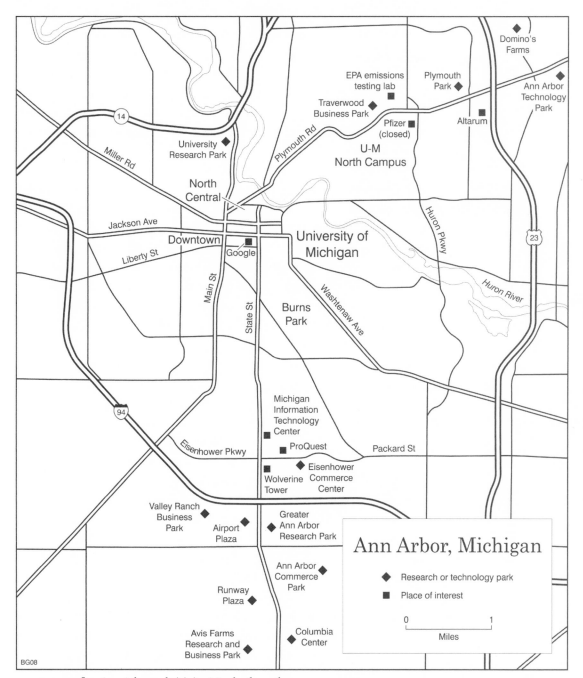

Domino's
Farms

EPA emissions
testing lab

Plymouth
Park

Ann Arbor
Technology
Park

Traverwood
Business Park

Pfizer
(closed)

Altarum

University
Research Park

U-M
North Campus

Plymouth Rd

Miller Rd

Huron Pkwy

North
Central

US 23

Jackson Ave

Huron River

Downtown

Liberty St

Google

University of
Michigan

Main St

State St

Burns
Park

Washtenaw Ave

Michigan
Information
Technology
Center

Eisenhower Pkwy

ProQuest

Packard St

Eisenhower
Commerce
Center

Wolverine
Tower

Valley Ranch
Business
Park

Airport
Plaza

Greater
Ann Arbor
Research Park

Ann Arbor, Michigan

◆ Research or technology park

■ Place of interest

0   1

Miles

Ann Arbor
Commerce
Park

Runway
Plaza

Avis Farms
Research and
Business Park

Columbia
Center

BG08

FIGURE 8.1. *Ann Arbor and vicinity. Map by the author.*

ing trails that encircle nine ponds, Avis Farms has a campus-like appearance. The buildings are sleek and ultramodern, many encased in mirrored glass and featuring little ornamentation. Loading docks are hidden from view. Avis erected a limestone obelisk near the park's entrance and imported swans to inhabit the ponds. Lease rates are higher than in nearby parks, so Avis Farms attracts companies for which image matters. When Avis Farms quickly filled, Avis built a second technology park, Avis Farms South, across the street. A map on the Avis Farms website labeled the area as the State Street Technology Corridor.[2] But was this a college town?

I drove north toward the University of Michigan campus in hopes of discovering a college town heart beneath Ann Arbor's business suit. I passed the eleven-story Wolverine Tower, home to the university's research division, which oversaw $800 million in research in 2006, and its technology transfer office, created to help commercialize the inventions of faculty. Coldly symbolic, Wolverine Tower is the antithesis of the ivy-covered college edifice. Nearby, ProQuest, one of Ann Arbor's oldest high-tech companies, moved into a new $34 million headquarters in 2006. North of it is the $20 million Michigan Information Technology Center (fig. 8.2), a high-tech conference center funded partly with state money that is so wired that even the coat room lockers include outlets for recharging laptops.[3]

Fatigued and discouraged, I drove downtown, parked, and wandered along State and Liberty streets, then walked around the campus. I ate lunch at Amer's Mediterranean Deli, full of students and professorial types. I climbed the stairs to browse the shelves at David's Books. I read with envy the schedule for the Ann Arbor Film Festival at the Michigan Theater. I made a mental note to have dinner at Seva, a vegetarian restaurant, and checked out the People's Food Co-Op on Fourth Avenue. A man asked me to sign a petition to get a medical marijuana initiative on the election ballot. Someone had plastered a "People Not Power" flyer over the Ann Arbor police department sign. Chain businesses like McDonald's failed in downtown Ann Arbor, but Shaman Drum bookstore recently celebrated its twenty-fifth anniversary and the Blind Pig nightclub has booked obscure blues and rock artists since 1971. It was no surprise that when iconoclast icon Google decided to open an office in Ann Arbor in 2006 it located downtown, with its vibrant street life and alternative capitalism.

Reinvigorated by what I saw downtown, I drove north across the Huron River, past the gargantuan University of Michigan hospital, and through the university's North Campus, which resembles a research park. Developed after World War II to be the focus of Michigan's growing science and technology research, the North Campus was envisioned as a place where

FIGURE 8.2.
Michigan
Information
Technology Center,
a high-tech
conference center
funded partly
with state money.
Photograph
by Balthazar
Korab; used with
permission, MAV
Development.

scientists and business could work together. To encourage collaboration, U-M occasionally sold chunks of land there to research-oriented companies. Today, it is unclear where the campus ends and the grounds of multinational corporations and private research bodies begin. The largest corporate facility built on former university land was the Ann Arbor research center of Pfizer pharmaceuticals (fig. 8.3), the world's largest drug company. Pfizer's Ann Arbor laboratories grew to encompass 177 acres and employ 2,100 people. It was there scientists developed the blockbuster drug Lipitor, which rang up $13 billion a year in sales. When I visited, the Pfizer complex was being enlarged yet again. Perpetual construction at the site over the last two decades made its future fate seem inconceivable, but in 2007, Pfizer announced it was closing the facility. The decision underscores the volatility of the global economy and the risks college towns face when they attempt to become something more than seats of learning.[4]

Security vehicles watched me as I walked around the edge of the Pfizer property, so I got back into my car and traveled east on four-lane Plymouth Road toward the city limits. Large office buildings line Plymouth Road and

FIGURE 8.3.
*Ann Arbor labora-
tories of Pfizer
pharmaceuticals,
which grew to
employ 2,100
people in the city,
but closed in 2007.
Photograph by the
author, 2001.*

are scattered along intersecting streets. Where the State Street corridor has traditionally been home to Internet and biotech startups, Plymouth Road has long been the center of Ann Arbor's defense industries, although the end of the Cold War and cuts in U.S. government defense spending have left some buildings vacant and forced defense contractors to reinvent themselves. One such organization is Altarum, which now specializes in health care and information technology research but in an earlier era, when it was the deceptively named Environmental Research Institute of Michigan, employed eight hundred people doing top secret military work. Also located in this area is a U.S. Environmental Protection Agency automobile emission testing laboratory, which has attracted research labs for several foreign auto makers to the area. Beyond the city limits are Domino's Farms, an office complex created by Domino's Pizza founder Tom Monaghan, and the Ann Arbor Technology Park, which was predicted to one day employ 12,000 people, but like so many high-tech projects in Ann Arbor never fulfilled its ambitions.[5]

Motoring in and out of office complex parking lots, I again felt as if I had left a college town and entered someplace decidedly more conservative and corporate. Plymouth Road is a car-oriented landscape, a sea of parking lots and uninhabited green spaces, its buildings private and uninviting, the sidewalks deserted. A week spent interviewing high-tech executives and venture capitalists intensified my alienation and made me fear for the future of college towns. High-tech Ann Arbor is like your punk rock buddy who grew up and went to work for a bank. Researching and writing this chapter has been a struggle. A summer spent reading and thinking about high-tech demoralized me. I recognize the importance of economics to understanding places, but I hate money and what it does to us. I am drawn to the idea of cooperatives and cohousing. I suppose one reason I am attracted to college towns is because they are generally places where money seems less important than elsewhere.

When this book took longer than planned, I considered eliminating this chapter, but decided that if I was going to create a meaningful portrait of college towns, I must represent not only what I like about such places, but their other distinguishing features and ways they are changing. What is happening in Ann Arbor is happening in college towns from Charlottesville, Virginia, to Santa Barbara, California. Yet little has been said about college towns in the growing literature about high-tech. I came to recognize, too, that there is something fundamentally different about high-tech development in college towns. The distinctive college town way of life shapes the nature of the high-tech economy in places like Ann Arbor. High-tech entrepreneurs and workers drawn to college towns tend to be motivated by different factors than individuals who gravitate to established tech centers. College towns also impose limitations on high-tech growth. They may never become leading high-tech centers, but they serve as alternative sites for knowledge-based entrepreneurship and so might be thought of as high-tech valhallas, to borrow a usage applied by Joel Kotkin.[6]

This chapter will examine the development of a high-tech economy in Ann Arbor as a window into the ways knowledge-oriented industry can impact college towns. I will begin by discussing the types of industry that naturally emerge in university communities such as Ann Arbor. I will examine the growing relationship between academe and industry over time and trace efforts by public and private leaders to transform the city into "The Research Center of the Midwest." I will contemplate the advantages for high-tech development that exist in college towns and the obstacles to success intrinsic to such places. Finally, I will evaluate how high-tech growth has changed a college town like Ann Arbor, for better and worse.

EARLY UNIVERSITY-RELATED INDUSTRY

Most college towns have historically resisted smokestack industry because of a belief that factories are inappropriate in communities where the pursuit of knowledge is considered a higher calling. Although businessmen in Ann Arbor occasionally pushed for industrial development, the University of Michigan, which opened in 1841, came to dominate the city so thoroughly that those who did, according to Jonathan Marwil, "underestimated the inertial forces stymieing their dream." In 1866, for example, a businessmen's group won voter approval to impose a tax to raise money to attract new companies, but when they tried to collect the tax, a group of citizens obtained a court injunction halting it. A local newspaper, echoing sentiments still common in college towns, blamed "the element that fights all progress" and predicted Ann Arbor would stagnate "until dry-rot sets in."[7]

Yet, some industry did develop in Ann Arbor expressly because a university was located in the city, as it had in the earliest university towns in Europe. The first industries in Cambridge, England, for example, manufactured scientific instruments for professors at the university there. Cambridge also became a center for book publishing after a former faculty member established a printing house to supply books to students. Jena, a university town in Germany, developed into an optical center after a former student established the now famous Zeiss optical company to supply high-quality magnifying glasses to faculty. Similarly, the origins of book publishing in the United States can be traced to the granddaddy of U.S. college towns, Cambridge, Massachusetts, where the first publishing house in the colonies was established in 1638.[8]

Several industries in Ann Arbor have roots related to the university. The city has become a center for the printing of academic and small press books. In 2005, there were nine book printers in the area, and they employed more than 1,500 people. The oldest and largest is Edwards Brothers, begun in 1893 when two brothers who were law students began mimeographing lecture notes to sell to U-M students. When they graduated, their brother took over the business and expanded it to other universities. Early in the twentieth century, Edwards Brothers made the transition to book publishing. Today, it employs 500 people in Ann Arbor and prints books for university presses and academically oriented commercial publishers. Most other book printers in the area were established by former Edwards Brothers employees.[9]

Ann Arbor's most successful home-grown technology company emerged out of Edwards Brothers, developed to serve an academic market, and built a close alliance with the University of Michigan from its inception. Eugene Power, founder of University Microfilms, now part of ProQuest, an information company with annual revenues of nearly one half billion dollars, went to work for Edwards Brothers as a salesman in 1930 after earning an MBA from U-M. Although Edwards Brothers specialized in printing books in small numbers, Power built a company conceived on the notion of producing rare materials in even smaller quantities, or one at a time. His innovation was the medium he used to do this—microfilm, 35 mm film on which pages are photographed and then magnified for viewing and printing. Power is credited with turning microfilm into an "affordable and accessible medium" and, as a result of that work, has been compared to Johannes Gutenberg, inventor of printing.[10]

As a salesman for Edwards Brothers, Power called on faculty to solicit manuscripts for printing. He regularly visited the Clements Library on the Michigan campus and eventually arranged to produce a facsimile edition of a rare book from its collection. That project attracted the attention of a U-M English professor, who was compiling a dictionary of early modern English. He arranged through Power for Edwards Brothers to photograph 150 books listed in Pollard and Redgrave's *Short Title Catalogue* of books printed in Great Britain from 1475 to 1640. Edwards Brothers published facsimile editions of three of the books, but sales were insufficient to recover costs. Power thought there must be a better way to make available rare materials for which the market was too small to justify printing.[11]

In 1931, Power attended a conference at which he began to formulate his ideas for creating "editions of one." One of the conference organizers introduced Power to microfilm. He told Power about a camera devised by a New York banker that photographed canceled checks automatically, one after another. When Power was shown the film, "it was as if a great light had gone on in my mind." Power convinced Edwards Brothers to allow him to establish a commercial microfilming operation. He thought an ideal test project would be to photograph all books in the *Short Title Catalogue*, then sell copies of the film to libraries. He arranged with the British Museum to photograph the books. Edwards Brothers sold the microfilm to libraries on a subscription basis. Microfilming was so different from printing, however, that Edwards Brothers lost interest in the project and gave Power an ultimatum: Abandon it or leave the company. He left Edwards Brothers and in 1938 started University Microfilms.[12]

The story of University Microfilms provides an example of how intellect and industry come together naturally and profitably in a college town. Microfilm is old technology now—it is hardly sexy—but Power's use of it was visionary. His next idea was to persuade universities to permit doctoral dissertations to be published on microfilm rather than printed. He proposed that universities require dissertation authors to submit their manuscripts to his company, which would film them. Anyone wanting a copy of a dissertation could buy it on microfilm. Power demonstrated his scheme to the dean of Michigan's graduate school, who liked it and encouraged his counterparts at other universities to try it. The concept caught on and, in 1951, University Microfilms International was designated as publisher of record for all dissertations produced in the United States. Since then, it has filmed more than one million dissertations, and today 90 percent of U.S. dissertations are available through UMI.[13]

The outbreak of World War II posed a risk to the young company because fighting threatened to interrupt filming of books at the British Museum. In response, Power created several new products based on U.S. sources. In 1939, UMI began filming back issues of newspapers. The success of that work prompted the *New York Times* to ask UMI to film its back catalog and future issues. Two years later, the company unveiled four more microfilm series, including one containing every U.S. magazine published before 1800. The war also brought the company work. Fearing destruction of rare materials, a scholarly organization contracted with UMI to film six million pages of books and manuscripts in British collections. In addition, the U.S. government arranged for UMI to film enemy documents gathered by British spies. Following the war, University Microfilms continued to expand its product line. Power hatched a plan to film back catalogs of periodicals to sell to libraries. Today, UMI sells catalogs of 19,000 periodicals and 7,000 newspapers on microfilm. In 1958, Power helped adapt xerographic technology to produce paper copies from microfilm, which enabled UMI to begin offering out-of-print books on demand, fulfilling Power's dream of producing "editions of one."[14]

Since that time, the company has become an ever-more diversified information provider and changed its named to ProQuest to reflect its new orientation. It has created databases that enable easier access to periodicals and converted microfilm products to digital format. It is now possible to purchase dissertations online as Adobe Acrobat files and view every page of the *New York Times* ever published on the World Wide Web. The company is no longer locally owned—most of it was sold in 2006 to the Maryland-based Cambridge Information Group—but still has a major presence in Ann Arbor, employing about five hundred people there. Until his death in 1993, Power continued to act as an important conduit between academe and commerce in Ann Arbor, serving on the U-M Board of Regents, donating money for a performing arts center on campus, and sitting on the boards of several Ann Arbor corporations. He created a model that no other Ann Arbor technology company has been able to follow, keeping the company in the area after it grew, became successful, and was acquired from outside the region.[15]

One of Ann Arbor's most unusual high-tech business stories also had strong university connections. Argus Camera, founded in 1931, became the first American company to produce a 35 mm camera for popular use and was once the city's largest private employer. The company was created by Charles Verschoor, who came to Ann Arbor to attend U-M but never earned a degree. Verschoor, who continued to take classes, was an inveterate inventor but inept manager. *Fortune* called him a "colorful old-school promoter," while another writer said he had "a special knack for exploiting the technology of the moment."[16] He developed an early automobile but was never able to bring it to market. In 1925, with radio booming, he founded a company that produced the Arborphone radio, until a fire destroyed its factory. With $20,000 from a group of Ann Arbor businessmen, Verschoor then founded the International Radio Corp., predecessor to Argus. The company produced the first portable AC-DC radio.[17]

Argus's most important U-M link was Clinton Harris, an engineering graduate hired in 1935, who was responsible for many of the company's most successful designs. In 1936, Argus introduced the world's first low-cost, easy-to-use 35 mm camera. It was an immediate success. The company sold 30,000 cameras the first week, and its revenues topped $2.7 million the following year. But under Verschoor's leadership, the company's spending was lavish and its bookkeeping haphazard, profits declining even as sales increased. In 1938, Verschoor was forced to resign by its board of directors. New management stabilized Argus's finances. The following year, the company introduced the Argus C-3, which became the best-selling 35 mm camera in the world for the next two decades. *Fortune* wrote that "overnight" the Argus C-3 transformed photography in the United States "from a class hobby to a mass pastime."

After Harris became chief engineer, Argus diversified its product line. In 1940, it began manufacturing aircraft radio controls, producing equipment for the U.S. Army. When the United States entered World War II, Argus secured a rush contract to manufacture 1,000 telescopes for the Army even though it had never made such instruments. Impressed with its work, the U.S. government provided Argus $430,000 to build a new factory to produce gunsights, periscopes, and other optical equipment. It produced sights for an anti-tank gun that an Army officer said was responsible "in no small manner for the defeat of Rommel in North Africa."[18] By 1945, Argus employed 1,200 people. Yet, rather than build on its war experience to become a major defense contractor, a strategy that helped companies like Raytheon stimulate Boston's high-tech growth, Argus resumed making cameras and other consumer goods. It ceased to be an innovator and gradually lost market share to Kodak and Japanese imports. In 1957, Sylvania purchased the company and moved part of its operations out of Ann Arbor, a common sequence of events that has stifled high-tech growth in the city ever since. Today, Argus exists only as a line of cameras produced by the Chicago-based Hartford Computer Co.[19]

THE UNIVERSITY AS AN AGENT OF ECONOMIC DEVELOPMENT

Scholars examining the university's role in industrial development have emphasized the importance of a small number of major events. The Cold War that emerged following World War II spurred dramatic increases in U.S. government funding for defense research and nurtured increasing interaction between universities, the military, and private contractors. The Soviet Union's launch of the Sputnik satellite in 1957 created a crisis in U.S. science policy that stimulated even greater funding for academic scholarship. In the 1970s, state governments began to reduce their funding for higher education, which forced universities to develop alternate revenue sources. Congress in 1980 gave colleges ownership of patents resulting from federal grants, providing universities an added incentive to commercialize the results of faculty research and prompting many to step up efforts to stimulate business development.[20]

But the relations between academe and industry have deeper histories than is often supposed. The Land-Grant College Act of 1862, which provided federal money to establish agricultural colleges and extension offices to help farmers, provided a key precedent for the belief that one purpose of higher education is to facilitate economic growth. Professors in a variety of disciplines have long conducted research under contract to corporations or augmented their salaries by working as consultants. Companies and industrialists, in turn, have provided a disproportionate share of donations to universities, paying for new buildings, supporting academic programs that advance their interests, and establishing fellowships to support students in their fields.[21] Finally, regardless of the ideals of higher education, a central function of American colleges has always been to prepare young men and women for careers, so the goals of colleges and business have always been intertwined.

The University of Michigan has been typical in this regard. Parke, Davis & Co. of Detroit, now part of the pharmaceutical giant Pfizer, established a chemistry scholarship in 1895 that has continued to the present. U-M President James B. Angell in his 1899 annual report sought to remind Michigan's elected officials of the service provided by the university to the state, pointing out that the chemistry laboratory on campus did work for alkali plants, cement mills, and sugar beet refineries. In 1900, a group of young faculty founded a research club on campus. At the time, professors devoted most of their attention to teaching. Howard Peckham dates the beginning of the research orientation of the university to this event.[22]

Research universities now devote substantial energy to helping faculty start companies, but professors were involved in business formation long before the phrase "technology transfer" entered the lexicon. The earliest faculty start-up at U-M can be traced to at least 1919, when a professor and local businessmen formed the King-Seeley Co., which for decades was Ann Arbor's largest private employer. Horace King, one of the company's founders, joined the engineering faculty in 1900 after a career building dams. In 1918, King was hired by Detroit Edison to develop a method for measuring the depth of water crossing its hydroelectric dams. He developed a system that enabled the water depth in midstream to be monitored remotely. A bell jar was placed on the river bottom and connected by a tube to a gauge on the shore. As the river depth increased, pressure on the jar grew, causing air to be pushed through the tube to the gauge. King thought his system would be valuable for dam operators around the world, but it would prove to have even greater worth than he imagined.

King lived in Burns Park, Ann Arbor's faculty enclave. One of his neighbors was Hal Seeley, who ran a company that made automobile windshields. It was Seeley who recognized that the true commercial potential of King's invention was in automobiles. At the time, the only way to check a car's gas level was to insert a stick into the tank, but Seeley wondered if King's device could be adapted to enable a driver to monitor the gas level without leaving the driver's seat. King and Seeley formed a company to develop such a device. Over the next three years, King and a team of U-M graduate students devised the first auto gas gauge. Production began in 1922. Within a few years, King-Seeley auto gauges became standard equipment on all cars made in the United States.

Other U-M faculty and graduates were crucial to King-Seeley's growth. King was the brains behind the company's original technology, but he and Seeley hired another professor, John Airey, to run the business. Airey developed King-Seeley's first factory and hired many U-M graduates. One of the first people he hired was Ted Bandemer, a student of King's, who became a key architect of the company's success. They hired Neil Gustine, another

U-M graduate. Airey, Bandemer, and Gustine transformed King-Seeley into a huge company that made a variety of auto instruments, became a major defense contractor during World War II, and grew into a multifaceted corporation that made everything from thermoses to power tools. At its peak, King-Seeley employed 2,000 people in Ann Arbor. The company then disappeared almost as fast as it rose to prominence, selling its instrument business to Chrysler in 1968.[23]

Though the circumstances that led to the formation of King-Seeley were serendipitous, U-M became more actively engaged with industry following World War I. It sought to establish a relationship with industry comparable to the service function agricultural colleges provided to farmers. In 1920, it established a Department of Engineering Research to undertake research for industry on a contract basis. The department was slow to gain acceptance because companies were reluctant to pay for research unless guaranteed the right to use the results. When it created the program, U-M reserved the right to publicize research results, so technology developed under contract to one company could be patented by someone else. In 1924, however, it changed program rules to allow a research sponsor an irrevocable license to use any patent resulting from that research. Sponsors could obtain ownership of patents if they paid an additional 10 percent beyond costs. The department's research contracts grew as a result. Faculty working under contract to industry developed motors used in vacuum cleaners, improvements in fishing reels, and steel alloys for use in petroleum refineries.[24]

The Great Depression slowed the growth of contract research at U-M, and World War II forever changed the nature of university scholarship. Before 1941, most contract research was funded by industry. But after the United States entered the war, federal research expenditures rose dramatically. President Franklin D. Roosevelt appointed Vannevar Bush, former engineering dean at the Massachusetts Institute of Technology, to direct the federal Office of Scientific Research and Development, and he brought in a team of academic heavyweights to redirect federal science policy. It was during World War II that the U.S. government first developed a collaborative research relationship with top universities including Michigan. The scientific power of universities was put to the service of the state under a grants and contracts system that has shaped academic research ever since. During World War II, university scientists working under federal contracts developed penicillin, computers, and the atomic bomb.[25]

U-M's Department of Engineering Research won its first federal contract in 1940. Two years later, the university was engaged in thirty-seven U.S. government research projects, most of them classified. By the end of the war, U-M had conducted $6.6 million worth of war-related research. Four Michigan scientists were involved in the development of the atomic bomb. U-M researchers also helped devise a process for mass producing the explosive RDX, the most powerful explosive in existence until the atom bomb. Michigan engineers invented a device for jamming the radar of aircraft, while a chemistry professor created a water-and-cold-resistant fabric for soldiers' uniforms.[26] Wartime research conducted in Ann Arbor provided the foundation for many scientific discoveries made after the war, some of which would help stimulate growth in the city's high-tech economy.

Following World War II, U.S. government funding for research grew and grew. The value of U-M federal contracts increased from $1.8 million in 1944–45 to $9.3 million a decade later. Most government research funding in the early Cold War years was for military purposes. The Soviet launch of Sputnik in 1957, however, stimulated a shift in federal science policy. Sputnik convinced elected officials that the country was falling behind its nemesis in education and science. After Sputnik, the U.S. government devoted an increasing share of its budget to research and broadened the emphasis of research funding, providing greater support for "basic" science that did not have an immediate application. At U-M, expenditures for medical and biological research grew the fastest, with those fields' share of research spending increasing from 5.6 percent in 1957 to 25.6 percent in 1963, though research for defense purposes still made up the largest share. U-M's federal contracts more than doubled from 1955 to 1959.[27]

The most important impetus to high technology business development in Ann Arbor was the establishment by the university in 1946 of Willow Run Laboratories at a former U.S. Army Air Force bomber plant fourteen miles east of Ann Arbor. Two U-M engineering professors convinced the Air Force to fund a project to develop an antiballistic missile defense system and, as part of the deal, the Department of Defense sold Willow Run to U-M for a dollar. It was placed under control of the Department of Engineering Research. By the end of its first year, 171 scientists were working there.[28] Over the next twenty-five years, Willow Run, according to one scholar, "gained an international reputation as a center for highly sophisticated R&D" and spawned numerous companies in Ann Arbor.[29]

Willow Run (fig. 8.4) is best remembered as a pioneer in remote sensing, technologies for detecting information from satellites and airplanes first developed for military reconnaissance. Willow Run scientists developed synthetic aperture radar, which improved the range and resolution of radar images. They developed the first multi-spectral scanner, which can detect non-visible forms of energy. They devised the ruby maser, a precursor to

FIGURE 8.4.
Early computer at the University of Michigan's Willow Run Laboratories, 1954. Willow Run was an important breeding ground for high-technology companies in Ann Arbor. Used with permission, Bentley Historical Library, University of Michigan.

lasers, and produced the first working demonstration of holography. Technology developed at Willow Run has been used to create "smart" bombs and night vision optics. Willow Run researchers also created one of the earliest digital computers. At its peak, Willow Run Laboratories employed more than six hundred people. By 1966, it was receiving $13 million a year from the Department of Defense, one-third of all U-M federal contracts.[30]

Many of Ann Arbor's earliest high-tech companies traced their roots to Willow Run. One after another, Willow Run researchers who helped produce major scientific breakthroughs spun off companies based on that technology. Those companies, in time, spawned other companies. At least two dozen companies were started by Willow Run alumni.[31] Other Willow Run scientists went to work for existing companies, so the lab's influence spread widely through Ann Arbor's emerging high-tech community. One of the first Willow Run scientists to start a company was Keeve "Kip" Siegel, who in 1960 started Conductron Corp., which produced ceramics used in microwave technology. Conductron grew to employ four hundred people. Later, Siegel founded KMS Fusion, a leader in laser fusion energy research.

Many expected big things from Siegel, but he suffered a cerebral hemorrhage while testifying before Congress in 1975 and died. Another Willow Run scientist-turned-entrepreneur was Samuel Irwin, who came to U-M in 1947 to study electrical engineering and went to work at Willow Run after graduation. In 1966, Irwin founded Sycor, which manufactured computer terminals and grew to employ 2,000 people, becoming the city's largest private employer.[32]

U-M also became involved with industry in other ways. Following World War II, university officials searched for a means to pay tribute to the nation's war dead. In 1948, they created the Michigan Memorial Phoenix Project to develop peaceful uses for atomic energy. Industry was integral to planning and financing the project, and many of the uses envisioned were commercial in nature. In a proposal to General Electric, in fact, project planners predicted that atomic energy would stimulate a "second Industrial Revolution." More than half the donations for the project came from corporations such as Ford Motor Co., Dow Chemical, and Parke-Davis. Corey Dolgon has argued that through programs like the Phoenix project "universities soon became full partners in the evolving military-industrial complex."[33]

Other university programs catered more explicitly to corporations. In 1952, the College of Engineering began offering companies three-year subscriptions to quarterly reports describing faculty research. That same year, U-M created the Transportation Institute to conduct training and present conferences for automobile industry personnel. Most of its initial funding came from auto manufacturers.[34] In response to the Soviet launch of Sputnik, U-M in 1957 established an Institute of Science and Technology, which included an Industrial Development Division. Comparing the legislative act that created the institute to the Land-Grant College Act, the institute's first director said it "for the first time, provides for direct state support for industry." Over the next dozen years, the Industrial Development Division sponsored sixty-five conferences and published fifty-eight reports on industrial topics.[35]

New research centers on campus and high-tech business development off campus began to change Ann Arbor. When playwright Arthur Miller, author of *Death of a Salesman* and a U-M alum, returned to the city fifteen years after earning his degree, he did not like what he found. Miller first came to Ann Arbor from New York in 1934. "I fell in love with the place," he later wrote. Ann Arbor was still a city apart and, in the depths of the Depression, radical ideas took root. "The place was full of speeches, meetings and leaflets," he said. "It was jumping with issues." When Miller returned in 1953, he wrote, "I did not feel any love around the place." Gone was the sense of freedom and discovery. "It just seemed to me that everybody had turned into engineers," he commented. "The old separation between the university and commerce . . . is disappearing."[36] The changes Miller witnessed intensified in years to come.

BUILDING "THE RESEARCH CENTER OF THE MIDWEST"

The genesis of efforts by Ann Arbor to capitalize economically on the research of the university can be traced to 1945, when businessman William Brown was elected to the first of six terms as mayor. Brown, who came to the city in 1914 to attend U-M, had his hands in a half dozen different companies and was one of the investors who provided start-up money for Argus Camera.[37] Reflecting his perspective as a business owner, Brown promised to "run this city like a business." He also commented that "the division which has existed between business and university interests . . . can and should be broken down."[38] It was Brown who got government, business, and the university to work together.

To college towns, an absence of industry poses fiscal challenges. The tax-exempt status of colleges reduces city government's ability to raise revenue to fund services. If a town lacks an industrial base, most of the tax burden must be shouldered by homeowners. When Brown was first elected, more than half of all land in Ann Arbor was exempt from property taxes. U-M enrollment exploded after World War II, so the campus had to be enlarged, removing more land from tax rolls. Brown in response created a University Relations Committee, and that committee persuaded U-M to begin paying the city for police protection and to extend utilities to new buildings. But the university continued to grow, which made it increasingly difficult for the city to balance its budget. In response, the city planning commission recommended in 1950 that "tax bases must be 'broadened'—and not permitted to diminish."[39]

One way Brown and other civic leaders sought to enhance Ann Arbor's tax base was to work with the university to recruit research-oriented companies to the city. In 1956, Brown and U-M officials met with representatives of Detroit-based Parke, Davis & Co. to discuss the possibility of the drug maker building a research lab in the city. Parke-Davis had been a long-time supporter of U-M, funding fellowships and scholarships, providing research grants to the medical school, and contributing to the Memorial Phoenix Project. As inducement for Parke-Davis to locate in Ann Arbor, U-M officials offered to sell the company fifty-six acres on the North Campus and help pay to extend utilities to the site. The city agreed to annex the site and provide $500,000 worth of infrastructure. Ann Arbor was attractive to Parke-Davis because proximity to the university would enable company scientists to interact with faculty, particularly at the expanding medical school, and aid in recruitment of skilled employees. Parke-Davis decided to build its research laboratory in Ann Arbor and dedicated the facility in 1960.[40]

One month after the city and university began talking with Parke-Davis, a second company said it was considering locating in Ann Arbor. Representatives of Detroit-based Bendix Aviation met first with U-M administrators, then with a realtor who also chaired the city planning commission. "I assured them we would cooperate 100 percent," he said. In 1956, Bendix committed to establishing its new aerospace division in Ann Arbor. U-M sold the company fifty-five acres on North Campus. The location enabled the company to be near U-M's engineering faculty, many of whom were involved in military research at Willow Run. In fact, several Willow Run researchers left U-M to help organize the Bendix division, which specialized in weapons systems development. In time, Bendix (fig. 8.5) became an important stimulus to business formation in Ann Arbor. At least six companies were started by former Bendix employees.[41]

The successful courting of Parke-Davis and Bendix created excitement in Ann Arbor. The *Ann Arbor News* trumpeted the developments with headlines that stretched across its entire front page. The U-M student newspaper published a cartoon depicting Mayor Brown wearing a jacket imprinted with dollar signs and holding a large magnet, which was drawing a factory toward it. The Chamber of Commerce created a committee to develop strategies for attracting more industry to the city, not just any industry but industry that was "clean, quiet and odorless" with a "major emphasis on research." The committee included business leaders, city officials, and university administrators. It created a brochure to promote Ann Arbor to research-oriented companies and devised a plan to market the city as "the Research Center of the Midwest." Billboards with the slogan were erected on highways entering the city.[42]

What was happening in Ann Arbor reflected larger developments. The U.S. government continued to boost its funding for research; federal R&D expenditures tripled in the five years following Sputnik's launch. The value of U-M federal contracts increased from $23 million in 1959 to $42 million in 1964. From Boston to Palo Alto, faculty were starting companies and corporations were locating near campuses to take advantage of the brainpower they contained. In 1951, Stanford University created the Stanford Industrial Park to stimulate high-tech development in the area. It became the

FIGURE 8.5.
*Space chamber at
Bendix Aviation's
Ann Arbor
aerospace division,
1961. Detroit-
based Bendix
was one of the
first established
technology
companies to
locate in Ann
Arbor and helped
stimulate high-
tech development
in the city. Used
with permission,
Bentley Historical
Library, University
of Michigan.*

model for research parks everywhere. In 1959, Research Triangle Park was developed near three research universities in North Carolina. Clark Kerr, president of the University of California, observed that the modern university was no longer a "one-industry town," but was the engine that drove a "knowledge industry" that was becoming "the focal point for national growth." [43]

Anxious to make sure Ann Arbor continued to be part of this economic transformation, civic leaders in 1960 launched a drive to create the Greater Ann Arbor Research Park. The Chamber of Commerce coordinated planning. Chamber officials acquired 210 acres just south of the city, and the city agreed to annex the site and extended utility lines to it. U-M officials helped recruit park occupants. The research park very much represented a cooperative effort by the city, university, and business community. Promoters made lofty predictions about the impact of the park. Boasting that it was the first research park in the Midwest, they claimed it would create 15,000 jobs. In 1961, Federal-Mogul-Bower Bearings became the first company to acquire a site in the park. Completion of the Federal-Mogul facility was marked by a ceremony in which Michigan's governor used a U-M radio telescope to capture a signal from space, triggering a device that produced ceremonial medallions.[44]

A study published in 1963 reported that thirty-seven "science-based" companies had already been established in the Ann Arbor area, fourteen of them started by U-M faculty. Companies were spread throughout the city. The greatest concentrations were downtown and on Main Street north of the city center. Three of the companies proved to be among the city's most successful high-tech enterprises and still exist today—Applied Dynamics International, founded by four engineering professors who developed computer simulation technology; Gelman Instrument, producer of laboratory and air monitoring devices; and Sarns, maker of heart-lung machines. There were a half-dozen Willow Run spin-offs. Research-oriented companies employed nearly 2,500 people in the area, prompting a city official to call research "Ann Arbor's fastest-growing 'industrial' activity."[45]

The high-tech boosterism did not last, however, and the promise of the period was never realized. Some of the reasons high-tech growth slowed reflected larger trends. The Greater Ann Arbor Research Park never had the impact imagined, perhaps because its parcels were too expensive to attract young companies. As late as 1966, only four buildings had been erected on the park's sixty-three sites. Nationally, dozens of research parks have been built, but few have stimulated significant economic development. The U.S. government, meanwhile, reduced its funding for research and shifted the focus of its spending away from defense and aerospace. Federal research spending declined 21.6 percent from 1966 to 1974, when adjusted for inflation, in part because of rising costs for the Vietnam War and expanding social welfare programs. Support for defense and aerospace research was cut dramatically after the U.S. pullout from Vietnam in 1973 and the end of the Apollo space mission. Private contractors in Ann Arbor felt the impact. Bendix Aerospace, a major supplier to the Apollo program, cut staff and closed its Ann Arbor facility in 1981.[46]

Equally important, however, to understanding why high-tech growth stumbled in Ann Arbor were factors suggestive of the distinctive nature of college towns. During the 1960s, college towns became the focus of the anti-war movement and defense-related research on campuses came under attack. Ann Arbor was the birthplace of the militant Students for a Democratic Society. An anti-war rally at Michigan Stadium drew 20,000 protestors. Protestors picketed Willow Run Laboratories (local radicals even claimed Willow Run was responsible for the assassination of revolutionary Che Guevara). In 1967, demonstrators occupied the U-M administration building to protest a defense department contract that helped the Thai government establish a military reconnaissance system. The following year, a faculty committee recommended that the university limit its classified research contracts and reject any contracts "the specific purpose of which is to destroy human life or to incapacitate human beings."[47]

Responding to the changing mood, Michigan's Board of Regents in 1972 voted to divest Willow Run Laboratories, site of most of the university's secret military research. No other event was more significant in altering the future of Ann Arbor's high-tech economy, according to David Brophy, a U-M finance professor. "The baby that was thrown out with the bath water," he said, "was the greatest engine for converting university research into commercialized product." U-M turned over ownership of Willow Run to a nonprofit organization, the Environmental Research Institute of Michigan. ERIM continued to emphasize defense research, but it never had the commercial impact of Willow Run. The divesture of Willow Run also spurred an exodus of scientists from Ann Arbor. "I absolutely believe the Willow Run guys and women would have morphed into very heavy commercial applications of computing and all the other aspects of technology," Brophy said. "The hell of it is that we had it, we had the lead. Our horse led at the first turn so to speak and came up lame."[48]

Finally, the stories of several pioneering Ann Arbor companies suggest that college towns may lack fundamental attributes necessary for high-tech growth. One after another, fast-growing Ann Arbor technology companies experienced the same fate as Argus Camera: They disappeared after they were acquired by corporations from outside the region. Keeve Siegel sold Conductron in 1966 to aerospace giant McDonnell Aircraft, which relocated its operations to St. Louis. Sycor, founded by former Willow Run engineer Samuel Irwin, was acquired in 1978 by Northern Telecom, which eventually closed its Ann Arbor operations.[49] These examples indicate that college towns may be high-tech seedbeds, fertile ground for launching new companies, but lack the resources necessary to sustain technology companies as they grow.

THREE STEPS FORWARD, TWO STEPS BACK

There is no map to high-tech success, as the Ann Arbor story demonstrates. Countless cities have sought to replicate what happened in Silicon Valley and Boston, but few have succeeded. College towns like Ann Arbor have tried various strategies to create what Manuel Castells calls a "milieu of innovation" and nurture the development of synergies that scholars agree are essential for high-tech growth.[50] Yet much appears left to chance. Ann Arbor possesses many of the characteristics necessary for high-tech development—an elite research university, a high quality of life, proximity to a major airport—yet its history is punctuated equally by success and failure, hope and doubt.

Ann Arbor in 1981 hosted the first Michigan Technology Fair, and that event provided a snapshot of the city's high-tech economy at the time. The fair was sponsored by the Michigan Technology Council, a nonprofit group created to help the state reduce its dependence on the auto industry, which experienced devastating declines because of the 1970s energy crisis. The council grew out of a group formed to encourage greater cooperation between the University of Michigan and technology-based industry. U-M had new reasons to improve its relationship with business. The decline of the auto sector reduced tax revenues, forcing the state to cut funding for colleges. Between 1975 and 1982, Michigan fell from 19th to 50th in state funding for higher education. To survive in the new economic climate, U-M had to develop alternative revenue sources. It raised tuition. It built a new hospital. It sought greater external research funding. In 1980, Congress provided universities a new potential income source when it approved the Bayh-Dole Act, which gave universities ownership of patents resulting from U.S. government-sponsored research. In response, many universities created offices to help faculty apply for patents and seek commercial applications for technology developed on campus. In 1981, U-M established an intellectual property office. Two years later, it created the Michigan Research Corp., predecessor to today's Technology Transfer Office.[51]

The Michigan Technology Council utilized a variety of methods to advance high-tech. It organized seminars on topics such as "Starting a High-Tech Company." It recruited companies to the state. In 1981, it persuaded an Ohio robotics company to relocate to Ann Arbor; U-M's president was instrumental in closing the deal. It sought to promote the image of Michigan as a high-tech center, placing an eighteen-page advertising supplement in *Scientific American*. The organization's highest-profile effort was the Michigan Technology Fair. The 1981 fair attracted 10,500 people and featured seventy-five exhibits, most sponsored by Ann Arbor companies and groups. Reflecting the changing nature of the local high-tech economy, a reporter remarked that "computer terminals and laser beams set the tone" for the event. A computer-controlled auto transmission test device was the most popular exhibit. Another company showcased a robotic arm used to feed aluminum into a lathe. A U-M biologist explained how genes are spliced in DNA research.[52]

Ann Arbor continued to experience high-tech growth, but signs of progress were often counteracted by episodes that created concern. Key developments pointed to the advantages and disadvantages of doing business in a college town. In 1982, for example, Parke-Davis threatened to leave Ann Arbor as it planned a $60 million expansion. Parke-Davis officials asked for a tax abatement from the city in return for a commitment to stay. Tax breaks are a common development incentive, but are rare in liberal Ann Arbor, and the request faced major opposition from critics who decried it as a corporate subsidy. Ann Arbor's City Council ultimately approved the tax abatement, but the city's reluctance to provide tax breaks highlights a deficiency of college towns for economic development. Only once since 1982 has Ann Arbor granted another tax break.[53]

A ballot initiative two years later demonstrated anew how the liberal political culture of college towns can threaten high-tech growth. Anti-nuclear activists succeeded in placing on the election ballot an initiative that proposed to make Ann Arbor a "nuclear-free zone" (fig. 8.6). Numerous local companies and university researchers still relied on defense contracts, some of which involved nuclear research. Several Ann Arbor corporations said they would have to relocate if the initiative was approved. The measure was defeated, but some said the proposal nevertheless harmed Ann Arbor's image.[54] In fact, an unidentified Fortune 500 company, which had been considering building a plant in Ann Arbor, decided to go elsewhere because of the initiative. "What scared our client is that 40 percent of the people voted *for* the free-zone proposal," said a consultant to the company.[55]

Ann Arbor has also failed to capitalize on positive developments. The city can reasonably claim to be one birthplace of the Internet because the backbone for the computer network that evolved into the Internet was developed there. In 1987, an Ann Arbor–based computer network linking Michigan's universities, Merit Network, won a National Science Foundation contract to build the backbone for a high-speed network linking supercomputers across the country. The network went online in 1988 and four years later connected more than 6,000 networks around the world. The economic impact of this development on the city has been minimal. "We had our big hit," says Susan Lackey, longtime president of a local development agency. "We just didn't tell anybody about it."[56] In a similar way, the first easy-to-use browser for the World Wide Web was developed at the University of Illinois in the college town of Champaign-Urbana, but was commercialized in Silicon Valley as Netscape. These examples suggest that researchers in college towns, with their more academic orientation, may be slow to recognize the business potential of high-tech innovations.

FIGURE 8.6. *Anti-nuclear demonstration, University of Michigan campus, 1980. Four years later, activists in Ann Arbor succeeded in placing on the election ballot an initiative to make Ann Arbor a "nuclear-free zone." Voters rejected the referendum, but the proposal nevertheless prompted one Fortune 500 technology company that had been considering building a plant in Ann Arbor to go elsewhere and underscored how the liberal political culture of college towns can undermine high-tech growth. Used with permission, Bentley Historical Library, University of Michigan.*

Nevertheless, the presence of an elite research university and the yearly graduation of engineers, computer scientists, and biomedical researchers did stimulate economic growth in Ann Arbor. Faculty start-ups became more common after U-M revised its policies to give faculty a larger share of patent royalties. Parke-Davis continued to grow. ERIM boasted $70 million in contracts. Irwin Magnetics, maker of computer tape drives, employed 600 people. A 1991 survey found that 205 high-tech companies and institutions employed 11,307 people in the county.[57] One newspaper article observed that "a fast growing" high-tech sector "has increasingly replaced the U-M as the pacesetter of the local economy" and said that "the newcomers are having a powerful impact on the tone of the town."[58]

Quantifying the evolution of Ann Arbor's high-tech economy can be difficult since local data sources are inconsistent and often unreliable, and because there is no widely agreed-upon definition of what constitutes high-tech. Some organizations define high-tech narrowly and do not include industries such as automobile manufacturing, even though it has been at the forefront of factory automation and has incorporated computers into every aspect of auto design. Others take a broader view but in the process include workers who cannot reasonably be considered high-tech, such as those on auto assembly lines. For these reasons, the best way to measure high-tech is by occupation. Unfortunately, the Bureau of Labor Statistics, which compiles data by occupation, does not provide detailed data for small cities, such as college towns.[59] Employment data categorized by industry, therefore, is the best we can do.

Ann Arbor's high-tech economy has a strong relation to the auto industry, so it is essential when trying to measure the city's technology sector to use a high-tech definition that includes automobiles. For that reason, a 1999 BLS classification of high-tech industries is most useful. It includes thirty-one industries in which the number of technology workers was at least twice the U.S. average. It also identifies twelve industries as "high-tech intensive" in which the number of tech workers was at least five times the national average. The number of people employed in "high-tech intensive" industries in Washtenaw County, which includes Ann Arbor, nearly doubled from 1988 to 1993, when 10,000 workers were employed in those industries, 7 percent of the labor force. High-tech job growth was greatest in five industries. Employment with companies that made measuring and controlling devices grew most, increasing 1,123 percent. Employment in research and testing services increased 260 percent, spurred by the growth of Parke-Davis and ERIM. Employment doubled in computer and data processing, and medical instrument manufacturing. These numbers show that Ann Arbor's high-tech growth was real and significant.[60]

High-tech growth fueled the development of research parks and office buildings, most of them on Ann Arbor's periphery. Plymouth Road in 1984 was a "beehive of activity."[61] Two new office buildings were erected in the area. Parke-Davis and ERIM were expanding. Beyond the city limits, Tom Monaghan was building Domino's Farms. On the opposite side of Plymouth Road was the most ambitious project of all, the 820-acre Ann Arbor Technology Park, developed by the University of Michigan and a local attorney, which they hoped would employ 12,000 people. It was the first time U-M had a supervisory role in a commercial development. Significant development was also occurring on the south side of town. By 1985, there were eighteen research and industrial parks in Washtenaw County.[62]

Ann Arbor's high-tech economy continued to grow through the boom-boom 1990s, only to contract following the dot com bust of 2001.[63] High-tech employment increased 17 percent from 1993 to 1998, when one in five county workers was employed in BLS-defined high-tech industries. High-tech employment fell from 1998 to 2002, then leveled off over the next three years. The data are deceiving, however, because employment in many of the most tech-oriented sectors increased from 1998 to 2005, often dramatically. Employment in the software industry, for example, jumped from 295 in 1998 to 1,534 in 2005, an increase of 420 percent. Employment in scientific R&D more than tripled to 5,671 during the same period, propelled by the phenomenal growth of Parke-Davis and its successor, Pfizer. Employment in engineering services nearly doubled to 3,152. High-tech employment fell in other areas, such as computer and medical equipment manufacturing.[64]

Several trends stand out when changes in Ann Arbor's high-tech economy are analyzed. The greatest growth occurred at a single company, Pfizer, which in 2000 acquired Warner-Lambert, parent of Parke-Davis. After obtaining a tax break from the city in 1982, Parke-Davis embarked on a major expansion, enlarging its facilities and doubling its workforce. By 1993, it employed 1,400 people in the city. The success of Lipitor stimulated more growth. In 1998, the company launched a $270 million expansion. Two years later, Pfizer acquired Warner-Lambert. The company announced plans to quadruple its R&D budget over ten years and, in 2001, initiated a $600 million expansion of its Ann Arbor research center. With little room left to grow, it purchased fifty-five acres from U-M and twenty-nine acres from Altarum. By 2007, Pfizer employed 2,100 people in Ann Arbor.[65]

The influence of Pfizer, the growth of the U-M health system, and initiatives to make Michigan a life sciences leader have nurtured development of a biotech economy in Ann Arbor. In 2005, there were eighty-eight life sciences companies in the area. The sheer size of the U-M health system makes it a likely source for spin-offs. It operates a 500-bed hospital and a multitude of research centers, and employs 9,000 people in Ann Arbor, including 2,100 physicians. The enormous research budget of the medical school—it accounts for 42 percent of U-M's research spending—creates commercial potential. Technology developed by U-M physicians to produce cells for regenerating human tissues, for example, led to the establishment of Aastrom Biosciences, one of Ann Arbor's brightest biotech hopes.[66] In an effort to encourage collaboration between medical researchers, biologists, chemists and others, U-M in 1999 created the Life Sciences Institute and built a $100 million facility to house it. The state, meanwhile, used Michigan's share of a federal tobacco settlement to create the Michigan

Life Sciences Corridor to provide grants to life sciences companies and researchers. Most of the money awarded went to Ann Arbor companies and scientists, and it helped stimulate company formation.[67]

Although biotechnology has received more government funding and headlines, Ann Arbor's Internet economy has demonstrated more widespread success. Even before Google came to town, the area was home to a large number of website designers, content providers, software developers, and other Internet-dependent businesses. Successful Ann Arbor–bred Internet companies include Fry Multimedia, which develops e-commerce websites for companies such as Godiva and Eddie Bauer; Enlighten, a web design company created by a U-M computer science graduate whose clients include Audi and Reebok; and All Media Group, which produces popular online music and movie databases. More specialized Internet companies include Arbor Networks, started by a U-M engineering faculty member and one of his students, which produces security systems that protect Internet sites from hackers, and HealthMedia, an online medical counseling service formed by a U-M public health professor.[68]

As a college town, Ann Arbor has been less shaped by Michigan's big three auto makers than the rest of the state. Nevertheless, the city has developed a unique niche within the industry as home to numerous auto research laboratories, most of them owned by foreign auto makers. They were initially drawn to the city by the presence of the EPA's national emissions testing laboratory, which opened in 1971. The lab tests all auto models for compliance with federal standards, but also conducts other research. By 1993, ten foreign auto makers had established labs in the area. Initially, most were small and concentrated on making sure a company's cars met EPA standards, but over time several evolved into full-range R&D labs. Toyota, for example, established its first testing facility in an old garage near downtown, but in 1991 built a $45 million technical center in the Ann Arbor Technology Park (fig. 8.7). By 2004, it employed 700 people. That year, the Toyota Avalon, designed top to bottom under the direction of Ann Arbor engineers, became the first Toyota vehicle developed entirely in the United States. Toyota was expected to open a new $187 million research facility south of Ann Arbor in 2008 and expand its local workforce to 1,100. The South Korean car maker Hyundai recently built a 200,000-square-foot R&D center in neighboring Superior Township.[69]

The University of Michigan has intensified efforts to transfer technology developed on campus into the marketplace. The promotion of engineer James Duderstadt to president in 1988 accelerated a shift that began under the presidency of Harold Shapiro, an economist. Duderstadt said in

FIGURE 8.7. *The Toyota Technical Center is one of several automobile research centers that have been built in the Ann Arbor area, drawn by the presence of the Environmental Protection Agency's National Vehicle and Fuel Emissions Laboratory. Photograph by the author, 2001.*

1993, "Our objective should be nothing more than to make the city of Ann Arbor the economic engine of the Midwest."[70] It was under Duderstadt that U-M revised its policies to give faculty a larger share of patent royalties. The university has steadily expanded its intellectual property and technology transfer offices. In 1979, it had a single half-time employee to oversee patent work. By 2007, U-M's tech transfer office had a staff of twenty-eight. The university revised policies to make it easier for researchers to apply for patents and start companies. Efforts have begun to pay dividends. Patent royalties and equity sales rose from $452,000 in 1986 to $20 million in 2006. Faculty started fifty-five companies in six years.[71]

The university has also taken a more active role in local economic development. Faculty initiated efforts in 1997 to create an organization to work for high-tech job creation and wire the downtown area. It became the Ann Arbor IT Zone, which sponsored frequent events on high-tech topics and offered entrepreneurs a "launch pad" for starting businesses. Seeking to expand on the work of the IT Zone, U-M in 2005 helped launch Ann Arbor Spark, a business development group that has the lofty goal of doubling the number of technology companies and tripling high-tech employment in the region by 2010. Spark is modeled after the University of California–San Diego's successful Connect program. U-M president Mary Sue Coleman has been a visible promoter of Spark and committed $1 million to get the group started. She told a national meeting of university technology transfer managers, "We believe the university can partner with business, government and community leaders to make the Ann Arbor region a nationally-known center for business creation and talent." [72]

Yet Spark has its skeptics, who question how it will succeed when past organizations failed to elevate the city's status as a high-tech center. The Michigan Technology Council faded away. The IT Zone failed to achieve its goals. Progress continues to be masked by significant setbacks. High-tech employment has grown in some areas but declined in others. Many high-tech businesses have failed. More than half of "emerging IT" companies on the IT Zone's membership list in 2001 did not exist four years later. [73] Business and civic leaders have been trying for a half-century to turn Ann Arbor into a nationally recognized high-tech center, but the city appears no closer to that goal today than it was a generation ago. Some of the city's difficulties have implications for college towns.

Ann Arbor continues to lose companies when they grow or are acquired, which may mean college towns lack what is necessary to take technology to the next level. Irwin Magnetics, for example, which once employed 600 people, disappeared four years after it was sold to a California company. More recently, billing software company Bluegill Technologies, one of the city's fastest growing companies in 2000, was purchased by an Atlanta company that closed its Ann Arbor office. Other companies that have remained in the city have felt the need to relocate part of their operations elsewhere. Arbor Networks still maintains its research operations in Ann Arbor, but its management is based near Boston. "We recognized early on that the sales and marketing team had to be headquartered outside Ann Arbor," says the company's founder, Farnam Jahanian, a U-M professor. [74]

Universities in college towns have also been relatively poor performers in technology transfer. Manuel Castells and Peter Hall argue that "an urban university in a large city . . . where there is feedback from industry, offers better prospects for synergy than an ivy-walled college in a remote small town." Michigan has been such a laggard, in fact, that when the *Chronicle of Higher Education* in 2002 published a study about technology transfer, it singled out U-M as the most dramatic example of a "powerhouse" university that has achieved little success. Michigan is consistently among the top three universities nationwide in research expenditures, but ranked 65th out of 118 universities in licensing income per dollar of research spending from 1996 to 2000. Only four of the top twenty were located in college towns. U-M has improved its tech transfer performance since that time, but, as David Brophy says, "it's like trying to turn the Queen Mary with a canoe paddle."[75]

Ann Arbor high-tech has a thousand champions, but its critics make more sense. One who ought to know is James Duderstadt, who as U-M's president from 1988 to 1996 pushed it to be more entrepreneurial. It was Duderstadt who said in 1993 his goal was to turn the city into "the economic engine of the Midwest." But he conceded eight years later, "We've been very much an underachiever. The level of economic activity that has been stimulated in the vicinity of the university has been very modest." He and others point to high-profile failures. The Ann Arbor Technology Park was a bust. U-M's $100 million Life Sciences Institute, he said, "is a hollow shell," unable to attract top scientists or compete with established centers. Michigan's Life Sciences Corridor, whose budget was gutted when the state experienced hard times, "is a joke." He concluded that "Ann Arbor is not going to be an Austin or a Palo Alto." Duderstadt, who now directs a think tank on the future of higher education, is more pessimistic than most, but says that is because "I've been beating my head against the wall for thirty years on it."[76]

Two developments that occurred within seven months of each other demonstrated anew Ann Arbor's inability to sustain high-tech growth. In July 2006, Google chose Ann Arbor over several other cities as headquarters for its Adwords unit and said it would create as many as 1,000 jobs in the city within five years. The University of Michigan was instrumental in recruiting the company. Google co-founder Larry Page is a Michigan native and U-M graduate. In 2004, Michigan became the first university to enter into an agreement allowing Google to digitize all books in its libraries as part of the controversial Google Book Search project. Page is a member of the College of Engineering's advisory board and in 2005 spoke at the college's commencement. As Google considered locations for its Adwords unit, U-M president Mary Sue Coleman flew to California and visited Page at Google's Silicon Valley headquarters.[77]

Google's decision to locate in Ann Arbor inspired widespread euphoria, but even before that jubilation subsided, Pfizer announced in January 2007 it would close its Ann Arbor research center, eliminating 2,100 jobs and sending shockwaves throughout the region. Michigan governor Jennifer Granholm, who called the arrival of Google "huge, huge, huge, huge," said shortly after Pfizer's announcement, "This is a punch to the gut." The move surprised everyone, but could have been predicted. Pfizer's patent on Lipitor, which accounts for perhaps half its cash flow, will expire soon and the company recently canceled trials on its best hope for a new blockbuster drug. Concerns about two other successful Pfizer medicines have reduced sales. The company's stock price had fallen 39 percent since 2001. Pfizer had already cut its Ann Arbor workforce by eight hundred workers over the previous two years.[78]

Pfizer's departure will have a devastating impact on Ann Arbor. The company was the city's biggest private employer and taxpayer. U-M economists predicted that in addition to the 2,100 jobs eliminated at Pfizer, the closing would result in the loss of 3,723 spinoff jobs.[79] Optimists argue that the company's departure could have unexpected benefits, if some Pfizer scientists choose to remain in Ann Arbor and they start businesses or boost the fortunes of its existing companies. "If we release all that talent from the corporate octopus and put it loose," asked Tom Kinnear, a professor in U-M's Ross School of Business, "what could it do?"[80] Ann Arbor has now lost its last five largest private employers—all technology-based companies. That fact may suggest that the city can recover from Pfizer's departure because it overcame the loss of those companies, but it may also indicate something fundamental about the limitations of college towns.

OPPORTUNITIES AND OBSTACLES

Richard Florida has observed that "the presence of a major research university is the basic infrastructure component of the creative economy—more important than the canals, railroads and freeway systems of past epochs." But the presence of a research university, Florida acknowledges, is not alone sufficient to generate substantial high-tech development. Cities that hope to excel in a knowledge-based economy, he argues, must possess what he calls the "3 T's" of economic development: technology, talent, and tolerance. Research universities provide technology. They possess talent in the form of faculty and produce new talent in their graduates. Tolerance in Florida's framework is meant to stand for a range of characteristics, including cultural and ethnic diversity. To succeed in a creative economy, Florida contends, cities must also be exciting places to live and have a strong sense of place.[81]

Many college towns, including Ann Arbor, possess these attributes, so why have they not been more successful at generating high technology development? Why does there seem to be a limit to high-tech growth in college towns? Why do companies that start in college towns so often leave when they become successful? While the leading high-tech centers in the United States are all home to major research universities, none are college towns. I must reemphasize here that I do not consider Austin, Texas, a college town. It is also a state capital, an important advantage in a big state. Palo Alto, the psychic center of Silicon Valley, is part of a larger urban region with a long history of technology development.[82] Chapel Hill is part of North Carolina's Research Triangle, but most high-tech development in the area has occurred outside that city.

In trying to comprehend why college towns have not been more successful, it is instructive to contemplate why Google is not headquartered in Ann Arbor. Larry Page earned a bachelor of science in computer engineering from Michigan in 1995, then left Ann Arbor to pursue a Ph.D. at Stanford.[83] Three years later, he and a fellow Stanford grad student founded Google, now based in Mountain View, California. Page's move to Palo Alto explains why the company was founded in Silicon Valley. But could he have founded Google in Ann Arbor? Could it have been as successful if he had? Could he have kept the company in Ann Arbor as it grew? It seems unlikely that Ann Arbor could have supported Google's meteoric rise, and the reasons why help us understand the shortcomings of college towns as technology centers.

Before considering the obstacles to high-tech growth in college towns, let's first review a few of their advantages. The most obvious is the research conducted on campus and the intellect of faculty and graduate students. Few scholars produce any truly original research and even fewer develop marketable ideas, but those that do tend to work at research universities like Michigan. High-tech businesses are less likely to emerge in college towns that are home to other types of colleges. Faculty at research universities are expected to conduct research and obtain grants to support their research. U-M researchers in 2006 obtained $676 million in research funding from external sources.[84] At any given time at a university like Michigan, there is a huge volume of research in progress, and some of it is bound to have commercial potential.

Edward Malecki has argued that the influence of research universities on local economic development has been "distorted" because research "can be procured at a distance."[85] But faculty who develop marketable technologies may start companies and, if they do, some are likely to start those companies locally so they can keep an eye on them. University graduates may also start companies where they went to school. Some of Ann Arbor's most successful high-tech companies have been founded by U-M graduates. Faculty researchers, furthermore, may prefer to develop relationships with existing companies that are local, because face-to-face interaction is still preferred for certain types of communication. Distance does still matter. The presence of a university like Michigan also offers benefits to non-faculty entrepreneurs. It gives them access to university libraries and scientific expertise on campus. An Ann Arbor address also confers respectability because people know it as home to U-M.

High-tech companies in college towns also have access to highly educated workers. In towns like Ann Arbor, two-thirds of adults may be college graduates. The greatest source of skilled employees is the university. U-M awards 6,000 bachelor's and 4,000 graduate degrees every year. A Michigan professor who started a company with one of his doctoral students and employs several former students commented that the most important means by which a university transfers technology into the marketplace "is the students we produce."[86] As high-tech development in Ann Arbor has increased, it has become more feasible for U-M graduates to stay in town to pursue a career. Students who are still in school also provide a source of inexpensive but intelligent labor for local companies. Many have internship programs or hire students part-time as a way to scout the best young talent, with an eye toward hiring their brightest student workers full-time once they graduate.

Perhaps the greatest advantage college towns have over larger tech centers is a perception that they offer a superior quality of life. Leonard Alvarez has written about quality of life as a locational asset in the California college towns of San Luis Obispo and Santa Barbara. College towns possess lively arts scenes and vibrant downtowns, full of amenities that Florida has identified as critical for attracting the "creative class." They have less traffic and lower crime rates than big cities. They have good schools. They are small enough that many people walk or bike to work. Real estate is cheaper than in Boston or Silicon Valley. "College towns are nice places to be," says David Fry, founder of Fry Multimedia, who reluctantly moved to Ann Arbor from Boston for his wife's medical career, but never left. Because universities attract faculty and students from around the world, college towns are also sophisticated and tolerant. "You can't shock anybody in Ann Arbor," says Steve Glauberman, a U-M graduate who founded the web design firm Enlighten. "You can wear whatever you want. You can do whatever you want."[87]

So what prevents college towns like Ann Arbor from becoming more robust centers of high-tech growth? Plenty. The most important disadvantages can be grouped under what Albert Bruno and Tyzoon Tyebjee call "the environment for entrepreneurship," which includes the size of the skilled labor force, the presence of experienced entrepreneurs, the availability of investment capital, and the receptiveness of the population to business growth. While Ann Arbor has an educated labor force, its size is limited. So while it may be possible to start a high-tech company in a college town, it may be difficult to recruit enough workers as the company grows. Larry Page could have started Google in Ann Arbor, but it is doubtful Google could have recruited enough employees there to grow as fast as it did (from 4 employees in 1998 to 10,674 in 2006).[88] Corporate executives, meanwhile, say it is difficult to recruit workers to Ann Arbor from larger tech centers because they worry they will be unable to find another job if the first one does not work out. Development officials say they have difficulty persuading companies to relocate to Ann Arbor because the low unemployment rates of college towns could make it hard to hire sufficient staff.

While college towns have plenty of technological talent, they often lack the management expertise capable of transforming a good idea into a profitable enterprise. Michigan produces plenty of engineers and MBAs, but college towns lack what Gordon Moore and Kevin Davis call "the technologist-manager," individuals who understand technology but also know business. That explains why Arbor Networks chose to locate its R&D activities in Ann Arbor but base its top management in the Boston area. Larry Page and Sergey Brin developed the technology that made Google's search engine so powerful, but recognized they needed to hire expert management if the company was going to realize its potential. They hired executives with experience at Silicon Valley companies such as Netscape, Apple, Novell Networks, and Sun Microsystems. It is unlikely they could have recruited such big-name talent to a college town.[89]

The third critical ingredient for high-tech growth often lacking in college towns is investment capital. Venture capital firms, which have been key to financing technology companies, are highly concentrated geographically and have shown a preference for investing in companies located nearby. Sixty percent of the most active venture investors in 2004 were based in California or Massachusetts, and nearly half of venture funds were invested in Silicon Valley or New England.[90] Venture funds have become more available in college towns, but have grown even faster in established tech hubs. Ten venture firms are located in Ann Arbor, and Ann Arbor companies received $446.9 million in venture funding from 2000 to 2004, an increase of 45 percent compared to the previous five years. But those numbers pale compared to Silicon Valley, which received $27.5 *billion* in the same period. Only a handful of college towns other than Ann Arbor—Boulder, Colorado; Provo, Utah; Santa Barbara; and Boise, Idaho—have received significant venture funding recently.[91] An absence of venture capital in an area may prompt an entrepreneur to move before launching a company and can stifle the growth of a company or cause it to leave. Venture firms sometimes make investments in companies outside their area contingent on a company relocating. The Ann Arbor biotech company GeneWorks obtained $19 million in venture capital, but founder Bill MacArthur said it was difficult to attract investment because of the company's location. "Half the [venture capital] we recruited said don't bother because we're out of their range and they don't want to take a jet every time they want to check on the place," he said. Once one of the city's best biotech hopes, GeneWorks went out of business in 2005 because it was unable to obtain any additional funding. Like other successful technology companies, Google was dependent initially on "angel" investors and venture capital. Page and his partner obtained $25 million in venture funding in the company's first year.[92] It is doubtful that two unproven entrepreneurs could obtain so much money so fast in a college town.

The culture of a college town can also inhibit high-tech growth. Many residents of towns like Ann Arbor mistrust business and oppose growth. College towns often have unwelcoming regulatory environments for business and do little to encourage development, such as offer tax breaks. Rick Snyder, a U-M graduate who became president of Gateway Computers before returning to Ann Arbor to start a venture capital firm, says that when he moved back to town, "I felt like Darth Vader walking the streets. People would look at me and [act] like, 'well, you want to make money. You're kind of bad.'" College towns are comfortable places, with high incomes and low unemployment. "University towns are rarely hungry," says Susan Lackey. High-tech executives also notice a difference in the attitudes of their employees. Fry Multimedia is headquartered in Ann Arbor but has a New York office, and founder David Fry says his Ann Arbor employees are less aggressive than those in Manhattan. "I often find myself in contention with some of my staff who think some of the things I'm trying to achieve as a business person go against their philosophical beliefs," he says. "I think that's the culture."[93]

The shortcomings of college towns are well illustrated by the case of Village Ventures, a venture capital firm started in the college town of Williamstown, Massachusetts, with the goal of investing in college towns and other neglected markets. Forty percent of the cities it initially targeted for investment were college towns. Since that time, however, Village Ventures has altered its strategy. It still invests primarily in secondary markets, but now is less likely to invest in college towns. "We learned," said Matt Harris, one of the firm's founders, "that scale really is important. College towns are attractive up to a point, but they are limited by their sheer small size from growing an enormous company." One college town that lost its luster was Charlottesville, which received $404.3 million in venture funding from 1998 to 2001, but only $2.4 million over the next three years. "It gets hard when you've got a 100-person company in Charlottesville to recruit the next twenty people," Harris said. "And there's no particularly good airport. You can't fly direct anywhere. If you're going public, you're going to want a CEO of a certain caliber. What are the odds that CEO wants to live in Charlottesville?" Harris also encountered resistance there because of the college town culture. "Charlottesville isn't a very commercial town," he said. "It's a very self-satisfied place."[94] The same could be said about Ann Arbor.

TRANSFORMING THE COLLEGE TOWN WAY OF LIFE

College towns aspiring to high-tech success should consider the implications such changes could bring. Ann Arbor has changed dramatically over the last two decades. Its population has increased. It has become wealthier. Home prices have soared. Housing developments have spread further into the countryside. Many are full of assembly-line mansions that seem the antithesis of college town modesty. Working-class residents have been forced to leave town to find affordable housing. Many professionals who work in Ann Arbor do not live there, commuting every morning and night, intensifying traffic in the process. Rising incomes have also helped transform the city's downtown. It is full of upscale restaurants and stores, and pulses late into the night. The city's rhythm is shaped less by the university and academic calendar than ever before. Technology development is not the only factor stimulating these changes—Ann Arbor's emergence as a bedroom community for Detroit is also important—but high-tech growth has contributed to the city's metamorphosis.

High-tech workers often earn high salaries. Employees of Ann Arbor companies engaged in scientific R&D earned an average of $101,193 in 2005. Software industry employees were paid an average of $86,751. R. Douglas Armstrong, chief executive officer of publicly traded Aastrom Biosciences, earned $2.7 million. Entrepreneurs like David Fry and Steve Glauberman make much more than most professors. Faculty who start their own companies, such as Farnam Jahanian of Arbor Networks, can boost their incomes. Migration from Detroit and high-tech growth have pushed family incomes in Ann Arbor ever upward. Median family income in Ann Arbor increased 53 percent from 1990 to 2005, when more than one-third of families in the city had incomes in excess of $100,000.[95] "The whole city's becoming one big yuppie neighborhood," says Lou Belcher, a former mayor.[96]

Rising incomes are increasing the cost of living, forcing out lower-income residents, and turning Ann Arbor into a less diverse community. The median home value in Ann Arbor more than doubled from 1990 to 2005. The average sales price of homes in 2006 was $258,934. "Affordable housing is an oxymoron," says Coleman Jewett, a prominent member of the city's black community.[97] "Where do the people who do the work to keep things running, where are they living?" asks Chuck Warpehoski, who directs Ann Arbor's Interfaith Council for Peace and Justice.[98] Many longtime residents say they could not afford to live in the city if they had not purchased their homes long ago. Census data support claims that Ann Arbor is becoming more homogeneous. Since 1990, the proportion of the population that is black, lacks a college education, and works in blue-collar occupations has declined. One casualty of Ann Arbor's rising affluence and changing demographics has been the city's North Central neighborhood, historically the heart of the black community. It is now three-quarters white, and most are college educated and prosperous.[99]

The most conspicuous evidence of high-tech's impact on Ann Arbor is the technology parks and office complexes on the city's edge. There were thirty-six research and industrial parks in Washtenaw County in 2005, twice as many as twenty years before. As new research parks were being built a few years ago, the *Ann Arbor Observer* remarked that the "the corporate influx is so massive that the very identity of Ann Arbor as a university town may begin to blur." The suburban tech parks are most attractive to biotech startups that need lab facilities, companies that require significant space, and others who are not repelled by what one writer called the "soulless part of town."[100] High-tech companies are less noticeable downtown, but they are there, typically located above stores and restaurants. Downtown is most attractive to entrepreneurs drawn to the urbane lifestyle, abundant restaurants, and nightlife. "The talent wants to be able to walk down and get a double latte," said real estate broker Jeffrey Harshe, "and go to a brew pub after work." High-tech companies that locate downtown are most likely to be computer and Internet companies. Their employees are young, work odd hours, and may live nearby. "I just hate the whole office park sterile environment," said the owner of a computer game company. "I like being near everything." Google fit that profile and chose to locate downtown, leasing most of a former bank building on Liberty Street and redesigning its interior (fig. 8.8).[101]

The influx of technology companies has contributed to the revitalization

FIGURE 8.8.
*When Google
located the
headquarters for
its Adwords unit
in Ann Arbor in
2007, it chose to
locate downtown,
drawn by its
vibrant college
town lifestyle
and proximity to
the University of
Michigan campus.
Photograph
by Erin Leigh
Bedoun, 2007;
used with
permission.*

of Ann Arbor's downtown. Demand for offices stimulated development of several new office buildings. Nearly 500,000 square feet of office space was added between 1993 and 2007, boosting total space by 40 percent. More people working downtown has increased demand for housing in the area, so many of the new office buildings also include residences, usually in the form of condominiums. A Detroit developer, for example, built the nine-story Ashley Mews, which includes two floors of condos, plus forty-seven adjacent townhouses. Since it was completed, ten other housing developments have been constructed or approved downtown, six of them nine

FIGURE 8.9.
*Growth in Ann
Arbor's high-
tech economy
has helped to
revitalize the
city's downtown
and has nurtured
the development
of high-end
restaurants like
the West End
Grill. Photograph
by the author,
2001.*

stories or taller. If they are all built, they will add 750 residences to downtown. City officials hope to add 2,000 more. High-tech also impacts downtown in other ways. Tech workers hang out at coffee houses like Café Zola
and can afford to eat in pricey restaurants such as the West End Grill (fig.
8.9). They patronize downtown Ann Arbor's bars, bookstores, and high-
end boutiques. Because many tech workers are young and single, they help
support downtown's active nightlife. The arrival of Google will only intensify these changes.[102]

High-tech has also changed Ann Arbor in less tangible ways. U-M does
not dominate local life to the degree it once did. Important business developments are just as likely to be front page news as changes on campus. The
contrasts between the school year and holiday periods are less apparent in
Ann Arbor than they used to be. As the city attracts more people without
U-M connections, it has become more splintered socially. Old-timers are
less likely to run into acquaintances on the street and complain, "I don't
know who all these people are." The Ann Arbor farmers market is symbolic
in this regard. Close to campus and older residential neighborhoods popular with professors, it was for years "like . . . an informal faculty meeting,"
according to one academic, but now draws a more diverse crowd and no
longer serves that role. Longtime residents generally agree that the pace of

life in the city has quickened. "There's no question," says *Observer* editor John Hilton, "that Ann Arbor has become a more dynamic, less stable place with more aggressive, hard-charging individuals."[103]

The changes high-tech has helped to bring about have fundamentally altered the psyche of this midwestern college town. Is that a good thing? It depends on your perspective. Many curse the changes. "The heart and soul of Ann Arbor has disappeared," says one resident.[104] The city, comments another, is now full of "people who look through you and around you. The economic success has taken away their humanity."[105] It is becoming, many agree, "more ordinary."[106] But others believe the new Ann Arbor is a "much more interesting" and "exciting" place.[107] Bright and discontented techies, they argue, fit comfortably in the iconoclastic stew of a college town. They contend that the city must evolve if it wants to continue to attract creative people and will atrophy if it clings too tightly to an idealized past. Ann Arbor cannot decide whether it wants to be a storybook college town or a city of the future, but as it wrestles with the question of what it should be, it confirms what makes college towns unusual. Writing about Ann Arbor but speaking more generally about college towns, the novelist Charles Baxter observes that such places are full of mutterers, "opinionated about every feature of life."[108] In too many places, the questions that are part of the ongoing conversation in college towns are rarely even asked.

TOWN VS. GOWN

When David Athey bought his Colonial Revival house in the Kells Avenue neighborhood of Newark, Delaware, the seller told him that the best attribute about the house was the same as the worst—its proximity to the University of Delaware.[1] The house is one block from campus, so when Athey decided to pursue a graduate degree at night, he was able to walk to class. A major research library is five minutes from his door. He can attend plays and concerts in two campus performing arts venues. Foreign films shown nowhere else in the state are screened in the Trabant University Center. Residents can walk five minutes to watch UD football and basketball games. As in other college towns, the green spaces of campus act as parks for the nearby residents.

But the closeness of Athey's house to the campus also means the neighborhood is home to an ever-changing population of student renters, whose lifestyles sometimes bring them into conflict with other residents. Loud parties rattle windows, and residents are awoken when students return home noisily from bars and parties. There is the constant worry that homeowners will sell to landlords, who will turn houses into student rentals. Traffic is heavy during the school year, and parking is in short supply. The university itself is viewed as an adversary because it does not house most of its students, fails in the eyes of some to control their behavior off campus, and builds new facilities that are seen to undermine the local quality of life.

All around Athey's home are the battle sites in an undeclared but unresolved civil war. Next door is a house until recently occupied by undergraduates, one group of which so angered Athey, allowing their dog to defecate on his lawn and keeping his family up late playing loud music, that he considered moving. Around the corner is a former fraternity that was closed by the university after police were called to the house eleven times in one year. Nearby are the Ivy Hall Apartments, one of four Newark apartment complexes the city identified as "problem" properties because they are the source of a disproportionate share of alcohol and disorderly conduct complaints.[2] A few blocks away, the university has built an arts center and parking garage, the latest in a long list of development projects opposed by residents because of the fear they will increase traffic.

Such are the issues that create tension in college towns all over and are fundamental features of college town life. Much of the conflict is the simple result of what happens when so many young people, free from parental supervision for the first time, descend upon relatively small cities. The other critical characteristic that divides town and gown is the fact that higher education institutions located outside big cities often dominate a town physically, economically, and politically. Colleges are viewed with conflicting emotions—welcome because of the benefits they bring, but resented when they act with little regard to the interests of permanent residents and because students can make bad neighbors.

While many of the characteristics that make college towns distinctive are unique to the United States, animosity between town and gown has an ancient lineage that can be traced to the beginning of the university in Europe. The degree of privilege enjoyed by medieval universities and the intensity of town-gown conflict have no parallels in America. Hastings Rashdall has observed that the town of Oxford in England, site of Oxford University, "was practically governed by the university." The history of the university in Europe is full of stories of town-gown riots in which countless students and townspeople were killed. The St. Scholastica's Day massacre in Oxford in 1335, for example, left nearly one hundred dead. Fighting was "perpetually going on in the streets of Oxford," Rashdall said. "There is probably not a single yard of ground . . . which has not at one time or other, been stained with blood."[3]

Town-gown conflict, furthermore, is not limited to college towns, but the nature of problems is different in bigger cities, as Gordon Lafer demonstrates in his study of New Haven, Connecticut. The economic contrasts between colleges and the areas that surround them are often greater in big cities than in college towns, which heightens resentment of an institution. Urban universities have been accused of exploiting unskilled workers whose job opportunities diminished as manufacturing declined. Most colleges are exempt from property taxes, which creates an added burden for city governments hurt by an exodus of businesses and middle-class residents, making it difficult for them to provide services to an increasingly poor population.[4] Town-gown tensions in big cities can make issues in college towns seem petty by comparison, but higher education institutions in college towns exert a greater overall impact because they are bigger relative to the size of the cities.

Town-gown relations in Newark have been tense for decades, although they have eased somewhat recently. While the level of town-gown hostility has been unusual, the sources of conflict and the solutions attempted are common to college towns. Newark has been the site of educational institutions since Newark Academy was created there in the 1760s. That institution evolved into Newark College in 1833, which was later renamed Delaware College and became the University of Delaware in 1921.[5] Newark, meanwhile, has grown from a colonial market town into a city that is both a college town, and, in areas farthest from campus, a bedroom community for the Wilmington metropolitan area. Town-gown relations in Newark have more in common with those of other college towns than with relations in large university cities because Newark is separately incorporated and most students and staff live in the city.

Newark (fig. 9.1) has experienced town-gown tension since the colonial era, when students complained that local residents were charging them exorbitant rates for board.[6] Conflicts increased in frequency and intensity as the institution expanded, particularly after World War II. As the University of Delaware grew, student regulations were loosened, and a majority of students came to live off campus, disagreements between students, townspeople, the city, and university escalated. This chapter will trace the evolution of three sources of town-gown tension in Newark that are present in most college towns and will also consider how town and gown have sought to overcome their animosities and cooperate.

STUDENT ROWDINESS

The most persistent source of town-gown tension in college towns over the years has been student behavioral problems. At the University of Delaware, nearly all have fallen into one of three areas—conflicts between students and town youth, student pranks, and drinking. For most of the university's history, student rowdiness was comparatively innocent. It became more serious during the freewheeling 1960s and reached a crisis level in the 1980s, prompting UD and the city to work aggressively to rein in unruly undergraduates. Those efforts have reduced town-gown tensions, but the seemingly unsolvable problem of student drinking continues to undermine relations in Newark and other college towns.

In the early years of Delaware College, such a small percentage of youth

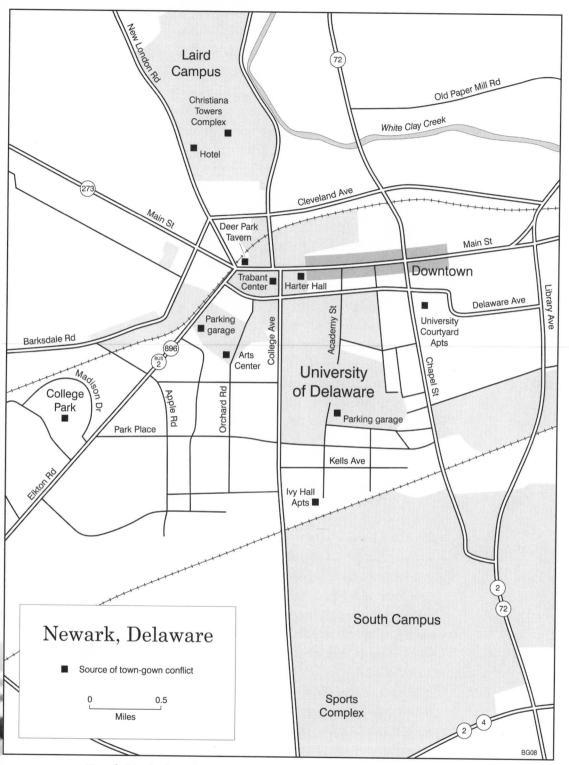

FIGURE 9.1. *Newark. Map by the author.*

attended college, and the collegiate way was so at odds with mainstream lifestyles, that the school and its students were natural objects of resentment and ridicule. Newark was a growing industrial town, and the rough and tumble mill workers and their children occasionally picked on students and caused trouble on campus. In 1852, for example, an undergraduate reported in his diary that a student went downtown and "a factory fellow licked him." Two years later, another student wrote that college boys "were beaten in a fight with the mill men."[7]

The diary of student William Cleaver provides a vivid glimpse of student life in Newark in the nineteenth century. In the first three months of 1854, Cleaver reported five confrontations between students and townspeople. In January, town boys "disturbed" a lecture by a professor. "At the end our boys tried to stampede them at the door," Cleaver wrote. In March, town youth created "a little disorder" at the annual Junior Exhibition. "The town boys," he wrote, "never come for any other purpose." Later that spring, a group of students out for a stroll "met a gang of unrecognized ruffians" who removed one of the student's clothes and burned them. Such confrontations continued. In 1921, a newspaper reported that "war was waged up and down Main Street" after a local boy insulted several females who were speaking to a male student. Hostility between students and townies, evocatively portrayed in the 1979 movie *Breaking Away*, still occurs in college towns, but is less common because students constitute a larger percentage of college town populations and their lifestyles are not so anomalous.[8]

Collegiate pranks have also been a source of irritation for Newark residents. Cleaver reported in his diary that in June 1854, a farmer's bull was found at the top of the stairs in the college building and its owner threatened to sue the college if "any harm comes to the bull." Later that year, a pig that belonged to a local widow was found at the bottom of the college well, and she demanded that the entire student body be "flogged" in punishment. One of the most famous incidents to stir town tempers occurred in 1951 when all students living in Harter Hall were expelled after they began to set off firecrackers nightly (fig. 9.2). The fracas made the pages of *Life* magazine, which reported that "citizens of the town . . . grew increasingly jittery from the volleys and pressed the dean of men . . . to put a stop to them."[9]

Problems caused by student drinking date to the earliest years of the college. Student damage to the college building, partly blamed on drunkenness, was so rampant that the college president suggested encasing the pillars in iron to prevent further destruction. His successor appealed to the Delaware legislature to enact a law prohibiting the sale of "intoxicating

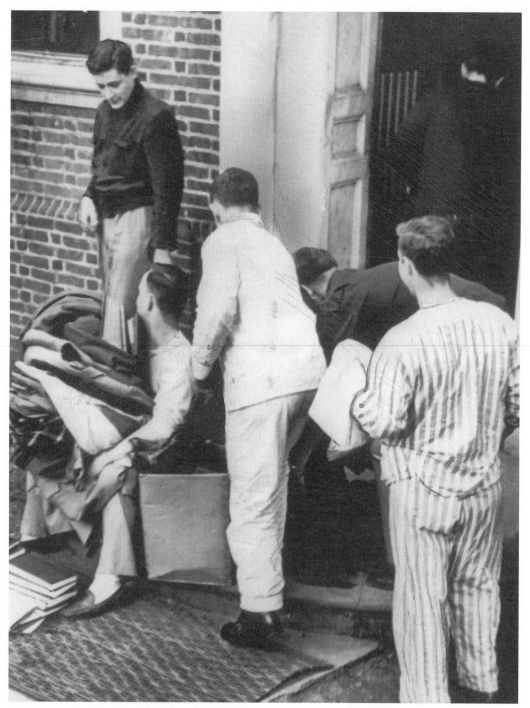

FIGURE 9.2. *Students are evicted from Harter Hall on the University of Delaware campus in 1951 after residents of the dormitory began to set off firecrackers nightly, disturbing residents of nearby neighborhoods and stirring a town-gown fracas that made the pages of* Life *magazine. Used with permission, University of Delaware Archives.*

drinks" to college students, arguing it "is much needed for the protection of such children as are away from their parents." In 1843, the legislature enacted a law prohibiting the sale of alcoholic beverages to students within two miles of the campus, but the law appeared to have had little impact. In 1854, a student admitted obtaining liquor from two hotels and a store in Newark. On another occasion, a college janitor was found to be supplying students with liquor, hiding bottles in their shoes when he returned them from being polished. Minutes of faculty meetings include regular mentions of "wild parties" in the college building. Sometimes such escapades spilled onto the streets of Newark. In 1855, one student was suspended after several drunken students were reported "creating disorder in the street at a very late hour of the night." [10]

Cleaver's diary provides the best evidence for the pervasive nature of student drinking in the nineteenth century. In September 1853, he reported that there was a "card and liquor party across the hall." Two months later, he wrote of a similar party and remarked that, because of it, "reading went badly." The next spring, following a temperance lecture, several students "celebrated with a very disorderly party." Students attended college year-round, so there was no reprieve from student antics in summer. In June 1854, Cleaver noted, "liquor was flowing freely" in one room. In July, he wrote that two students "are off on a spree." Other reports indicate that student drinking may have been even more widespread than Cleaver's diary suggests. The Delta Phi *Star*, published by a college literary society, commented in 1855 that "almost every week we behold some scene of drunkenness and disorderly conduct." [11]

Yet most student drinking appears to have taken place in the college building, and there is little indication it had much impact off campus. One reason student behavioral problems were largely confined to campus was because nineteenth-century colleges maintained tight control over all aspects of student life. Student drinking did not become a serious town-gown issue in college towns until after World War II. Several factors stimulated this change. Enrollment increased, so students were more numerous. The growth in enrollment created housing shortages on campus, which prompted many students to move off campus, where they had greater autonomy. Simultaneously, what students did for fun began to change, and undergraduates pushed for greater freedom. Although the most dramatic changes took place in the late 1960s and early 1970s, hints that a shift was occurring are noticeable a decade before. UD's dean of students noted in 1959 that there had been a "sudden sharp increase" in the number of misconduct cases, including violations of the university's alcohol policies. [12]

Enrollment at the University of Delaware grew rapidly after World War II, as it did at public universities all over. The initial surge was caused by the arrival of veterans, drawn by the free tuition provided by the GI Bill. But enrollment continued to grow after the veterans graduated, as their siblings came to appreciate the value of a college education. Undergraduate enrollment at Delaware was just 602 in 1939, as war broke out in Europe. One year after the war's end, enrollment swelled to 1,817. Undergraduate enrollment grew every year from 1951 to 1977, increasing to 11,253. By the 1970s, students came to represent about half the population of the city. Like most universities, Delaware struggled to accommodate the growth. It built fourteen housing complexes containing 6,400 beds, but the number of students living off campus also increased.[13]

As the university was transformed, so was the nature of extracurricular activities. Part of this change was stimulated by the enrollment of veterans, who were older than earlier students and had little patience for the rituals of college life. But subsequent generations of students also lost interest in the traditional aspects of undergraduate culture. Rules that in 1959 required freshmen to wear a "dink" the first week of class, learn the Delaware alma mater and fight song, and attend all pep-fests and home football games were soon forgotten.[14] By 1970, attitudes had been so transformed that students protested the tradition of electing a homecoming queen by electing a chicken. As Helen Lefkowitz Horowitz has noted, "the social order" on college campuses "seemed to be disintegrating."[15]

Inspired by the same spirit of social change that spurred the civil rights and anti-war movements, students demanded greater rights. Those efforts reached a climax at Delaware in 1967, when a female student accused UD of discrimination because it maintained different regulations for women, a member of the radical Students for a Democratic Society was elected student body president, and student leaders proposed a manifesto that called for greater freedom in all aspects of student life. The yearbook remarked that "a new spirit crackled over the campus—one of defiance, one of power." One by one, rules put in place to enable the university to act in place of parents—in loco parentis—were eliminated. The student dress code was abolished, ROTC was made voluntary, and a regulation prohibiting non-commuter students from bringing cars to Newark was ended. In time, the university also liberalized its residence hall regulations, and coed dorms became the norm. Female students were given the same rights as men. In 1971, UD revised its policy on alcoholic beverages, permitting students who were legally old enough to drink to consume alcohol in dorm rooms.[16]

As enrollment increased, students moved off campus, undergraduate cultures changed, and in loco parentis disappeared, alcohol came to occupy a central role in student life. Although the minimum drinking age in Delaware was twenty-one, it was eighteen in nearby Maryland, so alcohol was easy to obtain for all but the youngest students. Underage students were prohibited from drinking in dorms, but such activity was difficult to monitor so long as older students were allowed to drink. Student drinking was even harder to control off campus in apartments and rental houses. Student bars grew in number and popularity. Student drinking became excessive, and its consequences came under attack by Newark residents and city officials.

The Deer Park Tavern, built in 1851, is Newark's oldest bar. As the focus of student life shifted, it became the city's preeminent student hangout. "Everybody went to the Park," said a former student. Until relatively recently, it was easy for underage students to drink at the Deer Park because the owners "always seemed to know" when police would visit. Symbolic of the town-gown division in college towns, the Deer Park had two bars, separated by a wall. One catered to students; the other was patronized chiefly by "townies." "If you were a college kid, you didn't walk in there," said a longtime Newark merchant. "You didn't go through there unless you wanted to get in a fight." In 1972, a second student-oriented bar, the Stone Balloon, opened on Main Street. It was larger than the Deer Park and booked live music. In time, the Stone Balloon boasted that it sold more beer than any other bar in the East.[17]

The events of March 7, 1974, which began at the Deer Park but spread down the city's Main Street and to campus, demonstrated to Newark residents that student drinking had careened out of control. By this time, the nationwide streaking trend had reached the city. The night before, a man allowed two women to take off his clothes while he stood atop a table at the Deer Park, before "he streaked off into the night." Rumors circulating said there would be 1,500 streakers on campus the following night. By 10 p.m., the Deer Park was packed. On campus, a thousand people gathered. Shortly after midnight, ten nude males ran through the crowd. A few minutes later, a second group of streakers appeared. Then another and another. According to one eyewitness, there were about one hundred streakers in all.[18]

After the commotion ended on campus, many wandered to the Deer Park. Thousands filled Main Street. The scene turned violent when revelers began to loot a liquor store that adjoined the Deer Park and others threw empty bottles into the street. When police arrived, they were pelted with rocks and bottles. Two Newark police cars had all their windows broken, and five others were damaged. Newark police were no match for a crowd

FIGURE 9.3. *Police block Main Street in Newark during the city's 1974 Deer Park riot. Thousands of drunken young people filled the city's downtown following a mass streaking event on the University of Delaware campus, then turned violent, throwing rocks and bottles at police, damaging streetlights, and ripping trash receptacles from sidewalks. Used with permission, Newark Police Department.*

that grew to an estimated 4,000 people. The crowd moved down Main Street, throwing stones, breaking streetlights, and ripping trash containers from the sidewalk (fig. 9.3). Eventually, forty-two Newark police were joined by 193 officers from four other law enforcement agencies. Unable to disperse the mob, police fired tear gas into the crowd. A fog of tear gas spread throughout downtown and the campus. Thirteen people, including ten police officers, were injured and eleven arrested.[19]

Problems associated with student drinking intensified after Delaware in 1978 lowered the drinking age to twenty. In the three years after the drinking age was lowered, thirty-one new liquor licenses were granted in the city. The number of bars in a four-block area around Main Street increased from three in 1970 to fourteen in 1981. Unruly behavior became commonplace. During the first eighteen days of May 1980, for example, Newark police arrested 527 people, most for alcohol and related offenses, such as disorderly conduct and urinating in public. Weary residents threatened to take matters into their own hands. After a police crackdown on public drinking downtown displaced partiers to residential areas, one homeowner told the City Council, "If you don't do something, we're going to get permits for guns and do it ourselves." Another resident said he and his elderly neighbors were "scared to death."[20]

The public furor over student drinking inspired Newark's mayor in 1982 to create a commission to investigate the city's alcohol problems and recommend solutions. The commission—composed of government officials, UD administrators, and residents—represented the first effort by the city and university to work together to address the situation. The commission recommended seventeen actions, calling on the city to increase penalties for driving under the influence, require permits for large parties, and establish a training program for employees of businesses that sold alcohol. In the years following the commission's recommendations, Newark's City Council enacted a series of ordinances designed to reduce problems associated with drinking. It began charging businesses that sell alcohol a license fee to help pay for enforcement. It doubled its fines for noise violations, increased penalties for repeat offenders, and made landlords liable for tenant behavior. It amended Newark's housing code to require the eviction of tenants convicted twice of noise or disorderly conduct in one year. Following the example of another college town, Oxford, Ohio, Newark police adopted a "zero tolerance" policy for noise, alcohol and disorderly conduct violations.[21]

Delaware increased its drinking age to twenty-one in 1984 after Congress and President Ronald Reagan enacted a law requiring states to do so or lose federal highway funds. That change pushed student drinking out of bars and into houses and apartments in residential areas. Town-gown relations deteriorated still further as a result. William Hogan, the city's chief of police, remarked that "it was not uncommon for the police to confront parties in rental neighborhoods where 600 or more young adults were in attendance. Keg parties were the order of the day. The students would use the University of Delaware bus system as their means of transportation. Alcohol was everywhere." Several student apartment complexes and neighborhoods accounted for most noise and alcohol complaints.[22]

One such neighborhood was Madison Drive in College Park, one mile west of the Delaware campus. Built to provide starter homes to working-class residents, it had been transformed into a student-dominated neighborhood as UD's enrollment increased. The Delaware student newspaper in its "Best of Newark" issue selected Madison Drive as the site of the "Best Off-Campus Housing," justifying its selection by saying "parties are plentiful." Long-term residents found the student population intolerable. "People roam the street and carry on anytime at night," said a woman who had lived there for thirty-five years. "People race cars and throw beer bottles. Students have no respect for people's property." Repeated complaints prompted the university's dean of students to write a letter to 163 UD students living in the area, asking them to refrain from rowdy behavior.[23]

City officials and residents began to press the university to take more responsibility for the off-campus behavior of students. Because the most serious drinking problems were associated with younger students, city officials recommended that UD require not just freshmen but sophomores to live in university housing. They also demanded it tighten liquor law enforcement on campus. Over time, the university began to respond. The most fundamental change occurred in 1989 when UD expanded its judicial system to punish students for criminal offenses that occur off campus, reversing a policy adopted two decades before during the student rights movement that forbade it from practicing "double jeopardy" by penalizing students a second time for offenses for which they had been punished by civil authorities. Delaware was believed to be the only higher education institution in the country with such a policy at the time, but numerous colleges have implemented similar policies since.[24]

Increasing public concern about so-called binge drinking, Delaware's growing reputation as a party school, and the death of a freshman who fell thirteen floors from a dormitory after he had been drinking motivated the university to intensify its efforts. In 1996, it became one of six universities nationwide to receive a five-year, $770,000 grant from the Robert Wood Johnson Foundation to implement programs to reduce "high-risk" drinking. Two years before, a Harvard School of Public Health study reported that 44 percent of college students were "binge" drinkers. The study identified binge drinkers as males who drank five or more drinks consecutively and females who drank at least four in a row at least once in two weeks. In 1997, 60 percent of Delaware students were classified as "binge" drinkers.[25]

Most of the Robert Wood Johnson Foundation funds were spent on educational programs, public advocacy, and the creation of non-alcoholic social opportunities for students. UD created a poster campaign that mocks

Delaware's party school reputation and another, inspired by talk show host David Letterman's Top 10 lists, which identifies the "Top 10 Reasons Not to Get Drunk." It helped create a program called "UDo Live Here" that distributes to students and other residents "Good Neighbor" bags, which include "A Guide to Safe and Responsible Parties," a summary of alcohol laws, and a brochure that identifies alcohol-free restaurants. Other college towns, such as Durham, New Hampshire, have created similar programs. UD has helped organized alcohol-free social events. It donated two $2,500 electronic devices to Newark police that detect fake identification cards. In 2001, the Robert Wood Johnson Foundation awarded the university a $465,000 grant to continue its efforts. When it expired, UD won a $1.2 million grant from the federal government to combat student drinking.[26]

The university has also tightened student conduct rules, changed campus drinking policies, and implemented programs to improve behavior in fraternities. It implemented a "three strikes, you're out" program, under which students who violate school alcohol and drug policies three times are suspended for one year. It placed new restrictions on drinking in dormitories and serving alcohol at group events. In hopes of reducing drinking at football games, it began tighter enforcement of a policy requiring tailgating to end when the game begins and stopped providing "pass outs" that allowed fans to leave the stadium at halftime. Like Cornell University and many other colleges, UD also implemented strict regulations governing fraternity parties. It created a program that rates all Greek chapters each year and reduces party privileges of houses that do not meet standards. Delaware also now requires first-year students to complete a three-hour online alcohol education course.[27]

The most radical move made by the University of Delaware to rein in student behavior, however, was its decision in 1997 to notify parents of any student found guilty of violating its conduct code. When officials first contemplated parental notification they were told by lawyers that such a policy was illegal, a violation of the federal government's Buckley Amendment. "We decided to do it anyway," said David Roselle, UD's president from 1990 to 2007. At the time, no other college in the United States practiced parental notification, but in 1998 Congress approved an exception to the Buckley Amendment that allows higher education institutions to notify parents of students under age twenty-one who violate alcohol and drug laws or policies. Since that time, many colleges have begun parental notification.[28]

Parental notification and the tightening of student conduct rules represent a partial return to in loco parentis policies that were largely eliminated in the 1960s and 1970s. Roselle believes such a change was essential. "We did some things that didn't work," he said. "We put a group of nineteen-year-old boys in a house called a fraternity with absolutely no supervision and we expect a good result. There is a return to being willing to assume some measure of responsibility." Roselle contends, moreover, that a university's responsibility extends off campus. "You discipline people who misbehave," he said. "If they are misbehaving in the town, that's part of the university's responsibility." He cited a 1996 example in which the University of North Carolina disclaimed responsibility when a fire at a fraternity house off campus killed five students. "UNC tried to give the response that it wasn't their house, it was out in the town, it really didn't belong to them," Roselle said. "It was a public relations nightmare. Nobody buys that. They're your kids whether you like it or not."[29]

The university, meanwhile, pushed the city to tighten its liquor laws, and the city has done so. Many of the new policies have been an outgrowth of a new alcohol commission convened by Newark's mayor in 2001. At UD's request, the City Council added dormitories to its list of land uses covered by a law that prohibits the sale of liquor within 300 feet of a church, school, or residence. Newark also became the first city in the state to lower the minimum blood alcohol level at which a driver is considered drunk. It limited the time period in which bars could sponsor "happy hour" promotions and outlawed the use of banners to promote liquor sales, drink specials, and happy hours.[30]

Some argue the University of Delaware could do more to curb student drinking and contend its actions are inconsistent. City officials point out that, although the university pushed the city to outlaw bars within 300 feet of dorms, alcohol is still allowed in those residence halls. Others criticized the university for including a bar in a hotel it built on campus. UD also found itself in hot water when its bookstore featured a prominent display of shot glasses and beer mugs emblazoned with the school's logo and it allowed a "Taste of Newark" event held on campus to serve alcohol. A growing number of colleges, such as the University of Oklahoma, have banned alcohol use by students on campus completely.[31] But longtime UD president Roselle said such efforts are misguided. "It's dumb," he said. "It doesn't work. We tried prohibition way back. Trust me, there are kids at the University of Oklahoma who are drinking. Kids should be told, hey, it's okay to have a beer. What is a big deal is when you're not responsible. I think your rules and regulations should be made to address that group, the irresponsible group."[32]

Have the Robert Wood Johnson Foundation program and other university efforts to curb student drinking been successful? Have new laws imposed by the city reduced drunkenness and eased town-gown tension related to it? It depends on how you interpret the data and whom you ask. Annual surveys of UD students conducted by the Harvard School of Public Health show little change in student drinking habits. In 2003, 57 percent of Delaware students surveyed were classified as "binge" drinkers, a decline of only 3 percent in seven years since the Robert Wood Johnson Foundation program began. But underage students acknowledged alcohol was more difficult to obtain and believed they were more likely to be caught drinking and punished if caught using a fake ID. Data suggest students better understand the dangers of drinking but continue to drink anyway. "We haven't accomplished what we'd hoped," said Tracy Downs, who directed UD's Robert Wood Johnson Foundation–funded programs. "Students are still drinking to get drunk."[33]

Alcohol arrests in the city have risen dramatically, while noise and disorderly conduct arrests have also increased, but it's unclear whether the increases reflect an increase in activity or tighter enforcement. Arrests for alcohol violations more than tripled between 1996 and 2006, while arrests for noise or disorderly premises and disorderly conduct doubled. Although not all those charged are students, data on student liquor law violations referred to the university suggest most are. In 2005, Newark police arrested 1,034 people for alcohol violations and referred 1,020 cases to the university. A recent survey, furthermore, found that a majority of Newark residents believed there had been no improvement in behavior typically associated with students. Two-thirds of those surveyed in 2004 said irresponsible alcohol use, noise, and vandalism were as bad as they had been three years before, or worse.[34]

The story of a Newark resident who lived one block north of Main Street provides a graphic example of the problems that exist. In October 1999, he wrote to a local newspaper describing conditions he called "intolerable." During the previous twenty-four hours, he said, there had been four parties within earshot of his house. He called police repeatedly about the noise, which kept his family awake well past midnight. Males at a party next door urinated out a window below his thirteen-year-old daughter's bedroom window, witnessed by his daughter and a friend. At 2 a.m., guests at the party next door began throwing a baseball on his tin roof and watching it roll down. After police called to investigate a complaint nearby left, several drunken young people began shouting and cursing in the street. Someone spray painted obscenities on his car. The same car had been hit or vandalized four other times in the previous year. "We have footprints and dents in the roof of both of our cars," he said, "from times when the students feel that it is fun to jump up and down on other people's property." While he was writing the letter, his car was hit by another vehicle, which quickly drove off.[35]

Riotous behavior and tragedy have continued to punctuate town-gown debates. In April 1998, Newark police were forced to seek help from nine other law enforcement agencies to halt a party that attracted more than 2,500 people to a student house. Partyers threw bottles at police, injuring three officers and damaging two police cars. Ten people were arrested. Three years later, a crowd of 500 to 600 people celebrating the final night before the Deer Park Tavern closed for renovation turned malicious when police arrived to break up a fight. They looted the bar of alcohol and memorabilia before spilling onto Main Street, where they blocked traffic, damaged parked cars, and threw rocks and bottles at police. They also broke the gates on a railroad crossing and halted train service for ninety minutes. Then in 2004, a drunken UD freshman was killed by a train after leaving a fraternity party in the second week of school. Her blood-alcohol level was three times the legal definition of drunkenness.[36]

The Robert Wood Johnson Foundation program has been the frequent object of ridicule by students. Attendance at alcohol-free social events has been sparse. The posters and publicity campaigns were derided as propaganda. "The university and the RWJF just don't get it," said a columnist in the student newspaper. "Drinking is fun." In its annual "Cheers" and "Jeers" column, the *Review* singled out the grant as "most ineffective use of funds." But it has not only been students who have criticized the program. Roy Lopata, city planning director, called it "a total waste of money." Thomas Wampler, a former City Council member who has lived in Newark since 1966, said, "I don't think it's made the slightest bit of difference."[37]

Other students and residents, however, argue that city and university efforts to curb student drinking and disruptive behavior have altered the student party culture. A senior, reflecting on his undergraduate years, said Delaware's reputation as a party school had diminished. "If I was 18 and looking for a college," he said, "I'm not sure Delaware is the place I'd go." The student newspaper begrudgingly acknowledged that the Robert Wood Johnson Foundation program had made UD a safer place and, because of it, "a degree from the university is worth more than it was five years ago." A columnist observed that stepped-up liquor law enforcement has led to "a severe decline in campus social life" and remarked that "what makes for a 'good night' is not getting arrested or fined." Some residents have commended UD's efforts, even if results have been limited. David Athey, a Newark City Council representative who is one of the university's most vocal critics, said, "On this subject, the university has done a good job." He added, "If there was just one kid that one night decided he was going to go to a non-alcohol event instead of going and getting blind drunk, maybe there's one more kid that didn't get killed." [38]

Yet for all the disagreement, there is one point upon which students, townspeople, city officials, and university administrators agree—college students will drink regardless of the laws, penalties, and risks, they will get drunk and, when they do, they will disrupt the lives of others. "It's a battle that can't be won," said one Delaware undergraduate. Student drinking has been the one constant of college life since the first universities emerged in Europe. "New students away from home," said Newark city manager Carl Luft, "will always test the limits of their freedom." Youth drinking, scholars on the subject contend, is a societal problem that begins before college and will not be solved until addressed at a higher level, as with government and health industry efforts to reduce cigarette smoking. [39] In the meantime, student drinking and related behavior, more than any other issue, seem certain to keep town-gown tensions simmering in college towns.

EROSION OF SINGLE-FAMILY NEIGHBORHOODS

Student behavioral issues cannot be divorced from the geography of housing in college towns. Such problems are comparatively minor in towns that are home to private colleges, which house most of their students on campus where they can closely monitor behavior. College towns like Newark that are sites of public universities, moreover, had few problems before the bulk of undergraduates began to live off campus. Most observers in Newark, as in other college towns, chart the rise of student behavioral problems, and a corresponding increase in town-gown tension, to the increased migration of students into single-family neighborhoods beginning in the 1960s. In Newark, what started as a trickle became a flood by the 1980s as the University of Delaware stopped building dormitories but also because students sought the greater freedom off-campus living allows. College town governments, in response, have sought to regulate student housing as a way to restrain student behavior.

The earliest students at Delaware College were expected to live on campus or with their families. Then as now, a greater percentage of Delaware students lived with their parents and commuted to campus than do so in isolated college towns because of the college's proximity to Wilmington. [40] Delaware housed a minority of its undergraduates until the 1950s, but most students who did not live on campus lived at home. As enrollment surged following World War II, UD struggled to accommodate increasing housing demand, like colleges everywhere. A former hospital was converted to student housing. Old Army barracks were moved to the campus to provide temporary quarters. By 1951, university housing could accommodate only 17 percent of undergraduates. "Housing was badly needed," John Munroe, author of a history of UD, observed.[41]

In response, the University of Delaware embarked on a major dormitory building program that continued for more than twenty years and, in the process, was transformed from a commuter school to a residential university. Between 1951 and 1972, the university built fifty residence halls that could house 6,500 students. Like other colleges, Delaware was aided in those efforts by the federal government, which provided low-interest loans to colleges for that purpose. Between 1950 and 1956, Congress authorized $750 million for loans to colleges. All the new housing meant that by 1961, UD housed 60 percent of its undergraduates, a more than threefold increase in a decade. Although data on the number of students who lived in Newark are unavailable, students from the period say few undergraduates lived in apartments or houses in the city. Vance Funk, Newark's mayor, who attended UD from 1960 to 1966, said nearly all undergraduates "lived on campus or lived at home. I can't remember going to one person's house off campus, other than married students."[42]

Universities like Delaware that built much new housing after World War II did so because they had to in order to accommodate rapid enrollment growth, but once growth slowed, and the private housing market was able to meet demand, they stopped. UD's decision to stop building dormitories also reflected changes in philosophy about the role of colleges in the non-academic lives of students. As students pushed for greater freedom, Acting President John W. Shirley wondered in 1967 if the university still had a responsibility to provide housing for them. A campus development plan issued four years later said the university wished to "encourage the development of off-campus housing" and reduce the percentage of students housed on campus from 60 to 40 percent. The plan proposed no new dormitory construction, but recommended UD enrollment be allowed to grow to 18,300 students, double its size in 1971.[43]

No other factor has inflamed town-gown tension in Newark more than the University of Delaware's decision to stop building housing while allowing enrollment to grow, because it forced more and more students to seek housing off campus and in the town. But two other changes in university policy also heightened student demand for off-campus housing and so contributed to the problem. UD gradually eliminated the requirement that unmarried female students must live in dormitories or at home. It also began to seek more out-of-state students, who are less likely than Delawareans to commute. As state support for higher education has diminished nationwide, public universities have discovered that one way to offset declining appropriations is to admit more out-of-state students, who pay higher tuition and fees than state residents. The share of UD undergraduates who came from outside the state grew from 25 percent in 1965 to 60 percent in 1991.[44]

UD built no housing between 1972 and 1991, a period during which undergraduate enrollment grew by 4,414 students. Rising enrollment stimulated repeated housing crises on campus. In 1974, for example, Delaware admitted more students who requested housing than it could accommodate. Five hundred students were forced to look elsewhere for housing. In 1977, demand for on-campus housing again exceeded supply, and some students were forced to live three-to-a-room or in dormitory lounges.[45] By 1980, the university was able to house less than half its undergraduates, a 10 percent drop in a decade. Faced with increased competition for dorm rooms and the prospect of being forced into undesirable living situations, more students chose to rent apartments or houses with friends. Developers built apartment complexes aimed at the student market, and landlords recognized the profit potential of turning single-family homes into student rentals. Block by block, neighborhoods near the university were transformed (fig. 9.4). Longtime residents fought to prevent the conversion of their neighborhoods into student rental districts, and the city was forced to respond.

Longtime Newark residents first began to notice a change in the community stimulated by a shift in student housing in the 1970s. Bob Thomas, a lifelong resident, said when students began to move off campus, "immediately there were problems."[46] Thomas's family has lived in Newark since the early twentieth century, and its story illustrates how the expansion of student rental housing alters the social geography of college towns. When Thomas was born in 1950, his parents lived in a row house on Academy Street, one block from campus. His grandparents lived two doors down. Thomas's family knew every resident on the block, and often those friendships spanned multiple generations. Most residents lived there for years. Students did not begin moving into the single block of row houses until the mid-1970s, but, once they did, Thomas said, the neighborhood was transformed virtually overnight. When his grandparents moved in 1979, "they were the last [non-student] residents on the row." Students call the block "Skid Row" and now organize an annual "Skidfest" block party. In 2004,

FIGURE 9.4. *Students hang out in front of a typical student rental house in Newark. The conversion of single-family homes to student rental properties has been a major source of town-gown conflict in Newark and other college towns. Photograph by the author, 2000.*

the party grew so raucous police shut it down. After the party, the backyards of the houses, according to a student writer, looked "like a beer can massacre."[47]

Thomas's parents bought a townhouse on Cleveland Avenue, and he lived there until he graduated from high school in 1969. His parents remained on the street until 1995. Like the row houses on Academy Street, Cleveland Avenue when Thomas was growing up was a close-knit neighborhood and its residents had deep roots in Newark. Nearly all houses on the street were owner-occupied. "There were families in some houses that had been there for forty or fifty years," Thomas said. He delivered newspapers on the street. A corner grocery was a neighborhood hangout. Entire families sat on porches on summer evenings. "It was easy to get to know these people when you knew the families sometimes two or three generations," Thomas said. "They were more than neighbors."

Farther from campus, Cleveland Avenue was discovered by students later than Academy Street, but eventually it, too, was converted from a working-class neighborhood into a student ghetto. When Thomas's parents moved from the street in 1995, he said, 90 percent of residents were students and nearly all houses were rentals. Today, most houses on Cleveland Avenue are run down. Many have been split into apartments. Exterior fire escapes have been erected without regard to aesthetics. Bicycles and old couches occupy rotting porches. Grass is long and littered with beer bottles. "For Rent" signs are permanently nailed to shingles, including several from a company called "UD Cribs," whose name suggests its owners realize no one but students would live there. The Delaware student newspaper in 2002 crowned Cleveland Avenue "best place to party," calling it "a mega belt of seething house party jubilation."[48] Walking along the street of his youth, Thomas said, "Neighborhoods like this have been destroyed."

The city of Newark has aggressively sought to control the expansion of student rental housing and mitigate its negative consequences. Facing rising complaints from homeowners, the city in 1980 implemented a strategy that is ubiquitous in college towns—it imposed limits on how many people could live in a rental house. A 1989 survey of university communities found that 76 percent of cities with fewer than 100,000 residents had occupancy limits. Occupancy limits have two intended purposes. By limiting the number of people who can live in a rental house, planners hope to reduce the profit potential for landlords and make single-family homes less attractive to investors. Occupancy limits are also intended to minimize the problems associated with student rentals. Fewer occupants mean fewer cars, less trash and, neighbors and planners hope, fewer parties and less noise. When the city first enacted occupancy limits, no more than four un-related people could live in a single-family house.[49]

While occupancy limits had some impact, they did not halt the erosion of single-family neighborhoods by student housing or eliminate student behavioral problems in residential areas. The number of rental houses in the city increased from 155 in 1983 to 732 by the end of the decade.[50] Long-term residents continued to complain about the behavior of students, and friction between students and non-students became ever more acrimonious. Homeowners said police efforts to crack down on underage drinking in bars only pushed drinking into residential areas. Realizing occupancy limits had little influence on student behavior because they do not regulate how many guests an occupant can have, the city in 1985 implemented strict noise regulations and enacted a law making landlords responsible for the behavior of their tenants.[51]

Newark progressively tightened its housing regulations in ways that came to be viewed as hostile toward students. In 1985, the City Council amended the city's housing code to require eviction of tenants convicted twice in one year for noise or disorderly conduct. In 1989, it began requiring single-family rental houses to have at least two off-street parking spaces. It increased the annual permit fee for single-family rentals to $120 per unit. Landlords opposed the changes. John Bauscher, who owned ten rentals in the Madison Drive area, filed a complaint with the state Human Relations Commission charging that Newark's occupancy limits discriminated based on age and marital status. Students remained surprisingly silent in the debate, although one recent graduate said at a hearing, "I'm a renter. I might as well be a disease carrier for the way I've been treated."[52]

Undeterred, the City Council in 1992 reduced from four to three the number of unrelated people who could live in a single-family rental home. The reduction was adopted at the request of residents in the Kells Avenue neighborhood, south of the Delaware campus (fig. 9.5). One of the city's most affluent older neighborhoods, full of architecturally distinctive homes, it had resisted the invasion of student renters because its homes were large and comparatively expensive. But once most houses in other areas near campus had been converted to rentals, investors began to buy houses there. About 1985, Thomas Wampler, a resident of the neighborhood, founded the Old Newark Civic Association to fight encroachment of student housing on older neighborhoods and pressure the city to protect such areas. "We saw houses one by one being converted to student rentals," he said. "It was unstoppable." By 1990, so many students had moved into the Kells Avenue neighborhood, Wampler said, that "it was almost unlivable."[53]

FIGURE 9.5. *Bungalow in Newark's Kells Avenue neighborhood, where homeowners have organized to fight encroachment of single-family neighborhoods by student housing throughout the city. Photograph by the author, 2004.*

Despite the city's efforts, the number of single-family houses converted to rental properties continued to grow by about fifty a year throughout the 1990s. Although that number is not large, the impact was concentrated in a few areas near campus. Residents and city officials say university efforts to better control student behavior on campus have had unintended consequences. As it became harder for undergraduates to drink in dormitories, more students sought to move off campus because of the perception that apartments and, especially, houses allow greater freedom. A 1999 survey of housing preferences of UD undergraduates found that 54 percent who expressed a preference preferred to live off campus in houses. When students were asked why they moved out of university housing, 82 percent said houses and apartments offered more "freedom and privacy" than dorms. The undergraduate who conducted the survey concluded that "renting a single-family house with plenty of parking and room to party [is] a status symbol and rite of passage for students."[54]

The university's critics insist it should build more housing on campus and house a greater share of its students. UD in 1991 built 332 apartments on campus. In 2006, it finished construction on three dormitories that can house 1,000 students, but they replaced an existing dorm so the net increase in beds was only 250. Delaware has no plans to build additional housing or increase the percentage of students housed on campus. University officials believe students acquire greater responsibility by living off campus and are doubtful it could fill more beds. "People get tired of living in dormitories and going down the hallway with a towel over their shoulder," said David Roselle.[55] They point out that UD already houses a greater percentage of its undergraduates than comparable institutions. In 2006, Delaware housed 47 percent of its undergraduates, more than flagship state universities in three neighboring states.[56]

Unable to halt the erosion of single-family neighborhoods by student housing, Newark became more bold in its tactics. In 1999, the City Council approved an ordinance that prohibited new student rentals within a specified distance (typically about 500 feet) of existing student rentals in single-family neighborhoods. By that time, the number of rental houses had grown to 1,173, a sixfold increase since 1983. The ordinance was modeled after one in Pennsylvania, near Villanova University. Key to understanding the City Council's motivations for enacting the law was a provision that exempted parts of thirty-three streets, which already contained such high proportions of student rentals that they had reached a "tipping point" beyond which complete turnover from owner-occupants to renters is likely.[57] What is the tipping point for family neighborhoods in college towns? At what point, does the percentage of homes occupied by students become so high that the remaining owner-occupants seek to leave and conversion of the neighborhood seems assured? No one knows for sure, but Thomas Wampler believes it is about 25 percent student houses and fears his Kells Avenue neighborhood had nearly reached that point. "I noticed that once a neighborhood became 25 percent rental," he said, "the reputation that it got was that the neighborhood is all rental and it's a dump. The neighborhood took on the character of a place people were moving through and didn't care."[58]

The student home ordinance faced strong opposition from students and landlords. "Where do they expect students to live?" asked one undergraduate. "They're making one set of rules for students and one set of rules for everyone else," said Brenda Mayrack, president of the College Democrats. To many students, the ordinance was simply the latest in a long line of anti-student policies implemented by the city. A survey of undergraduates conducted as the ordinance was being debated found that more than half believed the city discriminated against students.[59] Landlords were even more vehement in their protests. John Bauscher, president of the Newark Landlord Association, insisted the student home ordinance was discriminatory because it applied only to unrelated students. Landlords have also condemned occupancy limits, which they argue fail to take into account the size of a house, and laws that make landlords liable for tenant behavior. "I have a thirty-one-year-old daughter," said one. "When she was home, I couldn't get her to do anything. How the fuck am I going to get four kids who aren't mine to do anything?" Bauscher also denounced the intolerance of permanent residents for students. "I never ceased to be amazed at how people move to a college town and they hate college students," he said.[60]

In November 1999, the Newark Landlord Association and seven landlords sued the city, claiming that the student home ordinance violated state law because it discriminated based on age, marital status, and occupation. Delaware Chancery Court in 2003 struck down the ordinance, saying it violated the Delaware Fair Housing Act because it discriminated based on marital status. The court did not address claims that the ordinance also discriminated based on age and occupation. The court also declared illegal a city ordinance that required leases to state that tenants would be evicted in seven days if convicted twice in one year of noise or disorderly conduct because state law requires tenants to be notified of eviction in writing, gives them more time to vacate, and allows them additional time if they demand a jury trial.[61]

But what initially seemed like victory for landlords and students did not turn out that way. Four days after the ruling, Newark's City Council imposed a two-month moratorium on new rental permits. Then it set out to rewrite the student home ordinance to comply with the court opinion. Three weeks later, the council approved a revised ordinance that changed the definition of a student home. The original ordinance defined a student home as any home occupied by two or more unrelated students. The new ordinance defined a student home as any home occupied by three or more students regardless of family relation. The ordinance is still in place, and the landlord organization said it had no plans to challenge the law. Newark planning director Lopata said that the landlords "won the battle, but we've won the war."[62]

At the same time that Newark sought to slow the expansion of student houses through regulatory means, it also began to actively encourage apartment construction as a way to reduce pressure for conversion of owner-occupied houses to rentals. Between 1987 and 2006, the city approved construction of 1,169 apartment units, most of them near campus and aimed at the student market. The biggest project was the University Courtyard complex (fig. 9.6), built one block from campus by a Georgia developer that has built similar complexes near twenty other colleges. It includes twelve buildings containing 266 apartments. City officials have also devised creative programs they hope will increase the number of owner-occupied homes. In 2005, the city began offering $50,000 interest-free loans to home buyers who buy rental houses, relinquish their rental permits, and live in them.[63]

Together, the student home ordinance and the increased availability of apartments have slowed the erosion of single-family neighborhoods by student housing. Between 1999 and 2005, the number of single-family rental permits increased by only sixty-six. Residents of the Kells Avenue neighborhood and other campus-adjacent areas say their neighborhoods have been saved. Students have abandoned some neighborhoods they used to dominate. The College Park neighborhood, once a major source of town-gown conflict, has few students today. The changing geography of student housing also reflects shifts in student housing tastes nationwide. University Courtyard and other new complexes offer amenities that beat-up old houses cannot, such as high-speed Internet access and fitness centers. Yet the problems associated with students living in family neighborhoods remain. Such tensions will always be present whenever significant numbers of students live off campus in college towns.[64]

FIGURE 9.6. *The University Courtyard apartment complex, built one block from the Delaware campus as part of a city effort to encourage apartment construction as a way to relieve pressure for conversion of single-family homes to student rentals. Photograph by the author, 2004.*

CAMPUS EXPANSION AND DEVELOPMENT

As typically the largest landowner and most active developer in a college town, a college or university exerts a profound influence over the city where it is located that is more direct than its role in conflicts caused by student behavior and rental housing expansion. Most higher education institutions are exempt from local property taxes, so when they grow in area they reduce the tax revenues of city governments. Most colleges and universities are also exempt from local zoning laws, so they enjoy much greater autonomy in building than private developers. Because colleges and universities are normally only subject to housing and safety codes, they can build what they want, where they want, and when they want no matter how vocal and widespread the opposition from city officials and residents.

Significant town-gown conflict over campus expansion is a comparatively recent phenomenon because most colleges were relatively small until after World War II. The original campus of Newark College was just six acres. After Delaware College was designated the state's land-grant college, the campus grew in area. In 1907, the state provided the college $20,000 to develop an experimental farm on 212 acres south of the main campus. This became the nucleus for what is now South Campus, which encompasses 500 acres and is the site of most of the university's agricultural and athletics facilities. Residents and town officials were mostly supportive of the college—a historian in 1917 observing that "town and gown at Newark were always on good terms"—but when its expansion began to pose financial challenges to the town, local government reacted. In 1910, the town council requested that the college curb, gutter, and install a sidewalk along a portion of a street that bordered the college grounds because it paid no property taxes.[65]

The college continued to expand. In 1913, the state created a separate women's college and purchased nineteen acres south of Delaware College for its campus. The state also granted the college right of eminent domain, and those powers have worried residents and public officials ever since. To bridge the gap between the Delaware College grounds and the women's campus, chemical company magnate Pierre S. du Pont bought for the college a parcel one-half mile long and up to one-quarter mile wide. By 1921, the campus encompassed eighty-eight acres, plus the college farm. Still, there is little evidence to suggest campus growth caused much consternation in Newark, although the same commentator who earlier characterized town-gown relations as uniformly cordial, observed a few years later that "jealousies and suspicions . . . have of late poisoned the local atmosphere."[66]

Animosity inspired by university expansion grew as enrollment mushroomed following World War II and buildings were erected to accommodate that growth. In the sixteen years following the war, the campus grew from 295 to 650 acres. The added real estate enabled the university to embark on the most ambitious building program in its history. It built fifty-six new buildings in twenty years. UD's growth strained the city's ability to provide services and reduced its income, so much so that a local newspaper observed that "Newark suffers acute growing pains, especially in the region of the purse." Whenever the university purchased land or bought existing buildings, the city's tax revenues were cut, since those properties became tax exempt. At the same time, increased enrollment and population inflated the city's costs. Heightened traffic meant streets had to be enlarged. Construction on campus created more work for city building inspectors and engineers. Utility lines had to be installed. The police force had to be expanded. More people meant more trash to collect. Rapid growth created "an explosion in demand for city services," wrote a later Newark city planner, "in a community whose taxing potential was eroded by university growth."[67]

In response, Newark in 1951 obtained a new municipal charter from the state that doubled the city's acreage, increasing the territory from which it could collect property taxes. It also adopted a policy that continues to the present of annexing new land to compensate for any property acquired by the university. While those changes helped Newark avert financial disaster, they did not eliminate the city's financial woes. The university continued to acquire land. The campus grew 50 percent in the 1950s alone. In response, Newark's City Council in 1959 asked the Delaware General Assembly to require the state to pay municipalities to compensate for tax-exempt properties. It refused. Local attitudes toward the university were changing. *Delaware Today* magazine observed, "There is a vitality in Newark that is exciting," but added, "there is also one great, consuming frustration to its citizens. There is a very large fly in the ointment of success, and that fly is the University of Delaware."[68]

Unable to obtain fiscal relief from the state, Newark appealed directly to the university for aid, arguing that the city provided it services for which it was not paid. In 1965, UD agreed to pay the city an annual subvention of $105,000. That money was intended to pay for police and fire protection, engineering services, and street maintenance. College towns nationwide have sought payments from universities for similar purposes. A 1989 survey of university cities found that 11 percent received direct payments from colleges or universities in lieu of property taxes. Subventions were most common in smaller university cities, like Newark, where colleges typically occupy a greater percentage of city land. Thirty-eight percent of cities with fewer than 25,000 residents received such payments. Many other college towns, such as Ann Arbor, Michigan, have sought payment recently without success.[69]

As the University of Delaware campus grew, specific building projects began to face opposition, and the city challenged in court the university's exemption from land-use regulations. The court challenge was inspired by a university plan to build the high-rise Christiana Towers housing complex adjacent to a residential neighborhood. The university eventually built three high-rise residences, the tallest of which is seventeen stories (fig. 9.7). City zoning laws prohibit buildings taller than three stories except downtown and in industrial areas. Homeowners in the area opposed the project because they feared student residences would reduce their property values.

FIGURE 9.7.
Construction
of the high-rise
Christiana Towers
housing complex
on the Delaware
campus in 1971
was opposed by
residents in the
vicinity and the
City of Newark,
which sued the
university in an
effort to force it
to comply with
zoning laws. Used
with permission,
University
of Delaware
Archives.

In 1969, the city sued the university in an effort to force it to comply with zoning laws. Four years later, Delaware Chancery Court rejected the city's suit, ruling that the university's board of trustees has exclusive jurisdiction over development of the campus and declaring that UD was subject only to local regulations designed to protect the health and safety of building occupants. In other words, the university is subject to city building codes, but not zoning.[70]

Active opposition to campus building projects became more common after the Christiana Towers controversy, but most subsequent efforts to stop such projects and reduce the university's autonomy also failed. In 1973, the city opposed a UD plan to build a parking lot adjacent to one of Newark's wealthiest neighborhoods, claiming that traffic it would generate posed a safety hazard. The lot was built as planned. Three years later, the city petitioned the state legislature to require UD to submit its building plans to the city ninety days before starting construction and hold public hearings on all building projects. The petition was denied. In 1989, residents protested a UD plan to build three residence halls because the project required the removal of several homes. The dorms were built anyway. One exception to the lack of success in halting campus building projects occurred in 1979, when UD canceled plans for a new bookstore. The bookstore was to be built in the same residential area where the parking lot was developed a few years before. Critics of the plan argued that the bookstore would choke traffic, compete with downtown businesses, and have inadequate parking, which would prompt customers to park on residential streets. At first, university officials dismissed criticism, but as opposition mounted, President E. A. Trabant canceled the project.[71]

Protests over university developments became more heated as the tenor of town-gown debates turned more contentious. Campus building projects draw greatest opposition when they take place on the fringes of campus. One such project was the building in 1996 of the Trabant University Center on Main Street (fig. 9.8). The student center includes a food court with several national chains, bookstore, copy shop, movie theater, and travel agency. Merchants opposed the project because they said a public institution should not be in the commercial real estate business and because they feared it would hurt existing businesses on Main Street, which most agree it did. "It very, very seriously damaged Main Street," said the owner of a book and record store, who saw his business decline and later sold it.[72]

Newark residents and elected officials have also consistently opposed campus parking projects because of concerns they will increase the volume of cars on city streets. Traffic is a perpetual source of complaints in college towns because so many students bring cars with them to college. When the university in 1999 announced plans to build a 500-space parking garage on the east edge of campus, the plan drew vehement protests. Residents asked the university to delay the project so its impacts could be studied, but it refused. Elected officials expressed frustration with the university. "The citizens of this community," City Councilman Jerry Clifton said, "are the last to know about major construction projects that are going to impact quality of life." A 750-space garage built to provide parking for a new arts center on the west side of campus inspired the same sort of outrage in 2003. The controversy sounded awfully familiar. Once again, residents complained the garage would increase traffic near their homes. Once again, city officials denounced the university for failing to adequately consider the project's impacts. Once again, the university built the garage despite the protests.[73]

(opposite)
FIGURE 9.8. *Newark merchants opposed the building on Main Street of the Trabant University Center, which includes this food court and other businesses, because they feared it would hurt downtown businesses. Photograph by the author, 2000.*

The dogged opposition to campus building projects by a small but vocal group of Newark activists, though seldom successful, has nevertheless had an impact, and improved town-gown relations are the result. The university is more open than ever before about its plans. In 2001, it began notifying the public once a year about all building projects. UD's lobbyist to the state legislature now attends most City Council meetings and the council reserves a regular spot on its agenda for a university representative to speak and respond to questions. The university insists, moreover, that it has no plans to increase its enrollment or enlarge the campus, and has few building projects on the drawing board, though one cannot help but wonder if its present posture is partly a response to all the criticism it has faced. UD officials note, however, that the university's 2006 enrollment of 18,657 is very near the "optimum size" projected in a 1971 campus master plan.[74]

Yet, indicative of the tensions that exist in college towns, the university's critics insist it could do more to ameliorate concerns. There is a persistent fear that UD is concealing its true intensions, since it refuses to divulge any plans until a project has been approved by its trustees. David Athey has emerged as the university's chief public nemesis since his election to City Council in 2003. He led opposition to the two parking garages. He is representative of a type of individual present in most college towns. Educated, politically adept, combative, and ever watchful, they seek to counterbalance the dominating influence of a university. UD and city officials say privately that Athey's ideas are extreme and unrealistic, yet his reelection in 2005 by a 161–9 margin shows he has strong support. In response to the dispute over the arts center parking garage, Athey proposed that the city and university sign a memorandum of understanding to prevent future conflicts. In it, he asked UD to pledge to keep enrollment at its current level or commit to build more housing, contribute to the city's comprehensive plan, follow the city's subdivision planning process, and notify the city six months before it intended to apply for any building permits. UD officials dismissed the proposal. "We're not going to do that," said Rick Armitage, UD's director of government relations. David Roselle, university president at the time, said, "His idea that we should plan with him just doesn't work. The governance structure of the university has the trustees at the top. When we get an idea and a way that we might be able to pay for it, we talk to the trustees. If the trustees say it looks good, then we tell the city about it." Why should a university be exempt from city oversight and most regulation? "We're here to serve all the citizens of the state," Armitage said, "not just the people in Newark."[75]

Over time, the subvention paid by UD to the city in lieu of property taxes has once again become a point of contention because the university has not boosted the amount it pays in nearly forty years, even though it has continued to enlarge the campus and the growth of the university has raised the cost of providing city services to it. UD pays the city $122,537 each year for police and fire protection, street maintenance, and other basic services, the same amount it has paid since 1970.[76] If the basic subvention amount were adjusted for inflation alone, it would have been $684,161 in 2008.[77] Such an increase would not take into account the expansion of the university since 1970, which has been substantial. UD has enlarged its Newark campus from 670 to 970 acres. It has added more than 8,000 students. It has built dozens of new buildings. The subvention is a small fraction of what UD would pay for city services if it paid property taxes based on the value of its property. In 2007, the university's tax-exempt property within the city had an assessed value of $541.5 million. If UD paid property taxes on its holdings, its tax bill that year would have been $2.8 million.[78]

Elected officials have repeatedly pressed UD to increase the subvention. They did so in 1979. The university refused. They tried again in 1982 without success. Current Newark mayor Vance Funk, soon after he was elected in 2004, commented, "That's something we're going to have to visit." University officials, in response, point out that UD has added to its payments to the city in recent years for special purposes and now pays the city $135,021 in addition to the basic subvention. UD pays the city $46,021 annually to compensate it for revenues lost when parking meters were removed near two campus buildings. It pays the city $60,000 a year to support one police officer and $5,000 for the fire department. UD officials argue, furthermore, that the city provides fewer services to the university than it did when the subvention was first negotiated. UD's public safety department, for example, now has full policing powers. They add that the university pays $10 million a year to the city for electricity, water, and sewer service, roughly one-third of the city's budget. When asked if the university would consider increasing the basic subvention, longtime president Roselle said, "If they'd reduce our electric rates."[79]

One reason the city has not pushed the university harder to increase the basic subvention is because the payment is voluntary and some fear that if the city is too demanding, the university may eliminate the subvention altogether or stop buying electricity from the city. "We don't want to alienate them so much that they say, 'Screw it, next time around we're going to buy our electricity directly from DP&L [Delaware Power & Light]," Planning Director Lopata said. Nevertheless, the city in 2000 conducted a financial analysis of what it costs to provide the university services and compared that amount to payments it receives from the university. The study concluded that those services cost the city $930,240 more a year than it receives. The issue remains unresolved.[80]

GOOD WITH THE BAD

My analysis has focused on town-gown conflict rather than cooperation because it is conflict that drives the relationship between a city and its college, because cooperation is often a response to such conflict, and because conflict has the greatest potential to undermine the quality of life for residents, young and old, permanent and transient. Yet it is critical to acknowledge that universities like Delaware provide many benefits for the towns in which they are located, and cities and universities work together more than they spar. Town-gown hostility is occasional, not constant. In dozens of e-mail exchanges with me, Roy Lopata, Newark's planning director and sometimes a critic of UD, regularly prodded me to recognize the "symbiotic relationship" that exists between the city and the university. "This is a company town," Lopata said, "and the university is the company." David Athey, UD's most strident adversary in recent years, acknowledged he lives in Newark in part because the university is located there. "It's fantastic to live right next door to a college," Athey said, "but you're going to have traffic. You're going to hear noise at night. The good with the bad."[81]

For most of the University of Delaware's history, however, there was little cooperation between town and gown. Cooperation was so rare that writers noted even the smallest examples when they occurred. Before the town established a library, for example, campus literary societies allowed local residents to borrow their books. Soon after Delaware College reopened as the state's land-grant college in 1870, students, faculty, and townspeople joined together to stage a play. "It was truly a community project," Carol Hoffecker wrote. "Unfortunately, this brave beginning . . . had no sequel." Not until nearly a half-century later did the college and town again cooperate to sponsor a cultural event, when in 1916, they presented a two-day Shakespeare Festival at the Newark Opera House. John Munroe, historian of the university, called it "a rare case of town gown cooperation."[82]

Cooperation increased as the university grew, problems resulted, conflict intensified, and compromise was sought. When the city first created a comprehensive plan to respond to rapid post–World War II growth, it contracted with the university's Division of Urban Affairs to prepare the plan, prompting a newspaper to comment that "there are encouraging signs the university is willing to cooperate with the city." When enrollment growth led to increasing clashes between students and motorists, the university and city jointly pushed the state to construct pedestrian overpasses over major streets and UD built one such overpass. Heightened traffic prompted the university to initiate a free shuttle bus service for students, and it eventually opened the shuttle bus service to Newark residents. When a regional public transit agency discontinued one of its Newark routes, the city and university jointly created the Unicity Bus System, which is free for residents and students.[83]

The university has worked most closely with the city to combat student behavioral problems. The most significant UD effort in this regard was its decision to extend its student judicial system to include off-campus offenses. Newark's mayor and police chief spoke at a Faculty Senate meeting to express their support for that change. UD's efforts to combat student binge drinking also show a willingness to address problems associated with student drinking beyond the campus. UD president David Roselle and Newark mayor Vance Funk went door to door together to distribute "Good Neighbor" bags to students and other residents. UD has also significantly tightened its controls on fraternities, which are located off campus. In recent years, at least eleven fraternities have lost university recognition, and several others have been suspended. When a former Newark mayor demanded that UD help city police control unruly students off campus, furthermore, the university agreed to pay the city $60,000 a year so it could hire additional personnel. City and university officials say Newark police and the university's public safety department cooperate in many other ways, formal and informal.[84]

The University of Delaware has also become actively involved in efforts to revitalize Newark's Main Street business district, recognizing that the character of downtown can influence prospective students and their parents. Main Street in the 1980s was full of empty lots and vacant storefronts, the victim of a suburbanization of shopping that hurt downtowns everywhere. When the city hired a consultant to develop a plan for reinvigorating Main Street, UD provided $6,500 to help pay for the $37,500 study. Among the consultant's recommendations was that an organization be formed to oversee downtown planning that recognized the common interests of the city, university, and business community. The Downtown Newark Partnership was the result, and the university contributes $24,000 annually to the organization, nearly half its budget. UD president Roselle sat on the organization's board of directors and attended most of its meetings. Main Street is once again a vibrant shopping district, albeit with a stronger student orientation than before.[85]

Other efforts at town-gown cooperation have been less problem-oriented. The university and city jointly operate a refuse transfer station. Newark's annual Community Day festival is co-sponsored by the university and held on campus (fig. 9.9). The city and university sponsor an annual Taste of Newark food festival. The university donated $15,000 to the city's volunteer fire department so it could buy pagers for firefighters. The city and UD built a wall beside railroad tracks that run through the heart of the city to reduce the potential for accidents, and they jointly developed a bike path. The city created a Town & Gown Committee that includes city officials, university administrators, students, and residents to encourage greater communication, though most say it is ineffective because it has little power. More successful, many say, was the annual "Town Conversation," organized by the city and university with the help of a geography faculty member, April Veness, which gives residents, students and others an opportunity to speak about civic issues of their choice.[86]

It is important to recognize, too, that the University of Delaware provides significant economic benefits to Newark. A growing number of universities in recent years have produced economic impact studies to demonstrate that their benefits outweigh their costs to the cities and states where they are located.[87] Higher education institutions provide jobs and, along with their employees and students, spend money locally. Those expenditures, in turn, have a multiplier effect because they stimulate spending by others. UD produced an economic impact study in 2003. The study reported that it employed 3,641 people in Newark, and students, staff, and the university spent $408.4 million annually in the state (much of that, presumably, in Newark). If each of those dollars was recirculated 1.8 times, then the total economic impact of the university on the state, the study concluded, was $735.2 million, seven times the amount that UD received in appropriations from the state that year. Unlike other universities, Delaware has not separately calculated its economic impact on the city in which it is located, though it did conduct a survey of Newark businesses as part of the 2003 study. Twenty-six percent reported that one-quarter to one-half of their income came from the university community.[88]

People on all sides of the town-gown debate in Newark agree that town-gown relations are substantially better than they were a quarter-century ago. When Roy Lopata was hired as the city's planning director in 1977, the city and university "barely spoke," he said. "The university," said longtime UD administrator Joan Odell, "thought of itself as an island." Many credit President Roselle for showing a willingness to listen to city and resident concerns. Others praise city government for aggressively seeking to con-

FIGURE 9.9. *The city and university jointly sponsor Newark's annual Community Day festival on the University of Delaware campus, an example of town-gown cooperation of the sort that is often overshadowed by city-university conflict in college towns. Photograph by Kevin Quinlan, 2006; used with permission, University of Delaware.*

trol student behavior and housing. The election of a student to Newark's City Council for the first time in 2004 was seen as a positive sign (though he declined to seek a second term). Problems persist, however. Some local residents still perceive the university as aloof and domineering. They curse the bad behavior of students. Many students, in turn, still perceive Newark as anti-student.[89]

Some degree of town-gown conflict seems inevitable and unavoidable in college towns, the result of what happens when a single institution is so large and powerful, and young adults constitute such a disproportionate share of the population. In some college towns, residents and public officials begrudgingly accept college dominance and student unruliness with little objection. In other places, townspeople oppose a college and its students no matter what they do. In Newark, there have been meaningful attempts to communicate and cooperate. Where significant disagreements exist between a town and college, tensions rise and fall, but never really go away. That ebb and flow may be explained by the personalities of the individuals involved, the behavior of a particular group of students, or economic conditions. "Heck, it could be the full moon," said the University of Delaware's Rick Armitage.[90] But that seemingly ceaseless give and take, push and shove, accuse and argue, has been a defining feature of college towns since medieval times and will likely be an integral component of college town life as long as higher education institutions exist as material features on the urban landscape.

THE FUTURE OF THE COLLEGE TOWN

What does the future hold for college towns? Some say that the growth of online education will mean the extinction of the bricks-and-mortar university, which would mean the end of the college town as I've described it. Others believe that college towns are representative of a new kind of geography that is the result of a changing U.S. economy and may become magnets for growth in an information age. College towns have also been discovered as nice places to live by people with no formal connection to a university—from young professionals disenchanted with suburban living to senior citizens seeking alternatives to traditional retirement destinations. The attractions of college towns have become so widely known that a growing number of larger cities have sought to market themselves as college towns or initiate developments that replicate the more distinctive elements of college town life. College towns continue to evolve in response to other changes in higher education and American society. The purpose of this concluding chapter is to contemplate the potential impact of these and other changes on the college town.

There has been no shortage of would-be prophets offering grand pronouncements about the potential impact of technology on higher education. Management consultant Grady Means went so far as to say "a child born in 2003 will probably never see the inside of a university."[1] Such commentators criticize traditional universities as inefficient and say they will be unable to compete against for-profit institutions and online education. They insist that college students in the future will take their classes via the Internet, without leaving home. Perhaps I fear for my survival, but such a prediction seems preposterous. Enrollment at traditional colleges continues to grow. Classrooms are full. Though I've occasionally had students take online courses to overcome scheduling problems or last-minute deficiencies, I've never had a student drop out or decide not to enroll in order to pursue an online degree, nor have I ever heard about a student doing that. Technology has changed how I teach and how my university does business, but most learning still takes place in classrooms located in buildings on a real (not virtual) campus, just as it did one hundred years ago. Students still stroll across campus in front of my office window, still fill the sports arena on Saturday night, still live nearby, and still patronize bars and businesses in the college town where I work. If my university is any indication, online learning has not revolutionized higher education.

Data on the growth of online and distance education would seem to argue against my view, but there's more to the story than the numbers reveal on the surface. Sixty-two percent of U.S. colleges offered distance education courses in 2005, up from 35 percent seven years before. Enrollment in distance education courses in the United States quadrupled from 1995 to 2001. More than 11 percent of students in fall 2002 took online courses. Thirty percent of colleges that taught distance education courses in 2001 offered degree programs that could be completed entirely at a distance. Eighty-eight percent of colleges, furthermore, said they planned to increase their number of online courses. Nevertheless, the percentage of students who take all their courses online is small—just 2.6 percent in 2002.[2] Even more telling for our purposes here are the characteristics of students who enroll in distance education courses. The students most likely to take courses online or at a distance are non-traditional students, who have never attended traditional colleges and universities located in college towns in large numbers.

A U.S. Department of Education study published in 2003 found that older, working adults participate in distance education at higher rates than other students. Married students, especially those with children, single parents, and students who receive no financial support from their parents are also more likely to enroll in distance education courses than others.[3] Such students have historically been more likely to attend community colleges and urban universities that cater to non-traditional students than schools in college towns. Young people without such constraints still prefer to go away to college—to get away from mom and dad, have fun and live relatively free from responsibility for a few years, and experience the non-academic aspects of college life. Many prefer to do that in a college town. Going away to college is a phenomenon that is so deeply ingrained in middle-class American culture that it won't be easily undermined by the advent of online teaching.

While some are predicting the end of the university as we know it and by extension the college town, others envision a very different future. Rich Karlgaard, publisher of *Forbes* magazine, has written and spoken widely about the economic advantages of college towns. "Youth and technology will inherit the world," he says. "College towns are a likely place to find this potent combination." Because many have strong research infrastructures, comparatively cheap real estate, and the cultural amenities necessary to attract creative people, Karlgaard believes they are poised to become the winners in our increasingly knowledge-based economy. "If I were an entrepreneur hoping to run technology and talent together to start a company," he writes, "I'd do it in a college town."[4] Although my research shows there are limits to the potential for high-tech growth in college towns, university communities from Blacksburg, Virginia, to Bozeman, Montana, show that the role of college towns in the U.S. economy is changing. No longer are they merely places where future business leaders are educated before they head out into the "real world." College towns are becoming important sites of innovation and entrepreneurship in their own right.

Karlgaard's proselytizations also demonstrate another important development that is altering college towns. They have been discovered, even by the mainstream. The peculiar charms of college towns have long been known by artists, musicians, slackers, and bookish sorts, but now even the publisher of a magazine that calls itself the "Capitalist Tool" wants to move to one. He's not alone. It used to be that the only people who chose to relocate to a college town were students and professors, but that has changed. Nowhere is this more apparent than in the college town where I went to school. During my years as an undergraduate from 1977 to 1983, Lawrence, Kansas, was a sleepy midwestern college town. Most residents had some connection to the University of Kansas. Accordingly, the town went into hibernation during school breaks and over the summer. The city's downtown was more like other small-city downtowns than Harvard Square or Berkeley's Telegraph Avenue. Although it showed some influence of a collegiate culture, you could easily overlook that. I lived above a maternity store downtown my last years in Lawrence and could find an open parking space in front of my building any time, day or night. I remember strolling through downtown on Saturday nights with my girlfriend. We were often the only people on the street. Lawrence was anything but hip.

Lawrence when I went to school had 50,000 residents, including students. KU had an enrollment of about 25,000. Downtown was still where most people shopped for anything but groceries, gas, and other staples. The city was compact. I could walk or bike anywhere I needed to go. Lawrence's geography in those days was defined by a rectangle of four streets, the main commercial thoroughfares in town, which measured just over a mile from east to west. For an undergraduate, there wasn't much reason to venture beyond that rectangle. The KU campus sat in the middle. A five-minute drive in any direction would have taken you into the countryside. Sixth Street, home to run-down motels and tepee-shaped restaurants, defined the northern edge of the rectangle. Massachusetts Street, the heart of downtown, marked the eastern side. Twenty-third Street, fast food row, defined the south. Iowa Street, along which the first suburban shopping centers were built, represented what was then the western edge of the city. There were a few newish residential areas beyond Iowa Street, but not much else.

In the quarter century since I graduated, however, Lawrence has transmogrified. Massachusetts Street bustles day and night (fig. 10.1). The city has expanded in every direction. The population has grown by more than 30,000 since 1980, even though enrollment at the university remains about the same. Going back to Lawrence expecting to rekindle memories of youth is like returning home only to discover your parents have moved and your house has been demolished. Contemporary Lawrence is shocking and almost unrecognizable. The single most important factor that is stimulating change has been the migration to the city of people with no connection to the university other than an affinity for the way of life it inspires. They prefer the college town lifestyle to big-city problems or the monotony of suburban living, even if they have to commute somewhere else for work. Many of the newcomers are commuters, traveling daily to Kansas City or Topeka, the state capital. One-quarter of Lawrence workers in 2000 commuted to jobs outside the city.[5] The influx of commuters has stimulated massive homebuilding west of Iowa Street. The developed portion of Lawrence occupies twice as much land as it did when I went to school.

Lawrence has changed so dramatically that the *New York Times* in 2005 chose to focus on the city for its weekly "36 Hours" travel feature.[6] The *Times* called Massachusetts Street "the strip of hip." Downtown has been transformed from an all-purpose shopping area with a locally owned department store, hardware stores, and barber shops to a happening entertainment and specialty shopping district full of coffee houses, gourmet restaurants, martini bars, and pricey boutiques.[7] In my day, a breakfast of waffles and eggs at Drake's Bakery was the pinnacle of downtown dining, but restaurants today offer French toast made from challah soaked in brandy-nutmeg batter and prosciutto omelets with leeks and Gorgonzola. The changes to Lawrence are most conspicuous downtown, but are evident all over. Although Massachusetts Street is still the symbolic heart of the city, most shopping is now done elsewhere. My friend Steve Wilson, a Lawrence native who runs a downtown record store, says that the city's true central business district is now centered on 31st and Iowa streets, an area one writer calls "consumption junction," which is located well outside the defining rectangle of my

FIGURE 10.1.
Young people gather on Massachusetts Street in downtown Lawrence, Kansas, which the New York Times *has called "the strip of hip." Photograph by Bob Travaglione, www.FoToEdge .com, 2007; used with permission.*

college years,[8] It includes a Wal-Mart Supercenter, Home Depot, Best Buy, Old Navy, and a twelve-screen movie complex. The westward shift of shopping reflects the direction of population growth, most of which has occurred west of Iowa Street. Lawrence now sprawls four miles beyond Iowa Street, which was essentially the western edge of town when I was a student. Out west are a new high school, a corporate research park, a few small shopping centers, countless medical offices, a softball complex, and endless nondescript subdivisions with names like Stonegate Park and Quail Run. As such changes suggest, Lawrence has become more like everywhere else.

What is happening in Lawrence is occurring in other college towns. It is happening in Athens, Ann Arbor, and Boulder. It is happening in Chapel Hill, Missoula, and Davis. Although average enrollment at colleges in my sixty study towns rose only 3 percent from 1980 to 2000, the average population of those towns increased 25 percent. Some of that difference is because the size of the non-teaching staff at elite universities is growing faster than the teaching faculty because of rising research spending. Some of that has to do with high-tech business development in college towns. Some population growth is also the result of students who stay in the towns where they went to school after they graduate. But the dramatic expansion of certain college towns is most directly the result of their discovery as attractive places to live. The population of Athens, for example, has increased four times as fast as enrollment at the University of Georgia since 1980. Ann Arbor has added 75,000 residents during the same period, even though the University of Michigan has grown by only 4,000 students. Davis has grown three times as fast as the University of California campus there. Not all college towns are experiencing rapid growth. This phenomenon is most common in college towns that possess major research universities, especially those within commuting distances of bigger cities.

James Shortridge and Barbara Shortridge, writing about Lawrence, have observed that the movement of lifestyle migrants to college towns threatens to erode the characteristics that made such communities attractive in the first place. The fastest-growing college towns are acquiring some of the negative attributes they long resisted, such as traffic, sprawl, high housing prices, and chain-store culture (fig. 10.2). Will such college towns become merely the enlightened exurbs of the information age, David Brooks's quintessential "latte towns," where hip and well read is a marketing niche, and the buying of organic produce and carbon credits merely the expected choices of the affluent progressive? Perhaps, but as the Shortridges have also noted, migrants to college towns are a self-selected group, drawn to them because "they match the existing image" and "want to be part of it." It could be argued that newcomers to places like Lawrence only help to intensify those characteristics for which college towns are known.[9] If my views were untainted by nostalgia, I might love what Lawrence has become since it has so much of what I desire—weird movies, adventurous bookstores, contrary people. Most college towns, it is worth noting, are too remote and obscure to experience significant non-university-related growth.

A third dimension to the changing demographics of college towns is their emergence as retirement destinations.[10] College towns are being promoted as alternative retirement locations for baby boomers and others who desire an active and intellectually stimulating retirement and for whom the sun, sand, and sedentary lifestyles of Florida and Arizona hold little appeal. College towns are attractive to seniors because they are comparatively inexpensive and safe, and offer abundant cultural and recreational opportuni-

FIGURE 10.2.
*College towns like
Charlottesville,
Virginia,
have begun to
acquire some
of the negative
characteristics
they long resisted,
including chains
like Starbucks.
Photograph by the
author, 2002.*

ties. Many major universities have medical schools and teaching hospitals, so provide the high-quality health care that seniors prize. The youthful vigor of college towns is also appealing. "When you get out of the bus and there are all these kids walking around," said one senior who retired to State College, Pennsylvania, "it just makes you feel so alive." College towns are especially popular with alumni seeking to revive memories of their college years. They are also appealing to college faculty and staff, who do not always choose to stay in the college towns where they worked, sometimes retiring to college towns halfway across the country where they always wished they could live.[11] Colleges have encouraged the migration of retirees to college towns by creating continuing education programs for seniors, allowing elderly to audit classes and use campus facilities, and even building retirement housing or partnering with private developers to do so.

The influx of retirees to college towns can be easy to overlook because senior citizens are so outnumbered by young people and are less conspicuous, but data substantiate the growth of the elderly population. The number of residents 65 years and older in my sixty study towns grew 15 percent from 1990 to 2000, 25 percent faster than in the country as a whole. Some of this growth reflects the aging of the professoriate and retirement of faculty, but many of the elderly residents are newcomers or have returned to the college towns where they went to school. The elderly population has grown fastest in college towns that are home to major universities or elite liberal arts colleges. It grew 84 percent from 1990 to 2000 in Auburn, Alabama; 76 percent in Athens, Georgia; and 66 percent in College Station, Texas. Although the fastest growth has been in Sun Belt college towns, growth is not limited to warm-weather locales. The 65-plus population grew 60 percent in chilly Hanover, New Hampshire.[12] The trend has mostly missed lesser-known college towns, though that may change if seniors discover that living costs are lower in more out-of-the-way college communities.

One builder of retirement developments, the Pennsylvania-based Kendal Corp., specializes in developing retirement communities in college towns. Kendal built its first retirement community in a college town in Hanover in 1998. Since then, it has built four more—in Oberlin, Ohio; Ithaca, New York; Lexington, Virginia; and Granville, Ohio.[13] Kendal has developed close relationships with the schools in the towns where it has planted communities. Oberlin College acquired the land on which Kendal's community there was built and helped recruit residents from its alumni. About half of the original residents were Oberlin alumni or former employees. Dale Corson, a former president of Cornell University, helped found Kendal at Ithaca. Retired Cornell faculty and staff make up a sizable portion of residents. The joke around Ithaca is that Kendal, full of retired Cornell scientists, has the best physics department in the country. Big-name developers have also built retirement communities in college towns. Marriott Corp. built one near the University of Virginia in Charlottesville. Hyatt Corp. developed a retirement community in Palo Alto, California, on land leased from Stanford University.[14]

A growing number of colleges are helping to develop retirement communities. Thirty college-affiliated retirement communities already exist, and two dozen more are planned. The nature of the relationship between colleges and retirement communities varies. In a few cases, colleges own the developments. In others, the only link is that a college owns the land on which the community was built. The University of Michigan, for example, developed the University Commons retirement community with a private developer on university-owned land (fig. 10.3). Residence was originally limited to U-M alumni, faculty, and staff (now it is open to alumni and retired staff of other colleges). U-M provides residents with high-speed Internet access and U-M e-mail addresses. Music students regularly play recitals there. A former Pennsylvania State University president first proposed the idea of creating a retirement community near the university's campus in

FIGURE 10.3. *The University of Michigan developed the University Commons retirement community with a private developer on university-owned land. It is one of a growing number of retirement communities developed in college towns, many with cooperation of a college or university. Photograph by the author, 2001.*

State College. The Village at Penn State was built on eighty acres leased from the university, and the developers included Penn State football coach Joe Paterno and a former university administrator. Residents can take one class on campus each semester for free. They get priority access to tickets for Penn State sports and cultural events. They can use the university swimming pool and tennis courts.[15]

The incentives to colleges to help develop retirement communities are numerous. Retirement developments can generate revenue in an era of declining government support for higher education. Seniors provide a new pool of potential students and patients for university hospitals. Alumni and faculty close at hand may be more likely to donate money or think of a college in their wills. Retirees provide an available group of volunteers for campus activities and can serve as research subjects. Retirement communities also provide work and internship opportunities for students. Not all college-affiliated retirement communities have been successful, however. Indiana University in Bloomington, for example, developed a retirement community in 1980, but sold it when it experienced cost overruns and construction delays. Moody's Investors Service, in fact, warned in a 2006 report that retirement communities present significant financial and other risks for universities.[16]

The discovery of college towns is also having impacts beyond their borders. Recognizing the appeal of college towns, larger cities with colleges or universities have sought to promote themselves as college towns. A New York City organization composed of business and civic leaders called the Association for a Better New York, which created the city's famous "I Love NY" marketing campaign, in 1999 embarked on a campaign to promote New York as a college town and published a thirty-two-page booklet, *New York: It's a Great College Town*, that was distributed as a supplement to the *New York Times*. A private company that helps market colleges to prospective students has launched a website promoting Boston as "America's College Town." Organizations in Baltimore; Newark, New Jersey; and Spartanburg, South Carolina, have initiated similar campaigns.[17]

Some cities and universities have gone even further, instigating building projects intended to emulate the defining features of college towns. Rochester Institute of Technology in New York is developing a campus-adjacent commercial and residential area to enable students to live closer to the school and provide more activities near its campus. RIT's "college town" project will mimic a traditional pedestrian-oriented downtown, with gridded streets, dense retail, and varied architecture. The University of British Columbia in Vancouver has embarked on an ambitious "University Town" project to enliven the area surrounding its suburban campus. It calls for the development of eight neighborhoods, each compact, walkable, and containing a mix of housing, retail, and open space.[18] The University of Kentucky and the city of Lexington, where it is located, are jointly planning a "college town concept" to be developed between the university's campus and the city's downtown. Proposals have called for development of a retail corridor, the building of condos and other residences, and enhancing the streetscape to make the area more attractive as a public space. Observing that traditional college towns like Ann Arbor and Chapel Hill "just feel different," UK president Lee Todd said, "It is critical for us to create that here." Such efforts seem naïve and are more about marketing than planning. They are designed to make areas around urban campuses livelier so that urban universities can compete for students who otherwise might go to college in a college town. But they ignore the fundamental differences between college towns and other places. College towns like Ann Arbor and Chapel Hill emerged organically over long periods of time in response to a multitude of forces, most of which are not present in the same form in larger urban areas. A college town cannot be manufactured, created in an instant from an architect's plans or a developer's specifications. True college towns are living organisms that are born with a college, grow with it, and evolve in ways no college or government body can control.

Throughout this book, I have sought to identify, describe, and explain those characteristics that make college towns distinctive. In contemplating the future of college towns, then, let's revisit those themes and reflect on whether there is any reason to believe that they may change in important ways. Certain characteristics seem unlikely to change. College towns will remain youthful places (fig. 10.4), though the increasing propensity of undergraduates to stay in school longer and the influx of retirees may alter the age structure slightly. College towns will continue to be among the most highly educated places on earth, and the growth in some of a high-tech economy will only intensify that attribute. So long as the principal business of college towns is education and new industry in them tends to be knowledge-based, college towns will remain largely white-collar places. Since attending college is a temporary process, college towns will continue to be unusually transient and contain high proportions of renters. College students living away from their parents will always experiment and test life's boundaries, so college towns will remain bohemian islands where new expressions flourish and eccentrics feel at home. Although there have been countless calls to reform college athletics, they have had little impact and the public's appetite for college sports only seems to grow. The influence of big-time

FIGURE 10.4.
A couch in the snow in front of a fraternity house in the college town of Geneseo, New York. Photograph by the author, 2002.

sports, therefore, will remain perhaps the single feature that most distinguishes U.S. college towns from university cities elsewhere.

Other features of college town life may change somewhat, though it is unlikely that any of these changes will fundamentally alter the nature of such places. As college towns continue to be discovered by lifestyle migrants and high-tech development occurs in some of them, living costs will increase. Housing prices in college towns like Lawrence, Ann Arbor, and Davis have risen substantially, which has the potential to reduce their attractiveness and make them less socially diverse. High-tech development in college towns seems certain to increase and will probably spread to a greater number of college towns, particularly as spending on academic research escalates. The growth of high-tech industries could make college towns less economically stable, since private businesses are more susceptible than colleges to economic fluctuations and the inherent uncertainty of business, as the recent decision by Pfizer to close its mammoth Ann Arbor research laboratories shows.

Heightened restrictions on international students and immigration by foreign-born faculty implemented following the September 2001 attacks on the United States could make college towns less cosmopolitan, though such restrictions may be dismantled when Democrats regain control of the White House. Two terms of George W. Bush as president and the nation-wide swing to the right have had strong political reverberations in college towns, helping to radicalize residents and increase the political differences between college towns and the rest of the country. Nowhere has the opposition to Bush and the Iraq war been stronger and more outspoken than in college towns. But such changes tend to be cyclical and will shift as power fluctuates. Tension between higher education institutions and the towns that surround them may be the most enduring feature of college town life, but recent efforts by American universities to increase their control over student behavior and reinstitute in loco parentis policies could quiet conflicts, unless the chains on students become too tight and they rebel, as they have before.

The role of college campuses as public spaces in college towns will likely intensify as higher education institutions continue to build concert halls, museums, arenas, and other non-academic facilities in an effort to compete for students and money. The student presence on campuses may diminish because cell phones, e-mail, and the World Wide Web make it easier for students to communicate and do research from home, and less necessary to go to campus for anything but classes. Campus-adjacent commercial areas, like older shopping areas everywhere, will continue to evolve. Bars will become less central to student life, replaced by coffee houses and restaurants. Bookstores, whose prevalence has long been a characteristic feature of college towns, will shrink in number because of the growth of online booksellers. Downloading of music may lead to the disappearance of record stores. To remain vital, college-oriented shopping areas will have to become entertainment and specialized shopping districts, develop market niches for products and services less suitable for online sales, and continue to adapt to the changing tastes of young people. Fewer undergraduates desire to live in college-owned housing, which will lead to expansion of off-campus student housing areas and stimulate the building of high-priced housing geared to student tastes, with high-speed Internet access, fitness centers, and other modern amenities. Heightened student demand for housing could lead to further erosion of single-family neighborhoods, particularly if homeowners and city officials are not vigilant about preserving such areas. Student membership in Greek-letter societies is declining, which could lead to a contraction in the size of fraternity districts and significantly alter social lives for a portion of undergraduates, though fraternity membership has declined before only to rebound, so it is uncertain if that trend will be permanent.

College towns have changed. Many of the adjectives once commonly used to describe them—words like sleepy, idyllic, and unhurried—are no longer accurate. College towns continue to evolve in response to modifications in higher education, youth culture, and American society, but most do so slowly. The transformations that are occurring in a small number of college towns like Lawrence are atypical. College towns changed more dramatically earlier in history than they do today because American society and education changed more rapidly. Higher education, the single biggest influence on college town life, seems to have reached a steady state, and so the college town, too, has settled into a period of relative equilibrium. As a result, the convulsive changes that occurred on campuses and in college towns as recently as the 1960s no longer seem possible. College towns will continue to change incrementally, but the characteristics that make them unusual and compelling are likely to persist. Time, tradition, geography, and culture seem to have cemented in place their most fundamental features. By and large, the American college town will remain a place apart, a unique type of urban community that has been a critical but under-recognized part of American life.

NOTES

Preface

1. This view is echoed in Michael Moffatt, *Coming of Age in New Jersey: College and American Culture* (New Brunswick: Rutgers University Press), the most accurate and penetrating scholarly depiction of undergraduate student life in America I have found.

2. William Least Heat Moon, *Blue Highways: A Journey into America* (Boston: Little, Brown, 1982); Jane and Michael Stern, *Road Food* (New York: Random House, 1978).

3. See, for example, John S. Garner, *The Company Town: Architecture and Society in the Early Industrial Age* (New York: Oxford University Press, 1992); Gary Kulik, Roget N. Parks, and Theodore Z. Penn, *New England Mill Village, 1790–1860* (Cambridge: MIT Press, 1982); Robert R. Dykstra, *The Cattle Towns* (New York: Knopf, 1968); and Norman L. Crockett, *The Black Towns* (Lawrence: University Press of Kansas, 1979).

4. See, for example, Hildegarde Hawthorne, *Rambles in Old College Towns* (New York: Dodd, Mead, 1917); Roland M. Harper, "Some Demographic Characteristics of American Educational Centers," *Scientific Monthly* 30:2 (February 1930): 164–69; Charles Morrow Wilson, "Anatomy of a College Town," *North American Review* 237 (1934): 506–13; David Cort, "In Search of Athens, U.S.A.," *The Nation*, January 23, 1960, 72–76; Delbert Miller, "Town and Gown: The Power Structure of a University Town," *American Journal of Sociology* 68:4 (January 1963): 432–43; John Miller, "Living in a Small College Town," *Mother Earth News*, September 1971, 62–65; John A. Jakle and Richard L. Mattson, "The Evolution of a Commercial Strip," *Journal of Cultural Geography* 1:2 (Spring/Summer 1981): 12–25; John A. Jakle, "Twentieth Century Revival Architecture and the Gentry," *Journal of Cultural Geography* 4:1 (Fall/Winter 1983): 28–43; Matt Kane, *Issues and Opportunities for University Communities* (Washington: National League of Cities, 1989).

5. Edmund W. Gilbert, *The University Town in England and West Germany*, University of Chicago Department of Geography Research Paper No. 71 (Chicago: University of Chicago Press, 1961); Henry Seidel Canby, *Alma Mater: The Gothic Age of the American College* (New York: Farrar & Rinehart, 1936), 3; Wilbur Zelinsky, *The Cultural Geography of the United States* (Englewood Cliffs, N.J.: Prentice Hall, 1973), 136.

6. William Carlos Williams, *Imaginations* (New York: New Directions, 1970), 358.

7. U.S. Bureau of the Census, 2005 Population Estimates, http://factfinder.census.gov (accessed February 28, 2007).

8. I chose not to include any towns that are the site of women's colleges because many have gone co-ed, most that remain female-only are located in big cities, and nearly all are small, and so exert a limited influence on the places where they are located. I did not consider towns that are the sites of two-year colleges because the latter are distinct from four-year institutions and their impact on local communities is much smaller.

1. Defining the College Town

1. I am indebted to Molly Ivins for this analogy. She wrote about "the university universe" in

the *New York Times Magazine*, November 10, 1974, 36–47, 51–58.

2. In 2000, 411 cities and towns in the United States met the 20 percent threshold. Analysis was based on comparison of college enrollment in 2000 for all four-year colleges with enrollments of at least 1,000 and 2000 population for the cities in which they were located. Population data are taken from U.S. Bureau of the Census, *Census 2000*, http://factfinder.census.gov (accessed May 31, 2006). Enrollment data is drawn from institutional sources and U.S. Bureau of Education, National Center for Educational Statistics, *Integrated Postsecondary Education Data System*, http://nces.ed.gov/ipeds/ (accessed May 31, 2006). I did not use Census data on college student population because they include students at two-year colleges, do not include students who go to school in a place but reside elsewhere, and do include students who reside in a place but attend school somewhere else. Enrollment data provide a more accurate representation of the number of students who attend college in a particular city or town.

3. Brian J. L. Berry, *City Classification Handbook: Methods and Applications* (New York: Wiley-Interscience, 1971), 41; Edmund W. Gilbert, *The University Town in England and West Germany*, University of Chicago Department of Geography Research Paper No. 71 (Chicago: University of Chicago Press, 1961), 6.

4. Except as noted, data in the rest of this section are drawn from U.S. Bureau of the Census, *Census 2000*.

5. American Library Association, *American Library Directory 2005–06* (New York: Bowker, 2005); U.S. Bureau of the Census, *2002 Economic Census*, http://www.census.gov/econ/census02/ (accessed June 2, 2006).

6. Southern Illinois University, "Staffing Breakdown by Campus and EEO6 Categories,"

http://www.irs.siu.edu/webRoot/factsonline/Staff/hcount_cam_brkdwn.pdf (accessed June 2, 2006).

7. Comparison is to U.S. Bureau of the Census–defined "urban clusters" with populations from 25,000 to 49,999.

8. U.S. Bureau of Labor Statistics, "Unemployment Rates for Metropolitan Areas," April 2002, http://www.bls.gov/web/laummtrk.htm (accessed June 3, 2002); Ford Fessenden, "College Towns Escape the Pain," *New York Times*, November 4, 2007; *Sperling's Best Places*, http://www.bestplaces.net (accessed June 2, 2006). Data for twelve-month job growth were reported in October 2005.

9. Robin Wagner, "The Plight of the Trailing Partner," *Chronicle of Higher Education*, August 3, 2001; Donna Martin, "The Wives of Academe," *Change*, Winter 1972–73, 67–69.

10. *Sperling's Best Places*; Coldwell Banker, "Coldwell Banker College Market Home Price Comparison Index Evaluates Cost Variances in 59 U.S. College Towns," http://hpci.coldwellbanker.com/hpci_press.aspx (accessed April 25, 2006).

11. University of Illinois, University Office for Planning and Budgeting, Student Databook, Fall Term 2004, http://www.pb.uillinois.edu/dr/databook.asp (accessed June 5, 2006); Will Counts, James H. Madison, and Scott Russell Sanders, *Bloomington: Past & Present* (Bloomington: Indiana University Press, 2002), 7.

12. Austin, Boulder, Cambridge, Iowa City, Ithaca, and Madison are also known as "[Insert number] square miles surrounded by reality."

13. The Boulder slogan was actually imported from Austin by the owner of Boulder Bookstore, but its use has since spread widely. Befitting the age, there is now a "Keep Boulder Weird" website (http://www.keepboulderweird.org/), with photos of naked pumpkin runs, marijuana smoking protests, and

prairie dog statues, and information about famous local pranks, eccentric individuals, and wacko organizations.

14. Religious data by county and metropolitan area obtained from http://ext.nazarene .org/rcms/ (accessed April 14, 2006). Data were derived from Dale E. Jones and others, *Religious Congregations and Membership in the United States 2000: An Enumeration by Region, State, and County Based on Data Reported by 149 Religious Bodies* (Nashville: Glenmary Research Center, 2002).

15. Alice Evans, "Our Share of Churches: Religion and Values in Eugene, 1945–2000," in *Eugene 1945–2000: Decisions That Made a Community*, ed. Kathleen Holt and Cheri Brooks (Eugene, Ore.: City Club of Eugene, 2000), 255.

16. Radio ratings data are from Eastlan Resources, an Oregon-based ratings research company that produces ratings for radio stations in several college towns; Radio Research Consortium, http://www.rrconline .org/arbitron/ (accessed April 13, 2006), which provides Arbitron ratings data to non-commercial radio stations; and Radio Online, http://ratings.radio-online.com/ ARBFC.HTM (accessed June 5, 2006).

17. *Dave Leip's Atlas of U.S. Presidential Elections*, http://www.uselectionatlas.org (accessed June 5, 2006); The Co-Op Network, *National Co-op Directory, 2005: A Guide to the Cooperative Natural Food System* (Bethel, Vt., 2005).

18. See, for example, Bert Spelling and Peter Sander, *Cities Ranked & Rated: More Than 400 Metropolitan Areas Evaluated in the U.S. and Canada* (Hoboken, N.J.: Wiley, 2004); Richard L. Fox, *America's Best Places to Retire* (Houston: Vacation Publications, 1995); Kurt Badenhausen, "Best Places for Business and Careers," http://www.forbes .com/lists/2005/5/Rank_1.shtml (accessed July 26, 2006).

19. Bill King, "Here's How to Evaluate the Public Schools in a Metro Area," *Expansion Management*, April 2006, 15; Bill King, "How Well Are We Educating Our Future Workers?" *Expansion Management*, December 2005, 4–13; Federal Bureau of Investigation, *Crime in the United States, 2004*, http://www .fbi.gov/ucr/cius_04/ (accessed June 5, 2006); Spelling and Sander, *Cities Ranked & Rated*, 97.

20. Observations about the relative absence of college-dominated cities outside the United States are based on comparisons of college enrollments and city populations in eighteen countries. Enrollment data compiled from Association of Universities and Colleges of Canada, "Full-Time and Part-Time Fall Enrolment at AUCC Member Institutions by Level, 2001," www.aucc.ca/en/research/ enr_inst.htm (accessed May 28, 2002); International Association of Universities, *International Handbook of Universities*, 15th ed. (New York: Grove's Dictionaries, 1998); and *World of Learning* (London: Europa Publications, 2001). Population data compiled from Statistics Canada, *2001 Community Profiles*, http://www12.statcan.ca/english/profil01/ (accessed June 8, 2006); and the *World Gazetteer* website, www.world-gazetteer.com (accessed June 5, 2002).

21. Gilbert, *University Town in England and West Germany*; Oxford City Council, *A Preliminary Case for Unitary Status*, http://www.oxford .gov.uk/files/seealsodocs/35445/OCCUnitary -seb.pdf (accessed June 8, 2006); Nomis, "Labour Market Profile: Oxford," http:// www.nomisweb.co.uk (accessed June 8, 2006); United Kingdom, Office of National Statistics, 2001 Census, Oxfordshire Profile, http://www.statistics.gov.uk/census2001/ profiles/38.asp (accessed August 4, 2007).

22. Henry Srebrnik, "Football, Frats, and Fun vs. Commuters, Cold, and Carping: The Social and Psychological Context of Higher Education in Canada," in *Canada and the United*

States: Differences That Count, ed. David Thomas (Peterborough, Ontario: Broadview Press, 1993), 396.

23. Charles Homer Haskins, *The Rise of Universities* (New York: Henry Holt, 1923), 6–7, 12, 20–22; Walter Rüegg, "Themes," in *A History of the University in Europe*, vol. 1: *Universities in the Middle Ages*, ed. Hilde de Ridder-Symoens (Cambridge: Cambridge University Press, 1992), 11–13, 18–19; Jacques Verger, "Patterns," in *A History of the University in Europe*, vol. 1, 51–58, 96–97; Rainer Christoph Schwinges, "Student Education, Student Life," in *A History of the University in Europe*, vol. 1, 204, 207; Laurence Brockliss, "Gown and Town: The University and the City in Europe, 1200–2000," *Minerva* 38 (2000): 151; Donald G. Tewksbury, *The Founding of American Colleges and Universities before the Civil War* (New York: Teachers College, Columbia University, 1932), 16–17, 78; Colin B. Burke, *American Collegiate Populations: A Test of the Traditional View* (New York: New York University Press, 1982), 38, 97, 111–12, 192.

24. Tewksbury, *Founding of American Colleges*, 3–4; Burke, *American Collegiate Populations*, 25, 55, 66–76; Frederick Rudolph, *The American College & University: A History* (1962; repr., Athens: University of Georgia Press, 1990), 185.

25. Tewksbury, *Founding of American Colleges*, 22; Samuel Eliot Morison, *The Founding of Harvard College* (Cambridge: Harvard University Press, 1935), 181–92; Samuel Eliot Morison, *Three Centuries of Harvard, 1636–1936* (Cambridge: Harvard University Press, 1936), 6; Paul Venable Turner, *Campus: An American Planning Tradition* (Cambridge: MIT Press, 1984), 23; S. B. Sutton, *Cambridge Reconsidered: 3 1/2 Centuries on the Charles* (Cambridge: MIT Press, 1976), 6.

26. Rudolph, *American College & University*, 8; Alexander Leitch, *A Princeton Companion* (Princeton: Princeton University Press, 1978), 75; Tewksbury, *Founding of American Colleges*, 14.

27. Tewksbury, *Founding of American Colleges*, 15, 93, 112, 121, 129–30; William D. Snider, *Light on the Hill: A History of the University of North Carolina at Chapel Hill* (Chapel Hill: University of North Carolina Press, 1992), 11; Theodore Francis Jones, ed., *New York University: 1832–1932* (New York: New York University Press, 1933), 13; Charles Francis Adams, *Three Phi Beta Kappa Addresses* (Boston: Houghton Mifflin, 1907), 112.

28. Daniel J. Boorstin, *The Americans: The National Experience* (New York: Random House, 1965), 152–61; Turner, *Campus*, 38; Leitch, *A Princeton Companion*, 75.

29. David B. Potts, "American Colleges in the Nineteenth Century: From Localism to Denominationalism," *History of Education Quarterly* 11:4 (Winter 1971): 367. See also David B. Potts, "'College Enthusiasm!' As Public Response, 1800–1860," *Harvard Educational Review* 47:1 (February 1977): 28–42.

30. Stanley D. Brunn, *Geography and Politics in America* (New York: Harper & Row, 1974), 113; Boorstin, *The Americans*, 159; Henry C. Dethloff, *A Centennial History of Texas A&M University, 1876–1976* (College Station: Texas A&M University Press, 1979), 16–19; Deborah Lynn Balliew, *College Station, Texas, 1938/1988* (College Station: Intaglio Press, 1987), 11; Mary Clare Fabishak, "'Single Industry' Boom Town: The Rise and Decline of a Dependency Relationship—College Station, Texas" (diss., Boston University, 1986), 101–2; Clifford S. Griffin, *The University of Kansas: A History* (Lawrence: University Press of Kansas, 1974), 25; Raymond Bial, *Champaign: A Pictorial History* (St. Louis: G. Bradley, 1993), 45; Roger L. Geiger, "The Era of Multipurpose Colleges in American Higher Education, 1850 to 1890," *History of Higher Education Annual* 15 (1995): 59.

31. Harry Christopher Humphreys, *Factors Operating in the Location of State Normal Schools* (New York: Teachers College, Columbia University, 1923), 6–14, 22–25, 32–34, 84, 97–98, 115, 118–43.

32. Michael Bezilla, *Penn State: An Illustrated History* (University Park: Pennsylvania State University Press, 1985), 5, 154, 176; Peirce Lewis, "College Town USA," paper presented the annual meeting of the Association of American Geographers, Miami, 1991.

33. Except as noted, data in the rest of this section are drawn from U.S. Bureau of the Census, *Census 2000*.

34. Carll Everett Ladd, Jr., and Seymour Martin Lipset, *The Divided Academy: Professors and Politics* (New York: McGraw-Hill, 1975), 60; Richard F. Hamilton and Lowell L. Hargens, "The Politics of the Professors: Self-Identifications, 1969–1984," *Social Forces* 71:3 (1993): 603–27; Stanley Rothman, S. Robert Lichter, and Neil Nevitte, "Politics and Professional Advancement among College Faculty," *Forum* 3:1 (2005), http://www.bepress.com/forum/vol3/iss1/art2/ (accessed March 14, 2007); *Dave Leip's Atlas of U.S. Presidential Elections*.

35. The gay population can be estimated using a formula that includes data on the number of same-sex couples (available in the decennial U.S. Census of Population and Housing), scholarly estimates on the percentage of homosexuals who are in coupled relationships at any time (I used 23.5 percent for gays and 42.7 percent for lesbians), and theories about the percentage of homosexuals typically undercounted by surveys because of the reluctance of some gays to reveal any information that could disclose their sexual orientation (I assumed a 25 percent undercount). For discussion of these methodological questions and a detailed examination of the geography of U.S. gays and lesbians, see Gary J. Gates and Jason Ost, *The Gay &*
Lesbian Atlas (Washington: Urban Institute Press, 2004).

36. Religious data from http://ext.nazarene.org/rcms/. Data were derived from Jones, *Religious Congregations and Membership in the United States 2000*.

37. Circulation figures for the Sunday edition of the *New York Times* substantiate this claim. Ten of the twenty-five metropolitan areas in the United States outside New York, New Jersey, and Connecticut where market penetration of the Sunday edition of the *Times* was greatest in 2000 were small cities with flagship state universities. Audit Bureau of Circulations, *Audit Report: The New York Times* (Schaumburg, Ill.: Audit Bureau of Circulations, 2000).

38. *Sperling's Best Places*.

39. Edward Danforth Eddy, Jr., *Colleges for Our Land and Time: The Land-Grant Idea in American Education* (New York: Harper, 1957); Kansas State University, Office of Planning and Analysis, "Comparison of All Undergraduate Students by County from Fall 1996 to Fall 2001" (Manhattan: KSU, 2002); University of Kansas, Office of Institutional Research and Planning, *University of Kansas Profiles, 2002*, http://www.ku.edu/~oirp/profiles.shtml (accessed June 11, 2002).

40. Kansas State University, Office of Planning and Analysis, *2002 Fact Book*, http://www.k-state.edu/pa/statinfo/factbook/ (accessed June 11, 2002); KU, *University of Kansas Profiles, 2002*; University of Kansas, College of Liberal Arts and Sciences, *A Year in Review 2000–2001* (Lawrence: University of Kansas College of Liberal Arts and Sciences, 2001); *Dave Leip's Atlas of U.S. Presidential Elections*; Stewart Frescas (resident, Lafayette, Indiana, and laboratory technician, Purdue University), e-mail to the author, June 4, 2006.

41. E. Alden Dunham, *Colleges of the Forgotten Americans: A Profile of State Colleges and Re-*

gional Universities (New York: McGraw-Hill, 1969).

42. An average of 14 percent of students at regional state universities located in study towns graduated in the top 10 percent of their high school class, compared to 39 percent for flagship universities, 40 percent for land-grant institutions, and 68 percent for private liberal arts colleges. Bondan Romaniuk and Verne Thompson, eds., *College Blue Book*, Narrative Descriptions, 33rd ed. (Farmington Hills, Mich.: Thomson Gale, 2006).

43. Leslie Anders, *Education for Service: Centennial History of Central Missouri State College* (Warrensburg, Mo.: 1971); Central Missouri State University, Office of Institutional Research, *Central Fact Book 2001*, http://www.cmsu.edu/rsearch/ (accessed June 12, 2002); *Dave Leip's Atlas of U.S. Presidential Elections*.

44. Romaniuk and Thompson, *College Blue Book*; *Sperling's Best Places*; U.S. Bureau of Labor Statistics, Local Area Unemployment Statistics, http://data.bls.gov/PDQ/outside.jsp?survey=la (accessed June 21, 2006); U.S. Bureau of the Census, *2002 Economic Census*; ALA, *American Library Directory, 2005–06*; Williams College, Institutional Research Office, "Common Data Set, 2002–03," http://www.williams.edu/admin/provost/ir/2002–03cds.pdf (accessed June 15, 2002).

45. Brigham Young University, Honor Code Office, "Abstain from Alcoholic Beverages, Tobacco, Tea, Coffee, and Substance Abuse" and "Dress and Grooming Standards," http://honorcode.byu.edu (accessed June 21, 2006). For a history of BYU's student behavior standards and honor code, see Gary James Bergera and Ronald Priddis, *Brigham Young University: A House of Faith* (Salt Lake City, Utah: Signature Books, 1985), 93–130. The book is a probing and frank examina-

tion of the school's unusual history and exceptional nature.

46. Religious data from http://ext.nazarene.org/rcms/. Derived from Jones, *Religious Congregations and Membership in the United States 2000*.

47. U.S. Bureau of the Census, *2002 Economic Census*; *Dave Leip's Atlas of U.S. Presidential Elections*;.

48. *Economic Diversity of Colleges*, http://economicdiversity.org (accessed June 21, 2006); U.S. Bureau of the Census, *2002 Economic Census*; Robert J. Norrell, *Reaping the Whirlwind: The Civil Rights Movement in Tuskegee* (Chapel Hill: University of North Carolina Press, 1998), 213; V. S. Naipaul, "Reflections: How the Land Lay," *New Yorker*, June 6, 1988, 100. Naipaul's essay formed one chapter in his 1989 book, *A Turn in the South*.

49. Regional comparisons are based on regional definitions used by the U.S. Bureau of the Census in decennial Census of Population and Housing reports.

50. Just 21 percent of UNH faculty and staff lived in Durham in 2006. University of New Hampshire, Office of Institutional Research, "Geographic Distribution, UNH Faculty and Staff by Permanent Address," unpublished table, January 26, 2006. Just 7.7 percent of students and 34.7 percent of employees at the University of Rhode Island in 2005 lived in South Kingston, the town where URI is located. University of Rhode Island, Office of Institutional Research, "Statewide Distribution of URI Alumni, Faculty and Staff, and Students Who Are R.I. Residents (Fall 2005)," http://autocrat.uri.edu/fileadmin/ir/infobank/Distributionstudents/2005_URI_Map.pdf (accessed July 4, 2006).

51. Town of Durham, New Hampshire, *Master Plan*, 2000, 10.2, http://www.ci.durham.nh.us/DEPARTMENTS/planning/masterplan.html (accessed July 3, 2006); Everett

B. Sackett, *New Hampshire's University: The Story of a New England Land Grant College* (Somersworth: New Hampshire Publishing Co., 1974), 124; Stephen Hornsby (associate professor of geography, University of Maine), e-mail message to the author, March 18, 2006.

52. Michael Bérubé, "Blue Towns in Red States," *Chronicle of Higher Education*, March 9, 2007, B10.

53. Rudolph, *American College and University*, 1–22; Tewksbury, *Founding of American Colleges*, 32–33; Beverly McAnear, "College Founding in the American Colonies, 1745–1775," *Mississippi Valley Historical Review* 42:1 (June 1955): 24–44; Oscar Handlin and Mary F. Handlin, *The American College and American Culture: Socialization as a Function of Higher Education* (New York: McGraw-Hill, 1970), 3–12; W. H. Cowley, "European Influences upon American Higher Education," *Educational Record* 20:2 (April 1939): 165–90.

54. Bainbridge Bunting, *Harvard: An Architectural History*, completed and edited by Margaret Henderson Floyd (Cambridge: Belknap Press of Harvard University Press, 1985), 38; Sutton, *Cambridge Reconsidered*, 24–29; Alan Seaburg, Thomas Dahill, and Carol Rose, *Cambridge on the Charles* (Cambridge, Mass.: Anne Miniver Press, 2001), 18–19; Kenneth Chorley, *Williamsburg in Virginia: Proud Citadel of Colonial Culture* (New York: Newcomen Society in North America, 1953), 11; Carl Bridenbaugh, *Seat of Empire: The Political Role of Eighteenth-Century Williamsburg* (Charlottesville: Dominion Books/University Press of Virginia, 1958), 1; Nathaniel Bouton, ed., "Census of 1773," *Miscellaneous Documents Relating to New Hampshire at Different Periods*, vol. 10 (Concord, N.H.: State Printer, 1877), 634; Stearns Morse, "The Place," in *The College on the Hill: A Dartmouth Chronicle*, ed. Ralph Nading Hill (Hanover:

Dartmouth Publications, 1964), 88–91; John Hurd, "Victualing and Lodging," in *Hanover, New Hampshire, a Bicentennial Book: Essays in Honor of the Town's 200th Anniversary* (Hanover: Hanover Bicentennial Committee, 1961), 126.

55. Tewksbury, *Founding of American Colleges*, 16; Burke, *American Collegiate Populations*, 14, 21, 57; John S. Brubacher and Willis Rudy, *Higher Education in Transition: A History of American Colleges and Universities*, 4th ed (New Brunswick, N.J.: Transaction Publishers, 1997), 154; James J. Murray III, *American Universities and Colleges*, 16th ed. (New York: Walter de Gruyter, 2001), vol. 1, 3–4; W. Earl Armstrong, "Teacher Education," *Higher Education* 10:8 (April 1954): 125; Morris Bishop, *A History of Cornell* (Ithaca, N.Y.: Cornell University Press, 1962), 55; Geiger, "The Era of Multipurpose Colleges," 51; David F. Allmendinger, Jr., *Paupers and Scholars: The Transformation of Student Life in Nineteenth-Century New England* (New York: St. Martin's, 1975), 8, 81.

56. William H. Pierson, "Making a Living," in *Williamstown: The First Two Hundred Years, 1753–1953, and Twenty Years Later, 1953–1973*, ed. Robert R. R. Brooks (Williamstown, Mass.: Williamstown Historical Commission, 1974), 83, 97; Frances Taliaferro Thomas, *A Portrait of Historic Athens & Clarke County* (Athens: University of Georgia Press, 1992), 30; Mary D. Beaty, *A History of Davidson College* (Davidson, N.C.: Briarpatch Press, 1988), 39; Scott Meacham, *Halls, Tombs, and Houses: Student Society Architecture at Dartmouth*, http://www.dartmo.com/halls/index.html (accessed September 5, 2006); Jonathan Marwil, *A History of Ann Arbor* (Ann Arbor: University of Michigan Press, 1991), 44.

57. Eddy, *Colleges for Our Land and Time*, 35; Janet St. Cyr Henderson and John Fraser Hart, "The Development and Spatial

Patterns of Black Colleges," *Southeastern Geographer* 11:2 (1971): 134; Paul Woodring, "A Century of Teacher Education," in *A Century of Higher Education: Classical Citadel to Collegiate Colossus*, ed. William W. Brickman and Stanley Lehrer (New York: Society for the Advancement of Education, 1962), 158; Brubacher and Rudy, *Higher Education in Transition*, 174–78, 376; Geiger, "Era of Multipurpose Colleges"; Burke, *American Collegiate Populations*, 215, 221; National Center for Education Statistics, *Digest of Educational Statistics: 2003* (Washington: NCES, 2004), 54, 221; Thomas D. Snyder, ed., *120 Years of American Education: A Statistical Portrait* (Washington: NCES, 1993), 76; Woodrow Wilson, "What Is College For?" *Scribner's Magazine*, November 1909, 576; Helen Lefkowitz Horowitz, *Campus Life: Undergraduate Cultures from the End of the Eighteenth Century to the Present* (Chicago: University of Chicago Press, 1987), 98–117.

58. James Shortridge and Barbara Shortridge, "Yankee Town on the Kaw: A Geographical and Historical Perspective on Lawrence and Its Environs," in *Embattled Lawrence: Conflict & Community*, ed. Dennis Domer and Barbara Watkins (Lawrence: University of Kansas Continuing Education, 2001), 14, 16; John A. Jakle, "Twentieth Century Revival Architecture and the Gentry," *Journal of Cultural Geography* 4:1 (Fall/Winter 1983): 36; Gorman Beauchamp, "Dissing the Middle Class: The View from Burns Park," *American Scholar* 64:3 (Summer 1995): 335–49; Carol U. Sisler, "Village of Cayuga Heights: Its Development by Newman and Blood," in *The Towns of Tompkins County: From Podunk to Magnetic Springs*, ed. Jane Marsh Dieckmann (Ithaca, N.Y.: DeWitt Historical Society of Tompkins County, 1998), 31–36; City of Champaign, Illinois, Planning Department, *Campustown Existing Conditions Report* (Champaign: City of Champaign, 1998), 4;

Bois Burk, "Military Training," in *Exactly Opposite the Golden Gate: Essays on Berkeley's History, 1845–1945* (Berkeley, Calif.: Berkeley Historical Society, 1983), 125.

59. Brubacher and Rudy, *Higher Education in Transition*, 230; Bezilla, *Penn State*, 206; Ann F. Scheuring, *Abundant Harvest: The History of the University of California, Davis* (Davis: University of California, 2001), 69; Mickey Logue and Jack Simms, *Auburn: A Pictorial History of the Loveliest Village*, rev. ed. (Auburn, Ala.: n.p., 1996), 186; Snyder, *120 Years of American Education*, 76; Horowitz, *Campus Life*, 185; Geiger, "Ten Generations of American Higher Education," 61; Edith Efron, "The Two Joes Meet—Joe College, Joe Veteran," *New York Times Magazine*, June 16, 1946, 21, 55; Sackett, *New Hampshire's University*, 127; William L. Stimson, *Going to Washington State: A Century of Student Life* (Pullman: Washington State University, 1989), 165.

60. Snyder, *120 Years of American Education*, 79; University of Massachusetts, Amherst, Office of Institutional Research, "Headcount Student Majors by Degree Program Level and Gender, Fall 1867–Fall 1976," http://www.umass.edu/oapa/publications/factbooks/04–05/enrollment/FB_en_02_2004.pdf (accessed September 14, 2006); Charles F. Frederickson, "A Brief History of Collegiate Housing," in *Student Housing and Residential Life: A Handbook for Professionals Committed to Student Development Goals*, ed. Roger B. Winston, Jr., Scott Anchors, and Associates (San Francisco: Jossey-Bass, 1993), 167–83; Arnold H. Diamond, "The College Housing Program: Its History and Operations," *Educational Record* 38:3 (July 1957): 204–29; Margaret Pugh O'Mara, *Cities of Knowledge: Cold War Science and the Search for the Next Silicon Valley* (Princeton: Princeton University Press, 2005), 5–6, 118; Hugh Davis Graham and Nancy Diamond,

The Rise of American Research Universities: Elites and Challengers in the Postwar Era (Baltimore: Johns Hopkins University Press, 1997), 33–34; Mickey Logue and Jack Simms, *Auburn . . . The Loveliest Village: A Pictorial History* (Norfolk, Va.: Donning, 1981), 157; Woodring, "Century of Teacher Education," 158–59; Karl W. Bigelow, "The Passing of the Teachers College," *Teachers College Record* 58:8 (May 1957): 409–17; Georgia Southern University, Office of Strategic Research and Analysis, "Fall Enrollment History, 1906–Present," unpublished table; Balliew, *College Station, Texas, 1938/1988*, 41.

61. Marwil, *History of Ann Arbor*, 161–62; "Drugs: Grass in Eugene," *Newsweek*, October 27, 1975, 28; James Grauerholz, "Williams S. Burroughs: Did Lawrence Matter?" in Domer and Watkins, *Embattled Lawrence*, 254; John Lofland, "The Youth Ghetto: A Perspective on the 'Cities of Youth' around Our Large Universities," *Journal of Higher Education* 29:3 (March 1968): 121–43; William L. Partridge, *The Hippie Ghetto: The Natural History of a Subculture* (New York: Holt, Rinehart, and Winston, 1973), 19; Hugh Moffett, "Sexy Movies? Chadron, Neb. Tries Gentle Persuasion," *Life*, May 30, 1969, 51–56; Clark Kerr, "Clark Kerr Calls It the Exaggerated Generation," *New York Times Magazine*, June 4, 1967, 33.

62. NCES, *Digest of Educational Statistics, 2003*, 222; "Change at Colleges: Away from the Barricades, Back to the Books," *U.S. News & World Report*, December 2, 1974, 70–74; Kent Christopher Owen, "Reflections on the College Fraternity and Its Changing Culture," in *Baird's Manual of American College Fraternities*, 20th edition, ed. Jack L. Anson and Robert F. Marchesani Jr. (Indianapolis: Baird's Manual Foundation, 1991), I-23; Frederick Iseman, "Nothing Happened," *Esquire*, September 1977, 74.

63. Graham and Diamond, *Rise of American Research Universities*, 85; Roger L. Geiger, *Knowledge and Money: Research Universities and the Paradox of the Marketplace* (Stanford: Stanford University Press, 2004), 43–44; Linda Sandler, "Schools Upgrade Their Social Centers with the Help of Big-Name Architects," *Wall Street Journal*, April 28, 1999; Michael J. Lewis, "Forget Classrooms: How Big Is the Atrium in the New Student Center?" *Chronicle of Higher Education*, July 11, 2003, B7–B9; Greg Winter, "Jacuzzi U.? A Battle of Perks to Lure Students," *New York Times*, October 5, 2003.

64. Carolyn J. Palmer and others, "Parental Notification: A New Strategy to Reduce Alcohol Abuse on Campus," *NASPA Journal* 38:3 (Spring 2001): 372–85.

65. The sixteen college towns designated metropolitan areas since 1994 are: Ames, Iowa; Auburn, Alabama; Blacksburg, Virginia; Bowling Green, Kentucky; Corvallis, Oregon; Fairbanks, Alaska; Flagstaff, Arizona; Harrisonburg, Virginia; Hattiesburg, Mississippi; Ithaca, New York; Logan, Utah; Missoula, Montana; Morgantown, West Virginia; Pocatello, Idaho; Salisbury, Maryland; and Valdosta, Georgia. See U.S. Bureau of the Census, "Historical Metropolitan Area Definitions," http://www.census.gov/population/www/estimates/pastmetro.html (accessed November 27, 2007); U.S. Office of Management and Budget, "Metropolitan Statistical Areas," http://www.whitehouse.gov/omb/inforeg/statpolicy.html#ms (accessed March 13, 2007).

2. The Campus as a Public Space

1. Alksander Gieysztor, "Management and Resources," in *A History of the University in Europe*, vol. 1:, *Universities in the Middle Ages*, ed. Hilde de Ridder-Symoens (Cambridge: Cambridge University Press, 1992), 137; Paul Venable Turner, *Campus: An American*

Planning Tradition (Cambridge: MIT Press, 1984), 12–21.

2. Turner, *Campus*, 27.

3. Gieysztor, "Management and Resources," 218–19.

4. John Womack, *Norman—An Early History, 1820–1900* (Norman: self-published, 1976), 24–25, 42, 47–51, 76, 116, 132; Bonnie Speer, *Cleveland County: Pride of the Promised Land* (Norman: Traditional Publishers, 1988), 28; U.S. Bureau of the Census, *Census of Population: 1950;* vol. 1 *Number of Inhabitants* (Washington, D.C.: U.S. Bureau of the Census, 1952), 36–38.

5. Roy Gittinger, *The University of Oklahoma, 1892–1942: A History of Fifty Years* (Norman: University of Oklahoma Press, 1942), 8; David W. Levy, *The University of Oklahoma: A History*, vol. 1, *1890–1917* (Norman: University of Oklahoma Press, 2005), 22–26; *Norman* [Oklahoma] *Transcript*, March 5, 1892, 4, March 19, 1892, 4–5, March 21, 1892, 5, April 16, 1892, 1.

6. For a more detailed account of early tree-planting efforts in Norman, see Blake Gumprecht, "Transforming the Prairie: Early Tree Planting in an Oklahoma Town," *Historical Geography* 29 (2001): 116–34.

7. George Milburn, "Planting a University: First Varsity President Recounts How He Did It," *Sooner Magazine*, November 1938, 39.

8. Barzilla "Dill" Boyd, "Biography of David Ross Boyd," Edward Everett Dale Papers, Box 212, Folder 9, Western History Collections, University of Oklahoma, Norman [hereafter WHC].

9. Oklahoma House of Representatives, *Journal*, 1893, 336; *Norman Transcript*, November 18, 1892, 5, June 9, 1893, 12; Milburn, "Planting a University," 39–40; Edward Everett Dale, "Notes of an Interview with David Ross Boyd and Jennie Boyd, August

1936, Glendale, Calif.," Edward Everett Dale Papers, Box 212, Folder 7, WHC.

10. *El Reno* [Oklahoma] *News*, March 19, 1897, 4; *University Umpire* [University of Oklahoma], May 1, 1898, 6; *Norman Transcript*, December 30, 1898, 1.

11. Clifford S. Griffin, *The University of Kansas: A History* (Lawrence: University Press of Kansas, 1974), 116; Deborah Hardy, *Wyoming University: The First 100 Years, 1886–1986* (Laramie: University of Wyoming, 1986), 79.

12. *University Umpire*, June 15, 1900; *Norman Transcript*, May 15, 1902, 1.

13. *University Umpire*, May 15, 1900, 11; *The Sooner* [University of Oklahoma annual], 1912, 18; *Oklahoma State Capital* [Oklahoma City], May 29, 1904, 3.

14. University of Oklahoma, *General Information and Announcements for 1903 and 1904* (Guthrie: State Capital Co., n.d.), 15.

15. V. L. Parrington, "On Recent Developments in American College Architecture," April 25, 1908, 21, 23–24, unpublished manuscript, WHC.

16. Glenn Patton, "American Collegiate Gothic: A Phase of University Architectural Development," *Journal of Higher Education* 38:1 (June 1967): 1–8; Peter Ferguson, James F. O'Gorman, and John Rhodes, *The Landscape and Architecture of Wellesley College* (Wellesley, Mass.: Wellesley College, 2000), 152. For an examination of the meaning of Collegiate Gothic to its leading proponent, architect Ralph Adams Cram, see Albert Bush-Brown, "Cram and Gropius: Traditionalism and Progressivism," *New England Quarterly* 25:1 (March 1952): 3–22.

17. Shepley, Rutan, & Coolidge to W. E. Rowsey, Board of Regents, December 5, 1908, A. Grant Evans Presidential Papers, Box 1, Folder 3, WHC; Carolyn S. Sorrels, "Eight Early Buildings on the Norman Campus of

the University of Oklahoma," March 1985, 64, unpublished manuscript, WHC; A. Grant Evans to W. J. Clark, Shepley, Rutan, & Coolidge, February 13, 1909, A. Grant Evans Presidential Papers, Box 1, Folder 6, WHC.

18. Sorrels, "Eight Early Buildings," 95; Carol J. Burr, "A Stadium for Oklahoma," *Sooner Magazine*, Winter 2001, 17–19; Carol J. Burr, "Under Construction," *Sooner Magazine*, Summer 2002, 2–7.

19. Turner, *Campus*, 204; "University Campus, Once Ugly Ranch, Is Now State's Most Beautiful Flower Garden," *Daily Oklahoman* [Oklahoma City], October 9, 1921, B5; Zona Moore, "Making the Campus Beautiful," *Sooner Magazine*, January 1929, 117–19; "Record Breaking Attendance Expected at O.U. As Many Seek Rooms in Norman," *Daily Oklahoman*, September 12, 1920, B3.

20. Judy Day, "University of Oklahoma Land Acquisition, 1891–1976," unpublished paper, GEOG 6430, Department of Geography, University of Oklahoma, 1977, WHC; Oklahoma Center of Urban and Regional Studies of the University of Oklahoma Research Institute, *Physical Development Plan: The University of Oklahoma and Environs, 1965–1985* (Norman, 1966), 12–14, 17; "Oklahoma University Goes Modern," *Architectural Forum*, September 1945, 104–14; Joye R. Swain, "Friends of the Duck Pond," *Sooner Magazine*, Summer 1984, 4–10.

21. "Sports for All Students," *Sooner Magazine*, July 1937, 278–79; J. Lewie Sanderson, R. Dean McGlamery, and David C. Peters, *A History of the Oklahoma State University Campus* (Stillwater: Oklahoma State University, 1990), 184; Van Dorn Hooker, *Only in New Mexico: An Architectural History of the University of New Mexico* (Albuquerque: University of New Mexico Press, 2000), 100.

22. Turner, *Campus*, 140–50; Dober, *Campus Landscape*, 45.

23. "A Beautiful Campus Means Work to Landscapers at O.U.," *Sooner Magazine*, August 1947, 21; Margaret French, "Cultivating the Perfect Setting," *Sooner Magazine*, Spring/Summer 1992, 14.

24. For examinations of the post–World War II expansion of American universities, see, for example, Clark Kerr, *The Great Transformation of Higher Education, 1960–1980* (Albany: State University of New York Press, 1991); John Hardin Best, "The Revolution of Markets and Management: Toward a History of Higher Education since 1945," *History of Education Quarterly* 28:2 (Summer 1998): 177–89; John R. Thelin, *A History of American Higher Education* (Baltimore: Johns Hopkins University Press, 2004).

25. Arthur Tuttle (retired director, Architecture and Engineering Services, University of Oklahoma, and Norman resident since 1969), interview by the author, Norman, June 14, 2001; "Landscape Service Cuts Back Employees," *Oklahoma Daily* [University of Oklahoma], November 13, 1974, 2.

26. Carol J. Burr (editor, *Sooner Magazine*, and Norman resident since 1955), interview by the author, Norman, June 25, 2001.

27. "Landscaping Improvements Underway," *Oklahoma Daily*, April 16, 1979, 9; "Campus Bulletin Board" [advertisement], *Oklahoma Daily*, October 1, 1979, 15; Bob Crouch, "System to Help Grass," *Oklahoma Daily*, February 15, 1980, 1; "Banowsky Begins Ambitious Tree-Planting Project," press release, University of Oklahoma, February 12, 1981, William Banowsky Presidential Papers, Box 86, Folder 15, WHC; "The David Ross Boyd Tree Planting Program," brochure, William Banowsky Presidential Papers, Box 86, Folder 15, WHC; Richard T. Mason, "OU's Improvements Numerous," *Oklahoma Daily*, August 27, 1982, 2.

28. Kathryn Jenson White, "If Statues Could

Speak," *Sooner Magazine*, Spring 1998, 4–8; Chip Minty, "Planting for a Green Future at OU," *Daily Oklahoman*, March 20, 1998, Norman Oklahoman section, 7; University of Oklahoma Foundation and University Development, *Excellence Reached: The University of Oklahoma Reach for Excellence Campaign, 1995–2000; A Report to Donors* (Norman, 2000), 22.

29. For an example of one university's early efforts to protect its wooded lands and create an arboretum, see Archibald Henderson, *The Campus of the First State University* (Chapel Hill: University of North Carolina Press), 53–63.

30. David Boren, "Decision to Remove Trees Made by Experts [letter to the editor]," *Oklahoma Daily*, September 23, 1996.

31. Susan Grossman, "New OU Campus Fountain to Echo French Gardens," *Norman Transcript*, August 3, 1999, 1; Summer DuFran, "Benches Beautify Landscape," *Norman Transcript*, June 13, 2000, 1; Carol J. Burr, "Fountains among the Flowers," *Sooner Magazine*, Winter 2000, 14–17; Mary Lynne Weeks, "A Front Door Welcome," *Sooner Magazine*, Winter 1997, 19–23; University of Oklahoma, *Historic Campus Guide* (Norman: University of Oklahoma, n.d.).

32. Jerry Fowler (Norman resident, 1956–80), e-mail message to the author, May 7, 2003.

33. Bob Goins (Norman native and emeritus professor of architecture, University of Oklahoma), interview by the author, Norman, June 30, 2001.

34. Nancy Rimassa (Norman resident), e-mail message to the author, March 2, 2003.

35. Burr, interview.

36. Vicki Dollarhide (Norman resident since 1969), interview by the author, Norman, July 9, 2001.

37. David Littlejohn, " 'Scattering of Buildings Softened by Landscape,' " *Architecture*, December 1985, 77; David Robertson (resident,

Newark, Delaware), interview by the author, March 12, 2000; Jo Chesworth, *The Story of the Century: The Borough of State College, Pennsylvania, 1896–1996* (State College: Borough of State College/Barash Group, 1995), 194.

38. Burr, interview.

39. Charles F. Long and Carolyn G. Hart, *The Sooner Story: Ninety Years at the University of Oklahoma, 1890–1980* (Norman: University of Oklahoma Foundation, 1980), 12.

40. Harold Keith, *Oklahoma Kickoff: An Informal History of the First Twenty-Five Years of Football at the University of Oklahoma, and of the Amusing Hardships That Attended Its Pioneering* (Norman: The author, 1948), 13, 20, 29.

41. John F. Rooney, Jr., and Richard Pillsbury, *Atlas of American Sport* (New York: Macmillan, 1992), 62; Keith, *Oklahoma Kickoff*, 123, 148, 151; Dorothy H. Bodell, "Blacksburg Social Life and Customs," in *A Special Place for 200 Years: A History of Blacksburg, Virginia*, ed. Clara B. Cox (Blacksburg: Town of Blacksburg, 1998), 41.

42. Jesse Frederick Steiner, *Americans at Play: Recent Trends in Recreation and Leisure Time Activities* (New York: McGraw-Hill, 1933), 91. At the University of North Carolina, attendance at football games exceeded seating capacity at the school's small football field, so that by 1921, "thousands of spectators had to be turned away." Henderson, *The Campus of the First State University*, 318.

43. Tom Blumbaugh (assistant athletics director, ticket operations, University of Oklahoma), e-mail to the author, February 4, 2004; Long and Hart, *The Sooner Story*, 50; Louis G. Geiger, *University of the Northern Plains: A History of the University of North Dakota, 1883–1958* (Grand Forks: University of North Dakota Press, 1958), 322.

44. For other examples of the important role campuses play in providing cultural opportunities to the surrounding community,

see Griffin, *University of Kansas*, 293–97, 590–91; Mary Kay Mason, ed., *Laramie: Gem City of the Plains* (Dallas: Curtis Media, 1987), 155; Roger Bjerk, "Pullman: From Farming Frontier to Urban Center," *Bunchgrass Historian* 9:3 (Fall 1981): 31–32.

45. "Classic Gems of Music Fall Flat at O.U.," *Daily Oklahoman*, December 24, 1922, 36.

46. "Celebrity Series Association [advertisement]," *Sooner Magazine*, August 1947, 26; Tracy Silvester, "University Celebrity Series Books Six Major Attractions," *Daily Oklahoman*, September 26, 1948; Jim Dolen, "OU Bans Rock Festivals," *Daily Oklahoman*, December 10, 1970, 10; Joe Salwell, "Mud Rally Tells a Story of Man," *Oklahoma Daily*, May 24, 1984, 4; Hanna Bolte, "Concerts Keep Lloyd Noble in Black," *Oklahoma Daily*, October 23, 1984, 3.

47. Fowler, e-mail.

48. Suzanne Eder (former Norman resident), e-mail to the author, February 28, 2003.

49. David Levy (professor of history, University of Oklahoma, and Norman resident since 1967), interview by the author, Norman, June 27, 2001.

50. David Athey, who lives one block from the University of Delaware campus in Newark, said he moved to the neighborhood in part because of the cultural opportunities the university provides. "They're real intangibles that you only get living next to a university," he said. Athey, telephone interview by the author, February 7, 2005.

51. Scott Carlson, "Dazzling Designs at High Prices," *Chronicle of Higher Education*, January 26, 2001, A29–A35; Michael J. Lewis, "Forget Classrooms: How Big Is the Atrium in the New Student Center?" *Chronicle of Higher Education*, July 11, 2003, B7–B9; David Dillon, "Starchitecture on Campus," *Boston Globe Magazine*, February 22, 2004, 12–15, 21–23; Oklahoma Center of Urban and Regional Studies, *Physical Development*

Plan, 36; Ben Fenwick, "New Catlett Music Building Opens to a Fanfare of Trumpets," *Oklahoma Daily*, September 8, 1986, 1; Paula Baker, "Playing to Rave Revues," *Sooner Magazine*, Fall/Winter 1986, 24.

52. Ann Hester, "Opera Singer Packs Hall," *Daily Oklahoman*, September 16, 1998; Kathryn Jenson White, "The Halls of Music," *Sooner Magazine*, Winter 1999, 15–20; Kenneth Fuchs (director, University of Oklahoma School of Music), interview by the author, Norman, June 18, 2001; Lynette Lobban, "A Grand Revival," *Sooner Magazine*, Summer 2005, 4–9.

53. "A Student Shock Absorber," *Sooner Magazine*, October 1928, 12–13; "Union Building Nearly Ready," *Sooner Magazine*, January 1929, 115, 140; Long and Hart, *Sooner Story*, 53; Burr, interview; Andy Rieger (Norman native and managing editor, *Norman Transcript*), interview by the author, Norman, June 21, 2001; "Union Hums with Visitors," *Sooner Magazine*, May 1935, 181; "Conventions, Short Course," *Sooner Magazine*, May 1940, 31.

54. Paul A. Andres, "Another Dream Takes Concrete Form," *Sooner Magazine*, November 1948, 16–20; John Wagoner, "For the Union, a New Look," *Sooner Magazine*, June 1950, 7–10; "The Fabulous Union," *Sooner Magazine*, December 1951, 28–44; Pat West, "OU's Ming Room Staff Keeps Busy," *Daily Oklahoman*, September 16, 1957, 15; James "Tuffy" McCall (Norman real estate agent, former food director, Oklahoma Memorial Union), interview by the author, Norman, July 9, 2001.

55. McCall, interview; Rieger, interview.

56. Jack Copeland, "The Union," *Sooner Magazine*, Fall 1983, 4–10; Robert Ferrier, "New Life for a Grand Old Girl," *Sooner Magazine*, Fall 1998, 9–13.

57. University of Kansas, *The Campus Plan* (Lawrence: University of Kansas, 1997), D–1;

Andrew Phelan, "University of Oklahoma College of Fine Arts," http://art.ou.edu/dept/history/cfahistory.pdf (accessed April 8, 2004); Gittinger, *University of Oklahoma*, 155–56.

58. James D. Watts, "A French Collection," *Tulsa World*, December 17, 2000; "Exhibit on View Tuesday," *Tulsa World*, November 10, 2000; Ryan Chittum, "Art Exhibit Breaks Museum Records," *Oklahoman Daily*, June 2, 2001; Eric Lee (director, Fred Jones Jr. Museum of Art), interview by the author, Norman, June 21, 2001.

59. W. Eugene Hollon, "A History of the Stovall Museum of Science and History, University of Oklahoma" (Norman: n.p., 1956), 2, 12–13; Michael Mares, "Miracle on the Prairie: The Development of the Sam Noble Oklahoma Museum of Natural History," *Museologia* 2 (2002): 36, 47.

60. Hollon, "History of the Stovall Museum," 13–18; Stephan F. De Borhegyi, "The Student and the Museum," *Sooner Magazine*, January 1956, 6; Carol J. Robinson, "With an Eye toward Greatness," *Sooner Magazine*, May 1961, 4–6; Kyle Gilliland, "Stovall Facilities Thrust for New Director," *Oklahoma Daily*, July 30, 1980, 1.

61. Mares, "Miracle on the Prairie," 39.

62. Michael A. Mares, *Heritage at Risk: The Oklahoma Museum of Natural History, Oklahoma's Hidden Treasure* (Norman: Oklahoma Museum of Natural History, 1988); Eve Sandstrom, "Preserving a Priceless Past," *Sooner Magazine*, Fall/Winter 1990, 14.

63. Chip Minty, "Museum Petition Drive Completed," *Daily Oklahoman*, July 22, 1991, 49; Chip Minty, "Voters OK Bond Issue for Norman Museum," *Daily Oklahoman*, November 20, 1991, 1; Brian Ford, "Health-Care Tax Rejected, Education Bond Approved," *Tulsa World*, November 4, 1992, A1; Mares, "Miracle on the Prairie," 43–47.

64. Mares, "Miracle on the Prairie," 50; Peter Tirrell (associate director, Sam Noble Oklahoma Museum of Natural History), interview by the author, Norman, June 25, 2001.

65. Eliphalet Nott, president of Union College from 1804 to 1866, quoted in Turner, *Campus*, 71; Le Corbusier, *When Cathedrals Were White: A Journey to the Country of Timid People* (New York: Reynal & Hitchcock, 1947), 135. Stefan Muthesius writes about the connections between the utopian philosophies of American colleges and universities and the design of campuses in *The Postwar University: Utopianist Campus and College* (New Haven: Yale University Press, 2000).

66. Turner, *Campus*, 4, 101, 216.

67. Milburn, "Planting a University," 39; David Ross Boyd to J. O. Blakeney, April 10, 1903, Boyd Presidential Papers, Box 2, Folder 2, WHC.

68. Lisa Chase, "Imagining Utopia: Landscape Design at Smith College, 1871–1910," *New England Quarterly* 65:4 (December 1992): 566, 573; Kit Anderson, "Ira's Acres," *Vermont Quarterly*, Summer 2002, 20.

69. "Banowsky Begins Ambitious Tree Planting Project," press release, February 12, 1981, Banowsky Presidential Papers, Box 86, Folder 15, WHC; Yi-Fu Tuan, *Topophilia: A Study in Environmental Perception, Attitudes, and Values* (Englewood Cliffs, N.J.: Prentice-Hall, 1974), 115; Simon Schama, *Landscape and Memory* (New York: Vintage Books, 1995), 16.

70. Richard Dober, *Campus Planning* (n.p: Reinhold Publishing Corp., 1963), 27; Parrington, "Developments in American College Architecture," 21, 23–24; Woodrow Wilson, "President Wilson's Address," *Princeton Alumni Weekly*, December 13, 1902, 199.

71. W. B. Bizzell, "Discovery and Learning," *Sooner Magazine*, November 1932, 40–42; Littlejohn, " 'Scattering of Buildings Softened By Landscape,' " 81.

72. Ernest L. Boyer, *College: The Undergraduate*

Experience in America (New York: Harper &
Row, 1987), 16–17; Jack Ahern et al., *Campus
Physical Master Plan, University of Massa-
chusetts, Amherst* (Amherst: University of
Massachusetts, 1993), 2.

73. Patricia C. Sherwood and Joseph Michael
Lasala, "Education and Architecture: The
Evolution of the University of Virginia's
Academic Village," in *Thomas Jefferson's
Academical Village: The Creation of an Archi-
tectural Masterpiece*, ed. Richard Guy Wilson
(Charlottesville: Bayly Art Museum of the
University of Virginia, 1993), 43; University
of Oklahoma, *Catalogue, 1902–1903* (Nor-
man: University of Oklahoma, n.d.), 11; "The
Way to College [advertisement]," *University
Umpire*, June 1904.

74. University of Oklahoma, *Campus Preview:
For Students Entering 2004–2005* (Norman:
University of Oklahoma, n.d.); University
of Oklahoma Recruitment Services website,
http://www.go2.ou.edu (accessed February
17, 2004).

75. University of Oklahoma Visitor Center website, http://www.ou.edu/visitorcenter/index
.html (accessed February 19, 2004); Todd
Gitlin, "Berkeley's Right Angles: A Social
Science Ideal in Perpendicular Stucco,"
American Scholar 69:4 (Autumn 2000):
107–12.

76. "An Outline of Some Points to Be Discussed
at a Conference on a Museum for the
University of Oklahoma," March 24, 1944,
Stovall Museum vertical file, WHC; David
Dollarhide (investment banker, RBC Dain
Rauscher, Oklahoma City, and longtime
Norman resident), interview by the author,
Norman, July 9, 2001.

77. Neil Dutcher, "Hey, I Really Do Love the
Place," *Daily Oklahoman*, March 26, 1998,
Norman Oklahoman section, 5.

78. Howard F. Stern and Robert F. Hill, "The
Culture of Oklahoma: A Group Identity and
Its Image," in *The Culture of Oklahoma*, ed.

Howard F. Stern and Robert F. Hill (Norman: University of Oklahoma Press, 1993),
208; "Art Donation Puts OU among Elite
Campus Galleries," *Tulsa World*, September
29, 2000.

79. *Norman Transcript*, December 2, 1898, 4;
Norman Convention and Visitors Bureau,
Norman 2003 Visitors Guide (Norman: Con-
vention and Visitors Bureau, 2003); Andy
Rieger, "Envy of the State," *Norman Tran-
script*, January 21, 2001, A2.

3. Fraternity Row, the Student Ghetto,
and the Faculty Enclave

1. Dan Snodderly, "Downtown," in *Ithaca's
Neighborhoods: The Rhine, the Hill, and The
Goose Pasture*, ed. Carol U. Sisler, Margaret
Hobbie, and Jane Marsh Dieckmann (Ithaca,
N.Y.: DeWitt Historical Society of Tompkins
County, 1988), 36–37; Clayton W. Smith,
"South Hill," in *Ithaca's Neighborhoods*,
85–87; Ithaca College, "Common Data Set,
2003–2004," http://www.ithaca.edu/ir/
cdsindex.html (accessed April 13, 2004).

2. Gretchen Sachse, "Ithaca: An Overview," in
Ithaca's Neighborhoods, 9, 14; Smith, "South
Hill," 83–84; Amy Humber, "Fall Creek," in
Ithaca's Neighborhoods, 41–46.

3. Manufacturing's share of total employment
in Tompkins County, where Ithaca is located,
declined from 45.7 percent in 1948 to 9.4
percent in 2001. Tompkins County Area
Development, *Economic Development Strategy*
(Ithaca, 1999), 7; Tompkins County Area Development and Tompkins County Planning
Department, "Tompkins County Economic
Development Strategy: Phase One, The Data-
base and Comparisons" (Ithaca, 1992), 23;
U.S. Bureau of the Census, *County Business
Patterns*, Tompkins County, New York, 2001,
http://censtats.census.gov/cbpnaic/cbpnaic
.shtml (accessed April 20, 2004).

4. Cornell University, Institutional Research
and Planning, "Total Cornell Workforce,

1993–94 to 2003–04," http://dpb.cornell
.edu/irp/pdf/FactBook/HR/workforce.pdf
(accessed April 15, 2004); Ithaca College,
Institutional Research, "Facts in Brief,"
http://www.ithaca.edu/ir/factsfigs.html (accessed April 15, 2004); U.S. Bureau of the
Census, "Census 2000," http://factfinder
.census.gov (accessed April 15, 2004);
Cornell University, Institutional Research
and Planning, "Cornell University Enrollment, Total Registration, Ithaca Campus,
Fall 1868–Current," unpublished table.

5. Jack L Anson and Robert F. Marchesani
Jr., eds., *Baird's Manual of American College
Fraternities*, 20th ed. (Indianapolis: Baird's
Manual Foundation, 1991).

6. Leo Reisberg, "Fraternities in Decline,"
Chronicle of Higher Education, January 7,
2000, A59–A62. Estimates on the proportion of students who belong to fraternities
and sororities are based on data obtained
from a variety of sources about the sixty college towns that are the focus of this book.

7. For a sympathetic but objective history of
Greek letter societies, see Kent Christopher
Owen, "Reflections on the College Fraternity
and Its Changing Nature," in Anson and
Marchesani Jr., *Baird's Manual of American
College Fraternities*, I-1–I-24.

8. Richard Ford, "Rules of the House," *Esquire*,
June 1986, 231.

9. Helen Lefkowitz Horowitz, *Campus Life:
Undergraduate Cultures from the End of the
Eighteenth Century to the Present* (Chicago:
University of Chicago Press, 1987), 274;
Simon J. Bronner, *Piled Higher and Deeper:
The Folklore of Student Life* (Little Rock, Ark.:
August House, 1995), 128; Toby Merchant
(president, Sigma Nu fraternity, Cornell
University), interview by the author, Ithaca,
May 3, 2000; Michael Tranter (member, Psi
Upsilon fraternity, Cornell University), inter-
view by the author, Ithaca, April 28, 2000.

10. Frederick Rudolph, *The American College and

University: A History* (New York: Alfred A.
Knopf, 1968), 138–41; Owen, "Reflections on
the College Fraternity," I2, I14.

11. Rudolph, *American College and University*,
p, 146; Andrew Dickson White, "College Fraternities," *Forum*, May 1887, 251; Waterman
Thomas Hewett, *Cornell University: A History*, vol. 3 (New York: University Publishing
Society, 1905), 13.

12. Horowitz, *Campus Life*, 111–12; James H.
Goodsell, "The College Homesteads of
Greek Letter Men," in *Greek Letter Men
of Central New York, South*, comp. Will J.
Maxwell (New York: College Book Co., 1901),
39–48; Scott Meacham, *Halls, Tombs and
Houses: Student Society Architecture at Dart-
mouth*, http://www.dartmo.com/halls/index
.html (accessed January 22, 2004); White,
"College Fraternities," 246; Morris Bishop,
A History of Cornell (Ithaca: Cornell Uni-
versity Press, 1962), 81–82, 95, 138; Kermit
Carlyle Parsons, *The Cornell Campus: A His-
tory of Its Planning and Development* (Ithaca:
Cornell University Press, 1968), 91, 101, 219.

13. Meacham, *Halls, Tombs and Houses*; Willard
Austin, "Fraternities at Cornell University,"
College Fraternity, April 1893, 14; G. H.
Hooker, "Cornell Fraternities: A Sketch,"
Cornell Era, April 1901, 315; Hjalmar H.
Boyesen, "Chi Chapter," in *The Annals of
Psi Upsilon, 1833–1941*, ed. Peter A. Babauer
(New York: American Book–Stratford Press,
1941), 232–33; H. William Fogle, Jr., *The Cor-
nell Deke House: A History of the 1893 Lodge*
(Ithaca: The Delta Chi Association, 1993), 1;
Knight Kiplinger, "The History of the Chap-
ter [Alpha Delta Phi, Cornell University],"
unpublished manuscript, no date; Bishop,
History of Cornell, 138, 206.

14. Kiplinger, "The History of the Chapter";
A. L. Reed, ed., *Alpha Delta Phi: The History,
Function & Structure of the Fraternity, Cornell
Chapter, Founded 1869* (Ithaca: n.p., n.d.), 27.

15. Cornell University, *Proceedings of the Board of

Trustees of Cornell University, April 1965–July 1885 (Ithaca, 1940), 223; Hewett, Cornell University, 20; Carol U. Sisler, "East Hill," in Sisler, Hobbie, and Dieckmann, Ithaca's Neighborhoods, 59, 66; Minutes, Cornell chapter, Alpha Delta Phi, April 20, 1900, Alpha Delta Phi chapter records, #37\4\2101, Department of Manuscripts and University Archives, Cornell University; Sanborn Map. Co., fire insurance maps for Ithaca, N.Y., 1893, 1898, 1904.

16. Kiplinger, "The History of the Chapter"; Edward R. Alexander, Alpha Delta Phi Home, Cornell University (Ithaca, N.Y.?, 1902?), 6; Cornell University, Sixth Annual Report of President Schurman, 1897–98 (Ithaca, 1898), 59–60; Minutes, Cornell chapter, Alpha Delta Phi, April 20, 1900.

17. Kiplinger, "History of the Chapter"; Hewett, Cornell University, 20; "Psi. U. Chapter House," Ithaca Daily Journal, June 23, 1884, 3; Ithaca Democrat, June 18, 1891, 5; "Fraternity Houses," Ithaca Daily Journal, January 2, 1892, 3; Fogle, Cornell Deke House, 6; "Sigma Chi House," Ithaca Daily Journal, December 15, 1900, 3; Sanborn Map Co., fire insurance maps for Ithaca, N.Y., 1893, 1898; Parsons, Cornell Campus, 119, 122; "Receptions," Ithaca Daily Journal, February 1, 1899, 6; Jane Marsh Dieckmann, A Short History of Tompkins County (Ithaca: DeWitt Historical Society of Tompkins County, 1986), 47; Geoffrey M. Gyrisco, "A Guide to the Works of William Henry Miller, Ithaca's Architect," typescript, December 1978, Fine Arts Library, Cornell University.

18. Minutes, Cornell chapter, Alpha Delta Phi, April 20, 1900.

19. "Alpha Delta Phi," Ithaca Daily Journal, April 10, 1902, 8. Both the Chi Psi and Alpha Delta Phi chapter houses were destroyed by fire, but were rebuilt, although in different styles. See "Fire in Chi Psi Fraternity House Results in the Loss of Seven Lives," Ithaca Daily Journal, December 7, 1906, 3; "Chi Psi House Plans Completed," Ithaca Daily Journal, August 3, 1907; Reed, Alpha Delta Phi, 62.

20. "Alpha Delta Phi's Unique Building," Ithaca Daily Journal, July 14, 1908, 7; Kiplinger, "History of the Chapter"; Meacham, Halls, Tombs and Houses; "Three New Fraternity Houses," Cornell Daily Sun, October 2, 1903, 1; "Fraternity House Changes," Cornell Daily Sun, September 26, 1902, 3.

21. Horowitz, Campus Life, 131, 138–40, 144; Owen, "Reflections on the College Fraternity," 13; O.D. von Engeln, Concerning Cornell (Ithaca: Geography Supply Bureau, 1917), 299; Bishop, History of Cornell, 293, 304–5, 403, 420; Hewett, Cornell University, 20–21; "New Buildings Being Erected," Cornell Era, October 24, 1891, 37–39; "Chi Psi Reception," Ithaca Daily Journal, November 21, 1896; Kenneth L. Roberts, "Far Above Cayuga's Waters," Saturday Evening Post, February 2, 1929, 57.

22. M. G. Lord, "The Greek Rites of Exclusion," The Nation, July 4, 1987, 12; Lawrence Bancroft (Cornell chapter, Alpha Phi Alpha), e-mail message to the author, April 27, 2004; Bishop, History of Cornell, 404.

23. Cornell, Directory, 1925–26, 109; Bishop, History of Cornell, 448; Charles Thompson, Halfway Down the Stairs (New York, 1957), 99–101.

24. Cornell University, Office of the Dean of Students, "A Report on Some Aspects of Fraternity Life at Cornell University," September 1960, 5, 10; Owen, "Reflections on the College Fraternity," 122–123; Horowitz, Campus Life, 239, 244; Cornell University, Student Directory, October 1960 (Ithaca, 1960), 2; Cornell University, Student Directory, 1975–1976 (Ithaca, 1975), 6–7; Deborah Huffman, "Trustees Implement Anti-Bias Legislation for All Living Units," Cornell Daily Sun, February 23, 1968, 1; Richard

M. Warshauer, "White Attempt to Break In Sparks Dispute over Cops," *Cornell Daily Sun*, April 20, 1969, Extra edition, 1; Cornell University, University Faculty Committee on Student Affairs, "Fraternities at Cornell (The Muller Report)," March 1, 1961, 6, Fraternity and Sorority Affairs Records, #37/4/3027, Box 2, Division of Rare and Manuscript Collections, Cornell University Library. G. Armour Craig, former president of Amherst College, commented that the reason many small colleges do not abolish their Greek systems is because of a fear that such reforms will reduce alumni giving: Lord, "Greek Rites of Exclusion," 12.

25. Ernest L. Boyer, *College: The Undergraduate Experience in America* (New York: Harper & Row, 1987), 208; Bronner, *Piled Higher and Deeper*, 127; Owen, "Reflections on the College Fraternity," 123; Lynn Hirschberg, "Greek Don't Want No Freaks," *Rolling Stone*, October 1, 1981, 55; "Fraternities Are Making a Comeback," *Ithaca Journal*, October 12, 1973; Cornell University, *Student Directory, 1975–1976* (Ithaca, 1975), 6–7; Cornell University, *Student Directory, 1985–1986* (Ithaca, 1985), 8; Dan Meyer (member, board of directors, Cornell chapter of Phi Kappa Psi), telephone conversation with the author, October 25, 2002; Bill Noon, "The 1980s," unpublished manuscript, Lambda Chi Alpha, Cornell University, 1999, http://www.iswza.org/culture/history/oracle1980s.html (accessed May 30, 2003); William L. Simson, *Going to Washington State: A Century of Student Life* (Pullman: Washington State University Press, 1989), 256.

26. William A. Bryan, "Contemporary Fraternity and Sorority Issues," in R. B. Winston, Jr., W. R. Nettles III, and J. H. Opper, eds., *Fraternities and Sororities on the Contemporary College Campus* (San Francisco: Jossey-Bass, 1987), 37–56; George D. Kuh and James C. Arnold, "Liquid Bonding: A Cultural Analysis of the Role of Alcohol in Fraternity Pledgeship," *Journal of College Student Development* 34 (September 1993): 327–34; Peggy Reeves Sanday, *Fraternity Gang Rape: Sex, Brotherhood, and Privilege on Campus* (New York: New York University Press, 1990); Hank Nuwer, *Wrongs of Passage: Fraternities, Sororities, Hazing, and Binge Drinking* (Bloomington: Indiana University Press, 1999).

27. Cornell University, Fraternity and Sorority Affairs, "Social Responsibility Policy," http://www.dos.cornell.edu/dos/fsa/socialpol/SocialPolicy.html (accessed January 22, 2004); Scott Conroe, "Fraternities Forever," *Cornell Magazine*, May/June 1999, 30–37; Chris Koza (president, Cornell University Interfraternity Council, member, Chi Psi fraternity), interview by the author, Ithaca, April 28, 2000.

28. In fall 2003, 82 percent of members in fraternities and sororities that were part of Cornell's Interfraternity Council or the Panhellenic Association were white, compared to 59.4 percent of all undergraduates. Cornell University, Fraternity and Sorority Affairs, "Membership Demographics," Fall 2003, unpublished table; Cornell University, Institutional Research and Planning, "Common Data Set, 2003–2004," http://dpb.cornell.edu/irp/pdf/CDS/cds_2003–04.pdf (accessed April 29, 2004).

29. Reisberg, "Fraternities in Decline," A59; Conroe, "Fraternities Forever," 34; comment from unidentified fraternity member, Chi Psi fraternity, Cornell University, Ithaca, April 28, 2000; Cornell University, Fraternity & Sorority Advisory Council, *2001–2002 Annual Report* (Ithaca, 2002), 29–30; Cornell University, Fraternity & Sorority Advisory Council, *2005–2006 Annual Report* (Ithaca, 2006), 15.

30. Horowitz, *Campus Life*, 250; Avikam Wygodski, "Neighborhood Analysis of the Student

Ghetto" (master's thesis, University of
Florida, 1979), 3.

31. Lynn A. Staeheli and Albert Thompson,
"Citizenship, Community, and Struggles for
Public Space," *Professional Geographer* 49:1
(February 1997): 28–38; Jason Kobylarek
et al., "Past, Present, and Future Relation-
ships between the University of Kansas and
Adjacent Neighborhoods," student research
paper, UBPL 502/802, University of Kansas,
July 2001, http://www.users.muohio.edu/
karrowrs/College/sTU_rESEARCH_ku.pdf
(accessed January 22, 2004); William L.
Partridge, *The Hippie Ghetto: The Natural
History of a Subculture* (New York: Holt,
Rinehart, and Winston, 1973); Beth Kassab,
"Mayor Envisions Improved 'Student Ghet-
tos' Near U. Florida," *Independent Florida
Alligator* [University of Florida], January 14,
1999; Nick Madigan, "Peace Plan in Boulder
Bans Sofas on Porches," *New York Times*,
May 30, 2002, A14.

32. Dieckmann, *Short History of Tompkins
County*, 43; Jane Marsh Dieckmann, "The
University and Collegetown," in Sisler, Hobbie, and Dieckmann, *Ithaca's Neighborhoods*,
157–58.

33. Bishop, *History of Cornell*, 92.

34. Parsons, *Cornell Campus*, 91, 102.

35. W. H. Cowley, "The History of Student
Residential Housing," *School and Society*
40:1040 (December 1, 1934): 710–11; Charles
F. Frederiksen, "A Brief History of Collegiate
Housing," in *Student Housing and Residential
Life: A Handbook for Professionals Committed
to Student Development Goals*, ed. Roger G.
Winston, Jr., Scott Anchors, and Associates
(San Francisco: Jossey-Bass, 1993), 169.
Increasing opposition to dormitories showed
the strong influence of German universities
from the Civil War until the early 1900s.
Many American higher education leaders
during this period were educated at German
universities, which did not believe it was
the responsibility of universities to provide
housing for students.

36. Bishop, *History of Cornell*, 80.

37. "A Word to Wise Ithacans," *Cornell Era*,
March 13, 1869, 5; Parsons, *Cornell Campus*,
105; Bishop, *History of Cornell*, 98.

38. Parsons, *Cornell Campus*, 104; Dieckmann,
"University and Collegetown," 164, 169;
"Editorial," *Cornell Era*, April 26, 1889, 1;
Bishop, *History of Cornell*, 359.

39. Romeyn Berry, "Now in *My* Time!," *Cornell
Alumni News*, February 15, 1945, 323; Par-
sons, *Cornell Campus*, 105; Bishop, *History of
Cornell*, 293, 343.

40. Cowley, "History of Student Residential
Housing," 711; Frederiksen, "Brief History
of Collegiate Housing," 169; Boyesen, "Chi
Chapter," 234; Berry, "Now in *My* Time";
"Eating in Ithaca," *Cornell Alumni News*,
February 4, 1926, 222–23; S. Lovell, "The
Crime of the Boarding Houses," *Cornell
Era*, November 1910, 47–54; H. H. Crum,
"Inspect the Boarding-Houses," *Cornell
Era*, October 1911, 29–30; Bishop, *History of
Cornell*, 405, 422; Michael Doucet and John
Weaver, *Housing the North American City*
(Montreal: McGill-Queen's University Press,
1991), 388, 391.

41. "Where the Students Live," *Cornell Alumni
News*, February 7, 1912, 207; Sanborn Map
Co., fire insurance maps for Ithaca, N.Y.,
1904, 1910; H. A. Manning, comp., *Manning's Ithaca (New York) Directory for Year
Beginning January, 1930* (Schenectady, N.Y.,
1930).

42. Morris Bishop, "On Boarding-Houses and
Landladies," *Cornell Era*, October 1912,
38–41; "Report of the Freshman Advisory
Committee," *Cornell Alumni News*, December 18, 1913, 155–56; "Tackling Rooming
House Problems," *Cornell Alumni News*, May
21, 1914, 406.

43. Bishop, *History of Cornell*, 403; Thompson,
Halfway Down the Stairs, 128.

44. Roger Geiger, "The Ten Generations of American Higher Education," in *American Higher Education in the Twenty-first Century*, ed. Philip G. Altbach, Robert O. Berdahl, and Patricia Gumport (Baltimore: Johns Hopkins University Press, 1999), 61; John Harp and Philip Taietz, "The Cornell Student, 1950 and 1962: A Comparative Report" (Ithaca: Cornell University, 1964), 25. Between 1950 and 1962, the percentage of Cornell students living in rooming houses declined from 23 to 8 percent, while the percentage living in apartments increased from 7 to 29 percent.

45. Jim Myers, "Collegetown," *Ithaca Journal*, August 22, 1975, Welcome Students issue, 6–8, 13; John Lofland, "The Youth Ghetto: A Perspective on the 'Cities of Youth' around Our Large Universities," *Journal of Higher Education* 39:3 (March 1968): 121–43; Partridge, *Hippie Ghetto*; Clark Kerr, "Clark Kerr Calls It the Exaggerated Generation," *New York Times Magazine*, June 4, 1967, 33; Richard Fariña, *Been Down So Long it Looks Like Up to Me* (New York: Random House, 1966); John Marcham, "A Question of Turf," *Cornell Alumni News*, July 1972, 25.

46. Myers, "Collegetown," 5.

47. Ibid., 8–11.

48. Joseph Masci and Robert A. Molofsky, "Police Gas C-Town Crowd," *Cornell Daily Sun*, May 14, 1972, Extra edition, 1; Dick Brass, "Town vs. Gown," *Cornell Alumni News*, July 1972, 16–23.

49. Jan Mireles, "Is Collegetown Development a Boon or Bust?" *Ithaca Journal*, May 21, 1990, 9A.

50. Cornell, "Cornell University Enrollment, Fall 1868–Current"; Sol L. Erdman, "FCSA Allows Coeds to Live Off Campus," *Cornell Daily Sun*, February 9, 1965, 1; "Residence Rules Are Suspended," *Ithaca Journal*, June 5, 1969; David F. Maisel, "Housing Shortage Plagues University," *Cornell Daily Sun*,

September 20, 1965, 1; Patricia Nordheimer, "University Ready to Enforce Housing-Approval Ruling," *Ithaca Journal*, January 17, 1966, 9; Sue Strandberg, "Tenants Union Becoming Active," *Ithaca Journal*, February 6, 1969; Ithaca Tenants Union, *Tenants Arising: A Case Study of Dynamic Management of Existing Buildings* (Ithaca, 1974); Allison Walzer, "Fane Tenants to Strike," *Cornell Daily Sun*, March 24, 1974, 1.

51. Rob Simon, "A Moveable Lease," *Cornell Daily Sun*, October 6, 1975, 5.

52. Carol Irene Chock, "Collegetown Redevelopment: An Analysis of a Public/Private Partnership in Ithaca, New York" (master's thesis, Cornell University, 1985); H. Matthys Van Court (director of planning and development, city of Ithaca), interview by the author, Ithaca, May 4, 2000.

53. Mireles, "Collegetown Development," 9A; Alex Leary, "Second City," *Ithaca Times*, May 22, 1997, 27–29.

54. "New Student Housing Helps Ease Local Rental Market," clipping of unknown origin, September 1989; Diane Heath, "From Homes to High Rises," *Cornell Daily Sun*, February 11, 1988, 1, 7; Nina Fox, "New Housing Complex Gains Interest among Iowa State U. Students," *Iowa State Daily* [Iowa State University], January 12, 2000; Jeff Johncox, "Apartments Offer Students a Better Life," *Oklahoma Daily* [University of Oklahoma], June 4, 2003; Sterling University Housing web site: http://www.sterlinghousing.com (accessed January 22, 2004); Ben Gose, "Colleges Invest Millions on Improvements to Keep Upperclassmen in Campus Housing," *Chronicle of Higher Education*, February 13, 1998; Alex Kellogg, "Facing More, Possibly Pickier Students, Colleges Renovate and Add Housing," *Chronicle of Higher Education*, October 19, 2001, A37.

55. Myers, "Collegetown," 6; Eli Lehrer, "New

Era Dawns in Collegetown," *Ithaca Journal*, July 30, 1997, 2A; Jason Fane, comments prepared for conference on student housing, Cornell University, April 18, 2000; Jason Fane (real estate developer, Ithaca Renting Company), interview by the author, Ithaca, May 1, 2000; Ithaca Renting Co. web site, http://www.ithacarenting.com (accessed March 16, 2007); 312 College Avenue web site, http://www.312collegeave.com (accessed February 16, 2007).

56. Data are for Census Tract 2, Tompkins County, the boundaries of which roughly approximate those of Collegetown. U.S. Bureau of the Census, "Census 2000." Comparisons for 1980 and 2000 are based on U.S. Bureau of the Census, *1980 Census of Population and Housing*, Neighborhood Statistics Program: New York (Ithaca) (Washington, 1983); City of Ithaca, Department of Planning and Development, "Neighborhood Statistics Program, Census 2000, SF1 & SF3 Releases, April 2004, http://www.ithacamaps.org/download/census/2000NeighborhoodStatistics.pdf (accessed May 14, 2004).

57. John A. Jakle, "Twentieth Century Revival Architecture and the Gentry," *Journal of Cultural Geography* 4:1 (Fall/Winter 1983): 37; Gorman Beauchamp. "Dissing the Middle Class: The View from Burns Park." *American Scholar* 64:3 (1995): 337.

58. U.S. Bureau of the Census, "Census 2000"; Margaret Hobbie (real estate agent, Ithaca), interview by the author, Ithaca, April 29, 2000; George J. Staller (professor, Department of Economics, Cornell University), telephone interview by the author, July 25, 2002.

59. Alfred M. Brooks, "Houses for College Professors," *School and Society* 18:448 (July 28, 1923): 116–18; Deborah Lynn Balliew, *College Station, Texas: 1938/1988* (College Station,

1987), 18; Everett B. Sackett, *New Hampshire's University: The Story of a New England Land Grant College* (Somersworth, N.H.: New Hampshire Publishing Co., 1974), 124; Durham Planning Board, *Town of Durham Master Plan 2000* (Durham, N.H., 2000), 10.3.

60. Parsons, *Cornell Campus*, 113–15; John Roger Ahlfeld, "The First Century of the Physical Development of Ithaca, New York" (master's thesis, Cornell University, 1966), 150.

61. "A Word to Wise Ithacans"; "Cornell Heights," *Ithaca Daily Journal*, May 10, 1899, 8.

62. Carol U. Sisler, *Enterprising Families, Ithaca, New York: Their Houses and Businesses* (Ithaca: Enterprise Publishing, 1986), 87, 90; Carol U. Sisler, "Cornell Heights," in Sisler, Hobbie, and Dieckmann, *Ithaca's Neighborhoods*, 178; Historic Ithaca, *Cornell Heights Historic District: An Architectural Walking and Driving Tour* (Ithaca, 1998), 8.

63. Sisler, "Cornell Heights," 180–81, 186; Sisler, *Enterprising Families*, 94–95; Parsons, *Cornell Campus*, 217.

64. "White Park," undated brochure, Jared Treman Newman Papers, #2157, Box 38, Division of Rare and Manuscript Collections, Cornell University Library; Sisler, *Enterprising Families*, 105–6; A. Robert Jaeger, "Cayuga Heights and the American Suburb," unpublished manuscript, History 333, Cornell University, May 1983, 15, 21; Kenneth T. Jackson, *Crabgrass Frontier: The Suburbanization of the United States* (New York: Oxford University Press, 1985), 79–81.

65. Jared T. Newman, "To Alumni Intending Sometime to Locate in Ithaca," *Cornell Alumni News*, October 21, 1915, 47; "White Park"; Agreement between Jared T. Newman and Charles H. Blood and Karl McKay Wiegand, September 29, 1914, Jared Treman Newman Papers, #2157, Box 9, Division of

Rare and Manuscript Collections, Cornell University Library.

66. Jared T. Newman to Charles Gray Co., December 15, 1920; Letter from Jared T. Newman for which first page is missing, February 23, 1921; Jared T. Newman to John T. Parson, July 17, 1928; Jared T. Newman to W. W. Fisk, May 31, 1922. All letters from Cayuga Heights Collection, History Center in Tompkins County, Ithaca.

67. Minutes, Board of Trustees, Cayuga Heights, 1923–2002, Marcham Hall [Village Hall], Cayuga Heights; F. G. Marcham, "Cayuga Heights Memories," prepared by John Marcham, unpublished manuscript, 26, 29, 37, 92; "Annexation Rejected by Heights," *Ithaca Journal*, December 30, 1954, 3.

68. M. H. Abrams (professor of English emeritus, Cornell University), interview by the author, Cayuga Heights, N.Y., April 30, 2000.

69. Marcham, "Question of Turf," 24; Ronald Anderson (former Cornell faculty member and mayor, village of Cayuga Heights), interview by the author, Cayuga Heights, N.Y., April 28, 2000.

70. Margaret Hobbie, "Belle Sherman," in Sisler, Hobbie, and Dieckmann, *Ithaca's Neighborhoods*, 193; "New Residence Tract," *Ithaca Daily Journal*, September 19, 1908, 2; Rebecca Bernstein, "A History of the Bryant Park Neighborhood, Ithaca, New York: An Architectural and Social Study of Household Use" (master's thesis, Cornell University, 1988), 21–25, 30; Bryant Park Civic Association records, 1941–1951, #3627, Department of Manuscripts and University Archives, Cornell University Library.

71. "New Residence Tract"; Deed, Lot 168, Bryant Park, agreement between Harold E. Ross and Bryant Park Land Co., June 15, 1910, Jared Treman Newman Papers, #2157, Box 9, Division of Rare and Manuscript Collections, Cornell University Library.

72. Bryant Park Civic Association records, 1941–1951.

73. U.S. Bureau of the Census, *Census of Population: 1950*, Volume 1: Number of Inhabitants (Washington, 1952); U.S. Bureau of the Census, *1970 Census of Population*, Characteristics of the Population, Number of Inhabitants (Washington, 1972); John Munschauer, "Village of Cayuga Heights, 1940 to Present," in *The Towns of Tompkins County*, ed. Jane Marsh Dieckmann (Ithaca: DeWitt Historical Society of Tompkins County, 1998), 37, 42.

74. Ellen McCollister (resident, Bryant Park neighborhood), interview by the author, Ithaca, August 11, 2002.

75. Susan Blumenthal (former alderperson, Ithaca Common Council), interview by the author, Ithaca, August 5, 2002.

76. Joel Savishinsky (professor of social sciences, Ithaca College, resident, Bryant Park neighborhood), interview by the author, Ithaca, August 9, 2002.

77. Ibid.

78. Alison Lurie, *The War between the Tates* (New York: Random House, 1974), 36–37.

79. Abrams, interview.

4. Campus Corners and Aggievilles

1. *Flagpole Guide to Athens, 2007–2008*, http://flagpole.com/Guide/ (accessed March 19, 2008).

2. James C. Carey, *Kansas State University: The Quest for Identity* (Lawrence, Kans.: Regents Press of Kansas, 1977), 25; A. Thornton Edward, "A Brief History of On-Campus Residence Halls and Apartments," unpublished paper, Department of Special Collections, Hale Library, Kansas State University, 4.

3. Julius Terrass Willard, *History of the Kansas State College of Agriculture and Applied Science* (Manhattan, Kans.: Kansas State College Press, 1940), 85; Mamie Alexander Boyd,

Rode a Heifer Calf through College (Brooklyn, N.Y.: Pageant-Poseiden, 1972), 88; "From Swamp to City in 20 Years," *Morning Chronicle* [Manhattan, Kans.], December 16, 1923, Aggieville section, 1.

4. "Dr. J. W. Evans Remembers Manhattan of Early Days," *Mercury-Chronicle* [Manhattan, Kans.], July 29, 1945, 7; J. W. Evans, "Reader Writes," newspaper clipping of unknown origin, Riley County Historical Museum, Manhattan, Kansas; advertisement for College Barber Shop, *Students' Herald* [Kansas State Agricultural College], November 24, 1897; "Local Matters," *Students' Herald*, November 24, 1897, 1; advertisement for Hansen's Laundry, *Students' Herald*, January 12, 1899.

5. Advertisement for Manhattan Transfer Company, *Students' Herald*, September 14, 1899, 19; Willard, *History of the Kansas State College*, 115–16.

6. Carey, *Kansas State University*, 78–79; J. D. Walters, *History of Kansas State Agricultural College* (Manhattan, Kans.: Kansas State Agricultural College, 1909), 139.

7. Carey, *Kansas State University*, 79–83; Leslie Anders, *Education for Service: Centennial History of Central Missouri State College* (n.p.: n.p., 1971), 37.

8. *Students' Herald*, September 14, 1899, 17, 20; "The Expanding Harvard Coop," *New York Times*, November 11, 1980, D1.

9. "From Swamp to City in 20 Years," 5; *Manhattan* [Kans.] *Mercury*, February 4, 1903, 7; advertisement for College Grocery, *Students' Herald*, September 11, 1903; "Students Co-Operative Association," *Royal Purple*, 1909 (Manhattan, Kans.: Kansas State Agricultural College, 1909), 213; Dan Walter, *Aggieville, 1889–1989: 100 Years of the Aggieville Tradition* (Manhattan, Kans.: Varney's Book Store, 1995).

10. Winifred N. Slagg, *Riley County, Kansas: A Story of Early Settlements, Rich Valleys, Azure Skies, and Sunflowers* (Manhattan, Kans.: The author, 1968), 71; "The Car Line," *Students' Herald*, August 18, 1909, 12; "New Residence District," *Students' Herald*, October 8, 1910, 6.

11. "From Swamp to City in 20 Years," 5; Wareham Telephone Co., *Directory, 1914* (Manhattan, Kans.: The Nationalist Press, 1914); Sanborn Map Co., fire insurance maps for Manhattan, Kans., 1912 (New York: Sanborn Map Co., 1912; microfilm edition, Alexandria, Va.: Chadwyck-Healey, 1983); Kansas State University, Department of Planning and Analysis, "Kansas State University Enrollment, 1863–2003," unpublished table; J. G. Emery Directory Co., *Republic-Mercury Directory of Manhattan for the Year 1911* (Manhattan, Kans.: Kimball-Vernon, 1911).

12. "Aggieville, the Thriving College Suburb," *Manhattan Daily Mercury*, August 13, 1913, Industrial edition, 69; advertisements for Varsity Shop and Palace Drug Store, *Students' Herald*, August 13, 1910, 5, 7; "Bungalow Dry Goods and Notion Store," *Manhattan Daily Mercury*, August 30, 1913, Industrial edition, 71; advertisement for College Book Store, *Manhattan Daily Mercury*, August 30, 1913, Industrial edition, 73; "The Baker," *Manhattan Daily Mercury*, August 30, 1913, Industrial edition, 72.

13. "From Swamp to City in 20 Years," 5; Sanborn Map Co., fire insurance maps for Manhattan, Kans., 1923 (New York: Sanborn Map Co., 1923; microfilm edition, Alexandria, Va.: Chadwyck-Healey, 1983); "Aggieville Business Directory," *Morning Chronicle*, December 16, 1923, 1; "Banking Facilities Now at A.V. 'Front Door,'" *Morning Chronicle*, December 16, 1923, 6; "Aggieville, the 'City of Youth,'" *Morning Chronicle*, December 16, 1923, 1.

14. "Make Rules for Students," *Kansas State*

Collegian [Kansas State Agricultural College], September 16, 1919; "Betas Dance at Harrison's," *Kansas State Collegian*, September 18, 1915; Dan Walter, *The Harrison Building Scrapbook: 1915–1998* (Manhattan, Kans.: Varney's Book Store, 1998), 23, 27; "A Restriction on Dance Hall Crowd," *Manhattan Mercury*, November 15, 1940; "Doors of Miller Theatre Will Open This Evening," *Morning Chronicle*, May 1, 1926, Miller Theatre Section, 1. The Avalon Ballroom closed in 1948 after attendance at dances declined. By that time there were three bars in Aggieville and other dance halls in Manhattan. Nichols Gym on campus replaced the Avalon as the site of many large college dances. See "Avalon to Close after 33 Years," *Kansas State Collegian*, March 15, 1948.

15. The editors, "Somehow," *Royal Purple*, 1932 (Manhattan, Kans.: Kansas State Agricultural College, 1932).

16. Robert Smith Bader, *Prohibition in Kansas: A History* (Lawrence: University Press of Kansas, 1986), 229; advertisements for Shamrock Tavern, *Royal Purple*, 1937, 1949 (Manhattan, Kans.: Kansas State Agricultural College, 1937 and 1949).

17. KSU, "Kansas State University Enrollment, 1863–2003"; "More Than 20 New Businesses in Aggieville," newspaper clipping of unknown origin, September 5, 1946, Riley County Historical Museum; Sanborn Map Co., fire insurance maps for Manhattan, Kans., 1947 (New York: Sanborn Map Co., 1947; microfilm edition, Alexandria, Va.: Chadwyck-Healey, 1983); R. L. Polk & Co., *Manhattan (Riley County, Kans.) City Directory*, 1946, 1951 (Kansas City, Mo.: R. L. Polk & Co, 1946, 1951).

18. Dick Morgan, quoted in Peg Braasch, "Growth of Aggieville Meets Campus Needs," *Kansas State Collegian* [Kansas State University], April 21, 1972, 10A.

19. The Students' Co-Operative Book Store appears to have ceased to be a true cooperative organization about 1912. It changed its name from the Co-Op Book Store to the Campus Book Store in 1947. See advertisement for Campus Book Store, *Kansas State Collegian*, September 12, 1947, 6.

20. Walter, *Aggieville, 1889–1989*; advertisement for Yeo & Trubey Electric Co., *Kansas State Collegian*, September 12, 1947, 6; "Aggieville Rocks n' Rolls to Bands and Jamboree," *Kansas State Collegian*, September 24, 1956, 1.

21. Kansas State Agricultural College, *Royal Purple*, 1950 (Manhattan, Kans.: KSAC, 1950), 97; *Manhattan City Directory, 1951*; "Those Were the Days," *Manhattan Mercury*, October 30, 1994; Bernie Butler (owner, Pizza Hut, Aggieville), interview by the author, Manhattan, June 8, 2004; Charles Hostetler (Manhattan native, KSU graduate, and partner, Charleson & Wilson Insurance Agency, Manhattan), interview by the author, Manhattan, June 7, 2004.

22. *Kansas State Collegian*, September 24, 1918; "Canteen Serves K-Staters and Uniformed Men during Two Wars," *Kansas State Collegian*, June 10, 1943; Cynthia A. Harris, "Mary Louise Pierce Van Zile: First Dean of Women at Kansas State Agricultural College," research paper, HIST 586, Kansas State University, Fall 1998, Department of Special Collections, Hale Library, Kansas State University; Willard, *History of the Kansas State College*, 258; Bob Rousey (1953 KSAC graduate and longtime Manhattan resident), telephone interview by the author, July 19, 2004; advertisement for College Canteen, *Royal Purple*, 1947 (Manhattan, Kans.: KSAC, 1947), 396.

23. Kansas State Agricultural College, "Constitution and SGA Regulations," *Student Directory, Kansas State College, 1950–1951* (Manhattan, Kans.: KSAC, 1950), 143–45; Kansas State University, *Kansas State University Directory, 1965–1966* (Manhattan,

Kans.: KSU, 1965), 14; Joyce Jenkins, quoted in Daryl Jepson, "Burger Joints Boom in the 50s," *Kansas State Collegian*, April 21, 1972, 4A.

24. Edwin Olson (Manhattan native and owner, Olson's Shoe Service), interview by the author, Manhattan, June 7, 2004; Charles Hostetler, e-mail message to the author, July 19, 2004; Rousey, interview; Becky Ballard (Manhattan resident and co-owner, Ballard's Sporting Goods, Aggieville), interview by the author, Manhattan, June 7, 2004.

25. Terry Ray (former owner of Kite's and four other Aggieville bars), telephone interviews by the author, July 9 and 20, 2004; Bob Sands, "Kite's Gone, but Memories Still Flow," *Manhattan Mercury*, January 29, 1995, C7; Bill Colvin, "Cancer Claims Kite Thomas," *Manhattan Mercury*, January 8, 1995, A1.

26. Butler, interview; Hostetler, interview; Ray, interviews; Walter, *Aggieville, 1889–1989*; Mike Kuhn (Manhattan resident and former Aggieville bar owner), interview by the author, Manhattan, June 11, 2004; Olson, interview.

27. "Damage by Staters Estimated at $700," *Kansas State Collegian*, March 8, 1956; "Remember When?" *Kansas City Star*, February 4, 1988.

28. Walter, *Aggieville, 1889–1989*; Ellie Brent (retired owner, Woody's Lady's Shop, Aggieville), interview by the author, Manhattan, June 9, 2004.

29. Carey, *Kansas State University*, 226–34; Jenn Davoren, "Up in Smoke," *Kansas State Collegian*, November 10, 1999, 1.

30. Jonah Boone, "Ein Kleines Nachttraum," in *Cows Are Freaky When They Look at You: An Oral History of the Kaw Valley Hemp Pickers*, ed. David Ohle, Robert Martin, and Susan Brosseau (Wichita, Kans.: Watermark Press, 1991), 12; Rusty L. Monhollon, "Lawrence, Kansas, and the Making of the Sixties," in *Embattled Lawrence: Conflict and Community*, ed. Dennis Domer and Barbara Watkins (Lawrence, Kans.: University of Kansas Continuing Education, 2001), 212; Louie Louis, "Picking Hemp in Douglas County," in *Embattled Lawrence*, 244; Carey, *Kansas State University*, 244.

31. Carey, *Kansas State University*, 224–34; Bob Kirk, "Nixon Visit Not a Compliment [letter to the editor]," *Kansas State Collegian*, September 15, 1970, 2; Calvin Trillin, "U.S. Journal: Manhattan and Atchison, Kans.," *New Yorker*, June 12, 1971, 90.

32. Larry Reynolds, "Clenched Fist Baffles Police," *Kansas State Collegian*, September 14, 1970, 4; John Heritage (former owner, Texas Star Café and Hibachi Hut, Aggieville), interview by the author, Manhattan, June 8, 2004; Alvan Johnson (Riley County Commissioner and retired director of Riley County Police Department, Manhattan), interview by the author, Manhattan, June 9, 2004; Butler, interview.

33. Carey, *Kansas State University*, 223; Cece Jones, "Women's Self-Limited Hours Adopted According to Needs," *Kansas State Collegian*, August 7, 1970, 5; Edward, "A Brief History of On-Campus Residence Halls," 14; Leete Coffman, "Co-ed Halls Step to Natural Living," *Kansas State Collegian*, March 20, 1969, 7.

34. Advertisement for The Door, *Kansas State Collegian*, February 27, 1970, 3; advertisements for Whitewater Leather Co. and Earthshine, *The Mushroom* [Manhattan, Kans.] 2:3, n.d., Riley County Historical Museum; Roger Zerener, "American Dream, Thumbs Down to Big Business," *Kansas State Collegian*, April 29, 1970, 6; advertisement for Treasure Chest, *Kansas State Collegian*, October 7, 1968; Jules Asher, "New Food Store Deals in Exotic Eatables," *Kansas State Collegian*, September 10, 1970, 7; advertisement for Experimental Light Farm, *Kansas*

State Collegian, October 2, 1969, 2; Heritage, interview; R. L. Polk & Co., *Manhattan (Riley County, Kans.) City Directory*, 1975 (Kansas City, Mo.: R. L. Polk & Co., 1975).

35. Ballard, interview; Jon Levin (owner, Varney's Book Store), interview by the author, Manhattan, December 6, 1999; advertisement for Waggoner's, *Kansas State Collegian*, October 21, 1969, 10; advertisement for Campus Theater, *Kansas State Collegian*, September 26, 1969, 2; Hugh Moffett, "Sexy Movies? Chadron, Neb. Tries Gentle Persuasion," *Life*, May 30, 1969, 52B–57.

36. Johnson, interview.

37. "Mescin' Around," *The River* [Manhattan, Kans.] 3, n.d, Department of Special Collections, Hale Library, Kansas State University.

38. R. L. Polk & Co., *Manhattan (Riley County, Kansas) City Directory*, 1964, 1972, 1980 (Kansas City, Mo.: R. L. Polk & Co., 1965, 1972, 1980); Becky Howard, "Barber Tells of 62 Years in Aggieville," *Kansas State Collegian*, July 2, 1986, 2.

39. KSU, "Kansas State University Enrollment, 1863–2003"; "Aggieville Area's Fame Known throughout the State," *Manhattan Mercury*, August 20, 1978, D5; Jenny Dean, "Aggieville: A Neon World Corrals Youths Fresh Off Farm," *Kansas City Star*, September 9, 1984, 1A; Deborah Neff, "Higher Drinking Age Affects College Town's Business, Social Habits," *Kansas City Times*, September 7, 1985, B1.

40. Advertisement for the Jon, *Kansas State Collegian*, September 29, 1969, 11; advertisement for Kite's and Mr. K's, *Kansas State Collegian*, February 24, 1970, 6; advertisement for Mother's Worry, *Kansas State Collegian*, September 15, 1981, 10; advertisement for Kite's, *Kansas State Collegian*, September 18, 1981; advertisement for Alpha Tau Omega Chug-A-Thon, *Kansas State Collegian*, April 23, 1971, 10; advertisement for Mother's

Worry, *Kansas State Collegian*, June 16, 1976, 5; Dan Walter (longtime Manhattan resident and textbook manager, Varney's Book Store), interview by the author, Manhattan, December 1, 1999.

41. Press release for Kite's, no date, Riley County Historical Museum; Diane Webb, "Football Victories, Defeats Determine Taverns' Business," *Kansas State Collegian*, October 30, 1973, 10; Ray, interviews.

42. Kuhn, interview.

43. Lori Bergen, "It Beats to a Nocturnal Drummer," *Kansas State Collegian*, April 29, 1983; Diane Meredith (KSU student during 1980s and owner, Dusty Bookshelf and Acme Gift, Aggieville), telephone interview by the author, June 23, 2004; Randy Griffin (KSU undergraduate, 1977–83), e-mail message to the author, July 23, 2004; William L. Stimson, *Going to Washington State: A Century of Student Life* (Pullman: Washington State University Press, 1989), 254.

44. Mark R. Edwards, "Dazed Aggievillians Ask: 'It Couldn't Happen Again, Could It?'" *Manhattan Mercury*, October 16, 1972, A1; Patti Urosevich, "Aggievillians Take Storm in Stride," *Manhattan Mercury*, November 20, 1978, A1.

45. Valerie Strauss, "College Towns, School Officials Seek End to Post-Game Rioting," *Washington Post*, April 4, 2001, B9; Brian Dekoning, "More Arrests Likely for UNH Rioting," *Foster's Daily Democrat* [Dover, N.H.], April 14, 2003, 1; Dave Curtin and Courtney Lingle, "Melee Tests Hill's Resolve," *Denver Post*, December 3, 2001, B1; John D. McCarthy, Andrew Martin, and Clark McPhail, "The Policing of U.S. University Campus Community Disturbances, 1985–2000," paper presented at the workshop "Policing Public Protest after Seattle," May 1–5, 2004, Fiskebackekil, Sweden.

46. Kellee Miller, "Riot in the 'Ville," *Kansas State Collegian*, December 1, 1999, 1; Wayne

T. Price, "Police Arrest 15 K-State, 2 KU Students," *Kansas State Collegian*, October 15, 1984, 1; Lucy Reilly, "Riots in Aggieville Stun Local Officials," *Kansas State Collegian*, October 15, 1984, 8; Wayne Price, "Crowd Vents Anger in Attack on Police," *Kansas State Collegian*, October 15, 1984, 8; "Plans Being Made to Prevent Future Clashes with Students," United Press International, October 15, 1984, AM cycle.

47. Mike Doucey, "Aggieville: A Night of Turmoil," *Manhattan Mercury*, October 20, 1986, B8; Lillian Zier, "Owners Pick Up Pieces from Horde's Rampage," *Kansas State Collegian*, October 20, 1986, 1; "K-State Melee Shows Signs of Becoming Tradition," United Press International, October 20, 1986, AM cycle; "Regional News," United Press International, November 6, 1986, BC cycle; "Regional News," United Press International, November 21, 1986, BC cycle; Tim J. Janicke, ed., *A Week at Kansas State* (Manhattan, Kans.: Student Publications, 1987), 157; Miller, "Riot in the 'Ville."

48. Kansas State University, Office of the President, press release, October 27, 1987, Department of Special Collections, Hale Library, Kansas State University; Bill Felber, "RCPD Is Ready For Saturday," *Manhattan Mercury*, November 2, 1987, A1; "Aggieville Crowded but Basically Calm," *Manhattan Mercury*, November 8, 1987, A1; "Regional News," United Press International, November 8, 1987, BC cycle; Johnson, interview; Bill Felber (executive editor, *Manhattan Mercury*), interview by the author, Manhattan, June 10, 2004.

49. R. L. Polk & Co., *Manhattan (Riley County, Kansas) City Directory*, 1965, 1970–71 (Kansas City, Mo.: R. L. Polk & Co., 1966, 1970); Walter, *Aggieville, 1889–1989*; Paul Rhodes, "'Ville Growing, but . . . ," *Manhattan Mercury*, October 16, 1983, C1; R. L. Polk & Co., *Manhattan, Kansas, City Directory*, 1985

(Kansas City, Mo., 1985); "New Complex to Offer Variety of Services," *Kansas State Collegian*, September 18, 1987.

50. Chad L. Sanborn, "'Ville Raises Its Head Again after Near Death," *Kansas State Collegian*, April 17, 1989.

51. See, for example, Debra F. Erenberg and George A. Hacker, *High-Risk Bar Promotions That Target College Students: A Community Action Guide* (Washington: Center for Science in the Public Interest, 1997); Leo Reisberg, "Some Experts Say Colleges Share the Responsibility for Recent Riots," *Chronicle of Higher Education*, May 15, 1998; Leo Reisberg, "2 Years after Colleges Started Calling Home, Administrators Say Alcohol Policy Works," *Chronicle of Higher Education*, January 19, 2001, A34–A36; Henry Wechsler and Bernice Wuethrich, *Dying to Drink: Confronting Binge Drinking on College Campuses* (New York: St. Martin's Press, 2002); Henry J. Wechsler et al., "Secondhand Effects of Student Alcohol Use Reported by Neighbors of Colleges: The Role of Alcohol Outlets," *Social Science and Medicine* 55 (2002): 425–35.

52. Kansas Legislative Research Department, "Kansas Liquor Laws," 2001, http://www.ksrevenue.org/pdf/Kansas_Liquor_Laws_2001.pdf (accessed August 12, 2004).

53. Kuhn, interview; Jola Murphy, "Local Beer Tavern Soon to Shut Down," *Kansas State Collegian*, June 16, 1987; Steve Walker, "Dark Horse Tavern to Close Doors May 14," *Kansas State Collegian*, May 4, 1988, 3; Lisa Stevens, "Changes in Aggieville Aid Business," *Kansas State Collegian*, University edition, August 1988, 2B; Bill Felber, "Aggieville: Transition," *Manhattan Mercury*, June 12, 1988, A1; Renee Beaudoin, "Where Have All the Kids Gone," *Manhattan Mercury*, August 17, 1986, KSU edition; John Meirowsky, "Kite's Name Auctioned to Bar Owner," *Kansas State Collegian*, April 11, 1994, 1.

54. Bill Colvin, "Rays Seek Chapter 11 Protec-

tion," *Manhattan Mercury*, September 1, 1991, A1; Blake Gumprecht, "Drinking Bill Passage Would Reflect National Trend," *University Daily Kansan* [University of Kansas], February 27, 1980, 1; Ray, interviews.

55. "Manhattan Town Center Stands Out in Kansas," *Chain Store Age Executive*, January 1987, 72–76; R. L. Polk & Co., *Manhattan (Riley County, Kans.) City Directory*, 1963 (Kansas City, Mo.: R. L. Polk & Co., 1964); Hammer, Siler, and George Associates, *Community Market Strategy: Manhattan, Kansas* (Manhattan, Kans.: City of Manhattan Community Development Department, 2002); Mike Dorcey, "Downtown: A Re-Fill," *Manhattan Mercury*, June 12, 1988, A1.

56. R. L. Polk & Co., *Manhattan (Riley County, Kans.) City Directory*, 1970–71, 1977, 1978, 1982, 1983, 1984 (Kansas City, Mo., 1977, 1978, 1982, 1983, 1984); Karen Rainey, "Shopping Bag Appeal: Several Aggieville Stores Sell Unusual Goods and Services," *Kansas State Collegian*, April 29, 1983, Dimensions section; Mark Scott, "Aggieville . . . Theaterless," *Manhattan Mercury*, July 17, 1998, A1.

57. Gwyn Riffel (owner, Riffel Property Management, Manhattan), interview by the author, Manhattan, June 10, 2004; Felber, "Aggieville: Transition"; Brent, interview; Richard Andrade, "Hard Times in Aggieville," *Kansas State Collegian*, July 16, 1992, 12–13.

58. Meredith, interview.

59. R. L. Polk, *Manhattan City Directory*, 1980; author's fieldwork, 2004.

60. When asked why his business failed, the manager of a chain record store in Lawrence that closed in 2001, said, "We're owned by a corporation. We've gotten a bad name as a corporation. It's a college town: 'damn the man.'" "Chain Music Store to Close," *Lawrence Journal-World*, March 1, 2001.

61. Tom Monaghan with Robert Anderson, *Pizza Tiger* (New York: Random House,

1986), 113, 137; Robert Halasz and Suzanne L. Rowe, "Kinko's," in *International Directory of Company Histories*, ed. Thom Votteler (Detroit: St. James Press, 1988), 43: 261–62.

62. Don Dodson, "Champaign-Urbana Area Investors Open Sandwich Franchises across Country," *News-Gazette* [Champaign, Ill.], October 14, 2002; Don Nelson, "Small Business News," *Athens* [Ga.] *Banner-Herald*, February 8, 2004; History and locations, Pita Pit web site, http://www.pitapit.com (accessed July 28, 2004); "Corporate Information," Gumby's Pizza web site, http://www.gumbyspizza.com/corporateinfo.html (accessed July 28, 2004); Andrew Waters, "Street Talk," *Columbia* [Mo.] *Daily Tribune*, September 27, 2000; Store locator, Chipotle Mexican Grill website, http://www.chipotle.com (accessed July 28, 2004); Kathryn Mayes, "City to Help with Parking Garage Study," *Manhattan Mercury*, May 5, 2004.

63. KSU, "Kansas State University Enrollment, 1863–2003"; Kansas State University, *Fact Book 2007*, http://www.k-state.edu/pa/statinfo/reports/student/index.htm (accessed May 4, 2007); Scott Daugherty, "New Aggieville Designs Unveiled," *Manhattan Mercury*, July 15, 2004; Scott Daugherty, "Aggieville Gets Facelift," *Manhattan Mercury*, July 19, 2004; Abbie Whited, "City Sets New Housing Regulations," *Kansas State Collegian*, October 8, 2003; Michael Ashford, "Campus Edge Project at a Standstill," *Kansas State Collegian*, February 23, 2006; City of Manhattan, Planning Division, *Users' Guide to the Multi-Family Redevelopment Overlay District* (Manhattan, n.d.).

64. Kansas Department of Revenue, Alcohol Beverage Control, "Liquor Licensee Search" web page, http://www.kdor.org/abc/licensee/LicenseeDb.aspx (accessed May 9, 2007).

65. KSU, "Kansas State University Enrollment, 1863–2003"; KSU, *Fact Book 2007*; Alexander

C. McCormick and Laura J. Horn, *A Descriptive Summary of 1992–93 Bachelor's Degree Recipients: 1 Year Later; With an Essay on Time to Degree*, National Center for Educational Statistics Statistical Analysis Report NCES 96–158 (Washington: U.S. Department of Education, 1996), 11; Ellen M. Bradburn et al., *A Descriptive Summary of 1999–2000 Bachelor's Degree Recipients 1 Year Later; With an Analysis of Time to Degree*, National Center for Educational Statistics Statistical Analysis Report NCES 2003–165 (Washington: U.S. Department of Education, 2003), 21, 24; Kelly Simmons, "Colleges Face Crunch over Space," *Atlanta Journal-Constitution*, January 20, 2004, 8B; Kansas State University, Department of Planning and Analysis, "Big Twelve Longitudinal Retention Survey," 1995–2005, http://www.k-state.edu/pa/statinfo/retention/UnivTot.pdf (accessed May 4, 2006); Kansas State University, Department of Planning and Analysis, "Number by Age, Undergraduates, Fall 2005," unpublished table.

66. Michael Moffatt, *Coming of Age in New Jersey: College and American Culture* (New Brunswick, N.J.: Rutgers University Press, 1989), 50; statistics provided by Riley County Police Department, Manhattan; Rusty Wilson (owner, Kite's Bar and Grill, former owner, Rusty's Last Chance), interview by the author, Manhattan, June 11, 2004.

67. Wilson, interview; Karen Sottosanti, "Chance Encounter . . . A Playboy Pick," *Manhattan Mercury*, August 28, 1997, A1; Cori Muth, "Aggieville Is One Huge Street Party (with Beer)," *Manhattan Mercury*, November 15, 1998, A1.

68. Layton Ehmke, "Aggieville Empire: Popular Bar Continues to Grow in Aggieville," *Kansas State Collegian*, March 13, 2003; Jeremy Claeys, "Smoke-Free Bar Offers Aggieville Alternative," *Kansas State Collegian*, August 28, 2000; Jessica Pits, "New Stores,

Restaurants Open in 'Ville," *Kansas State Collegian*, September 3, 2002; Edie Hall, "Sports-Oriented Atmosphere Theme of New Aggieville Bars," *Kansas State Collegian*, January 28, 2003; Wilson, interview.

69. Description of the social geography of Aggieville's bars is based on the author's fieldwork in 1999, 2001, and 2004, and interviews with Rusty Wilson, owner of Kite's and former owner of Rusty's Last Chance, and Billy Porter, who co-owns five Aggieville bars.

70. Walter, *Aggieville, 1889–1989*; Walter, interview.

71. Ballard, interview; Olson, interview; Butler, interview; "Campus Fourum," *Kansas State Collegian*, August 26, 2003.

72. Meredith, interview; Riffel, interview.

73. See, for example, Derek Prater, "Lawrence City Officials Draw the Line with New Downtown Bars: Ordinance Designed to Prevent New Aggieville," *University Daily Kansan* [University of Kansas], November 29, 1999; Joel Mathis, "City Battle on Tap over Downtown Bars," *Lawrence Journal-World*, January 17, 2004.

74. Paul Schumaker, "Downtown Lawrence: Marketplace and Heart of a Political Community," in *Embattled Lawrence*, 299.

75. Lindsey Praechter, "Lawrence Offers Diversity Not Found in Manhattan," *Kansas State Collegian*, October 10, 2003.

76. Everett Carll Ladd, Jr., and Seymour Martin Lipset, *The Divided Academy: Professors and Politics* (New York: McGraw-Hill, 1975); Richard Hamilton and Lowell L. Hargens, "The Politics of the Professors: Self-Identifications, 1969–1984," *Social Forces* 71: 3 (1993): 603–27.

77. Schumaker, "Downtown Lawrence."

78. Wilson, interview.

79. Steve Wilson (manager, Kief's Downtown Music, Lawrence), e-mail to the author, July

16, 2004; Meredith, interview; Steve Wilson, e-mail to the author, July 13, 2004.

5. All Things Right and Relevant

1. Don Lotter, "The Davis Farmers' Market, Thirty Years On," *The New Farmer*, April 2004, http://newfarm.org/features/0404/davis/index.shtml (accessed March 7, 2006).

2. R. J. Ignelzi, "In Davis, California, No Ifs, Ands or Butts," *San Diego Union-Tribune*, May 8, 1994, D1.

3. See, for example, Everett Carll Ladd, Jr. and Seymour Martin Lipset, *The Divided Academy: Professors and Politics* (New York: McGraw-Hill, 1975); Richard F. Hamilton, "The Politics of the Professors: Self-Identifications, 1969–1984," *Social Forces* 71:3 (March 1993): 603–27; Daniel B. Klein and Charlotta Stern, "How Politically Diverse Are the Social Sciences and Humanities?" http://www.ratio.se/pdf/wp/dk_ls_diverse.pdf (accessed December 6, 2005).

4. Tom Hritz, "Weirdo Hunting in Davis, Calif.," *Pittsburgh Post-Gazette*, March 4, 1995, B1.

5. *Davis Enterprise* columnist Bob Dunning, who has made a career of lampooning Davis liberals, coined the phrase, which has since gained wide usage locally.

6. John Nichols, "Urban Archipelago: Progressive Cities in a Conservative Sea," *The Nation*, June 20, 2005, 13–16; Yvonne Abraham and Michael Paulson, "Wedding Day," *Boston Globe*, May 18, 2004, A1; Jon Spayde, "Our Kind of Town," *Utne Reader*, May–June 1997, 45–49; William Poole, "Inside Ecotopia," *Sierra*, January 1998; Mary Curtius, "Town Goes with the Low-Tech Flow," *Los Angeles Times*, November 30, 1998, A3; Chapel Hill Bicentennial Commission, *Chapel Hill: 200 Years—"Close to Magic"* (Chapel Hill, N.C.: Town of Chapel Hill, 1994), 79; Jonathan Marwil, *A History of Ann Arbor* (Ann Arbor: University of Michigan Press, 1991), 161–62;

George A. Pettit, *Berkeley: The Town and Gown of It* (Berkeley, Calif.: Howell-North Books, 1973), 142; Charles Wollenberg, *Berkeley: A City in History*, Berkeley Public Library, Berkeley, California, 2002, http://berkeleypubliclibrary.org/system/historytext.html (accessed November 29, 2005); Raymond Lee Muncy, *Searcy, Arkansas: A Frontier Town Grows Up with America* (Searcy, Ark.: Harding Press, 1976), 417.

7. California Secretary of State, *Statement of Vote: General Election, November 7, 1972* (Sacramento, 1972), 70; Ted Bell, "Davis Votes Dictated Prop. 187's Yolo Rejection," *Sacramento Bee*, November 16, 1994, B4; California Secretary of State, "Supplement to the Statement of Vote," 2000 General Election, President, Political Districts Within Counties, http://www.ss.ca.gov/elections/sov/2000_general/ssov/pol_dis.pdf (accessed December 5, 2005); *Dave Leip's Atlas of U.S. Presidential Elections*, http://www.uselectionatlas.org (accessed December 5, 2005); Christophe Olson, "Williams Should Focus on Real Problem," *The Missoulian* (Missoula, Mont.), December 27, 2000.

8. Ann F. Scheuring, *Abundant Harvest: The History of the University of California, Davis* (Davis: University of California, 2001), 16–20, 28, 48; Joann Leach Larkey, *Davisville '68: The History and Heritage of the City of Davis, Yolo County, California* (Davis: Davis Historical and Landmarks Commission, 1969), 46, 70.

9. Scheuring, *Abundant Harvest*, 58–60, 62, 77–78, 94–95, 110, 118; John Lofland, *Davis: Radical Changes, Deep Constants* (Charleston, S.C.: Arcadia, 2004), 110; John Lofland, *Davis City Council Elections, 1917–2000* (Woodland, Calif.: Yolo County Historical Society, 2001), 15.

10. Lofland, *Davis: Radical Changes, Deep Constants*, 132–34; James Stevens (former mem-

ber of Davis City Council and Yolo County Superior Court judge), telephone interview by the author, November 11, 2005.

11. Frank and Eve Child (former Davis residents), telephone interview by the author, November 7, 2005; Dale Lott (former professor, UC Davis, now deceased), interview by the author, Davis, May 25, 2005; John Knox, "They Brought Holland to Davis," *Daily Democrat* [Woodland, Calif.], September 30, 1976, B11.

12. University of California, Davis, *Long Range Development Plan* (Davis, 1963). It is not known exactly when UC Davis closed the central campus to autos.

13. Robert Sommer and Dale F. Lott, "Bikeways in Action: The Davis Experience," unpublished report, 1971; Frank and Eve Child, telephone interview; Lott, interview; Dale Lott, "How Our Bike Lanes Were Born," *Davis Enterprise*, July 27, 2003; Knox, "They Brought Holland to Davis"; Letter to the editor signed by "Just a Taxpayer," *Davis Enterprise*, March 7, 1966, 6; Dave Pelz (former public works director, city of Davis), interview by the author, Davis, May 22, 2001.

14. Maynard Skinner (former member of Davis City Council and two-time mayor), interview by the author, Davis, May 17, 2001; Lott interview; Lofland, *Davis: Radical Changes, Deep Constants*, 129.

15. Ed Goodykoontz, "Council Okays Pioneer Bike Path System for Davis," *Davis Enterprise*, April 12, 1966, 1; Knox, "They Brought Holland to Davis"; Lott, "How Our Bike Lanes Were Won"; "Bike Paths Bill Co-Authors Here to Check Lanes," *Davis Enterprise*, September 8, 1967, 1; Sommer and Lott, "Bikeways in Action."

16. Several American cities in the nineteenth century created bike paths separated from roads, and Homestead, Florida, in 1962 initiated a new era in bike path development, but Davis was the first city to designate a portion

of streets solely for bicycle use. Robert A. Smith, *A Social History of the Bicycle: Its Early Life and Times in America* (New York: American Heritage Press, 1972), 214–17, 249.

17. Larkey, *Davisville '68*, 79; "Emblem for Centennial Celebration Is Selected," *Woodland* [Calif.] *Daily Democrat*, April 11, 1968.

18. Pelz, interview; David Takemoto-Weerts (UC Davis bicycle program coordinator), e-mail message to the author, December 15, 2005; City of Davis, University of California, Davis, *Davis Bike Map*, 4th ed. (Davis, 2003); Tim Bustos and Ad Hoc Bicycle Task Force, *City of Davis Comprehensive Bike Plan* (Davis: City of Davis, 2001).

19. De Leuw, Cather & Company, "Bicycle Circulation and Safety Study" (San Francisco, 1972); City of Davis, *General Plan*, May 2001 (Davis, 2001), 114; Pelz, interview; City of Davis, *Municipal Code*, sec. 40.11.070, http://www.cityofdavis.org/cmo/citycode (accessed December 14, 2005); Tim Bustos (bicycle coordinator, city of Davis), interview by the author, Davis, May 21, 2005; Bustos and Ad Hoc Bicycle Task Force, *City of Davis Comprehensive Bicycle Plan*, 2; League of American Bicyclists, "Bicycle Friendly Communities," http://www.bicyclefriendlycommunity.org/list.htm (accessed December 13, 2005).

20. Beth Curda, "Is Davis' Top-Rated Bike Culture Starting to Backpedal?" *Davis Enterprise*, November 16, 2003; Bob Sommer, "Where Have All the Cyclists Gone?" *Davis Enterprise*, May 18, 2003, A11; David Takemoto-Weerts, letter to Bob Sommer, May 19, 2003, http://www.runmuki.com/paul/writing/takemoto.html (accessed December 14, 2005); U.S. Bureau of the Census, Census of Population and Housing, 1990 and 2000, http://factfinder.census.gov (accessed December 15, 2005).

21. Susan Strasser, *Waste and Want: A Social History of Trash* (New York: Metropolitan

Books, 1999), 72, 80–81, 103–5, 127–28, 212–13.

22. Richard Gertman (founder of original Davis recycling program; principal, Environmental Planning Consultants, San Jose, Calif.), telephone interview by the author, November 4, 2005.

23. Ibid.; Neil Seldman, "The Rise and Fall of Recycling," *Environmental Action*, January/February 1987, 12; Andrew Kirk, " 'Machines of Loving Grace': Alternative Technology, Environment, and the Counterculture," in *Imagine Nation: The American Counterculture of the 1960s and 1970s*, ed. Peter Braunstein and Michael William Doyle (New York: Routledge, 2002), 363–65; "Student Drive Launched for 44,000 Aluminum Cans," *Davis Enterprise*, April 3, 1970, 1.

24. Gertman, telephone interview; R. Gertman, "Recycling in Davis, California," *Waste Management & Research* 2 (1984): 293–302.

25. James J. Nagle, "One-Way Containers Make Further Gains," *New York Times*, September 1, 1968, F12; Frank Ackerman, *Why Do We Recycle? Markets, Values, and Public Policy* (Washington: Island Press, 1997), 125; Mark Pendergrast, *For God, Country, and Coca-Cola: The Definitive History of the Great American Soft Drink and the Company That Makes It* (New York: Basic Books, 2000), 295; Martin Melosi, *Garbage in the Cities: Refuse, Reform, and the Environment*, rev. ed. (Pittsburgh: University of Pittsburgh Press, 2005), 207; Gertman, telephone interview.

26. Bob Black, campaign brochures, 1972 Davis City Council election; David M. Cohen, *A National Survey of Separate Collection Programs* (Washington: U.S. Environmental Protection Agency, 1979), 10; Bob Black (former member of Davis City Council and Yolo County Board of Supervisors, present Del Norte County counsel), telephone interviews by the author, November 4 and 9, 2005.

27. Scheuring, *Abundant Harvest*, 119–23, 194;

Gertman, "Recycling in Davis," 294. Population data compiled by California Department of Finance and provided by City of Davis Community Development Department.

28. Black, telephone interviews; Gary Hyman, "City Backs Recycle Law," *Davis Enterprise*, November 6, 1973, 1; Cohen, *National Survey of Separate Collection Programs*, 10; Gertman, "Recycling in Davis," 294; Gertman, telephone interview.

29. Gertman, "Recycling in Davis," 295–301; Paul Hart (president, Davis Waste Removal), interview by the author, Davis, May 21, 2001; Mike Fitch, *Growing Pains: Thirty Years in the History of Davis*, 1998, chap. 4, http://www.city.davis.ca.us/pb/cultural/30years/ (accessed December 9, 2005).

30. Judy Breninger, "Davis Model for County Recycling Plans," *Davis Enterprise*, August 29, 1979, 3; Gertman, telephone interview; Nick Burdick, "Davis Cleans Up in Effort to Boost Recycling in California," *Sacramento Bee*, September 22, 1994, N2; Cory Golden, "City on Par with Recycling," *Davis Enterprise*, August 9, 2004; California Integrated Waste Management Board, "Jurisdiction Diversion Rate Summary," http://www.ciwmb.ca.gov/lgtools/mars/DrmcMain.asp (accessed December 19, 2005).

31. Black, telephone interviews.

32. Scheuring, *Abundant Harvest*, 143, 173; Black, telephone interviews.

33. Black, telephone interviews.

34. Ann F. Scheuring, "The First 75 Years: III," *UC Davis Magazine*, Spring 1984, 15; Scheuring, *Abundant Harvest*, 155–57; "The Quiet Campus," *UC Davis Magazine*, Fall 1996, 16–20; Joe White and Peter Magnam, "The City of Davis—What Lies in the Future," *Davis Enterprise*, January 21, 1969, 1.

35. Black, telephone interviews.

36. Lofland, *Davis: Radical Changes, Deep Constants*, 138; Skinner, interview; Black, telephone interviews.

37. Skinner, interview; Black, telephone interviews; Gregg Foster, "Davis Politics and the Progressive Coalition, 1972–1988," research paper, Political Science 193, University of California, Davis, 1988, 5, 12; Pat Fulton, "Students Reveal How They Did It," *Davis Enterprise*, April 14, 1972, 1.

38. William Endicott, "Slate Backed by UC Davis Students Wins Council Jobs," *Los Angeles Times*, April 13, 1972, 1, 27; Bob Black, campaign brochures, 1972 Davis City Council election; Pat Fulton, "Winners Buoyed by Landslides," *Davis Enterprise*, April 12, 1972, 1; Fitch, *Growing Pains*, chap. 2.

39. Lofland, *Davis City Council Elections*, 8; Greg de Giere, "All Four City Propositions Win Big Too," *Davis Enterprise*, April 12, 1972, 1; Endicott, "Slate Backed by UC Davis Students Wins Council Jobs," 1, 27; "Election Results Breakdown," *Davis Enterprise*, April 12, 1972, 3; Rich Moreno, "'72 Election: Effects in Retrospect," *Davis Enterprise*, October 1, 1981, 21.

40. "Council Votes to Let City Workers Off 2 Hours Friday to Attend Moratorium," *Davis Enterprise*, April 19, 1972, 1; Jim Adamek, "Council Supports Peaceful Protests," *Davis Enterprise*, May 9, 1972, 1; Black, telephone interviews.

41. Greg de Giere, "Councilman Plus 59 Other Anti-War Protestors Jailed," *Davis Enterprise*, May 10, 1972, pp, 1, 13; Pat Fulton, "The S.P. Train Incident," *Davis Enterprise*, May 10, 1972, 1, 13; Barbara Hooker, "Davis War Foes Halt Trains," *Sacramento Bee*, May 10, 1972, A1.

42. Because of the moratorium, fewer than two hundred housing units were built between 1973 and 1975. In the previous two years, 2,500 units had been added. Dwelling unit data compiled by California Department of Finance and provided by City of Davis Community Development Department.

43. City of Davis, *General Plan*, adopted 1973, 3, 5, 72–73; John Lofland, "Davis City Planning, 1925–2005," draft manuscript, 29; Peter M. Zorn, David E. Hansen, and Seymour I. Schwartz, "Mitigating Price Effects of Growth Control: A Case Study," *Land Economics* 62:1 (February 1986): 49; Lofland, *Davis: Radical Changes, Deep Constants*, 138.

44. Karen Seidel, "Coping with Growth," in *Eugene, 1945–2000: Decisions That Made a Community* (Eugene: City Club of Eugene, 2000), 52; Douglas Porter, *Managing Growth in America's Communities* (Washington: Island Press, 1997), 32.

45. Black, telephone interviews; Davis, *General Plan*, adopted 1973.

46. James Ridgeway, "A Community Energy Plan: Davis Leads the Way," *Organic Gardening & Farming*, December 1976, 31; Sandra Blakeslee, "A City Plans Code to Save Energy," *New York Times*, October 6, 1975, 32; "First Lady's Visit to Davis Top Story of '79," *Davis Enterprise*, December 31, 1979, 1; David Pauly, "The Thriftiest Town of All," *Newsweek*, April 18, 1977, 74.

47. Art Nauman, "Townsfolk Keep Davis Different," *Sacramento Bee*, April 9, 1978, A1; David Rosenberg (Yolo County Superior Court judge and former member of the Davis City Council and Yolo County Board of Supervisors), e-mail to the author, November 21, 2005; average City Council meeting length calculated from City Council minutes, http://www.city.davis.ca.us/meetings/oldagendas.cfm?CommissionID=18 (accessed December 27, 2005); David Weinshilboum, "City OKs General Plan," *Davis Enterprise*, May 24, 2001, 1.

48. Bob Dunning, "Private, Collective Actions Get All Mixed Up," *Davis Enterprise*, July 8, 2005, 2A; California Secretary of State, *Report of Registration, State of California*, November 3, 1970 (Sacramento, 1970), 86; California Secretary of State, "Report of Registration as of September 9, 2005,"

http://www.ss.ca.gov/elections/ror/090905/
pol_sub_09_09_05.pdf (accessed February
16, 2006).

49. Fitch, *Growing Pains*, chap. 5; Communi-
Care Health Centers website, http://www
.communicarehc.org (accessed December
29, 2005); Short Term Emergency Aid Committee website, http://www.dcn.davis.ca.us/
go/steac/ (accessed December 29, 2005).

50. The Co-Op Network, *National Co-op Directory, 2005: A Guide to the Cooperative Natural
Food System* (Bethel, Vt., 2005).

51. Robert Sommer, "More Than Cheap Cheese:
The Food Co-op Movement in the United
States," *Research in Social Movements,
Conflict and Change* 7 (1984): 72; Maria
McGrath, " 'That's Capitalism, Not a Co-op,':
Countercultural Idealism and Business Real-
ism in 1970s U.S. Food Co-ops," *Business
and Economic History On-Line* 2 (2004), 3
http://www.thebhc.org/publications/BEH
online/2004/McGrath.pdf (accessed March
7, 2006); Daniel Zwerdling, "The Uncertain
Revival of Food Cooperatives," in *Co-ops,
Communes, & Collectives: Experiments in So-
cial Change in the 1960s and 1970s*, ed. John
Case and Rosemary C. R. Taylor (New York:
Pantheon Books, 1979), 93.

52. Ann Evans (founder, Davis Food Co-op;
former member of Davis City Council and
mayor), interview by the author, Davis, May
20, 2001.

53. Ibid.; Chris Laning, "Looking Back: A Co-op
History," unpublished manuscript, revised
version of a study originally published in
three parts in the Davis Food Co-op newsletter, 1987–93.

54. Laning, "Looking Back"; Evans, interview.

55. Elisabeth Sherwin, "Davis Food Co-op,"
Davis Enterprise, April 22, 1980, 9; Laning,
"Looking Back."

56. Laning, "Looking Back"; David J. Thompson,
"A Choice of Futures Face the Davis Food
Co-op," *Winds of Change*, October 1981, 7.

57. Laning, "Looking Back"; Davis Food Co-op,
"Chronology," unpublished document.

58. Doug Walter (membership director, Davis
Food Co-op), interview by the author, Davis,
May 17, 2001; David Thompson, "Davis Food
Co-op: Turnaround Tale," *Cooperative Grocer*
22 (April–June 1989); Davis Food Co-op,
"Growth of Capital and Members," unpub-
lished table.

59. Dave Webb, "Marketing a Changed Co-op,"
and Dennis McLearn, "Managing a Turnaround," both in *Cooperative Grocer* 22
(April–June 1989); Walter, interview; David
Thompson (longtime Davis resident and cooperative promoter), interview by the author,
Davis, May 20, 2001.

60. Sales data provided by Davis Food Co-op;
Davis Food Co-op, "Growth of Capital and
Members"; Gillian Butler, "Davis Food
Co-op: Learning from a Failure," *Cooperative
Grocer* 57 (March–April 1985).

61. Dave Webb and Chris Laning, "Why Another
Logo?" *Davis Co-Op News*, March 1989, 6.

62. Davis Food Co-op, *'What's That Doing on the
Shelf?!?'* (Davis, 2004); "New Seafood Labeling Program Launched through Davis Food
Co-op," *Davis Enterprise*, April 24, 2005, 7C;
Walter, interview; Eric Stromberg (general
manager, Davis Food Co-op), interview by
the author, Davis, May 22, 2001.

63. Katherine Bishop, "Who'll Sell Tofu Puffs
after Co-ops Are Gone?" *New York Times*,
June 6, 1988, 14; Karen Zimbelman, "Berkeley: Lessons for Co-op Leaders," *Cooperative
Grocer* 38 (January–February 1992); Thompson, interview.

64. Doug Walter (Davis Food Co-op membership director), e-mail to the author, January
8, 2006; Dave Atkinson, "Davis Food Co-op
Has a Truly Giving Spirit," *Davis Enterprise*,
October 11, 1998, Celebration of Cooperation
section, 6; Caryn Cardello, "Coffee Co-op
Members Talk of Fair Trade," *Davis Enterprise*, April 20, 2000; Julie Cross and Doug

Walter, "Carrots in the Classroom," *Cooperative Grocer* 117 (March–April 2005); Corey Golden, "Co-op Adds High-Tech Solar Roof," *Davis Enterprise*, June 30, 2004, 1.

65. Fitch, *Growing Pains*, chap. 4; Lofland, *Davis: Radical Changes, Deep Constants*, 140–41; Jeff Loux and Robert Wolcott, "Innovation in Community Design: The Davis Experience," paper presented to the Make Cities Livable Conference, February 22–26, 1994, San Francisco; Ted Fourkas, "Designed to Be Partners with the Sun," *Sacramento Bee*, April 11, 1977, CL11–12; John Dreyfuss, "Developer's Social Values Go into Tract," *Los Angeles Times*, July 2, 1979, part 1, 1.

66. Village Homes has been the subject of four books: David A. Bainbridge, Judy Corbett, and John Hofacre, *Village Homes' Solar House Designs: A Collection of 43 Energy-Conscious House Designs* (Emmaus, Pa.: Rodale Press, 1979); Michael N. Corbett, Judy Corbett, and John Klein, *A Better Place to Live: New Designs for Tomorrow's Communities* (Emmaus, Pa.: Rodale Press, 1981); Judy Corbett and Michael Corbett, *Designing Sustainable Communities: Learning from Village Homes* (Washington: Island Press, 2000); and Mark Francis, *Village Homes: A Community by Design* (Washington: Island Press, 2003).

67. Cohousing Association of the United States, "United States Cohousing Communities," http://directory.cohousing.org/us_list/all_us.php (accessed January 6, 2005).

68. Scheuring, *Abundant Harvest*, 170; David Thompson, "Davis: A Guide to the City of Cooperatives," unpublished manuscript, 2000; Kevin Wolf (N Street Cohousing organizer), interview by the author, Davis, May 24, 2001; Kevin Wolf, telephone interview by the author, October 15, 2005.

69. The Danish communities were not known by the cohousing name, which was applied later by two American architects. They were called *bofællesskaber*, which translates as "living communities." Kathryn McCamant and Charles Durrett, *Cohousing: A Contemporary Approach to Housing Ourselves*, 2nd edition (Berkeley, Calif.: Ten Speed Press, 1994), 12.

70. Virginia Thigpen (longtime Davis developer), interview by the author, Davis, May 21, 2001; Kathryn McCamant and Charles Durrett, *Cohousing: A Contemporary Approach to Housing Ourselves* (Berkeley, Calif.: Habitat Press, 1988). All other citations in this chapter are to the second edition.

71. Kathleen Frances Smith, "Retrofit Cohousing: Redesigning Existing Neighborhoods to Meet the Changing Needs of Today's Society," master's thesis, University of California, Berkeley, 1998, 21; Tracey Jefferys-Renault, "Tearing Down Fences," *Farmer Bob's Sometimes News & Local Review*, June 1989, 1; Donna Spreitzer, "Living in My Thesis: Cohousing in Davis, California," master's thesis, School for International Training, 1992, http://wheel.dcn.davis.ca.us/go/nstreet/library/Spreitzer/thesis.html (accessed January 13, 2006); Wolf, interview, 2001; Wolf, telephone interview, 2005; Thigpen, interview.

72. McCamant and Durrett, *Cohousing*, 38, 209–10; Thigpen, interview; Don Stanley, "Davis Group Lucked Out with a Site for Planning," *Sacramento Bee*, September 29, 1991, E1; Don Stanley, "Once Again, Group Living Experiments Are Sprouting," *Sacramento Bee*, September 29, 1991, E1, E4.

73. See, for example, Eric Nee, "Davis, Calif.: 26 Units of Co-Housing," *New York Times*, May 26, 1991, sect. 8, 1; Claudia Morain, "Common Ground," *Los Angeles Times*, March 31, 1992, E1; Betsy Streisand, "Creating an Instant Extended Family," *U.S. News & World Report*, April 6, 1992, 82.

74. McCamant and Durrett, *Cohousing*, 38, 40; Streisand, "Creating an Instant Extended Family."

75. Thigpen, interview; Kate Markey (Muir Commons resident), interview by the author, Davis, May 23, 2001; Sumita Mukherji, "Co-housing Group Goes Solar," *Davis Enterprise*, June 30, 2002, 1A.

76. McCamant and Durrett, *Cohousing*, 38; Muir Commons, "Newcomer's Guide," August 1996; Charlie Thomsen (Muir Commons resident), interview by the author, Davis, May 23, 2001.

77. Rick Mockler (Muir Commons resident), e-mail to the author, January 11, 2006; Markey, interview.

78. Stanley, "Davis Group Lucked Out with a Site for Planning," E4; Melanie Turner, "A Sense of Community," *Davis Enterprise*, November 29, 1992, C1; Charlie Thomsen, interview; Holly Istas Thomsen (Muir Commons resident), interview by the author, Davis, May 23, 2001.

79. Wolf, interview, 2001; Wolf, telephone interview, 2005; Smith, "Retrofit Cohousing," 19–20; Spreitzer, "Living in My Thesis."

80. Wolf, interview, 2001; Wolf, telephone interview, 2005.

81. Smith, "Retrofit Cohousing," 21–23, 32; Teresa Simons, "Davis Neighbors Tear Down Their Fences to Build Extended Family," *Los Angeles Times*, April 23, 1989, 3; Tracy Jefferys-Renault, "Tearing Down Fences," *Farmer Bob's Sometimes News & Local Review*, June 1989, 13; Wolf, interview, 2001; Wolf, telephone interview, 2005; Kevin Wolf, e-mail to the author, January 12, 2006.

82. Wolf, interview, 2001; Wolf, telephone interview, 2005.

83. Wolf, interview, 2001; Wolf, telephone interview, 2005; Webb Hester (Muir Commons resident), conversation with the author, Davis, May 21, 2001.

84. Lofland, *Davis: Radical Changes, Deep Constants*, 137, 145; John Lofland and Lyn H. Lofland, "Lime Politics: The Selectively Progressive Ethos of Davis, California,"

Research in Political Sociology 3 (1987): 250–51, 253.

85. Lofland and Lofland, "Lime Politics," 250–51; Crystal Ross O'Hara, "Davis Considered Gay Friendly," *Davis Enterprise*, June 8, 2004; Nichols, "Urban Archipelago," 16; Living Wage Resource Center, "Living Wage Wins," http://www.livingwagecampaign.org/index.php?id=1959 (accessed January 17, 2005).

86. Gorman Beauchamp, "Dissing the Middle Class: The View from Burns Park," *American Scholar* 64:3 (Summer 1995): 340.

87. Gretchen Kell, "Davis Boldly Battles Rising Urban Tide," *Sacramento Bee*, June 2, 1985, 1; Zorn, Hansen, and Schwartz, "Mitigating the Price Effects of Growth Control," 56–57; Bob Dunning, "That Housing Shortage," *Davis Enterprise*, September 6, 1985.

88. California Department of Finance, "Population Estimates for California Counties and Cities," 1970–75, http://www.dof.ca.gov/HTML/DEMOGRAP/E4call.htm (accessed January 20, 2006); California Department of Finance, "Population Estimates for California State and Counties," 1981–90, http://www.dof.ca.gov/HTML/DEMOGRAP/90e-4.xls (accessed January 20, 2006).

89. Fitch, *Growing Pains*, chap. 6; City of Davis, *General Plan*, May 2001, 48.

90. Fitch, *Growing Pains*, chap. 6; Lofland, *Davis: Radical Changes, Deep Constants*, 139; Black, telephone interviews. Population data compiled by California Department of Finance and provided by City of Davis Community Development Department.

91. University of California, Davis, Planning and Budget Office, "Davis Campus, Net Campus Population," *Statistical Supplement to the Academic Plan* (Davis, 1989); Lofland, *Davis: Radical Changes, Deep Constants*, 145–47.

92. Lauren Obermueller, "Voters Say 'No' to Widening," *Davis Enterprise*, March 5, 1997, A1; Fitch, *Growing Pains*, chap. 8; Melanie Turner, "Davis Wants Say in Future Sprawl,"

Davis Enterprise, May 8, 2000; David Weinshilboum, "General Plan Is History," *Davis Enterprise*, May 22, 2001, A1; City of Davis, *General Plan*, May 2001, 88; University of California, Davis, *Neighborhood Master Plan* (Davis, 2003), http://www.westvillage .ucdavis.edu/development/masterplan.html (accessed January 25, 2005).

93. California Coalition for Rural Housing and Non-Profit Housing Association of Northern California, *Inclusionary Housing in California: 30 Years of Innovation* (Sacramento?, 2003), 2, 31–35; City of Davis, *General Plan*, adopted 1973, 73; Zorn, Hansen, and Schwartz, "Mitigating the Price Effects of Growth Control," 49; City of Davis, "Overview of the City's Affordable Housing Program," unpublished document; City of Davis, "Overview of the City's Inclusionary Ordinance," unpublished document; Katherine Hess (administrator, City of Davis Community Development Department), telephone interview by the author, November 18, 2005; Danielle Foster (housing programs manager, city of Davis), e-mail to the author, February 1, 2006; Claire St. John, "Housing Rules Win City's Okay," *Davis Enterprise*, December 14, 2005, A1.

94. Rob Weiner (executive director, California Coalition for Rural Housing), telephone interview by the author, November 22, 2005.

95. Covell Village Partners, "Covell Village: An Innovative Solar Village for Davis," http:// www.covellvillage.com (accessed January 26, 2005); Mike Corbett, "Covell Village: It's a Perfect Fit," *Davis Enterprise*, June 12, 2005, C5; Ken Wagstaff and others, "Davis Can't Afford Covell Village," *Davis Enterprise*, July 17, 2005, B7; Jeffrey M. Barker, "Is Davis Turning Red?" *Sacramento News & Review*, November 3, 2005; Claire St. John, "Voters Just Say No," *Davis Enterprise*, November 9, 2005, A1.

96. "We're Voting Yes on X" (advertisement),

Davis Enterprise, October 23, 2005, A3; Black, telephone interviews.

97. Eileen Samitz (longtime Davis resident and founder, Citizens for Responsible Planning), telephone interview by the author, November 21, 2005.

6. Paradise for Misfits

1. Rodger Lyle Brown, *Party Out of Bounds: The B-52's, R.E.M., and the Kids Who Rocked Athens, Georgia* (New York: Plume, 1991), 142.

2. Mark Maynard, "Pylon: Sounds, Utterances and Everything . . . ," *Crimewave USA* 14 (2003): 22.

3. Richie Unterberger, "Chapel Hill," *Music USA* (New York: Rough Guides, 1999), 127–31; John Hess, "Where Have All the Writers Gone? To Iowa City, That's Where," *Holiday*, June 1969, 61–63, 68; Holly Carver (director, University of Iowa Press), e-mail to the author, October 24, 2007; William Kittredge, "Montana Renaissance," in *The Last Best Place: A Montana Anthology*, ed. William Kittredge and Annick Smith (Helena: Montana Historical Society, 1988), 760–65; Betty Wetzel, *Missoula: The Town and the People* (Missoula: Montana Magazine, 1987), 48–53; John Villani, *The 100 Best Art Towns in America*, 4th ed. (Woodstock, Vt.: Countryman Press, 2005), 161, 234–35.

4. In addition to the people featured in this chapter, I also interviewed David Barbe, Barrie Buck, James Cobb, Tom Dyer, Tony Eubanks, Jim Herbert, Carol John, Bill "Gomer" Jordan, Judy Long, Deonna Mann, Carl Martin, Jim Payne, Andrew Rieger, Ella Silverman, and Rebecca Wood.

5. Pete McCommons, e-mail to the author, July 11, 2003; Pete McCommons, interviews by the author, Athens, October 5–6, 1999; Frances Taliafero Thomas, *A Portrait of Historic Athens & Clarke County* (Athens: University of Georgia Press, 1992), 199.

6. Thomas G. Dyer, *The University of Georgia:*

A *Bicentennial History, 1785–1985* (Athens: University of Georgia Press, 1985), 268, 337–45; Thomas, *Portrait of Historic Athens*, 224; McCommons, interviews.

7. Thomas, *Portrait of Historic Athens*, 224; Dyer, *University of Georgia*, 347–50; Mary Cantwell, "University of Georgia," *Mademoiselle*, August 1973, 275; McCommons, interviews.

8. For a reminiscence of the El Dorado's beginnings and Athens at the time, see John (Pat) Huie, "Even Hippies Have to Eat," *Flagpole*, September 15, 2004.

9. McCommons, interviews. McCommons and Searcy discuss the paper's first year in Charles Giddens, "Closeup: Pete McCommons . . . Chuck Searcy," *Athens Observer*, January 2, 1975, 2–3, 6.

10. Pete McCommons, telephone conversations with the author, July 16 and 18, 2003.

11. Art Harris, "Oh Little Town of Rock 'n' Roll," *Washington Post*, August 29, 1994, B1.

12. Pete McCommons, "What a Difference a Decade Makes," *Athens Magazine*, December 1989; McCommons, interviews.

13. Abe Peck, *Uncovering the Sixties: The Life and Times of the Underground Press* (New York: Pantheon, 1985), 29–30; Tim Wong, "The Wong Truth Conspiracy: A History of Madison Alternative Journalism," in *Voices from the Underground: Volume 1, Insider Histories of the Vietnam Era Underground Press*, ed. Ken Wachsberger (Tempe, Ariz.: Mica's Press, 1993), 269–92; Thomas Mead Jennings, "The Underground Press to the Alternative Press: A Case Study of the Athens News, 1977–1980" (master's thesis, Ohio University, 1993); Erik Cushman (publisher, *Monterey County Weekly*), e-mail to the author, September 13, 2007.

14. Pete McCommons, telephone interview by the author, June 7, 2007; Pete McCommons, e-mail to the author, June 14, 2007; Pete

McCommons, "Athens and How It Got This Way," *Flagpole*, August 17, 2005.

15. For a remembrance of Greenwood, see Steve Wilson, "A Tribute to Steve Greenwood," *Lawrence.com: Deadwood edition*, October 11, 2005, 6, http://www.lawrence.com/news/2005/oct/10/tribute_steve_greenwood/ (accessed June 20, 2007).

16. John Seawright, interview by the author, October 3, 1999.

17. Seawright, interview.

18. Brown, *Party Out of Bounds*, 51, 114.

19. "Jon Krakauer," *Contemporary Authors Online*, 2004, http://galenet.galegroup.com (accessed November 1, 2007); Roger Mummert, "In the Valley of the Literate," *New York Times*, November 16, 2007, D1.

20. Seawright, interview; Julie Phillips Jordan. "City Loses Friend, Historian," *Athens* [Ga.] *Banner-Herald*, May 15, 2001; Julie Phillips Jordan, "Vic Chesnutt: This Is What He Does," *Athens Banner-Herald*, June 28, 2001.

21. Michael Lachowski, interview by the author, Athens, October 5, 1999.

22. Ibid.; Bill King, "Athens: A City Attuned to the New Wave-Length," *Atlanta Journal & Constitution*, August 30, 1981, 1F; Brown, *Party Out of Bounds*, 156.

23. Maynard, "Sounds, Utterances and Everything"; Brown, *Party Out of Bounds*, 84–85; Lachowski, interview, 1999.

24. Brown, *Party Out of Bounds*, 86–90, 110–12; Lachowski, interview, 1999.

25. Karen Moline, "Temporary Rock," *New York Rocker*, March 1981, 15–17.

26. Michael Lachowski, interview by the author, Athens, July 30, 2003; Bo Emerson, "Pylon Pilots a Reunion as Athens Rock Fans Chomp Up the News," *Atlanta Journal & Constitution*, October 14, 1988; Jason Gross, "Pylon," *Perfect Sound Forever*, May 1988, http://www.furious.com/perfect/pylon.html (accessed August 14, 2003).

27. Carrie Lare, "Flicker Finds a Spot," *Flagpole*, February 23, 2000; "Flicker Society and Flicker Theater and Bar," *The Red and Black* [University of Georgia], March 2, 2000; Lachowski, interview, 1999.

28. Lachowski, interview, 2003; Michael Lachowski, telephone interviews by the author, June 1 and 4, 2007; Jonathan Reed, "Candy Sweetens Athens' Growing Turntable Scene," *Red and Black*. October 23, 1998; "DJ to Lend His Talents," *Red and Black*, April 24, 1998; Michael Ruppersburg, "Fashioning Electronic 'Candy,'" *Red and Black*, April 26, 2002; Jennifer Schultz, "The Big Lachowski," *Flagpole*, February 28, 2001; Lee Valentine Smith, "Feast on My Art," *Flagpole*, June 15, 2005.

29. Lachowski, telephone interviews, 2007; "Atomlook" website, http://atomlook.com (accessed June 18, 2007).

30. Lachowski, telephone interviews, 2007; Chelsea Cook, "Local Magazine 'Cool, Beautiful,'" *Red and Black*, April 30, 2007; Blake Aued, "Winning Bus Shelter Designs Chosen," *Athens Banner-Herald*, May 18, 2006; Chad Radford, "Pillar of the Community," *Flagpole*, December 29, 2004.

31. Lachowski, telephone interviews, 2007.

32. Tom Patterson, "Joni Mabe's Public Obsessions," *CRITS: Discourses on the Visual Arts*, 1990, 10–18.

33. Joni Mabe, interview by the author, Athens, October 5, 1999.

34. Pete McCommons, "Joni Mabe Finds Art in Elvis, Jesus, Rock and Roll, Sex, Death, Religion, and Sin," *Georgia Alumni Record*, June 1995, 33–38; Greg Freeman, "In This Art Exhibit, It's Not Their Eyes That Catch Yours," *Red & Black*, April 8, 1983, 1.

35. Pete McCommons, "Art Show Poster Causes a Stir," *Athens Observer*, May 26, 1983, 4A; Molly Read, "Controversial Art Ripped from Walls," *Red & Black*, June 1, 1983, 2; Chuck Reece, "Controversial Artist Trying to Point Out Southern Contradictions with Her Work," *Red & Black*, June 3, 1983, 6; Patterson, "Joni Mabe's Public Obsessions," 13.

36. Mabe, interview, 1999; Mabe, interview by the author, Athens, July 1, 2003; Joni Mabe, *Everything Elvis* (New York: Thunder's Mouth Press, 1996).

37. Joni Mabe, telephone interview by the author, June 13, 2007; Melissa Link and Mary Jessica Hammes, "Love Me Obsessive," *Flagpole*, August 19, 1998, 6.

38. Mabe, interviews, 1999, 2003.

39. Barrie Buck, interview by the author, Athens, October 2, 1999.

40. King, "Athens: A City Attuned to the New Wave-Length"; Jessica Greene, interview by the author, Athens, June 30, 2003.

41. Ted Hafer, interview by the author, Athens, October 5, 1999.

42. Greene, interview.

43. Barrie Buck, conversation with the author, Athens, June 30, 2003. For a reminiscence of the Grit's beginnings by one of its founders, see Melanie Hander Reynolds, "How the Grit Got Started," *Flagpole*, October 4, 2006.

44. Greene, interview.

45. Hafer, interview.

46. Greene, interview; Ballard Lesemann, "Athens Eatery Reveals All," *Flagpole*, November 28, 2001; Jessica Greene and Ted Hafer, *The Grit Cookbook: World-Wise, Down-Home Recipes* (Athens: Hill Street Press, 2001); Ted Hafer, telephone interview by the author, June 7, 2007. The Chicago Review Press in 2006 published an expanded edition of the cookbook to commemorate the restaurant's twentieth anniversary.

47. Mark Rozzo, "When Audible Meets Edible," *New Yorker*, July 1, 2002; Mollie Katzen (co-founder, Moosewood Restaurant, Ithaca, N.Y.), e-mail to the author, October 19, 2007; Josh Katzen (co-founder, Moosewood),

e-mail to the author, October 23, 2007; Ranae Gillie (co-owner, Gillie's Restaurant, Blacksburg, Va.), telephone conversation with the author, October 23, 2007; Melissa Trotman, "A Day in the Life of a Restaurant Owner," *Collegiate Times* [Virginia Polytechnic and State University], September 28, 2006; Elaine Ramseyer (general manager, Longbranch Coffeehouse, Carbondale, Ill.), telephone conversation with the author, October 23, 2007; Micah Sturr, "A Taste of Laramie," *Laramie Boomerang*, June 29, 2006; Karen Iacobbo and Michael Iacobbo, *Vegetarians and Vegans in America Today* (Westport, Conn.: Praeger, 2006), 42–43; Melissa Murphy (owner, Sweet Melissa's Restaurant, Laramie), telephone conversation with the author, October 23, 2007.

48. Rebecca McCarthy, "A Writer's Town," *Atlanta Journal and Constitution*, April 11, 1999, 1M; Judy Long (editor, Hill Street Press), e-mail to the author, July 2003; Rodger Lyle Brown, "Dance This Dusty Mess Around," *Creative Loafing Atlanta*, February 13, 2002; "Campus Music Scenes That Rock," *Rolling Stone*, February 20, 2003, 45–57.

49. Brown, "Dance This Dusty Mess Around"; *Flagpole Guide to Athens, 2007–2008*, http://flagpole.com/Guide/ (accessed March 19, 2008); Flagpole, *Athens Music Directory*, http://flagpole.com/MusicDirectory/ (accessed June 19, 2007); Patterson Hood, e-mail to Peter Jesperson (senior vice president, New West Records), July 21, 2003.

50. David Peisner, "The Phony Earth Below My Feet," *Creating Loafing Atlanta*, April 2, 2003; Vic Chesnutt, interview by the author, Athens, October 2, 1999.

51. Travis Nichols, "It Weren't Supernatural," *Flagpole*, October 20, 1999; Meegan Perry, "Vic Chesnutt," *Mote Magazine*, May 1999, http://www.moregoatthangoose.com/interviews/chesnutt.htm (accessed July 22, 2003); Vic Chesnutt, "Bio," http://www.vicchesnutt.com/bio.html (accessed July 22, 2003); Steve Dollar, "The Paraplegic Troubadour," *GQ*, August 1996, 57.

52. Vic Chesnutt, interview.

53. Miriam Chesnutt (Vic Chesnutt's mother), interview by Peter Sillen, *Speed Racer: Welcome to the World of Vic Chesnutt*, VHS, produced and directed by Peter Sillen (Dashboard Dog Pictures, 1993).

54. Michael Stipe, interview by Peter Sillen, *Speed Racer*.

55. Vic Chesnutt, interview.

56. MySpace.com pages for Superchunk, Southern Culture on the Skids, Less Than Jake, Against Me, Sister Hazel, and Green Day; Chris Stamey website, http://www.chrisstamey.com (accessed November 1, 2007); Phish, "Band History," http://www.phish.com/bandhistory/ (accessed November 1, 2007); Unterberger, *Music USA*, 431; Shayna Miller, "Butch Is Back," *Madison Magazine*, January 2006; Butch Vig Productions, "Butch Vig Biography," http://www.garbage.suite.dk/bio.html (accessed November 1, 1977).

57. Various artists, *Sweet Relief 2: The Songs of Vic Chesnutt*, Sony Records, 1996; Vic Chesnutt, interview; William Bowers, "Little Big Man," *No Depression*, May/June 2003, 66–79.

58. Lee Smith, "The Gospel According to Vic," *Creative Loafing Atlanta*, April 3, 2003.

59. Melissa Link, "Helping Our Pubs Enjoy? The Hope Scholarship Has Had a Big Impact on UGA and Athens," *Flagpole*, September 15, 1999, 10–11.

60. Vic Chesnutt, interview; Andrew Rieger (singer and Athens resident), interview by the author, Athens, October 3, 1999; U.S. Bureau of the Census, *2005 American Community Survey*, http://factfinder.census.gov (accessed June 1, 2007); U.S. Bureau of the

Census, "General Population and Housing Characteristics: 1990," http://factfinder .census.gov (accessed July 25, 2003).

61. Janis Reid, "Mayor: I'll Sign Rental Ordinance," *Athens Banner-Herald*, May 7, 2003.

62. Melissa Link, "Very Nice DJ Divas Discuss Cardboard, Polka and the Cost of Living in Athens," *Athens Banner-Herald*, August 16, 2001.

63. Melissa Link (writer, Athens), comment to Athens-Clarke County Commission, May 6, 2003.

64. Al Dixon (Athens resident), comment to Athens-Clarke County Commission, May 6, 2003.

65. Matt Thompson (Athens resident), comment to Athens-Clarke County Commission, May 6, 2003.

66. Janis Reid, "Rental Registration Ban Now Law," *Athens Banner-Herald*, June 5, 2003; Allison Floyd, "A-C Weights Next Move after Ruling," *Athens Banner-Herald*, February 21, 2004; Pete McCommons, "Bang the Drum Slowly," *Flagpole*, July 16, 2003; Allison Floyd, "Rental Regulation Passes," *Athens Banner-Herald*, August 6, 2003.

67. Rodrecas Davis (artist and Athens resident), e-mail to the author, July 21, 2003.

68. Julie Phillips, "Transcript: Interview with Pylon," http://onlineathens.com/stories/123004/roc_20041230005.shtml (accessed June 19, 2007).

7. Stadium Culture

1. Bob Hille, "The Best Sports Cities," *Sporting News*, August 11, 2006, 22–23.

2. Murray Sperber, *Beer and Circus: How Big-Time College Sports Is Crippling Undergraduate Education* (New York: Henry Holt, 2000).

3. Mike Fish, "No Easy Answers Can Explain Bowden's Departure at Auburn," *Atlanta Journal & Constitution*, October 31 1998, 1E; John Sayle Watterson, *College Football: History, Spectacle, Controversy* (Baltimore: Johns Hopkins University Press, 2000), 380.

4. John Bale, *Sports Geography* (London: E. & F. N. Spon, 1989), 20.

5. John F. Rooney, Jr., and Richard Pillsbury, *Atlas of American Sport* (New York: Macmillan, 1992), 62.

6. Auburn University implemented new regulations before the 2002 season that forbid the staking off of spaces earlier than 4 p.m. on the day before the game for safety reasons. See Auburn University, *The 2002 Guide to Game Day at Auburn University* (Auburn: Auburn University, 2002).

7. Southeast Research and Alabama Bureau of Tourism and Travel, unpublished study on fan spending at a 2003 Auburn-Tennessee football game.

8. The Auburn Grille closed in 2004 after sixty-eight years on College Street. Stan Bailey, "Auburn Landmark Closes," *Birmingham News*, March 31, 2004.

9. Al Reinert, *Rites of Fall: High School Football in Texas* (Austin: University of Texas Press, 1979), 8.

10. In response to security concerns raised by the September 11, 2001, attacks on the World Trade Center and Pentagon, Auburn University in October 2001 implemented new regulations that forbid the parking of RVs in the areas immediately surrounding Jordan-Hare Stadium. The regulations have altered somewhat the geography of tailgating described here. See Auburn University, *The 2002 Guide to Game Day at Auburn University*.

11. For a lively exploration of RVers who follow the University of Alabama football team, see Warren St. John, *Rammer Jammer Yellow Hammer: A Journey into the Heart of Fan Mania* (New York: Crown, 2004).

12. Toomer's lemonade was featured in Charles Pierce's "162 Reasons It's Good to Be an

American Man [In No Particular Order]," *Esquire*, December 2001, 112–15.

13. John Egerton, *The Americanization of Dixie: The Southernization of America* (New York: Harper's Magazine Press, 1974), 176.

14. Robert G. Murphy and Gregory A. Trandel, "The Relation between a University's Football Record and the Size of Its Applicant Pool," *Economics of Education Review* 13:3 (1994): 265–70.

15. Auburn University, Office of Institutional Research and Assessment, "Historical Enrollment Fall Terms, 1859–2006," http://www.panda.auburn.edu/factbook/enrollment/enrtrends/hefq.aspx (accessed March 26, 2007); Auburn University, Department of Athletics, Media Relations Department, *2006 Auburn Football Media Guide*, http://auburntigers.cstv.com/sports/m-footbl/spec-rel/06-fb-media-guide.html (accessed March 26, 2007).

16. Michael Bezilla, *Penn State: An Illustrated History* (University Park, Pa.: Pennsylvania State University Press, 1985), 277.

17. Mike Poorman, "It's A Wonderful Life, Joe Paterno," *Town & Gown*, December 1998, 26; St. John, *Rammer Jammer Yellow Hammer*, 209.

18. Jeff Beard, "Jordan-Hare Stadium, Down through the Years," unpublished manuscript, 1989, Special Collections and Archives Department, Ralph Brown Draughon Library, Auburn University, 2; "HomeComing of Old Auburn Men to Bring Many," *Opelika Daily News*, October 3, 1924, 1; "Auburn Beat Georgia, Saturday Winning Southern Championship," *Opelika Daily News*, November 24, 1913, 1.

19. For an interesting psychological study of the propensity for fans to identify with winning teams, see Robert B. Cialdini and others, "Basking in Reflected Glory: Three (Football) Field Studies," *Journal of Personality and Social Psychology* 34 (1976): 366–75.

20. Frederick Rudolph, *The American College and University: A History* (New York: Alfred A. Knopf, 1962), 379.

21. "The New Gymnasium," *Auburn Alumnus*, January 1914, 110; "Alumni Enjoy Home-Coming." *Plainsman* [Alabama Polytechnic Institute], October 10, 1924, 1.

22. Andrew Doyle, "Causes Won, Not Lost: Football and Southern Culture, 1892–1983" (diss., Emory University, 1998), 171–75; Dwayne D. Cox, "Academic Politics at Auburn University, 1872–1983," Special Collections and Archives Department, Ralph Brown Draughon Library, Auburn University, 2001, http://www.lib.auburn.edu/archive/auhy/au%5Fpolitics.htm (accessed March 26, 2007).

23. Spright Dowell, "A Report by the President to the Board of Trustees," *Bulletin, Alabama Polytechnic Institute* 12:8 (November 1927): 3–29; Doyle, "Causes Won, Not Lost," 177–78; Cox, "Academic Politics at Auburn University"; Watterson, *College Football*, 380.

24. Bradford Knapp, "Prexy's Page," *Auburn Alumnus*, October 1928, 8; "A Stadium at Auburn," *Auburn Alumnus*, April 1928, 14; "$20,000 in Donations Launches Stadium Drive," *Auburn Alumnus*, May 1930, 1, 10; Jesse Frederick Steiner, *Americans at Play: Recent Trends in Recreation and Leisure Time Activities* (New York: McGraw-Hill, 1933), 91.

25. Associated Press article reprinted as "Happy Football Days Are Here Again," *Auburn Alumnus*, October 1932, 7.

26. "Alumni Launch Drive to Increase Athletic Facilities," *Auburn Alumnus*, February–April 1937, 1; "Athletics at Auburn," *Auburn Alumnus*, February–April 1937, 10; "College Building Program Gets Regional PWA Okeh," *Lee County Bulletin*, September 1, 1938, 1; Elmer Salter, "New Athletic Era Will Start for Auburn with Dedication of Stadium," *Lee County Bulletin*, November 30, 1939, 6; Dru

McGowen, "Anniversary," *Inside the Auburn Tigers*, March 1989, 12–14, 23–24.

27. Salter, "New Athletic Era"; "Biggest Crowd in History of City Is Expected for Homecoming Program," *Lee County Bulletin*, November 23, 1939, 1; "Jaycees Out to Pack Stadium for Nov. 30 Tilt," *Lee County Bulletin*, November 2, 1939, 1; "Thousands Will Trek to Auburn from All Over South for Dedication of New Stadium," *Opelika Daily News*, November 28, 1939, 6.

28. Beard, "Jordan-Hare Stadium," 6; "Visitors Take Over Village," *Lee County Bulletin*, November 30, 1939, 1; "Homecoming Brings Thousands to Auburn," *Opelika Daily News*, December 1, 1939, 1; "Hundreds of Dollars Spent Here by Football Crowds," *Opelika Daily News*, December 1, 1939, 6.

29. Elmer Salter, "Tigers Retain Title of Gridiron Nomads, 6,858 Mile Journeys," *Opelika Daily News*, November 2, 1940; Beard, "Jordan-Hare Stadium," 7.

30. Cecil Stowe, "Plainsmen Squad Gets Rousing Welcome on Return Home Today," *Opelika Daily News*, January 4, 1938, 1; Neil O. Davis, "Passenger Trains to Bow Out at the End of the Year," *Auburn Alumnews*, September 1969, 17; Jack Simms (emeritus professor of journalism, Auburn University, and co-author of *Auburn: A Pictorial History*), interview by the author, Auburn, February 1, 2002.

31. "War Eagle!" *Auburn Alumnews*, January 1950, 1; Mickey Logue and Jack Simms, *Auburn: A Pictorial History of the Loveliest Village* (Auburn: n.p., 1996), 34.

32. Rooney and Pillsbury, *Atlas of American Sport*, 70; J. Steven Picou, "Football," in *Encyclopedia of Southern Culture*, ed. Charles Reagan Wilson and William Ferris (Chapel Hill: University of North Carolina Press, 1989), 1221–24; Andrew Doyle, "Turning the Tide: College Football and Southern Progressivism," *Southern Cultures* 3:3 (1997):

28–51; Patrick B. Miller, "The Manly, the Moral, and the Proficient: College Sport in the New South," in *The Sporting World of the Modern South*, ed. Patrick B. Miller (Urbana: University of Illinois Press, 2002).

33. Harold Keith, *Oklahoma Kickoff* (1948; repr., Norman: University of Oklahoma Press, 1978), 79, 180–81, 186, 211, 243, 304; Simon J. Bronner, *Piled Higher and Deeper: The Folklore of Student Life* (Little Rock, Ark.: August House, 1995), 110; Thomas D. Clark, *Indiana University, Midwestern Pioneer.* vol. 3: *Years of Fulfillment* (Bloomington: Indiana University Press, 1977), 337; Jo Chesworth, *Story of the Century: The Borough of State College, Pennsylvania, 1896–1996* (State College, Pa.: Borough of State College/Barash Group, 1995), 37; Howard H. Peckham, *The Making of the University of Michigan, 1817–1992*, ed. and updated by Margaret L. Steneck and Nicholas H. Steneck (Ann Arbor: University of Michigan, Bentley Historical Library, 1994), 218.

34. "Tickets Available," *Auburn Alumnews*, October 1950, 5; Mark Murphy, "Jordan-Hare," *Inside the Auburn Tigers*, January 1985, 21–25.

35. Rich Donnell, *Shug: The Life and Times of Auburn's Ralph "Shug" Jordan* (Montgomery, Ala.: Owl Bay Publishers, 1993), 96; Dru McGowen, "Home Schedule Godfather," *Inside the Auburn Tigers*, October 1988, 23–30.

36. "More Building Planned," *Auburn Alumnews*, May 1955, 4.

37. "Season Ticket Plan," *Auburn Alumnus*, March 1957, 5; Bill Beckwith, "Ticket Deadline Approaches Again," *Auburn Alumnus*, June 1951, 9; "30,000 Crowd Will Jam Auburn for Homecoming," *Lee County Bulletin*, November 3, 1955, 1; Southern Bell Telephone & Telegraph Co., *Telephone Directory: Auburn, Ala.* (N.p: Southern Bell, 1958); "56-Unit Holiday Inn Plus Restaurant to Be Built," *Lee County Bulletin*, September 29, 1955, 1; "Special Program for Sunday Night

Service at First Methodist Church," *Opelika Daily News*, November 4, 1955, 3.

38. "API Students Stage Big Rally after News of No. 1 Ranking," *Opelika Daily News*, December 3, 1957, 1; "Football Trophy Will Be Awarded Here Tuesday," *Lee County Bulletin*, December 5, 1957, 1A.

39. McGowen, "Home Schedule Godfather," 28.

40. Norman Brown, "Bids Asked for Stadium Project," *Opelika-Auburn News*, October 29, 1969, 2.

41. St. John, *Rammer Jammer Yellow Hammer*, 8; South Central Bell, *Auburn-Opelika, Ala. Telephone Directory* (N.p.: South Central Bell, 1975); Edwin H. Cady, *The Big Game: College Sports and American Life* (Knoxville: University of Tennessee Press, 1978), 62.

42. Watterson, *College Football*, 343, 348. From 1996 to 2005, Auburn appeared on television at least eight times each season. Over nine years, fifty-five of its games were televised nationally. Auburn University, *2006 Auburn Football Media Guide*.

43. John F. Rooney, Jr., and Audrey B. Davidson, "Football," in *The Theater of Sport*, ed. Karl B. Raitz (Baltimore: Johns Hopkins University Press, 1995), 221; "Stadium Work Progressing toward 1980," *Opelika-Auburn News*, September 23, 1979; Perry Ballard, "Trustees Vote to Expand Stadium," *Opelika-Auburn News*, December 4, 1984, 1.

44. Ronald A. Smith, *Sports and Freedom: The Rise of Big-Time College Athletics* (New York: Oxford University Press, 1988), 218; Karl B. Raitz, "The Theater of Sport: A Landscape Perspective," in Raitz, *The Theater of Sport*, 5; Michael Novak, *The Joy of Sports* (New York: Basic Books, 1976), 123–26.

45. Michael Oriard, *King Football: Sport and Spectacle in the Golden Age of Radio and Newsreels, Movies and Magazines, the Weekly & the Daily Press* (Chapel Hill: University of North Carolina Press, 2001), 70.

46. Wayne Atcheson, "The 41 Year Time-Out," *Alabama Heritage*, Fall 1992, 10–20.

47. Dru McGowen, "The Big Game," *Inside the Auburn Tigers*, November 1989, 8.

48. Clyde Bolton, "In '89, The Story Isn't Who, It's Where," *Birmingham News*, October 27, 1989, 1H; Perry Ballard, "Frenzied Atmosphere Expected This Weekend," *Opelika-Auburn News*, December 1, 1989, A6; Perry Ballard, "AU Fans Have the Day They've Long Waited For," *Opelika-Auburn News*, December 3, 1989, B1; Paul Cox, "Merchants Still Counting Money from Game," *Opelika-Auburn News*, December 11, 1989, A1; U.S. Bureau of Labor Statistics, Inflation Calculator, http://data.bls.gov/cgi-bin/cpicalc.pl (accessed June 16, 2008).

49. Ann Pearson (Auburn resident and daughter of former Auburn University president), telephone conversation with the author, October 7, 1999.

50. Douglas Watson (city manager, Auburn), e-mail to the author, January 9, 2002; Jan Dempsey (former mayor, Auburn), interview by the author, Auburn, October 11, 1999.

51. Douglas Watson, interview by the author, Auburn, February 1, 2002; Andrea Jackson (finance director and treasurer, city of Auburn), telephone conversation with the author, October 1999.

52. Robert Day, "A Clean, Turf Battling, Hard Driving Industry," *Business Alabama Monthly*, March 1998, 16–18; U.S. Bureau of Labor Statistics, Inflation Calculator. While considerable research has been conducted about the economic impact of professional sports teams, comparatively little research has been conducted about the impact of college sports on college communities. Exceptions include Neil J. Dikeman, "The Economic Impact of Sooner Football," *Oklahoma Business Bulletin* 56:6 (June 1988): 15–17; Kari Hawkins, "The Business of Ath-

letics," *Tuscaloosa County Business Source-book*, 1st/2nd quarter 1999, 5–7, 20; and Loren C. Scott, "It's Not Just Entertainment: The Impact of the LSU Athletic Department on the Baton Rouge Metropolitan Statistical Area," Louisiana State University Division of Economic Development and Forecasting, 1998. Findings in those studies were similar to those reported by Day. For examples of studies on the economic impact of professional sports, see John L. Crompton, "Economic Impact Analysis of Sports Facilities and Events: Eleven Sources of Misapplication," *Journal of Sport Management* 9 (1995): 14–35; and Roger G. Noll and Andrew S. Zimbalist, eds., *Sports, Jobs, and Taxes: The Economic Impact of Sports Teams and Stadiums* (Washington: Brookings Institution, 1997).

53. Mitch Sneed, "Where Do They All Come From?" *Opelika-Auburn News*, October 15, 2006; Auburn University Department of Athletics, "Five-Year Financial Summary," Auburn, 1998; Auburn University Department of Athletics, "Auburn Athletics Department: 6 Year Financial Summary," Auburn, 2002.

54. Ken Wesson (manager, Heart of Auburn Inn, Auburn), interview by the author, Auburn, October 7, 1999. The Heart of Auburn Inn has since been acquired by Days Inn.

55. John Wild (general manager, Auburn University Hotel and Dixon Conference Center, Auburn), telephone interview by the author, October 22, 1999; Rachel Norris, "Auburn to Add New Football Excitement for Next Season," *Auburn Plainsman* [Auburn University], September 3, 1998, 20.

56. Bob Binkley (owner, Auburn Grille, Auburn), interview by the author, Auburn, October 9, 1999; Ronnie Ware (owner, Ware Jewelers, Auburn), interview by the author, Auburn, October 7, 1999; Trey Johnston III (owner,

J&M Bookstore, Auburn), interview by the author, Auburn, October 7, 1999.

57. Daniel Jackson, "Home, Home on the Plains," *Auburn Plainsman* [Auburn University], September 21, 1999, 43; Olin Hill (longtime merchant and tailor, Auburn), conversation with the author, Auburn, October 10, 1999; David Rosenblatt (curator, Lovelace Museum, Auburn University; retired archivist, Auburn University Libraries), interview by the author, Auburn, January 31, 2002; Gregory Stone, "Sport as Community Representation," in *Handbook of Social Science of Sport*, ed. Günther R. F. Lüschen and George H. Sage (Champaign, Ill.: Stipes Publishing, 1981), 230.

58. Daniel Wallace, "University Town: Chapel Hill, North Carolina, and Its Many Degrees," *Sky*, March 2002, 37; Guy Maynard, "Go Ducks: How UO Sports Have Changed and Changed Us for Better and Worse," in *Eugene 1945–2000: Decisions That Made a Community*, ed. Kathleen Holt and Cheri Brooks (Eugene, Ore.: City Club of Eugene, 2000), 377, 385.

8. High-Tech Valhalla

1. Gorman Beauchamp, "Dissing the Middle Class: The View from Burns Park," *American Scholar* 64:3 (Summer 1995): 336.

2. Rick Haglund, "Warren Avis Launching His Tech Park," *Ann Arbor News*, October 12, 1986, C1; Avis Farms Research and Business Parks, "Location Map," http://www.avisfarms.com/large_avisfarms_map.jpg (accessed July 28, 2005).

3. Jennette Smith, "ProQuest to Build Ann Arbor HQ," *Crain's Detroit Business*, November 22, 2004, 3; Scott Anderson, "State Offers State of the Art," *Ann Arbor News*, January 30, 2005, F1.

4. Corey Dolgon, "Innovators and Gravediggers: Capital Restructuring and Class Forma-

tion in Ann Arbor, Michigan, 1945–1994"
(diss., University of Michigan, 1994), 98;
Corey Dolgon, "Rising from the Ashes: The
Michigan Memorial Phoenix Project and
the Corporatization of University-Based
Scientific Research," *Educational Studies* 24:1
(1998): 5–31; Howard H. Peckham, *The Making of the University of Michigan, 1817–1992*,
ed. Margaret L. Steneck and Nicholas H. Steneck (Ann Arbor: Bentley Historical Library,
1994), 270; Ken Garber and Eve Silberman,
"Rise and Fall: What Went Wrong at Pfizer,"
Ann Arbor Observer, May 2007, 29–35.

5. Don MacMaster, "Inside ERIM," *Ann Arbor
Observer*, December 1989, 52; Laura Bailey,
"Alter 'em: ERIM Changes Biz Plan—and
Even Its Name: Altarum," *Crain's Detroit
Business*, February 4, 2002, 31; "Auto Labs'
Building Boom," *Ann Arbor Observer*, December 1993, 17.

6. Joel Kotkin, *The New Geography: How the
Digital Revolution Is Reshaping the American Landscape* (New York: Random House,
2000), 11.

7. Jonathan Marwil, *A History of Ann Arbor*
(Ann Arbor: University of Michigan Press,
1991), 69, 85. For an example of the view
that the university sought to inhibit industrial development see W. F. Freakey, "Booming Ann Arbor!" *Ann Arbor Courier*, February
17, 1886, 2.

8. Edmund W. Gilbert, *The University Town
in England and West Germany*, University
of Chicago, Department of Geography,
Research Paper No. 71 (Chicago: University
of Chicago Press, 1961), 11, 65; David McKitterick, "Textbook Printing at Cambridge,"
Paradigm 1:7 (December 1991): 1–2; Martin
C. Cohen, "Carl Zeiss: A History of the Most
Respected Man in Optics," http://www
.company7.com/zeiss/history.html (accessed
August 3, 2005); S. B. Sutton, *Cambridge
Remembered: 3 1/2 Centuries on the Charles*
(Cambridge: MIT Press, 1976), 16, 65.

9. U.S. Bureau of the Census, County Business
Patterns, Michigan, Washtenaw County,
2005, http://www.census.gov/epcd/cbp/
view/cbpview.html (accessed July 13, 2007);
Edwards Brothers, *From Mimeograph to Life
of Title* (Ann Arbor: Edwards Brothers, n.d.);
John Serwach, "By-the-Book Success," *Crain's
Detroit Business*, August 5, 1996, 43; Edwards
Brothers family tree, unpublished chart.

10. George W. Cooke, "Eugene B. Power: Father
of Preservation Microfilming," *Conservation
Administration News*, July 1993, 6.

11. Eugene Power, *Edition of One: The Autobiography of Eugene B. Power, Founder of
University Microfilms* (Ann Arbor: University
Microfilms International, 1990), 11–15.

12. Ibid., 16–35; Alan Marshall Meckler, *Micropublishing: A History of Scholarly Micropublishing in America, 1938–1980* (Westport,
Conn.: Greenwood Press, 1982), 61.

13. Eugene B. Power, "University Microfilms,"
Journal of Documentary Reproduction 2:1
(March 1939): 25–27; Power, *Edition of One*,
166–68; ProQuest Co., "History and Milestones," http://www.infolearning.com/
division/pub-history.shtml (accessed August
4, 2005).

14. Power, *Edition of One*, 111, 118–19, 134–36;
Cooke, "Eugene B. Power," 7; American
Council of Learned Societies, "British
Manuscript Project," *PMLA* 59, Supplement
(1944): 1463; V. B. Tate, "Microphotography
in Wartime," *Journal of Documentary Reproduction* 5:3 (September 1942): 129–30; Philip
H. Power, "Eugene Barnum Power," *Proceedings of the American Philosophical Society*
139:3 (September 1995): 302; Power, *Edition
of One*, 161, 231; ProQuest Corp. "Serials in
Microfilm Catalog," http://www.il.proquest
.com/sim/info/introduction.shtml (accessed
September 12, 2005); Eugene Power, "O-P
Books: A Library Breakthrough," *American
Documentation* 9:4 (October 1958): 274.

15. Power, "Eugene Barnum Power"; Jenny

Rode, "ProQuest Plans to Grow," *Ann Arbor News*, June 19, 2007.

16. "The Fall and Rise of Argus," *Fortune*, January 1945, 235–40; John Hilton, "Amazing Argus," *Ann Arbor Observer*, October 1982, 43.

17. Winfield Scott Downs, ed., *Encyclopedia of American Biography*, N.S., vol. 19 (New York: American Historical Co., 1947), 104–6; Mary Hunt, "An Erratic Genius Put Ann Arbor on the Map," *Ann Arbor News*, March 23, 1975, 17; Henry Gambino, *Argomania: A Look at Argus Cameras and the Company That Made Them* (Doylestown, Pa.: Aeone Communications, 2005).

18. "Fall and Rise of Argus."

19. *Michigan Alumnus*, December 13, 1952, 211; Hunt, "Erratic Genius," 18; Power, *Edition of One*, 32; Gambino, *Argomania*; Manuel Castells and Peter Hall, *Technopoles of the World: The Making of Twenty-First-Century Industrial Complexes* (London: Routledge, 1994), 33; Hilton, "Amazing Argus," 46.

20. Margaret Pugh O'Mara, *Cities of Knowledge: Cold War Science and the Search for the Next Silicon Valley* (Princeton: Princeton University Press, 2005), 5–6; Hugh Davis Graham and Nancy Diamond, *The Rise of American Research Universities: Elites and Challengers in the Postwar Era* (Baltimore: Johns Hopkins University Press, 1997), 33–34; Roger L. Geiger, *Knowledge and Money: Research Universities and the Paradox of the Marketplace* (Stanford: Stanford University Press, 2004), 43–44, 181.

21. Edward Danforth Eddy, Jr., *Colleges for Our Land and Time: The Land-Grant Idea in American Education* (New York: Harper & Brothers, 1957); Roger L. Geiger, *To Advance Knowledge: The Growth of American Research Universities, 1900–1940* (New York: Oxford University Press, 1986), 175–91.

22. Peckham, *Making of the University of Michigan*, 101, 104–6.

23. Don Hunt, "The Last Downtown Factory," *Ann Arbor Observer*, March 1980, 32–35; A. K. Steigerwalt, "The Amazing Saga of King-Seeley," *Ann Arbor Observer*, July 1988, 53–62; Walter A. Donnelly, ed., *The University of Michigan: An Encyclopedic Survey*, vol. 3, parts 6 and 7 (Ann Arbor: University of Michigan Press, 1953), 1240.

24. Peckham, *Making of the University of Michigan*, 151–52, 162, 184; Bernhard A. Uhlendorf, "The Engineering Research Institute," in Donnelly, *The University of Michigan: An Encyclopedic Survey*, vol. 3, parts 6 and 7, 1243–47.

25. Graham and Diamond, *Rise of American Research Universities*, 28; Geiger, *To Advance Knowledge*, 264.

26. Uhlendorf, "Engineering Research Institute," 1248; Peckham, *Making of the University of Michigan*, 230–34; Marwil, *History of Ann Arbor*, 129.

27. O'Mara, *Cities of Knowledge*, 18–20, 45–46; Graham and Diamond, *Rise of American Research Universities*, 33–34; Ferol Brinkman, ed., *The University of Michigan: An Encyclopedic Survey*, vol. 6 (Ann Arbor: Bentley Historical Library, 1981), 19; Frank R. Bacon, Jr., and Kenneth E. Bayer, *Research Emphasis in Michigan Universities* (Ann Arbor: University of Michigan, Institute of Science and Technology, 1964), 14.

28. W. K. Pierpoint, "The Willow Run Airport," *Michigan Alumnus*, Winter 1949, 119–27; William G. Dow, "The Development of a Research Center," in Irvin J. Sattinger, *History of ERIM: The Environmental Research Institute of Michigan, 1946–1989* (Ann Arbor: ERIM, n.d.), 1–3.

29. John Walsh, "Willow Run Laboratories: Separating from the University of Michigan," *Science* 177:4049 (August 18, 1972): 594–96.

30. Sattinger, *History of ERIM*; Walsh, "Willow Run Laboratories," 594–96; Uhlendorf, "Engineering Research Institute," 1250; Don

MacMaster, "Inside ERIM," 49–57; Ken Gar-
ber, "ERIM's Gamble," *Ann Arbor Observer*,
January 1996, 23. See also Sean F. Johnston,
Holographic Visions: A History of New Science
(Oxford: Oxford University Press, 2006).

31. For a family tree of companies spawned
by Willow Run, see *Ann Arbor News*, April
19, 1983, F3. See also Janet Cohen, "Small
Research Pond Spawned a Sea of Marketable Ideas," *Ann Arbor News*, April 19, 1985,
F4; Max Gates, "The '60s Saw a Boom, '70s
a Downturn," *Ann Arbor News*, April 10,
1981, High Technology supplement, 4; Max
Gates and Tina Lam, "Mother ERIM and Its
'Children,'" *Ann Arbor News*, November 24,
1985, C1.

32. Larry Bush, "Three Success Stories That
Quickly Changed," *Ann Arbor News*, April
10, 1981, technology supplement, 20; John
Hilton, "The Late, Great Kip Siegel," *Ann
Arbor Observer*, September 1982, 55; Ray
Sleep, "Of Michigan's High Tech Future,"
Ann Arbor News, April 15, 1983, D5.

33. Michigan Memorial Phoenix Project, pro-
posal to General Electric Co., 1949, Box 1,
Michigan Memorial Phoenix Project Papers,
Bentley Historical Library, University of
Michigan; Dolgon, "Rising from the Ashes,"
12, 15.

34. Corey Dolgon, Michael Kline, and Laura
Dresser, "'House People, Not Cars!': Eco-
nomic Development, Political Struggle, and
Common Sense in the City of Intellect," in
Marginal Spaces, ed. Michael Peter Smith
(New Brunswick, N.J.: Transaction, 1995), 7;
Dolgon, "Innovators and Gravediggers," 70;
Peckham, *Making of the University of Michi-
gan*, 270.

35. University of Michigan, "The Industrial
Development Division of the Institute of
Science and Technology of the University
of Michigan: Fifteen Years, 1960–1974,"
unpublished report, 3–4.

36. Arthur Miller, "University of Michigan,"
Holiday, December 1953, 68–70, 128–34,
136–37, 140–43.

37. Grace Shackman, "The Unsinkable Mayor
Brown," *Ann Arbor Observer*, May 1990, 62.

38. "Brown's Views," *Washtenaw Post-Tribune*
[Ann Arbor, Mich.], February 9, 1945, 12.

39. Dolgon, "Innovators and Gravediggers," 8,
99.

40. Bob Schairer, "City May Get Huge Research
Center," *Ann Arbor News*, May 29, 1956, 1;
Dolgon, "Innovators and Gravediggers,"
99–100; Walter A. Donnelly, ed., *The Uni-
versity of Michigan: An Encyclopedic Survey*,
vol. 4, parts 8 and 9 (Ann Arbor: University
of Michigan Press, 1958), 1351, 1958; Wilfred
B. Shaw, ed., *The University of Michigan: An
Encyclopedic Survey*, vol. 2, parts 3, 4, and 5
(Ann Arbor: University of Michigan Press,
1951), 908; Samuel J. Eldersveld, *Party Con-
flict and Community Development: Postwar
Politics in Ann Arbor* (Ann Arbor: University
of Michigan Press, 1995), 18; "Parke-Davis
Dedicates Research Laboratories," *Ann Arbor
News*, April 19, 1960, 9.

41. Dolgon, "Innovators and Gravediggers," 101;
"Bendix Aviation Corp. Will Build Facility in
City," *Ann Arbor News*, November 16, 1956,
1; Lawrence M. Lamont, *Technology Transfer,
Innovation, and Marketing in Science-Oriented
Spin-Off Firms* (Ann Arbor: University of
Michigan, Institute of Science and Technol-
ogy, Industrial Development Division, 1971),
9; Marilyn Sauder McLaughlin, *Ann Arbor,
Michigan: A Pictorial History* (St. Louis:
G. Bradley, 1995), 64.

42. "'I Did It with My Little Magnet,'" *Michigan Daily*, March 24, 1957, 4; Ann Arbor
Chamber of Commerce, Economic Development Committee minutes, July 18, 1957,
Ann Arbor Chamber of Commerce Papers,
1926–1967, Bentley Historical Library, University of Michigan; Ann Arbor Chamber of

Commerce, "Memorandum on Economic Development," February 2, 1959, Ann Arbor Chamber of Commerce Papers; Economic Development Committee folders, Box 3, Ann Arbor Chamber of Commerce Papers; Greater Ann Arbor Research Park folders, Box 3, Ann Arbor Chamber of Commerce Papers; Ann Arbor Chamber of Commerce, *1961 Progress Report* (Ann Arbor: Chamber of Commerce, 1962).

43. O'Mara, *Cities of Knowledge*, 46, 118; Brinkman, *University of Michigan*, vol. 6, 13; Michael I. Luger and Harvey A. Goldstein, *Technology in the Garden: Research Parks & Regional Economic Development* (Chapel Hill: University of North Carolina Press, 1991), 77; Clark Kerr, *The Uses of the University* (1963; repr., Cambridge: Harvard University Press, 2001), 31, 66.

44. "Ann Arbor: Midwest's Research Center," *Michigan Alumnus*, April 8, 1961, 250; Robert M. Leary, "Ann Arbor Develops a Research Park," *Michigan Municipal Review*, February 1961, 35; Tom Kleene, "Industry Given New Research Tool," *Detroit Free Press*, February 26, 1961, C5; Thomas L. Dickinson, "Recipe for a Research Park," *Michigan Business Review*, November 1961, 3; University of Michigan, Office of Research Administration, "Ann Arbor: Research Center of the Midwest," *Information Bulletin for Michigan Industry* 6 (December 1, 1963): 6.4.; Ann Arbor Chamber of Commerce, *Ann Arbor, Michigan: Research Center of the Midwest* (Ann Arbor: Chamber, 1962), 610; Tom Kleene, "Signal from Star Will Dedicate First Lab in Ann Arbor Park," *Detroit Free Press*, February 24, 1963, C11.

45. U-M, "Ann Arbor: Research Center of the Midwest"; Jim Taylor, ed., *A Report on Research, Technology and Entrepreneurship* (Ann Arbor: Ann Arbor Chamber of Commerce, 1989), 18; City of Ann Arbor, Planning De-

partment, *Economic Base Report* (Ann Arbor, 1965), 31.

46. "Research Park Adds Buildings," *Ann Arbor News*, February 23, 1966; Luger and Goldstein, *Technology in the Garden*, 57, 74; Edward J. Malecki, *Technology and Economic Development: The Dynamics of Local, Regional, and National Competitiveness* (Essex, England: Longman, 1997), 270; National Science Foundation, *National Patterns of R&D Resources: 1994* (Washington: NSF, 1995), tables B-3 and B-14, http://www.nsf.gov/statistics/s2194/dst1.htm (accessed August 15, 2005); Graham and Diamond, *Rise of American Research Universities*, 85; Bush, "Three Success Stories," 20; Max Gates, "U-M Will Buy Bendix Corp.'s Vacant Aerospace Building," *Ann Arbor News*, January 21, 1983, D5.

47. Marwil, *History of Ann Arbor*, 152–54, 161–62; Sattinger, *History of ERIM*, 46–48; Peckham, *Making of the University of Michigan*, 313.

48. David Brophy (associate professor of finance, University of Michigan), telephone interview by the author, June 30, 2005; MacMaster, "Inside ERIM," 52; "Offspring of Willow Run Labs and ERIM," *Ann Arbor News*, April 19, 1985, F3.

49. Gates, "'60s Saw a Boom," 4; Hilton, "Late, Great Kip Siegel," 55; Sleep, "Michigan's High-Tech Future," D5.

50. Manuel Castells, *The Informational City: Information Technology, Economic Restructuring, and the Urban-Regional Process* (Cambridge, Mass.: Blackwell, 1989), 82–83.

51. University of Michigan, Institute of Science and Technology, "Progress Report of the Technology-Based Industry-University Committee," March 17, 1980, Box 1, Michigan Technology Council Papers, Bentley Historical Library, University of Michigan; Peckham, *Making of the University of Michigan*,

296, 328, 330, 339; Geiger, *Knowledge and Money*, 180; Association of University Technology Managers, *AUTM Licensing Survey: FY 2003* (Northbrook, Ill.: AUTM, 2004), 12; Taylor, *Report on Research*, 6.

52. "Michigan . . . Technology That Works," *Scientific American*, September 1982; Max Gates, "U-M Plays Cautious Hand in Its Dealings with Private Sector," *Ann Arbor News*, April 10, 1981, 12; Mary Hunt, "Technology on Parade," *Ann Arbor Observer*, May 1981, 37.

53. Owen Eshenroder, "Parke-Davis Tax Break Wins First OK," *Ann Arbor News*, June 29, 1982, A1; John Hinchey, "The Gift," *Ann Arbor Observer*, September 1982, 34; "Pfizer Announces Planned Expansion in Ann Arbor," Associated Press, November 20, 2001.

54. Bonnie DeSimone, "N-Free Proposal Could Affect Many Firms Here," *Ann Arbor News*, October 29, 1984, A1; Jane Myers, "Is the Welcome Mat Out?" *Ann Arbor News*, April 19, 1985, F20.

55. Jane Myers, "A Cautionary Tale," *Ann Arbor News*, April 19, 1985, F20.

56. Karen D. Frazer, *NSFNET: A Partnership for High-Speed Networking; Final Report, 1987–1995* (Ann Arbor: Merit Network, n.d.), http://www.merit.edu/nrd/nsfnet/final.pdf (accessed August 18, 2005); Susan Lackey (executive director, Washtenaw Land Trust, and former president, Washtenaw Development Council), telephone interview by the author, July 6, 2005.

57. John Cain, "The Gold Rush," *Ann Arbor Observer*, March 1982, 39; Paul Judge, "U-M Urges Inventors to Move Ideas into Industry," *Ann Arbor News*, March 22, 1988, Update, 18; Michael Kersmarki, "Parke-Davis Slated for Major Expansion," *Ann Arbor News*, October 10, 1980, D6; MacMaster, "Inside ERIM," 52; Ken Garber, "The Murder of Irwin Magnetics," *Ann Arbor Observer*,

March 1993, 37; Matt VanAuker, "Local High-Tech Data Hard to Find," *Ann Arbor News*, May 24, 1991, B5.

58. Eve Silberman and Jay Forstner, "The Busy Decade," *Ann Arbor Observer*, January 1990, 28.

59. Ross C. DeVol, *America's High-Tech Economy: Growth, Development, and Risks for Metropolitan Areas* (Santa Monica, Calif.: Milken Institute, 1999); American Electronics Association, *Cybercities* (Santa Clara, Calif.: American Electronic Association, 2000); Daniel Hecker, "High-Technology Employment: A Broader View," *Monthly Labor Review*, June 1999, 18–28; Karen Chapple and others, "Gauging Metropolitan 'High-Tech' and 'I-Tech' Activity," *Economic Development Quarterly* 18:1 (February 2004): 10–29; Patrick Kilcoyne, "High-Tech Occupations by Metropolitan Statistical Area," U.S. Bureau of Labor Statistics, 2001, http://www.bls.gov/oes/2001/tech.pdf (accessed August 19, 2005).

60. U.S. Bureau of the Census, *County Business Patterns, Michigan, 1988* (Washington: U.S. Government Printing Office, 1983); U.S. Bureau of the Census, *County Business Patterns, Michigan, 1993* (Washington: U.S. Government Printing Office, 1993).

61. "Plymouth Road Comes Alive," *Ann Arbor Observer*, December 1984, 26.

62. Teresa Blossom, "Path's Clear for High-Tech Park," *Detroit Free Press*, January 23, 1984, 1E; Ray Sleep, "Tech Park Update," *Ann Arbor News*, April 19, 1985, C5.

63. The U.S. Office of Technology Policy converted the 1999 BLS high-tech industry list, which was based on the Standard Industrial Classification (SIC) system, into the newer North American Industrial Classification System (NAICS) codes. See National Science Board, "High-Technology NAICS Codes," *Science and Education Indicators 2004*, vol. 1 (Washington: National Science Foundation,

2004), 8–54. Unfortunately, the revised list made no attempt to convert the BLS list of "high-tech intensive" industries to the new classification system.

64. U.S. Bureau of the Census, *County Business Patterns, Michigan, 1993* (Washington: U.S. Government Printing Office, 1995), 129–33; U.S. Bureau of the Census, County Business Patterns, Michigan, Washtenaw County, 1998, 2002, 2003, 2005, http://www .census.gov/epcd/cbp/view/cbpview.html (accessed July 13, 2007).

65. "Warner Lambert-Parke Davis: The Giant Keeps Growing," *Ann Arbor Observer*, April 1993, 9; Ken Garber, "Parke-Davis in Ann Arbor (Part Two)," *Ann Arbor Observer*, October 1995, 23–29; "Parke-Davis's Billion-Dollar Babies," *Ann Arbor Observer*, November 1997, 9; Paul Gargaro, "Parke-Davis Is Growing," *Crain's Detroit Business*, June 22, 1998, 1; Andrew Dietderich, "Pfizer Expanding Site Despite $4B Cutback," *Crain's Detroit Business*, April 11, 2005, 3.

66. Scott Anderson, "Biotech Takes Stock of Its Future," *Ann Arbor News*, February 9, 2002, A1; "Crain's List: Washtenaw County's Largest Employers," *Crain's Detroit Business*, August 15, 2005, 16; University of Michigan Health System, "UMHS: At a Glance," http://www.med.umich.edu/opm/ newspage/details.htm (accessed August 23, 2005); Andrew Dietderich, "Aastrom Gets $22M Financing Boost," *Crain's Detroit Business*, January 17, 2005, 3.

67. Michael Betzold, "Predator or Prey: The U-M Life Sciences Institute Is Still Looking to Lure Its First Big Fish—But the Bait Keeps Getting Eaten," *Ann Arbor Observer*, March 2005, 25–31; David Poulson, "Millions in Research Funds Awarded," *Ann Arbor News*, June 6, 2002, C1.

68. David Fry (founder, president, and chief executive officer, Fry Multimedia), telephone interview by the author, June 30, 2005; Steve Glauberman (president, Enlighten), interview by the author, Ann Arbor, March 23, 2001; Brian J. Bowe, "Make It or Break It," *Metro Times*, January 24, 2007; Tom Henderson, "Arbor Networks Software Keeps Hackers at Bay," *Detroit News*, April 18, 2004; Andrew Dietderich, "Clicking against the Current," *Crain's Detroit Business*, March 3, 2003, 3.

69. Bryce G. Hoffman, "Automotive Epicenter," *Ann Arbor News*, March 6, 2005; "Auto Labs' Building Boom"; Russell Grantham, "Area Attracts Japanese Tech Centers," *Ann Arbor News*, June 2, 1991, B1; Bryce G. Hoffman, "Homegrown Toyota," *Ann Arbor News*, November 9, 2004, C1; Bryce G. Hoffman, "Hyundai Is Looking Ahead," *Ann Arbor News*, July 17, 2005; Stefanie Murray, "Toyota Tech Center," *Ann Arbor News*, March 18, 2007.

70. Kim Clarke, "U-M Chief Proposes 'Incubator,'" *Ann Arbor News*, February 10, 1993, D8.

71. University of Michigan, Technology Transfer Office, "UM Tech Transfer Metrics Summary," 1995–2006, unpublished table.

72. Tom Walsh, "U-M Strives for Tech Growth," *Detroit Free Press*, May 23, 2005; Scott Anderson, "Optimistic Leaders Launch Spark," *Ann Arbor News*, May 27, 2005; Mary Sue Coleman, "Innovate or Bust: The Role of American Universities, and University Technology Transfer, in America's Future Competitiveness," keynote address to Association of University Technology Managers annual meeting, Phoenix, February 3, 2005, http://www.techtransfer.umich.edu/ aboutus/Coleman.html (accessed September 21, 2005).

73. Comparison based on search for all Ann Arbor companies listed on the IT Zone membership list on January 3, 2001 in Verizon Superpages, http://www .superpages.com/, July 15, 2005.

74. Garber, "Murder of Irwin Magnetics," 37; Joseph Serwach, "Venture Funding Brings BlueGill Clients Closer to Electronic Billing," *Crain's Detroit Business*, May 8, 2000, 13; Farnam Jahanian (founder and chairman of the board, Arbor Networks, professor of electrical engineering and computer science, University of Michigan), telephone interview by the author, July 14, 2005.

75. Castells and Hall, *Technopoles of the World*, 235; Goldie Blumenstyk, "U. of Michigan Finds Good Research Is Not Enough," *Chronicle of Higher Education*, July 19, 2002, A24–26, plus more detailed tables on *Chronicle of Higher Education* website, http://chronicle.com/stats/techtransfer/ (accessed May 19, 2005); Brophy, telephone interview.

76. James J. Duderstadt (president emeritus, University of Michigan, director of the Millennium Project), interview by the author, Ann Arbor, March 20, 2001; James J. Duderstadt, telephone interview by the author, June 28, 2005. See also: Jay Forstner and Tom Rieke, "Dick Wood: The International Connection," *Ann Arbor Observer*, May 1990, 43; Betzold, "Predator or Prey"; Rick Haglund, "Life Sciences Corridor Faces Big Challenges," *Ann Arbor News*, June 8, 2003, F1; "Insult to Injury," *Ann Arbor Observer*, July 2005, 9; Mary Morgan, "Michigan Faltering on Life Sciences Research," *Ann Arbor News*, July 17, 2005.

77. Mike Ramsey, "Net Giant Takes Ann Arbor," *Ann Arbor News*, July 11, 2006; Tom Walsh, "Google Coming to Ann Arbor," *Detroit Free Press*, July 11, 2006; Bill Shea, "UM Was Key in Getting Google to Pick Ann Arbor," *Crain's Detroit Business*, July 17, 2006, 35; Vickie Elmer, "Google U," *Ann Arbor Observer*, May 2006, 37–41.

78. Walsh, "Google Coming to Ann Arbor"; "Pfizer's Gut Punch," *Ann Arbor News*, January 23, 2007; Garber and Silberman, "Rise

and Fall"; Stephen T. Rapundalo, "Take It From Someone Who Knows: There's Life after Pfizer," *Ann Arbor News*, January 28, 2007.

79. Jenny Rode, "Michigan May Lose 6,000 Jobs," *Ann Arbor News*, February 7, 2007.

80. Jewel Gopwani, "Pfizer Job Losses Are Blow to Ann Arbor," *Detroit Free Press*, January 23, 2007.

81. Richard Florida, *The Rise of the Creative Class and How It's Transforming Work, Leisure, Community, and Everyday Life* (New York: Basic Books, 2002), 291–92.

82. Ward Winslow, ed., *The Making of Silicon Valley: A One Hundred Year Renaissance* (Palo Alto, Calif.: Santa Clara Valley Historical Association, 1995); Gordon Moore and Kevin Davis, "Learning the Silicon Valley Way," in *Building High-Tech Clusters: Silicon Valley and Beyond*, ed. Timothy Bresnahan and Alfonso Gambardella (Cambridge: Cambridge University Press, 2004), 16.

83. "Page by Page," *Michigan Engineer*, Spring/Summer 2001.

84. Stephen R. Forrest, *Research at the University of Michigan: A Report to the Regents*, 2007, http://www.research.umich.edu/research_guide/annual_reports/FY06/regents-FY06report.pdf (accessed July 17, 2007).

85. Malecki, *Technology and Economic Development*, 269; William C. MacArthur (founder and president, GeneWorks), telephone interview by the author, June 29, 2005.

86. Jahanian, telephone interview.

87. Leonard Alvarez, *New Money, Nice Town: How Capital Works in the New Urban Economy* (New York: Routledge, 2003), 73–76; Fry, telephone interview; Glauberman, interview.

88. Albert V. Bruno and Tyzoon T. Tyebjee, "The Environment for Entrepreneurship," in *Encyclopedia of Entrepreneurship*, ed. Calvin A. Kent, Donald L. Sexton, and Karl H. Vesper (Englewood Cliffs, N.J.: Prentice-Hall, 1982),

293; Google, "Google Announces Fourth Quarter and Fiscal Year 2006 Results," http://investor.google.com/pdf/2006Q4_earnings_google.pdf (accessed July 24, 2007).

89. Moore and Davis, "Learning the Silicon Valley Way," 13; Jahanian, telephone interview; John Battelle, *The Search: How Google and Its Rivals Rewrote the Rule of Business and Transformed Our Culture* (New York: Portfolio, 2005); "Google History," http://www.google.com/corporate/history.html (accessed August 31, 2005); Google, "Google Management," http://www.google.com/corporate/execs.html (accessed August 31, 2005).

90. Michael Horvath, "Imitating Silicon Valley: Regional Comparisons of Innovation Activity Based on Venture Capital Flows," in Bresnahan and Gambardella, *Building High-Tech Clusters*; PricewaterhouseCoopers, Thomas Venture Economics, and National Venture Capital Association, *Money Tree Survey: Full-Year & Q4 2004 Results*, http://www.pwcmoneytree.com (accessed September 1, 2005).

91. Data based on author's calculations from information provided Pricewaterhouse Coopers/Thomson Venture Economics/National Venture Capital Association Money-Tree Survey.

92. MacArthur, telephone interview; Ken Garber, "Scrambled Eggs: Biotechnology Takes on the Chicken," *Ann Arbor Observer*, June 2002, 33–37; Scott Anderson, " 'Drug-in-an Egg' Company Closes," *Ann Arbor News*, December 5, 2005; Google, "Google History."

93. Rick Snyder (founder and chief executive office, Ardesta, and chairman, Ann Arbor Spark), telephone interview by the author, July 7, 2005; Lackey, telephone interview; Fry, telephone interview.

94. Matt Harris (co-founder and managing general partner, Village Ventures, Williamstown, Mass.), telephone interviews by the author, July 1 and 6, 2005. Charlottesville data based on author's calculations from information provided by PricewaterhouseCoopers/Thomson Venture Economics/National Venture Capital Association MoneyTree Survey.

95. U.S. Bureau of the Census, County Business Patterns, Michigan, Washtenaw County, 2005; "Crain's List: Top-Compensated CEOs," *Crain's Detroit Business*, May 22, 2006; U.S. Bureau of the Census, 1990 Census of Population and Housing, Summary File 3, http://factfinder.census.gov (accessed July 18, 2007); U.S. Bureau of the Census, 2005 American Community Survey, http://factfinder.census.gov (accessed July 18, 2007).

96. Bonnie Brereton, "Looking Back, Looking Ahead," *Ann Arbor Observer*, July 1996, 29.

97. U.S. Bureau of the Census, 1990 Census; U.S. Bureau of the Census, 2000 Census of Population and Housing, http://factfinder.census.gov (accessed July 18, 2007); U.S. Bureau of the Census, 2005 American Community Survey; Ann Arbor Area Board of Realtors, "MLS Sales Report," December 2006, http://www.aaabor.com/downloads/News/PressRoom/06DEC.pdf (accessed July 2007); Coleman Jewett (retired Ann Arbor school teacher and administrator), interview by the author, Ann Arbor, March 19, 2001.

98. Tracy Davis, "Home Buyers Feel Pinch in Ann Arbor," *Ann Arbor News*, June 24, 2005.

99. William Ferrall, "Big Changes for North Central," *Ann Arbor Observer*, June 1988, 55–67; Corey Dolgon, "Soulless Cities: Ann Arbor, the Cutting Edge of Discipline; Postfordism, Postmodernism, and the New Bourgeoisie," *Antipode* 31:2 (1999): 135–36.

100. Washtenaw Development Council, "Washtenaw County Research and Industrial Parks," unpublished listing, 2005; "The

South Side Is Booming," *Ann Arbor Observer*, September 2000, 11; Bowe, "Make It or Break It."

101. Barton Wise, Jeffrey Harshe, and Michael Giraud (brokers, Swisher Commercial real estate, Ann Arbor), interview by the author, Ann Arbor, March 20, 2001; Mary Morgan, "Cyber City," *Ann Arbor News*, December 6, 1996, B1; Jeff Karoub, "Google Shows Off New Office Building in Ann Arbor," Associated Press, May 18, 2004.

102. Swisher Commercial, "Office and Flex Space Vacancy Trends," 1993–2007, unpublished table; "Big Plans Downtown," *Ann Arbor Observer*, February 2001, 11; Tom Gantert, "Downtown Residential Scene Set to Explode," *Ann Arbor News*, April 30, 2006; Peggy Page, "130—and Counting," *Ann Arbor Observer*, November 2006, 27–29; Stefanie Murray, "Loft Owners Open Their Doors," *Ann Arbor News*, March 3, 2007.

103. Marcy Westerman (longtime Ann Arbor resident), interview by the author, Ann Arbor, March 20, 2001; Gorman Beauchamp (adjunct associate professor, University of Michigan), interview by the author, Ann Arbor, March 24, 2001; John Hilton (editor, *Ann Arbor Observer*), telephone interview by the author, June 28, 2005.

104. Val Rasmussen (real estate agent and resident of Ann Arbor since 1964), interview by the author, Ann Arbor, March 20, 2001.

105. Web Kirksey, "Ann Arbor: Still a Good Place to Live," in *Ann Arbor (W)rites: A Community Memoir*, ed. Nicholas Delbanco (Ann Arbor: Ann Arbor District Library, 2004), 79.

106. Susan McGee and Adam Brook, quoted in Mary Jean Babic, "Talk of the Town," *Ann Arbor Observer*, September 2000.

107. John Woodford, quoted in Brereton, "Looking Back, Looking Ahead," 35; Joe Summers (pastor, Church of the Incarnation, Ann Arbor), interview by the author, Ann Arbor, March 22, 2001.

108. Beauchamp, interview; Karl Pohrt (owner, Shaman Drum Bookshop, Ann Arbor), telephone interview by the author, July 8, 2005; Ed Surovell (president, Edward Surovell Realtors, Ann Arbor), telephone interview by the author, July 12, 2005; Charles Baxter, "Hybrid City," in Delbanco, *Ann Arbor W(rites)*, 10–11.

9. Town vs. Gown

1. David Athey (Newark resident), interview by the author, Newark, March 11, 2000.

2. Terri Sanginiti, "UD Cracks Down on Frats," *News-Journal* [Wilmington, Del.], February 21, 2002; Newark Police Department, "Apartment Complex Report," Newark, September 2004.

3. Hastings Rashdall, *The Universities of Europe in the Middle Ages*, ed. F. M. Powicke and A. B. Emden (Oxford: Clarendon Press, 1936), vol. 1, 295, 335, vol. 3, 95–96, 100; Rowland Parker, *Town and Gown: The 700 Years' War in Cambridge* (Cambridge: Patrick Stephens, 1983), 44, 53, 89–90; Marilyn Yurdan, *Oxford: Town and Gown* (London: Robert Hale, 1990), 18.

4. Gordon Lafer, "Land and Labor in the Post-industrial University Town: Remaking Social Geography," *Political Geography* 22 (2003): 89–117. Other studies that show differences in the nature of town-gown relations in big cities vs. college towns include Kermit C. Parsons, "A Truce in the War between Universities and Cities," *Journal of Higher Education* 34:1 (January 1963): 16–28; Ira Fink, "University-Community Relationships," *Planning for Higher Education* 14:1 (1986): 23–30; and Matt Kane, *Issues and Opportunities for University Communities* (Washington: National League of Cities, 1989).

5. John A. Munroe, *The University of Delaware:*

A History (Newark: University of Delaware, 1986), 9, 18–19.

6. *Pennsylvania Gazette*, October 10, 1771, http://www.accessible.com/accessible/text/gaz3/00000497/00049733.htm (accessed March 7, 2005).

7. William Cleaver, "The Diary of a Student at Delaware College," ed. William Ditto Lewis, *Delaware Notes* 24 (1951): 32, 39.

8. Ibid., 35, 47, 52; "Second Fight Did Not Come," *Newark* [Del.] *Post*, October 19, 1921, 1; *Breaking Away*, directed by Peter Yates (20th Century Fox, 1979).

9. Cleaver, "Diary," 61, 72; "Who Flung a Torpedo Out of Harter Hall?" *Life*, May 14, 1951, 34–35.

10. Board of Trustees, Newark College, Minutes, September 22, 1840, University Archives, University of Delaware; Munroe, *University of Delaware*, 73–74; Memorial of the Prudential Committee of the Newark College Board of Trustees to the General Assembly of the State of Delaware, William Ditto Lewis Papers, Scrapbook 1834–1850, item 1843–6, University Archives, University of Delaware; State of Delaware, *Laws of the State of Delaware*, vol. 9 (Dover, Del.: S. Mimmey, 1843), 532; Cleaver, "Diary," 20; H. Clay Reed, "Student Life at Delaware College, 1834–1859," *Delaware Notes* 8 (1934): 45.

11. Cleaver, "Diary," 13, 22, 50, 59, 63; Delta Phi Star [University of Delaware], June 9, 1855.

12. John E. Hocutt, "Dean of Students' Report for 1958–1959," University Archives, University of Delaware.

13. Munroe, *University of Delaware*, 348. Other enrollment data provided by Office of Institutional Research and Planning and University Archives, University of Delaware. City population data is taken from the decennial U.S. Census of Population.

14. Office of the Dean of Students, University of Delaware, *Student Handbook*, 1959–1960

(Newark, 1959), 56. The last student handbook to include "freshman rules" was the 1964–65 edition.

15. Helen Lefkowitz Horowitz, *Campus Life: Undergraduate Cultures from the End of the Eighteenth Century to the Present* (Chicago: University of Chicago Press, 1987), 221, 236.

16. Carol E. Hoffecker, *Beneath Thy Guiding Hand: A History of Women at the University of Delaware* (Newark: University of Delaware, 1994), 100–102; "New Student Rights Statement Passed Unanimously by SGA; Goes to Faculty for Vote," *Review*, October 4, 1968, 1; University of Delaware, *1968 Blue Hen* (Newark: University of Delaware, 1968), n.p.; Munroe, *University of Delaware*, 409, 412, 418; Board of Trustees, University of Delaware, "Resolutions from the Standing Committees of the Board of Trustees, from Docket of Meeting of the Board of Trustees on January 6, 1970," volume for June 6, 1970, part 1, 21, University Archives, University of Delaware; Board of Trustees, University of Delaware, Minutes, May 22, 1971, 31–37, University Archives, University of Delaware.

17. Carrie Pazda, "That Was Then, This Is Now," *Review*, May 9, 1997; Vance A. Funk (attorney and mayor of Newark), telephone interview by the author, February 2, 2005; Joe Maxwell (former owner, Rainbow Books and Records, Newark), interview by the author, Newark, March 10, 2000; John Taylor, "Newark: The Small Town That Outgrew Itself," *Delaware Today*, July 1981, 45.

18. Jeff Crossan, "From Bottle Breaking at the Deer Park . . . to the 'Beach'. . . and Back to Violence," *Weekly Post* [Newark], March 13, 1974, 1A.

19. Hugh Cutler, "Newark Calm, Still on Edge in Wake of Riot," *Morning News* [Wilmington], March 9, 1974; Robert Hodierne, "It Was

Like a Party, Bottle-Thrower Recalls," *Morning News*, March 15, 1974, 1.

20. Taylor, "Newark," 47; Gail Marksjarvis, "Newark Seeking Controls on Bar Crowds," *Evening Journal* [Wilmington], October 11, 1979, Compass, 4; Bill Frank, "Newark Goes to War for Peace," *Morning News*, May 27, 1980; Jeffrey R. Welsh, "The Party's Not Over," *Evening Journal*, October 7, 1982, Compass, 2; Tom Conner, "Drinkers Remain . . . Newark Man Tells Council," *Weekly Post*, June 11, 1980; Michelle Barbieri, "Moving Up Life's Ladder: Analysis of University of Delaware Student Off-Campus Rental Housing Choices, 1990–2000" (Senior thesis, Department of Geography, University of Delaware, Spring 2000), 20.

21. Mayor's Committee on Alcohol Related Antisocial Behavior, "Final Report," June 14, 1982 (Newark: City of Newark, 1982); Michele Besso, "Newark's Alcohol Program in Danger," *News-Journal*, June 17, 2004, A17; Ted Caddell, "Noisy Parties Targeted," *Morning News*, October 29, 1985, A1; William A. Hogan (chief of police, city of Newark) to Carl F. Luft (city manager, city of Newark), "Response and Recommendations Concerning City Councils' [*sic*] Roomers and Boarders Workshop," March 17, 1997; Roy Lopata (planning director, city of Newark) to Carl F. Luft, "Summary of 'Roomers and Boarders' Regulations and Related Information," March 19, 1997.

22. Hogan to Luft, "Response and Recommendations."

23. John Bauscher (president, Newark Landlord Association, and owner of several Madison Drive rental properties), interview by the author, Newark, March 11, 2000; Hogan to Luft, "Response and Recommendations"; Stefanie Small, "Best Off-Campus Housing," *Review*, May 13, 1997; Dino F. Ciliberti, "Rowdy Renter Rift Reaches Madison Drive," *Morning News*, May 31, 1988, B1.

24. Carl L. Luft to Ronald L. Gardner (mayor, city of Newark) and Newark City Council, "Roomers and Boarders Workshop," March 25, 1997; Timothy Brooks (former dean of students, University of Delaware), interview by the author, Newark, March 10, 2000; Ron Kaufman, "Judicial System Seen as Model for University, City Relations," *Review*, April 3, 1990.

25. Laura Ungar, "UD Hopes to Dry Up Party Image," *News-Journal*, October 8, 1996, A1; Henry Wechsler and Bernice Wuethrich, *Dying to Drink: Confronting Binge Drinking on College Campuses* (Emmaus, Pa.: Rodale, 2002), xiii; "Survey Results from the Harvard School of Public Health College Alcohol Study for the University of Delaware: 1997–2003," Building Responsibility Coalition, University of Delaware, http://www.udel.edu/brc/research_statistics/hsph_survey.html (accessed March 17, 2005).

26. University of New Hampshire, "Durham: It's Where U Live" program website, http://www.diwul.org (accessed March 18, 2005); Michele Besso, "Newark Gets a New Tool," *News-Journal*, April 29, 2002, B1; Adam Taylor, "UD Receives Grant to Fight Alcohol Abuse," *News-Journal*, July 21, 2005, A1.

27. University of Delaware, *Student Guide to University Policies*, 2004, http://www.udel.edu/stuguide/04–05/disciplinary.html#alcohol (accessed March 18, 2005); Building Responsibility Coalition, University of Delaware, "Accomplishments," http://www.udel.edu/brc/news_events/accomplishments.html (accessed March 18, 2005); Kevin Tresolini, "UD Closing Gates Tighter on Its Tailgating Fans," *News-Journal*, April 27, 2001; University of Delaware Student Centers, "Summary of FIPG and University Policies for Hosting Events," http://www.udel.edu/student-centers/FandS/fipg.html (accessed May 2, 2005); University of Delaware Student Centers,

"Chapter Assessment Program," http://www.udel.edu/studentcenters/FandS/cap.html (accessed May 2, 2005); Mike Chalmers and Pat Walters, "For Some, College Kicks Off in Wild Style," *News-Journal*, September 3, 2006.

28. David Roselle (president, University of Delaware), telephone interview by the author, February 11, 2005; *Higher Education Amendments of 1998*, Public Law 105–244, *U.S. Statutes at Large* 112 (1998), 1836, http://frwebgate.access.gpo.gov/cgi-bin/getdoc.cgi?dbname=105_cong_public_laws&docid=f:publ244.105.pdf (accessed May 2, 2005); Carolyn J. Palmer and others, "Parental Notification: A New Strategy to Reduce Alcohol Abuse on Campus," *NASPA Journal* 38:3 (Spring 2001): 372–85.

29. Ray Gronberg, "5 Killed in Fraternity House Fire," *Chapel Hill* [N.C.] *Herald*, May 13, 1996, 1; Roselle, telephone interview.

30. City of Newark, Mayor's Alcohol Commission, "Report to the City Council," March 2002; Building Responsibility Coalition, "Accomplishments"; Mary Petzak, "Alcohol Limit Lowered in Newark," *Newark Post*, December 1, 2000; Richard Waibel, "Newark Is Cleaning Up the Alcohol Mess," *News-Journal*, January 23, 2001; Robin Brown, "Happy-Hour Signs Banned in Newark," *News-Journal*, May 16, 2001.

31. Roy Lopata (planning director, city of Newark), telephone interview by the author, February 8, 2005; Sasha Aber (Newark resident and co-owner, Homegrown Café), telephone interview by the author, February 9, 2005; Melissa Hankins, "Controversy with RWJ and Shot Glasses," *Review*, October 23, 1998; Michele Besso, "Alcohol at UD Fest Raises Eyebrows," *News-Journal*, September 6, 2004, B1; University of Oklahoma, "Student Alcohol Policy," http://www.ou.edu/studentcode/AlcoholPolicy.pdf (accessed May 2, 2005). A 2002 Harvard School of Public Health study found that one-third of U.S. colleges surveyed banned alcohol on campus for all students. See Henry Wechsler and others, "Colleges Respond to Student Binge Drinking: Reducing Student Demand or Limiting Access," *Journal of American College Health* 52:4 (2004): 161.

32. Roselle, telephone interview.

33. "Survey Results from the Harvard School of Public Health College Alcohol Study for the University of Delaware"; Michele Besso, "UD Vows Vigilant Anti-Drinking Effort," *News-Journal*, April 17, 2005, B3.

34. Data on alcohol, noise/disorderly premise, and disorderly conduct investigations and arrests for city of Newark, 1996–2006, provided by Newark Police Department; University of Delaware, Department of Public Safety, Crime Statistics, Newark campus, 2003–2005, http://www.udel.edu/PublicSafety/newark05.htm (accessed June 27, 2007); Building Responsibility Coalition, University of Delaware, "Summary of Findings for Newark Community Survey, June 2004" (Newark: BRC, 2004).

35. Buglass, letter to the editor, *Newark Post*, November 12, 1999, 13.

36. Vernica Fraatz, "Riot Ends Elkton Party," *Review*, April 24, 1998; Sean O'Sullivan, "Old Deer Park Goes Out With a Bang," *News-Journal*, May 16, 2001; Michele Besso, "UD Student Killed by Train Was Drunk," *News-Journal*, October 27, 2004, B1.

37. Stephanie Lane, "Sparse Turnout for RWJ-Balloon Event," *Review*, March 10, 2000, A4; Brenda Mayrack, "Administrators Can't Change the Fact That Drinking Is Fun," *Review*, April 14, 2000; "And Jeers," *Review*, May 15, 2001; Lopata, telephone interview, 2005; Thomas Wampler (Newark resident and former member, Newark City Council), interview by the author, Newark, March 10, 2000.

38. Shawn Mitchell, "Last Call," *Review*,

November 21, 1997; "Three V's Have Not Vanished," *Review*, March 17, 2000, A14; Brian Packett, "More Officers Mean No Social Life," *Review*, October 2, 2001; Sean O'Sullivan, "Drinking Habits Die Hard at UD," *News-Journal*, May 29, 2001; David Athey (Newark resident and member, Newark City Council), telephone interview by the author, February 7, 2005.

39. Charlotte Hale, "Bars Now UD's Ally in War on Drinking," *News-Journal*, January 10, 2000, A1; Luft to Gardner, "Roomers and Boarders Workshop"; Wechsler and Wuethrich, *Dying to Drink*, 71–72.

40. Munroe, *University of Delaware*, 36, 50, 67, 179, 219.

41. Ibid., 293, 345–56; Angela Zawacki, "A History of Nonresident Undergraduate Enrollment and Admission at the University of Delaware," Institutional Research Study 81–25 (Newark: University of Delaware, 1982), 10. The percentage of undergraduates who could be accommodated in university housing is based on comparing original bed capacity for campus residence halls and undergraduate enrollment by year. Residence hall data from "Undergraduate Residence Hall Data," unpublished table, University Archives, University of Delaware. Enrollment data provided by Office of Institutional Research and Planning, University of Delaware, and University Archives, University of Delaware.

42. "Undergraduate Residence Hall Data"; Arnold H. Diamond, "The College Housing Program: Its History and Operations," *Educational Record* 38:3 (July 1957): 204–19; Charles F. Frederiksen, "A Brief History of Collegiate Housing," in *Student Housing and Residential Life: A Handbook for Professionals Committed to Student Development Goals*, ed. Roger B. Winston, Jr., Scott Anchors, and Associates (San Francisco:

Jossey-Bass, 1993), 167–83; Funk, telephone interview.

43. Munroe, *University of Delaware*, 412; John Carl Warnecke and Associates, *University of Delaware Development Plan* (New York, 1971), 11, 18.

44. Zawacki, "History of Nonresident Undergraduate Enrollment."

45. Newark Planning Department, "Housing Analysis of the City of Newark, Delaware" (Newark, 1974), 60; University of Delaware, *Blue Hen 1984* (Newark: University of Delaware, 1984).

46. Bob Thomas (Newark native and president, Newark Historical Society), interview by the author, Newark, March 11, 2000.

47. Tina Hernandez, "Best On-Campus [*sic*] Festival: Skidfest," *Review*, May 11, 2004.

48. Adrian Bacolo, "Best Place to Party: Cleveland Avenue," *Review*, April 26, 2002.

49. Kane, *Issues and Opportunities for University Communities*, 33; Gail Marksjarvis, "Newark Council Stands Firm on Limits for Landlords," *Morning News*, June 24, 1980; Janine Jaquet, "Newark Plans to Tighten Housing Code Enforcement," *Sunday News-Journal*, September 27, 1981, B1.

50. Data on rental permits by year provided by City of Newark Planning Department.

51. Conner, "Drinkers Remain"; Caddell, "Noisy Parties Targeted."

52. Caddell, "Noisy Parties Targeted"; Lopata to Luft, "Summary of 'Roomers and Boarders' Regulations"; Claire Sanders, "Landlords Challenge Ordinance," *Review*, October 10, 1989; Tom Curley, "Newark Law Limits Renters in Single-Family Homes," *News-Journal*, February 25, 1992.

53. Curley, "Newark Law Limits Renters"; Wampler, interview.

54. Barbieri, "Moving Up Life's Ladder," 21, 43, 45.

55. Roy H. Lopata to Carl F. Luft, "Compre-

hensive Rentals Plan," February 17, 1999;
Prashant Gopal, "UD Frowns on City's
Request to Construct Dorms," *News-Journal*,
February 28, 1999, B1; Roselle, telephone
interview.

56. In 2006, Pennsylvania State University
housed 38 percent of its undergraduates,
Rutgers University housed 41 percent,
and the University of Maryland housed 42
percent. Data from "Common Data Set" for
each school, 2006–07.

57. Prashant Gopal, "Newark Votes to Restrict
Spread of Student Housing," *News-Journal*,
May 25, 1999. The law stated that new
student rental houses could not be located
closer to an existing student rental house
than ten times the required lot width for
single-family homes in a particular area.

58. Wampler, interview.

59. Melissa Ricci, "Student Rental Fate in Hands
of Pro-Cappers," *Review*, April 20, 1999,
A3; Prashant Gopal, "Student Housing Rule
Goes to a Vote," *News-Journal*, May 24, 1999;
Barbieri, "Moving Up Life's Ladder," 53.

60. John Bauscher, telephone conversation
with the author, February 28, 2000; Vince
D'Anna (Newark landlord and real estate
agent), interview by the author, Newark,
March 11, 2000; Bauscher, interview, 2000;
John Bauscher, telephone interview by the
author, March 9, 2005.

61. Charlotte Hale, "Newark Student-Rental
Housing Codes Discriminate, Lawsuit
Says," *News-Journal*, November 16, 1999,
B1; *Newark Landlord Association and others
v. City of Newark*, 2003 Del. Ch. Lexis 124,
http://www.lexisnexis.com (accessed May 5,
2005); *Newark Landlord Association and others v. City of Newark*, 2003 Del. Ch. Lexis 66,
http://www.lexisnexis.com (accessed May 5,
2005); Michele Besso, "Newark's Housing
Laws Ruled Illegal," *News-Journal*, June 18,
2003, A1.

62. Michele Besso, "Newark Council Suspends
New Rental Permits," *News-Journal*,
November 21, 2003, A1; Darrel W. Cole,
"Student Rentals Revised," *Newark Post*,
December 12, 2003; Lopata, telephone
interview, 2005.

63. Roy Lopata, e-mail messages to the author,
February 22, 2005, June 26, 2007; Katy
Ciamaricone, "Apartments Just Around
the Corner," *Newark Post*, July 28, 2000, 1;
Michele Besso, "Newark Adds Perks for Buyers of Homes," *News-Journal*, September 14,
2005, B1.

64. Athey, telephone interview, 2005; Bauscher,
telephone interview, 2005.

65. Munroe, *University of Delaware*, 54, 161, 190;
E. N. Vallandigham, "A Word from Brook-
line," *Newark Post*, September 12, 1917; New-
ark Town Council to Trustees of Delaware
College, "Street Improvement," *Newark Post*,
June 15, 1910, 4.

66. Hoffecker, *Beneath Thy Guiding Hand*, 24;
Munroe, *University of Delaware*, 216; William
D. Lewis, *University of Delaware: Ancestors,
Friends, and Neighbors* (Newark: University of
Delaware, 1962), 143; University of Dela-
ware, *Annual Catalogue, 1921–22* (Newark:
University of Delaware, 1922); Edward N.
Vallandigham to Walter Hullihen, June 15,
1920, quoted in Lewis, *University of Dela-
ware*, 142.

67. University of Delaware, *Catalogue Number,
1939–1940* (Newark, 1939); University of
Delaware, *Catalogue Number, 1950–1951*
(Newark, 1950); Munroe, *University of Dela-
ware*, 352–53, 359; University of Delaware,
"Newark Building Information," unpub-
lished table, June 27, 2000; "Newark Suffers
Acute Growing Pains Especially in the
Region of the Purse," *Sunday Star* [Wilming-
ton], October 7, 1951; Roy H. Lopata, "Small
Cities Planning from a Historic Perspective:
A Case Study of the Municipal Response to

Tax-Exempt Landholdings," *Public Historian* 4:1 (Winter 1982): 56.

68. Lopata, "Small Cities Planning from a Historic Perspective"; Newark City Council, Minutes, May 26, 1959, May 24, 1960, city of Newark records; Mary Lou Ponsell, "Newark Grapples with Prosperity," *Delaware Today*, January 1967, 7.

69. Randolph Meade, Jr. (vice president for business and finance, University of Delaware) to Albert K. Martin (finance director, city of Newark), March 11, 1969, city of Newark records; Peter S. Marshall (city manager, city of Newark) to J. Robert R. Harrison (treasurer, University of Delaware), July 17, 1975, city of Newark records; Susan Lamblack (city secretary/treasurer, city of Newark), e-mail message to the author, April 21, 2005; Kane, *Issues and Opportunities for University Communities*, 18; Patrick Healy, "Colleges vs. Communities: Battles Intensify over City Efforts to Win Payments from Tax-Exempt Institutions," *Chronicle of Higher Education*, May 5, 1995, A27.

70. "Donor Provides 65-Acre Tract for U. of D. North of Campus," *Newark Post*, December 26, 1968, 1; Munroe, *University of Delaware*, 384; "U.D. Free of Local Zoning, Court Rules," *Evening Journal*, March 15, 1973; *City of Newark v. University of Delaware*, 304 A.2d 347; 1973 Del. Ch. Lexis 145, http://www.lexisnexis.com (accessed May 5, 2005); *Delaware Code Annotated* 14 Del. C. § 5106 (2005), http://www.lexisnexis.com (accessed May 5, 2005).

71. "Newark to Sue University," *Evening Journal*, November 8, 1973; Prashant Gopal, "Newark Tries to Control UD," *News-Journal*, September 27, 1999, B1; Cathy Thomas, "UD Squeezes Newark Residents," *Newark Post*, August 3, 1989, 4A; Joann Leszczynsky, "UD Nixes Plans for Bookstore," *Weekly Post*, August 15, 1979, 1A.

72. Maxwell, interview.

73. Prashant Gopal, "UD Plan Angers Newark Leaders," *News-Journal*, August 22, 1999, B1; Murali Balaji, "Neighbors Worried about UD Expansion," *News-Journal*, November 7, 2003, B1.

74. Rick Armitage (director of government relations, University of Delaware), telephone interview by the author, February 16, 2005; Roselle, telephone interview; Warnecke and Associates, *University of Delaware Development Plan*, 11–12, 55; University of Delaware, Office of Institutional Research and Planning, *Facts and Figures, 2006–07* (Newark, 2006), http://www.udel.edu/IR/fnf/resid/resid.pdf (accessed June 26, 2007), 21.

75. "Clifton Makes History," *Newark Post*, April 15, 2005; David Athey (member, Newark City Council) to Mayor Vance A. Funk III, members of City Council, and City Manager Carl Luft, memorandum on proposed memorandum of understanding between the City of Newark and the University of Delaware, June 16, 2004; Armitage, telephone interview, 2005; Roselle, telephone interview.

76. Susan Lamblack (city secretary/treasurer, city of Newark), conversation with the author, Newark, March 8, 2000.

77. Calculated using the U.S. Bureau of Labor Statistics' "Inflation Calculator," http://data.bls.gov/cgi-bin/cpicalc.pl (accessed June 18, 2008).

78. Acreage data provided by University Archives, University of Delaware; University of Delaware, *Facts and Figures, 2006–07*, 42; James W. Smith (accountant, city of Newark), e-mail to the author, June 26, 2007.

79. Denise Antonelli, "Coverdale Rips Tax Exemption Policy," *Weekly Post*, April 25, 1979, 1A; Mark Walsh, "Newark Councilman Feels UD Should Pay City More," *Evening Journal*, February 11, 1982, Compass, 8; Funk, telephone interview; University of Delaware, "Financial Support for the City of Newark," unpublished table, February 14, 2005; City

of Newark, *City of Newark Operating Budget, 2005* (Newark: City of Newark, 2005), 14–15; Roselle, telephone interview.

80. Lopata, interview, 2000; City of Newark, Planning Department, "Fiscal Impact Model," December 2000.

81. Lopata, telephone interview, 2005; Athey, interview, 2000.

82. Reed, "Student Life at Delaware College," 54; Hoffecker, *Beneath Thy Guiding Hand*, 8; Munroe, *University of Delaware*, 226.

83. "Our Growing Partnership: University of Del.–City of Newark," *Newark Weekly*, February 24, 1965, 2B; Norma B. Handloff, "From Where I Sit," *Newark Post Weekly*, February 18, 1970, 4A; Celia Cohen, "University Opening Shuttle Bus Service to Newark Public," *Weekly Post*, March 23, 1977; "Trend to Cooperation Has Eased Many Town-Gown Frictions," *New York Times*, September 3, 1986, A8.

84. Brooks, interview; University of Delaware, Fraternity and Sorority Life, "Current Judicial Status," http://www.udel.edu/student-centers/FandS/reports/judicial.html (accessed April 25, 2005); Armitage, telephone interview, 2005; Lopata, telephone interview, 2005.

85. Maureen Feeney Roser (assistant planning director, city of Newark), e-mail to the author, April 29, 2005; HyettPalma, *Downtown Newark Economic Enhancement Strategy 1997* (Alexandria, Va.: HyettPalma, 1997), 82–83; Dale Dallabrida, "Main Street Makeover," *News-Journal*, January 15, 1996, D9; Stephen Chrzanowski, "Have a Sense of Purpose," *News-Journal*, February 21, 1997, B5.

86. Rick Armitage (director of government relations, University of Delaware), interview by the author, Newark, March 13, 2000; Charlotte Hale, "Newark Fire Station's Siren May Be Silenced," *News-Journal*, April 20, 2000, B1; Lopata, telephone interview, 2005; Roy Lopata, e-mail message to the author, April

25, 2005; Cory Abbey, "Town and Gown Hosts First Community Discussion," *Review*, November 12, 2004, A1.

87. A national organization representing state colleges and universities publishes regular compendiums of such studies. See for example, National Association of State Universities and Land-Grant Colleges, *Shaping the Future: The Economic Impact of Public Universities* (Washington: NASULGC, 2001). The study that stimulated colleges to begin studying their economic impacts is John Caffrey and Herbert H. Isaacs, *Estimating the Impact of a College or University on the Local Economy* (Washington: American Council on Education, 1971).

88. Allison M. Ohme, "The Economic Impact of the University of Delaware on Newark and the State of Delaware, Fall 2003," Institutional Research Study 04–03 (Newark: Office of Institutional Research and Planning, University of Delaware, 2004).

89. Lopata, telephone interview, 2005; Joan Odell (assistant secretary, University of Delaware), interview by the author, March 13, 2000; Michele Besso, "Youngest Newark Councilman Keeps Students in Mind," *News-Journal*, May 31, 2004, B1.

90. Armitage, telephone interview, 2005.

10. The Future of the College Town

1. Mick Mortland, "A-Digital: The End of the U," *The Public Manager*, Winter 2002–03, 58.

2. Laurie Lewis and others, *Distance Education at Postsecondary Institutions: 1997–98* (Washington: National Center for Education Statistics, 1999); E. D. Tabs, *Distance Education at Degree-Granting Postsecondary Institutions: 2000–2001* (Washington: National Center for Education Statistics, 2003); I. Elaine Allen and Jeff Seaman, *Sizing the Opportunity: The Quality and Extent of Online Education in the United States, 2002 and 2003*, The Sloan

Consortium, 2003, http://www.sloan-c.org/
resources/sizing_opportunity.pdf (accessed
January 2, 2007); National Center for Education Statistics, *The Condition of Education:
2006* (Washington: U.S. Department of
Education, 2006), 96.

3. National Center for Education Statistics, *A
Profile of Participation in Distance Education,
1999–2000* (Washington: U.S. Department
of Education, 2003), 5.

4. Rich Karlgaard, "Life Rich in College
Towns," *Forbes*, November 28, 2005, http://
www.forbes.com/forbes/2005/1128/
039_print.html (accessed January 3, 2006);
Rich Karlgaard, *Life 2.0: How People Across
America Are Transforming Their Lives by Find-
ing the Where of Their Happiness* (New York:
Crown Business, 2004).

5. U.S. Bureau of the Census, *Census 2000*,
http://factfinder.census.gov (accessed January 4, 2007).

6. Seth Sherwood, "36 Hours: Lawrence, Kan.,"
New York Times, February 25, 2005, F4.

7. Chad Lawhorn, "A Full Plate? Owners Serve
up Differing Views on Lawrence Restaurant
Growth," *Lawrence Journal-World*, June 9,
2002.

8. Echoes 1971 (author), "Lawrence, Kansas,"
http://everything2.com/index.pl?node=
Lawrence%2C%20Kansas (accessed January
4, 2006).

9. James R. Shortridge and Barbara G.
Shortridge, "Yankee Town on the Kaw:
A Geographical and Historical Perspective
on Lawrence and Its Environs," in *Embattled
Lawrence: Conflict & Community*, ed. Dennis
Domer and Barbara Watkins (Lawrence:
University of Kansas Continuing Education,
2001), 17; David Brooks, *Bobos in Paradise:
The New Upper Class and How They Got
There* (New York: Touchstone, 2000),
104–10.

10. This trend has received substantial media
attention. In fact, two books have been writ-
ten about the subject: Leon A. Pastalan and
Benyamin Schwarz, eds., *University-Linked
Retirement Communities: Student Visions of
Eldercare* (New York: Haworth Press, 1994);
and Joseph M. Lubow, *Choose a College
Town for Retirement* (Guilford, Conn.: Globe
Pequot Press, 1999).

11. Adam Geller, "Alumni Return to College
Towns, Drawn by New Campus Retirement
Communities," Associated Press, March 15,
2005; "Great Places to Retire," *Kiplinger's
Personal Finance*, Fall 2005 Retirement
Planning, 117; Ben Gose, "5 Inviting College
Towns for Retired Academics," *Chronicle of
Higher Education*, March 21, 2006, B14–17.

12. U.S. Bureau of the Census, 1990 and 2000
Census of Population and Housing, http://
factfinder.census.gov (accessed January 4,
2007).

13. Kendal Corp., *Values and Standards* (Ken-
nett Square, Pa.: Kendal, 2000). See also
Kendal's website: www.kendal.org.

14. Katherine S. Mangan, "Retiring to Alma
Mater," *Chronicle of Higher Education*, January 19, 1994, A31; Bill Luginger, "Back-to-
School Real Estate Sale: College Towns
Attracting Retirement Communities,"
Cleveland *Plain Dealer*, September 5, 1993,
1F; Shira J. Boss, "On Campus, the Living
Is Easy," *Christian Science Monitor*, September 21, 1999; Wendy Ann Larson, "Back
to School," *Washingtonian*, March 2005,
197–202.

15. Audrey Williams June, "Getting Smarter
with Age: New College-Affiliated Retirement
Communities Are Learning from Their Fore-
bears," *Chronicle of Higher Education*, July
14, 2006, A25; Francis X. Donnelly, "Aging
Boomers Head Back to College Towns,"
Detroit News, April 18, 2005, 1A; Geller,
"Alumni Return to College Towns"; "Penn
State Perks," Village at Penn State website,
http://www.villageatpennstate.com/perks
.htm (accessed January 9, 2007).

16. Moody's Investors Service, "Retirement Communities Present Opportunities and Risks for Universities," http://www .universitybusiness.com/uploaded/pdfs/ Hi-Ed_Retir_comms.pdf (accessed January 9, 2007).

17. Association for a Better New York, *New York: It's a Great College Town*, advertising supplement to the *New York Times*, 1999; Collegia, Inc., "Boston: America's College Town," website, http://www.bostonvisit .com (accessed January 10, 2007); "Baltimore: Collegetown" website, http://www .baltimorecollegetown.org (accessed January 10, 2007); "Newark IS a College Town" website, http://www.newarkcollegetown.org (accessed January 10, 2007); The Colleges of Spartanburg: A Consortium, website, http:// www.collegetownsc.org (accessed January 10, 2007).

18. Bob Finnerty, "College Town Concept Expands Life on Campus," *R.I.T.: The University Magazine*, Winter 2005; Pike Company, *College Town: Rochester Institute of Technology*, n.d.; Nicole Morgan, "University of Kentucky President Hopes to Give Town More 'Collegial' Feel," *Lexington Herald-Leader*, February 6, 2002; University of Kentucky and Lexington/Fayette, *Lexington, Kentucky, College Town Study* (Lexington, 2002); University of British Columbia, "University Town: A Vision for the 21st Century," http://www.universitytown.ubc.ca/pdf/fact_sheets/FS_Utown Vision_Jun2003.pdf (accessed January 10, 2006). See also UBC's "University Town" website, http://www.universitytown.ubc.ca/ (accessed January 10, 2006).

ACKNOWLEDGMENTS

Writing books would not be considered worth the effort if calculated by most standard measures. It is the loneliest of endeavors. For most authors, the monetary rewards are small. The work required is often overwhelming. The delay in gratification can seem interminable. The personal sacrifices are great. Why do it? It is the intangible benefits that make it worthwhile. One of the most satisfying is social. I have met and gotten to know many people in the process of writing this book. Some became friends. Existing relationships have also been strengthened. I am glad for all that. Now is the time to say thanks.

Several individuals have been steadfast in their belief in me and this project, and their support has been crucial to my completion of the book. Foremost among these has been Peirce Lewis, a professor of geography at Pennsylvania State University, whose perceptivity about the American landscape is unrivaled. As a longtime resident of State College, Pennsylvania, he recognized the need for a book about college towns. Richard Nostrand of the University of Oklahoma was an enthusiastic champion of this project when it was just an idea, provided helpful feedback, and suggested one of the chapter titles. Rick Musser, a professor of journalism at the University of Kansas, read several chapters in draft form, massaged my ego when it needed it, and provided advice on personal matters. Bret Wallach, my adviser at the University of Oklahoma, responded quickly whenever I asked his opinion and continues to push me in ways that have made me a better geographer and writer. Although I don't ever feel he really likes what I do, I respect his judgment so greatly that I will keep trying to earn his approval. John Hudson of Northwestern University gave me a venue for presenting versions of several chapters in the sessions he organizes at the Association of American Geographers' annual meetings. William Deverell of the University of Southern California offered comment and suggestions. My father, William Gumprecht, acted as my clippings service for the Newark chapter, read every page in manuscript form and gave detailed comments, and provided financial help when personal difficulties threatened to derail this project.

I developed close working relationships with a small number of college town residents, and they influenced this book in palpable ways. John Lofland, a sociologist at the University of California, Davis, contacted me after reading about my project and became a valued adviser. He steered me to essential sources on Davis history, counseled me on the worth of potential interview subjects, and patiently responded to my many queries. He offered me a bike to use while I was in Davis and even purchased me a subscription to the local newspaper. John Hilton, editor of the *Ann Arbor Observer*, possesses a deep knowledge about Ann Arbor and could always be counted on for suggestions and intelligent responses to my questions. Roy Lopata, planning director of the city of Newark, Delaware, is a candid and keen observer of college town life and helped me greatly. Steve Wilson, a lifelong resident of Lawrence, Kansas, and an old friend, was my most valuable source for information and insight about Lawrence and spent a weekend with me doing "fieldwork" in the bars of Manhattan, Kansas.

Publication was delayed when my original publisher, Routledge, changed direction in ways that no longer made it a good home for this book, and my editor, Dave McBride, left to take a job at Oxford University Press. Dave was the first editor to truly "get" my project, worked hard to secure me the best possible contract, and became a friend. I regret that the project took so long that he was unable to see it through to completion, but I benefited from his input and appreciate his help. Bruce Wilcox, director of the University of Massachusetts Press, stepped up when my publishing prospects were bleak, gave me the money I needed to get out of my Routledge contract, and has done everything in his power to speed publication while also producing the best possible book. Smaller is usually better, and the University of Massachusetts Press has impressed me in every way. Thanks also to Carol Betsch and Jack Harrison at the press, and Kay Scheuer, my copy editor. Although Sam Stoloff, my first (and probably last) agent, was unsuccessful at interesting a trade publisher in my book, he didn't make a penny off this project and I appreciate his efforts. Thanks to Sandy Coit for research and proofreading assistance.

Thanks to the many people I interviewed as part of my research and the hundreds of others who helped in myriad ways. I am also indebted to the authors of the books, articles, reports, and other sources cited in these pages and many others that informed me directly and indirectly about college towns. The following individuals were especially helpful to me in my research on the eight case study chapters:

Norman: Gail Anderson, Carol Burr, Kenneth Fuchs, Robert Goins, Eric Lee, David Levy, John Lovett, James McCall, Michael Moorman, Andrew Phelan, Andy Rieger, Peter Tirrell, Arthur Tuttle, Eleanor Weinel.

Ithaca: M. H. Abrams, Martha Armstrong, Leslie Chatterton, Scott

Conroe, Jane Dieckmann, Jason Fane, Margaret Hobbie, Carol Kammen, Chris Koza, John Marcham, Ellen McCollister, Suzy Nelson, John Novarr, Joel Savishinsky, Howie Schaffer, Carole Schiffman, John Schroeder, Carol Sisler, David Stewart, Thys Van Cort.

Manhattan: Bernie Butler, Richard Coleman, Cheryl Collins, Tony Crawford, Linda Glasgow, Charles Hostetler, Alvan Johnson, Diane Meredith, Pat Patton, Billy Porter, Terry Ray, Gwyn Riffel, Cheryl Sieben, Jeri Stroade, Dan Walter, Dan Weir, Rusty Wilson.

Davis: Bob Black, Debbie Davis, Dennis Dingemans, Bob Dunning, Ann Evans, Danielle Foster, Richard Gertman, Katherine Hess, Graham Meltzer, John Skarstad, Maynard Skinner, Bob Sommer, Virginia Thigpen, David Thompson, Doug Walter, Bob Wolcott, Kevin Wolf.

Athens: Terry Allen, David Barbe, Barrie Buck, Laura Carter, Vic Chesnutt, Tom Dyer, Jessica Greene, Peter Jesperson, Michael Lachowski, Joni Mabe, Pete McCommons, Andy Oblander, Julie Panebianco, Andrew Rieger, Rebecca Wood.

Auburn: Gail Alsobrook, Ron Anders Jr., Dwayne Cox, Andrew Doyle, Joyce Hicks, David Housel, Trey Johnston, Evelyn Jordan, Mickey Logue, David Rosenblatt, Jack Simms, Todd Van Emst, Terry Windle.

Ann Arbor: Lou Belcher, Gorman Beauchamp, David Brophy, Karen Chapple, Corey Dolgon, James Duderstadt, Henry Gambino, Steve Glauberman, Don Grimes, Matt Harris, Susan Lackey, Anne Martino, Ken Nisbet, Joshua Radler, Rick Snyder.

Newark: Kenneth Ackerman, Rick Armitage, David Athey, Michelle Barbieri, John Bauscher, John Burton, Tracy Downs, Vance Funk, Ian Janssen, John Munroe, James Owen, David Robertson, Gunter Shaffer, Bob Thomas, April Veness, Jennifer Wallace, Thomas Wampler.

I received financial assistance from the Graham Foundation for Advanced Studies in the Fine Arts, which provided a grant that paid for most of my travel, acquisition of illustrations and research materials, and assorted other expenses, and the Center for the Humanities at the University of New Hampshire, which awarded me a fellowship that relieved me of teaching responsibilities for one semester so I could devote all my time to the book. The Center also provided me a timely grant to help pay for illustrations and publication permissions. Thanks to Burt Feintuch, the Center's director, for his support.

Thanks to the following editors and journals that published my college town research and granted me permission to use in this book material published elsewhere: Craig Colten and *Historical Geography,* Jim Wheeler and

Southeastern Geographer, Douglas Johnson and the *Geographical Review*, David Goldfield and the *Journal of Urban History*, and David Robinson and the *Journal of Historical Geography*.

With mixed feelings, I thank my now ex-wife, Josephine Lenardi, who supported this project financially in the beginning and in other ways for years, but ultimately gave up on me in part because the book required too much of my time and energy. This project hastened the collapse of our marriage and I am sorry for that.

This book, like my first, is dedicated to my son Zeke, who, quite simply, is my reason for being. He is a joy and a challenge. He's also funny, fun, interesting, and smart. I am proud of him. He has changed my life in ways I could never have imagined a decade ago. He is a child of college towns: He shared in this research, added to it, and will benefit from it. I have occasionally cursed this book because it has taken time I would rather have spent with him and occasionally stretched me so thin that it negatively impacted our relationship. I hope he can forgive me for that and can understand that I did it partly for him.

Liz Halprin entered my life late in writing this book, but her love and support helped me finish and gave me something to look forward to at the end. She restored my faith at the most difficult time in my life and I will forever be indebted to her for that.

INDEX

Less Than Jake (musical group), 222
Levy, David, 57
Lewisburg, Pa., 6
Lexington, Ky., 345
Lexington, Va., 342
libraries: as amenities, xii, 107, 201–2,
    288, 296; circulation, 7, 26; in literary
    societies, 77, 330; university, 47, 47,
    49, 66, 69, 237, 254, 263, 285
Life, 300
Lismore, Australia, 17
literary societies, 75–76, 330
Littlejohn, David, 67
"living wage" laws, 182
location of colleges and universities:
    anti-urbanism as influence, 18–20,
    64; boosterism as influence, 20–22;
    competition between communities,
    21–22; outside United States, 16–17;
    politics as influence, 21–22; religion as
    influence, 17–20
Lofland, John, 94, 149–50, 152, 181
Lofland, Lyn, 181
Logan, Utah, 357n65
Lolita (Nabokov), 94
Lopata, Roy, 311, 321, 329–30, 332
Los Angeles, Calif., xiv, 222
Los Angeles Times, 162
Lott, Dale, 150–52, 158
Lott, Donna, 158
Luft, Carl, 312
Lurie, Alison, 107

Mabe, Joni, 210–14, *212*
MacArthur, Bill, 290
Madison, Wisc., 156, 198, 222, 350n12
Malecki, Edward, 287
Malibu, Calif., 51
Manhattan, Kans., 2, *6*, 10, 108–44;
    athletics celebrations, 119, *120*, 123,
    129–32, *131*; bars, 108, 117, 121, *122*,
    125, 127–31, *129*, 133–44, *139*; boarding
    houses, 114, 116, 119; bookstores,
    109, *111*, 112–14, *115*, 116, 119, 126,
    135–36, 143, 372n19; campus-adjacent
    business district, 108–44, *110*, *113*, *118*;
    counterculture, 123–27; downtown, 113,
    134–35; drug use, 125–27; housing, 112,

115–16, 119–20, 137; movie theaters,
    117, 119, 126, 135; nightclubs, 117, 119,
    126, 128, 371n14; restaurants, 114, 116,
    119–21, 123, 133, 136–37, 143; riots,
    130–32, *132*; shopping mall, 134–35. *See
    also* Kansas State University
Manhattan City Commission, 130
Manhattan Police Department, 126
Manhattan Mercury, 116, 133–34
Manning, Warren, 102
manufacturing: automobile, 267–68,
    277, 280; computer hardware, 271,
    279, 281, 284; defense-related,
    265–66, 268; employment, 9, 72,
    363n4; measuring devices, 275, 280;
    medical equipment, 275, 280–81;
    microwave technology, 270; opposition
    to, 261–62; photography, 265–66. *See
    also* high-technology industry; industry
Marburg, Germany, 16
Marcham, Frederick, 103
Marcham, John, 104
Mares, Michael, 61–62
marijuana, xvi, 94, 126, 199, 350n13;
    decriminalization, 36, 147; medical,
    258. *See also* drugs
marital status, 4, 317, 320, 336
Marwil, Jonathan, 262
Maryland, University of, 407n56
Massachusetts-Amherst, University of,
    35, 49, 67
Mayrack, Brenda, 320
McCall, James "Tuffy," 59
McCamant, Kathryn, 175–76, 180
McCommons, Pete, 193–98, *194*, 225
McGovern, George, 23, 28, 148
McKaig, Richard, 85
McMahon, Neil, 202
Meacham, Scott, 81
Means, Grady, 335
medicine: free clinics, 167; hospitals,
    258, 277, 281, 344; instrument
    manufacture, 280–81; medical
    marijuana, 258; medical schools,
    272–73, 281, 363; physicians, 26;
    research, 269–70, 281. *See also*
    biotechnology; Pfizer
Merge Records, 191

159–61, 166, 185, 188; demographic changes, impact of, 148–50, 156–57, 185, 189, 195; disciplinary differences in beliefs, 23, 142, 146; influence in college placement, 21–22; liberal culture, xvi, 1, 13, 15, 23–24, 28–29, 34, 36, 39, 99, 146–49, 152, 154, 159–70, 174–75, 179–83, 187–88, 189, 195–96, 258, 271, 278, 340, 347; progressivism, changing meaning of, 166, 182, 187–88; Republicans, 113, 146, 148, 159, 166; voting law changes, impact of, 36, 148, 160–61. *See also* activism; voting behavior; *specific issue names*

Pollard, A. W., 263

population: 1636–1775, 31; 1776–1861, 32; 1862–1945, 34, 237; 1946–1973, 36, 105, 152, 156, 160, 247; 1974–present, xix, 39, 74, 142, 165, 182–83, 185, 292, 337–38, 340; age structure, 4, 98, 107, 341, 345; Asian, 12, 29, 98; black, 12, 29, 292; foreign-born, 12, 25, 29; Hispanic, 12, 29; ratio of enrollment to, 2–3, 5, 16, 32, 34, 350n2

Porn Orchard (musical group), 215

Potts, David, 20–21

Poulos, Joan, 161–62

poverty rates, 9

Power, Eugene, 262–64

Presbyterian colleges, 18–20

Presley, Elvis, 210–13

Princess Anne, Md., *6*

Princeton, N.J., *6*, 10, 19–20, 31, 66

Princeton University, 18–20, 31, 63

private colleges, 28, 72; characteristics, 26–27, 354n42; college towns with, 26–27, 146, 312

ProQuest, 258, 262, 264. *See also* University Microfilms International

protests. *See* activism; anti-war activism; *specific issue names*

Provo, Utah, *6*, 27–28, 289

Psi Upsilon fraternity, 78, 83, 91

Pullman, Wash., *6*, 25, 74, 84, 129

Purdue University, 25

Puritans, 41

Pylon (musical group), 201, 203–4, 206–7, *206*, 210

quality of life, 15–16, 183, 207, 288

race: population by, 12, 29; multicultural fraternities, 82; school integration, 148

radio, non-commercial, xiii, 15, 148, 199, 222

Raitz, Karl, 249

Ramos, Frank, 183, 185

Ramparts, 159

Ramseyer, Elaine, 218

Rashdall, Hastings, 297

Ray, Terry, 128, 134, 139

Reagan, Ronald, 133, 306

record stores, 37, 108–9, 347, 376n60; characteristics, xii, 143; importance to alternative communities, xiii, 196, 200, 222. *See also* rock music

recreational facilities, 15; on campuses, 41, 49, 54, 106

recycling, 146, 155–59, *158*, 161, 165–66

Redgrave, G. R., 263

regional state universities, 36; characteristics, 25–26, 354n42; college towns with, 25–26, 109

Reinert, Al, 232

religion: athletics compared to, 232, 235, 249; campus-adjacent religious organizations, 109; religiosity, 13–14, 23, 28–30; role in college founding, 17–20

religious colleges and universities: characteristics, 27–28; college towns with, 27–28; founding, 18–20, 32

R.E.M. (musical group), 191, 197, 206–8, 214, 216, 219, 221

remote sensing, 269

rent control, 182

Republicans, 113, 146, 148, 159, 166. *See also* politics

research, 25, 36, 287; military, 260, 266, 268–70, 273, 275–76, 278; by private companies, 259–60, 272–73, 275–76, 282, 284–85; university, 258, 266–71, 275–76, 278, 281, 283–84, 287; U.S. government funding for, 36, 38, 266, 268–70, 273, 275

BLAKE GUMPRECHT is associate professor
and chair of the Department of Geography at
the University of New Hampshire in the college
town of Durham. He has published studies
about college towns in the *Journal of Urban
History, Geographical Review, Journal of Historical
Geography,* and other publications. He is the
author of *The Los Angeles River: Its Life, Death,
and Possible Rebirth,* winner of the Association of
American Geographers' J. B. Jackson Prize. He
has also produced studies about tree planting on
the Great Plains, the making of an Oklahoma city
as an international grain center, whiskey towns
of Oklahoma Territory, and the role of place in
the music of West Texas. Born and raised in
Wilmington, Delaware, he was educated at the
University of Kansas; Louisiana State University;
California State University, Los Angeles; and the
University of Oklahoma.